KARL MARX
FREDERICK ENGELS
COLLECTED WORKS
VOLUME
42

KARL MARX
FREDERICK ENGELS

COLLECTED
WORKS

INTERNATIONAL PUBLISHERS

NEW YORK

KARL MARX
FREDERICK ENGELS

Volume
42

MARX AND ENGELS: 1864-68

INTERNATIONAL PUBLISHERS
NEW YORK

This volume has been prepared jointly by Lawrence & Wishart Ltd., London, International Publishers Co. Inc., New York, and Progress Publishers, Moscow, in collaboration with the Institute of Marxism-Leninism, Moscow.

Editorial commissions:

GREAT BRITAIN: Eric Hobsbawm, John Hoffman, Nicholas Jacobs, Monty Johnstone, Martin Milligan, Jeff Skelley, Ernst Wangermann.

USA: Louis Diskin, Philip S. Foner, James E. Jackson, Leonard B. Levenson, Betty Smith, Dirk J. Struik, William W. Weinstone.

USSR: for Progress Publishers—A. K. Avelichev, N. P. Karmanova, V. N. Sedikh, M. K. Shcheglova; for the Institute of Marxism-Leninism— P. N. Fedoseyev, L. I. Golman, A. I. Malysh, M. P. Mchedlov, V. N. Pospelova, A. G. Yegorov.

Library of Congress Cataloging in Publication Data

Marx, Karl, 1818-1883.
    Karl Marx, Frederick Engels: collected works.

    1. Socialism—Collected works. 2. Economics— Collected works. I. Engels, Friedrich, 1820-1895. Works. English. 1975. II. Title.
HX39.5 A16 1975   335.4   73-84671
ISBN 0-7178-0542-5 (v. 42)

Printed in the Union of Soviet Socialist Republics

Contents

KARL MARX AND FREDERICK ENGELS
LETTERS
October 1864-March 1868

1864

1865

1866

1867

APPENDICES

NOTES AND INDEXES

ILLUSTRATIONS

TRANSLATORS:

CHRISTOPHER UPWARD: Letters 1-27, 29, 31-65,
67-72, 74-99, 101-08, 110-12, 114-39, 141, 145-52,
154-58, 160-83, 185, 188-220, 222, 224-38, 240-309;
Appendices 1, 2, 4-10

JOHN PEET: Letters 310-44; Appendices 11

Preface

Volume 42 of the *Collected Works* of Karl Marx and Frederick Engels contains their correspondence from October 1864 to March 1868. Chronologically, the volume covers the period, very important for the history of Marxism and the international working-class movement, of the founding and the early years of the International Working Men's Association (the First International). This period was also marked by the publication of Marx's most important work, Volume One of *Capital.*

With the foundation of the International the correspondence of Marx and Engels became particularly intense and ideologically rich, and the circle of people with whom they corresponded, active members of the working-class movement in various countries, grew wider. An important place in their letters is devoted to the pressing problems of the organisation and revolutionary tactics of the working class, to the theory and practice of the proletarian struggle.

Marx and Engels had countless ties with the working-class movement. This can be seen from the numerous letters published in this volume that deal with the activity of the International Working Men's Association, an organisation set up with Marx's direct participation. These letters are one of the most important sources revealing the history of the emergence of the International and the way that it turned under the guidance of Marx and Engels into a true centre for uniting the militant forces of the working class. All of Marx's previous activity had prepared him for the task of leading the movement of the international proletariat, and Engels was fully justified in writing later that among those who attended the meeting in St Martin's Hall,

London, on 28 September 1864 to proclaim the International 'there was only one person who was clear as to what was to happen and what was to be founded: it was the man who had already in 1848 issued to the world the call: "Proletarians of All Countries, Unite!"' (see Frederick Engels, 'Marx, Heinrich Karl', present edition, Vol. 27).

'Marx was the heart and soul of this organisation' is how Lenin described the role of the founder and leader of the first international mass organisation of the proletariat (V. I. Lenin, *Collected Works*, Vol. 21, Moscow, 1977, p. 49).

The letters included in this volume throw light on Marx's many-sided activity in the International Working Men's Association, his leading role on its guiding body, the Central (General) Council, his active participation in all the discussions that took place in the Council, the drafting of its decisions and the preparation of congresses of the International, their agendas and resolutions. From the letters it is also obvious that after the founding of the International Engels constantly helped Marx in guiding it. Until his move from Manchester to London in 1870, Engels could not take part directly in the work of the General Council, but during those years too Marx discussed all important questions concerning the International with him, kept him informed of the course of discussions in the Council and of the decisions being drafted, and made use of his recommendations. Engels helped to draw up the tactical line of the International, explaining it in letters to active members of the working-class movement, particularly in Germany, and frequently wrote to the press to present the position of the International Working Men's Association on various questions.

Marx guided the activity of the new organisation with characteristic confidence, skilfully overcoming the difficulties obstructing the path of the development of an independent proletarian movement. He constantly thwarted attempts by petty-bourgeois democrats and supporters of sectarian and reformist trends to deflect the International Working Men's Association from a revolutionary course and to subject it to tasks and aims alien to the interests of the working-class movement.

Marx's letters to Engels of 4 November, to Joseph Weydemeyer and Lion Philips of 29 November 1864 and others show what an effort it cost Marx, right from the foundation of the International, to counteract the constant attempts by petty-bourgeois elements to exert their influence over it. Thanks to Marx's endeavours the new organisation acquired a truly proletarian class character. The first considerable success in this respect, of historic significance, was the adoption by the Central Council of the Inaugural Address and Provisional Rules of the International drafted by Marx. As Marx himself admitted, it was no easy task to work out a common platform for all the different contingents of the working class, with their different levels of development, that had been drawn into the ranks of the International. But Marx, author of its first programme and its associated documents, performed this task brilliantly. Without making the slightest concession of principle to sectarian trends, these documents did not shut the doors of the international organisation to the British trade unions, the French and Belgian Proudhonists, or the German Lassalleans. On learning from Marx of the content of the Inaugural Address, Engels wrote that he could not wait to see it and that 'it must be a real masterpiece' (see this volume, p. 20).

While guiding the International and drafting all the most important documents that set out the strategy and tactics of the proletarian movement, Marx persistently did his utmost to ensure that in the daily battles for particular and purely economic demands the workers should gain an understanding of the common tasks of their class struggle against capitalism. The establishment of firm contacts by the International with the working-class organisations in various countries, the setting up of sections of the International in the main European countries, its active support of the strike movement in 1865-67, and the victories gained by striking workers in a number of industries in Britain and France thanks to this support—all this helped to enhance the authority of the International Working Men's Association and helped the workers to realise gradually the strength of proletarian solidarity.

As the correspondence shows, during this period Marx and Engels devoted considerable attention to the formation and ideological training of progressive militants of the working class. Marx sought to create a strong nucleus of proletarian rev- olutionaries on the General Council and administrative bodies of the International in various countries. Under his direct influence, the Germans Georg Eccarius, Friedrich Lessner and Karl Pfänder, the Frenchman Eugène Dupont, the Englishman Robert Shaw, the Swiss Hermann Jung and other members of the General Council acquired the necessary theoretical knowledge and became ac- quainted with scientific socialism. The letters from Marx and Engels to Wilhelm Liebknecht, Paul Lafargue, Johann Philipp Becker, Joseph Weydemeyer and other eminent figures in the working-class and socialist movement show how patiently and persistently they taught their friends and comrades, helping them with advice, responding to their requests and criticising their shortcomings and mistakes.

In the period of the activity of the International the need for an independent workers' press was particularly acute. 'It is impossible to have a movement here without its own press-organ,' Marx wrote to Engels on 2 December 1864. From the inception of the International Working Men's Association Marx and Engels directed their efforts towards setting up press-organs for it in Britain, France, Germany and Switzerland. They endeavoured to take part personally in the production of a number of newspapers and to lend them a revolutionary character. They also concerned themselves with the composition of the editorial boards and contributors and encouraged like-minded people to work on them (see Marx's letters to Engels of 2 December 1864, 9 May and 26 December 1865 and others). Thanks to this, the leaders of the International not only organised the widespread publication of its documents in various countries, but also trained a whole galaxy of working-class journalists who propagated its ideas.

Marx attached great importance to the establishment of close relations between the International and the British trade unions. He strongly supported the participation of their representatives in its founding, believing that this would help to disseminate the ideas of the International in Britain, then the citadel of the capitalist world and the country with the most developed and organised working-class movement (see Marx's letter to Ludwig Kugelmann of 29 November 1864). Marx saw the further drawing of the British trade unions into the ranks of the International as an important way of broadening its mass base in the British Isles, and also as a means of overcoming the narrow-mindedness typical of British trade unions, expressed in their efforts to limit their activity to the economic struggle. To arouse the political activity of the trade unions and turn them into real centres of resistance to the capitalist system—this was the task that Marx set before the International in including, among other things, the question of the trade unions in the agenda of the Geneva Congress (see Marx's letter to Hermann Jung of 20 November 1865). The General Council relied on the support of the trade unions, organising campaigns to aid strikers both in Britain and on the Continent and thereby helping to kindle a spirit of proletarian solidarity in British workers.

The leaders of the large London trade unions represented a considerable force on the General Council, and from the very beginning of the International Marx sought to use the authority of these 'real worker-kings of London' (p. 44) in order to strengthen the position of the International in Britain. At the same time, taking into account the ideological dependence of many trade union leaders on bourgeois liberals and radicals, he did his utmost to counteract any reformist tendencies shown by them. Marx's tactics aimed at removing obstacles to making the British working class a revolutionary force. He frequently managed to encourage reformist-minded trade union leaders to act in a revolutionary way.

One of the most striking episodes in the activity of the International in Britain was its participation in the broad movement for electoral reform that began in spring 1865. On Marx's advice, the British members of the General Council joined with representatives of the radical bourgeoisie in the leadership of the Reform League to campaign for the demand for universal suffrage. After beginning in London, the movement gradually gained strength, spreading to the provinces, and its powerful dimensions gave Marx grounds for hoping that it would be successful. 'If we succeed in re-electrifying the political movement of the English working class,' he wrote to Engels on 1 May 1865, 'our Association will already have done more for the European working class, without making any fuss, than was possible in any other way.'

Using the influence of the International on British workers, Marx strove to give the reform movement a radical nature, to turn it into a national struggle for a democratic political system in Britain, to encourage workers to stand for their own political platform, regardless of the position of the bourgeois parties (see Marx's letters to Kugelmann of 23 February 1865 and 9 October 1866, to Engels of 13 May 1865, and others). In this connection the drawing into the struggle for reform of those strata of British trade union workers who had previously been indifferent to politics both pleased Marx and encouraged high hopes. 'We have succeeded in attracting into the movement,' he wrote to Ludwig Kugelmann on 15 January 1866, 'the only really big workers' organisation, the English "*Trade Unions*", which previously concerned themselves *exclusively* with the wage question.'

The reform movement did not yield the expected results, however. The unity of its supporters was undermined by the bourgeois radicals who renounced the League's original programme calling for universal suffrage. After having come 'to a *compromise with the bourgeoisie*' (Marx to Johann Philipp Becker of 31 August 1866), the reformist trade union leaders began playing up to the radicals. This enabled the ruling circles in Britain to limit themselves to introducing a moderate reform in 1867 that extended the franchise to the top strata of the working class only. The need to assert a truly proletarian world outlook and principles of revolutionary tactics of the proletariat, to counter reformist ideology and practice had now become even more evident. It was to this end that the subsequent activity of Marx and his associates in the International in Britain was directed.

As can be seen from their correspondence, Marx and Engels focused their attention also on the prospects for the development of the German working-class movement. As Corresponding Secretary for Germany on the General Council, Marx hoped that the German proletariat would become one of the leading national detachments of the International Association. The objective prerequisites for this existed. The activity of the Communist League and the *Neue Rheinische Zeitung* during the revolution of 1848-49 prepared the ground for the dissemination of the ideas of scientific socialism in Germany. However, the propagation of these ideas and the principles of the International came up against serious obstacles there. Reactionary legislation prevented the formation of the sections of the International. On the other hand, the very ideas of the international class solidarity of workers encountered resistance from Ferdinand Lassalle's followers, who had inherited his sectarian dogmas and nationalistic approach to the working-class movement. 'As long as these abominable Lassalleans rule the roost in Germany, that country will be infertile ground for the "*International Association*",' Marx wrote to Engels on 13 February 1865.

A number of Marx's and Engels' letters written shortly after Lassalle's death in 1864 contain an assessment both of his services to the cause of the liberation of the German working-class movement from the tutelage of the liberal 'patrons' (Schulze-Delitzsch and others) and of the harm that his mistaken views and tactics had done to the development of the class consciousness of the German workers. In a letter to Kugelmann of 23 February 1865 and a number of other letters, Marx noted that Lassalle did not understand the real conditions for the liberation of the working class, had only a superficial knowledge of the ideas of scientific socialism, and tended to vulgarise economic theory. In campaigning for the solution of the social question by setting up producer associations with state help, Lassalle was fostering the illusion of the 'social mission' of the reactionary Prussian monarchy (see this volume, p. 101). At the same time he denied the expediency of the economic struggle of the working class and opposed the creation of trade unions, the true centres of organisation of the workers. By orienting the latter towards attaining their goals by reformist means, Lassalle began the opportunist trend in the German working-class movement.

In a number of letters Marx and Engels criticised Lassalle's political tactics. They condemned the absolute importance that he attached to the demand for universal suffrage, which he proclaimed as the most effective way of liberating the proletariat. The example of Bonapartism in France enabled them to foresee the demagogical use of this demand by the Prussian counter-revolution. They also strongly condemned Lassalle's policy of flirting with Bismarck and his attempt to form an alliance with the Prussian Junkers against the bourgeoisie, particularly after they learnt of Lassalle's direct negotiations with the head of the Prussian government. 'Objectively it was the act of a scoundrel, the betrayal of the whole workers' movement to the Prussians,' Engels wrote to Marx on 27 January 1865.

In opposition to the Lassalleans, Marx and Engels sought to set the German working-class movement on the revolutionary path. They attached great importance to bringing the General Association of German Workers, founded by Lassalle in 1863, into the International (see Marx's letter to Carl Siebel of 22 December 1864). The Association had many healthy proletarian elements within its ranks, including former members of the Communist League, and Marx hoped that if the General Association of German Workers joined the International this would be an important step towards overcoming Lassalleanism and that eventually it would be possible radically to reshape this organisation, to change its programme and tactics and also its organisational principles. However, the Lassallean leaders of the Association opposed its joining the International.

In the struggle against the influence of Lassalleanism on the German working-class movement an important part was played by Engels' pamphlet *The Prussian Military Question and the German Workers' Party* published in Germany in February 1865. Marx and Engels discussed its plan and content in detail in their letters. In them they denounce the social demagogy of the Prussian government and Bismarck's use of the Bonapartist tactics of manoeuvring between the bourgeoisie and the proletariat, reveal the inconsistency and cowardice of the bourgeois opposition Party of Progress and determine the tasks of the working class in the struggle for democratic transformations in Germany (see, for example, Marx's letters to Engels of 3, 10 and 18 February 1865). The ideas expressed in their letters were developed in the pamphlet, in which Engels stressed that the main thing in the tactics of the working class was to avoid compromise with reaction, to denounce the anti-revolutionary role of the bourgeoisie and to pursue the policy of creating an independent proletarian party.

An important milestone in the break by Marx, Engels and their supporters with the Lassalleans was the cessation of their short-lived cooperation on the Berlin *Social-Demokrat*. The letters of Marx and Engels reflect their relations with this newspaper of the General Association of German Workers quite fully. By agreeing to contribute to it, Marx and Engels hoped to influence the German working-class movement in the spirit of the principles of the International, and later Marx intended to make use of the *Social-Demokrat* to propagate the ideas of *Capital*. On 14 November 1864 he wrote to Engels: 'It is important for us to have a mouthpiece in Berlin, especially for the sake of the association I was involved in founding in London, and for the sake of the book I am planning to publish.' However, the *Social-Demokrat*'s servile attitude to Bismarck's government and the cult of Lassalle that was blown up out of all proportions in its columns caused Marx and Engels to review their decision. Convinced that, in spite of their warnings, the newspaper's editor Schweitzer was still trying to justify the policies of the Prussian ruling circles and to sing the praises of Lassalle, they both announced publicly that they refused to contribute to it (pp. 96-97, 98-99, 104-05, etc.).

After the break with the *Social-Demokrat* Marx and Engels continued to strengthen contacts with the German workers, relying on the progressive elements who were disillusioned with Lassalle's dogmas and the tactics of making advances to government circles, and helped a considerable section of the German proletariat to part company with Lassalleanism.

Marx and Engels gave constant support to Wilhelm Liebknecht and later to August Bebel in their struggle to consolidate the forces of the German working class on a revolutionary basis, on the platform of the International. This help was particularly great at the time when the question of the ways of the national unification of Germany was being decided and circumstances demanded that German proletarian revolutionaries should put up a firm challenge to Bismarck's policy of uniting the country from above, under the supremacy of Prussia, by opposing to it the policy of revolutionary democratic unification from below. At that juncture, as Marx and Engels frequently stressed in their letters, it was most important to denounce the militaristic regime of the united state being created by Bismarck, to support democratic demands and to rally militant detachments of the German proletariat on a national level (pp. 297-98, 300, etc.). Marx and Engels expressed their warm approval of Liebknecht's speeches criticising the policies of the Prussian ruling circles from the tribune of the North German Reichstag to which he was elected with Bebel in 1867. 'Liebknecht is doing very well,' Engels wrote to Marx on 13 October 1867 concerning one of the denunciatory speeches by this true parliamentarian of the working class. The activity of Liebknecht, Bebel and their supporters, the creation of German sections of the International, the increasing influence of its ideas among the German workers, and the growing opposition to the Lassallean leadership in the ranks of the General Association of German Workers—all this inspired Marx and Engels with the conviction that the working-class movement in Germany would take the path of revolutionary struggle and master the principles of scientific socialism.

Seeking to consolidate the position of the International in France, Marx did his utmost to counter the claims of bourgeois republicans to leadership of its local organisations. To this end, on his initiative the Central Council adopted decisions on the conflict in the Paris section (see Marx's letters to Engels of 25 February and 7 March 1865 and to Hermann Jung of 13 March 1865). At the same time Marx was constantly searching for ways of overcoming the belief of a section of French workers in utopian Proudhonist doctrines. This is why in the letters published in this volume so much space is devoted to criticism of Proudhon's petty-bourgeois views that had a perceptible influence during this period not only on the French, but also on the Belgian and to some extent on the Swiss working-class movement. A generalised criticism of Proudhon's views was provided by Marx in his letter to Kugelmann of 9 October 1866 where he sums up the results of the Geneva Congress at which the difference between Proudhon's views and the revolutionary line of the leadership of the International became particularly evident: 'Beneath the *cloak of*

freedom and anti-governmentalism or anti-authoritarian individualism these gentlemen, who for 16 years now have so quietly
endured the most wretched despotism, and are still enduring it,
are in actuality preaching vulgar bourgeois economics, only in the
guise of Proudhonist idealism!'

Analysing the causes of the spread of Proudhonist utopias,
Marx points to Proudhon's 'pseudo-critique' of the bourgeois
system, to his outwardly radical phraseology that impressed the
'jeunesse brillante' (brilliant youth) and students, and also the
backward, semi-artisan strata of workers engaged in small-scale
production (p. 326). Marx strongly condemns the Proudhonists
for their disparaging attitude to 'all *revolutionary* action, i.e. arising
from the class struggle itself, every concentrated social movement,
and therefore also that which can be achieved by *political means*
(e.g., such as limitation of the working day *by law*)' (ibid.). In a
letter to Engels of 20 June 1866 Marx describes the sharp reproof
which, in the course of a discussion on the Austro-Prussian war of
1866, he delivered to a number of French members of the
General Council of the International who were seeking in a spirit
of Proudhonist nihilism to call nations and nationalities 'obsolete
prejudices'.

Marx's letters in this volume also show what importance he
attached to the setting up of sections of the International in
countries like Belgium (see his letters to Léon Fontaine of
15 April and 25 July 1865) and Switzerland (see his letters to
Johann Philipp Becker of 13 January, Kugelmann of 15 January
1866 and others). For propagating the principles of the International Working Men's Association and founding its sections in the
USA Marx made use of contacts with Joseph Weydemeyer, Sigfrid
Meyer and other participants in the European revolutionary
movement who emigrated to America. Marx and Engels followed
closely the development of the working-class movement in the
USA, noting each of its successes with pleasure. Thus, Marx rated
the results of the workers' congress in Baltimore very highly: 'The
watchword there was organisation for the struggle against capital,
and, remarkably enough, most of the demands I had put up for
Geneva were put up there, too, by the correct instinct of the
workers' (p. 326).

During this period Marx and Engels paid great attention to
drafting the platform of the International on the national

question. They substantiated the tactics of the international proletarian organisation in relation to the national liberation movement, regarding the support of the working class for the liberation struggle of the oppressed nations as one of the most important conditions of its own liberation. The correspondence of Marx and Engels reveals how much energy Marx spent on organising public meetings and gatherings in defence of the fighters for Poland's independence. Unlike the Proudhonists, the leaders of the International regarded the demand that Poland should be reorganised on a democratic basis as an integral part of the struggle for the democratic transformation of Europe, in which the working class had a vital interest. Marx's consistently internationalist standpoint on the Polish question was also reflected in his polemic with the English radical journalist Peter Fox, one of the leaders of the British National League for the Independence of Poland. Although supporting Poland's national sovereignty, Fox shared the Francophile attitudes of the English radicals and the illusions of the Right bourgeois-aristocratic wing of the Polish national movement concerning 'assistance' to it from the ruling circles of the Western powers (see Marx's letters to Engels of 10 December 1864, 25 February and 4 March 1865, to Jung of 13 April 1865, and others). In his polemic with Fox Marx argued that the Polish revolutionaries should look not to the Western powers, who had treacherously betrayed the interests of insurgent Poland, but to the European proletariat, its true and selfless ally. In the opinion of Marx and Engels, the prime role in the liberation of Poland should be played by the united efforts of the representatives of the Polish national liberation and Russian revolutionary movements, their joint struggle against the common foe—Tsarist autocracy.

An important contribution to the elaboration of the national and colonial question and the substantiation of the principles of proletarian internationalism was made by Marx and Engels in connection with determining the International's position on the liberation struggle of the Irish people. Their letters that deal with this problem formulate a number of fruitful ideas concerning the interdependence and inter-connection of the national liberation and proletarian movements. The national liberation of Ireland and the revolutionary democratic transformation of its agrarian structure was regarded by Marx as an essential prerequisite for the successful development of the British proletarian movement and for ridding the British workers of reformist and chauvinistic prejudices. In his letters to Engels of 2 and 30 November 1867, he set out the basic demands of his proposed programme on the Irish question, which he trusted would receive the support of the British working class. The main ones were: Irish self-government and independence from Britain, an agrarian revolution and the introduction of protective tariffs to ensure the country's economic independence. Noting that the British ruling classes had virtually established colonial rule in Ireland, introducing the practice of 'clearing' estates, i.e. evicting Irish peasants from the land in the interests of English landlords and capitalists, Marx in a letter to Engels described this as a blatant manifestation of national enslavement mixed with social oppression: 'In no other European country has foreign rule assumed this form of direct expropriation of the natives' (p. 461).

On the initiative of Marx the General Council of the International conducted a campaign of support for the Irish people, while Marx himself in his public statements constantly defended the fighters for Irish independence, the Fenians. He stressed that the activity of these petty-bourgeois revolutionaries reflected the protest by the mass of the peasantry against the policy of eviction from the land, and also the discontent of the urban poor with the colonial regime. Describing Fenianism, Marx pointed out that it 'is characterised by socialist (in the negative sense, as directed against the appropriation of the soil) leanings and as a lower orders movement' (p. 486).

At the same time Marx and Engels were clearly aware of the weaknesses of Fenianism and emphasised that conspiratorial, adventurist tactics, and the use of terroristic methods of struggle did harm to the national liberation movement and prevented the establishment of international unity of action between the British proletariat and the Irish working people (see Marx's letters to Engels of 28 November and 14 December 1867 and of Engels to Marx of 29 November and 19 December 1867).

Commenting on the importance of the struggle to liberate Ireland and the participation of English workers in this struggle expressed in the letters of Marx and Engels, Lenin wrote in 1914: 'In the Irish question, too, Marx and Engels pursued a consistently proletarian policy, which really educated the masses in a spirit of democracy and socialism. Only such a policy could have saved both Ireland and England half a century of delay in introducing the necessary reforms, and prevented these reforms from being mutilated by the Liberals to please the reactionaries' (V. I. Lenin, *Collected Works,* Vol. 20, Moscow, 1977, pp. 441-42).

The correspondence of Marx and Engels illustrates Marx's truly colossal work on his main life's work, *Capital*. In a number of cases letters alone enable us to ascertain precisely what problems of economic theory were of interest to him at this or that point in time, to date the different preliminary versions of *Capital* and to determine the nature of non-extant manuscripts. From the letters we can get an idea of the way in which Engels helped Marx during the writing of *Capital*, of their constant exchange of views on problems of political economy, and of Engels' part in collecting factual material, determining the specific features of capitalist production and the influence of the economic situation, crises, etc., on it (see, for example, Engels' letters to Marx of 12 April 1865, 26 and 27 August 1867 and others).

Aware of the role that his work would have to play in the development of scientific socialism and the proletarian movement, Marx devoted all his energies to it, 'studying by day and writing by night'. 'I have *not an hour to spare*,' he wrote during this period (pp. 263 and 214). Marx hoped to 'deal the bourgeoisie a theoretical blow from which it will never recover' (letter to Carl Klings of 4 October 1864). Explaining to Ludwig Kugelmann the reasons for his refusal to attend the Geneva Congress of the International, Marx wrote on 23 August 1866: 'I consider that what I am doing through this work is far more important for the working class than anything I might be able to do personally at any *congrès quelconque* [congress whatsoever].'

In January 1866 Marx began to prepare Volume One of *Capital* for publication on the basis of the manuscripts of 1863-65. At first he assumed that it would contain the first two books 'The Process of Production of Capital' and 'The Process of Circulation of Capital', but already in the course of the work he decided that it would contain only the first book. And although he himself wrote that he had begun recopying it and '*polishing the style*' (Marx to Engels of 13 February 1866), much more than that was involved. Some chapters were considerably expanded by introducing new material. Thus, for the sections on the working day, machinery and the general law of capitalist accumulation, Marx made extensive use of factual data in the recently published Blue Books (containing the reports of parliamentary commissions, such as the Children's Employment Commission), about which he informed Engels on 21 July 1866 and in a number of other letters (p. 296).

The extreme exhaustion resulting from his scientific work and the performance of his numerous duties as a leader of the International and the constant material hardships had a serious effect on Marx's health. As can be seen from many letters, the preparation of the manuscript of the first volume of *Capital* for the publishers was frequently interrupted by acute bouts of ill health which forced Marx to put aside the work. 'Dear Mr Kugelmann, you can believe me when I tell you there can be few books that have been written in more difficult circumstances,' Jenny Marx confided in Kugelmann in a letter of 24 December 1867, 'and I am sure I could write a secret history of it which would tell of many, extremely many unspoken troubles and anxieties and torments' (p. 578). Nevertheless, in November 1866 Marx was able to send the first part of the manuscript to Hamburg, and on 2 April 1867 he informed Engels that he had completed the book and would take the manuscript to the publisher himself in a few days' time.

The Marx-Engels correspondence from May to August 1867 reflects the work of proof-reading the first volume. Marx systematically sent sheets of print to his friend in Manchester. Thus Engels was the first reader and most competent reviewer of Marx's great masterpiece. After reading the greater part of it, he congratulated the author on elucidating the most complex economic problems 'simply and almost sensuously merely by arranging them suitably and by placing them in the right context' (p. 405). 'The theoretical side is quite splendid,' Engels remarked in his letter of 1 September 1867, adding: 'The *résumé* on the expropriation of the expropriators is most brilliant and will create quite an effect.'

At the same time Engels made certain suggestions for improving the structure of the book and expounding a number of questions. In this respect, his letters to Marx of 16 and 26 June and 23 August and Marx's letters to Engels of 3, 22 and 27 June and 24 August 1867 are of considerable interest. Taking account of Engels' suggestions, Marx wrote a special appendix on the form of value.

Marx greatly appreciated Engels' opinion of *Capital*. He wrote: 'That you have been satisfied with it so far is more important to me than anything the rest of the world may say of it' (p. 383). A striking document revealing the collaboration between the two great thinkers and revolutionaries, and a moving testimony to Marx's profound gratitude to his friend, is Marx's letter to Engels written on 16 August 1867 at 2.0. a.m. when he had just finished correcting the last sheet of Volume One of *Capital*. 'So, *this volume is finished*. I owe it to **you** alone that it was possible! Without your self-sacrifice for me I could not possibly have managed the immense labour demanded by the 3 volumes. I embrace you, full of thanks!'

The publication of Volume One of *Capital* (September 1867) became an outstanding event in the history of human thought. As Lenin said, in his *Contribution to the Critique of Political Economy* and particularly in *Capital* Marx 'revolutionised' political economy (V. I. Lenin, *Collected Works*, Vol. 21, Moscow, 1978, p. 49). Volume One of *Capital* contains a thorough analysis and explanation of the essence of capitalist exploitation, reveals and expounds the economic laws of the motion of bourgeois society and shows the inevitability of capitalism being replaced by a new social system as a result of a revolution carried out by the working class. In this work Marx gave the proletariat a mighty ideological weapon in its struggle for the socialist transformation of society. 'Marx's economic theory alone has explained the true position of the proletariat in the general system of capitalism,' stressed Lenin (*Collected Works*, Vol. 19, Moscow, 1977, p. 28). History has confirmed the correctness of Marx's comparison of Volume One of *Capital* with 'the most terrible missile that has yet been hurled at the heads of the bourgeoisie (landowners included)' (p. 358).

The letters included in this volume also deal with the steps taken by Marx and Engels to popularise Volume One of *Capital* and its main ideas. On 27 April 1867 Engels wrote to Marx: 'I am convinced that the book will create a real stir from the moment it appears, but it will be very necessary to help the enthusiasm of the scientifically-inclined burghers and officials on to its feet and not to despise petty stratagems.' To attract attention to *Capital* Marx and Engels sent copies to their comrades and acquaintances, circulated notices through the publisher Otto Meissner announcing its publication, wrote reviews for various press organs and published extracts from the preface to Volume One in various periodicals.

Engels played a most important part in propagating Volume One of *Capital*. In order to thwart a possible 'conspiracy of silence' by bourgeois scholars, Engels suggested attacking 'the book *from the bourgeois point of view*'. Marx fully approved of his friend's plan, describing it as *'the best tactic'* (p. 427).

Engels prepared a series of brilliantly written reviews for liberal and democratic newspapers (see present edition, Vol. 20). Their publication made it impossible for bourgeois ideologists to ignore *Capital* and helped to expose attempts to belittle the importance of Marx's work and distort its content.

However, the main aim behind all the efforts by Marx and Engels to disseminate and propagate *Capital* was to equip the working-class movement with a revolutionary economic theory, to introduce workers to truly scientific ideas concerning ways of getting rid of capitalist exploitation. It is no accident that in his letter of 30 November 1867 Marx asked Kugelmann to explain to Liebknecht 'that it really is his duty to draw attention to my book at *workers' meetings'*. Engels in his turn wrote to Hermann Meyer on 18 October 1867: 'I hope you will be able to bring Marx's book to the attention of the German-American press and of the workers. With the 8-hour-agitation that is in progress in America now, this book with its chapter on the *working day* will come at just the right time for you over there, and, in other respects too, it is likely to clarify people's minds on a variety of issues.' Other letters in this volume also testify to the true party concern for the working-class movement and the practical application of the conclusions of Marx's economic theory.

The correspondence of Marx and Engels for this period shows what great importance they attached to the publication of *Capital* in other languages. Already on 31 July 1865, when the book was only being prepared for publication, Marx expressed the idea of making an English translation straightaway from the proofs of the German text. Subsequently, Marx and Engels returned frequently to the discussion of this question, looking for a translator and a publisher (see Engels' letters to Marx of 24 June and 23 August 1867; Marx's letters to Engels of 27 June and to Kugelmann of 11 October 1867 and 6 March 1868). Unfortunately, the English edition of Volume One of Marx's main work did not come out during his lifetime.

At the same time efforts were made to prepare a French translation of Volume One. Marx believed that a French edition of *Capital* would help the French workers to realise how invalid Proudhon's reformist projects were for solving the social question. 'I consider it to be of the greatest importance to emancipate the French from the erroneous views under which Proudhon with his idealised petty-bourgeoisie has buried them,' he wrote to Ludwig Büchner on 1 May 1867. The search for a translator and publisher, as several letters show (including those of Marx to Engels of 28 November 1867 and to Victor Schily of 30 November 1867), turned out to be no easy matter in this case too. Marx was not able to realise his intention of bringing out a French translation of Volume One of *Capital* until 1872-75.

The publication of Volume One of *Capital* was, as Marx

intended and the publisher insisted, to be followed by that of the two other volumes. Marx immediately set about revising his manuscripts of the second and third books of *Capital*, elaborating certain problems in greater detail as he went along. Thus, in his correspondence with Engels the question of the replacement of fixed capital is discussed (pp. 409-13); 'for the chapter on ground rent' (pp. 507-08) Marx asks Engels for help in selecting books and consultations on agro-chemistry, etc. 'We must keep a close watch on the recent and very latest in agriculture...,' he writes to Engels on 25 March 1868.

Marx showed a rare conscientiousness in his studies. Again and again he would return to what might appear to be sufficiently studied problems, making use of new material. This was one of the reasons for the delay in the preparation of the subsequent volumes of *Capital*. It was Engels who completed this task after Marx's death on the basis of Marx's manuscripts.

A subject of constant attention for Marx and Engels during the period under review was not only the state and level of development of the working-class movement in different countries, but also the general economic and political position of these countries, and the international situation. All this had to be taken into account in elaborating the tactics of the international working-class movement at different stages. Therefore, many of the letters in this volume contain a description of the most important events that took place during these years in Europe and beyond the Continent, new phenomena in economics, including those related to the economic crisis of 1866, and in political life. Marx and Engels discussed with each other and their acquaintances the details of the struggle of the political parties in England, the symptoms of the imminent bankruptcy of the Bonapartist regime in France, the situation in Germany produced by the growing rivalry between Prussia and Austria, Prussia's victory in the Austro-Prussian war of 1866 and the first steps to carry out Bismarck's plan for uniting the country by 'blood and iron'. The founders of Marxism made a thorough examination of the alignment of forces in the international arena, and of the positions of the European powers in the conflicts that followed one after another (the Luxemburg crisis of 1867, the international complications arising from the Rome expedition of Garibaldi and his followers, the Crete uprising, etc.) and testified to the growing danger of a new war. The assessments made by Marx and Engels of all these events are remarkable for their historical accuracy and depth. They were based on a dialectical-materialist analysis of the phenomena in question, which made it possible to reveal their class roots and essence, to expose the contradictory aspects, to determine the possible consequences and to conclude from this what tasks confronted the working class.

Marx and Engels made a close study of the course of the US Civil War, which entered its final stage during this period. Their letters contain assessments of military operations and forecasts on the future development of events, a profound ˙ analysis of which enabled Marx and Engels to conclude that things were coming to a head and that the economic, moral and political advantages of the North would lead to the defeat of the slave-owning South.

The revolutionising influence of the US Civil War on the development of the democratic and working-class movement was obvious to Marx and Engels. At the same time they also saw the limitations of the bourgeois democracy of the Northern states, and also the anti-democratic, sometimes downright counter-revolutionary trends in the policies of the bourgeois ruling circles of the North. Criticising President Johnson, who succeeded Lincoln, Marx and Engels noted that his policies reflected the desire of the big bourgeoisie in the North to ally with the defeated planters of the Southern states, and to continue the system of racial discrimination against the 'liberated' Black people, etc. Engels wrote to Marx on 15 July 1865 that renewed hatred towards blacks was 'coming out more and more violently' and that Johnson 'is relinquishing all his power vis-à-vis the old lords in the South.... Without coloured suffrage nothing can be done, and Johnson is leaving it up to the defeated, the ex-slaveowners, to decide on that. It is absurd.' That is why when Johnson was defeated in the 1866 elections Marx gave the main reason for this in a letter to François Lafargue in a single sentence: 'The workers in the North have at last fully understood that white labour will never be emancipated so long as black labour is still stigmatised' (p. 334).

This statement by Marx is yet further confirmation that the events of his day, including questions of international politics, were seen by him and Engels primarily from the viewpoint of the interests of the revolutionary proletariat. Already during the founding of the International Marx called on the working class to proclaim its own independent policy opposed to that of the ruling classes. In his letter of 25 February 1865 to Engels he emphasised: 'The working class has its own foreign policy, which is most certainly not determined by what the middle class considers opportune.'

It was from this standpoint that Marx and Engels elaborated the tactics of the working class in connection with the growing threat of war in Europe. They condemned with severity the wars unleashed by the ruling classes for territorial, dynastic and anti-popular ends, and linked the struggle against such wars and against militarism in general with the liberation movement of the proletariat against the capitalist exploitatory system. It is no accident that when the Austro-Prussian war of 1866 broke out, Marx did his utmost to see that the International dissociated itself from the aggressive, expansionist tendencies introduced by the ruling circles of Germany and Italy into the struggle for the national unification of these countries, which was objectively progressive in the given historical situation. Marx and Engels saw these tendencies as a source of further aggravation of international contradictions, of fresh military conflicts. They predicted that the war of 1866 would be fraught with new, even more extensive military conflicts, first and foremost between Prussia and France. In a letter to Engels of 27 July 1866 Marx stressed that the end of the war would not lead to a lasting peace in Europe. 'That we shall soon be back to bashing is clear enough,' Engels replied to him on 6 August 1866. All this required the further mobilisation of the forces of the working class for the struggle against the threat of war.

Criticising the pacifist illusions of the bourgeois-democratic League of Peace and Freedom, Marx and Engels at the same time supported the idea of joint action by the working class with all truly anti-militarist forces prepared to stand up for peace between nations in deeds and not just in words. Guided by Marx the International tirelessly carried on an energetic struggle for peace, consistently denouncing the foreign policy and diplomacy of the ruling classes in the capitalist countries.

From this volume it is clear that from 1864 to 1868 Marx and Engels continued to study the natural and social sciences, in particular world history, philology, ethnography and philosophy. Marx's letter to Engels testifying to Marx's interest in higher mathematics and his study of differential calculus was written at the end of 1865. In their letters Marx and Engels exchange views on books they have read, talk about discoveries in various spheres of science and assess new scientific hypotheses (see, for example, pp. 7-8, 184-85, 212, 232, 291-92, 304-05, 320-25, 495, 547-49, 557-59).

Their letters show the leaders of the proletariat to be men with an extraordinarily wide range of interests, capable of discerning and assessing fruitful ideas and discoveries marking the steady advance of science. These discoveries, as Marx and Engels so rightly assumed, served as further proof of the correctness of the proletarian revolutionary world outlook and dialectical-materialist views on the development of nature and society. Thus, in the research on the social system of ancient and mediaeval Germany by the German historian Georg Maurer, Marx saw the 'Mark theory' as factual confirmation of the view, expressed earlier by Marx himself, that communal property in land came first, that everywhere it preceded the emergence of private property in land (see his letter to Engels of 14 March 1868). The striving of Marx and Engels to make full use of the latest achievements of the various sciences shows that Marxism, both during its formation and throughout its subsequent development, rested on the finest achievements of human thought.

The biographical material contained in the letters in this volume gives a clear picture of the great thinkers and revolutionaries, and enables the reader to form a clear idea of the conditions in which they lived and struggled and the characteristic features of the theoretical and practical activity at the time when, after the founding of the International, they virtually became the leaders of the mass international proletarian movement. An important document in this respect that supplements the correspondence, is Marx's 'Confession' (answers to questions in a semi-humorous questionnaire) which reveals the richness and integrity of his personality (see Appendices).

From the material in the volume it is clear that both Marx and Engels were extremely high-principled and unwavering on scientific and political questions, yet possessed the necessary flexibility in solving the urgent tasks of the working-class movement, and also that they were exceptionally modest and lacked any trace of personal vanity. Marx who frequently wrote that the whole burden of the leadership of the International lay virtually on him, stated in a letter to Liebknecht of 21 November 1865 that he could not read out his report on the German working-class movement at the London Conference because, as he wrote, 'I was too personally introduced in it'. Resolute and high-principled in criticising the errors of friends and comrades, Marx and Engels were always ready to encourage and support them and to come to their assistance. On 8 December 1864 Marx wrote to Engels: '*Apropos Liebknecht*.... I have sent him money several times in the course of the last six months and now I want to send his wife something ... since I know they are in dire straits. I would appreciate it if you would make a contribution, too.'

Marx's service to the cause of the working class is exemplary. In a letter to Kugelmann of 9 October 1866, for example, he writes that if he were prepared 'to take up a practical trade' he could dispose of his pecuniary troubles entirely. But Marx never strove for personal well-being, although the hardships endured by his family caused him no little suffering. 'Working for the cause', for the party, for the liberation of the working class and the whole of the working people, that was Marx's aim throughout his life. 'I laugh at the so-called "practical" men and their wisdom,' he wrote on 30 April 1867 to Sigfrid Meyer, admitting what sacrifices the writing of *Capital* had cost him. 'If one wanted to be an ox, one could, of course, turn one's back on the sufferings of humanity and look after one's own hide. But I should really have thought myself *unpractical* if I had pegged out without finally completing my book....' And to his future son-in-law Paul Lafargue Marx wrote: 'You know that I have sacrificed my whole fortune to the revolutionary struggle. I do not regret it. Quite the contrary. If I had to begin my life over again, I would do the same' (p. 308).

The letters in this volume supplement the works written by Marx and Engels in the period in question. They provide an important source for studying Marxist ideas and the creative and revolutionary biographies of Marx and Engels, and for elucidating their leading role in the development of the working-class liberation movement at the stage when the foundations of the international proletarian struggle for socialism were being laid.

* * *

Volume 42 contains 344 letters from Marx and Engels, of which 159 are published in English for the first time and 185 were published earlier, most of them in part only. These publications are mentioned in the Notes. Of the 12 items included in the Appendices, two were written in English and the rest are published for the first time in this language.

During the work on the text of the volume and the notes and indexes to it the dating of some of the letters was established more accurately as a result of additional research. The two letters from Marx to Engels of 6 February 1865, printed earlier as independent ones, are published in this volume as one letter.

Obvious slips of the pen are corrected without comment. Proper names, geographical names and individual words contracted by the authors are given in full, except when these contractions were made for the sake of conspiracy or cannot be deciphered. Defects in the manuscript are indicated in the footnotes and passages with missing or illegible words are marked by three dots in square brackets. If the context allows a presumable reconstruction to be made of the missing or illegible words, these words are also given in square brackets. Passages crossed out by the authors are reproduced in the footnotes only in cases where there is a significant discrepancy. If a letter is a rough copy or a draft, a postscript to a letter of another person, or a fragment quoted elsewhere, this is marked either in the text itself or in the Notes.

Foreign words and expressions are retained in the form in which they were used by the authors with a translation where necessary in the footnotes and are italicised (if underlined by the authors, they are given in spaced italics). English words and expressions used by Marx and Engels in texts originally written in German, French and other languages are printed in small caps. Longer passages written in English in the original are placed in asterisks. Some of the words are now somewhat archaic or have undergone changes in usage. For example, the term 'nigger', which has acquired generally—but especially in the USA—a more profane and unacceptable status than it had in Europe during the 19th century.

Information on undiscovered letters mentioned in the text will be found in the Notes. If a fact or event is referred to in several letters, the same note number is used each time.

The volume was compiled, the text prepared and the Preface, Notes and the Subject Index written by Vladimir Sazonov and edited by Lev Golman (Institute of Marxism-Leninism of the C.C. C.P.S.U.). The Name Index, the Index of Quoted and Mentioned Literature and the Index of Periodicals were prepared by Natalya Kalennikova (Institute of Marxism-Leninism).

The translations were made by Christopher Upward and John Peet and edited by Eric Hobsbawm and Nicholas Jacobs (Lawrence & Wishart), Glenys Ann Kozlov, Lydia Belyakova, Elena Kalinina and Margarita Lopukhina (Progress Publishers), and Larisa Miskievich, scientific editor (Institute of Marxism-Leninism).

The volume was prepared for the press by the editors Svetlana Gerasimenko, Elena Kalinina and Anna Vladimirova (Progress Publishers).

KARL MARX
and
FREDERICK ENGELS

LETTERS

October 1864-March 1868

1864

1

MARX TO CARL KLINGS [1]

IN SOLINGEN

[Draft]

London, 4 October 1864
1 Modena Villas, Maitland Park,
Haverstock Hill [a]

Dear Friend,

I was glad to receive further signs of life from the workers of the Rhine Province, as conveyed in your letter of 28 September.[2]

B. Becker or *M. Hess*? I know them both; both are old members of the movement. Both are honest. Neither of them is capable of leading a movement of any import. Becker is a weak man, in fact, and Hess a muddle-head. It is therefore difficult to decide between the two. I also think it scarcely signifies which of the two you elect, as there will be no difficulty in finding the right people at the decisive moment.

Enquiries have reached me, e.g. from Berlin, as to whether I would accept the presidency?[3] I replied that it was *impossible,* because for the present I am still forbidden to take up residence in Prussia.[b] However, I would certainly think it a *good gesture by the party,* vis-à-vis both the Prussian government and the bourgeoisie, if the workers' congress were to *elect* me, to which I would make a public reply explaining why I can*not* accept the election. Such a step would be important for the following reason in particular: a big public MEETING of workers took place here in London on 28 September, with English, German, French and Italian workers participating. The Parisian workers had, moreover, sent over a special delegation, headed by Tolain, a worker, who was put up as

---

[a] The Marx family lived here from March 1864 to March 1875. - [b] At this point, the following passage is deleted from the manuscript: 'in any case, if I were to assume the leadership, the government would immediately suppress the whole thing.'

a candidate by the working class in Paris in the last elections for the Corps législatif.[4]

At this MEETING, a *Comité* was elected—an *international Comité* to represent the workers' interests, which is directly linked to the workers in Paris and includes the leaders of the London workers. I was elected as representative of the German workers (and my old friend Eccarius, the tailor, along with me).[a] If I were thus nominated by the German congress—although I would have to *decline* the election now—the *Comité* and with it the workers in London and Paris would regard this as a gesture on the part of the German workers. Next year, the *Comité* will be calling an *international workers' congress* in Brussels.[5] Unfortunately, I shall not be able to attend in person, as I am still exiled from the model state of Belgium, just as I am from France and Germany.

I shall send you some '*Manifestoes*'[b] at the first *safe* opportunity.

This letter will be brought to you by one of my friends[c] from Barmen.

I have been sick throughout the past year (being afflicted with carbuncles and furuncles). Had it not been for that, my work on *political* economy, '*Capital*', would already have come out. I hope I may now complete it finally in a couple of months and deal the bourgeoisie a theoretical blow from which it will never recover.

Farewell; you may count on my remaining ever a loyal champion of the working class.

Yours
K. M.

First published, in Russian, in *Bolshevik*,   Printed according to the original
No. 8, 1934

---

[a] At this point, the following passage is deleted from the manuscript: 'to establish a liaison between the German workers' movement and the English one.' - [b] K. Marx and F. Engels, *Manifesto of the Communist Party*. - [c] At this point in the manuscript, the following words are deleted: 'C. Siebel from Barmen or'.

2

MARX TO SOPHIE VON HATZFELDT[6]

IN BERLIN

[Copy]

London, 16 October 1864
Modena Villas, Maitland Park,
Haverstock Hill

My dear Countess,

In recent weeks I have been so seriously ill that I was obliged to keep to my bed and hence, unfortunately, to defer until now my reply to your friendly letter of 1 October.

I assure you that I still cannot bring myself to accept Lassalle's death as a *fait accompli*! I see him in my mind's eye so full of life, spirit, energy and plans, so very, very young, and now suddenly his voice is silenced and his breath departed—I find it impossible to reconcile the two, to conceive of both simultaneously, and the reality oppresses me like an awful, nightmarish dream.

You are quite right to imply that no one appreciated Lassalle's greatness and significance better than I. He himself was most aware of this, as his letters to me show. As long as the correspondence between us lasted, I always expressed to him my heartfelt appreciation of his achievements, on the one hand, while always frankly advising him of my criticisms and reservations regarding those things I considered faulty, on the other.

In one of his last letters to me he wrote, in that peculiarly forceful manner he had, of the satisfaction that this gave him. But, apart from all his abilities, I felt affection for him *as a person*. The pity is that we have always concealed this fact from one another, as if we were going to live for ever...[a]

First published in: *F. Lassalle. Nachgelassene Briefe und Schriften*, Bd. III, Stuttgart-Berlin, 1922

Printed according to the original

---

[a] The end of the letter is missing.

3

MARX TO ENGELS

IN MANCHESTER

[London,] 2 November 1864

Dear Engels,

Your long silence worries me. I presume you are back.[7] Why have we not heard from you?

I have all kinds of important things to tell you, which I shall do immediately as soon as you give some sign of life.

Salut.

Your
K. M.

First published in *MEGA*, Abt. III, Bd. 3, Berlin, 1930

Printed according to the original

Published in English for the first time

4

ENGELS TO MARX

IN LONDON

Manchester, 2 November 1864

Dear Moor,

The crisis and its innumerable vexations must be my excuse for not writing to you earlier. Never in my whole life have I had such a glut of Jewish chicanery as now, and you can just imagine how much correspondence that entails.

Later this week, I shall go and see Borchardt to complete the business of Lupus' legacy,[8] which is now about to be concluded.

My travels[7] took me as far as Sonderburg[a]; I did not go to Copenhagen, in part because I had neither the time nor a passport, and in part because Bille, the editor of the *Dagbladet,*

---

[a] Danish name: Sønderborg.

had just arrived in Lübeck when I was in Kiel, and so I had no contact in Copenhagen at all, never having seen any of the other papers anywhere.

Schleswig is a curious country—the east coast very pretty and prosperous, the west coast also prosperous, heath and moors in the middle. All the bays extremely beautiful. The people are decidedly one of the biggest and heaviest of all the human races on Earth, especially the Frisians on the west coast. One only needs to travel across the country to be convinced that the main stock of the English comes from Schleswig. You know the Dutch Frisians, in particular those colossal Frisian women with their delicate white and fresh red complexions (which also predominate in Schleswig). They are the ancestral types of the northern English, and in particular those colossal women, who are also found here in England, all are of decidedly Frisian type. There is no doubt in my mind that the 'Jutes' (Anglo-Saxon *eotena cyn*), who migrated to England with the Angles and Saxons, were Frisians, and that the Danish migration to Jutland, as to Schleswig, dates only from the 7th or 8th century. The present Jutland dialect is proof enough of this.

These fellows are great fanatics and, for that reason, really took my fancy. You must have read something by that extraordinary 'Dr K. J. Clement of North Friesland'. The man is typical of the whole race. These fellows are in deadly earnest about their struggle against the Danes, which is their whole purpose in life, and the Schleswig-Holstein theory is not an end but a means for them. They regard themselves as a physically and morally superior race to the Danes, and indeed they are. Bismarck was really kidding himself when he thought he could get the measure of such people by his own methods.[9] We have held out against the Danes for fifteen years and became consolidated on our territory, and are we supposed to let these Prussian bureaucrats get us down?—that's what these fellows were saying.

The situation regarding language and nationality is most bizarre. In Flensburg, where the Danes claim that the whole of the northern part is Danish, especially by the harbour, all the children, who were playing down by the harbour there in droves, spoke *Low German*. On the other hand, north of Flensburg the language of the people is Danish—i.e. the Low Danish dialect, of which I hardly understood a word. The peasants in the tavern at Sundewitt,[a] however, spoke Danish, Low German and High

---

[a] Danish name: Sundeved.

German by turns, and neither there nor in Sonderburg, where I always addressed the people in Danish, was I answered in any language but German. At all events, Germanisation has encroached considerably on North Schleswig, and it would be very difficult to make it entirely Danish again, certainly more difficult than German. I would rather it was more Danish, for one day something will surely have to be given up to the Scandinavians here, for decency's sake.

I have recently been doing some work on the philology and archaeology of the Frisians, Angles, Jutes and Scandinavians, and here, too, I have come to the conclusion that the Danes are no more than a nation of advocates, who will *knowingly and brazenly lie*, even in matters of scholarship, if it is in their interest. Mr Worsaae ON THE DANES ETC. IN ENGLAND TO WIT.[a] By way of contrast, next time you come here I will show you a book, which is in the main very good, by the lunatic Clement from North Friesland about Schleswig and the migration to England in the 6th to 8th centuries.[b] The fellow is certainly knowledgeable, despite his eccentricity. But he does appear to be a prodigious drinker.

To my surprise, the Prussians in Schleswig created a very good impression, particularly the Westphalians, who looked like giants at the side of the Austrians, but admittedly much more ponderous. The whole army went around entirely unshaven, with their buttons undone and generally bearing themselves in a most unsoldier-like fashion, so that the natty Austrians acted almost like Prussians here. Amongst the officers of the Prussian artillery and engineers I encountered several very agreeable fellows, who told me all kinds of interesting things, but the infantry and cavalry maintained a most dignified reticence and enjoyed a thoroughly bad reputation with the population. There was a notable lack of enthusiasm for Prince Frederick Charles' conduct of the war, and no one at all, not even those who had been decorated, had a good word to say about the distribution of rewards. The non-commissioned officers behaved well towards the older soldiers, and indeed generally when in company; on the other hand, I did see one of the Brandenburg sappers drilling recruits in Sonderburg, a real old infamous Prussian. It was, by the way, remarkable to observe the different tone that prevailed in the 3rd and 7th army corps in this respect. Your March Tribe, as Georg Jung has

---

[a] J. J. A. Worsaae, *An Account of the Danes and Norwegians in England, Scotland, and Ireland.* - [b] K. J. Clement, *Schleswig, das urheimische Land des nicht dänischen Volks der Angeln und Frisen und Englands Mutterland, wie es war und ward.*

it, submit to being kicked around and trampled on, whereas with the Westphalians (amongst whom there is a very strong admixture of Rhinelanders from the right bank) the non-commissioned officers mostly associate with their men *d'égal à-égal.*[a]

What do you think of the commercial crisis? I think it is all over, i.e. the worst is. It is a pity these things do not come to a proper head.

Can you explain: *Rüm Hart, klar Kimmang?*

Give my kindest regards to your wife and the girls.

Your
F. E.

First published in *Der Briefwechsel zwischen F. Engels und K. Marx*, Bd. 3, Stuttgart, 1913

Printed according to the original

Published in English for the first time

5

ENGELS TO HERMANN ENGELS[10]

IN BARMEN

Manchester, 2 November 1864

Dear Hermann,

No joy with the Niersteiner. The wine arrived here with a distinct sourness to it, it does not taste at all as it did at your house, and I shall therefore have to forgo any more orders.

The money crisis, I think, is over. Now only 3 things can have any effect:

1. possible major insolvencies owing to bad news from India. Such are, however, not expected by those most deeply involved. India had its crisis in the spring, when discount was at 32% in Bombay.

2. large deliveries of cotton arriving in Liverpool, say 100,000 bales in one week, which would mean the sudden completion of a mass of loss-making contracts and consequent insolvencies. This danger also appears to be receding. The Liverpool men know how deeply they are all implicated and are being extremely tolerant towards each other. Those who cannot pay the difference lost *in*

---

[a] as an equal among equals

full are offering part of it, and a settlement is usually reached. Moreover, the deliveries arriving are moderate, and the cotton now at sea (400,000 bales from India and China) will probably come little by little, and no one will be hit very hard.

A favourable factor in *both* cases is that the money market is experiencing a decided lift and confidence is returning.

3. if in America Lincoln were *not* elected. However, his re-election is as certain as anything ever can be in America. I have no doubt that the war will be continued until the South is totally subjugated,[11] irrespective of who becomes President, but if McClellan should be elected, at least 6 months of uncertainty would ensue, until people learned precisely what his policy was. But after the elections in the individual states, there can be no question of that happening.

The result of all this will, in my view, be as follows: the American war will continue, certainly, until late next year, and will end with bands of Southerners resorting to brigandry, as in Naples 2 years ago,[12] in the course of which much cotton will be burnt. We shall therefore remain dependent on the same sources for our cotton as in the past year. Supplies from these are only increasing slowly. However, since consumption has become more and more limited owing to high prices, stocks of finished goods, even in the hands of the individual consumers themselves, must now be exceedingly small, and as consumption after all absolutely requires a very large quantity of cotton goods, I believe that increased demand will fully accommodate the increased supply of raw cotton, and, consequently, not only will the downward trend cease to continue, but by next summer we ought, by and large, to see a general rise.

During the money crisis the price of cotton was not determined by the state of the cotton trade but by the state of the money market in general. I believe we've got over that now, and prices will once more be determined naturally by supply and demand, and then with the healthy state of business and the absolute deficiency in stocks, and with prices lower now, I am sure we can expect business to thrive with prices as a whole rising.

There may yet be sporadic shocks, perhaps from India, perhaps from Liverpool. We may, in consequence, again find ourselves momentarily somewhat depressed, but it cannot last, nor will it be of any import, and it would assuredly be an error to speculate *à la baisse*[a] on such evidence. Conversely, I am equally

---

[a] on prices falling

persuaded that any attempt to force prices up again rapidly would immediately be frustrated by the customers here and by the money market, too. This was already shown yesterday. Cotton has risen 3-3 $^1/_2$d. above its lowest point, yarns 1d., in some instances 1 $^1/_2$d. Yesterday, the spinners were demanding a further increase of approx. 1d., and business^a came to an immediate halt. If we succeed in forcing prices down another $^1/_2$ PENNY *à* 1 PENNY in Liverpool, the spinners will be able to accept the prices being offered; otherwise, the purchasers will presumably have to pay the extra in the end, as the demand is undeniably there.

SEWINGS were still very quiet, especially seven LEAS, for which there is not a buyer to be found.

This is my opinion. We are covered for one to two months and are expecting substantial ORDERS in a week or two.

Please pass on my regards to Emma, the little ones, Rudolf, the Blanks and the Boellings, and, if you are writing to Engelskirchen, then to mother^b and everyone there, too. The chicaneries arising from the fall in prices have caused me a deal of botheration.

Your
Frederick

First published in *Deutsche Revue*, Jg. 46, Bd. II, 1921

Printed according to the original and the *Deutsche Revue*

Published in English in full for the first time

6

MARX TO ENGELS [13]

IN MANCHESTER

[London,] 4 November 1864

Dear FREDERICK,

I was very pleased to hear from you again.

All well here. Myself included, since your departure from here⁷

---

^a The manuscript breaks off here. The end of the letter is printed according to the *Deutsche Revue*. - ^b Elisabeth Engels

until the day before yesterday, when yet another carbuncle appeared below my right breast. If the thing does not clear up quickly and others appear, I intend to use Gumpert's arsenic remedy this time.

I would translate your runic *rüm hart,* etc.[a] as Dutch-Frisian for open heart, clear horizon. But I fear that there may be a quite different explanation, so I give up the riddle.

You must send all the *enclosed papers* back to me as soon as read. *I still need them.* So that I do not forget any of the things I wanted to tell you, I am going to number them.

1. *Lassalle and Countess Hatzfeldt.*

The lengthy document is a copy of a circular that Herwegh's wife (*honi soit qui mal y pense*[b]), Emma, sent to Berlin immediately after the catastrophe,[14] so that EXTRACTS from it could be put in the newspapers. You will see from it how cleverly Emma manages to put herself and her spineless Georg in the limelight at the beginning, in the middle, and at the end of the report; how the account evades two important points, *firstly* Rüstow's meeting with Dönniges and daughter, when the latter must have *renounced* Lassalle before the scene recounted by Emma took place. *Secondly*: how the duel came about. Lassalle wrote the insulting letter. But then something happened which is *not* reported and which led directly to the duel.

The suppression of two such important and crucial points makes one sceptical of the accuracy of the account.

The Hatzfeldt letter. On her arrival in Berlin I got Liebknecht to take her a brief letter of condolence from myself.[c] Liebknecht wrote to me[d] that she was complaining 'I left Lassalle in the lurch', as if I could have done the man any greater service than by keeping my mouth shut and letting him do as he liked. (In his last speech before the Düsseldorf assizes, he played the part of Marquis Posa with handsome William as Philipp II,[e] whom he was trying to persuade to suspend the present constitution, proclaim universal direct suffrage and ally himself with the proletariat.[15]) You can see what is behind her letter and what she wants of me. I wrote a very amicable but diplomatically discouraging letter in reply.[f] The latterday Redeemer! That personage and the sycophants, who surround her, are mad.

---

[a] See this volume, p. 9. - [b] the shame be his who thinks ill of it (the motto of the English Order of the Garter) - [c] See present edition, Vol. 41, p. 563. - [d] on 30 September 1864 - [e] Marquis Posa and Philipp II are characters from Schiller's *Don Carlos*; William—King William I of Prussia. - [f] See this volume, p. 5.

Third page of Marx's letter to Engels of 4 November 1864

Apropos. A couple of NUMBERS of E. Jones' *Notes to the People* (1851, 1852) happened to fall into my hands again; as far as the economic articles are concerned, the main points in them had been written directly under my guidance and partly even in direct collaboration with myself.[a] WELL! What do I find in them? That at that time we conducted the same polemic—only better—against the co-operative movement, since it claimed, in its present narrow-minded form, to be the *last word,* as Lassalle conducted against Schulze-Delitzsch in Germany 10-12 years later.

In his last will and testament Lassalle has 'installed' Bernhard Becker, the unfortunate fellow, who was Juch's editor on the *Hermann* for a while, as his successor in the office of President of the General Association of German Workers[2]—in his 'last will and testament' (like a ruling prince). The Association's congress meets in Düsseldorf this month,[16] and strong opposition to this 'decree' by last will and testament is expected.

Also enclosed, letter from a worker in Solingen, Klings,[2] in fact the clandestine leader of the Rhineland workers (former member of the League[17]). *This letter is not to be returned but filed.*

2. WORKINGMEN'S INTERNATIONAL ASSOCIATION.

Some time ago, London workers sent an address to workers in Paris about Poland and called upon them to act jointly in the matter.[b]

For their part, the Parisians sent over a deputation headed by a worker named *Tolain,* who was the *real workers' candidate in the last elections in Paris,*[4] a thoroughly nice fellow. (His *compagnons* were quite nice lads, too.) A PUBLIC MEETING in St Martin's Hall was called, for 28 September 1864, by Odger (shoemaker, President of the local COUNCIL OF ALL LONDON TRADES' UNIONS and, in particular, also of the TRADES' UNIONS SUFFRAGE AGITATION SOCIETY,[18] which is connected with Bright) and Cremer, a MASON and secretary of the MASONS' UNION. (These two had arranged the big TRADE-UNION MEETING on North America chaired by Bright in St James's Hall, ditto the Garibaldi manifestations.[19]) A certain *Le Lubez* was sent to ask me if I would participate *pour les ouvriers allemands,*[c] and, in particular, whether I was willing to provide a German worker to speak at the MEETING, etc. I provided them with Eccarius, who put on a splendid

---

[a] E. Jones, 'A Letter to the Advocates of the Co-operative Principle, and to the Members of Co-operative Societies', 'Co-operation. What It Is, and What It Ought to Be' (see present edition, Vol. 11, pp. 573-89). - [b] 'To the Workmen of France from the Working Men of England', *The Bee-Hive Newspaper*, No. 112, 5 December 1863. - [c] for the German workers

performance, and I was also present myself in a non-speaking capacity on the PLATFORM. I knew that on this occasion 'people who really count' were appearing, both from London and from Paris, and I therefore decided to waive my usual standing rule to DECLINE ANY SUCH INVITATIONS.

(*Le Lubez* is a young Frenchman, i.e. in his thirties; however, he grew up in Jersey and London, speaks capital English and is a very good intermediary between the French and English workers.) (Music teacher and *leçons*[a] OF FRENCH.)

At the MEETING, which was *chock-full* (for THERE IS NOW EVIDENTLY A REVIVAL OF THE WORKING CLASSES TAKING PLACE), Major Wolff (Thurn-Taxis, Garibaldi's adjutant) represented THE LONDON *ITALIAN* WORKINGMEN'S SOCIETY.[20] It was resolved to found a 'WORKINGMEN'S INTERNATIONAL ASSOCIATION', whose GENERAL COUNCIL is to have its seat in London and is to 'intermediate' between the workers' SOCIETIES in Germany, Italy, France, and England. Ditto that a General WORKINGMEN'S CONGRESS was to be convened in Belgium in 1865. A PROVISIONAL COMMITTEE was set up at the MEETING, with Odger, Cremer and many others, some of them former Chartists, former Owenites, etc., representing England, Major Wolff, Fontana, and other Italians representing Italy, Le Lubez, etc. for France, Eccarius and myself for Germany. The COMMITTEE was empowered to co-opt as many people as it chose.

So FAR SO GOOD. I attended the first meeting of the committee. A *Sub-Committee* (including myself) was set up to draft a *déclaration des principes* and provisional rules.[21] Indisposition prevented me from attending the meeting of the Sub-Committee and the subsequent meeting of the full committee.

At these two meetings, which I did not attend,—that of the Sub-Committee and the subsequent one of the full committee— the following occurred:

Major *Wolff* had submitted the regulations (statutes) of the *Italian Workers' Associations* (which possess a central organisation, but, as emerged later, are essentially associated BENEFIT SOCIETIES) to be used by the new Association. I saw the stuff later. It was EVIDENTLY a concoction of *Mazzini's*, and that tells you in advance in what spirit and phraseology the real question, the labour question, was dealt with. As well as how the NATIONALITIES question intruded into it.[22]

What is more, an old Owenite, Weston—now a MANUFACTURER himself, a very amiable and worthy man—had drawn up a

---

[a] lessons

programme full of extreme confusion and of indescribable breadth.

The subsequent full committee meeting instructed the Sub-Committee to remodel Weston's programme, ditto Wolff's REGULA-TIONS. Wolff himself left to attend the congress of the ITALIAN WORKINGMEN'S ASSOCIATIONS in Naples and persuade them to join the central association in London.

A further meeting of the Sub-Committee, which again I did not attend, as I was informed of their rendezvous too late. At this meeting, 'une déclaration des principes' and a revised version of Wolff's rules were presented by Le Lubez and accepted by the Sub-Committee for submission to the full committee. The full committee met on 18 October. Eccarius wrote to me that it was a case of *periculum in mora*,[a] so I went along and was really shocked when I heard the worthy Le Lubez read out a fearfully cliché-ridden, badly written and totally unpolished preamble PRETENDING TO BE A DECLARATION OF PRINCIPLES, with Mazzini showing through the whole thing from beneath a crust of the most insubstantial scraps of French socialism. What is more, the Italian rules had by and large been adopted, whose aim, apart from all their other faults, was really something quite impossible, a sort of central government of the *European* working classes (with Mazzini in the background, of course). I remonstrated mildly, and, after prolonged debate, Eccarius proposed that the Sub-Committee should subject the thing to further 'editing'. However, the 'SENTIMENTS' expressed in Lubez' DECLARATION were carried.

Two days later, on 20 October, Cremer representing England, Fontana (Italy) and Le Lubez met at my house. (Weston was unable to be present.) I had not previously had the papers (Wolff's and Le Lubez') in my hands, so could not prepare anything; but I was absolutely determined that NOT ONE SINGLE LINE of the stuff should be allowed to stand if I could help it. To gain time, I proposed that before we 'edited' the preamble, we ought to 'discuss' the RULES. This was done. It was 1 o'clock in the morning before the first of the 40 RULES was adopted. Cremer said (*and that was my whole aim*): we have nothing to put before the committee that is to meet on 25 October. We must postpone it until 1 November. But the Sub-Committee can meet on 27 October and attempt to reach a definite conclusion. This was agreed and the 'papers' were 'bequeathed' to me for my perusal.

---

[a] danger in delay (Livy, *History of Rome*, Vol. XXXVIII, Chap. 25)

I could see it was impossible to make anything out of the stuff. In order to justify the extremely peculiar way in which I intended to edit the SENTIMENTS that had already been 'carried', I wrote AN ADDRESS TO THE WORKING CLASSES [a] (which was not in the original plan; A SORT OF REVIEW OF THE ADVENTURES OF THE WORKING CLASSES SINCE 1845); on the pretext that all the necessary facts were contained in this 'Address' and that we ought not to repeat the same things three times over, I altered the whole preamble, threw out the *déclaration des principes* and finally replaced the 40 RULES by 10. Insofar as INTERNATIONAL POLITICS is mentioned in the 'Address', I refer to COUNTRIES and not to NATIONALITIES, and denounce Russia, not the *minores gentium*.[b] The Sub-Committee adopted all my proposals. I was, however, obliged to insert two sentences about 'DUTY' and 'RIGHT', and ditto about 'TRUTH, MORALITY AND JUSTICE' in the preamble to the rules,[c] but these are so placed that they can do no harm.[23]

At the meeting of the General Committee my 'ADDRESS', etc., was adopted with great enthusiasm (UNANIMOUSLY). The debate on the form of publication, etc., is to take place next Tuesday.[d] Le Lubez has a copy of the 'Address' for translation into French and Fontana one for translation into Italian. (For a start there is a weekly CALLED *Bee-Hive*,[e] edited by Trade Unionist Potter, a sort of *Moniteur*.) I am to translate the stuff into German myself.

It was very difficult to frame the thing so that our view should appear in a form that would make it ACCEPTABLE to the present outlook of the workers' movement. In a couple of weeks, the same people will be having MEETINGS on the franchise with Bright and Cobden. It will take time before the revival of the movement allows the old boldness of language to be used. We must be *fortiter in re, suaviter in modo*.[f] You will get the stuff as soon as it is printed.

3. *Bakunin* sends his regards. He left today for Italy where he is living (Florence). I saw him yesterday for the first time in 16 years. I must say I liked him very much, more so than previously. With regard to the Polish movement, he said the Russian government had needed the movement to keep Russia itself quiet, but had not counted on anything like an 18-month struggle. They had thus provoked the affair in Poland. Poland had been defeated by two things, the influence of Bonaparte and, secondly, the hesitation of

---

[a] K. Marx, 'Inaugural Address of the Working Men's International Association'. - [b] smaller nations - [c] K. Marx, 'Provisional Rules of the Association'. - [d] 8 November - [e] *The Bee-Hive Newspaper*, No. 160, 5 November 1864. - [f] strong in deed, mild in manner

the Polish aristocracy in openly and unambiguously proclaiming *peasant socialism* from the outset.[24] From now on—after the collapse of the Polish affair—he (Bakunin) will only involve himself in the socialist movement.

On the whole, he is one of the few people whom after 16 years I find to have moved forwards and not backwards. I also discussed Urquhart's DENUNCIATIONS with him. (Apropos: the International Association will probably lead to a rupture between myself and these friends![25]) He inquired a great deal after yourself and Lupus. When I told him of the latter's death, he said straightaway that the movement had suffered an irreplaceable loss.

4. *Crisis.* By no means burnt out on the Continent yet (esp. France). Incidentally, what the crises have lost in intensity, they have now gained in frequency.

Salut.

Your
K. M.

First published in *Der Briefwechsel zwischen F. Engels und K. Marx*, Bd. 3, Stuttgart, 1913

Printed according to the original

Published in English in full for the first time

7

ENGELS TO MARX[26]

IN LONDON

Manchester, 7 November 1864

Dear Moor,

Your Frisian solution is quite right, but for one word. In *North Frisian*, *Kimmang* means: look, or eye; these North Frisians are of a speculative disposition and have substituted the *inward* horizon for the outward one, rather as Wagener is now calling for an 'inward Düppel'.[27] It is an old sailors' saying.

The Herwegh and Hatzfeldt papers returned enclosed. What was the further provocation you refer to which Lassalle inflicted on the Walachian[a] and was suppressed by Emma[b]? Lassalle's fatal error was obviously that he did not throw the hossy[c] straight on

---

[a] Janko von Racowiţa - [b] Emma Herwegh - [c] Helene von Dönniges

the bed in the boarding house and deal with her appropriately, it was not his fine mind but his Jew's pizzle she was interested in. It is yet another of these affairs that only Lassalle could get involved in. That it was *he*, who forced the Walachian into the duel, is doubly crazy.

Old Hatzfeldt's idea that *you* should write an *apotheosis* of the latterday Redeemer^a is really priceless.

The letter from the Solingen worker^b was *not* enclosed.

I cannot wait to see the Address to the Workers,^c it must be a real masterpiece, to judge by what you tell me of the people involved. But it is good that we are again making contact with people who do at least represent their class, which is what really matters ultimately. The effect on the Italians will be particularly good, as there is some chance that this will at last put an end to this *Dio e popolo*^d among the workers—it will come as quite a surprise to the worthy Giuseppe.^e Incidentally, I suspect that there will very soon be a split in this new association between those who are bourgeois in their thinking and those who are proletarian, the moment the issues become a little more specific.

Concerning Lupus' legacy, we had a meeting with the lawyer this morning.⁸ The sum still owing to you will amount to a little over £200; as soon as I have the money, I shall send most of it to you. There are still some details we do not know exactly, so we cannot finally calculate yet. The tax authorities want a list of all the books, and the exact value of the clock Lupus left. Please send me something itemising all the larger works and at the end just: so MANY PAMPHLETS ETC., everything IN ONE CLUMP.

I must close now, as I have to go to a Directors' meeting of the Schiller Institute,²⁸ of which I am chairman, as you know, to Mr Borchardt's annoyance. Happily, beer has been introduced.

Kind regards to your wife and the girls.

Your
F. E.

First published abridged in *Der Briefwechsel zwischen F. Engels und K. Marx*, Bd. 3, Stuttgart, 1913 and in full in *MEGA*, Abt. III, Bd. 3, Berlin, 1930

Printed according to the original

Published in English in full for the first time

---

^a Ferdinand Lassalle - ^b Carl Klings (see this volume, p. 15) - ^c K. Marx, 'Inaugural Address of the Working Men's International Association'. - ^d 'God and People' - ^e Mazzini

8

ENGELS TO MARX [29]

IN LONDON

Manchester, 9 November 1864

Dear Moor,

In respect of the legacy,[8] a further £200 enclosed in 2/2 à £100 banknotes. All being well, there will be approx. £40 to come. I'll send the other two halves as soon as you telegraph receipt.

You will have received the *Dagblätter*[a] with the celebrated article. Unfortunately, I could not find the 2nd section of the article, but there was not much in it.

The end appears to be approaching at Richmond.[30] However, as long as Lee is not obliged to stay entirely on the defensive, which in particular means pulling all his troops back from the Shenandoah Valley as well, and as long as Richmond is not *completely encircled*, all the advances Grant makes against the defences at Richmond or Petersburg will be of little importance. It is just as it was at Sevastopol, which was not encircled either.[31] I cannot imagine what Monsieur de Beauregard will do, probably no more than Hood before him, if as much. I have no confidence at all in this much-vaunted hero.

I am sending you yesterday's *Guardian*[b]; you must have a look at the Relief Committee's report in it, and see what a difference there is between Mr Marie's *ateliers nationaux* and those of your English gentlemen.[32] In the case of the former, tasks of doubtful utility were performed, but most of the money that was spent passed into the hands of the workers, who had lost their jobs. Here, tasks of similarly doubtful importance (but ultimately of definite utility to the bourgeoisie) were also performed, but of the £230,000 a mere £12,100 is going to pass into the hands of the FACTORY OPERATIVES, for whom the whole sum was intended (in other words, just that which is set down as being for UNSKILLED LABOUR). The ACT FOR THE RELIEF OF THE DISTRESSED FACTORY OPERATIVES is thus turned into one FOR THE RELIEF OF THE UNDISTRESSED MIDDLE CLASSES, who thereby save on rates.

All my regards.

Your
F. E.

---

[a] i.e. *Dagbladet* - [b] 'Central Executive Relief Committee', *The Manchester Guardian*, No. 5686, 8 November 1864

[Note by Marx]

Please return this letter, as I am going to file it on account of the remarks at the end.

First published in *Der Briefwechsel zwischen F. Engels und K. Marx*, Bd. 3, Stuttgart, 1913

Printed according to the original

Published in English in full for the first time

9

MARX TO ENGELS[33]

IN MANCHESTER

[London,] 14 November 1864

Dear Engels,

I have had to stay mainly *in bed* for almost a week on account of the carbuncle. The thing is now *healing up*. However, as the carbuncle is just below the breast, I still have trouble leaning forward in order to write. So, to keep it as brief as possible:

1. Please send the *enclosed* letters addressed to me back to me (both the one from Schweitzer and the one from Liebknecht) and reply *by return*, as the people need our reply as soon as possible.[34]

My view is that we should *promise* occasional contributions from time to time. It is important for us to have a mouthpiece in Berlin, especially for the sake of the association I was involved in founding in London,[a] and for the sake of the book[b] I am planning to publish. It is also important that whatever we do, we do it *together*.

If you agree with me, you can *send* me a few lines for these chaps, or say in a few lines what statement *I* am to make in your name.

2. You will receive the 'ADDRESS' along with the 'PROVISIONAL RULES', etc., in a few days. The thing was not quite so difficult as you think, because we are dealing with 'workers' all the time. The only LITERARY MAN in the Association is the Englishman, Peter Fox, a writer and AGITATOR who is, at the same time, one of the people from *The National Reformer* (atheist but anti-Holyoake). I am

---

[a] International Working Men's Association - [b] *Capital*

sending you the very kind note he passed on to me concerning the 'ADDRESS'. Mazzini is RATHER DISGUSTED that his people are among the signatories, *mais il faut faire bonne mine à mauvais jeu.*[a]

3. Your stuff from the *Guardian*[b] I find most valuable. I had already pieced this abomination together from the 'FACTORY REPORTS', but only in a most laborious and fragmentary fashion.

4. 2 COPIES received from the Manchester SOLICITOR for signing, etc. In a day or two, I shall send you the signed copies, along with the list (inventory), etc., which you will then have to record. Of course, I can no longer reel off a complete list of all the stuff we left in the flat, etc., and put a value on it.[8]

That old HUMBUG McCulloch has died. I hope the British Museum buys up his ECONOMICAL LIBRARY. But no doubt Edinburgh will get in first.

Salut.

Your
K. M.

I have just come across P. Fox's letter, which I am enclosing; please send it back as soon as you have had time to peruse it.

First published in *Der Briefwechsel zwischen F. Engels und K. Marx*, Bd. 3, Stuttgart, 1913

Printed according to the original

Published in English in full for the first time

10

ENGELS TO MARX

IN LONDON

Manchester, 16 November 1864

Dear Moor,

Glad that the carbuncle is getting better. Let us hope it is the last. But do take arsenic.

Acknowledgement from the charming private secretary[c] gratefully received.

---

a but one has to grin and bear it - b *The Manchester Guardian* (see this volume, p. 21) - c Laura Marx (a reference to Marx's receipt of money in respect of Wolff's legacy; see this volume, p. 20)

A few lines for Schweitzer enclosed.[35] It is a very good thing
that we shall again be getting a voice in the press; also very good
that Liebknecht is going to be co-editor (as long as he is under no
illusions); that does at least provide some safeguard. Meanwhile,
we shall do better if we conceal our enthusiasm, as 1. Liebknecht
is no diplomat, and one cannot rely too much on his CLAIRVOYANCE,
2. the countess[a] will, above all, be trying to swamp the paper from
beginning to end with a deliberate 'apotheosis',[b] and 3. we really
must find out first who else has been approached. Perhaps you are
better informed than I am, but in the letters from Liebknecht you
sent me there is no mention of the paper nor of this man
Schweitzer, so I am very much in the dark. For that reason, I have
asked for some clarification about the company we shall be seen to
be keeping. We might after all find ourselves cheek by jowl with
Mr Karl Grün or some such scum.

And what a dreadful title: *Der Socialdemokrat!* Why do these
fellows not simply call it the *Proletarier?*

Enclosed papers returned with thanks. Why haven't you sent the
Solingen letter[c] you promised?

Amid the nonsense written by Emma Herwegh,[d] I notice there is
a further attempt to turn Lassalle into a demi-god, as follows: only
his mighty spirit kept him alive for so long, anyone else would
have given up the ghost 2 hours after being wounded—but you
ask Allen some time about the way peritonitis develops following a
wound, and he will tell you inflammation hardly sets in at all
within 2 hours, and is scarcely ever fatal in *less than* 24 hours, and
usually not until much later. These people are really given to
deification.

Schaaffhausen in Bonn has given a pretty lecture on man and
apes, pointing out that Asiatic anthropoids have rounded heads,
like the human beings there, but in Africa both are long-headed,
and commenting that, with the present state of knowledge, this is
the strongest argument against the unity of the human race.
Someone ought to try saying that at a gathering of naturalists in
England!

It is splendid how Müller and the Rev. Cappell have made fools
of that gang Kinkel, Juch & Co. even from the gallows. It is a long
time since I have come across anything quite so absurd as the
conduct of these fellows. How fortunate Gottfried[e] is in the people
whose cases he takes up! First MacDonald, then Müller. And then

---

[a] Sophie von Hatzfeldt - [b] of Lassalle - [c] See this volume, pp. 15, 20. - [d] ibid.,
p. 12. - [e] Gottfried Kinkel

the way these gentlemen threw their weight around was the immediate cause of Koehl cutting that other lad's throat in the Thames marshes.[36] Just you wait and see what a mass of MARE'S NESTS they unearth concerning that affair, too.

Kindest regards to the family.

Your
F. E.

First published abridged in *Der Briefwechsel zwischen F. Engels und K. Marx*, Bd. 3, Stuttgart, 1913 and in full in *MEGA*, Abt. III, Bd. 3, Berlin, 1930

Printed according to the original

Published in English for the first time

11

MARX TO ENGELS

IN MANCHESTER

[London,] 18 November [1864]

DEAR FRED,

1. I am sending the stuff for the SOLICITOR. You will have to copy the enclosed inventory and put it into whatever shape you think fit.[a]

2. *Ad vocem*[b] Solingen. I had put the letter out READY when I sent you the *last but one* letter-package, and it hasn't been 'seen any more since then'.[c] I suspect it has ensconced itself in a notebook and WILL TURN UP one fine morning.

3. *Ad vocem Schweitzer.*

Is a Dr of Law, formerly of Frankfurt am Main. Published a confused pamphlet *against* Vogt in 1859.[d] Subsequently, a social novel I have not read.[e] Declared his vigorous support for Lassalle. Later, during Lassalle's lifetime, he got to know sundry writings of ours at Liebknecht's house while staying in Berlin and, even at that time, sent me a message through Liebknecht saying how amazed he was at finding that everything about Lassalle that he liked had been plagiarised.

---

a See this volume, pp. 20, 23. - b With regard to - c J. W. Goethe, 'Der Fischer'. - d J. B. Schweitzer, *Widerlegung von Carl Vogt's Studien zur gegenwärtigen Lage Europa's*. - e J. B. Schweitzer, *Lucinde oder Capital und Arbeit*.

I have written, like you, concerning the *prospectus of contributors.*[37] Have sent Liebknecht German translation of the address of the INTERNATIONAL COMMITTEE at the same time, with a view to eventual publication in the paper. (The stuff will appear today or tomorrow and will be sent to you.[a])

As far as Lassalle's apotheosis is concerned,[b] the Hamburg *Nordstern,* edited by that jackass Bruhn (who at the same time continues to print *Heinzen's* ELUCUBRATIONS, as though nothing had happened), is exclusively dedicated to this matter just as before, and the *Social-Demokrat* can scarcely compete with it in that respect.

Old Hatzfeldt seems to be most disappointed by the letter I sent in reply to her 'ploy',[c] although it was most delicate and considerate in tone. Since that time, she has—kept silence.

Social-Demokrat is a bad title. But there is no need to throw away the best titles immediately on things that may prove to be FAILURES.

Wilhelm Liebknecht is an unquestionably big man among the Berlin workers, as you can see from the Berlin correspondence of *The Morning Star.* I am only afraid he will soon be sent packing.

4. *Ad vocem Peritonitis,*[d] it says in *Andral: 'Clinique Médicale':* '*La Péritonite aiguë* ... en certains cas un petit nombre d'heures s'écoulent entre l'époque de l'invasion de la maladie et celle de la mort, tandis que d'autres fois la péritonite, toujours aiguë par ses symptômes, ne devient mortelle qu'au bout de 30 à 40 jours.'[e]

And under the rubric:

'*Péritonite par violence extérieure*'[f] he describes the case of a Parisian worker who was kicked in the stomach by a horse, in the region of his navel. Was only taken to the Charité[g] *le surlende-main,* 'offre tous les symptômes d'une phlegmasie aiguë du péritoine'[h] (later confirmed by *ouverture du cadavre*[i]). Died *du 5-ème au 6-ème jour,*[j] and amongst the general OBSERVATIONS concerning this case, it says: 'jusqu'au dernier moment, on n'observe aucun trouble des facultés intellectuelles et sensoriales.'[k]

---

[a] K. Marx, 'Inaugural Address of the Working Men's International Association'. - [b] See this volume, pp. 20, 24. - [c] ibid., p. 12. - [d] ibid., p. 24. - [e] '*Acute peritonitis* ... in some cases just a few hours elapse between the onset of the disease and death, whereas on other occasions peritonitis, which is always acute in its symptoms, does not cause death for from 30 to 40 days.' - [f] 'Peritonitis due to external violence' - [g] hospital in Paris - [h] two days later, 'exhibits all the symptoms of acute phlegmasia of the peritoneum' - [i] autopsy - [j] on the 5th or 6th day - [k] 'until the very last, no disturbance of the mind or senses is observed' (see G. Andral, *Clinique médicale, ou choix d'observations recueillies à l'hôpital de la Charité (clinique de M. Lerminier)*, t. 4, Paris, 1827, pp. 511, 532, 533)

5. *Take care to keep* the enclosed memorandum for student Blind published in a rag in which he has puffed himself up with surpassing zeal since 1859.[38] This '*Beobachter*' *est le 'grand' organe de la démocratie Suabaise*[a]!

6. Prof. Huber has held his 'labour convention' with ABOUT 100 workers' associations. He is conservative in politics but a co-operator as far as POLITICAL ECONOMY is concerned. His *Leipzig Convention* nearly ended in a real 'thrashing' for Huber and his comrades, with the great majority declaring themselves to be 'radical' in politics.[39]

7. I gather all kinds of things have been published by the COMMITTEE in Manchester about the COTTON-FAMINE[40].—I mean IN REGARD TO THE WORKINGMEN. Can you get hold of it for me?

8. My chest still hurts me when I write and lean forward. Hence this 'itemised' letter.

Regards to Gumpert.

Ditto to Madame Lizzy.[b]

Your
K. M.

[Enclosure: List relating to W. Wolff's Legacy]

SILVER WATCH	£2

BOOKS:

Schlosser, *Weltgeschichte*	£1	10s.
Schleiden, *Studien*		3s.
Schiller's Werke		10s.
Duller, *Geschichte des Deutschen Volkes*		5s.
Duncker, *Geschichte*	£1	
Mommsen, *Geschichte*		10s.
Schoemann, *Griechische Alterthümer*		5s.
Lange, *Römische Alterthümer*		3s.
Preller, *Griechische Mythologie*		5s.
Nösselt, *Weltgeschichte*		4s.
Völter, *Geographie*		5s.
Mortimer-Ternaux, *Histoire de la Terreur*, 2 v.		5s.
Arago, *Astronomie Populaire*		10s.
Müller, *Physik*		3s.
Baer, *Magnetismus*		1s.
Figuier, *Année scientifique*, 3 vol.		5s.

---

[a] is the '*grand*' organ of Swabian democracy - [b] Lizzy Burns

Mignet, *Révolution française*	5s.
Egli, *Handelsgeographie*	2s.
Ritter, *Europa*	3s.
Cotta, *Geologische Briefe*	2s.
Garrido, *Spanien*	1s.
Freytag, *Bilder aus dem Leben des Volkes*	2s.
Moleschott, *Lehre der Nahrungsmittel*	3s.
Harting, *Die Macht des Kleinen*	1s.
Grube, *Biographieen aus der Naturkunde*	1s.
Reisen des Marco Polo	1s.
Kiesselbach, *Gang des Welthandels*	1s.
Jacobs, *Hellas*	1s.
Smith, *English Latin Lexicon*	5s.
Rost, *Griechisch-Deutsches Lexicon*	5s.
Giebel, *Säugethiere*	5s.
Tschudi, *Thierleben der Alpenwelt*	5s.
Freytag, *Soll und Haben*	2s.
Pauli, *Bilder aus England*	1s.
Overbeck, *Pompeji*	10s.
Guhl, *Leben der Griechen und Römer*	10s.
Lau, *Sulla*	1s.
Macauley, *History of England*	10s.
Frankenheim, *Völkerkunde*	1s.
Stieler's Handatlas	£1 10s.
Berghaus, *Physikalischer Schulatlas*	5s.
Spruner, *Historischer Schulatlas*	5s.
Mozin, *Dictionnaire*	£1
55 PAMPHLETS	10s.
102 ELEMENTARY SCHOOLBOOKS	£31

I have put a much higher valuation on the stuff than it would fetch if sold, what with the selling-price of SECONDHAND BOOKS in England. On the other hand, all kinds of things are missing that I have not been able to remember. There is thus COMPENSATION. If you want to add anything regarding the other goods and chattels, please do so.

First published abridged in *Der Briefwech-sel zwischen F. Engels und K. Marx*, Bd. 3, Stuttgart, 1913 and in full in *MEGA*, Abt. III, Bd. 3, Berlin, 1930

Printed according to the original

Published in English for the first time

12

ENGELS TO MARX

IN LONDON

Manchester, 22 November 1864

Dear Moor,

I received enclosed today from Schweitzer.[41] Herwegh and Hess—fine company. As things stand and as I am not very familiar with the exact circumstances, I shall have to leave it to you to answer the man *on behalf of both of us*, as he wants his answer by return. Moses[a] of all people!

Please return the letter to me and let me know what you have written, and I can then confirm your statement to him later on.

Solicitor's stuff received.[8]

Kindest regards.

Your
F. E.

First published in *Der Briefwechsel zwischen F. Engels und K. Marx*, Bd. 3, Stuttgart, 1913

Printed according to the original

Published in English for the first time

13

MARX TO ENGELS

IN MANCHESTER

[London, 24 November 1864]

Dear Fredrick,

Letter from the old Hatzfeldt woman enclosed, which I would like sent back *by return.*[42]

Also enclosed the letter from the man in Solingen[b] which has turned up again, and Schweitzer's letter.

---

[a] Moses Hess - [b] See this volume, p. 15.

I sent off 3 'Addresses'[a] to you today, 1 for yourself, 1 for Gumpert and 1 for Ernest Jones. If you can distribute some more anywhere (gratis), you only have to ask.

As for Schweitzer, I have written—not to him but to Liebknecht—that we both dislike the company, but we intend FOR A NONCE to adopt *bonne mine à mauvais jeu*,[b] but to *disown* them *immediately* as soon as they do anything silly. I also ask why Bucher and especially *Rodbertus* are not among them![43]

Moses[c] and Herwegh (who are, incidentally, of some stature, compared with B. and Ph. Becker, IN A LITERARY SENSE) are, after all, more highly regarded by people in Germany than by us. At least, one cannot publicly denigrate them, as one can fellows like Grün, etc.

In great haste.
Salut.

Your
K. M.

I have just been obliged to write long letter to the old woman[d] to extricate myself from the Blind affair she has tried to involve me in. Student Blind has, of course, not let the opportunity slip by of puffing himself up, by issuing a 'protest' in the name of the Republic[e] and selecting a few passages from Lassalle's speeches which are indeed quite sickeningly royalist.[44] Also to advise her against reproducing the 'wanted' portraits of her enemies.[45]

First published in *Der Briefwechsel zwischen F. Engels und K. Marx*, Bd. 3, Stuttgart, 1913

Printed according to the original

Published in English for the first time

---

[a] K. Marx, 'Inaugural Address of the Working Men's International Association'. - [b] an attitude of grin and bear it - [c] Moses Hess - [d] Sophie von Hatzfeldt - [e] ['A Republican Protest',] *Neue Frankfurter Zeitung*, No. 270, 29 September 1864; 'Republikanischer Protest', *Hermann*, No. 2407, 8 October 1864; *Die Westliche Post*, October-beginning of November 1864.

14

MARX TO SOPHIE VON HATZFELDT

IN BERLIN

London, 24 November 1864
1 Modena Villas, Maitland Park,
Haverstock Hill

My dear Countess,

I have just informed you by telegraph[46] (to avoid all delay in reply) of my view that the two photograms of von R. *et* Co.[a] should, *in no circumstances*, appear together with Lassalle's in the pamphlet. It would, on the one hand, dishonour the deceased, and, on the other, give the publication a gaudy appearance which should be avoided completely. Furthermore, as you know, '*contra hostem vindicatio aeterna sit*'[b] is my motto too, but, for revenge to be successfully executed, it is advisable *not* to initiate the public in one's vindictive '*intent*'.[45]

'*Ex ossibus ultor*'[c] would seem to me the best title for Lassalle's portrait. They were also my *last words* spoken at the graveside of my never-to-be-forgotten friend W. Wolff[47] some six months ago.

As regards ex-student *Blind*, that fellow who made himself known before 1848 by peddling Heinzen's nonsense and as the *homme entretenu*[d] of the wife of the Jewish banker Cohen[e] (whom he later married in London), so I would ask you to remember that in my piece *Herr Vogt* (see pp. 58-69 and *Appendices* 9 and 11)[f] I do not merely describe this student Blind as a '*deliberate liar*', but I prove by reference to *legal documents* that this wretched man fabricated '*false witness*' to cast suspicion on myself and to extricate his neck from a noose that this creature had made for himself for the purpose of *merely making himself look big* (which is indeed this rascal's sole purpose in every public step, or rather crawl, he undertakes).[48]

Then Blind succeeded in deflecting the catastrophe of his

---

[a] Janko von Racowiţa and Helene von Dönniges - [b] A paraphrase of an article from the Twelve Tables (a code of law of ancient Rome) which says: 'Adversus hostem aeterna auctoritas [esto]' (III, 7); Marx uses the word *vindicatio* in the sense of revenge. - [c] 'Let the avenger rise' (Virgil, *Aeneid*, IV, 625: 'ex oriare aliquis nostrius ex ossibus ultor'). - [d] kept man - [e] Friederike Ettlinger, Cohen's and later Karl Blind's wife - [f] See present edition, Vol. 17, pp. 116-32, 315, 317-20.

political operations—by *simply saying nothing*. In this he was sustained firstly by the fact that *Freiligrath* (*this entre nous*[a]) unfortunately continued to parade publicly as his friend, and that *Lassalle*, although I had strongly urged him to do so, neglected to force my pillorying of Blind *d'une manière ou d'une autre*[b] on the attention of the German public.[49] This appeared necessary to me because the liberal press in Germany instinctively took the side of a scoundrel like Blind, and therefore sought to hush up my attack. Lassalle considered Blind too insignificant. It was only later that he discovered that there are times when one cannot decline a 'combat with a flea'.[c]

When Lassalle was here in London,[50] he sought to enlighten Louis Blanc and Mazzini about Blind on his personal visits to them, but in vain. The man is exactly what Mazzini, Ledru, etc., had hoped, but failed, to find in the other Germans of standing, a servile lackey and sycophant. Through his relations with these people he makes the English think that he represents Germany, and he impresses the Germans by his boasting here. Yet the whole of this fellow's activity consists in writing, in conjunction with 3 or 4 South Germans,[d] *from, for and about 'Karl Blind'* and, at every possible opportunity, to force on the English, Germans and Americans his 'unofficial judgment' as the self-appointed rep-resentative of '*German republicanism*' (a party, which is well known to exist only on the moon, since the German bourgeois is interested in a constitutional monarchy, the feudal lord in an aristocratic monarchy, and the worker in general not in *mere forms of state*, but in the form of state as the expression of economic social conditions, and, at all events, has never recognised ex-student Blind as representative). He is a true master of dictating letters to one of his 6 satellites,[51] in which they call on the said, etc., 'Karl Blind' to do this or that, or congratulate him on this or that, and then—by oversight or OTHERWISE—the replies from the same Karl Blind gain entry to the press.

As one of the 'YOUNG MEN' who were active in the service of F. Hecker, Blind learnt that art, which is by no means rare among the South Germans, of self-defamation and creating a spurious PUBLIC OPINION about people who are essentially nonentities. In London he thought himself far enough advanced along the road or to have served long enough in the 'Democratic cause' to

---

[a] between ourselves - [b] in one way or another - [c] Heinrich Heine, *Atta Troll. Ein Sommernachtstraum*, 11. - [d] Marx presumably has in mind, first and foremost, Eduard Bronner and Karl Heinrich Schaible.

exploit for himself those arts he had acquired in the service of others.

Regarding his education, it is, as I told Lassalle during his sojourn here, that of a *Baden publican*,[a] who has read Rotteck's *Weltgeschichte*, Welker's *Staatslexikon* and Mr Struve's republican Almanac.[b]

In his manoeuvres in Germany Mr Blind enjoys the particular support of Mr *Gustav Rasch* of Berlin.

Bernhard Becker, as the former SUBEDITOR of the London *Hermann*, best knows how Blind composed *with his own fair hand* the paeans of praise to himself that appeared e.g. in the *Hermann*. He does this mostly and on average. By way of variation he will occasionally get a certain *Dr Bronner* in Bradford or his *Schaible* (see '*Herr Vogt*') via London to put their names to *his* epistles. All the agitation of this person is nothing but a tissue of lies, self-deception and hot air. In this field, however, he has no rivals. He demonstrated the height of his dexterity when Garibaldi visited London.[19] He first spread the rumour in the English papers that he was an *intimate* friend of Garibaldi. Imposing himself as is his custom, he issued 'addresses' to Garibaldi from London and you know that in his kind-hearted naivety Garibaldi will write a nice letter back to anyone. Then he descends on the Isle of Wight (before Garibaldi made his ceremonial entry to London), and 'appoints' with him the date on which Garibaldi would receive the German deputation (Blind, you see, had so arranged things as to get a few Germans, including Kinkel and *unfortunately* my friend Freiligrath as well, to elect him as the leader of a deputation) and at the same time sends mysterious hints to some London papers[c] that Garibaldi WAS '*CLOSETED*' WITH 'HIS FRIEND' (Blind) and, of course, settled some very important affairs of state with him.[52] But Blind's masterstroke is still to come. As serving-man to the European 'kings of democracy'[d] (for so he designates Mazzini, Ledru Rollin, Louis Blanc, and indeed COMPARED WITH student Blind even they are 'great men'[e]), our Baden trickster manages so to arrange things that he, as a member of the society and a leader, fetches Garibaldi from the Duke of Sutherland's, where he is staying, and escorts him in the Duke's State Carriage

---

[a] An allusion to Karl Blind's father, Johann Adam Blind who was a publican in Mannheim. - [b] G. Struve, *Die neue Zeit. Ein Volkskalender auf das Jahr 1*. - [c] 'Interview of Karl Blind with Garibaldi', *The Morning Advertiser*, No. 22726, 11 April 1864. - [d] Marx quotes Karl Blind - [e] Cf. the title of Marx and Engels' pamphlet: *The Great Men of the Exile* (present edition, Vol. 11, pp. 227-326).

to Ledru Rollin and Louis Blanc. He seizes the opportunity to have the carriage stand for a while outside Mr Blind's house for Garibaldi to 'PAY HIS COMPLIMENTS TO Madame Karl Blind'. By skilful MANAGEMENT all this even appears in *The Times*,[a] and at the moment when Garibaldi is being idolized by all London. Perhaps you recall how 'Rameau', the nephew, in Diderot's wonderful piece, bursts out in admiration at the genius of Bouret, the general tax-collector, who cunningly devised a way to disaffect his little dog from himself and make it prefer the minister! This Garibaldi-farce was Blind's Bouret-prank! It is my belief that from that time on he began *bona fide* to think himself a great man! He has really got hold of something with Schleswig-Holstein! Did you not know then that for years Blind has been deriving his chief importance from acting as a 'representative' for Schleswig-Holstein against Denmark, saying 'he' had 'forced' the German tyrants into war against Denmark,[9] and that was why friend Rasch dedicated his piece about the 'orphaned' kith and kin[b] to him! Did you not know that in the Prussian House Prof. Virchow (probably at Mr Rasch's instigation) cited Blind's great influence in the Schleswig-Holstein affair[c] as proof of what a single man can do by his own efforts for a whole nation! The shameless man had made those German jackasses believe that he had got the English to change their view of Schleswig-Holstein! His feeble leaflets about Schleswig-Holstein are just about (and that is saying something) the most stupid thing that has appeared in this LINE. (Incidentally, Mr ex-student's best friend and associate is that lout Karl Heinzen in America, whose business for 20 years past has been to slander me in a manner such as even Lassalle never experienced. I have *never* thought it worth the trouble to reply to this fellow, but I was astonished that the *Nordstern*—for a long time also a major mouthpiece for student Blind—is *constantly* printing Heinzen's filth, which is extremely hostile to the principles of the workers' party, and generally makes propaganda for Mr Heinzen.)

But Garibaldi, Schleswig-Holstein, America, Lassalle, all are for the ex-student only a pretext for puffing up his own self-importance! The modest fellow wrote in his own fair hand a short while ago to the *'Glasgow Sentinel'* that the whole of Europe

---

[a] 'General Garibaldi', *The Times*, 19 April 1864. - [b] G. Rasch, *Vom verlassenen Bruderstamm. Das dänische Regiment in Schleswig-Holstein*, Bd. 1-3; *Vom verrathenen Bruderstamm. Der Krieg in Schleswig-Holstein im Jahre 1864*. Bd. 1-2. - [c] R. Virchow's speech in the House of Representatives on 9 December 1863. In: *Stenographische Berichte über die Verhandlungen der [...] beiden Häuser des Landtages, Haus der Abgeordneten*, 13 Sitzung, Bd. 1.

(literally) was not yet divided into two hostile camps with regard to 'Karl Blind', but that a *tiers parti* existed in this respect, too![a] In *The Observer* he describes himself as 'THE ILLUSTRIOUS CHIEF OF THE GERMAN REPUBLICANS'.[b]

A few more little touches to the description of this man, who, if one views him aright, is a *highly comical character.*

After his success with Garibaldi MR KARL BLIND JOINED THE SHAKESPEARE COMMITTEE,[53] as was stated in the *Athenaeum*![c] He had now clearly progressed to the status of 'literary' representative of Germany, too!

During the skirmish in Baden (1849),[54] Struve, as he himself recounts in a piece about the 'Baden revolution',[d] sent the 'young man', as he calls Blind, as Under-Secretary to Schütz, who had been appointed Secretary, from Mainz to Paris, to rescue ex-student Blind from conflict with Brentano. The government to which Blind was directed as Under-Secretary to Secretary Schütz,—the *provisional government no longer existed* when Secretary and Under-Secretary arrived in Paris. Nevertheless, in mysterious hints in English papers, he let it be understood that he held an important diplomatic post as agent of the German 'republican government' in Paris!

In the first few years after 1849 he lived in *Belgium* with his present wife. Since this woman has children from her marriage to the dead banker (and they inherited) and she also has children by Blind (at that time still illegitimate), a court in Baden ruled that Cohen's children should be taken away from his widow Cohen because of her 'immoral' relations with ex-student Blind. The court in Brussels gave this ruling legal force in Belgium, and this caused Blind to flee to England together with his wife and the children. He later got English papers to print (and was brazen enough to boast *publicly* of it on a visit to South Germany) that he had been *expelled* from Belgium for **political** reasons![e]

His next deed you will see from the enclosed cutting, which he had printed in many London papers. What provoked it was the report disseminated in some papers that Garibaldi had declared his support for the *slave-owners*! Blind used this to extort a short letter from Garibaldi with 'CORDIAL GREETINGS FOR MRS BLIND'. You can see what lies he told Garibaldi from his remark 'I THANK YOU FOR YOUR

a 'M. Karl Blind', *North British Daily Mail*, 30 March 1863. - b Marx refers to the reports on Blind's meetings with Garibaldi published in *The Observer*, Nos. 3804, 3805 and 3806, 10, 17 and 24 April 1864. - c *The Athenaeum*, No. 1902, 9 April 1864. - d G. Struve, *Geschichte der drei Volkserhebungen in Baden*. - e 'M. Karl Blind', *North British Daily Mail*, 30 March 1863.

GOOD NEWS'.[a] What on earth could this 'GOOD NEWS' have been in October 1864? Blind was obviously writing Garibaldi the most monstrous lies about the progress of 'republicanism' in Germany, which is presumably just awaiting Blind's arrival to lash out.

The most splendid aspect of the affair is that the London paper to which Blind is a regular contributor, the *mouthpiece of the publicans* (a most appropriate context to a 'Blind'), is a fanatical supporter of the Confederates![b] And by the by, the paper— *The Morning Advertiser*—is at one and the same time the mouthpiece of spirits, the Low CHURCH (English pietism),[55] the SWELL-MOB which is concerned with gambling, PRICEFIGHTS AND SO FORTH, and the most lickspittling poodle of Palmerston's. FROM A LITERARY STANDPOINT, it cannot be counted among the English daily press and is in general only read in TAPROOMS.

So much for the man.

In Lassalle's lifetime he issued an address casting doubt on the former's integrity.[56] But Lassalle—as far as I know—did not think it worth the trouble of a reply. I was only surprised that B. Becker, who is fully aware of Blind's doings, did not then take the opportunity to blazon abroad *my revelations about Blind.*[c]

One of the reasons why I have joined the International Working Men's Association here is to expose that man. After the statements I have made against Blind, branding him as a '*deliberate liar*' and a '*falsifier of evidence*', I cannot of course further involve myself in polemic against the fellow. I reserve the right to treat him as a *figure of comedy* should the occasion arise. If I should now take his scrawl against Lassalle, which I have incidentally *not seen,* as grounds for an attack on him, people here, who know of my implacable hostility to Blind, will think that in fact I am only using Lassalle's name as a pretext for personal spite.

But do send me the (printed) declaration by the workers. I shall ensure that it gets into a *German* paper here and if student Blind then makes any further moves, perhaps he will give me the opportunity to let me fall upon him.

At all events, you may depend on it that he will be shown *no* favours. In the meantime, the best thing you can do is to disseminate my revelations about Blind as a '*deliberate liar*' and '*falsifier*' as far as possible *in Germany.* (If his scrawl about Lassalle had set any mice stirring here, a word or two about it *at all events*

---

[a] Blind published Garibaldi's letter to him in *The Morning Advertiser*, 9 November 1864. - [b] i.e. the southern slave-owning states - [c] Marx means his revelations about Blind in *Herr Vogt.*

would have reached my ears.) This would force him to break his silence and so enable me to open my mouth again concerning a fellow whom I have *publicly* declared to be *atrocious.*

Apart from anything else, it would be quite impossible for me to travel to Berlin on account of the fresh outbreak of the fearful carbuncle disease that I have been struggling against for 14 months with slight interruptions.

You may, however, be sure that I shall seize whatever opportunity I find appropriate (but you will have to leave it to me to choose whatever moment appears favourable to me) to rebuff all malicious attacks on the friend who has been prematurely taken from me.

Yours very respectfully

K. M.

First published in *International Review of Social History,* Vol. XXVII, Assen, 1982

Printed according to the journal

Published in English for the first time

15

ENGELS TO JOSEPH WEYDEMEYER [57]

IN ST LOUIS

Manchester, 24 November 1864

Dear Weydemeyer,

I was most pleased to hear from you again at long last.[58] We have been without your address for years, otherwise you would already have received a reminder from me earlier on. My address is still Ermen & Engels and will probably continue to be so for five years or so yet, unless the storm breaks in Germany. Marx' address is No. 1, Modena Villas, Maitland Park, Haverstock Hill, London, but Dr Marx, London, will also suffice if need be.

Our plump little pig Blind is showing off here in Europe, wherever he can, just as he did over there, it is the only little pleasure the poor wee creature has, and he indulges it with an assiduity worthy of a better cause and greater success. However, ever since Marx belaboured him so thoroughly in *Herr Vogt,* he has been keeping out of our range.

As far as Lassalle's flirtations with Bismarck are concerned, they are beyond dispute. The passages quoted by Blind[a] were, of course, actually uttered by Lassalle in the speech he made in Düsseldorf in his defence and published by him, so there is nothing to be done there.[15] For all his distinctive qualities, Lassalle had that Jewish respect for momentary success, which made it impossible for him to deny Louis Bonaparte his respect, or to refrain from professing such overtly Bonapartist principles as he did. Those, who were more closely acquainted with him, knew that these things were not occasional happenings. You can readily imagine that this was as disagreeable to us as it was grist to the mill of piglet Blind, and that alone would have been sufficient ground for us to have had nothing to do with all Lassalle's agitation during his lifetime, although there were other reasons, too. Nevertheless, that is all over and done with now, and we shall have to see whether his agitation was just a flash in the pan, or whether there was really something to it.

You will have heard that our poor Lupus died here on 9 May of this year. His was a loss for the party of an altogether different order from Lassalle's. We shall never again find such a steadfast fellow, who knew how to talk to the people and was always there when things were at their most difficult. For 4 long weeks he had the most terrible headaches, his German doctor[b] neglected him, and at length a vessel burst in his brain from the colossal pressure of the blood, he gradually lost consciousness and died 10 days later.

Nothing of much interest is happening here in Europe. The suppression of the Polish uprising[24] was the last decisive event; for his assistance in this, the Tsar[c] gave Bismarck permission to take Schleswig-Holstein from the Danes. It will be a long time before Poland is capable of rising again, even with help from outside, and yet Poland is quite indispensable to us. The despicable behaviour of the liberal German philistines is to blame; if those curs in the Prussian Chamber had had more insight and courage, all might be well—Austria was ready to march in support of the Poles at any time, and it was only Prussia's attitude that prevented it, and the treachery of Mr Bonaparte, who was, of course, only prepared to keep his promises to the Poles if he could do so *safely*, i.e. if he was covered by Prussia and Austria.

That war of yours over there[11] is really one of the most

---

[a] 'Ein republikanischer Protest', *Die Westliche Post*, October-beginning of November 1864. - [b] Louis Borchardt - [c] Alexander II

stupendous things that one can experience. Despite the numerous blunders made by the Northern armies (enough by the South, too), the tide of conquest is rolling slowly but surely onward, and, in the course of 1865, at all events the moment will undoubtedly come when the *organised* resistance of the South will fold up like a pocket-knife, and the warfare turn into banditry, as in the Carlist war in Spain[59] and more recently in Naples.[12] A people's war of this kind, on both sides, has not taken place since great states have been in existence, and it will, at all events, point the direction for the future of the whole of America for hundreds of years to come. Once slavery, the greatest shackle on the political and social development of the United States, has been broken, the country is bound to receive an impetus from which it will acquire quite a differed position in world history within the shortest possible time, and a use will then soon be found for the army and navy with which the war is providing it.

It was incidentally quite understandable that the North had some difficulty in providing itself with an army and generals. From the outset, the South's oligarchy had brought the country's few military forces under its control, it supplied the officers and furthermore raided the arsenals. The North found itself with no resources other than the militia, while the South had been training for years. From the outset, the South had a population accustomed to the saddle for use as light cavalry, on a scale the North could not match. The North adopted the habit, introduced from the South, of filling positions with party supporters; the South, in the midst of a revolution and with a military dictatorship, could brush that aside. Hence, all the blunders. I do not deny that Lee is a better general than any the North has, and that his latest operations around the fortified camp at Richmond[30] are masterpieces from which our glorious Prince Frederick Charles of Prussia could learn much. But, ultimately, the determined attacks of Grant and Sherman made all strategy superfluous. It is clear that Grant is sacrificing a colossal number of men, but what else could he do? I have absolutely no idea of the level of discipline in your army, its cohesion under fire, its capacity and willingness to endure hardship, and in particular the nature of its MORALE, i.e. what can be demanded of it without its becoming demoralised. With such scanty reports and no proper maps, one needs to know all this before permitting oneself any judgment on this side of the water. What does seem certain to me, however, is that the army now commanded by Sherman is the best you have, as superior to Hood's as Lee's is to Grant's.

Your field-manual and elementary tactics are, as I hear, positively French—the basic formation thus presumably being the column with intervals between platoons. What kind of field artillery do you now have? If you can enlighten me on these points, I shall be greatly obliged. What has become of the great Anneke? Since the battle at Pittsburgh-Landing was all but lost [60] because he was not supplied with everything which he should have had, according to the Prussian field-manual, he has quite vanished from my view. Of the Germans who have joined in the war, Willich appears to have given the best account of himself, whereas Sigel has UNMISTAKEABLY demonstrated his mediocrity. And Schurz, the valiant Schurz, farting away amidst the shower of bullets and shells, what foes is he demolishing now?

Apropos. The Prussian cannons that smashed Düppel[a] and Sonderburg [61] from 6,500 paces were our old long bronze 24-pounders, rifled and rebuilt as breech-loaders, 54-pound shells with 4-pound-charge! I've seen them with my own eyes.

Kindest regards to your wife.[b]

Your
F. Engels

First published abridged in *Die Neue Zeit*, Bd. 2, Nr. 33, 1906-1907 and in full in: Marx and Engels, *Works*, First Russian Edition, Vol. XXV, Moscow, 1934

Printed according to the original

Published in English in full for the first time

16

MARX TO ENGELS

IN MANCHESTER

[London,] 25 November [1864]

Dear Frederick!

Weydemeyer's letter returned enclosed (how odd it should come at the same time as the one from the countess [c]) [58] with Schweitzer's letter,[d] which I forgot to enclose yesterday.

---

[a] Danish name: Dybböl. - [b] Louise Weydemeyer - [c] Sophie von Hatzfeldt - [d] See this volume, p. 29.

I still need to hold on to the 'clipping'.[a]

The position is now as follows:

1. It was not until after I wrote to you that I saw that Blind has sent an answer to the Swabian *Beobachter* via Dr Bronner (unsigned, of course, but dated Bradford; letter, naturally, *written by Blind himself*, in which he firstly proves that by his influence over '7' million Germans he in fact shaped American politics; secondly, he has the impudence to say that the Vogt affair has been disposed of by statements from all sides.[62] So, I have grounds here for replying and referring to the 'AFFIDAVITS',[63] and, at the same time, an extract from Weydemeyer's letter would kill two birds with one stone, firstly exposing Blind's influence on America and secondly giving the old countess some kind of satisfaction as far as Lassalle is concerned.

2. These 'Republican Protests', which Blind has sent with the *same date* to St Louis, Frankfurt am Main and the London *Hermann*, are only *identical* in their general drift. In the shit in the *Hermann* and the *Frankfurter Journal*,[b] which I shall try to send you later today, this *Baden publican*[c] has simply put together the passages which were *most damaging* to ourselves, whilst across the ocean he is more insolent and resorts to bare-faced lies.

But the *real* 'POINT' is this, a 'POINT' typical of the way he manufactures his pamphlets: in the *European* edition he says that the protest comes from *American and European republicans*, whilst in the American edition he calls upon the *American government* to protest. Here we have caught the dog *in flagranti*.[d]

3. Since Lassalle is dead and can do no more harm, we must of course—as far as possible, i.e. without compromising ourselves—defend him against these petty-bourgeois scoundrels.

My plan is therefore this: to reply (briefly) in the *Swabian Beobachter*; 1. putting the record straight about the '*statements from all sides*' in the Vogt affair; 2. giving an extract from Weydemeyer's letter about Blind's influence in America; 3. exposing the fellow afresh by comparing the European and American editions of his 'Republican Protest'; finally 4. concluding that it is NOT WORTH WHILE defending Lassalle against such a comical character.

If this seems all right to you, send me a wire and I will tie the whole business up tomorrow, amongst other things in order to have some peace with the 'old girl'. I said in my letter to her, by

---

[a] from *Die Westliche Post* with Blind's article 'Ein republikanischer Protest' - [b] *Neue Frankfurter Zeitung* - [c] See this volume, p. 33. - [d] red-handed

the way, that Lassalle only has himself to blame for being kicked by that jackass, because, although I strongly and repeatedly urged him to do so, he did not give all possible publicity in Germany to my denunciation of Blind in *Herr Vogt.*[a]

Salut.

Your
K. M.

First published in *Der Briefwechsel zwischen F. Engels und K. Marx*, Bd. 3, Stuttgart, 1913

Printed according to the original

Published in English for the first time

17

MARX TO SOPHIE VON HATZFELDT

IN BERLIN

[London,] Saturday, 26 November 1864

My dear Countess,

These few lines in the greatest of haste (there being just time before the last post goes) to inform you that I have been fortunate enough to be vouchsafed the opportunity to get a hold on Blind *immediately* and deliver him a vigorous kick for his attack on our Lassalle.[62]

I shall send you my attack on him on Monday which will appear in the form of a short letter to the Stuttgart *Beobachter.*[b] You will then learn of the circumstances of the case, too.

Yours very respectfully
K. M.

First published in: Marx and Engels, *Works*, Second Russian Edition, Vol. 31, Moscow, 1963

Printed according to the original

Published in English for the first time

---

[a] See this volume, p. 30. - [b] K. Marx, 'To the Editor of the Stuttgart *Beobachter*'.

18

MARX TO SOPHIE VON HATZFELDT

IN BERLIN

London, 28 November 1864

My dear Countess,

From the enclosed[a] you will see the circumstances that have presented me with the opportunity to renew my tussle with ex-student Blind and, at the same time, deliver him a kick in the name of Lassalle.

You must arrange for publication in the papers at your disposal, but *not before two days have elapsed* after you receive this, so that Mayer of Swabia—i.e. the editor of the *Beobachter* in Stuttgart— has no excuse for refusing it.[64]

Yours very respectfully

K. Marx

First published in: Marx and Engels, *Works*, Second Russian Edition, Vol. 31, Moscow, 1963

Printed according to the original

Published in English for the first time

19

MARX TO JOSEPH WEYDEMEYER[57]

IN ST LOUIS

London, 29 November 1864
1 Modena Villas, Maitland Park,
Haverstock Hill, N. W.

Dear Weiwi,

The whole household and myself were extraordinarily pleased to hear from you and your family again. My wife asserts that she wrote to yours[b] *last* and is thus expecting to have the first letter back from her.

---

[a] K. Marx, 'To the Editor of the Stuttgart *Beobachter*'. - [b] Louise Weydemeyer

I am, at the same time, sending you by mail 4 copies of a printed 'Address',[a] of which I am the author. The newly established INTERNATIONAL Workers' Committee, in whose name it has been put out, is not without significance. Its *English* members consist chiefly of the heads of the TRADE-UNIONS here, in other words, the real worker-kings of London, the same people who organised that gigantic reception for Garibaldi and who, by that monster meeting in St James's Hall (under Bright's chairmanship), prevented Palmerston declaring *war on the United States*, which he was on the point of doing.[19] On the French side, the members are unimportant figures, but they are the direct spokesmen of the leading 'workers' in Paris. There is likewise a link with the Italian associations, which recently held their congress in Naples.[22] Although I have been systematically refusing to participate in any way whatsoever in all the 'organisations', etc. for years now, I accepted *this time* because it concerns a matter by means of which it is possible to have a significant influence.

For the past 14 months I have been suffering almost constantly from carbuncles, which often threatened my life. More or less cured now.

Engels will have written to you of the loss of our friend Lupus.[b]

Curiously enough, I received a letter from Berlin last Friday, in which the old Hatzfeldt woman urged me to defend Lassalle against Blind's 'Republican Protest'.[42] The next day I received your letter to Engels, containing the *much amended American* edition of the same garbage. By a third coincidence, I was, at the same time, sent 2 numbers of the Swabian *Beobachter* (from Stuttgart) which I never see otherwise. In the first number the editor[c] was poking fun at a letter from Mr Blind to the American nation which had been translated from the English by 'Mr Blind' and sent to him and to other South German editors; in it, '*almost at official request*', as he puts it, he gives his inexpert opinion on Lincoln's election, etc.[d] In the same number, the editor said that one can see from my book attacking Vogt[e] what Blind's vanity leads to, etc. Whereupon, Blind sent the *enclosed* reply through his man-of-straw, Dr Bronner of Bradford, 1. setting out just how powerful his influence in America was, and 2. having the impudence to say that the Vogt affair was 'a put-up-job'.[62] This then enabled me (using your letter and copying the passages relating to Blind) to put out the

---

[a] 'Inaugural Address of the Working Men's International Association'. - [b] Wilhelm Wolff - [c] Karl Mayer - [d] 'Bescheidenheit—ein Ehrenkleid', *Der Beobachter*, No. 245, 21 October 1864. - [e] *Herr Vogt*

statement[a] as desired by the old Hatzfeldt woman against that clown, without identifying myself with those aspects of Lassalle's agitation[b] which are not to my liking. Write soon.

Your
K. Marx

The source of Blind's boastful epistle which I am copying out for you is No. 268 of the *Beobachter* (Stuttgart), 17 Nov., 1864.

It is absolutely essential that you write me a few lines, *suitable for publication*, about Mr Blind's *American* influence.

First published abridged in *Die Neue Zeit*, Bd. 2, Nr. 33, 1906-1907 and in full in: Marx and Engels, *Works*, First Russian Edition, Vol. XXV, Moscow, 1934

Printed according to the original

Published in English in full for the first time

20

MARX TO LUDWIG KUGELMANN[65]

IN HANOVER

London, 29 November 1864
1 Modena Villas, Maitland Park,
Haverstock Hill, N. W.

Dear Friend,

Today you will receive from me by post 6 copies of the 'ADDRESS OF THE WORKINGMEN'S INTERNATIONAL ASSOCIATION',[c] of which I am the author. Please be so good as to convey a copy with my kindest regards to Madame Markheim (Fulda). Give one to Mr Miquel as well.

The Association—or rather its Committee—is important because the leaders of the London TRADE-UNIONS belong to it, the same people who organised that enormous reception for Garibaldi and thwarted Palmerston's plan for a war with the United States by means of the monster meeting in St James's Hall.[19] The leaders of the Parisian workers are also in contact with it.

---

[a] K. Marx, 'To the Editor of the Stuttgart *Beobachter*'. - [b] See this volume, pp. 40-42. - [c] 'Inaugural Address of the Working Men's International Association'

In the last few years I have been much afflicted with illness (e.g., in the last 14 months by a recurrence of carbuncles). My private circumstances have improved in consequence of a legacy from the death of my mother.[a]

I think that my book on capital (60 sheets) will at last be ready for the press next year.[66]

You will doubtless understand the reasons for *not* allowing myself to become involved in Lassalle's movement in his lifetime, without my spelling them out in detail. However, that cannot deter me—the more so since persons close to him are urging me to do so—from taking up his defence, now that he is dead, against such despicable curs as the clamorous K. Blind.[b]

I am afraid that in mid-spring or early summer of next year there will be war between Italy, Austria and France. This will be very damaging for the movement in France and England, which is growing significantly.

I hope to hear from you soon.

Yours very respectfully

K. Marx

First published in *Die Neue Zeit*, Bd. 2, Nr. 1, Stuttgart, 1901-1902

Printed according to the original

21

MARX TO LION PHILIPS[67]

IN ZALT-BOMMEL

London, 29 November 1864
1 Modena Villas, Maitland Park,
Haverstock Hill

Dear Uncle,

I hope that you are in the best of health despite the ABOMINABLE weather. All is well here. Except that, to the great alarm of the whole family, I had a most malignant carbuncle below the left breast at the beginning of this month, which kept me in great pain for 2-3 weeks. Other than that, everything has been going well.

---

[a] Henrietta Marx (died 30 November 1863) - [b] See this volume, pp. 40-42.

The trade crisis, which I predicted to you long before its actual arrival,[a] has by this time long since lost its edge, although its consequences in the manufacturing districts proper are still very considerable. On the other hand, I believe a political crisis is to be expected in the spring or early summer. Bonaparte has again reached the point where he will have to make war again if he is to raise a loan. The Venetian business is being kept open (I am acquainted with some of the agents there) so that it can provide a point of contact if need be.[68] It is possible that Bonaparte will again find a way out, and then he will keep the peace (for he is no REAL Napoleon), but that is rather improbable.

The enclosed printed 'Address'[b] is written by myself. The matter hangs together like this: in September the Parisian workers sent a delegation to the London workers to demonstrate support for Poland. On that occasion, an international Workers' Committee was formed. The matter is not without importance because 1. in London the same people are at the head who organised the gigantic reception for Garibaldi and, by their monster meeting with Bright in St James's Hall, *prevented war with the United States*.[19] In a word, these are the real workers' leaders in London, with one or two exceptions all workers themselves. 2. On the Parisian side, Mr Tolain (*ouvrier*[c] himself, as well) *et* Co. are at the head, i.e., the same people who were prevented by a mere intrigue on the part of Garnier-Pagès, Carnot, etc., from entering the Corps législatif at the last elections in Paris as representatives of the workers there,[4] and 3. on the Italian side, it has been joined by the representatives of the 4-500 Italian workers' clubs which held their general congress in Naples some weeks ago,[22] an event which even *The Times* considered important enough to merit a few dozen lines in the paper.[d]

Courtesy toward the French and the Italians, who always require florid language, has obliged me to include a few superfluous turns of phrase in the preamble to the 'Rules',[e] though not in the 'Address'.[23]

A few days ago I received a letter from America from my friend Weydemeyer, Colonel in the regiment stationed at St Louis (Missouri). Amongst other things, he writes—and these are his exact words:

---

[a] Marx to Lion Philips, 17 August 1864 (present edition, Vol. 41). - [b] 'Inaugural Address of the Working Men's International Association'. - [c] worker - [d] *The Times*, No. 25021, 4 November 1864. - [e] K. Marx, 'Provisional Rules of the Association'.

'We are regrettably being detained here at St Louis, since, in view of the many "conservative" elements here, a military force is a continuing necessity to prevent a break-out and the possible release of the numerous Southern prisoners.... The whole campaign in Virginia is a BLUNDER, which has cost us innumerable men. But for all that, the South will not be able to hold out much longer: it has sent its last man into battle and has no fresh army to call upon. The present invasion of Missouri, like the incursions into Tennessee, has only the character of a RAID, a foray: there can be no thought of a lasting re-occupation of districts that have been lost.'[a]

When you reflect, my dear Uncle, how at the time of Lincoln's election 3¹/₂ years ago it was only a matter of making *no further concessions* to the slave-owners, whereas now the avowed aim, which has in part already been realised, is the *abolition of slavery*, one has to admit that *never* has such a gigantic revolution occurred with such rapidity. It will have a highly beneficial influence on the whole world.

At a public MEETING this week the fellow-member of our race *Benjamin Disraeli* has again made a dreadful laughing-stock of himself by assuming the mantle of guardian angel of the HIGH CHURCH[69] and CHURCH RATES, repudiating criticism in religious affairs.[b] He furnishes the best evidence of how a great talent unaccompanied by conviction creates rogues, albeit gold-braided and 'RIGHT HONORABLE' ones.

Those jackasses in Germany have again made a proper laughing-stock of themselves over the Müller affair,[36] with ex-parson Kinkel at their head.

With kindest regards from the whole family to you and from me to Jettchen, Dr, Fritz[c] *et* Co.

Ever your faithful nephew

K. M.

First published in *International Review of Social History*, Vol. I, Part 1, Assen, 1956

Printed according to the original

Published in English in full for the first time

---

[a] Marx quotes from J. Weydemeyer's letter to Engels written in October 1864. - [b] An account of Disraeli's speech at the meeting in Oxford on 25 November 1864 was published in *The Times*, No. 25040, 26 November 1864. - [c] Henriette van Anroij, Dr van Anroij and Friedrich Philips

22

MARX TO ENGELS[29]

IN MANCHESTER

[London,] 2 December 1864

DEAR FRED,

THANKS FOR THE *GUARDIAN*.[a]

I did send on a few COPIES of the 'Address'[b] to E. Jones afterwards, with a letter to him saying that he would probably receive one from you first. He writes today that he has neither seen nor heard anything from you. His address is 55, not 52, Cross Street. He says in his letter that, when the Assizes are over, he will form a branch association in Manchester amongst his acquaintances.

Could you by any chance dig up the address of the musician *Petzler* (maybe from the Manchester directory, or the Schiller Association[28])? He has *a lot of* contacts among the Manchester workers, and without ANY INTERVENTION ON YOUR PART I could put him in touch with E. Jones *from here*. You would only need to send me Petzler's address.

The worst thing about agitation of this kind is that one gets very BOTHERED as soon as one becomes involved in it. E.g. Address to Lincoln now on the agenda again, and again I had to compose the thing[c] (which is far more difficult than writing a proper work)—so that the phraseology to which that kind of writing is limited, is at least distinguishable from vulgar-democratic phraseology.[70] Fortunately, Mr Fox is doing the Polish business which is coming up in connection with 29 November, the anniversary of the Polish revolution of 1830.[71]

In the Committee, since the address for Lincoln is to be handed over to Adams, *some* of the English wanted to have the deputation introduced BY A MEMBER OF PARLIAMENT—as is CUSTOMARY. This desire was suppressed by the majority OF the ENGLISH and the unanimity of the continentals, and it was declared instead that such OLD ENGLISH CUSTOMS OUGHT TO BE ABOLISHED. On the other hand: M. Le Lubez, as a real *crapaud*,[d] wanted the address to be directed not to Lincoln but TO THE

AMERICAN PEOPLE. I made him look suitably foolish and made it clear to the English that FRENCH DEMOCRATIC ETIQUETTE is not worth a FARTHING more than MONARCHICAL ETIQUETTE.

Apropos. Naturally it is impossible to have a movement here without its own press-organ. *The Bee-Hive* (weekly, organ of the TRADES-UNIONS) was therefore declared to be the organ of the Association. By a stroke of ill-luck, to which the workers are particularly susceptible, a scoundrel called *George Potter* (in the BUILDING STRIKES[72] he acted as MOUTHPIECE in *The Times*, but with articles written not by *himself* but by *others*) has installed himself as MANAGER with a clique of shareholders, who have so far formed the majority. The COMMITTEE, whose English members are mostly *Bee-Hive* shareholders (a share costs only 5s., and no one can have more than 5 votes, even if he holds 5,000 shares; thus 1 vote per share up to a maximum of 5), has therefore decided that we should set up a share-fund here which will enable us to create shareholders AND TO SWAMP THE OLD MAJORITY. I would appreciate it if you would let us have a contribution for this purpose as well. The whole operation must, of course, be confined to the close friends of the members of the Committee, as otherwise counter-measures would be promptly taken by the other side (i.e. before the GENERAL MEETING OF SHAREHOLDERS which is not far off now).

Besides the *Hermann*, there was also another little paper here, the *Londoner Anzeiger*, which belongs to the worthy Jewish bookseller Bender. It is trying to build itself up as a competitor to the *Hermann*, as the editorship has been taken over by a certain L. Otto von Breidtschwerdt, although he writes under the name of L. Otto. I shall hardly become directly involved in the thing at all, as I had my fill with the *Volk*, but it is good for reprinting statements in London as soon as they appear in the German newspapers, e.g. like the one against Blind.[a]

This Otto first got to know Eccarius, at whose suggestion he became a German member of the INTERNATIONAL COMMITTEE. He is a Swabian, Stuttgarter born and bred. Quite a young fellow, ABOUT 27 OR 28. Very much like my wife's elder brother.[b] Began as a cadet in the Austrian army, where he learnt all kinds of languages and was stationed all over the place. Subsequently studied in Tübingen. As a person, he is a very pleasant, witty fellow and well-mannered. His head is still stuffed full of petty Swabianisms and Germanic nonsense. For all that, very good knowledge and ability. But he

---

[a] K. Marx, 'To the Editor of the Stuttgart *Beobachter*'. - [b] Ferdinand von Westphalen

seems to me to have more inclination than a gift for writing; dull, doctrinaire. He is useful as a go-between with South Germany and especially the Land of the Swabians. Also writes in the *Augsburger*[a] from time to time, which is, incidentally, entirely what you would expect from the Vogt standpoint.

I wrote to Mr Klings that it was difficult, but also quite unnecessary, to decide between Moses and Bernhard.[b] Both were honest and both incompetent. I said that, at the present moment, it was neither here nor there who has the title of President. When the time became decisive, there would be no difficulty in finding the right people.[c]

I am very much afraid I can feel another carbuncle starting on my right hip. Allen knows nothing about it as I have been treating myself for some time. If I went to him now about the arsenic business, which after all you cannot start without a doctor and to which he might perhaps not even agree, he would give me the most dreadful dressing down for having been carbuncling for so long behind his back!!

YOURS

K. M.

In his reply to Mayer the Swabian (via his man-of-straw Bronner),[d] Blind states that Lincoln and Frémont were fighting for his vote because it would decide the ELECTION.[62] And in an American newspaper, *The Radical Democrat*,[e] that *he* was responsible for the *Polish* revolution.

First published in *Der Briefwechsel zwischen F. Engels und K. Marx*, Bd. 3, Stuttgart, 1913

Printed according to the original

Published in English in full for the first time

---

a *Allgemeine Zeitung* - b Moses Hess and Bernhard Becker - c See this volume, p. 2. - d [K. Blind,] Article marked 'Bradford, 25. Oct.', *Der Beobachter*, No. 268, 17 November 1864 - e *Missouri Democrat*

23

MARX TO ENGELS

IN MANCHESTER

[London,] 8 December 1864

Dear Engels,

You will find enclosed

1. *Free Press.*[a]
2. Swabian *Beobachter.*

(With the latter, I have managed to get the fellow at least to adopt an ironical tone towards Blind again, whereas, as a result of the letter transmitted by Bronner,[b] he was so bowled over by Blind's boasting—I have sent the scrawl to *Weydemeyer*—that he absolutely drew in his horns and paid compliments to the '*excellent man*'. Incidentally, the editor—*hinc illae lacrimae*[c]—is the man whom I referred to in *Herr Vogt* as the 'garrulous Swabian, Karl Mayer',[d] and who is moreover the son of that Mayer the Swabian so incessantly derided by Heine.[73])

3. Letter enclosed from Red Becker.[e] I had, you see, sent a copy of the statement[f] to the *Rheinische Zeitung*. Please return Becker's letter to me.[74]

Apropos Liebknecht. At the end of the year he is, of course, in a very tight spot. I have sent him money several times in the course of the last six months and now I want to send his wife[g] something in the form of a Christmas present for the children, since I know they are in dire straits. I would appreciate it if you would make a contribution, too. But you must let me know quickly, as *periculum in mora.*[h] I would then send the whole lot to Frau Liebknecht at the same time.

Salut.

Your

K. M.

First published abridged in *Der Briefwechsel zwischen F. Engels und K. Marx*, Bd. 3, Stuttgart, 1913 and in full in *MEGA*, Abt. III, Bd. 3, Berlin, 1930

Printed according to the original

Published in English for the first time

---

[a] Presumably *The Free Press*, No. 12, 7 December 1864, with the article [C.D. Collet,] 'Russia's Designs on the Pope'. - [b] See this volume, p.51. - [c] hence these tears (Terence, *Andria*, I, 1, 99) - [d] See present edition, Vol. 17, pp. 120 and 205. - [e] Hermann Heinrich Becker - [f] K. Marx, 'To the Editor of the Stuttgart *Beobachter*'. - [g] Ernestine Liebknecht - [h] danger in delay (Livy, *History of Rome*, Vol. XXXVIII, Chap. 25)

24

MARX TO ENGELS[33]

IN MANCHESTER

[London,] 10 December 1864

DEAR FRED,

MY COMPLIMENT TO MRS LIZZY.[a]

You had already given me your PRIVATE ADDRESS some time ago, but not the 'FIRM' to which to write. I am very glad to have it now, as I sometimes find it desirable to drop you a few lines ON SATURDAYS.

The £5 for Wilhelm[b] is already on its way to Berlin today.

You have not sent me back the Becker.[74] However cunningly 'the Red' fancies he has extricated himself from the matter, his letter is a DOCUMENT WHICH ONE FINE MORNING HE MAY FIND TO TURN UP for unforeseen purposes. The old Hatzfeldt woman will, incidentally, ensure that the statement[c] gets to the right person.[64]

WHAT ABOUT SHERMAN'S EXPEDITION?[75]

Apropos. Your POOR-HOUSE *Purdy* is said to have published an absolutely disgraceful document during the COTTON-FAMINE,[40] recommending reducing support to a minimum, on the grounds that the HEALTH OF THE COTTON-OPERATIVES was said to have improved; as a result of this, FAMINE DISEASES are said to have broken out in the EAST OF LANCASHIRE. (That was in the early days of the COTTON-FAMINE.) Do you know anything about it? And, in general, can you obtain for me the OFFICIAL PAPERS in Manchester (of the Committee,[d] etc.) relating to the COTTON-FAMINE?

Lothario Bucher, whom Lassalle appointed executor to his will and to whom he left £150 a year pension, has, as you probably already know, gone over to Bismarck's camp. Baron Izzy[e] would perhaps have done the same himself as 'Minister of Labour', Marquis Posa to Philipp II of the Uckermark,[f] but not IN THE SMALL WAY OF Lothario, with whom the Hatzfeldt woman has fallen out and who can now shake hands with Edgar Bauer and the Prussian consul in Milan, Mr R. Schramm. The Prussians were looking for a post for Mr Schramm 'where yer don't need no exam'.[g] I also

---

a Lizzy Burns - b Wilhelm Liebknecht - c K. Marx, 'To the Editor of the Stuttgart *Beobachter*'. - d See this volume, p. 27. - e Lassalle - f Marquis Posa and Philipp II are characters from Schiller's *Don Karlos*. By 'Philipp II of the Uckermark' Marx means William I. - g Berlin dialect in the original here: 'wo ken Examen nicht netig.'

fancy Mr Rodbertus' intentions are 'none too 'onourable' because he is claiming to 'have *entirely divorced* the social question *from politics*',[a] a sure sign that he has got the ministerial itch. What a contemptible gang, all that riff-raff from Berlin, Brandenburg and Pomerania!

I fancy there is a SECRET UNDERSTANDING between Prussia, Russia and France for THE WAR AGAINST AUSTRIA IN NEXT SPRING. Venetia will, of course, provide the WAR-CRY.[68] The Austrians are behaving with abysmal cowardice and stupidity. This ensues from Francis Joseph himself interfering personally in Austrian politics. Buol-Schauenstein, etc., all the sensible *hommes d-état*,[b] are obliged to keep their traps shut, and the Russian agents, such notorious fellows as the present Austrian FOREIGN MINISTER,[c] are giving all the orders. For all that, the Austrians' behaviour would be inexplicable, unless these fellows either have faith in Prussia's perfidious promises or are determined to accept the long-standing promise of compensation in Turkey.

What do you say to Collet's profound discoveries—based on Urquhart—about Nebuchadnezzar and the Russians' Assyrian ancestry, and the further discovery, which is cited as 'Urquhart's', that IN ITALY THE POPE IS THE ONLY REAL THING?[d]

Today's *The Miner and Workman's Advocate*—the *Moniteur*[e] of the mineworkers in England and Wales—is printing the whole of my 'Address'.[f] The London 'BRICKLAYERS' (over 3,000 men) have announced they are joining the International Association, and they are fellows who have *never* before joined a MOVEMENT.

There was a SUB-COMMITTEE[21] meeting last Tuesday,[g] at which Mr Peter Fox (his real name is P. Fox André) presented his address on Poland[71] to us. (This kind of thing is always dealt with beforehand in the SUBCOMMITTEE before going to the GENERAL COMMITTEE.) The piece is not badly written and Fox has endeavoured to apply the concept of 'class', at least a semblance of it, although it is normally alien to him. His real forte is FOREIGN POLICY, and it is only as a propagandist of atheism that he has had dealings with the WORKING CLASSES AS SUCH.

But easy though it is to get the English workers to accept a rational approach, one has to be all the more careful the moment

---

a Marx quotes almost literally Liebknecht's letter to him of 2 December 1864. - b statesmen - c Alexander Mensdorff-Pouilly - d [C.D. Collet,] 'Russia's Designs on the Pope', *The Free Press*, No. 12, 7 December 1864. - e mouthpiece - f K. Marx, 'Inaugural Address of the Working Men's International Association', *The Miner and Workman's Advocate*, No. 93, 10 December 1864. - g 6 December

men of letters, members of the bourgeoisie or semi-literary people become involved in the movement. Fox, like his friend Beesly (Professor of Political Economy at the University of London, he took the chair at the founding MEETING in St Martin's Hall^a) and other 'DEMOCRATS', have a fanatical 'love' of France, which, as far as FOREIGN POLICY is concerned, they extend not only to Napoleon I but even to Boustrapa,[76] as opposed to what they call, not without justice, the English aristocratic tradition, and as a continuation of what they call the English democratic tradition of 1791/92. WELL! Not content in his address (which, incidentally, is not to appear as an address from the whole Association but as an address from the *English* section concerning the POLISH QUESTION, *endorsed* by the whole Committee) with telling the Poles, which is true, that the French people has been traditionally more sympathetic towards them than the English, Mr Fox WINDS UP HIS ADDRESS mainly by consoling the Poles with the passionate friendship that THE ENGLISH WORKING CLASSES have conceived FOR THE FRENCH DEMOCRATS. I opposed this and unfolded a historically irrefutable tableau of the constant French betrayal of Poland from Louis XV to Bonaparte III. At the same time, I pointed out how thoroughly *inappropriate* it was that the ANGLO-FRENCH-ALLIANCE should appear as the 'core' of the INTERNATIONAL ASSOCIATION, albeit in a democratic version. To cut matters short, Fox's address was accepted by the SUBCOMMITTEE on condition that he altered the '*TAIL*' in accordance with my suggestions. Jung, the SWISS SECRETARY (from French Switzerland), declared that, as a MINORITY on the GENERAL COUNCIL, he would move that the address be rejected as ALTOGETHER 'bourgeois'.[77]

Our *Major Wolff* has been locked up by the Piedmontese for the moment in the fortress of Alexandria.

Louis Blanc has written to the General Secretary *Cremer* that he approves the 'Address' and regrets not having been able to attend the St Martin's Hall MEETING, etc. ALTOGETHER, the sole purpose of his letter is to get him co-opted an HONORARY MEMBER. Foreseeing that attempts of this kind would be made, I had, however, fortunately got the BY-LAW accepted that no one (except workers' SOCIETIES) could be *invited* to join and that nobody at all could be an *honorary member*.[78]

Salut.

Your

K. M.

---

^a See this volume, pp. 15-16.

Gumpert will get the photograph as soon as he sends me the long-promised one of his wife.

First published in *Der Briefwechsel zwischen F. Engels und K. Marx*, Bd. 3, Stuttgart, 1913

Printed according to the original

Published in English in full for the first time

25

MARX TO ENGELS

IN MANCHESTER

[London,] 22 December 1864

Dear FREDERICK,

In great haste. Please send Becker's letter back to me.[a] I hope you have not lost it.

Happy New Year!

Your

K. M.

First published in *MEGA*, Abt. III, Bd. 3, Berlin, 1930

Printed according to the original

Published in English for the first time

26

MARX TO SOPHIE VON HATZFELDT

IN BERLIN

[Draft]

London, 22 December 1864
1 Modena Villas, Maitland Park,
Haverstock Hill

My dear Countess,

A few days ago, a friend in Hamburg sent me the *Nordstern* containing my statement against Blind,[b] duly emended with misprints.

---

[a] See this volume, pp. 52, 53. - [b] K. Marx, 'To the Editor of the Stuttgart *Beobachter*'.

It was at your request that I made this statement, although its composition did not come easily to me as I did *not* agree with Lassalle's *political tactics*. However, all my scruples were removed by Blind's shameless outburst against the deceased in the *St Louis 'Westliche Post'*.[44] I had not the slightest idea which papers you would send the statement to. The *Nordstern* was the furthest from my mind. Mr Bruhn has now seized upon this opportunity to make an 'indecent gesture' in my direction, by hinting to his readers in the commentaries that I had sought access to his emporium through the back door and had been granted it as an act of extreme graciousness only because a third party had intervened especially on my behalf.[64] I have no doubt that his accomplice in America[a] will make use of this. Is it Mr Bruhn's desire that I should be forced into exposing him publicly for the conceited nonentity that he is?

If Bruhn, Bernhard Becker and *tutti quanti* set out to oppose me and my efforts in any manner whatsoever that I consider harmful to the workers' movement itself, a storm will break about these gentlemen's heads that will take their breath away. Reasons of long-standing personal friendship and party interest, which held me back vis-à-vis Lassalle, can no longer have the slightest force in respect of these *dii minorum gentium*.[b] This I am stating once and for all, so that I cannot later be charged with ambiguity or inconsiderateness.

In no circumstances, do I wish the *Eighteenth Brumaire* to be published, and, if steps have already been taken to this end, they are to be checked forthwith.[79]

I scarcely dare express any good wishes for the New Year, knowing as I do that the old year has left you, my dear Countess, only with memories.

Yours very respectfully

K. M.

First published in: *F. Lassalle. Nachgelassene Briefe und Schriften,* Bd. III, Stuttgart-Berlin, 1922

Printed according to the original

Published in English for the first time

---

[a] Karl Blind - [b] Literally: minor gods; here, creatures of a lesser kind.

27

MARX TO CARL SIEBEL

IN ELBERFELD

London, 22 December 1864
1 Modena Villas, Maitland Park,
Haverstock Hill

Dear Siebel,

A Happy New Year!

You will perhaps have seen that Engels and I have agreed to become contributors to the Berlin *Social-Demokrat*.[80] Nevertheless—this *entre nous*[a]—either that paper will have to dissociate itself from the apotheosis of Lassalle, or we shall dissociate ourselves from it. But the poor devils have a lot to contend with.

You will have received the 'Addresses'[b] sent to you and have no doubt guessed I am the author. For the sake of the movement *here*, it is important for us that German workers' associations should join the Central Committee here. (As has happened in many cases with the Italians and the French.) Now Liebknecht has written to me that the Berlin printers' association will be joining, but that it is very doubtful whether the 'General Association of German Workers'[2] will join, on account of the intrigues of Mr Bernhard Becker, whose importance was *'invented'* by Lassalle. (*Entre nous* this is perhaps Lassalle's *only invention*.)[81]

Today I wrote the old Hatzfeldt woman a kind of threatening letter, *sub rosa,*[c] of course.

Now it would be highly desirable for you to pay a brief visit to Solingen to explain on my behalf to the cutler, *Klings,* how exceedingly important it is that the Association of German Workers should decide to join the INTERNATIONAL ASSOCIATION at its congress in Düsseldorf on 27 December of this year.[82] You might surreptitiously hint that, for such nonentities as B. Becker, etc., what matters is, naturally, not the cause but the *'infiniment petit',*[d] i.e., their own persons. But such a hint must be dropped *diplomatically,* without implicating me.

You understand that it is necessary that the General Association of German Workers should join only for a start, on account of our

---

[a] between ourselves - [b] K. Marx, 'Inaugural Address of the Working Men's International Association'. - [c] allusively (see previous letter) - [d] infinitely small

opponents here. At a later date, the whole organisation of this association will have to be broken up, as its basis is fundamentally wrong.

If you do not now at last write me a few lines, I shall presume that you have become totally disloyal to me, and will proclaim you excommunicated.

Your

K. M.

First published in *Deutsche Zeitung,* Nr. 473, 16 October 1920

Printed according to the original

Published in English for the first time

1865

28

MARX TO HERMANN JUNG [83]

IN LONDON

Manchester,[84] [about 8 January 1865]
58 Dover Street, Oxford Street

My dear Jung,

I felt rather shocked at reading in the 'Beehive' and the 'Miner' of this week that at our last Committee-sitting

'It was *unanimously* agreed to invite Messrs Beesly, *Grossmith*, Beales and Harrison, to the soirée which is to be held on the 16th'.[a]

I do not mention the mere anachronism, that no such resolution was taken on *last Tuesday's* sitting.[b]

What I object to is the positive falsehood that *Mr Grossmith* was invited.

This *Grossmith*, although he seldom or never attends our sittings, figures as a member of the Committee under all our addresses.

How could *our* Committee invite a *member of our Committee* to a soirée *given by our Committee*? Shall this, perhaps, form a sort of *premium* to be gained by regular absence from our weekly séances?

Since I cannot return to London before the end of next week, you'll much oblige me

By asking at next Tuesday's sitting, who is the *writer* of the report in the 'Beehive' and the 'Miner'?

Who empowered that writer to make our Committee the *'unconscious'* instrument of exalting *Mr Grossmith*?

You will understand at once how important it is to nip in the bud any attempt at turning our Committee into the tool of local ambitions, or any sort of intrigues.

---

[a] *The Bee-Hive Newspaper*, No. 169, 7 January 1865; *The Miner and Workman's Advocate*, No. 97, 7 January 1865. - [b] on 3 January

You will oblige me, by informing me, under the above
address,—and supposing you to make the interpellation—what
answer was given to you.[85]
Salut et fraternité.

K. Marx

First published in: Marx and Engels,
Works, First Russian Edition, Vol. XXV,
Moscow, 1934

Reproduced from the original for
the first time

29

ENGELS TO RUDOLF ENGELS[10]

IN BARMEN

[Manchester,] 10 January 1865

Dear Rudolf,

My view of the American war[11] is this: the South is gradually
becoming exhausted and cannot replace its armies. The North has
not yet mobilised the half of its resources. The South is limited to
defence, so much so in fact that counter-attacks such as, e.g.,
Longstreet undertook in the Shenandoah Valley, are now a thing
of the past. Hood attempted yet another one, but, in so doing,
revealed his own impotence and decided the whole campaign at
one stroke.[86] The North is superior to its Southern opponents at
all points and, furthermore, has Sherman's 40,000 men at its
disposal who can go wheresoever they please, everywhere destroying the South's forces, communications, resources and supplies
deep in the South's own territory.[75] Charleston is certain to fall in
4-6 weeks at the latest, once Sherman has encircled it on land.[87]
The South has but one army left, that at Richmond.[30] That will
assuredly be quite decisively beaten in the present year, and with
that the defence of the South *by armies* will be at an end. A
guerrilla war, brigandry, etc., may then ensue and will probably do
so into next year.

If the South arms its Negroes, that will be so much the better
for the North. However, they will take good care not to. At the
last moment, if at all. The Negroes are not so stupid as to allow
themselves to be massacred for the whip that flays their backs.

There will certainly still be moments when things look better for the South than they do now, but we have seen that happen too often before, and I shall not be deceived by that. Such moments are merely *a respite.*

I do not believe we shall get cotton from America; but I do believe we shall see a temporary fall. Cotton is at present so subject to speculation that prices are affected by every vicissitude of public opinion. There are, moreover, 500,000 bales in Liverpool, and the people here do have a tendency to fly to extremes immediately and shout: the South is done for, is bound to surrender in 14 days, etc.—a rise is thereby inconceivable. We shall be at the mercy of whatever news we receive, though always with the proviso that we know the STOCK in Liverpool to be double what it was last year. I also believe we shall see the year 1865 close below present prices, as we must expect more cotton from all parts.

Your
Friedrich

First published in *Deutsche Revue*, Jg. 46, Bd. II, 1921

Printed according to the original

Published in English in full for the first time

30

MARX TO HIS DAUGHTER JENNY

IN LONDON

Manchester, 11 January 1865
58 Dover Street

My sweet child,

I wanted to leave Manchester tomorrow, but I'll be hardly able to do so before Sunday (15th Jan.) next.[84] Ernest Jones, whom I am anxious to speak, is busily engaged in the neighbouring towns and has invited me (and Engels) for next *Friday* evening when he'll be at home. I have not yet seen him, and could not see him before that day. This is one cause of delay. There are others, but at all events I shall not stay longer than until Sunday.

The German translation of the 'Address to the Working Classes'[a] has been reprinted in the *Mainzer Zeitung,* the 'Address to Lincoln'[b] in the *Berliner Reform* and the London *Hermann.* The latter honour is probably due to Mr Juch's anxiety lest his rival Bender might monopolize 'our protection'.

The weather here was abominable. Today 'the sun shines', as Müller has it, but its rays are reflected by the ice drops covering the dirty streets. Even the sunbeams must here always have something disagreeable to fall upon.

I have not yet seen a Borchardt, and as to the Gumperts, I had only a few minutes' conversation with the Dr yesterday evening.

On my arrival I did not find Frederick, but in his stead a letter informing me that he would be back from fox-hunting at 6 o'clock. Meanwhile he had taken all precautionary measures for making my *'entrée joyeuse'*[c] (with your great historical knowledge you'll not be at a loss as to the *'entrée joyeuse'*). Whether his change of domicile is an improvement, seems a rather debatable question. At all events, the people are less impudent.

Apropos. There is much *'chronique scandaleuse'* just now in the Freiligrath world, as far as it is connected with the General Bank of Switzerland. There has appeared a pamphlet at Genève, disclosing the scandalous mismanagement of Fazy,[d] Freiligrath's 'natural superior'. He has been forced to resign his post as supreme director of the bank, and *'um zu retten, was zu retten ist'*[e] (*literally* this) Jew *Reinach* has been put into his place, assisted by a Frenchman and— *Karl Vogt* who has the despicable meanness of betraying, and denouncing, and publicly declaring against Fazy, his old idol, the man in fact of whom he is a mere 'creature'.

I suppose you are aware that the first *'abonnement number'*[f] of the 'Social-Democrat' has been *confiscated* by the police at Berlin.[88] This is a rather favourable accident. Those fellows stand in need of some small political martyrdom.

I hope all is right at home. The cat being gone, the mice ought to dance. Pay my compliments to Ma, 'Success', 'Mine Own' and the 'Prophet'.[g] As to yourself, my dear Aaron, I dreamt of you last

---

[a] K. Marx, 'Inaugural Address of the Working Men's International Association'. - [b] K. Marx, 'To Abraham Lincoln, President of the United States of America'. - [c] 'joyful entrance' (a French medieval expression used to welcome the arrival of a prince or king into one of his own towns). - [d] *James Fazy. Sein Leben und Treiben. (Von einem Westschweizer), Neue Zürcher-Zeitung,* Nos. 321-360, 16 November - 25 December 1864. - [e] to save what can yet be saved - [f] regular issue for the subscribers - [g] Mrs Marx, Laura, and Eleanor Marx and Helene Demuth

night, and saw you in your bloomer costume, performing the most wonderful jumps, almost flying through the air, after you had before done the Davenport trick in the most admirable manner.[89] I felt quite proud and chuckled in my sleeves over the success of my old acquaintance, and had the most lively remembrance of the rather unplastic dance you had in bygone times executed before the golden calf, in the desert.[a]

Show Ma the inclosed. She will remember Bochum-Dolfs, from Paris. He is now the happy father of 10 children with whom he 'vagabonds' through the world.

First published, in Russian, in *Voinstvuyushchy materialist*, Book 4, 1925, and in the language of the original, English, in *The Socialist Review* (London), No. 44, September 1929

Reproduced from the original

31

MARX TO JOHANN BAPTIST VON SCHWEITZER[1]

IN BERLIN

[Draft]

To. J. B. v. Schweitzer ('Social-Demokrat')

London, 16 January 1865

Sir,

Despite its brief existence, your *Social-Demokrat* has already carried *two attacks* on the *'International Association'*. I am only awaiting the *'third'* before my friends and I *publicly* dissociate ourselves from any connection with your paper. In the event of such a dissociation, I should be compelled to deal *'critically'* with certain things which, in deference to party interests, I have hitherto not aired, and this may not be at all to the liking of certain gentlemen. The first attack on the 'International Associa-

---

[a] Here a strip of paper is cut off at the bottom of the page, presumably bearing Marx's signature. The paragraph that follows is a postscript in the left-hand corner of the first page of the letter.

tion' was contained in an inane passage in B. Becker's 'Message'.[90] I did not hold you responsible for it for the very reason that it was a 'message' and you unfortunately have an official connection with the 'General Workers' *Association*'[2] (emphatically not to be confused with the working *class*).

The bare-faced, lying gossip of Mr Moses Hess[a] is another matter; if you had had the slightest consideration for me and my friends you would *under no circumstances* have accepted it, you could only have accepted it *with the intention of provoking me.*

With regard to Moses' fabrication itself, I shall be making a public statement about it *after* I have obtained certain information from Paris.[91] Regarding your acceptance of that abomination of an article, I should be obliged if you would inform me *whether I am to consider same as a declaration of war by the 'Social-Demokrat'?*

Your most obedient servant
K. Marx

First published in: Marx and Engels, *Works*, First Russian Edition, Vol. XXV, Moscow, 1934

Printed according to Marx's Notebook for 1865

32

MARX TO ENGELS[92]

IN MANCHESTER

[London,] 25 January 1865

Dear Frederick,

Letters enclosed
1. from Weydemeyer,
2. from Schily,
3. from Liebknecht. I must have all 3 back.
4. from Schweitzer and 5. a scrawl about *Vogt*, which I would also like back.

By way of explanation for letters 2, 3 and 4, the following: I do not know whether you get the *Social-Demokrat* (or have taken out a

---

[a] [Moses]H[ess], 'Paris, 10. Jan. [Arb.-Associationen. Internat. Arb.-Assoc. *Avenir national*], *Der Social-Demokrat*, No. 8, 13 January 1865.

subscription to it). (If neither should be the case, Bender can always send you one from here, as he has ordered 6 copies on the off-chance.)

There was a contribution in the *Social-Demokrat* from that jackass Moses Hess,[a] in which he related how *we* had approached *L'Association* (paper of the Paris associations) asking them to print a translation of our address[b] (on the contrary, Massol had made Schily an *offer* to that effect) and join our Association; they are said to have refused, however, because *we* had originally approached Tolain and others who were Plon-Plonists.[93] Tolain himself had admitted as much, etc.

I discovered this scrawl on the day after my return from Manchester.[84] Therefore wrote furious letters to Paris[94] and Berlin.[c] From Schily's and Schweitzer's letters it emerges that the whole thing can be blamed on Hess' asininity (mixed with a certain amount of MALICE, perhaps) and on Liebknecht's asininity *toute pure.*[d]

The affair created a great furore in the *Comité* here yesterday. Le Lubez, entirely on Tolain's side, declares the whole thing to be slanderous, since fellows like Horn (Einhorn, rabbi) and that gas-bag Jules Simon (of *La Liberté*[e]) are on the *Comité* of *L'Association.* However, at my suggestion, it was resolved not to send the 500 CARDS OF MEMBERSHIP to Paris until Schily had reported further from Paris.[95]

The Association is doing famously here. At its soirée,[f] which I did *not* attend, ABOUT 1,200 people (they would have had 3× as many if the hall had been big enough) gathered, which brought approximately £15 into our exceedingly depleted EXCHEQUER.

Letter has come from Geneva about joining,[96] and from DIFFERENT PARTS OF ENGLAND.

There will be a MEETING for the Poles in the course of February (especially to collect money for the *new* émigrés, which also explains *Lord* Townshend as CHAIRMAN), organised by the (English) POLISH LEAGUE, the *Polish* society here and our Association.[97]

What do you say to Lassalle's 'bequest', as described by Liebknecht?[98] Is it not exactly like his own Sickingen, who wants to compel Charles V to 'assume the leadership of the movement'?[g]

---

a [Moses] H[ess], 'Paris, 10. Jan. [Arb.-Associationen. Internat. Arb.-Assoc. *Avenir national*], *Der Social-Demokrat,* No. 8, 13 January 1865. - b K. Marx, 'Inaugural Address of the Working Men's International Association'. - c See this volume, pp. 64-65. - d pure and simple - e *La Liberté de penser* - f See this volume, p. 60. - g Sickingen and Charles V are characters in Lassalle's *Franz von Sickingen.*

Yesterday, I sent *Article on Proudhon*[a] to Schweitzer, in response to his urgent request (and also to make up to him for having bitten his head off instead of Liebknecht's for the BLUNDER in the *Soc.-Dem.*). You will see from it that several very savage blows, ostensibly aimed at Proudhon, strike home at our '*Achilles*'[b] and were intended to do so.

Apropos. Each secretary of our Association will receive a package of CARDS OF MEMBERSHIP next week (for the 'Association', not for the '*Comité*', of course) for distribution (ls. for annual subscription, ld. for the CARD). You must get rid of a few in Manchester. It will not be many. But let me know about HOW MANY I can send for this purpose? It is IN FACT ONE OF THE WAYS AND MEANS OF THE ASSOCIATION.

MY COMPLIMENTS TO MRS BURNS. WILL SHE, PERHAPS, BECOME A MEMBER? LADIES ARE ADMITTED.

YOURS TRULY

K. M.

P.S. I left a pair of winter BOOTS (shoes) at your house in Dover Street, ditto new pair of knitted stockings, and probably the 2 silk handkerchiefs as well. I only mention it so that you can DROP A WORD to your landlords 'some time or other' so that they know that an eye is kept on them.

By means of a most ingenious experiment Prof. Tyndall has managed to separate out the rays of the sun into a *heat-ray*, which even melts platinum, and a *cold light-ray which has no heat at all*. This is ONE OF THE FINEST EXPERIMENTS OF OUR DAYS.

P.S. II

Liebknecht has also sent me a note from the editors, urgently asking for a contribution from you. For the moment they are thinking either of the YANKEE WAR or the *Prussian Army Reform*, as they say their paper is read by more people of standing than any other Berlin paper.

Now, as far as the YANKEE WAR is concerned, you explained to me before that it was not suitable for the *Social-Demokrat*.

Regarding the *Prussian Army Reform*, the paper would be a very good place for it. Only QUESTION for *me* is *this*: would not an analysis of this topic involve you in a one-sided conflict with the men of Progress,[99] which would be undesirable at this moment and on *this* topic, since the King[c] has declared he will not give way

---

[a] K. Marx, 'On Proudhon [Letter to J. B. Schweitzer]'. - [b] Ferdinand Lassalle - [c] William I

on any point, so has naturally turned the question into a burning constitutional issue?[100] Or can you treat the question, in accordance with your military view, in such a way as to kill *both* birds, which is what is *wanted*?

At all events, as I have already sent the paper an article DIRECTLY (signed by me), you can be published there, too. And you ought to do so, while there is still an organ in existence at all.

First published abridged in *Der Briefwechsel zwischen F. Engels und K. Marx*, Bd. 3, Stuttgart, 1913 and in full in *MEGA*, Abt. III, Bd. 3, Berlin, 1930

Printed according to the original

Published in English in full for the first time

33

ENGELS TO MARX [101]

IN LONDON

Manchester, 27 January 1865

Dear Moor,

I will send the letters back to you tomorrow or on Sunday, as I simply have to read this dreadful handwriting and these pale inks by daylight; yesterday evening I was only able to skim through them.

Moses[a] really has been extraordinarily tactless (no doubt the *head of the party*[b] took a certain malicious pleasure in it), but Liebknecht even more so. But I am surprised the latter has not already committed more such gaffes, it always was his FORTE.

I am sending the fellows the little Danish folksong about Tidmann, who is struck dead by the old man at the Thing for imposing new taxes on the peasants.[c] It is revolutionary but not indictable, and above all it is directed against the feudal nobility, which the paper[d] *absolutely must condemn*. I am making a few remarks to that effect. I shall probably be able to do the article on the reorganisation of the army[e] as soon as I get the new military budget proposals, etc.; I am writing to ask them to send them to

---

[a] Moses Hess (see this volume, pp. 65, 66) - [b] Bernhard Becker - [c] F. Engels, 'Herr Tidmann. Old Danish Folk Song'. - [d] *Der Social-Demokrat* - [e] F. Engels, *The Prussian Military Question and the German Workers' Party*.

me and am telling them at the same time that I shall be coming out against the government—PAST AND PRESENT—just as much as against the men of Progress,[99] and that the article must *not be published* if the first point is unacceptable to them.[102] As far as the American war is concerned, perhaps something can be made of it at a later date after all. The present phase is not yet complete, the calm, to use J. Grimm's term, is 'inorganic'.

Good old Lassalle is after all gradually being unmasked as a common or garden scoundrel. It has never been our practice to judge people by what they thought but rather by what they were, and I do not see why we should make an exception in the late Izzy's case. Subjectively, his vanity may have made the affair seem plausible to him, but objectively it was the act of a scoundrel, the betrayal of the whole workers' movement to the Prussians. Throughout, the stupid fop does not seem to have obtained from Bismarck anything at all in return, nothing specific at all, let alone guarantees[98]; he seems just to have taken it for granted he would *definitely* do Bismarck in the eye, in exactly the same way as he could not fail to shoot Racowiţa dead. That's Baron Izzy all over for you.

Incidentally, it will not be very long now before it becomes not merely desirable but *necessary* to make this whole affair public. We can only gain from it, and, if the business with the Association[a] and the paper in Germany bears fruit, the fellow's heirs will have to be thrown out soon enough now. Meanwhile, the proletariat in Germany will soon see what it has got in Bismarck.

Kind regards to the LADIES.

Your

F. E.

I can only see my way to disposing of approx. $^1/_2$ dozen cards; I will see Jones about it, I'm very busy just now.

First published abridged in *Der Briefwechsel zwischen F. Engels und K. Marx*, Bd. 3, Stuttgart, 1913 and in full in *MEGA*, Abt. III, Bd. 3, Berlin, 1930

Printed according to the original

Published in English in full for the first time

---

[a] General Association of German Workers

34

MARX TO ENGELS [103]

IN MANCHESTER

[London,] 30 January 1865

Dear Engels,

Tout d'accord.[a] As far as your anxiety about confiscation is concerned, what you must do is to announce quite briefly, as a foreword to the first article,[b] that you are firstly going to throw light on the subject from the military point of view, secondly you are going to criticise the bourgeoisie and, thirdly, the reaction, etc., and the attitude of the workers' party to the question, etc., whereby *the drift* can already be narrowly outlined or hinted at. This will, *de prime abord,*[c] make it more difficult for the government to confiscate. If it does so in spite of that, the *Social-Demokrat* will thereby be hurled into a new phase (for the fellows cannot at present confiscate without releasing the confiscated material, or taking it to court), and, at the same time, you must keep a copy of the manuscript of No. III. It is then the easiest thing in the world to publish it in the one of the 2 German papers *here*[d] and then send COPIES of it to Hamburg, etc., where one or other of the bourgeois papers is sure to print it.

It seems to me that Schily has allowed himself to be duped by M. Hess. This is quite evident from all Moses' epistles to the *Social-Demokrat.* (CF. F.I. No. 15 of the *Social-Demokrat*[e] which has just arrived and is, on the whole, full of the most revolting 'Lassalleanism'. The gentlemen from Iserlohn speak of 'Lassalle-Lincoln'.[f]) Moses is our *adversary,* has forgotten neither our 'expulsion from Brussels' nor our 'ejection from Cologne' [104] and always counts it to Lassalle's credit that he had the 'tact' so necessary for a 'leader of the people' to take M. Hess seriously.

By the way, being the 'organ of the General Association of German Workers', the *Social-Demokrat* finds it extremely difficult to extricate itself from the apotheosis-soup.

---

[a] In complete agreement (see previous letter) - [b] F. Engels, *The Prussian Military Question and the German Workers' Party,* Chapter 1. - [c] from the outset - [d] The reference is presumably to the *Hermann* and the *Londoner Anzeiger.* - [e] A reference to Hess' report 'Paris, 25. Jan. [Associationswesen. Clerus. Der oppositionelle Wahlsieg]', *Der Social-Demokrat,* No. 15, 29 January 1865. - [f] Quoted from the report 'Iserlohn, 25. Januar', *Der Social-Demokrat,* No. 15, 29 January 1865.

Incidentally, since we now know that Izzy planned to trade off the workers' party to Bismarck[98] (we were previously quite unaware of *how*) so that he might become known as the 'Richelieu of the Proletariat', I shall not now have any scruples about making it *sufficiently plain* in the preface to my book that he is a parrot and plagiarist.[105]

I wonder whether the 'poems': 'To follow Lassalle is our every wish'[a] and other nonsense which *the workers* are sending to the *Social-Demokrat,* do not emanate directly or indirectly from the old lady.[b] At all events, I have already told the editors several times in writing that this nonsense has got to stop BY and BY.[106]

What sort of fellows the men of Progress[99] are is evident yet again from their conduct regarding the combination question.[107] (*En passant,* the Prussian Anti-Combination Law, like all continental laws of this kind, has its origin in the decree of the *Assemblée Constituante of 14 June 1791,*[108] by which the French bourgeois imposed the most severe penalties on ANYTHING OF THE SORT, in fact workers' associations of any kind,—e.g. loss of civil rights for a year—on the pretext that this constituted *restoration of the guilds* and is in contravention of *liberté constitutionelle*[c] and the '*droits de l'homme'.*[d] It is so characteristic of Robespierre that, at a time when it was a crime punishable by the guillotine to be 'constitutional', as defined by the *Assemblée* of 1789, all of its laws directed *against* the workers remained in force.)

Here in London Mr Bright has again spoiled his whole rapport with the workers by his SPEECH opposing the application of the Ten Hours' Bill[109] to the BIRMINGHAM TRADES.[e] A bourgeois of that kind really is INCORRIGIBLE. And the fellow does that at a moment when he wants to make use of the workers to beat the oligarchs!

Apropos. As I have now told the *Social-Demokrat* twice that they must purge their paper of this infantile 'apotheosis' as far and as quickly as possible, it will doubtless do no harm if you make similar remarks to the editors when you send your article.[f] If we allow them to use our names, then we can, at the same time, demand that *now,* when people are *aware of Lassalle's intended treachery,* they should not help to throw dust in the eyes of the

[a] Quoted from an anonymous poem published in the section 'Einsendungen von Arbeitern' in *Der Social-Demokrat,* No. 15, 29 January 1865. - [b] Sophie von Hatzfeldt - [c] constitutional liberty - [d] 'rights of man' - [e] J. Bright's speech in the Birmingham Chamber of Commerce on 19 January 1865. In: *The Times,* No. 25087, 20 January 1865. - [f] *The Prussian Military Question and the German Workers' Party*

workers or turn themselves into a vehicle for just any kind of loutish rubbish.

Salut.

Your

K. M.

First published abridged in *Der Briefwech-sel zwischen F. Engels und K. Marx*, Bd. 3, Stuttgart, 1913 and in full in *MEGA*, Abt.III, Bd. 3, Berlin, 1930

Printed according to the original

Published in English in full for the first time

35

MARX TO ENGELS [101]

IN MANCHESTER

[London,] 1 February 1865

Dear FREDERICK,

Enclosed letter from Strohn to be returned; write to me and let me know your thoughts about the publishing business at the same time. [110]

This 'Siebold' is the Siebold of champagne fame, NO DOUBT ABOUT THAT. I really am rather afraid that he did not merely find my reception of his bubbly enthusiasm very dry, but THAT HE CAUGHT SOME QUEER WORDS AT GUMPERT'S DOOR, AS I TOLD YOU AT THE TIME. At all events, it is nice of the fellow and quite typical of wine-salesman politics to go straight from us to Karl Blind and run as his MESSENGER to Hamburg. Has Blind perhaps also placed an order for 'sparkling wines' and granted his most gracious protection to scum-scoundrelism as well? I hope for the sake of bubbly's good reputation that Siebold is no such VENAL scum, although there was no mistaking that while one of his eyes was sparkling with enthusiasm, the other HAD AN EYE TO BUSINESS. Regarding Freiligrath, I FEEL SURE that he is much TOO CAUTIOUS to agree *publicly* in any way to collaborate (*in partibus*,[a] it goes without saying) with Blind. HOWEVER, I SHALL TRY TO ASCERTAIN THE FACT. At all events, it is very good that Strohn has so gratifyingly baulked Ruge and Blind. I sent off

---

[a] to all appearances (*In partibus infidelium*—literally: in parts inhabited by unbelievers. The words are added to the title of Roman Catholic bishops appointed to purely nominal dioceses in non-Christian countries).

a few sarcastic marginalia to him earlier today,[111] intended specifically for Meissner, concerning the *nobile par*[a] of antagonistic brothers.

You must excuse the scraps of English in my epistle as there was a SITTING OF THE COUNCIL yesterday which lasted until ONE O'CLOCK. ('Liquor' and 'smoke' are *banned* from these 'SITTINGS'.) The first thing was the answering epistle from Lincoln, which you may find in tomorrow's *Times*[112] and certainly in *The Daily News* and *The Star*.[b] In the reply to the LONDON EMANCIPATION SOCIETY [113] (which counts among its members such illustrious figures as Sir Charles Lyell and the 'Voice of World History', alias K. B.[c]), published in yesterday's *Evening Star*, the old man drily dismisses the fellows with two formal clichés, exactly as he had done in his earlier answer to the *Manchester* branch of the EMANCIPATION SOCIETY; whereas his letter to us is in fact everything we could have asked for, and, in particular, the naive assurance that the *United States* could not involve itself directly in 'PROPAGANDISM'. At any rate, it is the only answer so far ON THE PART OF THE OLD MAN that is more than a strictly formal one.

Secondly, a delegate was there from the Poles (*aristocrats*), who have links with the 'LITERARY SOCIETY',[114] through whom these gentlemen conveyed their solemn assurance, with an eye to the forthcoming MEETING on Poland, that they are *democrats* and that every Pole is *now* a democrat, since the aristocracy has dwindled away to such a degree that they would be *mad* not to recognise the *impossibility* of restoring Poland without a peasant rising. WHETHER or not these fellows believe what they say, at all events, the last lesson they had does not seem to have been entirely wasted on them.[24]

Thirdly, there were statements from various TRADES UNIONS about their joining. Ditto from an association in *Brussels* which is promising to organise branches throughout Belgium.[115]

I then handed over an issue of the *Daily St. Louis Press* which had arrived just yesterday containing leader about our 'ADDRESS TO THE WORKINGMEN'[d] and an excerpt from it which had obviously been arranged by Weydemeyer.[e]

But now the most remarkable thing of all.

Cremer, OUR HONORARY GENERAL SECRETARY, had received a written invitation for the 'COUNCIL', as well as a private visit, from a PROVISIONAL COMMITTEE which is meeting *privatim* at the London

---

[a] noble pair (Horace, *Satires*, II, III, 243) - [b] *The Morning Star* - [c] Karl Blind - [d] K. Marx, 'Inaugural Address of the Working Men's International Association'. - [e] *St.-Louis Daily Press*, No. 22, 10 January 1865.

Tavern next Monday. Object: MONSTER MEETING for MANHOOD SUFFRAGE. *Chairman:—Richard Cobden!*

The point is this: as E. Jones told us previously, these fellows have been a complete failure in Manchester. They have therefore adopted A BROADER PLATFORM, in which REGISTRATION 'FOR PAYING POOR-RATE' figured instead of MANHOOD SUFFRAGE, however. That is what is stated in the printed circular sent to us. However, since various indications made it clear to them that nothing less than MANHOOD SUFFRAGE can attract ANY CO-OPERATION WHATEVER ON THE PART OF THE WORKING CLASSES, they have announced they are prepared to accept the latter. A *big* demonstration in London would lead to similar ones in the provinces, write the provincials 'yet once again', having 'all ready' realised that they are not able TO SET THE BALL A-GOING.

The next question raised yesterday was this: should our SOCIETY, I.E. COUNCIL, agree to what these fellows want (they include all the old SHAM CITY AGITATORS such as Sam. Morley, etc.) and send a few delegates to attend the transactions of their provisional committee as 'watchmen'? Secondly, if these fellows pledge themselves *directly* to the slogan of MANHOOD SUFFRAGE and the PUBLIC MEETING is being called under this slogan, should we promise our support? *The latter* is, you see, just as crucial to these fellows as it was in the American business.[113] Without the TRADES UNIONS, no mass MEETING is possible, and without us, the TRADES UNIONS are not to be had. This is also the reason why these gentlemen have come to us.

Opinions were *very* divided, for which *Bright's* latest silly tricks in Birmingham were much to blame.[a]

On my motion, it was decided that: 1) the delegation should be sent (in my motion, I excluded FOREIGNERS from it; but Eccarius and Lubez were elected on to it as 'Englishmen' and *silent* witnesses) just as 'observers'[116]; 2) SO FAR AS THE MEETING IS CONCERNED, we should act with them *firstly* if MANHOOD SUFFRAGE is proclaimed directly and publicly in the programme, and *secondly* if people *selected by us* are included on the *permanent* committee, so that they can keep an eye on those fellows and compromise them in the event of fresh treachery, which, as I made plain to all of them, is *at any rate* intended. I am writing to E. Jones about the matter today.[117]

Your
K. M.

First published in *Der Briefwechsel zwischen F. Engels und K. Marx,* Bd. 3, Stuttgart, 1913

Printed according to the original

Published in English in full for the first time

---

[a] See this volume, p. 71.

36

MARX TO ENGELS[118]

IN MANCHESTER

[London,] 3 February 1865

DEAR FREDERICK,

Enclosed

1. Letter from Siebel[119] reporting on his meeting with Klings, with which I had 'charged' him.[a] My only comment on it is that I am not going to interfere in the affair *any further*. If Klings succeeds—without *our* help—in getting rid of B. Becker and his testamentary importance, together with the beastly old girl,[b] that suits me. There is nothing to be done with the Workers' Association[2] as bequeathed by Baron Izzy.[c] The sooner it is disbanded, the better.

2. *Rheinische Zeitung* with leading article,[120] probably by Red Becker.[d] It amounts to an APPEAL *ad misericordiam*[e] from the 'men of Progress'.[99]

My opinion is now that *the two of us* must issue a statement, and that this crisis particularly gives us the opportunity to reoccupy our 'LEGITIMATE' position. ABOUT 10 days ago, I wrote to Schweitzer that he must stand up to Bismarck and the workers' party must drop even the appearance of flirting with Bismarck, etc.[121] By way of thanks, he has 'all ready' been philandering with Pissmarck more than ever.

'Yet again' Moses Hess is 'all ready' *denouncing* the 'International Association'[122] for the second time in No. 16 of the *Social-Demokrat*, which contains the letter I wrote about Proudhon,[f] bristling with misprints. I wrote a furious letter to Liebknecht about it yesterday,[111] telling him that this was the **very last** warning; that I do not give a FARTHING for 'good will' when its actions are those of ill-will; that I cannot make it clear to the members of the 'INTERNATIONAL COMMITTEE' here that things like that occur *in bonne foi*[g] out of pure stupidity; that while their gutter rag continues to eulogise Lassalle, even though they know what treachery he had up his sleeve,[98] and while it conducts this

---

a See this volume, pp. 58-59. - b Sophie von Hatzfeldt - c Ferdinand Lassalle - d Hermann Heinrich Becker - e for mercy - f K. Marx, 'On Proudhon [Letter to J. B. Schweitzer]'. - g good faith

cowardly flirtation with Bismarck, it has the effrontery to let the Plonplonist[93] Hess accuse us here of Plonplonism, etc.

My opinion is now that we should take up Moses' denunciation or insinuation in order *d'abord*[a] to issue a brief declaration of war against Bonaparte Plon-Plon, at the same time making honourable mention of Moses' friend, the Rabbi Ein-Horn. Then we should use this to declare ourselves ditto against Bismarck, as well as against the rogues or fools who are dreaming or drivelling about an alliance with him for the sake of the working class. Then, of course, in conclusion the beastly men of Progress should be told that they have, on the one hand, run their cause into the ground by their political cowardice and helplessness, and that, on the other hand, if they are demanding an alliance with the working class against the government—which at the moment is, of course, the only correct line—then they would at least have to make the concessions to the workers that accord with their own principle of 'FREETRADE' and 'DEMOCRATISM', in other words, repeal of all the exceptional laws against the workers, which in addition to the combination laws quite specifically include the present Prussian legislation on the press. They would ditto have to proclaim, at least in principle, the restoration of universal suffrage, which was abolished by the coup d'état in Prussia.[123] This would be the minimum to be expected of them. Maybe something ought to be put in about the military question as well. At all events, the thing needs to be tied up quickly. And you must get your 'ideas' about the whole statement down on paper. I will then add mine to it and knead it all together, will send the whole thing back to you once again AND SO FORTH. The moment seems to me to be favourable for this 'coup d'état'. We cannot miss this moment for our *'restitutio in integrum'*[b] out of consideration for Liebknecht or for anyone else.

AT THE SAME TIME, you must not fail to let the *Social-Demokrat* have your article on the military question[c] SO SOON AS POSSIBLE.

I would of course write to them—*quoad*[d] statement—that, if they do *not* accept same immediately, same will 'all ready' appear in other papers.

If they do accept it, well and good, and it will not even matter if it blows them sky high. (Although Bismarck will take care not to resort to forcible measures at the present moment.) If they do not accept it, we have a decent excuse for getting rid of them.[e] At all

---

a first of all - b restitution to full rights - c F. Engels, *The Prussian Military Question and the German Workers' Party.* - d regarding - e See this volume, pp. 79-80.

events, the air must be cleared and the party purged of the stench
left behind by Lassalle.

Your

K. M.

First published abridged in *Der Briefwech-*
sel zwischen F. Engels und K. Marx, Bd. 3,
Stuttgart, 1913 and in full in *MEGA*,
Abt. III, Bd. 3, Berlin, 1930

Printed according to the original

37

ENGELS TO MARX [101]

IN LONDON

[Manchester,] 5 February 1865
Mornington St[reet]

Dear Moor,

I fully agree about the statement.[a] But you will have to do it
yourself, or I shall never get the military article[b] done. I fear the
thing is getting to be so long that it will only be feasible in
pamphlet form. I and II are finished (except for revision), III not
yet. I have had a lot of interruptions, Blank was here, etc., etc. So,
you do the statement. The exceptional law also includes the
restriction on the right of association and assembly, all the
legislation concerning *journeymen's road books*[124] and finally Article
100 of the penal code: Incitement of citizens to hatred and
contempt (another Napoleonic legacy). Then, if you can work it in,
some indication that in a predominantly agricultural country like
Prussia it is despicable to attack only the bourgeoisie in the name
of the industrial proletariat, without even mentioning the brutal
patriarchal exploitation of the rural proletariat by the big feudal
aristocracy. It is less important to say anything about the military
question, but the *budget question* should be given prominence: what
use is it to the workers to have a parliament elected by universal
suffrage, if it is as powerless as Bismarck wants to make the

---

[a] See previous letter. - [b] F. Engels, *The Prussian Military Question and the German
Workers' Party*.

present bourgeois parliament—whose successor it would after all be? And if it cannot even reject new taxation?

Those are my thoughts *ad hoc*.[a] So, get going and sent the thing to me straightaway.

Meissner. SO FAR SO GOOD. You should go there yourself, of course. *Conto a metà*[b] has its advantages if you reserve the contractual right to inspect the books and documents and if Meissner is prepared to make you an interest-free advance equal to $^2/_3$ of the fee you are claiming anyway. Strohn's letter seems to suggest that Meissner WOULD RATHER NOT PART WITH ANY MONEY IF HE COULD HELP IT.[66] At all events, you must go there yourself with the manuscript[c] and settle it.

Moreover, get on with it quickly now. The time is really ripe for the book, and our names again command respect in the public eye. You know how fashionable it is to procrastinate in publishing in Germany. So, do not miss the moment—it may make an enormous difference to the impact it produces.

Siebold. I have told you before that lads like that are not to be trusted and I was sure from the beginning that he would call on Blind in London. The assumption that he had picked up some odd remarks *ad portam Gumperti*[d] is quite unnecessary. The fellow has always done that and will always do so. But it is a good thing we have our eye on him 'all ready'.

I gather from Siebel's letter,[119] which I am keeping here, that the Lassalle Association[2] will very soon be ruined, thanks to its officers' roguish tricks and embezzlement, and a very good thing too that it 'will have turned out thus'. The beastly old girl[e] and her cliques will do the rest. The less we concern ourselves about the whole filthy business, the better. LET IT ROT AND BE DAM'D TO IT.

I find the *Social-Demokrätchen*[f] more repugnant with every passing day. That shitty Hess, who is, in relation to us, really acting like a secret employee of Lassalle, with his protectorial airs; Mr Schweitzer's bloody pretentious articles on the encyclical and Bismarck, flirting with every kind of trash and only scolding the bourgeoisie,[g] the complete lack of sparkle and talent, and the absence even of any common sense, with just a few exceptions, it is all a bit too much for me. Lassalle-worship three times a week,

---

a on the subject - b a joint account - c of *Capital* - d at Gumpert's door (see this volume, p. 72) - e Sophie von Hatzfeldt - f Literally: *Little Social-Demokrat* - g Engels is referring to the following articles by Schweitzer published as leaders in *Der Social-Demokrat* (Nos. 5, 6 and 14; 6, 8 and 27 January 1865): 'Das Kirchenthum und die moderne Civilisation', 'Das Ministerium Bismarck und die\Regierungen der Mittel- und Kleinstaaten' and 'Das Ministerium Bismarck. I'.

the devil can stomach that, and it is good that the crisis is coming.
I shall tell these gentlemen so in my next letter as well, have had
no opportunity to do so until now. Apropos, how are you
addressing your letters to *Liebknecht?* I would like to give him a
telling-off from time to time as well, or encourage him, *s'il y a
lieu.*ᵃ

I must stop now. Best wishes and do send the statement
straightaway. I shall have finished the article by Wednesday or
Thursday.

Your
F. E.

I have tried to sound out my brother-in-law ᵇ about Siebel, but I
could discover nothing except that he is 'always drunk', runs
around with actresses, and his wife wants to divorce him.
Mʏ ʙᴇsᴛ ᴄᴏᴍᴘʟɪᴍᴇɴᴛs ᴛᴏ ᴛʜᴇ ʟᴀᴅɪᴇs.

First published abridged in *Der Briefwech-
sel zwischen F. Engels und K. Marx,* Bd. 3,
Stuttgart, 1913 and in full in *MEGA,*
Abt. III, Bd. 3, Berlin, 1930

Printed according to the original

Published in English in full for the
first time

38

MARX TO ENGELS [101]

IN MANCHESTER

[London,] 6 February [1865]

Dear Engels,

As good luck would have it, in the feuilleton section in the
Social-Demokrat which arrived today your call for the crushing of
the aristocracy comes right after my article ᶜ condemning even a
'pseudo-compromise'.

In the first instance, I now believe it is better to send in the few
lines below,[125] instead of the statement I had originally intended.ᵈ
They will inevitably provide the *occasion* for a *further statement.* But

---

ᵃ if there are grounds for doing so - ᵇ Karl Emil Blank - ᶜ F. Engels, 'Herr
Tidmann. Old Danish Folk Song', K. Marx, 'On Proudhon [Letter to
J. B. Schweitzer]'. - ᵈ See this volume, pp. 75, 76-77.

my 'aesthetic' sense tells me—on further reflection—that the latter would not be entirely appropriate, because it would come *too soon* after Becker's APPEAL.[120] These few lines, on the other hand, will *quite certainly* provoke a real tussle between Schweitzer and Red Becker etc., in which we can then intervene and declare *our* policy briefly, forcefully and *without any beating about the bush*.

I enclose letter from the unfortunate Liebknecht[126] and note sent him by the old Hatzfeldt woman; there is still not enough 'Lassalle' in the paper[a] for her liking.

As TO Klings, I am not going to answer at all. Let the fellows manage by themselves.[b]

Letter from Schily just received (can only send it to you in a few days time), from which it emerges:

1. that Moses'[c] insinuations were pure invention,

2. that our plan will have a 'fantastic' effect in Paris, and the workers there are not taking any notice whatsoever of *L'Association*, which Mr A. Horn, Löb Sonnemann and other riff-raff use to indulge their self-importance.[95]

If the attached statement meets with your approval, make a copy of it and sign it. Then send it back. I will then put my name to it as well and post the thing to Berlin.

Apropos. Lincoln's answer to us is in today's *Times*.[112]

[Postscript]

Liebknecht's private address is: '13 Neuenburger Strasse, *Berlin*'. You can send to *Mrs* Liebknecht at that address whenever you want to write privately. Poor W. Liebknecht is obviously in an exceedingly embarrassing situation. He will have to be told that it is a case of either bending or breaking. In the latter case, I should think he could certainly earn an honest living as a schoolmaster in Manchester.

First published (without Postscript) in *Der Briefwechsel zwischen F. Engels und K. Marx*, Bd. 3, Stuttgart, 1913

Printed according to the original

Published in English in full for the first time

---

[a] *Der Social-Demokrat* - [b] See this volume, p. 82. - [c] Moses Hess

39

ENGELS TO MARX [29]

IN LONDON

Manchester, 7 February 1865

Dear Moor,

Statement[a] enclosed. They will take exception to the fact that we refer to Moses[b] *by name*, which, when published, could be regarded as a breach of editorial secrecy. Do not forget to give Liebknecht instructions about this, so that a justifiable technical objection of this kind does not delay the matter again.

Liebknecht is becoming more and more stupid. He calls it a compromise that we should not merely sanction in silence every stupid thing that appears in the paper[c] but also tolerate the paper *casting aspersions* on our own affairs and actions,[126] in defiance of every convention. But we always have a fine LOT of agents to act for us and will certainly not be such jackasses as Lassalle and 'bequeath' anything to them, *s'il y avait de quoi*.[d] If things go wrong in Berlin, Liebknecht would do best to come over, leaving his family behind, we will then see what can be done, he will be able to make acquaintances soon enough at the Schiller Institute[28] here, and whatever else can be done, will be; I think he might very well manage to settle down here like that, and if not, nothing is lost, and if it works out all right, he can bring his family over later. If he brings his family along straightaway, he will *certainly* go to the dogs here, because the cost will then be so much greater that the attempt cannot possibly last long. It will not be easy to obtain work teaching children, as Lupus did; but he can, of course, explore the possibilities.

Bender has sent me a bill for 5s. per quarter for my subscription to the *Social-Demokrätchen,* which seems exorbitant to me.

The devil knows how one's work here is subject to all kinds of interruptions. Another committee meeting of the Schiller Institute yesterday, so this evening is the first time since Friday that I have managed to get down to the military question.[e]

---

[a] K. Marx and F. Engels, 'To the Editor of the *Social-Demokrat*'. - [b] Moses Hess - [c] *Der Social-Demokrat* - [d] if there were anything to bequeath - [e] F. Engels, *The Prussian Military Question and the German Workers' Party.*

The attempt by Hatzfeldt and Klings to throw out Bernhard Becker has been a complete fiasco, and Klings has been thrown out. Whatever happens we must avoid soiling our hands in *that* dirty business; it is just as the worker said in the Gürzenich[a] in 1848: they may fall as they will, a rogue will always come out on top.

What mad German Schweitzer writes 'as who'! This second LEADER on Bismarck's ministry is once again as pretentiously abstruse as it could possibly be, even though there is no longer any direct flirtation with Bismarck, and it is good that he openly calls Prussia's policy *anti-German*.[b] But how naive of Liebknecht that he demands that *we* ought to make clear to them what their attitude to the government should be, whereas what he should do is to ask above all for a categorical statement from Mr Schweitzer as to *what attitude he intends to adopt towards the government.*

It looks to me as if a compromise is at hand in Prussia now, with the Prussian Chamber rescuing its prerogative regarding the budget, *but giving way on everything else.* Bismarck will certainly not think of seriously disputing the budget-prerogative in the long run, since, if he did so, he would get neither money nor credit and he is badly in need of both. Meanwhile, the affair can still founder on any number of trivial details.[100]

In America, the start of the Richmond campaign in March or April will probably be decisive for the whole year.[30] If Grant succeeds in driving Lee out, the CONFEDERACY is PLAYED OUT, their armies will break up, and only bandit-warfare, like that already rife in West Tennessee now and in general nearly everywhere, will remain to be overcome. In reality, the only army the SOUTHERNERS now have is Lee's; everything depends on its destruction. Now we can already assume that the area from which Lee procures his supplies is confined to South Virginia, the Carolinas and at most part of Georgia.

Salut.

                                                          Your
                                                          F. E.

First published abridged in *Der Briefwech-sel zwischen F. Engels und K. Marx*, Bd. 3, Stuttgart, 1913 and in full in *MEGA*, Abt. III, Bd. 3, Berlin, 1930

Printed according to the original

Published in English in full for the first time

---

[a] A hall in Cologne used for public meetings during the 1848-49 revolution. -
[b] [J. B. Schweitzer,] 'Das Ministerium Bismarck. II', *Der Social-Demokrat*, No. 18, 5 February 1865.

40

ENGELS TO MARX

IN LONDON

Manchester, 9 February 1865

Dear Moor,

Manuscript enclosed, now swollen to the dimensions of a full-sized pamphlet[a] and no doubt now quite unsuitable for the little paper.[b] So far, it has only been very cursorily revised and will have to be gone through again. Regarding the military question, some statistics about the population fit for military service have yet to be inserted, and some more about the petty bourgeoisie at the end, which I quite forgot in the 'heat of battle'. You will notice, by the way, that the piece has been thrown together straight out of my head, without any kind of literary sources, since it had to be finished quickly. I now await your comments on it.

But where next with it? To Liebknecht or to Siebel, to find a publisher? What do you think? Best outside Prussia, probably, or do you think there is nothing in it that might lead to confiscation? I have lost all my instinct for the publishing situation in Prussia. Let me know your opinion on this point, too—the possibility of publication in Prussia.

Another S. D. (Sow's Dirt)[c] has just arrived. What a lot of feeble whining about the position of the party. No cut or thrust at all. For ever keeping the little back-door open for Bismarck. Peaceful collaboration! And then Moses,[d] who has come round to the point of view that the bourgeoisie and the government in France are vying with each other to do the *right thing* by the workers. France these days is a real paradise for Moses. It is a bit too much even for Schweitzer to stomach, he has put a ? after it.

Should I leave that section in III in, about the present workers' movement?

It seems to me that Roon's speech really does imply compromise. The man is prepared to negotiate.[127] For that reason, the piece

---

a *The Prussian Military Question and the German Workers' Party* - b *Der Social-Demokrat* - c Engels is referring to *Der Social-Demokrat*, No. 19, 8 February 1865, containing Schweitzer's article 'Die deutsche Social-Demokratie' and Hess' article 'Paris, 4. Febr. [Neue Gesetzvorschläge betr. Cooperativ-Associationen. Die internationale Arbeiter-Association. Unterrichtsfrage]'. - d Moses Hess

must come out *fast*. So, do let me know soon what you think with respect to publisher.

Your

F. E.

First published in *Der Briefwechsel zwischen F. Engels und K. Marx*, Bd. 3, Stuttgart, 1913

Printed according to the original

Published in English for the first time

41

MARX TO ENGELS[29]

IN MANCHESTER

[London,] 10 February 1865

Dear FREDERICK,

The thing[a] is good. Although the style is too slapdash in places, it would be NONSENSE to polish or elaborate it at all now, as the main thing is to get it out IN THE NICK OF TIME, as the conflict[100] is 'all ready' on the point of being resolved.

My advice therefore is this:

Send the pamphlet straight to *Meissner* in Hamburg and tell him that *speed of publication* is paramount; and he should let you know immediately whether he will take it (leaving him to decide the fee), because then you would attract attention to the thing in advance in the Berlin and Rhineland papers.

The thing is much too long and 'too cheeky' for the *Social-Demokrat* in present circumstances. But I would arrange for notices, short ones, in the *Social-Demokrat* (through Eccarius), in the *Düsseldorfer Zeitung* through Siebel, and maybe even send a notice to the *Rheinische Zeitung*, to the effect that a pamphlet by you is being published at such and such a place, in which you are simply setting out our position on this specific question, as opposed to that of the Reaction, men of Progress[99] and Lassalleans, along with treatment of the PURELY MILITARY QUESTION.

Even if there are still things you have got to add to it, send the manuscript IMMEDIATELY ad Meissnerem (Hamburg) all the same and tell him that a few additions are to follow relating to such-and-such page (you can mark the places). There should have been

---

[a] F. Engels, *The Prussian Military Question and the German Workers' Party*.

rather more mention of the *country people*, which your German lout is far too inclined to ignore as non-existent. To judge by Strohn's last letter, he himself is probably away from Hamburg again, so that the piece cannot be sent to him but will have to go direct to Meissner.

An evil wind of reconciliation is blowing in Berlin, fanned from the direction of *Russia* this time and further strengthened by the turn for the worse in the business with Austria. The *Petersburger Zeitung* advises unconditionally making concessions to the chamber in the matter of *budget-approval* and *two-year military service*. It says, amongst other things:

'The present time appears to us, if not an alarming one, then, nevertheless, a grave one, and if circumstances do not become especially advantageous, it is still to be feared *that the future will be dismal*. In times of distress and danger, however, as history has proved only too often, *the strict enforcement of discipline in the army and the civil service is rarely enough on its own*. The real power of the state is then based, as it always is in general, far more on the unity of government and people. Although we do not underestimate the *conciliatory manner*, in which the government approached the people's representation in this year's session, nevertheless, in view of what we have just said, we cannot suppress the desire that this conciliatory spirit may *also spread to action*.' [a]

It appears that the Muscovites need their Prussians for the wheeling-movement they are about to execute *against* Austro-*Galicia*, as announced in the *Moscow Newspaper*.[b] According to the same *Moscow Newspaper, this* final subjugation of Poland, which however necessarily means the ruthless continuation of Muraviov's policy, would '*open a hole into the heart of Germany*'. Our good 'men of Progress' and equally good 'Lassalleans' are missing all that by sleeping.

Letter from Schily enclosed.

To Moses'[c] great distress, the 'INTERNATIONAL ASSOCIATION' is creating a great stir amongst the workers in Paris. As a result of Moses' gaffe, Tolain has stepped down. (We have *not* formally accepted his resignation.) H. Lefort (editor of the *Avenir*,[d] etc.), who is also on the editorial committee of *L'Association*, has at his request been appointed LITERARY DEFENDER (ATTORNEY GENERAL) of *our* Association in Paris. The latter is already under attack from *Horn* (a paragraph in the Rules[128]). This Jew Horn will soon notice that Moses Hess is not the only German around. *Fribourg* has opened a

---

[a] Quoted (with some digressions) from the article 'Die Eröffnung der preussischen Landtags-Session' published in *St.-Petersburger Zeitung*, No. 10, 14 (26) January 1865. Italics by Marx. - [b] *Московскія вѣдомости* - [c] Moses Hess - [d] *L'Avenir national*

bureau de renseignement[a] for us; CARDS OF MEMBERSHIP were sent to him the day before yesterday.

At the preparatory session for the Polish meeting,[97] I also saw OLD Oborski again, who does *not* send his regards.

Salut.

Your

K. M.

Apropos. The fact that Lincoln answered us[112] so courteously and the 'BOURGEOIS EMANCIPATION SOCIETY'[113] so brusquely and purely formally[b] made the *The Daily News* so indignant that they did *not* print the answer to us. However, since they saw, to their dismay, that *The Times* was doing so, they had to publish it *later* in *The Express*.[c] Levy also had to eat humble pie. The difference between Lincoln's answer to us and to the bourgeoisie has created such a sensation here that the West End 'clubs' are shaking their heads at it. You can understand how gratifying that has been for our people.

First published in *Der Briefwechsel zwischen F. Engels und K. Marx*, Bd. 3, Stuttgart, 1913

Printed according to the original

Published in English in full for the first time

42

MARX TO ENGELS[118]

IN MANCHESTER

[London,] 11 February [1865]

DEAR FRED,

It being Saturday today, I am assuming you won't be sending off your thing[d] this very day, so there will still be time for these 'supplementary' suggestions for changes:

1. In the passage where you *ask what the workers want?* I would not answer as you do that the workers in Germany, France and

---

[a] information bureau - [b] See this volume, p. 73.- [c] 'President Lincoln and the International Working Men's Association', *The Express*, 6 February 1865. - [d] F. Engels, *The Prussian Military Question and the German Workers' Party*.

England are demanding this and that. The answer sounds as though (at least, that's what it will be *taken to mean*) we have accepted Izzy's[a] slogans. I would be inclined to say rather[b]:

It would seem that the demands put forward at the present moment by the most advanced workers in *Germany* amount to the following, etc. This doesn't commit you at all, which is all to the good, as later on you yourself criticise universal suffrage if not accompanied by the requisite conditions. (Morever, in England e.g., etc., the word 'direct' would indeed be meaningless, it is after all only the opposite of the 'indirect' suffrage invented by the Prussians.) The form in which the louts in Germany conceive of state intervention *à la* Lassalle is such that one must ANYHOW take care not to identify oneself with 'same'. It would be a lot more dignified (and safer), if you took the louts at their word and *let them say for themselves* what *they* want. (I say the *louts* because they are the really argumentative section who have been *infected by Lassalle*.) [129]

2. I would not say that the 1848-49 movement failed because the bourgeois opposed *direct universal suffrage*. What happened was rather that this was proclaimed by the people of Frankfurt to be an ancient German right and proclaimed by the Imperial Regent[c] with all due formality.[130] (In my opinion, too, as soon as the matter comes up for serious discussion in dear old Germany, this franchise must be treated as a rightfully *existing* law.) As that is no place for a lengthy exposition, I would make do with the following phrase: that the bourgeois at that time preferred peace and servitude to the mere *prospect* of struggle and freedom, or something of that sort.

Taken as a whole, it's a very good piece, and 'Oi' am particularly tickled by the passage which shows that the present louts' movement IN FACT only exists *par la grâce de la police*.[d]

In great haste.

Salut.

Your

K. M.

I have crossed out the bit where you console the reactionaries, I DON'T KNOW WHY, by saying that a soldier does not turn reactionary in

---

a Lassalle's - b A sentence deleted by Marx follows here: 'This is not the place for you to set out your own view—or alternatively you could drop the introductory section and just say the following:'. - c Archduke John of Austria - d by gracious permission of the police

the 3rd year—or not for long—although you later say the opposite.

First published abridged in *Der Briefwech-sel zwischen F. Engels und K. Marx*, Bd. 3, Stuttgart, 1913 and in full in *MEGA*, Abt. III, Bd. 3, Berlin, 1930

Printed according to the original

43

ENGELS TO MARX [118]

IN LONDON

[Manchester,] 13 February 1865

Dear Moor,

Your SUGGESTIONS came just in time yesterday and have both been used. How necessary the one about the demands of the louts in particular was,[a] was further brought home to me by Nos. 20 and 21 of the Sow's-Dirt[b] which arrived today.

By the by, our attitude seems to be bearing fruit in spite of everything. There is a certain revolutionary note in No. 21 which was entirely absent before. By the by, I've written to Liebknecht that there's no point in raising a storm, they must just drop their flirting with reaction and make sure the aristocracy and reaction get their SHARE, too, but for the rest *abuse* neither them nor the bourgeoisie, which is superfluous in quiet times.[131]

But one can see that Izzy[c] has given the movement a Tory-Chartist character,[132] which it will be difficult to get rid of and which has given rise to a tendency in Germany which was previously unheard of among the workers. This nauseating toadying to the reaction comes through everywhere. WE SHALL HAVE SOME TROUBLE WITH THAT. You wait and see, the louts will be saying, what's that Engels after, what has he been doing all the time, how can he speak in our name and tell us what to do, the fellow's up there in Manchester exploiting the workers, etc. To be sure, I

---

[a] See previous letter. - [b] *Der Social-Demokrat* - [c] Lassalle

don't give a damn about it now, but it's bound to come, and we shall have Baron Izzy to thank for it.

Your
F. E.

First published in *Der Briefwechsel zwischen F. Engels und K. Marx*, Bd. 3, Stuttgart, 1913   Printed according to the original

44

MARX TO ENGELS

IN MANCHESTER

London, 13 February 1865
1 Modena Villas, Maitland Park,
Haverstock Hill

Dear Engels,

You'll see from the enclosed how things stand with regard to our statement[a] about Moses.[133] At the same time, you will have read Moses' scrawl in the last *Social-Demokrat*.[b]

This time I believe Liebknecht is right: Mr von Schweitzer is pretending to see in our statement only a personal attack on Moses; he 'overlooks' the stand against Bonapartism, etc., probably knowing full well WHAT HE IS ABOUT. It might perhaps not come amiss to Schweitzer if a public *break* (who knows whether he has committed himself to something which will soon force one or not?) were occasioned by this Moses business, *instead of ad vocem*[c] *Bismarck*? I have therefore written him letter (copy retained[134]) in which I *d'abord*[d] give him a summary of our relations to date and ask him where in all this we for our part have gone 'beyond the bounds'? And I analyse the Moses CASE once more. I then say that because of Moses' latest silly outburst, our statement is TO A CERTAIN DEGREE out-of-date, and the matter can therefore be allowed to rest.

---

[a] K. Marx and F. Engels, 'To the Editor of the *Social-Demokrat*'. - [b] [Moses] H[ess], 'Paris, 7. Febr. [Amerika.—Der Orient.—Italien.—Die Internationale Arbeiter-Association]', *Der Social-Demokrat*, No. 21, 12 February 1865. - [c] concerning - [d] firstly

As far as the *other point* in the statement is concerned, the hint to the workers, we would be setting out our position at length *elsewhere* on the attitude of the workers towards the Prussian government. At the same time, I took the opportunity—apropos of the telegram in today's *Times* about the Prussian ministerial statement—to make our opinion *quoad*[a] Bismarck and Lassalle [135] clear to Mr von Schweitzer once again.

(I would in fact not be at all surprised if Bismarck were to *reject outright* the repeal of the Combination Laws to the extent that some of the men of Progress [99] have now been obliged to demand. The right of combination, and all that it entails, interferes too much with police domination, the Rules Governing Servants, [136] the flog-'em and birch-'em rural aristocracy and bureaucratic tutelage in general. As soon as the bourgeoisie (or some of them) appear to turn serious, the government will certainly make a joke and do a *volte-face*.[b] The Prussian state can *not* tolerate COALITIONS and TRADES UNIONS. That much is certain. On the contrary, *government support* for a few lousy co-operative societies suited their dirty game to a tee. Officials becoming even more nosey, control of 'new' money, bribery of the most active of the workers, emasculation of the whole movement! However, since the Prussian government is so short of money just now, this plan is scarcely more to be feared than the Order of the Swan of old! [137]

Nota bene, Lassalle was *opposed to the campaign for the right of combination*. Liebknecht improvised it among the Berlin printers against Lassalle's wishes. That was the starting-point of the whole affair that beau Becker[c] has now taken over.[138])

For the present we should—in my opinion—exercise 'restraint' *quant au*[d] the *Social-Demokrat.* I.e. write *nothing* (Eccarius excepted). Things will soon reach such a pass that we shall either have to break *openly* with it, or we shall be able to collaborate with it in a proper manner. Moses will have to receive his chastisement on some later occasion.

MEANWHILE, I am *delighted* that you have got into the swing again. You are by nature always able to get back to working at speed. I take it my letter came in time?[e]

As long as these abominable Lassalleans rule the roost in Germany, that country will be infertile ground for the '*INTERNATIONAL ASSOCIATION*'. For the present, we must be patient. The

---

a concerning - b about-turn - c Bernhard Becker - d with regard to - e See this volume, pp. 86-88.

Prussian government will put an end to this foul morass of Izzyness[a] soon enough.

Apropos. Cutting from the latest *Hermann* enclosed. You must make a few bad jokes about this notice from Messrs Blind-Wolffsohn, for me to pass on to Eccarius for insertion *in his London correspondence*.[139] I have been so put out by this lousy correspondence with Berlin (apart from the amount of time the INTERNATIONAL ASSOCIATION inevitably takes up) that I absolutely must make up the lost ground.

Tyndall has succeeded in using a simple mechanical technique to break down sunlight into heat-rays and pure light-rays. The latter are cold. You can *light your cigar straight* from the former, and through a burning-glass they can melt platinum, etc.

* My best compliments to Mrs Burns. I am indeed very glad to hear that the *o* was an inorganic intrusion upon her name, and that she is a namesake of the great poet.[b] If Mrs Gumpert declines becoming a member of a *Workingmen's* Association, I hope Mrs Burns will not follow that example, but will believe with her namesake that 'a man is a man for all that'.[c]*

Salut.

Your
K. M.

HAVE AN EYE UPON JONES! HE IS A FELLOW 'TOO CLEVER BY HALF'!

Apropos. I think I should be in a position to send you the cards by Tuesday. I SEND ABOUT 2 DOZEN, which you don't need to dispose of all at once. But give *some of them to E. Jones.*

The latter has written to me about the electoral agitation (whereupon I wrote him that he should write me a 2nd letter[117] which I could read out *at the Comité.* Which he duly did).[140] But he didn't say *anything* in his letter about the INTERNATIONAL ASSOCIATION. As he is a *fox* and I want to pin him down, you should insist that he forms A BRANCH COMMITTEE immediately (the number of MEMBERS doesn't matter *for the present*) and that he and his friends take out CARDS OF MEMBERSHIP. They must realise that the '*INTERNATIONAL*' is the only means and method of establishing co-operation (political) *between London and the provinces*!

Concerning the cards, our RULES are as follows: *existing societies* (UNIONS, etc.) who wish to affiliate *in that capacity* need only take out *corporate membership.* That doesn't cost them anything, or they can

---

[a] Lassalleanism - [b] Robert Burns - [c] R. Burns, *Is There for Honest Poverty.*

make a voluntary donation. On the other hand, *every member* of such a society who wishes to become an INDIVIDUAL MEMBER of the Association, must take out his annual membership card at 1s. 1d. In France and Belgium, because of the laws there, it has 'turned out' that they will all *have to* become 'INDIVIDUAL' MEMBERS of the *English* society, since they are not able to join as societies. Every branch society or affiliated society *outside* London and ENVIRONS elects a secretary to correspond with us. We can 'reject' people we disapprove of.

First published abridged in *Der Briefwech-sel zwischen F. Engels und K. Marx*, Bd. 3, Stuttgart, 1913 and in full in *MEGA*, Abt. III, Bd. 3, Berlin, 1930

Printed according to the original

Published in English for the first time

45

MARX TO VICTOR LE LUBEZ[1]

IN LONDON

London, 15 February 1865

My dear Lubez,

The very success of our association warns us to be cautious. In my opinion, M. Beales joining our council would spoil the whole affair.[a] I believe him an honest and sincere man; at the same time, he is nothing and can be nothing save a Bourgeois politician. He is weak, mediocre and ambitious. He wants to stand for Marylebone at the next Parliamentary election. By that single fact he ought to be excluded from entering our committee. We cannot become *le piedestal* for small parliamentary ambitions.

You may be sure that if Beales is admitted *le ton cordial, sincère et franc*[b] that distinguishes now our Debates, will be gone, and make place to *word-mongering*. In the wake of Beales will follow *Taylor*, this unbearable nuisance and tufthunter.

In the eyes of the world, Beales' admission will change the whole character of our society, we will diminish into one of the numerous societies which he favours with patronage. Where he has driven in the wedge, others of his class will follow, and our

---

[a] See this volume, pp. 109-10. - [b] the cordial, sincere and frank atmosphere

efforts, till now successful at freeing the English working class movement from all middle class or aristocratic patronage, will have been in vain.

I know beforehand that if Beales be admitted, there will arise questions mainly of a social sort, which will force him to tender his demission. We will have to issue manifestos on *the land question*, etc., which he *cannot* sign. Is it not better not to let him instead of giving him afterwards an opportunity of denying us.[a]

I know that after the foolish step taken by Mr Dell,[b] there will be certain difficulties in ensuring this candidature.

I would think that by means of quiet talks with the chief English members, the whole question could be [settled][c] before it is put before the committee again.

Yours fraternally

K. Marx

Apropos. For all his enthusiasm for Poland, Mr Beales has as yet done nothing other than follow the Duke ...[d] in throwing all the demonstrations for Poland into confusion. Yesterday, he attempted the same trick again, under similar instigation.

First published abridged in the language of the original (English) in: I. Tchernoff, *Le Parti républicain au coup d'état et sous le Second Empire*, Paris, 1908 and in full in: Marx and Engels, *Works*, Second Russian Edition, Vol. 31, Moscow, 1963

Reproduced from the text of Tchernoff's book, verified with the manuscript copy in French written in an unknown hand

46

MARX TO ENGELS

IN MANCHESTER

[London, 16 February 1865]

Dᴇᴀʀ Fʀᴇᴅᴇʀɪᴄᴋ,

Jones has written, asking me to send him ABOUT 1 DOZEN CARDS; I am sending you 1 DOZEN for him and 1 for yourself. What you can't

---

[a] The rest of the letter, missing in the English original, has been translated from the extant French manuscript. - [b] See this volume, p. 110. - [c] Manuscript damaged - [d] An omission in the original; Marx presumably means Duke Townshend.

dispose of WITHIN A REASONABLE period of time you can send back. Price 1s. 1d. PER CARD.

I remind you AGAIN that *Petzler* may, in my opinion, be very useful in *this matter*. For years now he has had many PERSONAL RELATIONS (as SINGMASTER and socialist) with the Manchester workers.

You must return enclosed letter (to Lessner) when you have read it. How do you think we should MANAGE this business? *I* shall keep my mouth shut, of course, but *Lessner* won't be able to do that.[141]

I am pleased to see in today's *Times* that the Prussian Chamber has accepted the motion *against* the Combination Laws. The government will now arrange for it to be rejected in the LORDS HOUSE. Red Becker[a]—no doubt spurred on by your literary contribution[b]—has brought in the amendment about the rural population.[142]

Salut.

Your

K. M.

First published in *Der Briefwechsel zwischen F. Engels und K. Marx*, Bd. 3, Stuttgart, 1913

Printed according to the original

Published in English for the first time

47

MARX TO ENGELS[101]

IN MANCHESTER

[London,] 18 February 1865

DEAR FRED,

Enclosed 2 letters from Liebknecht, 1 to you and 1 to me. Ditto an *earlier* one from Schweitzer.

My view is this:

Once Liebknecht has given in his notice,[143] *il faut en finir.*[c] If he had put the matter off, we could have done so, too, since your pamphlet[d] is on the stocks.

---

[a] Hermann Heinrich Becker - [b] F. Engels, 'Herr Tidmann. Old Danish Folk Song'. - [c] we must put an end to it - [d] F. Engels, *The Prussian Military Question and the German Workers' Party*.

I consider Schweitzer to be incorrigible (probably has a secret arrangement with Bismarck).

What confirms me in that view is

1. the passage I have underlined in his letter of 15th enclosed [144];

2. the *timing* of the publication of his 'Bismarck III'.[145]

To do justice to both points, I shall now *copy out* for you *word for word* a passage from my letter to him [134] of 13 February:

'...since our statement [a] has become partially out-of-date, following the correspondence from M. Hess in No. 21 received today, we will allow the matter rest there.[125] Our statement did, of course, contain another point as well: praise of the anti-Bonapartist stance of the Parisian proletariat and hint to the German workers that they should follow this example. We regarded this as more important than our sally against Hess. Meanwhile, we shall set out our views in detail elsewhere on the relation of the workers towards the Prussian government.[b]

'In your letter of 4 February you say that I warned Liebknecht myself not to overstep the mark, so that he would not be sent to the devil. Quite right. But I wrote to him at the same time that one could say *anything* if one put it in the right way.[c] A form of polemic *against* the government which is "possible" even for the Berlin meridian is certainly very different from flirting with the government or even pretending to compromise with it! I wrote to you myself that the *Social-Demokrat* must eschew even the appearance of doing so.[121]

'I see from your paper that the ministry is making ambiguous and procrastinatory statements with regard to the repeal of the Combination Laws. On the other hand, a *Times* telegram reports that it was in favour of the proposed state aid for the co-operative societies.[d] It would not surprise me at all if *The Times* had for once telegraphed a correct report!

'Combinations and the TRADES UNIONS they would give rise to are of the utmost importance not merely as a means of organising the working class for the struggle against the bourgeoisie—just how important is shown among other things by the fact that even the workers of the United States cannot do without them, in spite of franchise and republic—but in Prussia and indeed in Germany as a whole the right of combination also means a breach in the domination of the police and the bureaucracy, it tears to shreds

---

[a] K. Marx and F. Engels, 'To the Editor of the *Social-Demokrat*'.- [b] See this volume, pp. 89-90. - [c] ibid., pp. 75-76. - [d] *The Times*, No. 25107, 13 February 1865.

the Rules Governing Servants [136] and the power of the aristocracy in rural areas, in short, it is a step towards the granting of full civil rights to the "subject population" which the Party of Progress, [99] i.e. any bourgeois opposition party in Prussia, would be crazy not to be a hundred times more willing to permit than the Prussian government, to say nothing of the government of a Bismarck! As opposed to that, however, the aid of the Royal Prussian government for co-operative societies—and anyone who is familiar with conditions in Prussia also knows in advance its necessarily minute dimensions—is worthless as an economic measure, whilst, at the same time, it serves to extend the system of tutelage, corrupt part of the working class and emasculate the movement. Just as the bourgeois party in Prussia discredited itself and brought about its present wretched situation by seriously believing that with the "New Era" the government [146] had fallen into its lap by the grace of the Prince Regent,[a] so the workers' party will discredit itself even more if it imagines that the Bismarck era or any other Prussian era will make the golden apples just drop into its mouth, by grace of the king. It is beyond all question that Lassalle's ill-starred illusion that a Prussian government might intervene with socialist measures will be crowned with disappointment. The logic of circumstances will tell. But the *honour* of the workers' party requires that it reject such illusions, even before their hollowness is punctured by experience. The working class is revolutionary or it is nothing.'

WELL! He replied to this letter of mine of 13th with his letter of 15th, in which he demands that in all 'practical' questions I should subordinate myself to *his* tactics; he replies with '*Bismarck III*' as a fresh specimen of these tactics!! And really it now seems to me that the *impudent* manner in which he raised the question of confidence apropos of the statement against Hess was not due to any tenderness for Moses but to the *firm resolution* not to give space in the *Social-Demokrat under any circumstances* to our hint to the German workers.

So, as a break must be made with the fellow after all, it had best be done at once. As far as the louts in Germany are concerned, they can scream as much as they like. Those of them who are any good will after all have to rally round us sooner or later. If the statement given below seems all right to you, make a copy of it, sign it and send it to me. As it was scrawled in great haste, alter

---

[a] William I

anything that seems unsuitable to you, or re-write the whole thing, just as you wish.

Your

K. M.

To the Editor of the 'Social-Demokrat'

The undersigned promised to contribute to the *Social-Demokrat* and permitted their being named as contributors on the express condition that the paper would be edited in the spirit of the brief programme submitted to them. They did not for a moment fail to appreciate the difficult position of the *Social-Demokrat* and therefore made no demands that were inappropriate to the meridian of Berlin. But they repeatedly demanded that the language directed at the ministry and the feudal-absolutist party should be at least as bold as that aimed at the men of Progress.[99] The tactics pursued by the *Social-Demokrat* preclude their further participation in it. The opinion of the undersigned as to the royal Prussian governmental socialism and the correct attitude of the workers' party to such deception has already been set out in detail in No. 73 of the *Deutsche-Brüsseler-Zeitung* of 12 September 1847, in reply to No. 206 of the *Rheinischer Beobachter*[a] (then appearing in Cologne), in which the alliance of the 'proletariat' with the 'government' against the 'liberal bourgeoisie' was proposed. We still subscribe today to every word of the statement **we** made then.

I'll send the Weydemeyer back to you tomorrow. What do you say to the 'Freiligrath-Blind' *Eidgenossenschaft*.[b][147]

For a couple of days now, I have had a carbuncle on my posterior and a furuncle on my left loin. All very nice.

First published in *Der Briefwechsel zwischen F. Engels und K. Marx*, Bd. 3, Stuttgart, 1913

Printed according to the original

Published in English in full for the first time

---

[a] A reference to Marx's article 'The Communism of the *Rheinischer Beobachter*'. -
[b] confederation

48

ENGELS TO MARX

IN LONDON

[Manchester,] 20[-21] February 1865

Dear Moor,

The letter from Matzeratt enclosed.[a]

Quant à[b] Petzler, so the photographer is an altogether different Petzler from the other one. I saw the photographer, you know, the day before yesterday, at a scientific soirée at the Schiller Institute,[28] and the fellow is at least 20 years younger and looks quite different. Heaven knows what has become of the musician.

Your
F.E.

[Pencilled note on the reverse of the letter]

Quite forgot to post the letter yesterday. No ANSWER YET FROM HAMBURG.[c]

First published in *Der Briefwechsel zwischen F. Engels und K. Marx*, Bd. 3, Stuttgart, 1913

Printed according to the original

Published in English for the first time

49

ENGELS TO MARX

IN LONDON

Manchester, 22 February 1865

Dear Moor,

In great haste, herewith the statement.[d] Schweitzer's letter is 'rotten to the core'.[e] The fellow has the job of compromising us,

---

[a] See this volume, p. 94. - [b] With regard to - [c] from Meissner (see this volume, pp. 84-85. - [d] K. Marx and F. Engels, 'To the Editor of the *Social-Demokrat*'. - [e] See this volume, pp. 94-95.

and the longer we have our dealings with him, the deeper we'll sink into the mire. So, the sooner the better! Liebknecht's and Schweitzer's letters likewise returned. You must have given Liebknecht a terrible dressing down if my letter appeared 'kind' to him! [131]

Enclosure from Meissner. This time it really is full steam ahead with the publication,[a] and that's what really matters. I replied to his proposal to fix the number of copies himself as follows: suits me, but he must then *tell* me how many there are to be, he only gets the *first* impression for 2 *louis-d'or*. (N.B. In the meantime, he will have had to make up his mind and get things ready for printing.)

In haste.

Your

F. E.

First published in *Der Briefwechsel zwischen F. Engels und K. Marx*, Bd. 3, Stuttgart, 1913

Printed according to the original

Published in English for the first time

50

MARX TO ENGELS

IN MANCHESTER

[London, before 22 February 1865]

232244

Dear FREDERICK,

Enclosed some secret contributions to the *crème bonapartiste* as a Sunday *treat* and *pour la bonne bouche*.[b][148]

You must keep these scraps of paper. MY COMPLIMENTS TO MRS LIZZIE.[c]

Your

K. M.

First published in: Marx and Engels, *Works*, Second Russian Edition, Vol. 31, Moscow, 1963

Printed according to the original

Published in English for the first time

---

[a] F. Engels, *The Prussian Military Question and the German Workers' Party.* - [b] as a special delicacy - [c] Lizzie Burns

51

ENGELS TO OTTO MEISSNER

IN HAMBURG

Manchester, 22 February 1865

Dear Sir,

Your kind letter of 17th inst. has only just been delivered to me, since postal communication via Ostende has been interrupted for three full days, and I am greatly obliged to you for your prompt agreement to publish, and more especially for your rapid prosecution of the printing.[a]

I accept your fee of 2 *louis-d'or* per sheet of print and likewise leave it to you to decide the number of copies to be printed, under the condition, however, that you inform me of it in your next letter; it goes without saying [that I] am only making [over the first impression][b] for this fee.

Announcements in the n[ewspapers shall be] attended to forthwith.

The apparent delay in [despatch] here, to which you justifiably allude, arose from the following: I finished on Saturday evening, 11 February, and wrote the accompanying letter late that night; the letter was taken to the post on Monday 13th at 10.00 a.m. and went by the mail-boat from Dover that Monday evening—no later than it would have done if I had posted it on Saturday evening. The pious English do not allow mail-steamers to leave on Sunday evening, at least not to Ostende.

Yours respectfully

Fr. Engels

I hope to receive 12 copies by post here on 27th or 28th inst.

First published in: Marx and Engels, *Works*, First Russian Edition, Vol. XXV, Moscow, 1934

Printed according to the original

Published in English for the first time

---

[a] Engels refers to his pamphlet *The Prussian Military Question and the German Workers' Party*. - [b] The manuscript is damaged; here and below the words in square brackets are reconstructed according to Engels' letter to Marx of 22 February 1865.

52

MARX TO WILHELM LIEBKNECHT [149]

IN HANOVER

[London, 23 February 1865]

In the few brief excerpts, which Eccarius gives from my speech at the workers' society, there are certain things *that convey precisely the opposite of what I said.*[150] I have written to him about it, leaving it to him whether to correct it or not in the next piece he contributes, as it is not very important in the present circumstances.[111]

First published in *Der Briefwechsel zwischen F. Engels und K. Marx*, Bd. 3, Stuttgart, 1913

Printed according to the original

Published in English for the first time

53

MARX TO LUDWIG KUGELMANN [65]

IN HANOVER

London, 23 February 1865
1 Modena Villas, Maitland Park,
Haverstock Hill

Dear Friend,

Yesterday I received your letter, which I found most interesting, and will now reply to the various points.

First of all, I shall briefly describe my attitude towards *Lassalle*. Whilst he was pursuing his agitation, our relations were suspended, 1. on account of his bombastic self-adulation, which he managed to combine with the most shameless plagiarism of writings by myself and others; 2. because I *condemned* his *political* tactics; 3. because, even *before* he began his agitation,[50] I had fully explained and 'proved' to him here in London that direct *socialist* intervention by a '*Prussian state*' was an absurdity. In his letters to me (from 1848 to 1863), as well as when we met personally, he had always declared himself a supporter of the party I represent.

As soon as he had become convinced in London (at the end of 1862) that he could not play his game *with* me, he resolved to set himself up as 'workers' dictator' *against* me and the old party. In spite of all that, I acknowledged his merits as an agitator, although towards the end of his brief career even that agitation appeared to me in an increasingly dubious light. His sudden death, our friendship of old, the grief-stricken letters from Countess Hatzfeldt, my indignation at the *cowardly impudence* of the bourgeois papers towards the man they had feared so much while he was alive, all these things induced me to publish a short statement attacking that wretch Blind[a] but not dealing with the *substance* of Lassalle's doings (Hatzfeldt sent the statement to the *Nordstern*[b]). For the same reasons, and in the hope of being able to drive out those elements whom I thought dangerous, Engels and I promised to contribute to the *Social-Demokrat* (it has published a translation of the 'Address',[c] and, at its request, I wrote an article about Proudhon[d] when the latter died) and allowed our names to be put out as contributors, after Schweitzer had sent us a *satisfactory programme of its editorial board*.[34] We had a further guarantee in W. *Liebknecht* being an unofficial member of the editorial board. In the meantime, it soon became clear—the proof of this came into our possession—that *Lassalle* had in fact *betrayed* the party. He had entered into a formal contract with Bismarck (with *no* guarantees *of any kind* in *his* hands, of course). At the end of September 1864, he was to go to Hamburg and there (together with the crazy Schramm and the Prussian police spy Marr) '*force*' Bismarck to incorporate Schleswig-Holstein, i.e. to proclaim such in the name of the 'workers', etc., in return for which Bismarck promised universal suffrage and a few spurious socialist measures.[98] It is a pity that Lassalle was unable to play this farce through to its conclusion! It would have made him appear deuced foolish and an utter gull! And it would have put paid to all such attempts for ever!

Lassalle got on the wrong path because he was, like Mr Miquel,[151] a '*realistic politician*', only on a larger scale and with grander aims! (By THE BYE, I had long ago seen through Miquel sufficiently to explain his conduct to myself[e] by the fact that the National Association[152] offered a splendid excuse for a petty

---

[a] K. Marx, 'To the Editor of the Stuttgart *Beobachter*'. - [b] See this volume, pp. 56-57. - [c] K. Marx, 'Inaugural Address of the Working Men's International Association'. - [d] K. Marx, 'On Proudhon [Letter to J. B. Schweitzer]'. - [e] See this volume, pp. 107 and 112.

Hanoverian lawyer to make himself heard beyond his own four walls, in Germany at large, and then to exploit the enhanced *'reality'* of his own self retrospectively in his native Hanover, playing the *'Hanoverian'* Mirabeau under *'Prussian'* protection, furthermore.) Just as Miquel and his present friends eagerly seized hold of the 'New Era'[146] inaugurated by the Prussian Prince Regent in order to national-associate and to fasten on to the 'Prussian leadership',[153] just as in general they cultivated their 'pride of citizenship' under *Prussian protection,* so Lassalle wanted to play the Marquis Posa of the proletariat to the Philipp II of the Uckermark,[a] with Bismarck as intermediary between himself and the Prussian monarchy. He was merely imitating the gentlemen of the National Association. But, if the latter were invoking Prussian 'reaction' in the interests of the middle class, he was shaking hands with Bismarck in the interests of the proletariat. Those gentlemen had more justification than Lassalle, inasmuch as the bourgeois is accustomed to regard the interest he perceives immediately in front of his nose as 'reality', and as this class has, in fact, compromised everywhere, even with feudalism, whereas the working class must in the nature of things be genuinely 'revolutionary'.

For a histrionically vain character like Lassalle (who was not, however, to be bribed with such paltry things as office, mayoralties, etc.), it was a most seductive thought that he, Ferdinand Lassalle, might perform a deed for the direct benefit of the proletariat! He was, in fact, too ignorant of the real economic conditions required for such a deed to be critically self-consistent! The German workers, on the other hand, had *'demoralised'* too far in consequence of the despicable *'realistic politics'* with which the German bourgeoisie had tolerated the reaction of 1849-1859 and watched the people's minds being stultified, for them not to hail such a mountebank of a saviour who was promising to help them reach the promised land with one bound!

So, to take up the thread where I left off above! Hardly had the *Social-Demokrat* been established when it became clear that the old Hatzfeldt woman was planning to execute Lassalle's 'testament' posthumously. She had contact with Bismarck through Wagener (of the *Kreuz-Zeitung*[b]). She placed the 'Workers' Association' (Gen. German),[2] the *Social-Demokrat,* etc., at Bismarck's disposal. The

---

[a] Marquis Posa and Philipp II are characters in Schiller's drama *Don Carlos.* Here Marx calls William I of Prussia 'the Philipp II of the Uckermark'. - [b] *Neue Preussische Zeitung*

annexation of Schleswig-Holstein was to be proclaimed in the *Social-Demokrat*, Bismarck to be generally acknowledged as patron, etc. The whole of this fine plan was *frustrated* because we had Liebknecht in Berlin and on the editorial board of the *Social-Demokrat*. Although Engels and I disliked the editorial board of the paper, its lickspittling cult of Lassalle, its occasional flirting with Bismarck, etc., it was, of course, more important publicly to stay with the paper for the time being in order to thwart the intrigues of the old Hatzfeldt woman and prevent the workers' party from being totally compromised. We therefore put on *bonne mine à mauvais jeu*,[a] although *privatim* we were constantly writing to the *Social-Demokrat* telling them that they should stand up to Bismarck just as much as to the men of Progress.[99] We even tolerated that affected fop, Bernhard Becker, who is taking the importance bequeathed to him in Lassalle's testament quite seriously, intriguing *against* the INTERNATIONAL WORKINGMEN'S ASSOCIATION.[b]

In the meantime, Mr Schweitzer's articles in the *Social-Demokrat* were becoming more and more Bismarckian. I had earlier written to him to say that, although the men of Progress can be *intimidated* over the 'Combination question', the *Prussian government* would *never under any circumstances* concede the complete abolition of the Combination Laws because that would entail breaching the bureaucratic system, giving freedom of thought and expression to the workers, tearing up the Rules Governing Servants,[136] abolishing flogging and birching by the aristocracy in rural areas, etc., etc., which Bismarck could never allow, it being altogether incompatible with the Prussian *bureaucratic* state.[c] I added that, if the Chamber were to repudiate the Combination Laws, the government would resort to empty *phrases* (such as e.g. that the social question requires 'profounder' steps to be taken, etc.) in order to preserve them. All this has come to pass. And what did Mr von Schweitzer do? He wrote an article *in support of* Bismarck[145] and is reserving all his heroism for such *infiniment petits*[d] as Schulze, Faucher, etc.

I believe that Schweitzer, etc., mean it *sincerely*, but they are '*realistic politicians*'. They wish to take due account of the *existing* state of affairs and not leave this *privilege* of 'realistic politics' to Messrs Miquel *et* Comp. alone. (The latter seem to wish to reserve the right of INTERMIXTURE with the Prussian government.) They know that the workers' papers and the workers' movement in

---

[a] a brave face on it - [b] See this volume, pp. 64-65. - [c] ibid., p. 90, 95-96. - [d] nonentities

Prussia (and hence in the rest of Germany) only exist *par la grâce de la police*.[a] They thus want to take the circumstances as they are, not to irritate the government, etc., quite as our *'republican'* realistic politicians want to 'put up with' a Hohenzollern *emperor*. As I am not a 'realistic politician', however, I found it necessary together with Engels to serve notice on the *Social-Demokrat* in a public statement[b] (which you will probably soon see in one paper or other).

You will see at the same time why there is *nothing* I can do in Prussia at the moment. The government there has flatly refused to restore my Prussian citizenship.[154] I should only be permitted to *agitate* there in a manner agreeable to Mr von Bismarck.

I prefer my agitation here through the *'International Association'* a 100 times. The effect on the *English* proletariat is direct and of the greatest importance. We are now STIRRING the GENERAL SUFFRAGE QUESTION here, which is, naturally, of *quite different significance* here than in Prussia.[155]

As a whole, the progress made by this 'Association' has *exceeded all expectations* here, in Paris, in Belgium, Switzerland, and Italy. Only in Germany, of course, I am opposed by Lassalle's successors who 1. are stupidly afraid of forfeiting their own importance; 2. are aware of my avowed opposition to what the Germans call 'realistic politics'. (It is this sort of *'reality'* that puts Germany so far behind all civilised countries.)

Since any person who takes out a card at 1 SHILLING can become a MEMBER OF THE ASSOCIATION; since the French have chosen this form of INDIVIDUAL MEMBERSHIP (ditto the Belgians) because the law prohibits them from joining us as an 'association'; and since the situation is similar in Germany, I have now resolved to ask my friends here and in Germany to form small SOCIETIES, regardless of how many MEMBERS there may be in each locality, each member of which will acquire AN ENGLISH CARD OF MEMBERSHIP.[156] Since the English society is *public*, there is no obstacle to this procedure even in France. I should appreciate it if you, too, would get in touch with London in this way in your neighbourhood.

My thanks to you for your prescription. Oddly enough this vile disease had broken out once more 3 days before it arrived. So, the prescription was most timely.

In a few days I shall send you another 24 ADDRESSES.[c] I have just been interrupted in my writing by a friend, and, as I very

---

a by the grace of the police - b K. Marx and F. Engels, 'To the Editor of the *Social-Demokrat*'. - c K. Marx, 'Inaugural Address of the Working Men's International Association'.

much want to send off this letter, I shall take up the other points in your letter next time.

Yours

K. M.

First published in *Sozialistische Aus-landspolitik*, No. 18, 1918   Printed according to the original

54

ENGELS TO MARX

IN LONDON

Manchester, 24 February 1865

Dear Moor,

I'm a bit concerned at not having heard from you today, in view of the furuncles and carbuncles you mentioned, in the most interesting places (or rather most interested). I hope you are not LAID UP.

I was particularly disappointed as I hoped to get the explanation—as well as the Weydemeyer—about the unspeakable mess the *Social-Demokrat* fellows made of your speech at the London Workers' Society festivity. They make you speak pure *S.-D.* Eccarius never reported that to them.[150] This piece of infamy and the reprint of the article from the *Norddeutsche Allgemeine Zeitung* in the following number, *ostensibly about universal suffrage, about which it says not a word*,[157] is proof enough for me that the fellow[a] has simply been bought and has the job of compromising us. I hope the statement[b] is on its way. We must not delay a moment longer.

But *quelle bête notre ami*[c] Liebknecht, who is supposed to keep an eye on the newspaper and *never reads it on principle*!

Your

F. E.

First published in *Der Briefwechsel zwischen F. Engels und K. Marx*, Bd. 3, Stuttgart, 1913   Printed according to the original

Published in English for the first time

---

[a] Schweitzer - [b] K. Marx and F. Engels, 'To the Editor of the *Social-Demokrat*'. - [c] what a fool our friend

55

MARX TO ENGELS[33]

IN MANCHESTER

[London,] 25 February 1865

Dear FRED,

I quite forgot—*you must excuse me—to send back Weydemeyer's letter. I enclose it. Ditto a letter of Dr Kugelmann with enclosure of wiseacre Miquel's letter.[151] Ditto a prescription* from Kugelmann. Oddly enough the prescription arrived just after the disease had broken out afresh. (Nota bene, the passage in Kugelmann's LETTER, saying I wrote that I wanted to defend Lassalle, referred to *Blind's* attack.[62] I have now told him (Kugelmann) the plain truth.[a] Return the letters from Kugelmann and Miquel.) I have had the prescription made up and have already taken the POWDER, but I would still like Gumpert's opinion of it. It's a most troublesome business. Unlike last year, however, my faculties are *not* affected and (*to the extent that sitting down for a long time is not physically troublesome*) I am perfectly able to work. Incidentally, I have the feeling in every part of my CADAVER that the stuff is about to burst out all over.

Strohn passed by here. He was still in Hamburg when your manuscript[b] came in, in the nick of time to recommend to Meissner that he should accept it. Strohn was informed that a manuscript from Rüstow on the same topic was rejected. Apropos. Have you taken any steps yourself regarding your pamphlet in the newspapers, or AM I TO DO IT? On this occasion, Eccarius himself was responsible for the incomprehensible BLUNDER.[150] When his article arrived, I wrote to him at once (22 February) enquiring whether the thing had been *falsified* by Schweitzer?[111] *Quod non.*[c]

When I sent our statement[d] to that jackass Wilhelm[e] (23 February), I wrote this to him:

'In the few brief excerpts, which Eccarius gives from my speech at the workers' society,[f] there are certain things that *convey precisely the opposite of what I said.* I have written to him about it, leaving it

---

[a] See this volume, pp. 101-05. - [b] F. Engels, *The Prussian Military Question and the German Workers' Party.* - [c] Not so. - [d] K. Marx and F. Engels, 'To the Editor of the *Social-Demokrat*'. - [e] Wilhelm Liebknecht - [f] German Workers' Educational Society in London

to him whether to correct it or not in the next piece he contributes, as it is not very important in the *present* circumstances.'[a]

My letters to Eccarius and Liebknecht have been written so that, if Schweitzer (who from the private letter he had just previously received from me[b] VERY WELL KNEW WHAT HE WAS ABOUT, of course) should try to use Eccarius' BLUNDER to defend himself, we could *if necessary* cut off this *retraite*.[c] MEANWHILE, I HAVE TOLD ECCARIUS PRIVATELY not to make any BOTHER about the whole filthy business until such time as Schweitzer's own behaviour requires it. Eccarius was very unwell, and that is probably to blame for the NONSENSE. On the other hand, I imagine that Schweitzer, who already had Wilhelm's resignation[143] in his possession and was therefore prepared for a statement from us, was delighted to accept the report, 1. so as to show by means of the passage about *Prussia* what *extravagant* demands we were making of *him,* and 2. by means of the conclusion to the report that we did IN FACT share *his* views. The *galantuomo*[d] is forgetting, by the way, that I have kept copies of my *private letter to him.*[134]

I have informed Liebknecht that, if Schweitzer should turn it down, he should put the thing in the *Berliner Reform* and tell Schweitzer about this at the same time, and also that I have simultaneously sent the statement to two Rhineland papers, so that Schweitzer cannot *procrastinate* this time. I have in fact sent 2 COPIES to Siebel, instructing him to insert the thing in the *Rheinische Zeitung* and the *Düsseldorfer Zeitung* (the latter being the workers' paper) *two days after receipt of my letter,* and to send us a report on any comments in the local press.[158] So, this time there is nothing Schweitzer can do about it any more. I would not be surprised if the Lassalleans, especially in the Hamburg *Nordstern,* declared we had *sold ourselves to the bourgeoisie.* BUT NEVER MIND!

The 'INTERNATIONAL ASSOCIATION' has managed so to constitute the majority on the committee to set up the new REFORM LEAGUE that the *whole leadership* is in our hands.[155] I have put the full details in a letter to E. Jones.[111]

Such a conflict has broken out in Paris between our own representatives that we have sent Lubez to Paris to clarify matters and effect conciliation.[95] His CREDENTIALS state that Schily has been attached to him as an adjunct, and I have given Schily private instructions.[159] We could have sold 20,000 cards in Paris, but since one group was accusing the other of having Plon-Plon behind

---

[a] See this volume, p. 101. - [b] ibid., pp. 95-96.- [c] retreat - [d] honourable man

them, etc., the distribution of cards has had to be suspended for the time being. Under this military despotism, people are naturally highly suspicious of each other (my impression is that this time both sides are doing each other an injustice), and they are not capable of sorting out their differences and reaching an understanding by MEETING or through the press. A further factor is this: the workers seem to want to take things to the point of *excluding* any LITERARY MAN, etc., which is absurd, as they need them in the press, but it is pardonable in view of the repeated treachery of the LITERARY MEN. Conversely, the latter are suspicious of *any workers' movement,* which displays hostility towards them.[160]

(Apropos these 'LITERARY MEN', I am reminded that the workers here (*English*) want *to make me editor* when *The Bee-Hive*[a] is transformed, which is to happen in 3 months time, and have already informed me of this. However, I shall mull over the matter in all its multifarious aspects, before making a move in one direction or another.)

So, what we have in Paris is, on the one hand, *Lefort* (a LITERARY MAN, well-to-do into the bargain, in other words 'bourgeois' but with an unsullied reputation, and, as far as *La belle France*[b] is concerned, the real founder of our Association), and, on the other, *Tolain, Fribourg, Limousin,* etc., who are workers. WELL, I shall let you know the outcome. At all events, Wolff, an acquaintance, who has just returned from Paris, tells me that there is growing interest in the 'INTERNATIONAL ASSOCIATION'. The *Débats*[c] has also intervened in the matter.

As far as the London UNIONS, etc., are concerned, every day brings about new ADHESION, so that BY AND BY we are becoming a force to be reckoned with.

But that is where the difficulty begins as well. Already MR BEALES (THE REGISTERING BARRISTER *of Middlesex,* one of the *most popular* people in London at present, President of the POLISH LEAGUE,[97] co-founder of the NEW REFORM LEAGUE, IN FACT THE GO-BETWEEN between WORKING-MAN and MIDDLE CLASS, *honest* and well-meaning to boot) has got himself proposed as MEMBER for our COUNCIL. The opportunity arose because as a SUB-COMMITTEE together with him we were to prepare the Polish MEETING (Marquis Townshend in the chair) for next Wednesday.[161] This was most unfortunate for me. I could, of course, have prevented the matter *by force,* as all the CONTINENTALS would have voted with me. BUT I DID NOT LIKE ANY SUCH DIVISION. So, by

---

[a] See this volume, pp. 154-55. - [b] beautiful France - [c] *Journal des Débats politiques et littéraires*

means of private letters^a to the PRINCIPAL ENGLISH MEMBERS, I have managed to persuade Beales' PROPOSER ^b *not* to bring forward his MOTION again. The *'official'* reason given was: 1. that Beales WILL STAND FOR MARYLEBONE at the next parliamentary elections and that our Association must by all means avoid appearing TO SERVE THE INTERESTS OF ANY PARLIAMENTARY AMBITION; 2. that Beales and we ourselves can be of greater assistance to each other, if we sail our separate ships. Thus, the danger has been temporarily averted. Incidentally, other parliamentarians, such as Taylor, etc. (fellows, who have close links with Mazzini), had taken it into their heads to tell us that the TIME *was not* OPPORTUNE for a Polish meeting. I answered through our COUNCIL that the WORKING CLASS has ITS OWN FOREIGN POLICY, which is most certainly not determined by what the MIDDLE CLASS considers OPPORTUNE. They always considered it OPPORTUNE TO GOAD ON THE POLES AT THE BEGINNING OF A NEW OUTBREAK, TO BETRAY THEM DURING ITS PROGRESS BY THEIR DIPLOMACY, AND TO DESERT THEM WHEN RUSSIA HAD THROWN THEM DOWN. In fact, the chief purpose of the MEETING is to raise money to support them. Are the poor émigrés (*this time mostly* WORKINGMEN and PEASANTS and thus not in the least PROTECTED BY PRINCE ZAMOYSKI *et* Co.) to starve because it appears to the ENGLISH MIDDLE CLASS JUST NOW INOPPORTUNE TO MENTION EVEN THE NAME OF POLAND?

Cutting enclosed by *Mr Blind from The Morning Star.*[162] Mazzini, who did tell Fontana that Blind was a *liar,* was absolutely furious that *his Italian Workers' Association*[20] here sent out the Italian version of my 'Address'^c into the world without the omissions Mr Mazzini had *expressly* demanded, e.g. the passages attacking the MIDDLE CLASS.

Your
K. M.

Apropos. Some port wine and claret would do me a world of good UNDER PRESENT CIRCUMSTANCES.

First published in *Der Briefwechsel zwischen F. Engels und K. Marx,* Bd. 3, Stuttgart, 1913

Printed according to the original

Published in English in full for the first time

---

^a See this volume, pp. 92-93. - ^b William Dell - ^c K. Marx, 'Inaugural Address of the Working Men's International Association'.

56

ENGELS TO CARL SIEBEL

IN ELBERFELD

Manchester, 27 February 1865

Dear Siebel,

Marx has sent you our statement denouncing the *Social-Demokrat* in Berlin.[a] In the meantime, to do something positive to prevent the people from lumping us together with Bismarckery, I have written a pamphlet,[b] and O. Meissner in Hamburg has accepted it. I should be grateful if you would arrange for a notice concerning it to be placed in the *Düsseldorfer Zeitung* and other papers to which you have access, with something like the following content:

A pamphlet by *Fr. Engels* entitled *The Prussian Military Question and the German Workers' Party* will shortly be published by Otto Meissner in Hamburg. It originated at the request of a so-called 'social-democratic' paper[c] to the author to express his views on the subject in that paper.[d] Detailed treatment of the subject, however, required more space than a newspaper could command; the pro-Bismarck direction adopted by the latest 'Social-Democracy' furthermore made it impossible for the people at the *Neue Rheinische Zeitung* to collaborate with the organs of *this particular* 'Social-Democracy'. In these circumstances, the above-mentioned work is being published *independently* in pamphlet-form...[163]

You will need to act quickly as Meissner has written that the pamphlet was already going to be *distributed* on 24 February. It will vex the Lassallean clique most dreadfully, the men of Progress[99] no less so, and not least Monsieur Bismarck. There are some most impudent things in it which have previously, for the most part, been passed over with tactful timidity. As long as the press does not again totally ignore the thing[164] with its fulminations against all and sundry, the story will have some effect.

So, be quick now! This is all important. For the *Rheinische Zeitung* I shall supply the necessary material through Dr Klein in Cologne.

Best wishes to your wife.

Your

F. E.

---

[a] K. Marx and F. Engels, 'To the Editor of the *Social-Demokrat*'. - [b] F. Engels, *The Prussian Military Question and the German Workers' Party*. - [c] *Der Social-Demokrat* - [d] See this volume, pp. 67-69.

N.B. You can further add: and sets out the views of the 'Social-Democrats' of 1848 with regard to both the government and the Party of Progress.

First published in *Deutsche Zeitung*, No. 473, 16 October 1920

Printed according to the original

Published in English for the first time

57

ENGELS TO MARX

IN LONDON

Manchester, 27 February 1865

Dear Moor,

As you had *positively* promised to take the necessary steps regarding the newspapers[a] *immediately* Meissner sent a positive reply, I counted on it that this had been done. Meanwhile, today I dispatched the necessary to Siebel,[b] Liebknecht and Klein in Cologne (for the *Rheinische Zeitung*),[163] as there is no time to lose. If you have anyone else who can do anything, please write to them—PERHAPS Kugelmann? His letter returned enclosed, ditto Miquel whose high-faluting refashioning of the theory into a platform for mayoral dignity and bourgeois benevolence greatly amused me.[151] It is more or less how Heinrich Bürgers will view the world if he should ever become mayor of Nippes or Kalscheuren.

Jones has got SESSIONS again, I have not been able to see him yet. More tomorrow, 7 o'clock has just struck and I must post this letter.

Your

F. E.

---

[a] Engels refers to the publication of a notice about his pamphlet *The Prussian Military Question and the German Workers' Party* (see this volume, p. 84). - [b] See this volume, pp. 111-12.

I have no port wine in the WAREHOUSE and will have to get hold of some first, but will do so immediately.

First published in *Der Briefwechsel zwischen F. Engels und K. Marx*, Bd. 3, Stuttgart, 1913

Printed according to the original

Published in English for the first time

58

ENGELS TO MARX

IN LONDON

Manchester, 3 March 1865

Dear Moor,

You must excuse me for neglecting my correspondence this week. Borkheim was here and took up a lot of my time; he left this evening; then there is COTTON-PANIC following Sherman's advance,[75] with endless letter-writing and vain attempts to dispose of our STOCK. I think Richmond will be abandoned within a fortnight, and, unless by some miracle Lee manages to get a fresh respite of 2-3 months, the final, decisive battle will be fought within 4 weeks.[30]

I must go home now and write to Meissner and Siebel, who is putting himself to a lot of trouble—he says he has sent you the statement.[a] I am glad the thing is finally published; *still nothing* in the damned *Social-Demokrat* of 1 March—presumably, they tried to go back on it?[165] It's a load off my mind that we have at last made the break with that gang. So, now we have the grand concluding article on Bismarck[b] which was supposed to patch everything up. *O, jerum, jerum, jerum!*[c]

Your
F. E.

---

[a] K. Marx and F. Engels, 'To the Editor of the *Social-Demokrat*'. - [b] A reference to the fifth article of the series 'Das Ministerium Bismarck', *Der Social-Demokrat*, No. 28, 1 March 1865. - [c] *O, jerum, jerum, jerum! O quae mutatio rerum!* (Oh, dear me, dear me, dear me. A crazy world. Lord, hear me!)—part of the refrain from a student song attributed to Höfling.

I have in my hurry not managed to find any decent port, but sent claret yesterday. Will keep looking for some port.

First published in *Der Briefwechsel zwischen F. Engels und K. Marx*, Bd. 3, Stuttgart, 1913

Printed according to the original

Published in English for the first time

59

MARX TO ENGELS

IN MANCHESTER

[London,] 4 MARCH 1865

DEAR FRED,

Our statement[a] is in today's *Social-Demokrat.* Although claiming that the statement from these 'gentlemen' requires no further comment, Mr Schweitzer has, nevertheless, '*anonymously*' devoted one of his 'bloody pretentious' LEADERS[166] to us. Lassalle and B. Becker, 'President of Mankind', FOR EVER! At all events, I have Mr Schweitzer's exceedingly humble letter of invitation, etc. in my possession. Siebel has sent 5 newspapers (the *Barmer,* the *Elberfelder,* the *Düsseldorfer,* the *Rheinische* and the *Neue Frankfurter*) carrying the statement.[158] The enclosed cutting is from the *Elberfelder.* I am glad, firstly, that we are 'out' and, secondly, that we were 'in'. If we had not been, we would never have penetrated the '*mystères* of Lassalle'.

I have written to Kugelmann (please send his prescription back to me) about your pamphlet[b] (it looks *very good* in print; if there is a 2nd impression, only a sentence here and there would need to be altered). Can you send me another 2 COPIES? I would like to use Eccarius' good offices to put two short notices in Bender's rag[c] (London) and in the *Hermann,* but that will hardly be possible unless I let them have 2 copies.[167]

The '*Polish Meeting*' (WEDNESDAY) went off very well, and *full,* although the BOURGEOIS had done everything they could to wreck it by declaring it 'INOPPORTUNE'.[d 168]

---

[a] K. Marx and F. Engels, 'To the Editor of the *Social-Demokrat*'. - [b] F. Engels, *The Prussian Military Question and the German Workers' Party. - [c] Londoner Anzeiger - [d] See this volume, pp. 109-10.

Affairs in France are very complicated.[95] I will tell you about it and send you Schily's REPORT (I have to translate extracts from it this very day and accordingly inform the SUBCOMMITTEE of it) in my next letter. For the moment, I shall just mention that there is A FIGHT between our original workers' representatives and the politico-social gentlemen (including the boss of the *Association*[a] so admired by Moses[b]) as to *who* is to be in contact with us. The [French],[c] particularly the *Parisian* workers (although already links with 25 other French cities, too) literally regard the London COUNCIL as a workers' government 'abroad'.

Major Wolff has returned after serving his sentence in Alessandria.

Apropos: did I tell you that *Mazzini* later secretly communicated his 'displeasure' to Fontana after all (and his predilection for K. Blind, whom he had himself branded as a 'liar'[d])?

Your wine came yesterday; received with THANKS.

For the past week my brother-in-law[e] from the Cape[f] has been here again; he leaves next Tuesday. My niece[g] from Maastricht came with him (daughter of my sister, widow Schmalhausen); I shall have to take her back IN ABOUT A WEEK LATER.

My old trouble is plaguing me in various sensitive and 'aggravating' places, so that sitting down is difficult.

Apropos: is the Lupus affair[8] still not quite wound up? Ditto I never heard a word from Mr Borchardt about the outstanding money he was going to collect in. You will see from the enclosed scrawl, which is just one example, how I am being sent claims of every conceivable kind, things I had totally forgotten about. This is the most recent to have raised its head from the days of the *Neue Rheinische Zeitung.* It is something I have to take into account in every possible way because otherwise the fellows will make a public scandal.[h]

It seems all up with CONFEDERACY.

Salut.

Your

K. M.

---

a See this volume, p. 118-19. - b Moses Hess - c Manuscript illegible - d See this volume, p. 110. - e Johann Carl Juta - f Cape of Good Hope - g Caroline Schmalhausen - h See this volume, pp. 117-18.

I wonder if you could send me the papers from the Manchester press relating to the COTTON-CRISIS?[40]

First published abridged in *Der Briefwechsel zwischen F. Engels und K. Marx*, Bd. 3, Stuttgart, 1913 and in full in *MEGA*, Abt. III, Bd. 3, Berlin, 1930

Printed according to the original

Published in English for the first time

60

ENGELS TO MARX

IN LONDON

Manchester, 6 March 1865

Dear Moor,

Yours of the day before yesterday received, as was the *Social-Demokrat* today containing that droll article excommunicating us.[166] It really makes one laugh.

I have been at home with 'flu most of today, but I shall go and see the lawyer about the Lupus affair[8] as soon as possible. Everything will be straight as soon as the fellow completes; Borchardt has been paid his £100 (i. e. less the money he has already had), and the Schiller Institute[28] its £100, too; furthermore, I gave the lawyer approx. £150 to cover tax and am only waiting for his account now before remitting the rest to you directly. I shall put together a provisional balance sheet for you in a day or two so that you can see how things stand.

Things from Siebel and a certain Lange enclosed.[a] *Qu'en penses-tu?*[b] Send the stuff back, as well as the letter from *Meissner*, which I must have for my correspondence with him. I am sending him the cuttings for him to see that we have also got people to push things along.

The *Kölnische Zeitung* has also printed our statement,[c] but only up to the words that the *Social-Demokrat*'s tactics preclude our further participation in it.

Bruhn returned enclosed. How THE HELL CAME YOU TO OWE THAT FELLOW ANY BRASS?[d] However much it is, I shall send it to you at once.

---

[a] See this volume, pp. 135-38. - [b] What do you think of it? - [c] K. Marx and F. Engels, 'To the Editor of the *Social-Demokrat*'. - [d] See this volume, pp. 117-19.

2 COPIES of the pamphlet[a] despatched herewith. They are the last
ones. But I have ordered some more. There is an announcement
about the pamphlet in the *Kölner Zeitung.*[b]

What kind of 'PAPERS from the Manchester *press* relating to the
COTTON-CRISIS' are you talking about? Surely you mean from the
RELIEF COMMITTEE [32]? I have not seen Maclure for some time; as soon
as I encounter him, I shall have a word with him about it.

Gumpert does not think much of Kugelmann's phosphate of
lime. At all events, it is not a specific remedy. He says you ought
to take arsenic. Returned enclosed.

I must now go to the Schiller Institute to chair the *Comité.* By
the by, one of the fellows there, a chemist,[c] has recently
explained Tyndall's experiment with sunlight[d] to me. It is really
capital.

Your
F. E.

First published abridged in *Der Briefwech-
sel zwischen F. Engels und K. Marx,* Bd. 3,
Stuttgart, 1913 and in full in *MEGA,*
Abt. III, Bd. 3, Berlin, 1930

Printed according to the original

Published in English for the first
time

61

MARX TO ENGELS

IN MANCHESTER

[London,] 7 March[e] 1865

DEAR FRED,

My brother-in-law[f] is leaving today to return to the Cape. I've
got to accompany him onto the ship. So, I'm very short of
time—hence just the following in the utmost brevity:

1. *Ad vocem*[g] *Bruhn.* A worker in Paris received a letter from a
worker in Hamburg saying that Bruhn is slandering us in every
way he can. Firstly, he says I owe him 60 talers which I never

---

[a] F. Engels, *The Prussian Military Question and the German Workers'* Party. - [b] *Kölnische
Zeitung* - [c] probably Carl Schorlemmer - [d] See this volume, p. 91. - [e] In the original:
May. - [f] Johann Carl Juta - [g] As regards

repaid. Secondly, you and I are said to have sold the Prussian government, or rather 'Police-Chief Stieber', a manuscript about the refugees.[169] The Parisian sent the letter to Lessner, who passed it on to me. I replied to Lessner by return of post, for communication to the Parisian, that I had *never* had any financial dealings with Bruhn (which I believed at that time to be the case), and in general considered that for Bruhn to ever have 60 talers to his name was like something out of Munchausen. Furthermore, I explained the affair of Bangya and the manuscript, in which connection our declaration of April 1853[a] in the *New-Yorker Criminal-Zeitung*[b] and references to it in *Herr Vogt* page such and such[c] were to be consulted. WELL! Then Bruhn's letter arrived. So, I racked my brains and think I remember the following: in the spring of 1849 I came to Hamburg to collect money for the *Neue Rheinische Zeitung*. I had just enough in my POCKET to get to Hamburg. However, stayed 14 days in a FIRST-RATE hotel. I explained to Baron Frisch, who later intended to send us donations, that I needed money to pay the hotel bill and my return fare. I now have a dim recollection that since I didn't want to take the money as a 'PRESENT' from him and he for his part didn't want it back, it was agreed that *Bruhn,* who was just as much a scoundrel then as now, should receive it. I had forgotten the whole bloody business; however, I now wrote to Bruhn[111] that I couldn't remember any financial transaction with *him.* Since the *Neue Rheinische Zeitung* was banned when I got back to Cologne from Hamburg and I myself was kicked out of Prussia, it was possible that in the whirl of events at the time *I* had forgotten.[170] It is still striking that he waited from 1849 to 1865 to *remind* me. But it was a simple matter. He should let me know by letter how much he thought he had on me and send me Grübel's address. I would then write to Grübel myself. If the latter *confirmed* what he said, his demand would be satisfied. This procedure is absolutely essential, as I am *still* uncertain about the matter *even at this moment,* and the way I have been fleeced by claims of this kind is really scandalous.

2. From the *enclosed from Schily* you will see what transpired in Paris whither we sent Le Lubez to settle the disputes that had broken out there. (We had given *Schily* ditto FULL POWER to negotiate,[d] as we were aware of Le Lubez's bias towards Lefort.[95] Here I should just mention in passing that *Béluze,* President of the

---

[a] In the original: January 1852. - [b] K. Marx, 'Hirsch's Confessions'. - [c] See present edition, Vol. 17, pp. 219-20. - [d] See this volume, pp. 108-09.

People's Bank,[171] who controls the few Paris Associations and their organ *L'Association,* is *with* Lefort.) *What else happens*—which will only be concluded this evening, as far as our intervention is concerned—in the *next letter.*[a]

3. The things from *Siebel* returned. It strikes me as *most unfortunate* that he gives *London* as the origin of the notice put in the *Düsseldorfer Zeitung,*[b] thus exposing *me* as the presumed author.

4. Letter from Liebknecht enclosed.

5. One copy of the circular from the Geneva Branch-Association[c] enclosed.

6. The letter from Meissner enclosed.

7. *Lange*: not to be directly rebuffed.[d] Write and tell him that he would do best to post the thing to you, 2 copies, and you would send one to me each time. As he rightly realises himself, after our recent experience we would have to hold back *for the present* from making contributions to any German paper. He would, of course, have the same right as any other editor of a journal to reprint whatever extracts he liked from your pamphlet.[e]

Salut.

Your
K. M.

The first numbers (2 sheets) of Blind's *Eidgenosse* have come, with the only contributions by Blind, Struve and Rasch.[172] Trivia. Emblem consisting of hand with dagger, to kill the 'tyrants'.

First published abridged in *Der Briefwechsel zwischen F. Engels und K. Marx,* Bd. 3, Stuttgart, 1913 and in full in *MEGA,* Abt. III, Bd. 3, Berlin, 1930

Printed according to the original

Published in English for the first time

---

a See this volume, p. 130 - b [F. Engels,] 'Notice Concerning *The Prussian Military Question and the German Workers' Party'.* - c 'Aufruf an alle Arbeiter, Arbeitervereine und Arbeiterassociationen in der Schweiz zum Beitritt der "Internationalen Arbeiter-Association"'. - d See this volume, p. 116. - e F. Engels, *The Prussian Military Question and the German Workers' Party.*

62

MARX TO ENGELS

IN MANCHESTER

[London,] 10 MARCH [1865]

DEAR FRED,

I can only write these few lines today, as I have much else to do.

The statement from Herwegh and Rüstow[a] is good. The impudence of Mr Schweitzer, who knows perfectly well that all I need to do is publish his own letters, is fantastic. Though what else can the wretched cur do?

As you will already have guessed, the scrawl he quotes from the *Neue Frankfurter Zeitung* is from student 'Blind'.[173] I'm sending you the first No. of this '*lackey*'[b] of the deposed Kings of Democracy and Holloway-type 'SELFADVERTISERS' and 'PUFFERS'. You must arrange for a few jokes about the fellow to reach Siebel, for him to hawk around to the various papers.

By the by, if there should be a 2nd impression of your pamphlet,[c] we can, in a short preface, make a brief official statement on *our* position with regard to the Lassalle shit and the *Social-Demokrat*. It would be, of course, *beneath* our dignity to take up the cudgels directly with that gang of riff-raff in minor journals.

Salut.

Your
K. M.

First published in *Der Briefwechsel zwischen F. Engels und K. Marx*, Bd. 3, Stuttgart, 1913

Printed according to the original

Published in English for the first time

---

[a] concerning the breach with *Der Social-Demokrat* - [b] *Der Deutsche Eidgenosse* - [c] F. Engels, *The Prussian Military Question and the German Workers' Party.*

63

ENGELS TO JOSEPH WEYDEMEYER[57]

IN ST LOUIS

Manchester, 10 March 1865

Dear Weydemeyer,

At last I have got down to answering your letter of 20 January. I had sent it to Marx who—partly because he was indisposed— kept it a very long while, IN FACT did not return it until a week ago today,[a] so that my letter could no longer catch the STEAMER; I was too occupied with business on that day.

My best thanks for your detailed answers to my questions.[b] With the negligent reporting on militaria[c] in the papers here, I had lost the thread of all the 'combined' operations; I found the Red River expedition[174] quite puzzling and I was not much wiser about Sherman's move eastward from Vicksburg,[75] as there was no mention here of the Southern corps advancing from New Orleans. These combined operations with a point of meeting up not merely in the enemy's territory but even behind his very lines show precisely how crude are the ideas of strategy of a nation that has no experience of war whatever. And yet if the noble Wrangel and Prince Frederick Charles had not been 2 to 1 in the Danish war[9] they would have got up to much the same tricks. The battle at Missunde[175] and the 2 inexplicable 'demonstrations' (to give a nameless thing some kind of name, nevertheless) against Düppel[27] before the assault were, if anything, even more childish.

As to Grant's conduct at Richmond,[30] I am trying to explain it in another way. I am completely of the same opinion as you that *strategically* the only correct thing was to attack Richmond from the *west.* However, it seems to me—insofar as one can form a judgement from such a distance and from such vague reports— that Grant preferred the eastern side for 2 reasons:

1. because he could provision himself more easily there. Whilst on the western side he commanded only the roads to Fredericksburg and to Tennessee (both crossing areas that had been exhausted), on the eastern side he had the Fredericksburg line, and the York and James RIVERS as well. Since the difficulty of supplying large armies with provisions has played an important part

---

[a] See this volume, p. 107. - [b] ibid., pp. 39-40. - [c] military matters

throughout the war, I would not like to condemn Grant out of hand until I am clear on that score. You reproach him with having turned his back to the *sea.* But if one controls the sea and has secure points of embarkation (Monroe and Norfolk), then that is an *advantage.* Compare Wellington's campaigns in Spain and the Crimean campaign, where the Allies, who had been victorious on the Alma, positively *ran away from the enemy* in order to ensure their rear the protective cover of the sea south of Sevastopol.[176] That the possession of the Shenandoah valley was the best way to secure Washington is clear. But? The question arises

2. did Grant (and Lincoln) *want* to have Washington completely secure? On the contrary, it seems to me that with the loose constitution of the Federation and the great indifference to the war in some parts of the North, Lincoln never seriously wanted to drive the Confederates out of Richmond, that, on the contrary, he just wanted to pin them down in a position where they represented something of a threat to Washington, Pennsylvania and even New York. I believe that without that he would have got neither the recruits nor the money to finish the war. I certainly believe that Grant would have very much liked to have taken Richmond in the last 3-4 months, but he has not sufficient forces to do so. I see them estimated at from 70-90,000 men and Lee at 50-70,000. If this ratio is approximately correct, then, with his attack acknowledged to be strategically wrong, he has done everything possible to frustrate any offensive defence by Lee, and to encircle Richmond on at least 3 sides out of 4. For, after distinguishing himself amongst all the other generals of North and South in the last 2 years just by his brilliant use of counter-attacks, I cannot believe that Lee would now abandon this tactic unless *forced to.* It was, however, a stupendous gain for the North if it succeeded in pinning down the South's best army at Richmond, in one corner of the southern territory, because of a childish *point d'honneur,*[a] until the whole hinterland was cut off and militarily disrupted for the South, firstly by conquest of the Mississippi valley and then again by Sherman's campaign, until finally, and this seems to be the case now, all the Union's available troops are marching on Richmond and one decisive blow can put an end to the whole business.

The latest news we have is from New York, dated 25 February, i.e. it includes the taking of Charleston and Wilmington, and Sherman's advance from Columbia to Winnsborough. This Sher-

---

[a] prestige

man appears to be the only fellow in the North who knows how to use his men's legs to win battles. But he must, incidentally, have splendid lads under him. I can't wait to see what will happen. If Lee assesses his desperate situation aright, he has no choice but to pack up and go south. But where to? The only way *open* to him is to Lynchburg and Tennessee; but that would be exceedingly hazardous to march into such a narrow mountain valley with just one railway, and Knoxville and Chattanooga fortified ahead of him. Besides, that would probably mean sacrificing Beauregard, Hardee and all other Confederate troops positioned in North Carolina, and exposing his flank to Sherman. Or he could advance from Petersburg, turn Grant's left flank and march directly south against Sherman? Daring, but better; the only way to draw to himself the remnants of the fleeing armies, delay Grant by destroying the railways and bridges, and fall on Sherman with superior strength. If the latter offers battle to this combined force, he will certainly be beaten; if he falls back toward the coast, he will open up the road toward Augusta for Lee who will there be able to make his first respite. But Sherman and Grant would then surely join forces and Lee would then again be faced by a superior force, this time as good as in open country; for I do not believe the Confederates can again concentrate so many heavy guns in any one place inland as to organise another Richmond there. And even if they were to do so, they would only be jumping out of the frying-pan into the fire. Or else—invasion of the North? Jefferson Davis would no doubt be capable of this, but that would also spell the end within a fortnight.

Now, however, Lee can only send some of his forces southwards as well to join with Beauregard and company and stop Sherman, and this seems to me the most probable course. In this case, Sherman will probably give them a proper 'drubbing', as they say in South Germany, and then Lee will really be stuck. But even if Sherman were to be defeated, Lee would only have gained one month's respite, and the troops advancing from every part of the coast—not to mention Grant's successes in the meantime against the weakened Richmond army—would soon make his position as bad as it had been before. One way or another, the game is up, and I look forward to the arrival of each STEAMER with expectancy; there is a positive deluge of exciting news just now. The strategic speculations of the numerous SOUTHERN SYMPATHISERS here are most comical to listen to, they are all epitomised by the remark made by the Polish general Sznayde in the Palatinate who said after every rout, 'We are doing exactly what Kossuth did.'

Incidentally, I am most grateful to you for your explanations about military organisation in America, it was only as a result of them that I obtained a clear picture of many aspects of the war there. I have been familiar with the *canons Napoléon* for many a long year, the English had *already replaced them* (light, smooth-bore 12-pounders with a charge weighing $^1/_4$ of the ball) when Louis Bonaparte re-invented them. You may have any number of Prussian howitzers, as they have all been withdrawn now and replaced by rifled 6-pounders and 4-pounders (which fire 13-pound and 9-pound heavy shells). I am not surprised that the ELEVATION of your howitzers is only 5°, it was no higher with the old long howitzers the French had (until 1856), and, if I am not mistaken, the English ones were only a little more. In general, the high-angle fire from howitzers has been used for a long time only by the Germans; its great unreliability in range-finding in particular had brought it into disrepute.

Now to other matters.

A Frankfurt lawyer 'von Schweitzer' had indeed established himself in Berlin with a little paper called *Der Social-Demokrat* and asked us to write for it. As Liebknecht, who is in Berlin, was to join the editorial board, we accepted.[a] But then, firstly, the little paper embarked on an insufferable cult of Lassalle, whilst we meanwhile received positive proof (the old Hatzfeldt woman told Liebknecht about it and urged him to work for the same ends) that Lassalle was *much more deeply* implicated with Bismarck than we had ever realised. There was an actual alliance between the two which had gone so far that Lassalle was to go to Schleswig-Holstein and there to advocate the annexation of the duchies by Prussia, while Bismarck had rather less definitely consented to the introduction of a sort of universal suffrage and more definitely to the right of combination and concessions regarding social policy, state support for workers' associations, etc.[98] The foolish Lassalle had *no guarantee whatever* from Bismarck, *au contraire*[b] he would have been put in prison *sans façon*[c] as soon as he became troublesome. The gentlemen on the *Social-Demokrat knew this*, but, for all that, they continued to intensify their cult of Lassalle. In addition to that, the fellows allowed themselves to be intimidated by *threats* from Wagener (of the *Kreuz-Zeitung*) into paying court to Bismarck, flirting with him, etc., etc. That was the last straw. We published the enclosed statement[d] and made our exit, with

---

[a] See this volume, pp. 22, 23-24. - [b] on the contrary - [c] without ceremony - [d] K. Marx and F. Engels, 'To the Editor of the *Social-Demokrat*'.

Liebknecht doing likewise. The *Social-Demokrat* then declared that we did not belong to the Social-Democratic Party,[166] which excommunication naturally did not bother us. The whole Lassallean General Association of German Workers[2] has taken such a wrong road that nothing can be done with it; however, it will not last long.

I was asked to write about the military question, which I did, but, in the meantime, relations between us became more strained, and the article turned into a pamphlet,[a] which I have now had published separately; I am now sending you a copy of it by the same STEAMER. To judge by the newspapers I receive, the thing appears to be creating quite a furore, especially on the Rhine, and it will, at any rate, make it very difficult for the workers to ally themselves with reaction just now.

The INTERNATIONAL ASSOCIATION in London is going from strength to strength. In Paris especially, in London no less so. It is also going well in Switzerland and Italy. Only the German Lassalleans are refusing to bite, and in present circumstances least of all. However, we are again receiving letters and offers from all sides in Germany, a decisive change has taken place, and the rest will turn out right.

The only reply I can make to your wife's[b] question is that I have not yet entered into a state of *holy* matrimony.

Photographs enclosed, of Lupus and myself, I have come out a little too dark; but it is the only one I have left.

Schimmelpfennig has taken Charleston—Hurrah!

Write soon.

Your
F. Engels

First published abridged in *Die Neue Zeit,* Bd. 2, No. 33, 1906-1907, and in full in: Marx and Engels, *Works,* First Russian Edition, Vol. XXV, Moscow, 1934

Printed according to the original

Published in English in full for the first time

---

[a] F. Engels, *The Prussian Military Question and the German Workers' Party.* - [b] Louise Weydemeyer's

64

ENGELS TO MARX

IN LONDON

Manchester, 11 March[a] 1865

Dear Moor,

Schweitzer's brazenness really is ludicrous. But it does show how hard he has been hit by our withdrawal[b] and how well he knows that *very much* depends on it for his petty paper. After Herwegh and Rüstow have come out in *support* of **our** statement,[c] anything can happen. Schweitzer will soon become aware of the effect his big talk has had, especially on the Rhine. Siebel has done a capital job in circulating the pamphlet.[d] The *Bonner Zeitung* has twice published long extracts already and is intending to produce still more. The *Rheinische*[e] has also got a long extract as well. Our standing with the Rhineland workers being what it is, this agitation-by-clique against us won't get very far.

Siebel had already sent me the little piece from the *Neue Frankfurter Zeitung*.[173] Student Blind as always. He is having to make a couple of phrases of Lassalle's last a whole year. I haven't received the *lackey*[f] yet.

The legacy business is complete, the LAWYER will send the statement of account next week, he has still got approx. 10s. to collect in or pay out, he wasn't sure which. So, I can send you the money on Monday then.[8] Meanwhile, *my* statement of account enclosed, according to which another £[g] approx. are due to you.

The ideas Liebknecht has about Manchester! He has got nothing to gobble and asks me what a house '*with garden*' costs here! The fellow is simply soft in the head. Schweitzer, he said, *could* not sell himself to Bismarck because he would have been *obliged* to use the good offices of the beastly old woman.[h]

I'm finding the new movement a terrible fag, by the way. It's the devil's own job letter-writing in the evening as well for the party and publisher, etc., until 1 or 2 o'clock, after letter-writing all day at work.

---

[a] The original has: February. - [b] from the *Social-Demokrat* - [c] K. Marx and F. Engels, 'To the Editor of the *Social-Demokrat*'. - [d] F. Engels, *The Prussian Military Question and the German Workers' Party.* - [e] *Die Rheinische Zeitung* - [f] *Der Deutsche Eidgenosse* - [g] No figure in the original. - [h] Sophie von Hatzfeldt

Siebel has sent me Lange's pamphlet.[a] Confused, Malthusian with some Darwinian ingredients, flirting with all and sundry, but several good passages against Lassalle and the bourgeois consumers' co-op fellows. I'll send it to you in the next few days.

Schily's letter also returned enclosed which I found most entertaining. Our old comrade is turning himself into a very useful diplomat.[159] How did the two of you settle the dispute?

It's impossible to get anywhere with Jones. Hardly are the SESSIONS over when the Assizes begin. THE TRADE IN CRIME SEEMS HIGHLY FLOURISHING.

Adios, and my kindest regards to the LADIES.

Your
F. E.

EXECUTION of Will W. Wolff

Debit

Payment from Steinthal & Co. incl. interest	£1,083-9-3
" " " Heywood BROTHERS incl. interest	" 234-14-9
Debts collected by Dr Borchardt	" 66-13-0
	£1,384-17-0

Credit

To payment to Marx	£234-14-9	
" " " do	" 350-0-0	
" " " do	" 200-0-0	
" " " do	" 40-0-0	
	£824-14-9	
" " to Borchardt	£ 100-0-0	
" " Schiller Institute[28]	" 100-0-0	
" " Engels	" 100-0-0	
" " Wood, Solicitor	" 150-0-0	
Paid by Borchardt { Payment to LANDLORD	" 13-4-9	
" funeral expenses	" 57-11-0	
" of 2 bills	" 1-2-4	
" of PROBATE DUTY .	" 30-0-0	1,376-12-10
	Balance	8-4-2

---

[a] F. A. Lange, *Die Arbeiterfrage in ihrer Bedeutung für Gegenwart und Zukunft.*

There is also a certain amount in interest I have got to make over to you for the period from 9 November (when I received the balance of approx. £633 from Steinthal but only sent you £200 in the first place and also held back other payments). I can't attend to it today as the cashier has already left and locked away the relevant book; you will receive it along with Wood's statement of account; but it won't be much. Most of the interest due arose from the fact that the £633 remained with Steinthal from May until November, which produced approx. £16 extra for you.

First published abridged in *Der Briefwechsel zwischen F. Engels und K. Marx*, Bd. 3, Stuttgart, 1913 and in full in *MEGA*, Abt. III, Bd. 3, Berlin, 1930

Printed according to the original

Published in English for the first time

65

MARX TO ENGELS [33]

IN MANCHESTER

[London,] 13 March 1865

Dear Engels,

There are mistakes in your financial statement, viz. you sent me £235 on *8 June*, £350 at the beginning of *July* (the letter enclosing the money isn't dated, but I can tell from a letter of 5 July which said it was about to be sent) and £200 on *9 November 1864*; on the other hand, the last *£40* itemised on the statement *you said would eventually follow* (in the enclosed letter dated 9 November) but you *never sent it.* I hope that you will be able to convince yourself of this on checking your books again, and if so, that you will send me the money by return of post, before I leave for the continent (with my NIECE[a]), which will probably be at the end of this week.[177]

With regard to *Schweitzer's brazenness,* I have decided on a different course. There are some things about which one would be glad to enlighten the public but can only do so *in response to direct provocation,* and then one must not miss the OPPORTUNE TIME OF A REPLY. And such is the case with Schweitzer's comments connected with

---

[a] Caroline Schmalhausen

the garbage from Blind.[173] I intend to reply in the *Düsseldorfer Zeitung* actually on behalf of *both of us*, but I shall sign in *my name* alone, as it would be *ludicrous to imply you shared responsibility for 'Achilles'*,[178] and as I shall be quoting mainly (*exclusively*, if my plan works out) from Schweitzer's letters to me anyway.

My plan therefore is this:

Schweitzer is reproducing, in print, the lies put out by the *Neue Frankfurter Zeitung*, knowing them to be lies. (Is the article in the form of an editorial in the paper, or what?) Viz.: 1. neither Lassalle's name nor any mention of Lassalle appeared in the prospectus we received 'printed as manuscript'. (Liebknecht had prevented that.) 2. In note of 30 December Schweitzer *most humbly* asks my pardon for so brazenly using passage from private letter of condolence, as both introduction and conclusion to his hymn of adulation. 3. By means of short extracts from Schweitzer's letters from 30 December 1864 to 15 February 1865 (his last letter), I shall show that the conflict over '*tactics*' was a lasting one from the *first*, trial number[a] right up until we announced our withdrawal,[b] and was by no means a quarrel suddenly picked, as man-of-honour Schweitzer pretends, with his support for Blind's shit. At the same time, this little mosaic of excerpts from Schweitzer's letters will show with what *servility* this selfsame brute behaved towards us, until he suddenly turned *vicious* on being kicked. This will make salutory reading for bourgeois and workers alike (and for Rüstow). All in all, good *introduction* for the break with 'Lassalleanism', which is in any case inevitable. (Of course, as far as student Blind is concerned, if that water-newt should ever COME OUT again, I shall always treat Lassalle as a dead lion set beside a live ass. It is indecent that such an 'uneducated' Baden publican should even presume to put himself on a level with a man who has studied Heraclitus and the Roman law of inheritance.)

Let me know by return if you approve of my plan, as I can't afford to lose any time.[179] (And don't forget to tell me in what form Blind's twaddle appeared in the *Neue Frankfurter Zeitung*.) In my opinion, it's necessary.

Although, unlike you, I don't have the pleasure of corresponding with the Too-Clever-By-Half,[c] nor of being able to foul his nest for him, nevertheless I've been infernally HARASSED just recently, quite apart from the furuncles, which won't go away; e.g., last night I didn't get to bed until 4 o'clock in the morning.

---

[a] of 15 December 1864 - [b] K. Marx and F. Engels, 'To the Editor of the *Social-Demokrat*'. - [c] Gottfried Ermen, Engels' partner

Besides my work on the book,[a] the INTERNATIONAL ASSOCIATION takes up an enormous amount of time, as I am IN FACT the HEAD of it. And what a waste of time! (And it would come just now, with the French business[95] and the election business[155] here, etc., all at the same time.) E.g. the French shit:

28 February. Tolain and Fribourg here from Paris. Meeting of the CENTRAL COUNCIL, where they state their case and bicker with Le Lubez until 12 o'clock at night. Then reconvene in Bolleter's tavern, where I had another 200 odd cards to sign. (I have now got them to change this stupid practice by having our handwriting engraved on the plate, and only the GENERAL SECRETARY[b] signs by hand. Meanwhile, the remaining 1,000 cards OF THE OLD EDITION had to be signed IN THE OLD STYLE.)

1 March. Polish MEETING.[168]

4 March. SUBCOMMITTEE[21] *meeting about the French question* until 1 o'clock in the morning.

6 March. SUBCOMMITTEE *meeting* about ditto until 1 o'clock in the morning.

7 March. SITTING OF THE CENTRAL COUNCIL until 12 o'clock at night. *Resolutions passed.* (*I enclose resolutions,* along with the private instructions which the CENTRAL COUNCIL is sending to Schily, who, as you can see from resolution V, *has been appointed* CENTRAL COUNCIL DELEGATE (AMBASSADOR) AT *Paris.*)[180]

(This meeting of 7 March, in which Le Lubez was utterly *culbuté,*[c] was very embarrassing and stormy, and left the English in particular with the impression THAT THE FRENCHMEN STAND REALLY IN NEED OF A BONAPARTE!) In between times, people *dashing this way and that* to see me in connection with the conference with Bright which was held last Saturday (11 March), etc. Reported briefly on same to Jones (he had enquired beforehand about it on Friday), instructed him to convey the letter to you.[181]

WELL, *mon cher, que faire?*[d] He who says 'A' must also say 'B'.

You will see from the enclosed *Nordstern* (SEE THE 2 FIRST LEADERS) that, despite his hatred for us, Bruhn immediately seized the opportunity to *attack* Schweitzer, out of sheer *professional jealousy.*[182] This is most important since Bruhn's paper is of longer standing, and this has at least sowed *dissension in the camp of these fellows themselves.*

A short notice about your pamphlet will appear in Bender's *Anzeiger*[e] this week. I sent one to the *Hermann* (Juch), saying he

---

[a] *Capital* - [b] William Cremer - [c] overturned - [d] what is to be done, my dear fellow? - [e] *Londoner Anzeiger,* 17 March 1865

should form his *own* opinion of it, etc.[a] This he will do. I chose this approach because with Juch I'd always poked fun at the notices sent to the *Hermann* by Blind, for Blind and about Blind, and the two of us here are generally regarded as *one* person.

   Salut.

Your
K. M.

First published abridged in *Der Briefwech-sel zwischen F. Engels und K. Marx*, Bd. 3, Stuttgart, 1913 and in full in *MEGA*, Abt. III, Bd. 3, Berlin, 1930

Printed according to the original

Published in English in full for the first time

66

MARX TO HERMANN JUNG

IN LONDON

[London,] 13 March 1865

My dear Jung,

   Mr Cremer has quite *misunderstood* me (and I shall write him *immediately* upon that point). I was so far from any intention of moving new amendments on Tuesday evening[b] to the old resolutions[183] that, before the arrival of your letter, I had to-day posted to Schily a letter *containing the very same resolutions.* I wrote him at the same time to wait with their communication until Thursday next, so as to give Mr Le Lubez the time to fulfil his functions, viz. to communicate himself the resolutions.

   What I said to Cremer, and to Fox ditto, was, that if Le Lubez and Mr Wolff, by their foolish behaviour, had not excited the feelings, and killed the time, the resolutions would and might have been *rédigées* in a way more polite on the one, and more *logical,* on the other hand; [so that] f.i. Resolution II (concerning Lefort's [defensive ways]) might, by a short phrase, have lost its aspect, while Resolution IV concedes *too much* to Lefort etc. All this might have been mended, and I expressed to Mr Cremer my regret that it had, after the vote on the *contents* of the resolutions, not been left to the subcommittee[21] to give it the convenient stylistic *form.*

---

a See this volume, p. 134. - b 14 March

Yet, I should consider it the *greatest folly* to reopen the questions once settled, and which, as far as the *substance* of the resolutions goes, have been settled in the most fair spirit. I should consider it, particularly, quite unworthy of the Central Council to *rescind one single word* after the exhibitions Le Lubez and Wolff have made of themselves. Moreover, by my letter to Schily such a course has become *impossible.*

You will, of course, oblige me by communicating to me your *résumé historique*—but I beg you to understand me well. I shall like to read it, as the thing itself interests me, but not in order to control your writing.[184] I am convinced beforehand that you will not embitter the spirits. I fear Mr Le Lubez has already sent to *his* friends private despatches in that childish spirit.

Yours fraternally

K. Marx

First published in: Marx and Engels, *Works*, First Russian Edition, Vol. XXV, Moscow, 1934

Reproduced from the original

Published in English for the first time

67

ENGELS TO MARX

IN LONDON

[Manchester,] 14 March 1865

Dear Moor,

The business of the £40 is based solely on a statement of the business I made out in November, in which this £40 figures as 'CASH' to you, but undated. I had the impression myself that I had *not yet* sent you this £40, but as I had no opportunity to check, I could only go by the memorandum. Today I checked my account in the ledger, but I couldn't deduce anything relevant from that either. But if you've not had the £40 and, at the same time, I too have the vague feeling that that is the position, that's good enough, and I've already given the cashier instructions to have the money ready tomorrow.

On the question of the statement in the *Düsseldorfer Zeitung*,[a] I'm in complete agreement. Though on the whole it doesn't matter at all if Mr Schweitzer occasionally takes it into his head to indulge in such barefaced effrontery, I did, nevertheless, find it galling that this vulgar upstart rogue should be allowed to get away with such behaviour towards us. Furthermore, if his smarmy letters aren't published *now*, they won't be any use at all later. It's always nice when someone like that gets the scolding he deserves for once. So, do it straightaway, and please ask Dresemann to send 2 COPIES, so that I can have one.

In haste.

Your
F. E.

First published in *Der Briefwechsel zwischen F. Engels und K. Marx*, Bd. 3, Stuttgart, 1913

Printed according to the original

Published in English for the first time

68

MARX TO ENGELS

IN MANCHESTER

[London,] 18 March 1865

DEAR FRED,

There are a lot of things, some of them important, that I want to write to you about. But as there's A VERY GREAT DEAL OF BUSINESS to do in connection with my departure tomorrow,[177] just the following bare facts:

The remaining HALVES of the notes received.

You can send the POST OFFICE order to my wife.

I've sent off a note from Bender asking for 50 copies, etc., of your pamphlet,[b] etc., to O. *Meissner* direct, as I had to write to him today. It is possible that Meissner's answer may arrive *too late* for the *next Londoner Anzeiger*. Since Bender does at present

---

[a] See this volume, p. 129. - [b] F. Engels, *The Prussian Military Question and the German Workers' Party.*

without doubt know best how to disseminate things of this kind in England, you should send him *a note about the price of the pamphlet* **by return** if you can (i.e. if you know it yourself). He will then advertise it straightaway in the next number. His address is 8 Little Newport St., Leicester Square.

I did a short, highly condensed little article for Bender, such as I thought would be suitable for his paper,[a] a kind of prospectus of contents, and sent Juch conversely, contrariwise and notwithstanding, just your pamphlet itself, asking him to do a critique of it in his own way and according to his own point of view.[b] Then I received enclosed note from Juch (*to be kept*). There certainly wasn't the time for a critical review. So, I sent the notice originally intended for Bender (in today's *Hermann*) to Juch[c] (and the enclosed message to Bender instead[d]). At the same time, I wrote to Juch—diplomacy becoming increasingly important—that I couldn't meet his request because I was going away, that he should print copious extracts in a later number; I would discuss his difficulty in finding contributors with him when I returned to London. (I am thinking of placing Eccarius there, instead of with the *Social-Demokrat*.) I sent him ditto a copy of my statement against Schweitzer, although the *Hermann* won't be able to print it until next Saturday's edition (copies sent at the same time to *Reform* in Berlin and to the *Düsseldorfer Zeitung*[e]); no amendments in the version for the *Hermann* except a stab at Blind inserted at the beginning.

Bender has written to me ditto:

'Most obliged and grateful for notice you sent; but we now need a review as well.'

I've passed this on to Eccarius.

Also enclosed a number of the *Rheinische Zeitung* sent to me by Liebknecht with HIS SPEECH.[185] His wife[f] has written to mine; they are really down on their luck. He still owed the *Social-Demokrat* £5, etc. I can't send him anything at the present moment.

Nordstern enclosed. You must *keep* this document. You can see these gentlemen are now trying to make out that that wretch Schweitzer completely *falsified* Lassalle.[186] So, my statement against Schweitzer, which also repudiates Lassalle, even though very

---

[a] *Londoner Anzeiger* - [b] See this volume, pp. 130-31. - [c] K. Marx, 'Review of Engels' Pamphlet *The Prussian Military Question and the German Workers' Party*'. - [d] K. Marx, 'Synopsis of Engels' Pamphlet *The Prussian Military Question and the German Workers' Party*'. - [e] K. Marx, 'Statement [Regarding the Causes of the Breach with the *Social-Demokrat*]'. - [f] Ernestine Liebknecht

indirectly, comes at a most opportune moment. It will all come out in the wash by and by.

It appears from the enclosed letter from Bruhn that I was right about Frisch.[a] I've sent him the 6 talers (not 60!), although I'm not convinced by it, at the same time saying that I would 'make further enquiries' regarding the 50, etc.

Salut.

Your
K. M.

Apropos. *Klings* called in on his way to America. He had all kinds of interesting things to report to me. A real 'Rhineland' worker.

On *5 March* the *Cologne* branch of the *General Workers' Association*[2] decided to issue a protest (along the lines of our statement[b]) against the *Social-Demokrat,* and *against B. Becker* as well, who is a kind of Biscamp Secundus. They have STOPPED THE MONEY SUPPLIES. And this refusal to pay taxes is catching.

First published abridged in *Der Briefwechsel zwischen F. Engels und K. Marx,* Bd. 3, Stuttgart, 1913 and in full in *MEGA,* Abt. III, Bd. 3, Berlin, 1930

Printed according to the original

Published in English for the first time

69

ENGELS TO FRIEDRICH ALBERT LANGE[101]

IN DUISBURG

[Copy]

Manchester, 29 March 1865
7 Southgate

Dear Sir,

I must offer you my profound apologies for allowing your kind letter of the 2nd-4th inst. to remain unanswered for so long. I

---

[a] See this volume, pp. 117-18. - [b] K. Marx and F. Engels, 'To the Editor of the *Social-Demokrat*'.

only hope you will not condemn me unheard. My excuse is that for the first few days I was greatly preoccupied in part with an accumulation of current business, but in part also with the large amount of urgent correspondence, which one always faces when one suddenly appears before the public again after long *otium cum (vel sine) dignitate*ᵃ and at the same time has such merry adventures as we have had with the *Social-Demokratchen*.³⁴ In addition to all that, I moved house, and that momentarily threw my papers into some disarray, in which your letter was mislaid; I only found it again the day before yesterday and I now hasten to reply to you.

I am most grateful to you for so kindly offering to send your *Sphinx* and other publications¹⁸⁷ to Marx and myself. My bookseller here is Mr Franz Thimm, Manchester, through whom you may send everything to me. Sending things via the bookseller requires 3-4 weeks as a rule; if you would send me at least the first few Nos. in a simple open wrapper by post (it does not cost much), I should be obliged to you and will gladly reimburse you. Communications for Marx should be sent to me here, and he will receive them within 12 hours of arrival. As you yourself rightly realise, I could not commit myself at all at this stage regarding possible future contributions; let us leave the question open for the time being, although, in your case, we are at least not running the risk of incurring the suspicion of wishing to rule over any section of the proletariat in Germany from England.

Meanwhile, the involuntary delay in my reply has given me the opportunity to obtain your publication on the working-class question ᵇ; I read it with great interest. I, too, was immediately struck on first reading Darwin ᶜ by the remarkable similarity between his description of the vegetable and animal life and the Malthusian theory. Only my conclusion was different from yours, viz.: that it is to the everlasting disgrace of modern bourgeois development that it has not yet progressed beyond the economic forms of the animal kingdom. The so-called 'economic laws' are not eternal laws of nature but historical laws that appear and disappear, and the code of modern political economy, insofar as the economists have drawn it up correctly and objectively, is for us merely a summary of the laws and conditions in which modern bourgeois society can exist, in a word: its conditions of production

---

ᵃ honourable (or dishonourable) leisure (Cicero, *Oratio pro Sextio*, 45) - ᵇ F. A. Lange, *Die Arbeiterfrage in ihrer Bedeutung für Gegenwart und Zukunft.* - ᶜ Ch. Darwin, *On the Origin of Species by means of Natural Selection....*

and exchange expressed and summed up abstractly. For us, therefore, none of these laws, insofar as it is an expression of *purely bourgeois relations*, is older than modern bourgeois society; those which have been more or less valid for all previous history, are thus only an expression of such relations as are common to all forms of society based upon class rule and class exploitation. Amongst the former we may count the so-called Ricardian law,[188] which is valid neither for serfdom nor for the slavery of antiquity; amongst the latter, whatever part of the so-called Malthusian theory can be sustained.

The parson Malthus filched this theory, like all his other ideas, directly from his predecessors; the only part of it which is truly his is the purely arbitrary application of the two progressions.[189] The theory itself has long since been reduced by the economists in England to rational dimensions; the population exerts pressure on the means—not of subsistence, but of *employment*; mankind could multiply more rapidly than modern bourgeois society can stand. For us yet another reason to proclaim this bourgeois society to be a barrier to development which must fall.

You yourself raise the question of how the increase in the means of subsistence can be made to keep pace with the increase in population; but excepting one sentence in the preface, I find no attempt at an answer. We start from the premise that the same forces which have created modern bourgeois society—the steam engine, modern machinery, mass colonisation, railways and steamships, world trade—and which through the unending commercial crises are already now working towards its ruin and ultimate destruction—that these means of production and exchange will also be sufficient to reverse the relationship in a short while and to raise the productive power of every individual to such an extent that he will produce enough for the consumption of 2, 3, 4, 5, or 6 persons, that enough people will become superfluous to urban industry to devote far more manpower than before to agriculture, that science will at last be applied to agriculture on a large scale as well and as systematically as in industry, that those areas of South Eastern Europe and Western America which have been inexhaustibly fertilised for us by nature itself will be exploited on a far mightier scale than before. Not until all these areas have been turned by the plough and there is then dearth, will it be time to say *caveant consules.*[190]

Not enough is being produced, that is the root of the whole matter. But *why* is not enough being produced? Not because the limits of production have been reached—even for today and by present-day means. No, but because the limits of production are determined not by the number of hungry bellies, but rather by the number of purchasers with full *purses*. Bourgeois society has no desire, and can have no desire, to produce more. Those impecunious bellies, the labour which cannot be utilised *with profit* and is thus incapable of purchasing, fall prey to the mortality figures. Let us assume that there is a sudden boom in industry, such as is constantly occurring, to enable this labour to be employed with profit, then the labour will acquire the money with which to purchase, and the means of subsistence have as yet always been found. It is the endless *circulus vitiosus*[a] in which the whole political economy revolves. One takes bourgeois conditions in their entirety as one's premise, and then proves that each separate part is a necessary part thereof—ergo, an 'eternal law'.

I was greatly amused by your description of the Schulzian co-operatives.[191] We have been through all that here in a different form, although it is now more or less a thing of the past. People in Germany have yet to develop their proletarian pride.

There is a remark about old Hegel which I cannot let pass without comment: you deny him any deeper knowledge of the mathematical sciences. Hegel knew so much mathematics that none of his disciples was capable of editing the numerous mathematical manuscripts he left behind. The only man who, to my knowledge, has enough understanding of mathematics and philosophy to be able to do so is Marx. That the detail of the philosophy of nature is full of nonsense I will of course gladly grant you, but his *real* philosophy of nature is to be found in the second part of the *Logic*, in the theory of Essence, the true core of the whole doctrine.[b] The modern scientific theory of the interaction of natural forces (Grove's *Correlation of Forces*, which I think first appeared in 1838) is, however, only another expression or rather the positive proof of Hegel's argument about cause, effect, interaction, force, etc. I am no longer a Hegelian, of course, but I still retain a deep feeling of piety and devotion for the titanic old fellow.

Yours very respectfully
Friedrich Engels

First published in *Die Neue Zeit*, Bd. 1, Nr. 5, 1909

Printed according to a copy made by an unidentified person

Published in English in full for the first time

---

[a] vicious circle - [b] G. W. F. Hegel, *Wissenschaft der Logik.* Erster Theil. *Die objektive Logik.* Zweites Buch. *Das Wesen.*

70

MARX TO SOPHIE VON HATZFELDT

IN BERLIN

London, 10 April 1865

My dear Countess,

I shall be obliged if you would hand the copy of the '18th Brumaire' with my marginal amendments, i.e., corrections, to Mr Wilhelm Liebknecht.[79]

I have read Becker's[a] attacks on you with the greatest indignation, and, to judge from letters I have received from people of the most divergent views, the scoundrel has thereby generally done harm not to you, but only to himself. I am in entire agreement with Mr Rüstow that it is incomprehensible that any section of the Association of German Workers could calmly listen to such scandalous talk. The most elementary sense of decency should make such infamy impossible.[192]

Yours most respectfully

Karl Marx

First published in: Marx and Engels, *Works*, Second Russian Edition, Vol. 31, Moscow, 1963

Printed according to the original

Published in English for the first time

71

MARX TO ENGELS[33]

IN MANCHESTER

London, 11 April [1865]

Dear Fred,

Returned home some twenty-four hours ago.[177] So, for the moment just a few lines to let you know.

---

[a] Bernhard Becker

7*

Letter from Wilhelmchen[a] enclosed. I sent him the STAMPS he asked for.

Quoad[b] B. Becker, I didn't get to see his dirty work until I got here. But thought reply really was needed.[c] (Rüstow and Herwegh have replied in the *Nordstern* on behalf of Hatzfeldt. Rüstow calls B. Becker a '*police-spy*'.[192]) Sent it to *Rheinische* and *Düsseldorfer*.[d] As soon as copies arrive, 1 for you.

I shall attend a SITTING of the 'INTERNATIONAL' this evening for the first time for 3 weeks. In the interval, revolution. Le Lubez and Denoual gone, Dupont APPOINTED FRENCH SECRETARY. As a result of Le Lubez's intrigues, and more particularly those of Major Wolff who is A TOOL in Mazzini's hand, the Italian delegates Lama and Fontana have left. Pretext: Lefort (who has meanwhile announced his departure in the journal *L'Association*[193]) must keep his post as DEFENDER GENERAL IN THE PARIS PRESS. The Italian WORKING MEN'S CLUB [20] has not withdrawn from the Association, but no longer has a REPRESENTATIVE on the COUNCIL. Meanwhile, I shall get Bakunin to lay some counter-mines for Mr Mazzini in Florence. The English SHOEMAKERS' UNION—5,000 strong—has joined the Association during my ABSENCE.[194]

How's the COTTON-CRISIS? I WANT INFORMATION ON THAT POINT.

In great haste.

Your

K. M.

First published in *Der Briefwechsel zwischen F. Engels und K. Marx*, Bd. 3, Stuttgart, 1913

Printed according to the original

Published in English in full for the first time

72

ENGELS TO MARX

IN LONDON

Manchester, 12 April 1865

Dear Moor,

It's good to have you back again, and I certainly hope this lousy squabble will soon be over. Letters from Dronke and Borkheim

---

[a] Wilhelm Liebknecht - [b] With regard to - [c] K. Marx, 'The "President of Mankind"'. - [d] *Rheinische Zeitung* and *Düsseldorfer Zeitung*

enclosed. I had told the latter how it was possible to work with Kolatschek's great-German organ supporting Austrian rule in Hungary, Poland and Italy, as we would immediately have all our friends in the other countries down on us, hence the vague reply.[195]

I had always half expected that the naive *fraternité* in the INTERNATIONAL ASSOCIATION would not last long. If there were an active *political* movement among the workers here, just the same SPLITS would occur. It will pass through a lot more such phases and will take up a great deal of your time. But it does still remain something quite different from Lassalle's Association.[2]

I couldn't resist a hearty laugh when I read in Wilhelmchen's[a] letter that the *official* Berlin community of that Association consists of 5 people, as there was recently a perfectly serious report in the *Social-Demokrat* of their transactions, in which they congratulated each other on *such a large* turn-out.[b]

Ad vocem[c] COTTON-crisis, things are looking quite cheerful here. Cotton (MIDDLING Orleans) stood at $31^3/_4$d in July, was quoted at $14^3/_4$d last Thursday, and today, if one is selling, it hardly fetches 14d. So, it has depreciated by more than half. It was still worth 27d on 30 December, which is a fall of $12^1/_2$-13d in 3 months! On top of that, there's been a fall in flax, wool, sugar and all IMPORTS GENERALLY, which makes a loss of at least £40-50 mill. stg. You will readily understand that all the philistines are in a cold sweat. In Liverpool, *bankruptcy has altogether gone out of fashion now.* Anyone who becomes insolvent goes to his creditors (generally people there have only a couple), notifies them and offers them such and such an amount, which is always accepted at once as they are glad to get *anything at all* and have got to avoid any scandal so that the whole rotten edifice doesn't collapse. Hundreds of such settlements are said to have been reached on the quiet, and today rumour even has it here that one of the biggest Stockport manufacturers, who owns 3 big factories and is reputed to have made £200,000 over the last few years in COTTON-SPECULATION alone, has just come to a similar understanding on the quiet. But what we've seen so far is nothing. The bills, which were drawn from India against the white cotton, run out in the next 6 weeks, and there will be many more besides Joyce who will come to grief. A lot of people in Scotland are finished as well, and one fine day it's bound to be the turn of the banks, and that'd be the end of the

---

[a] Wilhelm Liebknecht's - [b] *Der Social-Demokrat*, No. 43, 5 April 1865. - [c] Regarding

matter. The spinners and manufacturers are becoming bankrupt by the dozen in Austria, too—in the whole of Bohemia only 'the great Liebig' is still on his feet, all the others have gone bust—and in Poland it's all just starting as well.

Industry itself is not much affected. The small fry mostly went bust ages ago or quietly melted away, and the big ones can operate reasonably profitably once more, if they can get any orders at all. Among them, the only ones who are going bust are those who have bad machinery or who couldn't keep their fingers out of COTTON. Everyone is making a loss on their stocks of cotton yarns and fabrics. We too could sing you a woeful song about that, twice as woeful for me in particular as it would have been if droned out last year. That's what comes of being an *associé*.[a]

Glorious is also the ethics of trade, as at present. You buy something today, and by the time it's delivered, it is worth 3, 4, or 5d a pound less. This leads to all kinds of dirty tricks and repudiations, as people try to get out of these unprofitable contracts at any cost, and that lands you in interminable altercations and squabbling correspondence. I'm sick to the teeth with it. You can have no idea how much letter-writing and aggravation this entails.

I hope your wife got the £3? Final statement of account enclosed, I'll send the £12 in a few days, it's too late for a POST OFFICE order today.

Best wishes.

Your
F. E.

First published in *Der Briefwechsel zwischen F. Engels und K. Marx*, Bd. 3, Stuttgart, 1913

Printed according to the original

Published in English for the first time

---

[a] partner

73

MARX TO HERMANN JUNG

IN LONDON

London, 13 April 1865
1 Modena Villas, Maitland Park,
Haverstock Hill, N. W.

Dear Jung!

* In No. 30 of *Der weisse Adler, 223 Münstergasse, Zürich* there is a report of our Polish Meeting of 1 March.[168] This report must have been translated from the *Daily News* or some other English *middleclass paper* which, intentionally, suppressed the Resolution, proposed in the name of the 'International Association', and unanimously adopted by the St Martin's Hall Meeting.

As you are the *Swiss Secretary*, it belongs to you to rectify the report, and to request the *Editor* of the paper to print the notice[196] which I translate literally from the Report in *The Bee-Hive.*[a]

Yours fraternally *
K. Marx

It goes without saying, dear Jung, that you can change the concluding words at your discretion. Since you are *plus ou moins*[b] a Frenchman, I simply wanted to draft the scheme for you in German.

First published in *Archiv für die Geschichte des Sozialismus und der Arbeiterbewegung,* Jg. 6, Leipzig, 1916

Reproduced from the English original. The last paragraph translated from the German

Published in English for the first time

---

[a] *The Bee-Hive Newspaper,* No. 177, 4 March 1865. - [b] more or less

74

MARX TO LÉON FONTAINE[197]

IN BRUSSELS

[Draft]

London, 15 April 1865

Dear Citizen,

At its last sitting (see enclosure) the Central Council appointed me *pro interim*[a] to be secretary for Belgium in place of Citizen Le Lubez, whose resignation as Council Member was unanimously accepted. Citizen Dupont has taken his place as secretary for France.

I will, if you wish, later give you a brief account of the disagreeable incidents which occurred within the Central Council. In my opinion, they were really instigated by a person alien to our Council, well known as an Italian patriot[b] but an inveterate enemy of the interests of the proletariat, without which republicanism could be no more than a new form of bourgeois despotism. Did he not, as one of his most blindly faithful followers[c] confessed to me, go so far as to demand that all the passages hostile to the bourgeoisie should be deleted from the Italian translation of our '*Address*'.[d]

Despite these regrettable incidents and the more or less voluntary resignation of several individuals, our Association is making glorious headway. Founded only a few months ago, today it already numbers almost 12,000 members in England alone.

The Central Council will be much obliged to you if you send me *an official report on the present state of our society in Belgium.*

In your correspondence please be so kind as to keep the official letters, which are destined for the Central Council's archives, separate from such private communications as you may be good enough to send me.

---

[a] provisionally - [b] Giuseppe Mazzini - [c] Giuseppe Fontana - [d] K. Marx, 'Inaugural Address of the Working Men's International Association'.

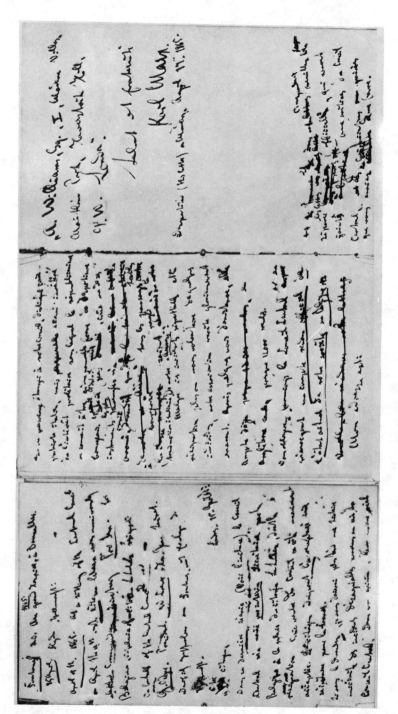

Pages of Marx's Notebook for 1864-65 with the rough draft
of his letter to Léon Fontaine of 15 April 1865

My address is: A. Williams,[a] Esq., 1 Modena Villas, Maitland Park, Haverstock Hill, N. W. London.
Greetings and fraternity.

Karl Marx

First published, in Russian, in *Bolshevik*, No. 11, 1934

Printed according to the original

Translated from the French

Published in English for the first time

75

ENGELS TO MARX [29]

IN LONDON

[Manchester,] 16 April 1865

Dear Moor,

The *Nordsterns* returned enclosed. Herwegh and Rüstow have certainly acquired a funny Dido[b] dog in Reusche. The fellow is a real comic turn with his solemn declarations. The inevitable oath beside Lassalle's dead body makes a precious counterpart to Willich's apple-tree.[198] It's a real blessing that these people live so far away and that they still show a certain reserve in their attempts to approach us.

I haven't received No. 43 of the *Social-Demokrat*, so let me have it some time if there's anything particular in it.

Your
F. E.

What do you say about Richmond?[30] I had expected that Lee would act like a *soldier* and surrender, instead of taking to his heels, at least so as to secure better terms for the army. But it's better the way it is. He has ended like a scoundrel, and the tragedy closes on a comic note.

First published in *MEGA*, Abt. III, Bd. 3, Berlin, 1930

Printed according to the original

Published in English in full for the first time

---

[a] Marx's conspiratorial pseudonym - [b] A reference to Engels' dog.

76

MARX TO ENGELS

IN MANCHESTER

[London,] Saturday, 22 April 1865

Dear Fred,

The scribble from the *Rheinische Zeitung* enclosed.

I'll write a detailed letter to you tomorrow. I'm as limp as a wet rag today, partly from working late at night (nothing practical), partly from the diabolical muck I've been taking.

Dronke would be ALL RIGHT, if I could turn copper into gold like he does. As IT IS, we must utilise the moment when the bourgeois papers are competing to print denials of SLANDER which tomorrow, if the struggle is being fought in earnest, they perhaps wish to have endorsed.

Salut. My compliments to Mrs Lizzy.[a]

Your
Moor

First published in *Der Briefwechsel zwischen F. Engels und K. Marx*, Bd. 3, Stuttgart, 1913

Printed according to the original

Published in English for the first time

77

MARX TO HERMANN JUNG[1]

IN LONDON

[London,] 25 April 1865

Dear Jung,

I hope I may have the pleasure of your company at my house on Monday evening (ABOUT 8 O'CLOCK or LATER, if that hour is too early for you) for a MEETING with Ernest Jones and a small SUPPER. Apart from yourself, *only* Odger, Cremer and P. Fox. Had I

---

[a] Lizzy Burns

wished to invite *more* guests, I should have had to ask *too many* for the purpose of the evening. This *entre nous*.[a]

I have just written to Cremer [111] that he should issue the letter of authority for P. Vinçard immediately, which Dupont must then deliver to Vinçard forthwith. It would be best if Dupont could despatch the thing to Vinçard *direct* without it having to go by way of Fribourg.

Vinçard had already written to Lubez that he would *not* accept if he did not receive the POWERS *direct* from London.[199] In a letter to Fribourg Lubez promised to inform the 'CENTRAL COUNCIL' of this, but did not do so. I have reason to believe that Fribourg subsequently '*forgot*' the matter, not unintentionally.

I shall give you a verbal account of what further occurred in Paris (which was for the most part good); but in the meantime you should tell Dupont.

Salut et fraternité.

K. Marx

First published in: Marx and Engels, *Works*, First Russian Edition, Vol. XXV, Moscow, 1934

Printed according to the original

78

MARX TO ENGELS [29]

IN MANCHESTER

[London,] 1 MAY 1865

DEAR FRED,

You must excuse me for not writing until today and thus breaking my LAST PROMISE. It happened not because it is 'sheer delight to break one's word',[b] but because I really am OVERWORKED, as completing my book,[c] on the one hand, and the 'INTERNATIONAL ASSOCIATION', on the other, are making very heavy demands on my time.

Today is little Jenny's birthday, and this evening I shall be having Ernest Jones to my house along with Odger, Cremer, Fox

---

[a] between ourselves - [b] Paraphrased quotation from F. Rückert's poem 'Die Weisheit des Brahmanen'. - [c] *Capital*

and Jung, so it will be a political birthday party. Laura HAD 'THE QUESTION POPPED' by one Charles Manning, born in South America, English father, Spanish mother. He's rich and generally a nice fellow, BUT LAURA 'DOES NOT CARE A PIN FOR HIM'. 'SHE HAS ALREADY KNOWN HOW TO DAMP' the passionate southern temperament. However, as my girl is a friend of his sisters, and he is frightfully IN LOVE, it is A DISAGREEABLE CASE.

I enclose a '*curiosity*'. The *Nordstern's* correction makes it a worthy organ of the German louts.

I am also enclosing for you THE LATTER END of a letter from Schily, whose report on the Moses woman[a] will amuse you.

The great achievement of the 'INTERNATIONAL ASSOCIATION' is this: The REFORM LEAGUE is OUR WORK. On the inner committee of 12 (6 MIDDLECLASSMEN and 6 WORKINGMEN), the WORKINGMEN are ALL MEMBERS OF OUR COUNCIL (including Eccarius).[155] WE HAVE BAFFLED all attempts by the middle class TO MISLEAD THE WORKING CLASS. This time the movement in the provinces is completely dependent on that in London. Ernest Jones, e.g., had DESPAIRED TILL WE SET THE BALL A-GOING. If we succeed in re-electrifying the POLITICAL MOVEMENT of the ENGLISH WORKING CLASS, our ASSOCIATION will already have done more for the European working class, WITHOUT MAKING ANY FUSS, than was possible IN ANY OTHER WAY. And there is every prospect of success.

You know that the *Italian* society[20] has not withdrawn from the ASSOCIATION, but its DELEGATES have from the COUNCIL.[b] We now have *Spaniards* on it instead. ONE ROMAN NATION FOR THE OTHER. If those fellows don't appoint new delegates soon, as we have asked them to, Bakunin will have to arrange FOR SOME LIFE ITALIANS.

Weber junior[c] has been thrown out of the workers' society here for making false reports to the *Social-Demokrat* and for stirring up trouble in the branch society 'Teutonia', which is run by two fanatical Prussians by the name of Klinker.[200]

Our joint statement[d] really was successful beyond all expectation. Not merely have we blown apart the 'General Association of German Workers'[2] as an organ of the Prussian government and in SIX WORDS generally cleared the heads of the German workers of their intoxication with royalty. The present *split in the Party of Progress*[99] was also the direct result of our stand.

The CHIVALRY OF THE SOUTH has ended worthily. In addition, Lincoln's ASSASSINATION was the most stupid act they could have committed. *Johnson* is STERN, INFLEXIBLE, REVENGEFUL and as a former

---

a Sibylle Hess - b See this volume, p. 140. - c Louis Weber - d K. Marx and F. Engels, 'To the Editor of the *Social-Demokrat*'.

POOR WHITE has a deadly hatred of the oligarchy. He will make less fuss about these fellows, and, because of the treachery, he will find the TEMPER of the North commensurate with his INTENTIONS.

Did you see how Blind HEADS the letter of condolence from the 'influential' Germans?[201] Blind is a genius in his way. IN THE VERY NICK OF TIME he does not merely go running to Freiligrath, etc., but has enough presence of mind to realise that, of the other signatories, ALPHABETICALLY 'Berndes' would open the list. So, he runs first to Freiligrath, etc., and gets him first of all to form a group and, after that worthy (who is now at one with Ruge as well), certain other INFLUENTIALS, I almost said INFINITESIMALS, such as Heintzmann and Kinkel, and puts himself 'alphabetically' at the top. Then he goes running to Berndes and gets him to start a second column next to himself, so that another lot of names, Trübner, etc., follows on. That is how the matter appears in *The Times*. In the same day's *Morning Star* the second column is added to the bottom of the first, with Blind AT THE TOP OF THE WHOLE, AND HIS FOOTMAN Freiligrath after him, etc. And not content with that, at his instigation, the *Star* of the same number also carries a notice on the front page THAT 'KARL BLIND HEADS, ETC.'.

Isn't that genius for you?

Salut.
                                                                Your
                                                                K. M.

First published abridged in *Der Briefwechsel zwischen F. Engels und K. Marx*, Bd. 3, Stuttgart, 1913 and in full in *MEGA*, Abt. III, Bd. 3, Berlin, 1930

Printed according to the original

Published in English in full for the first time

79

ENGELS TO MARX[29]

IN LONDON

Manchester, 3 May 1865

Dear Moor,

A belated many happy returns to little Jenny on her—20th?—birthday. THE OTHER AFFAIR LOOKS JUST LIKE LAURA ALL OVER.[a] But what else

---

[a] See this volume, p. 150.

can one say except repeat the verdict of the Stalybridge jury: SERVES HIM RIGHT.

I'll be sending all the things back to you in a few days time. I was very pleased to see in the *Nordstern* that something has at last been started against Becker[a] and Schweitzer in Solingen, too.[202] As all I have seen concerning this business *since your departure* has been the *Social-Demokrat* and two letters from Liebknecht, I am not at all clear as to what has come to pass on the Rhine in this connection; from the miserable silence maintained by the *Social-Demokrat* about developments in the General Association of German Workers, I could only *deduce* that things must be looking bad for these gentlemen. But it is understandable that I really do need to know how things stand on the Rhine, especially since in the beginning the scoundrels had some momentary success there. If you've got any material on it, please let me have it, I'll send everything back to you, and in general I will as a rule send all the documents back in future because now you need to have this stuff together.

Have you taken out a subscription to the *Nordstern?* It would be a good thing if you did, because we've got to know what's happening.

It is vital for us to have some contacts with the workers on the Rhine so that in future we can counter intrigues of that kind from the outset. Apropos, peculiar things seem to have been happening to Klings. Some jackass gave him my address as *58 Dover Street.* Klings goes there, does not find me, of course, and goes to see Rode in Liverpool, and the latter tells Eichhoff I'd pretended to be out when Klings called, did not wish to see him, what is this supposed to mean, etc., to a man like Klings who was after all going to 'organise everything' in America with Weydemeyer and the others (which others?), etc., etc. Monsieur Rode, whom I've never met, did thereby express his surprise that I had 'not yet' sent him a copy of my pamphlet.[b] Can you understand that?

The statement attacking the President of Mankind is very good.[c] Just what was needed and no more.

The worst of it is that the people in Germany will now demand that someone assumes the leadership over them, and who can do it? Eccarius would be the man, but he won't want to leave London.

The International Association really has gained an enormous amount of ground in such a short time and with so little to-do. But

---

[a] Bernhard Becker - [b] F. Engels, *The Prussian Military Question and the German Workers' Party.* - [c] K. Marx, 'The "President of Mankind"'.

it is a good thing it is at present occupied in England, instead of eternally having to deal with the disorders in France. So, you have something to compensate you for the time it's cost you.

How's the book[a] going?

As far as the strategic situation is concerned, at Richmond Grant has achieved a precise replica of the battle of Jena,[203] and with the same result: the whole of the enemy army is trapped.[30] Only he didn't have so far to march to gather the fruits.

Johnston has now surrendered, too, so I've won my wager of 2 months ago: that by 1 May the SOUTHERNERS would have no army left. Whoever still offers resistance will be taken in as a BRIGAND, and rightly so. At any rate, Johnson will insist on confiscation of the great estates, which will make the pacification and re-organisation of the South rather more acute. Lincoln would scarcely have insisted on it.

The SOUTHERN SYMPATHISERS here are consoling themselves for the hypocritical wailing they were obliged to put on over the assassination,[b] by prophesying that it'll be Grant I, Emperor of America, within 4 weeks. What jackasses they have made of themselves!

Incidentally, their 'Majesties'[c] must be absolutely furious that Lincoln's assassination has made such a colossal impact throughout the world. None of them has yet had such an honour.

Best wishes to your wife and the girls.

Your
F. E.

First published abridged in *Der Briefwechsel zwischen F. Engels und K. Marx*, Bd. 3, Stuttgart, 1913 and in full in *MEGA*, Abt. III, Bd. 3, Berlin, 1930

Printed according to the original

Published in English in full for the first time

---

[a] *Capital* - [b] of Abraham Lincoln - [c] Engels uses the South-German dialect here: 'Färschten'.

80

MARX TO ENGELS[29]

IN MANCHESTER

[London,] 9 May 1865

Dear Fred,

You need not send anything back (except Schily's letter[a]). Just keep the things safely. I enclose one *Free Press* (the queer article on the 'Reconstruction of Italy' is from the pen of the High Priest himself, from Urquhart[b]), also two *Nordsterns* (one of them somewhat out of date). I've got a subscription to the latter, but no longer to the *Social-Demokrat*. The latest *Nordstern* will give you some idea of the situation on the Rhine.[204] Incidentally, the *total number* of the faithful whom B. Becker still commands is barely 1,000.

Before I forget: there were several allusions to your pamphlet[c] in the debate in the Prussian Chamber. *Gneist*, for instance, said the Minister of War[d] would not persuade them, even if his statistics spoke with the tongue of *'Engels'*. (Laughter.) (That is how the affair appeared in the *Berliner Reform*.[e])

As everywhere, the London workers, of course, also include a knot of asses, fools and rogues, rallying round a scoundrel. The scoundrel in this case is 'George Potter', a rat of a man, supported by a venal but witty Irishman by the name of *Connolly*, who is a dangerous stump-orator. Although the bourgeoisie hate the said Potter as chief strike-manager, they do, nevertheless, support him against our people because they smell venality in him, whereas they know that our people are true men. This Potter derives his power particularly from the fact that he is presently the manager of *The Bee-Hive*, the official organ of the trades unions, although he uses it against the official council of these unions which is in our hands.[18] Since the paper is based on shares, the idea is now to distribute as many shares as possible (5sh. per share) amongst our workers. For my part I have undertaken to collect the money for about 30 shares. For this, I'm counting on you (single handed or with friends) for £5, I write to Dronke for £1 and I will pay the rest myself. (Although my function with the Central Council costs me a *lot* of money,

---

a See this volume, p. 150. - b D. Urquhart, 'Construction of the "Kingdom of Italy"', *The Free Press*, 3 May 1865. - c F. Engels, *The Prussian Military Question and the German Workers' Party*. - d von Roon - e [Account of Gneist's speech in the House of Deputies,] *Berliner Reform*, No. 69 (supplement), 22 March 1865.

compared with what I can afford.) The money must already be AT HAND *this* week, as the General Meeting of the SHAREHOLDERS is next week. If we are only strong enough (and Odger, for instance, has guaranteed 50 SHARES) to elect the *DIRECTORS*, we shall have that rogue Potter (who is only the *MANAGER*) UNDER OUR THUMBS. This matter is of decisive importance for the whole movement.[205]

E. Jones was here, very charming SOCIALLY SPEAKING. But between ourselves, *he* is *only* trying to use our Association for electoral agitation. Of the 12 cards I sent him, he returned 11, he had not sold a single one, whereas POOR Schily, for instance, paid for 24 for himself alone. I told him he should just put them back in his pocket again, I would dispose of them later, but I could not appear in front of the English workers and tell them that. BY AND BY HE *WILL* FIND OUT that if only for speculative reasons he should not have treated the business so lightly and RATHER CONTEMPTIBLY. I will write to him and tell him to hand over the 'ADDRESSES'[a] to you. You can give them to whomsoever you please. They are just dead weight with him. Incidentally, I don't take kindly to the fact that he was here to wangle a job as *RECORDER* out of Sir G. Grey either.

Today I am to submit an '*ADDRESS TO PRESIDENT JOHNSON*.'[206] Mr *Le Lubez* wants to return to the COUNCIL as—DELEGATE FOR DEPTFORD, the same fellow as resigned as *DELEGATE FOR FRANCE*,[b] BUT HIS ADMITTANCE (WE HAVE TO *CONFIRM* THE DELEGATES) WILL NOT RUN QUITE SO SMOOTHLY AS HE SEEMS TO FANCY. I would be pleased if you could form even just A BRANCH OF 6 MEN in Manchester, and could get yourself elected as their CORRESPONDENT FOR LONDON. For THE CORRESPONDING people are *eo ipso*[c] MEMBERS OF THE CENTRAL COUNCIL, and have a seat and a vote on it, WHEN AT LONDON.

New BRANCHES have been formed in Lyon, Neufchâteau (*département des Vosges*) and St Denis. The French BRANCHES (apart from Paris) are not linked with Paris, in view of the existing laws, but directly with London.

I'm hoping to put the finishing touches to my book[d] by 1 September (despite numerous interruptions). It's going ahead well, although I am still not quite well.

Your

K. M.

First published in *Der Briefwechsel zwischen F. Engels und K. Marx*, Bd. 3, Stuttgart, 1913

Printed according to the original

Published in English in full for the first time

---

[a] K. Marx, 'Inaugural Address of the Working Men's International Association'. - [b] See this volume, p. 140. - [c] of themselves - [d] *Capital*

81

ENGELS TO MARX

IN LONDON

Manchester, 12 May 1865

Dear Moor,

Schily's letter returned enclosed. That passing glimpse of the family life of Moses and the Moses woman[a] was most entertaining. Many thanks for the *Nordsterns*. The reports in them provide a check on the negative evidence of the *Social-Demokrat*, which I am keeping on until June (and if it is not being taken anywhere in London accessible to you, I am willing to continue taking it, one never knows what may happen).

By the by, the rag in question—i.e., the *Social-Demokrat*—has now gone into such decline that one really feels sorry for it. Poor Schweitzer's heroic soul is at its last gasp, every shred of an idea and all the fruits of his reading have already been used up and he hasn't even a fart left in him to serve up to his readers. Nor is Mauses[b] producing anything any more, Mauses, the last hope of the new 'party'.[207] 'News of the Association' is a complete blank, too—literary section re-printed from the Augsburger *Allgemeine Zeitung*.[208] After four months editorship during one of the most turbulent periods we have known since 1848, that milksop has been pumped dry, right down to the dregs, and those are the fellows who wanted to annex the whole German proletariat by one trick.

Ad vocem[c] Potter: five pounds encl., you can take some, i.e., five of the SHARES in my name and five in Samuel Moore's, whom I've admittedly not yet seen, but he's sure to take some; we'll send you PROXY for the general meeting.[d] If Gumpert also wants 5 SHARES, you can pass some of those 20 on to him—so: 5 for me, 5 for Moore, the remaining 10 to be distributed to other people, but make sure that, if the people are *not quite reliable*, you reserve the right to take them back again.

As for the suggestion that *I* should form a BRANCH of the International Association here, it's quite out of the question. Apart

---

[a] Moses and Sibylle Hess. See this volume, p. 150. - [b] Moses Hess. Engels makes a pun on the name *Moses* and the word *Maus* (mouse). - [c] concerning - [d] See this volume, pp. 154-55.

from Moore and Gumpert, I see no one here, as I can't broach that kind of thing with the Kyllmanns or we would have a squabble at once. Besides, my position as its correspondent for London would impose all kinds of obligations on me, which I would be unable to fulfil as soon as real contacts with the workers were found or arose here. *Et à quoi bon?*[a] I wouldn't be able to take any of the burden off your shoulders anyway.

Apropos. Moses is still up to his tricks against the International Association in the *Social-Demokrat*[209]; if you haven't read the piece, I'll send it to you.

The number of the banknote is: B/C 48498, Manchester, 4 January 1864.

The tongues of Engels, etc., are not a reference to me, as I thought myself at first, but to the statistician Privy Councillor *Engel* in Berlin who sorted out the things for Roon which I *criticised*.[b]

Jones must be allowed to go his own way. He doesn't seem to me to have any real confidence in the proletarian movement any more. I can never find him here anyway, he's always away.

Your
F. E.

First published abridged in *Der Briefwechsel zwischen F. Engels und K. Marx*, Bd. 3, Stuttgart, 1913 and in full in *MEGA*, Abt. III, Bd. 3, Berlin, 1930

Printed according to the original

Published in English for the first time

82

MARX TO ENGELS[33]

IN MANCHESTER

[London,] 13 May 1865

Dear Fred,

The £5 received with THANKS. Will be invested as suggested.

You are right about the COMMITTEE IN MANCHESTER.[c]

Quoad[d] E. Jones, it is necessary to march with him for the time being. He and his people will be figuring at the next Manchester

---

a And what would be the use? - b See this volume, p. 154. - c ibid., pp. 155, 156. - d Regarding

CONFERENCE (NEXT TUESDAY) together with our DELEGATES (Odger and Cremer ON THE PART OF THE INTERNATIONAL ASSOCIATION), Howell as secretary of the REFORM LEAGUE (BRICKLAYER, ONE OF THE MEMBERS OF OUR COUNCIL) and Beales and Mason Jones as bourgeois representatives of the same LEAGUE.[210]

Without us this REFORM LEAGUE would never have come into existence, or else it would have fallen into the hands of the MIDDLECLASS. The glorious failure of BAINES'S BILL (which will result in a CHANGE OF MINISTRY and the COMING IN of the Tories), originally SUPPORTED BY THE GOVERNMENT, WHICH WANTED SOME SUCH SMALL MEASURE FOR THE HUSTINGS, occurred in the Lower House itself with direct reference to the 'extravagant' demands recently put up by the WORKING CLASS (I.E. OUR MEN).[211]

As Dronke wrote me, Reinach I, who is now MANAGING DIRECTOR of the BANK OF SWITZERLAND, will be ruthlessly putting an end to the OFFICE in London, which is causing nothing but expenses. Reinach I is, of course, not bound by the same political and personal considerations as Fazy[212] and Klapka were.

A ghastly carbuncle has broken out again on my left hip, NEAR the INEXPRESSIBLE PART OF THE BODY.

Regards to Mrs Lizzy.[a]
Salut.

Your
K. M.

Apropos. Monsieur Le Lubez, who had miscalculated about how important and dangerous he is, WANTS NOW TO RETURN TO THE CENTRAL COUNCIL IN THE CAPACITY OF A REPRESENTATIVE 'FOR GREENWICH'! We replied that *d'abord*[b] we had to wait for certain letters to come, which he had written to France at the time of the CONFLICT.[213]

I hardly think the *Social-Demokrat* will see out another quarter. Moses[c] believed himself safely ensconced and didn't want to give up his prestigious position as Lassalle's really secret agent at any price.[207] *Le pauvre diable!*[d]

Lassalle's will is now proven. He has left **nothing** to B. Becker apart from his 'NOMINATION', accompanied by rules of conduct dictated 'with all severity and authority'.

First published abridged in *Der Briefwechsel zwischen F. Engels und K. Marx*, Bd. 3, Stuttgart, 1913 and in full in *MEGA*, Abt. III, Bd. 3, Berlin, 1930

Printed according to the original

Published in English in full for the first time

---

[a] Lizzy Burns - [b] first of all - [c] Moses Hess - [d] The poor devil!

83

MARX TO ENGELS[101]

IN MANCHESTER

[London,] 20 MAY 1865

DEAR FRED,

Cutting ENCLOSED which includes my address to Johnson.[a]

Edgar's[b] reappearance did, of course, surprise us greatly. QUITE THE FELLOW I THOUGHT HIM, and his career quite as I expected it. IT IS A PITY that he could not always have been right-hand to Garibaldi. He would have suited him to a tee. But the poor devil is still very weak. He will be staying here for some time, apropos of which you could be doing A GOOD WORK by contributing to the replenishment of my *wine-cellar*.

I am working like a horse at the moment, as I must make use of the time when I am fit for work, and the carbuncles are still with me, though they only trouble me locally and do not disturb the brain-pan.

In between times, since one cannot always be writing, I am doing some DIFFERENTIAL CALCULUS $\frac{dx}{dy}$. I have no patience to read anything else at all. Any other kind of reading always drives me back to my writing-desk.

Special meeting of the 'INTERNATIONAL' this evening. A good old codger, an OLD OWENIST, *Weston* (CARPENTER), has put up the following two propositions that he is constantly defending in *The Bee-Hive*:

1. that A GENERAL RATE IN THE RISE OF THE RATE OF WAGES would be of no benefit to the workers;

2. that the TRADES-UNIONS for that reason, etc., are *harmful.*

If these two propositions, in which *he* alone in our SOCIETY believes, were to be accepted, we should be in a terrible mess, both in respect of the TRADES-UNIONS here and the INFECTION OF STRIKES now prevailing on the Continent.

He will be supported in the matter by a native Englishman— since non-members are also admitted to this meeting—who has written a pamphlet to the same effect.[c] I am, of course, expected

---

a K. Marx, ['Address from the Working Men's International Association to President Johnson']. - b Edgar von Westphalen's - c T. J. Dunning, *Trades Unions and Strikes: Their Philosophy and Intention.*

to produce a refutation. I ought therefore really to have worked out my *réplique* for this evening, but I thought it more important to get on with writing my book,[a] and so I shall have to rely on improvisation.

I know in advance, of course, what the two main POINTS will be:
1. that *wages* determine the value of commodities;
2. that if the capitalists pay 5s. today instead of 4, tomorrow they will sell their commodities for 5s. instead of 4 (being ENABLED to do so by the increased demand).

Trite though that is, and however little it penetrates the topmost surface of things, it is, nevertheless, not easy to explain to the ignorant all the competing economic questions involved. YOU CAN'T COMPRESS A COURSE OF POLITICAL ECONOMY INTO 1 HOUR. BUT WE SHALL DO OUR BEST.[214]

Edgar regards it as a GOOD OMEN that he met you first in England. He liked Lizzy[b] very much.
Salut.

Your
K. M.

It is a most strange irony of fate that this Edgar, who never exploited anyone other than himself and was always a WORKMAN in the strictest sense of the word, went through A WAR OF and WITH STARVATION for the slave-owners. Ditto that both brothers-in-law have for the moment been ruined by the American war.

First published in *Der Briefwechsel zwischen F. Engels und K. Marx*, Bd. 3, Stuttgart, 1913

Printed according to the original

Published in English in full for the first time

84

MARX TO WILHELM LIEBKNECHT

IN BERLIN

[London, about 25 May 1865]

Dear LIBRARY,

I should prefer it if the translation of the Address[c] could appear in the *Reform*[d] and the *Rheinische Zeitung*. It will, of course,

---

[a] *Capital* - [b] Lizzy Burns - [c] K. Marx, ['Address from the Working Men's International Association to President Johnson']. - [d] *Berliner Reform*

be necessary to say that the original is in English, and it will do no harm if I am named as the author.[215] The bourgeois papers are still holding it against us that of *A. Lincoln*'s replies to the various messages of congratulations on his RE-ELECTION, only the reply to ours[a] was more than a *formal* ACKNOWLEDGEMENT of RECEIPT.[112]

Salut.

Your
K. M.

First published in: Marx and Engels, *Works*, First Russian Edition, Vol. XXIX, Moscow, 1946

Printed according to the original

Published in English for the first time

85

MARX TO ENGELS [29]

IN MANCHESTER

[London,] 24 June 1865

DEAR FRED,

You must excuse my long silence. The whole time I have been suffering throughout from bilious nausea (probably on account of the heat), had all kinds of other TROUBLES as well, and apart from that I have used the time, when fit to write, for official work on my book.[b] You know how, when one is in such a condition, one is always resolving to send letters but never manages to.

Not much new to report. The valiant *Nordstern* did not appear since my last despatch to you, probably for lack of money. I received it again today, and it does not mention the interval at all. As you will see, the rag is nothing but a dungheap of loutism. In their denunciation of B. Becker, these fellows are now declaring everyone a 'traitor' who dares to lay a finger on even one syllable of the truth as revealed by Lassalle.[216] Meanwhile, Mr B. Becker has provisionally ceded his chairmanship to that lout Fritzsche (of Leipzig) and set up his residence in Berlin in order to do business with Mr Bismarck directly.

---

[a] K. Marx, 'To Abraham Lincoln, President of the United States of America'. -
[b] *Capital*

A pretty shambles Baron Izzy's whole movement has degenerated into! But the fellow obviously had the right instinct for how to make himself Saviour of the German louts! Meanwhile, the 'unfaithful one'[a] is living in blissful happiness as a boyar lady with her Wallachian[b] in Bucharest.

I have had no letters from Liebknecht for some while. But that is no doubt because for a long time, while my correspondence was suspended, I did not answer the notes that used to come in almost daily from him, none of them having anything to say, and each successive one invariably confirming the nullity of its precursor.

In respect of the 'INTERNATIONAL ASSOCIATION', I will just mention the following here:

The Italian gentlemen have *come back* and indicated to us last Tuesday[c] that they have yet once again nominated Major Wolff as their delegate. Mr Mazzini appears to have convinced himself that he may need us, whereas we care not a FARTHING for him.

A YANKEE by the name of Leon Lewis (in Paris at the moment) has become the American secretary. In my opinion, he is worthless, although he has plenty of money and even more ambition. The fellow imagined that by founding a paper, *The Commoner,* he could revolutionise England in 24 hours or in 6 months at the very least. He offered this paper-to-be to us as our organ, but found that we are setting very business-like and by no means enthusiastic conditions, and so he has 'temporarily' left for France with his wife, who is also a great politician, I suspect to see if he can apply his 'LEVER' there with any more success.

I should like your advice on the following point:

I read a PAPER (which would perhaps cover two printed sheets) at the CENTRAL COUNCIL about the question raised by Mr Weston[d] as to the effect of A GENERAL RISE OF WAGES, etc.[214] The first part of it is a reply to Weston's nonsense; the second A THEORETICAL exposition, insofar as it was appropriate for the occasion.[e]

Now they want to have it printed. On the one hand, that could perhaps be useful to me, since they are in contact with J. St. Mill, Professor Beesly, Harrison, etc. On the other hand, I have my doubts:

1. to have 'Mr Weston' as adversary is not exactly 'vairy-flettering';

2. the second part of the paper contains, in an extraordinarily condensed BUT RELATIVELY POPULAR FORM, many new ideas which are

---

[a] Helene von Dönniges - [b] Janko von Racowiţa - [c] 20 June - [d] See this volume, pp. 159-60. - [e] K. Marx, *Value, Price and Profit.*

anticipated from my book,[a] whilst at the same time it does, of necessity, have to skate over a lot of problems. The question is, whether it is advisable to anticipate things of that kind in such a way? I think you can decide on this better than I can because you can look at the matter with more detachment from a distance.

I also had a lot of trouble TO PUT OFF the CONGRESS announced for this year, in the face of pressure from Schily, J. Ph. Becker, and some of the Paris COMMITTEE. I did, however, succeed—and that was decisive—in persuading the COUNCIL here that in view of the electoral agitation, etc., there should only be a preliminary (private) *conference in London* this year, to which the CENTRAL FOREIGN COMMITTEES would each send one delegate (not the AFFILIATED SOCIETIES BUT THEIR ADMINISTRATIVE COMMITTEES). I am certain that the Brussels Congress would come to nought. The time was not yet ripe for it.[217]

Our Eccarius has become one of the main London electoral agitators and would have accepted the invitation to agitate in the country (on £2 per week), if this were not the height of the tailoring SEASON. He has a peculiarly dry, humorous manner of speaking which particularly appeals to the English.

Edgar[b] is already much recovered. An odd fish for whom fodder and fancy clothes really are the only things of account; as egotistical as a dog or a cat, BUT A KIND-NATURED ONE. His brain has also begun to display certain activity.

Johnson's policy likes me not. A ludicrous AFFECTATION of severity towards individuals; hitherto excessively VACILLATING and weak when it comes down to it. The reaction has already set in in America and will soon be much fortified if the present lackadaisical attitude is not ended immediately.

What do you say to the debates in the Prussian Chamber? At any rate, the revelations about the judicial system, etc., following in rapid succession were splendid. Ditto the obvious blow which the National Association Great-Prussia men[152] received, as was shown particularly in the Polish debates.

Ad vocem[c] Poland, I was most interested to read the work by *Elias Regnault* (the same who wrote the 'histoire des principautés danubiennes'), 'La Question Européenne, faussement nommée La Question Polonaise'. I see from it that Lapiński's dogma that the Great Russians are *not Slavs* has been advocated on linguistic, historical and ethnographical grounds in all seriousness by Monsieur *Duchiński* (from Kiev, Professor in Paris); he maintains

---

[a] *Capital* - [b] Edgar von Westphalen - [c] Regarding

that the real Muscovites, i.e., inhabitants of the former GRAND DUCHY OF MOSCOW, were for the most part Mongols or Finns, etc., as was the case in the parts of Russia situated further east and in its south-eastern parts. I see from it at all events that the affair has seriously worried the St Petersburg cabinet (since it would put an end to *Panslavism* in no uncertain manner). All Russian scholars were called on to give responses and refutations, and these in the event turned out to be terribly weak. The purity of the Great Russian dialect and its connection with Church Slavonic appear to lend more support to the Polish than to the Muscovite view in this debate. During the last Polish insurrection [24] Duchiński was awarded a prize by the National Government for his 'discoveries'. It has ditto been shown geologically and hydrographically that a great 'Asiatic' difference occurs east of the Dnieper, compared with what lies to the west of it, and that (as Murchison [a] has already maintained) the *Urals* by no means constitute a dividing line. Result as obtained by Duchiński: *Russia* is a name usurped by the Muscovites. They are not Slavs; they do not belong to the Indo-Germanic RACE at all, they are *des intrus*,[b] who must be chased back across the Dnieper, etc. Panslavism in the Russian sense is a cabinet invention, etc.

I wish that Duchiński were right and AT ALL EVENTS that this view would prevail among the Slavs. On the other hand, he states that some of the peoples in Turkey, such as Bulgars, e.g., who had previously been regarded as Slavs, are non-Slav.

Salut.

Your

K. M.

Philistine Freiligrath descended on us with wife and daughter[c] 2 weeks ago! He now has his immediate superior Reinach on his back who is here 'to investigate' and is giving him a proper roasting.

First published abridged in *Der Briefwechsel zwischen F. Engels und K. Marx,* Bd. 3, Stuttgart, 1913 and in full in *MEGA,* Abt. III, Bd. 3, Berlin, 1930

Printed according to the original

Published in English in full for the first time

---

[a] R. I. Murchison, E. de Verneuil, Count Alexander von Keyserling, *The Geology of Russia in Europe and the Ural Mountains.* - [b] intruders - [c] Ida and Käthe Freiligrath

86

MARX TO WILHELM LIEBKNECHT

IN BERLIN

[London,] 24 June 1865

Dear Liebknecht,

You must explain to yourself my long silence by continuing indisposition and much work in intervals when I have been capable of it. Your letters, moreover, contained nothing which would have required urgent reply.

The *Nordstern* has most likely been suspended for a while owing to lack of money? At least, it has not arrived here for a couple of weeks. A fine gutter rag, to be sure! The declaration by various associations[a] that anyone who so much as lays a finger on the articles of faith as revealed by Lassalle is guilty of high treason, is priceless. *Haut-goût,*[b] INDEED!

What is Mr B. Becker doing in Berlin, and how is the *Social-Demokrat* 'surviving'?

You have quite the wrong notion of Dr Kugelmann. I have been in correspondence with him for years past. He was a socialist back in 1848, in Düsseldorf. As TO Pieper, the VERY NAME OF Kugelmann was not known to him when he was here.[218]

I have not yet written to Stumpf because I have not been writing any letters over this period. As regards the letter he entrusted to Bruhn, I have not, of course, ever set eyes upon it.[219]

The INTERNATIONAL ASSOCIATION is making great strides *despite* the 'ENORMOUS SUPPORT' it is receiving from Germany.[220]

As regards the 'Louis Bonaparte',[c] I could see from your DROPPING OF THE SUBJECT that the matter has come to nothing.[79] I am RATHER glad of this, as I shall later be having it re-printed in the essay-collection all the same.

What is old Hatzfeldt doing? And the fracas over the will?[221] *Salut.*

Your

K. M.

---

[a] A reference to the various branches of the General Association of German Workers (see this volume, p. 161). - [b] strong meat - [c] K. Marx, *The Eighteenth Brumaire of Louis Bonaparte.*

What are Messrs E. Bauer, Bucher *et* Co. up to?
Edgar[a] will probably be staying here a while longer yet.[b]

First published in: Marx and Engels, *Works*, First Russian Edition, Vol. XXIX, Moscow, 1946

Printed according to the original

Published in English for the first time

87

MARX TO ELEANOR MARX

IN LONDON

[London,] 3 July 1865
Maiden Tower

Dear Miss Lilliput!

You must excuse the 'belated' character of my answer. I belong to that sort of people who always look twice at things before they decide one way or the other. Thus I was rather startled on receiving an invitation on the part of a female minx, quite unknown to me. However, having ascertained your respectability, and the high tone of your transactions with your tradespeople, I shall feel happy to seize this rather strange opportunity of getting at your eatables and drinkables. But, pray, don't neglect the latter, as spinsters usually have bad taste of doing. Suffering somewhat under an attack of rheumatism, I hope you keep your reception room clear of anything like draught. As to the ventilation required, I shall provide for it myself. Being somewhat deaf in the right ear, please put a dull fellow, of whom, I dare say, your company will not be in want, at my right side. For the left, I hope you will reserve your female beauty; I mean the best-looking female amongst your guests.

I am somewhat given to tobacco-chewing, so have the stuff ready. Having from former intercourse with Yankees taken to the habitude of spitting, I hope spittoons will not be missing. Being rather easy in my manners, and disgusted at this hot and close English atmosphere, you must prepare for seeing me in a dress

---

[a] Edgar von Westphalen - [b] See this volume, p. 159.

rather adonistic. I hope your female guests are somewhat in the same line.

Adieu, my dear unknown little minx.

Yours for ever
Doctor Crankey

No British wines, I hope!

First published, in Russian, in *Voin-stvuyushchy materialist,* Book 4, 1925 and in the language of the original, English, in *The Socialist Review* (London), No. 44, September, 1929

Reproduced from the original

88

ENGELS TO MARX [29]

IN LONDON

[Manchester,] 15 July 1865

Dear Moor,

Liebknecht has been expelled from Prussia; has he written to you since and given you his address? The poor devil will probably need money, and a few pounds will be more valuable to him at this moment than otherwise. But where should they be sent to?

M<small>R</small> Johnson's policy is less and less to my liking, too. NIGGER[a]-hatred is coming out more and more violently, and he is relinquishing all his power vis-à-vis the old lords in the South. If this should continue, all the old secessionist scoundrels will be in Congress in Washington in 6 months time. Without COLOURED SUFFRAGE nothing can be done, and Johnson is leaving it up to the defeated, the ex-slaveowners, to decide on that. It is absurd. Nevertheless, one must still reckon on things turning out differently from what these barons imagined. After all, the majority of them have been completely ruined and will be glad to sell land to immigrants and speculators from the North. The latter will arrive soon enough and make a good number of changes. I think the MEAN WHITES will gradually die out. Nothing more will become of this RACE; those who are left after 2 generations will merge with the immigrants to make a completely different RACE.

---

a See p. XL of the Preface.

The NIGGERS will probably turn into small SQUATTERS as in Jamaica. Thus ultimately the oligarchy will go to pot after all, but the process could be accomplished immediately at one fell swoop, whereas it is now being drawn out.

I don't think that you would win many laurels by a disputation with Mʀ Weston, and it would certainly not make a good début in English economic literature.[a] Otherwise, I cannot see it would do much harm to anticipate a few odd points from your book[b]— N. B. if the latter is *really* almost finished now—how does it stand? The ultimate and final date for completion was 1 September, and the price, you remember, is 12 bottles of wine.

In the elections here Jones has been working BODY AND SOUL for Heywood, but as a TEETOTALLER and PERMISSIVE BILLS man [222] he won't pull much with the workers. Moore has been working hard, too. The Manchester SNOBS will be gladdened by James, the fellow wants to become a JUDGE and nothing more. The election is costing him a pretty penny, just for the champagne his committee and cronies have swigged. TALK ABOUT BRIBERY, CORRUPTION AND TREATING, fellows like that fat Knowles came in droves to the Queen's Hotel, where the headquarters was, gorged their fill and swigged rivers of champagne, and everything was settled with a slip of paper on which a committee-member wrote: valid for 2 LUNCHEONS and 3 BOTTLES CHAMPAIGN. In Lancaster, the 3 candidates together disbursed £20,000, and there was free booze for a whole week in every pub. I was here in the Queen's Hotel at 5 o'clock in the afternoon, the elegant SMOKING ROOM looked like the old den in Windmill Street,[223] and customers were served by CELLAR BOYS in white shirt-sleeves and aprons, instead of BARMAIDS in satin dresses. The whole company was drunk, and at half past six the landlord had to have the hotel cleared by a police patrol. My task consisted in getting James' committee people to tipple until they were incapable of doing their job, and in several cases I was successful beyond expectation.

I've had a very hard time at the office, Charles[c] was away, Franz Ermen ditto, and a colossal amount of work to boot. Things are better now. I am now on Grimm's Fairy Tales, German heroic epic, ancient Frisian law, etc. As soon as I have got through that somewhat, I'll have a serious go at Old Norse. The poetry in it is a tough nut because of its deliberate obscurity and all the many names in the mythology, and I can see it's NO USE doing this just as

---

[a] See this volume, pp. 159-60, 162. - [b] *Capital* - [c] Charles Roesgen

a side line; I need to spend 4 weeks all at once on it and nothing else, when I have little to do.

Many regards to the LADIES.

Your
F. E.

Moore has been asking me about the SHARES for *The Bee-Hive*; how do things stand? AND HOW DID YOU GET ON WITH POTTER? [205]

First published abridged in *Der Briefwechsel zwischen F. Engels und K. Marx*, Bd. 3, Stuttgart, 1913 and in full in *MEGA*, Abt. III, Bd. 3, Berlin, 1930

Printed according to the original

Published in English in full for the first time

89

ENGELS TO MARX

IN LONDON

[Manchester,] 25 July 1865

Dear Moor,

How do you like our Prussian Mirabeaus in—the **Zoological Gardens**? Harkort and Co. as wild animals, Bismarck himself could not have thought that up.[224]

By the by, it seems certain to me that Mr Bismarck decidedly wants to have a collision. For me the most convincing evidence of this is the behaviour of Schweitzer's shit-rag,[a] which is being confiscated every day now. The workers are now suddenly expected to take the part of the Deputies, after being called on for 6 months not to get excited; there are to be mass meetings, etc., and every effort is to be put into agitating against the government. Further corroboration is provided by the unanimous refrain from the reactionary press, which is comparing the banquet with the February banquets in Paris,[225] and finally the government's whole proceeding, the pointless provocations, etc. Meanwhile, it was to be expected that Bismarck would come a cropper. Wasn't cleverly enough organised anyway.

---

[a] *Der Social-Demokrat*

On the other hand, Schweitzer-Becker seem to want to take the opportunity to make a decent EXIT. The *Social-Demokrat* and the Association[a] are to be suppressed so that those gentlemen can be whitewashed. I've stopped reading that rag as of lst inst., incidentally. Bismarck seems to have had his fill of paying for it, and so have I. So, if anything should happen, I shall have to rely on you for information.

32° Réaumur in the shade in Germany! They say people are still only living in the cellars. It's as sultry as the tropics here, too.

Kindest regards.

Your
F. E.

First published in *Der Briefwechsel zwischen F. Engels und K. Marx*, Bd. 3, Stuttgart, 1913

Printed according to the original

Published in English for the first time

90

MARX TO LÉON FONTAINE[226]

IN BRUSSELS

[Draft]

[London,] 25 July 1865

Dear Citizen,

Some considerable time ago I sent a letter to you by an Englishman, who was to visit Germany and travel through Brussels. Since then I have had no news, either from you or from my Englishman. I shall not refer back to my reply to your letter, but will deal solely with current matters.

Mr Le Lubez has rejoined the Central Council as delegate from an English branch,[b] and the Italian society in London[20] has reinstated Mr Wolff as its representative on the Council.[c]

Mr Charles Limousin, one of our correspondents in Paris and editor of the *Tribune ouvrière*..., following the seizure of the *Tribune ouvrière*, and being unable to find another printer in Paris, went to Brussels in an attempt to bring out the paper there. Whilst

---

[a] General Association of German Workers - [b] in Greenwich (see this volume, p. 158) - [c] See this volume, p. 162.

there, he investigated the state of our affairs. He was told that, after it had unanimously approved your proposal that it should amalgamate with our Association, the Société Fédérative had withdrawn:

1. because it insisted on the right to choose its own correspondents and not have them imposed on it by the Central Council;

2. because it refused to pay for the membership cards, although it remitted lf. 50 just as before.

According to Mr Limousin's letter, you had then approached the Société typographique, but with the same result owing to the same difficulties.

With regard to the election of correspondents, the Central Council has acknowledged the right of affiliated societies to choose their own representatives. It has only retained the power to confirm them. Things were different in Brussels because no society had yet been constituted there. Would it not be possible to reach a compromise, whereby the societies would accept you as their correspondent, but they would, for their part, choose an administrative committee, as was done in Paris and Geneva?

With regard to the dues, the societies will readily realise that the Central Council would be prevented from any general action if all the affiliated societies claimed the right not to pay dues. It appears that the objection is to paying dues *twice*. Would it not be possible to find an amicable solution to these matters? The Central Council will make any concession compatible with its responsibilities.

For my part, I am convinced that your actions were dictated solely by your zeal for the common cause, and I am appealing to this same zeal in asking you to work for reconciliation and restoration of relations. You would oblige me greatly by replying immediately, firstly because I have to give the Central Council a report on this affair, and secondly because a *preliminary conference* of members of the various administrative committees will be taking place in London on 25 September.[217]

The Central Council is persuaded that the congress cannot take place this year, but the preliminary conference in London will make preparations for it.[a]

With fraternal greetings
Ch. Marx

First published in: Marx and Engels, *Works*, First Russian Edition, Vol. XXV, Moscow, 1934

Printed according to Marx's Notebook

Translated from the French

---

[a] See this volume, pp. 173-74.

91

MARX TO ENGELS [101]

IN MANCHESTER [a]

[London,] 31 July 1865

Dear Engels,

As you may have suspected, the reasons for my prolonged silence are not the most pleasant.

For two months I have been living solely on the pawnshop, which means that a queue of creditors has been hammering on my door, becoming more and more unendurable every day. This FACT won't come as any surprise to you when you consider: 1. that I have been unable to earn a FARTHING the whole time and 2. that merely paying off *the debts* and furnishing the house cost me something like £500. I have kept accounts (AS TO THIS ITEM) PENCE for PENCE, as I myself found it unbelievable how the money disappeared. To top that, I have been sent every conceivable, antediluvian IOU from Germany where God knows what rumours had been circulated.

To begin with, I wanted to come up to you to discuss the matter with you in person. But, at the present moment, any time lost cannot be made up as it is not good to interrupt my work. Last Saturday I told the Sub-Committee of the 'INTERNATIONAL' [21] that I was going away, so as at least to have a fortnight for once completely free of disturbance for PUSHING ON with my work.

I assure you that I would rather have had my thumb cut off than write this letter to you. It is truly soul-destroying to be dependent for half one's life. The only thought that sustains me in all this is that the two of us form a partnership together, in which I spend my time on the theoretical and party side of the BUSINESS. It is true my house is beyond my means, and we have, moreover, lived better this year than was the case before. But it is the only way for the children to establish themselves socially with a view to securing their future, quite apart from everything they have suffered and for which they have at least been compensated for a brief while. I believe you yourself will be of the opinion that, even from a merely commercial point of view, to run a purely proletarian household would not be appropriate in the cir-

---

[a] The letter bears the stamp: International Working Men's Association / Central Council / London.

cumstances, although that would be quite all right, if my wife and I were by ourselves or if the girls were boys.

Now, regarding my work, I will tell you the plain truth about it. There are 3 more chapters to be written to complete the theoretical part (the first 3 books). Then there is still the 4th book, the historical-literary one,[227] to be written, which will, comparatively speaking, be the easiest part for me, since all the problems have been resolved in the first 3 books, so that this last one is more by way of repetition in historical form. But I cannot bring myself to send anything off until I have the whole thing in front of me. WHATEVER SHORTCOMINGS THEY MAY HAVE, the advantage of my writings is that they are an artistic whole, and this can only be achieved through my practice of never having things printed until I have them in front of me *in their entirety.* This is impossible with Jacob Grimm's method which is in general better with writings that have no dialectical structure.[228]

The *English* version will be dealt with differently on the other hand. Fox has no doubt that he can find me a publisher as soon as I get the first sheets of print back. I would then arrange with Meissner that, in addition to the proofs for correcting, he would also send me the clean proof of each sheet, so that the German could be corrected at the same time as it is being translated into English. Regarding the latter, I shall of course need your assistance. I am expecting my real earnings from this work to come from the English edition.[229]

As far as the 'INTERNATIONAL' is concerned, the position is as follows:

I made over the £5 to Cremer to buy shares in *The Bee-Hive.* But since Cremer, Odger, etc., were going up to Manchester at that time, nothing came of it, and Potter HAD THE BETTER OF IT.[205] They decided to postpone the matter until the next meeting of shareholders (actually, the annual one). But I don't think that anything will come of it. Firstly, because the squabble between Odger and Potter has become a public scandal. Secondly, because *The Miner and Workman's Advocate* has offered its columns to us.[230] (Apropos. At a recent meeting with the *Miner* we undertook to let it have contributions gratis. So, if you have time to write a little article on FOREIGN POLITICS (**Prussian,** etc.), now and then, send it to me to be passed on to the paper.)

According to our Rules a public *congress* ought to be held in Brussels this year. The Parisians, Swiss and some of the people here, too, are going for it hammer and tongs. In the present circumstances—especially since I have so little time to write the necessary documents for the CENTRAL COUNCIL as well—I can only foresee a disgrace. Despite considerable opposition from the other side, I have succeeded in turning the public congress in Brussels into A PRIVATE PREALABLE CONFERENCE in London (25 September) which only DELEGATES OF THE ADMINISTRATIVE COMMITTEES will attend and at which the future congress is to be *prepared*. *Official* reasons given for postponing the congress were:

1. The need for PREALABLE UNDERSTANDING between the EXECUTIVE COMMITTEES.

2. The obstacles to the Association's propaganda arising from the STRIKES IN FRANCE, the elections, REFORM MOVEMENT and WORKINGMEN'S EXHIBITIONS IN ENGLAND.[231]

3. The ALIEN BILL RECENTLY PRESSED in Belgium[232] which rules out Brussels as a RENDEZVOUS for an INTERNATIONAL WORKINGMEN'S CONGRESS.[217]

I do not see the *Social-Demokrat* any more, as the Workers' Society[a] has also stopped it.[200] Nor am I taking the *Nordstern* any more, but I do see it occasionally at the Society. It said the Rhineland branches had on the main question deserted Bernhard.[b]

Edgar[c] is a very expensive guest for us, especially in the present circumstances, and he does not seem in the least inclined TO DECAMP.

In consequence of the hot weather and related biliousness, I have again been vomitting nearly every day for the past 3 months, as I did previously in Brussels.

Salut.

Your

K. M.

First published in *Der Briefwechsel zwischen F. Engels und K. Marx*, Bd. 3, Stuttgart, 1913

Printed according to the original

Published in English in full for the first time

92

MARX TO ENGELS

IN MANCHESTER

Dear Engels,   London, 5 August 1865

MY BEST THANKS FOR THE £50 AND the speed with which the help came. I was greatly amused by the part of your letter[131] which deals with the 'work of art' TO BE.[d] But you misunderstood me. The only

---

[a] German Workers' Educational Society in London - [b] Bernhard Becker (see this volume, p. 152) - [c] Edgar von Westphalen - [d] *Capital*

POINT IN QUESTION is whether to do a fair copy of part of the manuscript and send it to the publisher,[a] or finish writing the whole thing first? I have decided in favour of the latter for many reasons. No time is lost by it, AS FAR as the *work itself* is concerned, although some time is lost in printing; however, on the other hand, once begun, that cannot then be interrupted in any way either. Furthermore, in view of the level of the thermometer, progress with it has been as fast as anyone could have managed, even having no artistic considerations at all. BESIDES, as I have a MAXIMUM LIMIT of 60 printed sheets, it is absolutely essential for me to have the whole thing in front of me, to know how much has to be condensed and crossed out, so that the individual sections shall be evenly balanced and in proportion within the prescribed limits.[233] In any case, you can be sure that I shall spare no effort to *complete as soon as possible*, as the thing is a nightmarish burden to me. Not only does it prevent me from doing anything else, but it is also DAMNEDLY irksome to have the public kept entertained with the expectation of laurels to come (not by me, to be sure, but by Liebknecht and others). And furthermore, I know that time will not stand still for ever just as it is now.

Eichhoff has written a few lines to me, but couldn't call on me owing to pressure of business. In his letter he said Dronke would visit (he was here yesterday) but in such a confused way there was no making sense of the *scriptum*.[b] That 'treatise' is sticking to POOR Eichhoff like his own skin, and no operation will detach it from him.

What do you make of Siebel's productions as a patriotic-liberal poet? The thing appears to have been written during extremely depressing hangover. It is utter nonsense and surpasses EVERYTHING our friend has previously produced.

The *Social-Demokrat*'s attempt to commit itself in support of the bourgeoisie is a sign of complete and utter fiasco, although I share your view that the first calls in Berlin did not occur without some ministerial prompting.[c] However, the other Lassallean faction, which executed a *volte face*[d] against the *Social-Demokrat* as a result of our statement,[e] are also quite a pitiful rabble. These fellows are not merely at loggerheads with B. Becker and Co. as to whose faith in Lassalle is the true one, but several of their branches have published that phrase inspired by OLD Hatzfeldt and coined specifically with us in mind, that anyone who tried to overturn or

---

[a] Otto Meissner - [b] what he had written - [c] See this volume, pp. 169-70. - [d] about-turn - [e] K. Marx and F. Engels, 'To the Editor of the *Social-Demokrat*'.

change even one syllable of the truths as revealed by Lassalle, was declared a *traitor* to the 'people'.[216]

It is ages since I last answered Liebknecht, despite various notes he sent me; however I am going to do so now. He is in Hanover for the time being now, but his wife[a] is still in Berlin. The reason why I did not write was partly that I was very busy, and also I had enough on my hands with my own TROUBLES. On the other hand, I was furious with him for the nonsense which he had been retailing about me at the Berlin Lassalle-Association and which is there for all to read in the scrap of a pamphlet about B. Becker's expulsion from that association which the old sow got someone called Schilling to publish (Farthing would have been a more appropriate name).[234] With his usual talent for being too lazy to acquaint himself with the facts, he drivels the greatest nonsense about the Bangya-manuscript[169] and my intercession for Becker *quoad*[b] Vienna *Botschafter,*[c] etc. And, moreover, the whole way in which he plays the part of my 'PATRON' and 'apologises' for me to the louts of Berlin for *them* not knowing my works; and generally behaves as though so far I had done nothing in affairs of action. So, I allowed some time to elapse, so as not to say anything rude to him and to pacify myself with the thought that Liebknecht will be Liebknecht and that his intentions are 'good'. The 30,000 members of the old Berlin Journeymen's Association, and ditto the Association of Printers there organised a kind of ovation for him when he was expelled. With his usual optimism, Wilhelmchen sees 'the proletariat of Berlin at my (that is, his) and our (yours and mine) feet'.[235] At the same time, he has not managed even to form a single BRANCH of 6 members for the INTERNATIONAL ASSOCIATION in Germany, although the sanguine fellow must surely realise that I cannot serve up his DELUSIONS to the English as true coin. He also kept on writing to me about my 'book'.[d] But however often I sent him 'books' (first the whole remainder of '*Vogt*,'[e] then the whole remainder of the '*Communist Trials*'[f]) at his most sanguine request, from the moment he received them, I never heard a dying word more about them.

Mr *Groote*, Party of Progress[99] deputy for Düsseldorf, has written to him saying that what he did in Berlin has had more effect than the actions of 100 Party of Progress deputies.

---

[a] Ernestine Liebknecht - [b] with regard to - [c] The original has: *Beobachter.* - [d] *Capital* - [e] K. Marx, *Herr Vogt.* - [f] K. Marx, *Revelations Concerning the Communist Trial in Cologne.*

Edgar[a] has just recently caught a cold which has gone to his nose, which, as a result of this ACCIDENT, looks positively Bardolphian.[b]

During the warm weather I have been regularly working day and night by the open window. Outcome: an attack of rheumatism in my right arm, particularly the shoulder blade, which is very painful and makes writing, especially any *lifting-movement*, difficult. I instinctively cry out if I unintentionally raise my arm in bed at night, which tells you how nasty the thing is. Does Gumpert know of any kind of NOSTRUM for it?

You probably know that at the Gymnastic Festival in Paris, the worthy Gottfried Kinkel refused the laurel crown he was offered by a Jew who was presiding, with the words: 'I want no crown, not even a crown of laurel', but at once added in fairly unvarnished words that he had by no means yet given up his claims to the Presidency of the German Republic, the 'office' that was his due. The *Nordstern* ridiculed him rather effectively as much for this bit of melodrama, and for his whole SPEECH, which was *disgusting*.[c] The Festival opened with a toast to Badinguet.[d]

Where is Strohn?

As soon as you have time and inclination, do not forget to send me something 'continental' for the *Miner*.[e]

Kindest regards to you from the whole family, and from me to MRS Lizzy.[f]

Your
K. Marx

First published abridged in *Der Briefwechsel zwischen F. Engels und K. Marx*, Bd. 3, Stuttgart, 1913 and in full in *MEGA*, Abt. III, Bd. 3, Berlin, 1930

Printed according to the original

Published in English for the first time

---

[a] Edgar von Westphalen - [b] Bardolph—a character from Shakespeare's *The Merry Wives of Windsor* and *King Henry IV*. - [c] *Nordstern*, Nos. 315 and 316, 8 and 15 July 1865. - [d] nickname of Napoleon III (the name of a bricklayer in whose clothes Napoleon fled from prison in 1846) - [e] *The Miner and Workman's Advocate* - [f] Lizzy Burns

93

ENGELS TO MARX [26]

IN LONDON

Manchester, 7 August 1865

Dear Moor,

I have got a remedy for your rheumatism that Gumpert once used to cure me with within 24 hours, and from a much more severe attack, too. Get yourself 2 big bags of flannel made, big enough to cover the affected part completely and a bit over; have these bags filled with BRAN and heated each in turn in the oven, just as hot as you can bear it; you put each in turn on the place, changing them as often as ever you can. All the while keep yourself warm and quiet in bed, and you will soon feel very considerable relief, but you mustn't discontinue the treatment on that account until all the pain has gone (say 24-36 hours).

Eichhoff has just called; he has got himself made DIRECTOR of a LIMITED COMPANY in London; it is crystal clear to me from the whole affair that the idea is for him to be duped of a substantial sum again, but there's absolutely no helping the fellow, with his mania for seeing everything *couleur de rose*.[a] He has now gone so far as believing that the silk-trade here in England absolutely could not go on without him.

I'm so pleased the book[b] is making rapid progress, for I had really begun to suspect from one or two phrases in your last letter that you had again reached an unexpected turning-point which might prolong everything indefinitely. The day that manuscript is sent off, I shall drink myself to kingdom come, that is, unless you come up here the next day so that we can seal it together.

Many thanks for the *Free Presses*.

Our worthy Liebknecht simply cannot help putting his foot in it, or writing off to people just whenever the mood takes him. We shall always be annoyed with him for 10 months out of 12, as soon as he is by himself and has to act on his own initiative. In the meantime *que veux-tu*?[c] Liebknecht does as Liebknecht is, and all the exasperation and all the grumbling will not help matters. And after all, when all's said and done, at the moment he is the only reliable link we have in Germany.

---

[a] through rose-coloured spectacles - [b] *Capital* - [c] what would you have?

A WORKINGMEN'S CONGRESS in Brussels would certainly be the greatest stupidity in present circumstances.[217] Just remember our own experiences in that little country.[236] That sort of thing can only be done in England, the FRENCHMEN ought to know that. It would just be throwing away money and time and trouble to attempt anything of that kind in Belgium.

Have you got Schilling's pamphlet on B. Becker?[a] You might let me have it for a couple of days.

I don't know whether Strohn is in Hamburg or Bradford, I haven't heard anything from him for quite a long time now.

The Rhineland philistines are supposed to be frightfully angry with Bismarck; it is splendid that those jackasses are having their 'historical development on a legal basis' so nicely demonstrated. Have you seen Bismarck's latest dodge to raise money? The Cologne-Minden Railway had granted the state the right to *buy up its shares at par* in return for an interest-guarantee from the state (100-taler shares are now standing at over 200 talers); he has bartered away this right to the Railway for 13 million talers, and the *Kölner Zeitung* calculates that in this way he *got hold of 30 million talers,* including sale of the shares already owned by the state, etc. The question is, will the Cologne-Minden Railway pay up without the Chamber's approval for the deal. If it does so, Bismarck will again have a clear road for years ahead, and the philistines will have been atrociously shitted upon. We shall soon see.[237]

Lizzy[b] says Edgar[c] can't have been wearing his Texan hat, or he couldn't possibly have caught a cold in the nose.

Your
F. E.

First published in *Der Briefwechsel zwischen F. Engels und K. Marx*, Bd. 3, Stuttgart, 1913 and in full in *MEGA*, Abt. III, Bd. 3, Berlin, 1930

Printed according to the original

Published in English in full for the first time

---

[a] C. Schilling, *Die Ausstossung des Präsidenten Bernhard Becker aus dem Allgemeinen Deutschen Arbeiter-Verein und der 'Social-Demokrat'.* - [b] Lizzy Burns - [c] Edgar von Westphalen

94

MARX TO ENGELS[238]

IN MANCHESTER

[London,] 9 August 1865

DEAR FRED,

Letter from Mr Siebold enclosed.[239] You need not send it back. Secondly, I am sending you the Hatzfeldt rubbish.[a] Do *not* send it back, but store it. Don't show it to *anyone* either. Fortunately, this rubbish has left no trace in the German press. The only thing relating to it which appeared publicly in the press was a statement by *Metzner* (ex-authorised representative of the Berlin branch[b]) and *Vogt*[c] (STILL its treasurer), countersigned *W. Liebknecht*, in which they stated:

1. that Schilling had falsified the report, suppressed some resolutions and made others their direct opposite;

2. that that old girl Hatzfeldt could have spared her comments SINCE the Association had forbidden her to interfere in any way. That appeared in *Reform*[d] and *Volks-Zeitung*.[234]

I have been medicating myself for a couple of days now and am feeling utterly rotten, quite incapable of working. But Allen tells me that I shall be up and about again in a few days. It's the bilious trouble and a consequence of the 'bitter' labour of thinking in the HOT WEATHER. *Officially* I'm now *away from home* on account of the *'INTERNATIONAL'*.

Edgar[e] is vegetating. In his hermit-like existence he has become accustomed to the narrowest kind of egotism, pondering the needs of his stomach from morn till night. But as he is a good-natured sort, his egotism is that of a KIND-NATURED CAT or a friendly dog. To the devil with hermit-life. He has even lost all interest in women, and his sex-urge has gone to his belly, too. At the same time, he is constantly anxious about his precious health, that same lad who was, on the other hand, used to feeling 'safe' amongst snakes, tigers, wolves, and leopards.

He now wishes he was back in Texas again. But there is no escape from the confrontation with his *cher frère*.[f]

---

[a] C. Schilling, *Die Ausstossung des Präsidenten Bernhard Becker aus dem Allgemeinen Deutschen Arbeiter-Verein und der 'Social-Demokrat'.* - [b] of the General Association of German Workers - [c] August Vogt - [d] *Berliner Reform* - [e] Edgar von Westphalen - [f] dear brother (Ferdinand von Westphalen)

You can tell what his back-to-nature thinking is like from the fact that his present ideal is to set up a STORE—a cigar or wine STORE—obviously secretly hoping that this will be the surest way to apply oneself to the cigars and wine.

He likes to pretend to be an OLD GENTLEMAN who has settled his accounts with life, has nothing more to do and is only living 'for his health's sake'.

Besides, he is preoccupied with his *attire* as well, and the 'OLD GENTLEMEN' in Rotten Row[240] make him very sad because he cannot keep up with them. Queer cove! Laura, who HAS a small CARBUNCLE on her left cheek JUST NOW, SAYS THAT 'HER MOTHER'S BROTHER IS AN EXCEEDINGLY BRIGHT FELLAH!' Tussy[a] 'THAT SHE LIKES HIM, BECAUSE HE IS SO FUNNY' and little Jenny that Lina Schöler and he can congratulate each other 'TO HAVE SAFELY GOT RID OF EACH OTHER'. WELL, THEY ARE A BAD LOT. The girls have also SEVERELY CROSS-EXAMINED me AS TO THE 'MRS Burns'. *Salut.*

Your
K. M.

First published abridged in *Der Briefwechsel zwischen F. Engels und K. Marx*, Bd. 3, Stuttgart, 1913 and in full in *MEGA*, Abt. III, Bd. 3, Berlin, 1930

Printed according to the original

Published in English in full for the first time

95

ENGELS TO MARX

IN LONDON

Manchester, 16 August 1865

Dear Moor,

That unctuous trash from the Hatzfeldt woman[b] really is unctuous trash with all that is in it about Lassalle the only saviour, Liebknecht, etc. Dear old LIBRARY[c] has really surpassed himself this time in his customary spinelessness, lack of imagination and

---

[a] Eleanor Marx - [b] C. Schilling, *Die Ausstossung des Präsidenten Bernhard Becker aus dem Allgemeinen Deutschen Arbeiter-Verein und der 'Social-Demokrat'*. - [c] Wilhelm Liebknecht

forgetfulness, that is, unless the whole report is a fabrication. The devil take such an advocatus.

Ditto our sparkling-wine enthusiast Siebold. With what self-assured naivety the fellow tried to 'reconcile' you to Blind![239] And then those interesting 'old Swedes' whom nobody has ever heard of and whom we're supposed to write to, to make 'contact'. Quite à la Harro Harring. I'm increasingly coming round to think that from the most southerly latitude of North Friesland onwards everything beyond urban bourgeois and peasant politics is pure Harro Harring.[a] But no doubt you will be having that dolt on your back every year.

Next week (about Friday 25th inst.) Moore and I are going to Germany and Switzerland for a fortnight, and maybe we shall also 'cast a casual glance' over Italy.[241] If I can so arrange it, I shall call in briefly at Modena Villas[b] on my way back.

The 28th of this month, i.e. Monday week, is the date of the General Meeting of the Cologne-Minden shareholders, which will decide Prussia's politics for the next few years. I can't imagine that those fellows will be such jackasses as to pay out 13 mill. talers in cash to Bismarck without having the approval of the Chambers.[237] But your liberal Rhineland burgher is capable of a good many tricks the moment he has a chance of swindling the state, and thinks that in his capacity as Deputy he can obtain indemnity for himself afterwards. But if the deal were to fall through, or if it were made conditional on authorisation by the Chambers, that would be more or less the end for Monsieur Bismarck; even that adventurer would not survive such a defeat *in financialibus*[c] and after such a desperate attempt. But the fact that he is momentarily coming to terms with Austria again, shows that intellectually and morally he is *au bout de son latin*.[d] He knows only too well that he can't start a war without being brought down immediately, so he goes on lashing out with big talk, chalking up little gains and turning Germany into the laughing stock of the world. But the philistine is almost as much impressed by him as by Boustrapa.[76] The philistine now no longer requires even ephemeral victories from his idols, but only that they can brag. This is how Classen-Kappelmann became the idol of Cologne as well, because he took to his heels at the crucial moment.[224]

---

[a] See K. Marx and F. Engels, *The Great Men of the Exile* (present edition, Vol. 11, pp. 284-90). - [b] the street in London, where Marx lived - [c] in financial transactions - [d] at the end of his strength

It was also a nice thought of Siebold's to put in a good word for C. V. Rimestad in Copenhagen, who is one of the *Dagbladet* people! The so-called Workers' Association is a propaganda organisation of the Scandinavian Eider-Danes and the Hall ministry.[242]

What will Father Urquhart be saying next month about the legal advisers to the Prussian throne? What splendid lads they are!

Kindest regards to the LADIES and Edgar.[a]

Your
F. E.

First published abridged in *Der Briefwech-sel zwischen F. Engels und K. Marx*, Bd. 3, Stuttgart, 1913 and in full in *MEGA*, Abt. III, Bd. 3, Berlin, 1930

Printed according to the original

Published in English for the first time

96

MARX TO ENGELS[243]

IN MANCHESTER

[London,] 19 August 1865

DEAR FRED,

Since you are setting off on your travels,[241] I *must* tell you that I have to pay a BILL for £10 to BUTCHER on 28 August, and the LANDLORD is also becoming very TROUBLESOME. BY THE BY, the English state appears HARDPRESSED FOR MONEY. At all events, the TAXGATHERERS were more pressing this MONTH than ever before and have unexpectedly 'relieved' me.

I am still SICK, although Allen is getting rid of the LIVER troubles. But now I have caught a kind of INFLUENZA, which, he says, will last 5-6 days and which really is the biggest nuisance of all, AS FAR AS MENTAL ACTIVITY IS CONCERNED. I hope that with that I shall have settled MY DEBT TO NATURE.

Löhrchen[b] is not really very well either. For the past year she has been getting much thinner than she ought to be. But she is a strange child and only today agreed to go to the Dr with my wife.

---

[a] Edgar von Westphalen - [b] Laura Marx

I HOPE IT IS NOTHING SERIOUS. Little Jenny and Tussy[a] are very well. (Ditto Edgar's[b] STATE OF HEALTH much improved.) My wife had bitten out the 2 front teeth in the middle of her lower jaw, and yesterday had 4 teeth fitted by way of replacement. These are more or less the only 'events' that have occurred here.

Being unwell, I am unable to write much, and then only BY FITS AND STARTS. In between, I am just dabbling in irrelevancies, although with the INFLUENZA I cannot even read properly. I 'took the opportunity' to 'take up' a little astronomy again, amongst other things. And one thing I would like to mention that was new to me at least, but perhaps you have known about it for some time. You know Laplace's theory of the formation of the CELESTIAL SYSTEMS and how he explains the rotation of the various BODIES about their own axis, etc. Proceeding from there, a YANKEE, Kirkwood, has discovered a kind of law concerning the *differences* in the rotation of the planets, which had previously appeared quite abnormal. The law is as follows:

* 'The *square of the number of times* that each planet rotates during one revolution in its orbit, is proportioned to the *cube of the breadth of a diameter of its sphere of attraction.*' *

This means that between two planets there must be a point at which their power of attraction is equally strong; so that a body at this point would remain stationary between them. On the other hand, the body would fall towards one planet or another on either side of that point. This point thus forms the LIMIT of the SPHERE OF ATTRACTION of the planet. This SPHERE OF ATTRACTION is, in turn, the measure of the breadth of the GAZEOUS RING from which, according to Laplace, the planet was formed when it first became separated from the GENERAL GAZEOUS MASS. Kirkwood concluded from this that, if Laplace's hypothesis is correct, a specific relationship must exist between the VELOCITY OF THE PLANET'S ROTATION and the BREADTH OF THE RING from which it was formed or its SPHERE OF ATTRACTION. And he has expressed this in the above law, and proved it by analytical calculations.

Old Hegel made some very good jokes about the 'sudden reversal' of centripetal to centrifugal force, right at the moment when one has attained 'preponderance' over the other; e.g., centripetal force is greatest near the sun; *therefore*, says Hegel, centrifugal force is greatest, since it overcomes this *maximum of centripetal* force and vice versa. Moreover, the forces are in

---

[a] Eleanor Marx - [b] Edgar von Westphalen

equilibrium when half way between the apsides.[244] *Therefore* they can *never* depart from this equilibrium, etc. Incidentally, taken as a whole, Hegel's polemic amounts to saying that Newton's 'proofs' added nothing to Kepler, who already possessed the 'concept' of movement, which I think is fairly generally accepted now.[a]

You know that the *President* of the Bank of Switzerland is now Mr *Karl Vogt*, who betrayed his friend Fazy as soon as the latter left Geneva,[212] and cheated together with Reinach (the real ACTING DIRECTOR). I asked Freiligrath how Mr Vogt, who is otherwise of ill repute as a FINANCIER in Switzerland, had come by this honourable post. *Answer*: the Swiss have hardly a share left in the 'Bank of Switzerland'. The Jews in Berlin and Frankfurt a. M. take the decisions. And they support Vogt. Meanwhile, Reinach has been teasing our POOR Freiligrath so much that the latter wrote him the right-thinking rejoinder that even the Prussian police never persecuted him quite so much. They say Fazy swindled the bank out of $1^{1}/_{2}$ mill. frs.

A few weeks ago, Professor Beesly had an article about Catiline in *The Fortnightly Review*, vindicating the latter as a man of revolution.[b] Much of it is uncritical (as one would expect from an Englishman, e.g. wrong information on Caesar's position at that time), but his intense rage at the oligarchy and 'respectable people' is very nice. Likewise his sallies against the professional English 'DULL *littérateur*'. Mr *Harrison* had an article in the same *Review* expounding why 'political economy' can adduce '*nothing*' in refutation of communism.[c] It seems to me that *now* there is more MOVEMENT amongst English thinkers than amongst the Germans. The latter are sufficiently preoccupied with celebrating Classen-Kappelmann.[224]

Regards to Mrs Lizzy.[d] The children are depending on you not to pass through London without stopping on your way home.

Your
K. M.

You cannot have the remotest conception of the utter nonsense contained in the PARLIAMENTARY REPORTS of 1857 and 1858 on banking, etc., which I recently had to refer back to.[e] As in the monetary

---

[a] See G. W. F. Hegel, *Vorlesungen über die Naturphilosophie als der Encyklopädie der philosophischen Wissenschaften im Grundrisse*, Zweiter Theil, § 270. - [b] E. S. Beesly, 'Catiline as a Party Leader', *The Fortnightly Review*, Vol. I, 15 May to 1 August 1865. - [c] F. Harrison, 'The Limits of Political Economy'. - [d] Lizzy Burns - [e] *Report from the Select Committee on Bank Acts*

system, capital=gold. In the midst, shame-faced recollections of A. Smith and excruciating attempts to reconcile the chaos of the MONEY MARKET with his 'enlightened' ideas. MacCulloch, who has at last now gone the way of all flesh, distinguishes himself most of all. The fellow was obviously in receipt of a substantial *douceur*[a] from Lord Overstone, who is consequently '*facile maximus argentariorum*'[b] and has to be cleared, come what may. I shall have to reserve my critique of this whole unsavoury stew for a later paper.[245]

First published abridged in *Der Briefwechsel zwischen F. Engels und K. Marx*, Bd. 3, Stuttgart, 1913 and in full in *MEGA*, Abt. III, Bd. 3, Berlin, 1930

Printed according to the original

Published in English in full for the first time

97

ENGELS TO MARX

IN LONDON

Manchester, 21 August 1865

Dear Moor,

Encl. £20, first half, B/G 56794, Manchester, 9 January 1864, second to follow as soon as you acknowledge receipt. I cannot send more until I know how the final accounts work out, and I shall not know that until my return or even later.

That business of Kirkwood's law was new to me, as it was to Moore. But is it really proven, or is it not perhaps just a hypothesis?[c] Surely it ought to be possible to verify a thing like that.

I hope you are all restored to health now. That trouble with Laura is probably of no more consequence than with little Jenny that time, but it really is absurd of you to allow yourself to continue in such a way. In such circumstances, you should put your foot down as master of the house. I expect you have shaken off your INFLUENZA now, with the warm weather, that kind of thing really takes it out of you, but at least it is easily cured now.

---

[a] sweetener - [b] without doubt the greatest banker - [c] See this volume, p. 184.

The old women are just coming to sweep out the office and drive me from my post; so I must quickly finish.
Kindest regards.

Your
F. E.

First published abridged in *Der Briefwechsel zwischen F. Engels und K. Marx*, Bd. 3, Stuttgart, 1913 and in full in *MEGA*, Abt. III, Bd. 3, Berlin, 1930

Printed according to the original

Published in English for the first time

98

MARX TO ENGELS

IN MANCHESTER

[London,] 22 August 1865

DEAR FRED,

BEST THANKS FOR THE £20, FIRST HALF of which received. I most certainly would not BOTHER you, but the end of the quarter, whose bills have been put off, is a very difficult time.

Regarding Kirkwood's law, there is no doubt that it explains the difference in the ROTATORY MOVEMENTS, e.g., between those of Jupiter and those of Venus, which hitherto appeared entirely fortuitous.[a] But *how* he finds out and proves the law itself, I do not know, but on my next visit to the British Museum I will try to get to the bottom of the original work and will tell you more about it then. The only 'problem' attached to the matter, as far as I can see, consists in mathematically determining the SPHERE OF ATTRACTION of each planet. The only *hypothetical* thing about it is probably the assumption of Laplace's theory as a premise.

My INFLUENZA has invaded my nose to such an extent that the TEXAN BOY's[b] 'nozzle' has reproduced itself in me, accompanied by a frightful cold and a muzziness in the head such as must have filled the whole of Laplace's universe of incandescent gas.

The fellows and friends of the 'INTERNATIONAL' have now discovered after all that I am *not* away, and I have therefore

---

[a] See this volume, pp. 184, 186. - [b] Edgar von Westphalen's

received a SUMMONS TO ATTEND a meeting of the SUBCOMMITTEE today. The 4 weeks of my disappearance have been totally SPOILT for me by the DOCTOR'S prescriptions.

Amongst the books from Lupus' legacy I have in my possession there is a copy of Egli's *Neue Handelsgeographie*. This Swiss says in the preface that into the 'biographies of commercial geography' he has now and again

'woven a view from life, a view in contemplation of which the soul may lose itself for a moment, in comfortable repose ... genre miniatures woven in ... a piece of life shall here unfold before our eyes. Life evolves from life alone'.

The following shows you what this naive Swiss means by 'views from life':

'Markgräfler wine grows on the sunny hills of Mühlheim and Badenweiler. It was not for nothing that our dearly beloved Hebel sang:

> "At t'Mill by t'Post
> Tallyho, mine host!
> Drink up lads: a grand wine flows,
> Smooth as olive oil it goes!
> At t'Mill by t'Post."''[a]

To prove 'that I have not taken the easy path', this same naive Swiss refers to the list of works he has used. This list numbers precisely 20 items, where along with naive 'children's literature' as the *Buch der Erfindungen*, etc., there are two works by the self-same Mr Egli.[b]

Kindest regards from the WHOLE FAMILY.

Your
K. M.

First published abridged in *Der Briefwechsel zwischen F. Engels und K. Marx*, Bd. 3, Stuttgart, 1913 and in full in *MEGA*, Abt. III, Bd. 3, Berlin, 1930

Printed according to the original

Published in English for the first time

---

[a] J. P. Hebel's poem 'Der Schwarzwälder im Breisgau'. - [b] J. J. Egli, *Praktische Erdkunde mit Illustrationen* and *Praktische Schweizerkunde für Schule und Haus*

99

MARX TO WILHELM LIEBKNECHT

IN LEIPZIG

London, 11 September 1865

Dear Liebknecht,

As soon as I know whether you are still in Hanover, I shall report to you the reasons for the interruption in correspondence, and indeed write at greater length.

On 25 September, a (PRIVATE) *conference* between the COUNCIL of the International here and the DELEGATES of the ADMINISTRATIONS in Switzerland, France, and Belgium will take place here. Can you not send yourself over here as DELEGATE from Germany?[246]

Salut.

Your
K. M.

First published in: Marx and Engels, *Works*, First Russian Edition, Vol. XXIX, Moscow, 1946

Printed according to the original

Published in English for the first time

100

MARX TO WILHELM LIEBKNECHT

IN LEIPZIG

[London,] 20 September 1865

Dear Miller,[a]

I received yours yesterday afternoon, too late to post a letter here. *Illness* had much to do with my protracted silence. There were other reasons which I think useless now to dwell upon. Much business pressing upon my time just now, I can only return these few lines.

----

[a] Liebknecht's conspiratorial pseudonym

A *Report*[247] (English, of course) on your part is very important. It must be here on Monday next (25 September). It cannot arrive timely unless you send me the letter *directly* by the Leipzig post.

The Swiss have chosen two delegates, Mons Dupleix, a Frenchman, and Mr *Philipp Becker,* a German.

Old Hatzfeldt dwells at Paris, where the old hag is intriguing with the 'horn-bearing' father of 'Socialism', *Moses,*[a] her most cringing slave. It was at her instigation, that he inserted his 'warning' in the *Nordstern* and his slander into the *Social-Demokrat.*[248] She is now concocting with him the 'Apotheosis' of her own belated 'Oedipus'.[b] The London correspondent of the *Social-Demokrat* seems to be cracked Weber.[c] All these things have been reported to me from Paris. As to myself, I carefully abstain from taking any notice whatever of what is going on in the Berlin and Hamburg 'organs' of the movement.[d] This so-called movement is so disgusting a thing that the less you hear of it the better.

We have founded here a *weekly* paper of our own *The Workman's Advocate.* You will oblige by sending correspondence (English) for it to my address.

Yours truly
A. Williams[e]

First published in the language of the original, English, in *Wilhelm Liebknecht. Briefwechsel mit Karl Marx und Friedrich Engels,* The Hague, 1963

Reproduced from the book

101

ENGELS TO WILHELM LIEBKNECHT

IN LEIPZIG

Manchester, 21 September 1865

Dear Liebknecht,

It was bad luck that you chose to write to me just as I was leaving for 3 weeks on the Continent,[241] so that I only found your

---

[a] Moses Hess - [b] Ferdinand Lassalle - [c] Louis Weber - [d] *Der Social-Demokrat* and *Nordstern* - [e] Marx's conspiratorial pseudonym

letter[a] waiting for me on my return. The £5 banknote B/V 68754, Manchester, 16 January 1865, encl. as requested.

I cannot write much today, as I want to get the banknote sent off as well; but I will just say that Marx has, of course, every reason to be angry with you. The manner in which you rebutted Becker's[b] absurd allegations against Marx in your Berlin defence-speech was exceedingly weak and incompetent, and in respect of both the Bangya-affair[169] and several others you twisted the facts as much as did Mr Becker, although you could easily have gained better knowledge by referring to *Herr Vogt*.[234] These are extremely disagreeable matters, which Madame Hatzfeldt will now purvey to the world in this distorted form, and with your seal of approval,[c] and you demand that Moor should take all that so calmly?

Your
F. E.

First published in: Marx and Engels, *Works*, First Russian Edition, Vol. XXIX, Moscow, 1946

Printed according to the original

Published in English for the first time

102

MARX TO HERMANN JUNG[1]

IN LONDON

[London,] 30 September [1865]

Dear Jung,

I am expecting you tomorrow (Sunday) for DINNER (A VERY FRUGAL ONE); I have also asked De Paepe and Becker.[d] Please be so kind and invite *Kaub in my name*. This morning I am SO PRESSED BY BUSINESS OF ALL KIND THAT I CANNOT AFFORD TO WRITE TWO LETTERS.

YOURS FRATERNALLY
K. Marx

First published in: Marx and Engels, *Works*, First Russian Edition, Vol. XXIX, Moscow, 1946

Printed according to the original

---

[a] of 30 August 1865 - [b] Bernhard Becker - [c] See this volume, p. 176. - [d] Johann Philipp Becker

103

ENGELS TO MARX

IN LONDON

Dear Moor,   [Manchester,] 4 October 1865

I always strike unlucky with my plans for coming to London. I met my mother[a] just 3 days before my return here, in Ostende, to be exact, and I couldn't make it an hour shorter, of course. Nor could I have met her any earlier, as neither of us knew where she would be 2-3 days before. But I was DUE here on 15 September,[241] as Charles[b] had to leave on that day, as he in fact did. Since then, as always when I come back from a journey, the very devil has got into the cotton market, I have had to look after Charles' work as well as my own, and that is no trifle when cotton goes up in a fortnight from 18 to 24 $1/_2$d. per pound, yarns on the other hand by 8-9d. per pound, and telegrams of every description pour in. I hope that is all over now, and besides Charles will come back at the beginning of next week, so that I can gather my wits again at last. This horrible rush has made it positively impossible for me to write even 2 lines to you, in fact, since I've been back, I've not been able to write a line of private correspondence at all. As soon as ever I can, I will write at greater length; meanwhile do let me know how you all are and how the 'book'[c] is getting on. I think I should manage to come over some time for 3×24 hours, as soon as we have got things in order here. But our office is looking like a pigsty, Gottfried[d] has taken on 3 fellows for me who are absolutely hopeless, and is holding me to the contract which says I am to make something of them. So, you can see the way things are here. I shall have to sack one or two of them.

Your
F. E.

Kindest regards to all.

I was also 'all ready' among the Swabians; however, they are not creating any School of Poetry but are cotton-spinning, or emigrating.

First published in *Der Briefwechsel zwischen F. Engels und K. Marx*, Bd. 3, Stuttgart, 1913

Printed according to the original

Published in English for the first time

---

[a] Elisabeth Engels - [b] Charles Roesgen - [c] *Capital* - [d] Gottfried Ermen

104

MARX TO ENGELS

IN MANCHESTER

[London,] 19 October 1865

DEAR FRED,

I shall arrive in Manchester ABOUT 4.40 tomorrow afternoon and will make my way to your official dwelling.[249]

Your
K. M.

First published in *Der Briefwechsel zwischen F. Engels und K. Marx*, Bd. 3, Stuttgart, 1913

Printed according to the original

Published in English for the first time

105

MARX TO ENGELS[6]

IN MANCHESTER

[London,] 8 November 1865
1 Modena Villas, Maitland Park,
Haverstock Hill

Dear FREDERICK,

I arrived here on Friday[a] evening. Strohn had pressed me very strongly to spend some days with him, but I had too much on my mind. I knew things were awry in London and thus wanted to be on the spot.

The DISAPPOINTMENTS Mrs Lizzy[b] prophesied for me came true with a vengeance. *D'abord,*[c] on arrival at King's Cross,[d] my case had gone, and I still have not got it back even now, which is particularly annoying because of the 'papers' it contained, for which I am responsible. Then I found my child[e] was still very unwell. Finally, the LANDLORD had been round, had made threats, and my wife had only calmed him down with *promises of my return.* The man talked of putting the '*BROKER*' into the house and also of

---

[a] 3 November - [b] Lizzy Burns - [c] Firstly - [d] railway station in London - [e] Laura Marx

terminating the LEASE, which the contract admittedly entitles him to do. All the other riff-raff appeared in the LANDLORD'S wake, some of them in person, and some in the form of threatening letters. I found my wife SO DESOLATE that I *had not the COURAGE* to explain the TRUE STATE OF THINGS to her. And I *really do not know what to do!* And we also have to get coals in, etc.

As well as these DISAPPOINTMENTS ONE GOOD NEWS. One of the two aunts in Frankfurt (the one who is 73,[a] the other[b] is two years younger) has passed on, but *ab intestato*[c] (being afraid of dying if she should make a will). I shall therefore have to share with the other heirs, which would not have been so if there had been a will, as she cared nothing for the others. And then another pleasant circumstance—we have to wait for the power of attorney from Mr Juta from the CAPE OF GOOD HOPE.

All these pleasant circumstances have rather gone to my stomach, so that I at once had myself made up some more of Gumpert's medicine.

Salut (to MRS Lizzy, too).

Your
K. M.

First published in *Der Briefwechsel zwischen F. Engels und K. Marx*, Bd. 3, Stuttgart, 1913

Printed according to the original

106

MARX TO SALOMON FULD [250]

IN FRANKFURT AM MAIN

London, 9 November 1865

Dear Dr Fuld,

As I have lost my aunt's private address, I am taking the liberty of sending you the enclosed letter[111] for forwarding to Madame Babette Blum.

Yours respectfully
Dr K. Marx

First published in: Marx/Engels, *Werke*, Bd. 31, Berlin, 1965

Printed according to the original

Published in English for the first time

---

[a] Esther Kosel - [b] Babette Blum - [c] intestate

107

ENGELS TO MARX

IN LONDON

[Manchester,] 13 November 1865

Dear Moor,

You should receive herewith at the same time a registered letter with £15, which I made out on Friday and gave to our errand-boy to attend to. I received no answer from you on Sunday, which I found somewhat surprising, and it occurred to me that the boy did not give me the ticket for the letter on Saturday morning. When I looked into it today, it turned out that the wretch had messed up the whole business with his procrastinating and still had the letter in his pocket. That was the last straw as far as his slovenliness was concerned, and he was sacked. I am extremely annoyed about this, as you must meanwhile have been thinking I had quietly put your last letter in my pocket and left things to take their course, without writing a single word to you.

Your
F. E.

Has Edgar^a gone?

First published in *Der Briefwechsel zwischen F. Engels und K. Marx*, Bd. 3, Stuttgart, 1913

Printed according to the original

Published in English for the first time

108

MARX TO ENGELS

IN MANCHESTER

[London,] 15 November 1865

Dear Fred,

You must excuse me for not most gratefully acknowledging receipt of the £15 until today and for not writing to you until *tomorrow*. I am so pressed that I cannot manage it today.

---

^a Edgar von Westphalen

Little Jenny has diphtheria, but I hope it will soon be over.

As soon as you have read the enclosed letter—whose manner and style do, incidentally, stand out most favourably from those of the Rhineland workers—please be so good as to send it back. Courtesy requires that it should be answered.[251]

Salut.

Your

K. Marx

First published in *Der Briefwechsel zwischen F. Engels und K. Marx*, Bd. 3, Stuttgart, 1913

Printed according to the original

Published in English for the first time

109

MARX TO HERMANN JUNG

IN LONDON

[London,] 15 November 1865

My dear Jung,

On my return from Manchester,[249] I find your letter from which I am deeply concerned to see that you are still suffering. I fear very much that you have been always interrupting your cure by a premature application to work.

I shall call upon at your house on *Sunday afternoon.* I should like to find Dupont there since I must communicate to him different things.

My whole family takes the most earnest interest in everything concerning you and sends you the best wishes for your reconvalescence.

My compliments to Mrs Jung.

Yours fraternally

K. Marx

First published in: Marx and Engels, *Works,* First Russian Edition, Vol. XXV, Moscow, 1934

Reproduced from the original

Published in English for the first time

110

ENGELS TO MARX

IN LONDON

Manchester, 17 November 1865

Dear Moor,

Your letter was only passed on to me yesterday evening, and I shall be making enquiries as to how it was left lying around for so long.

I hope little Jenny is ALL RIGHT again and at least has got over the acute stage of the illness and the danger therewith. I'm sending her a case of port, sherry and claret this evening, to restore her strength. It gave me a real fright when I read the word diphtheria; it is not something to be made light of.

The letter from the Berliners really took me aback.[251] It has obviously been written by someone with a lot more to him than Wilhelmchen [a] and his references to the latter do not appear to be without a certain irony. Now the letter has certainly not been written by a worker, the mere fact that Grimm's rules of orthography are impeccably observed shows that, and I am just a mite suspicious as to how genuine the thing is. At any rate, we ought to obtain more information about the 3 signatories, Wilhelmchen should know them at least, if the business is *bona fide*. It is rather the form of the document that makes me suspicious, the content most definitely implies the contrary. But as you won't in any case be going to Berlin to found a new organisation there, it will not signify if you write to these people. Letter returned encl.

What do you say to the NIGGER-rebellion in Jamaica and the atrocities perpetrated by the English?[252] *The Telegraph* says today:

* 'We should be very sorry if the right was taken away *from any British officer to shoot or hang all and every British subject found in arms against the British Crown!'* *[b]

Your
F. E.

First published abridged in *Der Briefwech-sel zwischen F. Engels und K. Marx*, Bd. 3, Stuttgart, 1913 and in full in *MEGA*, Abt. III, Bd. 3, Berlin, 1930

Printed according to the original

Published in English for the first time

[a] Wilhelm Liebknecht - [b] *The Daily Telegraph*, No. 3249, 17 November 1865.

111

MARX TO ENGELS [253]

IN MANCHESTER

[London,] 20 November[a] 1865

Dear Engels,

Little Jenny is on the mend again now and thanks you very much for the wine.

Regarding the financial questions, it would be futile to approach Dronke about it. To have some peace with the LANDLORD, and that is at the root of it all, I have persuaded him to take a bill of exchange up till the middle of February for the current quarter, for which I owe him $\frac{2}{3}$. As for the other creditors, I have satisfied the most pressing with the £15 and am considering ways and means of putting together at least an instalment for the others. Your offer is very generous, and as soon as my work[b] is finished and out, the remainder will have to be made up through other commitments, or if that should not succeed, *although I fully expect it will*, we shall have to move somewhere cheaper, perhaps to Switzerland.

The Berlin letter is genuine.[251] Some days after it arrived, I received a letter about it from Liebknecht, who is in continuous contact with the Berliners. It also emerges from Liebknecht's letter that those curs from the *Social-Demokrat* would oh so dearly love to resume their ties with us. The kind of illusions Liebknecht is for ever indulging in can be seen from the following passage:

*'The people that have applied to you from Berlin, are *our* friends. If you could come, show yourself but once—the gain would be immense. Come if it is possible.'*

Surely Liebknecht ought to know that even if I could go to Berlin AT PRESENT, just as a VISITOR, I would have to be completely quiet and keep myself to myself and not address workers' clubs![254]

Liebknecht also writes:

*'Professor *Eckardt*'* (now the 'principal' radical in the south, as a letter from Stumpf in Mainz makes clear) *'of Mannheim places the *Wochenblatt*[c] at our disposal. He would be delighted if you and Engels were to write for it a few articles, but not too strong.'*

The Workman's Advocate is as weak as ever. However, it must have some appeal as it appeared in a larger format last week. I know no more details, as I shall be present at the Association

---

[a] In the original: October. - [b] *Capital* - [c] *Deutsches Wochenblatt*

again for the first time tomorrow. The Parisians have published a report on the *conference* together with the *programme* we drew up for the next congress. It appeared in *all* the liberal, quasi-liberal and republican papers in Paris.[255] You will see what a friendly reception it had from the following report by Fox on the last meeting of our Council which I am cutting out of *The Workman's Advocate* for you. Our Parisians are somewhat taken aback that the para. on Russia and Poland which they did *not* wish to have, is the very one to create the biggest stir.[256] I hope that you will now use some of your leisure time to write the occasional article on one subject or another for the *Advocate.*

The Paris publication absolves me from the trouble of writing a report on France.

The Jamaican business is typical of the utter turpitude of the 'TRUE ENGLISHMAN'.[252] These fellows are as bad as the Russians in every respect. But, says the good old *Times,* these DAMNED ROGUES ENJOYED 'ALL THE LIBERTIES OF AN ANGLO-SAXON CONSTITUTION'.[a] I.e. they ENJOYED THE LIBERTY, amongst others, of having their hides taxed to raise money for the PLANTERS to import COOLIES and thus depress their own labour market below the minimum. And these English curs with their sensibilities sent up an outcry about 'BEAST Butler' for hanging *one* man! and refusing to allow the former planters' diamond-spangled yellow womenfolk to spit in the faces of the FEDERAL SOLDIERS! The Irish affair[257] and the Jamaica BUTCHERIES were all that was needed after the American war[11] to complete the unmasking of English hypocrisy!

Please do not forget to obtain the necessary data from Knowles for me (and *as soon as possible*). AVERAGE WEEKLY WAGES, either for a MULE SPINNER, or for a female THROSTLE spinner; *how much* yarn (or *cotton,* that is, *including* the *déchet*[b] that is lost in spinning) is spun *per week* ON AVERAGE by an AVERAGE NUMBER (or, for that matter, any number) by each individual; and then, of course, an arbitrary (corresponding to the labour-wage) *price* for the cotton and the *price of yarn.* I cannot write out the second chapter[c 258] until I have these details.

Ernest Jones' address is now 47 Princess Street.

Salut.

Your
K. M.

First published in *Der Briefwechsel zwischen F. Engels und K. Marx,* Bd. 3, Stuttgart, 1913

Printed according to the original

Published in English in full for the first time

---

[a] *The Times,* No. 25347, 20 November 1865. - [b] waste - [c] of *Capital*

112

MARX TO HERMANN JUNG [259]

IN LONDON

[London,] 20 November 1865

*My dear Jung,
The following are the questions:
  I. *Questions relating to the Association*
  1) Questions relating to its organisation.*
  2) The establishment of friendly societies for the members of the Association.—Moral and material support to be given to the Association's orphans.
  II. *Social Questions*
  1) Co-operative labour.
  2) Reduction of the hours of labour.
  3) Female and children's labour.
  4) *Trades Unions.* Their past, their present, and their future.
  5) Combination of efforts, by means of the International Association, in the struggle between capital and labour.
  6) *International Credit:* foundation of international credit institutions, their form and their mode of operation.
  7) *Direct and Indirect Taxation.*
  8) Standing armies and their effects upon production.
  III. *International Politics*
  The need to eliminate Muscovite influence in Europe by applying the right of self-determination of nations, and the re-establishment of Poland upon a democratic and social basis.
  IV. *A Question of Philosophy*
  The religious idea and its relation to social, political, and intellectual development.
  *The other *resolutions* as to the Congress etc. you find in the number of *The Workman's Advocate* which contains the report on the three days' sittings of the Conference. [260]
  Don't forget to ask for an *official* report on Vésinier.
  Send me the *address* of *Kaub* which I have mislaid.

Yours fraternally*

K. Marx

First published in: Marx and Engels, *Works*, First Russian Edition, Vol. XXV, Moscow, 1934

Printed according to the original Passages enclosed between asterisks are reproduced from the English original, the remaining text is translated from French

113

MARX TO WILHELM LIEBKNECHT

IN LEIPZIG [a]

[London,] 21 November 1865

My dear Miller,[b]

Since the conference[246] held at this place I fell again very sick. Afterwards I had to leave London for family affairs.[249] Hence my protracted silence. As to your report, I could *not* lay it before the conference, because I was too personally introduced in it.[261] As to your Berlin speech, there were some very disagreeable blunders in it which could only emanate from yourself, because they alluded to facts only known to you, but half forgotten and wrongly reproduced by you.[c] But this is a thing of the past.

I have received the Berlin letter, and I shall answer to it.[251] I have at present neither the *time* nor the means to go to Berlin. Even if I could, you know very well that all and every sort of agitation would be out of the question. The Prussian government has not in vain declared that the amnesty, as far as I was concerned, still excluded me from Prussia, and only gave me leave to travel as a Foreigner through the Bismarckian world.[154]

The Workman's Advocate I shall send you one of these days some numbers of. You can write to it on *every* subject you please, social or political. Till now it is a paper of good will, but very mediocre still. Of course, myself had and have not yet the time to contribute to it, although I am one of its Directors.[230] (By my continual relapse into damned ill health I was forced to interrupt the finishing of my book[d] and must now apply to it all my time, part of which is, with all that, absorbed by the International Association.) Engels has promised to contribute[e] but not yet done so. And the same is the case with other people.

The Conference has resolved that a *Public Congress* is to take place at the end of May, at Geneva. A programme of questions to be there debated, has been resolved upon.[f] But nobody can assist who does not belong to a society connected with us, and being sent as a delegate of such society. I now call upon you *very seriously* (I

---

[a] The letter bears the stamp: International Working Men's Association / Central Council / London - [b] Liebknecht's conspiratorial pseudonym - [c] See this volume, p. 176. - [d] *Capital* - [e] See this volume, pp. 198-99, 205. - [f] See previous letter.

shall do the same at Mayence through Stumpf, and shall write to the Berliners[a] on it) to enter the Association with some men, few or many, we do not care. I shall send you *cards* which I have prepaid, so that you can *give them away.* But now work! Every *society* (whatever its number) can enbody itself by paying 5 shilling in the block. The *cards,* on the contrary, which cost each 1 shilling, give the right of *individual* membership, which is important for all workingmen going to Foreign countries. But treat this money matter as quite secondary. The principal thing is to get up members, individual or societies, in Germany. On the congress, *Solingen* was the only place represented (they had given power of delegation to our old friend Becker,[b] whom you are very mistaken in if you consider him as a tool of Megära Hatzfeldt).

The programme (of questions to be lead before Congress) I shall send you in my next letter. All the Paris liberal and republican papers have made great fuss about our Association. *Henri Martin,* the well known historian, had a most enthusiastic leader about it in the *Siècle!* [256] I have heard nothing of *Quenstedt.* [262]

A thing which will rather surprise you, is this: Shortly before the arrival of workingmen's letter from Berlin, I received from that very same place—'*centre et foyer des lumières*',[c] of course—a letter on the part of—*Lothar Bucher,* inviting me to become the London money article writer of the *Preussische Staatsanzeiger,* and giving me to understand that everybody, der noch bei Lebzeiten im Staat wirken will, 'sich an die Regierung ralliiren' muss.[d] I have answered him by a few lines which he is not likely to exhibit.[263] Of course, you must not *publish* in the papers this affair, but you can communicate it, under the seal of discretion, to your friends.

Freiligrath's London shop—viz. the London branch of the Bank of Switzerland—will be shut up, never to be opened again, before 1866.[e]

Give my best compliments to Madame and Alice.[f]

Yours truly

A. Williams[g]

---

[a] August Vogt, Sigfrid Meyer, Theodor Metzner - [b] Johann Philipp Becker - [c] centre and hearth of enlightenment - [d] who wishes to be active in the state during his lifetime must 'rally to the government' - [e] See this volume, p. 208. - [f] Ernestine and Alice Liebknecht -[g] Marx's conspiratorial pseudonym

Some curious letters, written long time since, during his stay at London, by Bernhard Becker to Dr Rode have fallen into my hands.

I have opened this letter again, and by that operation somewhat torn it, in order to add that, during the past spring I had sent a letter to Dr Kugelmann, together with cards of membership for our Association.[a] I have received *no answer* on his part.[264] The letter of which you speak has never arrived at my hands. Please, write him on this affair. If he writes to me, let him do so under the address of '*A. Williams, Esq.*', and not the other one.

First published in: Marx and Engels, *Works*, First Russian Edition, Vol. XXIX, Moscow, 1946 and in the language of the original, English, in: *Wilhelm Liebknecht. Briefwechsel mit Karl Marx und Friedrich Engels*, The Hague, 1963

Reproduced from the original

114

MARX TO CÉSAR DE PAEPE[265]

IN BRUSSELS

[London, about 25 November 1865]

I. Questions relating to the Association

1) Question of organisation.

2) System of friendly societies for the members of the Association. Moral and material support for the Association's orphans.

II. Social questions

1) Co-operative labour.

2) Reduction of the hours of labour.

3) Children's labour.

4) [Trades' Unions,] their past, their present, and their future.

5) [Combination] of efforts, by means of the International Association, in the struggle between capital and labour.

6) International credit, banking institution, mode of operation.

7) Direct and indirect taxation.

8) Standing armies and their effects upon production.[b]

---

[a] Marx is referring to his letter to Kugelmann of 23 February 1865 (see this volume, pp. 101-06). - [b] The French text mistakenly has here: 'Association'.

III. Questions of International Politics

The need to reduce Muscovite influence in Europe by applying the rights of self-determination of nations, and the re-establishment of Poland upon a democratic and social basis.

IV. Question of Philosophy

The religious idea and its relation to social, political and intellectual development.

First published in: Marx and Engels, *Works*, Second Russian Edition, Vol. 31, Moscow, 1963

Printed according to the Minutes of the meeting of the Brussels section of the International Working Men's Association of 25 November 1865

Translated from the French

Published in English for the first time

115

ENGELS TO MARX [253]

IN LONDON

Manchester, 1 December 1865

Dear Moor,

Enclosed on the new month's account a further two five-pound notes, please to confirm receipt to me at 86 Mornington Street or if possible telegraph tomorrow early in the morning to 7 Southgate, as I'm not registering the letter this time because of the fuss.

As far as I can tell from the German newspapers, Prof. *Eckardt*[a] is a South German democrat, one of the Swabians and Bavarians who seceded from the National Association.[152] It is not clear to me how we are supposed to collaborate with him, it's something like Kolatschek.

That the gentlemen from the *Social-Demokrat* would like to resume their ties with us is typical of that riff-raff. They think everyone is as much of a swine as they are. Bismarck seems to have realised how powerless they are and therefore to have thrown them out, so at last there's a trial and Schweitzer has been

---

[a] See this volume, p. 198.

sentenced to 1 year of imprisonment.[266] B. Becker has now also detached himself from Schweitzer and given up his post as President of Mankind, so that everything is now falling apart just splendidly. So that it was not our intervention, but our non-intervention that put paid to the whole caboodle. This no doubt means that 'Lassalleanism' in its official form will soon come to the end of the line.

Every post brings news of worse atrocities in Jamaica.[252] The letters from the English officers about their heroic deeds against unarmed NIGGERS are beyond words. Here the spirit of the English army is at last expressing itself quite uninhibitedly. 'THE SOLDIERS ENJOY IT.' Even *The Manchester Guardian* has had to come out against the authorities in Jamaica this time.

Regarding *The Workman's Advocate*, I will see what can be done, meanwhile perhaps you could send the paper to me. You have no notion at all of the TROUBLE and chasing around involved here in obtaining these PENNY WEEKLY PAPERS which are not worth the bother to the NEWSAGENTS. You still do not get them even if you order and pay for them in advance. Or put MRS Burns down for a subscription with an order for the PAPER to be sent here by post.

Every good wish to MRS and MISSES.

Your
F. E.

G/P 62563. London, 4 August 1865—£5

E/M 35757. Liverpool, 15 May   "—" 5

How much is the bill for that you accepted, and when is it due?

First published in *Der Briefwechsel zwischen F. Engels und K. Marx*, Bd. 3, Stuttgart, 1913

Printed according to the original

Published in English in full for the first time

116

MARX TO ENGELS

IN MANCHESTER

[London, 2 December 1865]

Dear FRED,

I found your letter just as I arrived home (I was at the Museum[a] where I had some things to look up). I've just TIME to

---

[a] the British Museum Library

acknowledge the £10 with best thanks. I shall write more tomorrow.

Salut and COMPLIMENTS to Mrs Lizzy.[a]

Your
K. M.

First published in *Der Briefwechsel zwischen F. Engels und K. Marx*, Bd. 3, Stuttgart, 1913

Printed according to the original

Published in English for the first time

117

MARX TO ENGELS[33]

IN MANCHESTER

[London,] 26 December 1865

DEAR FRED,

Please forgive me for not thanking you on behalf of the FAMILY for the CHRISTMAS present until today, and indeed for not writing at all for so long. I have been so very BOTHERED ALL THAT TIME OVER and have wasted so much time dashing this way and that, transactions right and left to satisfy A, and thereby falling into the clutches of B, etc., that my work has been chiefly confined to the night, and the good intention to deal with correspondence the next day comes to grief every day.

With regard to the INTERNATIONAL ASSOCIATION and all that that entails, it has consequently been weighing down on me like an INCUBUS, and I would be glad to be able to get rid of it. But that is impossible, least of all at the present time. On the one hand, sundry bourgeois—Mr. Hughes, M.P., at their head—have conceived the idea of turning *The Workman's Advocate* into a proper *funded* paper, and as one of the DIRECTORS I MUST WATCH THE TRANSACTIONS, to prevent FOUL PLAY.[230] On the other hand, the Reform League, one of the organisations we founded, has had a triumphant success at the St Martin's Hall MEETING, the largest and most purely working-class MEETING that has taken place since I have been living in London. The people from *our* COMMITTEE were at the head

---

[a] Lizzy Burns

of it and put forward our ideas.[267] If I resigned tomorrow, the bourgeois element, which looks at us with displeasure in the wings (FOREIGN INFIDELS), would have the upper hand. With the complete failure of the workers' movement in Germany, the workers' elements in Switzerland have grouped themselves all the more around the sections of the INTERNATIONAL ASSOCIATION there. In the middle of this month first number of the *Journal de l'Association Internationale des Travailleurs. Section de la Suisse Romande* appeared in Geneva, and a German organ[268] will shortly appear under the editorship of Becker,[a] which has a chance on account of the *Nordstern*'s demise and the discrediting of the *Social-Demokrat*. (Old Becker is desperate for articles and has asked me to write *urgently to you* about it, as *pro nunc*[b] he has *no* contributors.) Finally, in France the Association is making great progress, in the absence of any other centres of movement. So, if I were to resign in these circumstances, I should be doing very serious damage to the cause; but, on the other hand, since I have so little time just now, it is no trifle for me: ABOUT 3 MEETINGS in the West End or the City, EVERY WEEK first a session of the INTERNATIONAL COUNCIL, then of the STANDING COMMITTEE,[21] then of the DIRECTORS or SHAREHOLDERS of *The Workman's Advocate*! And in addition all manner of writing to do.

I have had a few lines from Liebknecht. He is living at 2 Gerichtsweg, Leipzig, to be addressed as J. Miller,[c] Esq. Things seem to be going badly with him as usual, but he seems to have some prospect of getting a position as a lexicographer, as well as of being granted civic rights in Leipzig, and becoming one of Beust's subjects.

Dr Kugelmann has also written to me.[264] Justus Möser's successor, the present mayor of Osnabrück, Mr Miquel, has now openly turned renegade; for the moment with bourgeois leanings, but 'already' veering in the aristocratic direction. A certain Wedekind, formerly consul SOMEWHERE, rolling in money and an enthusiastic National-Association member,[152] has rewarded him for his merits by making him his son-in-law. Kugelmann has seen 'gentle Heinrich'[d] in Cologne. He is now cosily installed as editor of the *Rheinische Zeitung*. He complained that I had not visited him in Cologne and was treating him as a 'turncoat', etc. He claimed always to have 'kept faith with the "cause"' and only to be working with the bourgeoisie against the aristocracy now 'to promote the evolution and clarification of the *class contradictions*'

---

a Johann Philipp Becker - b at present - c Liebknecht's conspiratorial pseudonym - d Heinrich Bürgers (which in a speech in Cologne scarcely a year ago he declared NON-EXISTENT), etc.

Bonaparte appears to me shakier than ever. The business with the students[269] is symptomatic of ominous signs of conflict in the army itself, but above all the Mexico affair[270] and that original sin of the LOWER EMPIRE,[a] *debts*! Nor has the fellow managed to pull off a single coup in the past year. Indeed things have reached such a pass with him that Bismarck figures as a rival to him!

Palmerston's death has obviously been a blow here. If he were still alive, Governor Eyre would have been awarded the *ordre pour le mérite*!

Freiligrath is also ending the year with tremendous bad luck. Jew Reinach has closed down the business here, with a great brouhaha, coming to London expressly for the purpose.[b] Freiligrath, who owed the bank money anyway, suffered the further misfortune that 3 days before the ARRIVAL of the mighty Reinach one of his clerks absconded with £150. But still the old boy has got powerful protection TO FALL BACK UPON. His Plonplonist[93] friends in Paris (e.g. EX-COLONEL Kiss, who married the daughter of the former French minister Thouvenel, a millionaire, and is now at the head of an enormous company) will find a new position for him soon enough.

Happy New Year! To Mrs Lizzy,[c] too.

Your
K. M.

First published in *Der Briefwechsel zwischen F. Engels und K. Marx*, Bd. 3, Stuttgart, 1913

Printed according to the original

Published in English in full for the first time

118

MARX TO ENGELS[271]

IN MANCHESTER

[London, end of 1865-beginning of 1866]

Appendix

While I was last staying in Manchester[249] you once asked me to explain differential calculus. The thing will be quite clear to you

---

[a] the designation of the Byzantine Empire; used figuratively it means any state experiencing decline - [b] See this volume, pp. 158, 164. - [c] Lizzy Burns

from the following example. The whole of differential calculus arose originally from the task of drawing *tangents* through any point on any curve. So, that is the example I am going to use for you.

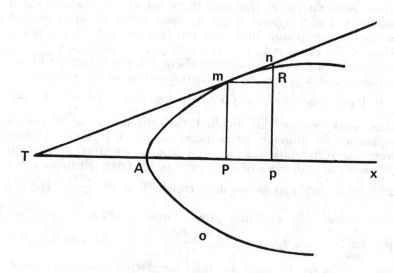

Assume that the line *nAo* is any curve whose nature (whether it's a parabola, ellipse, etc.) is *unknown* to us and on which a tangent is to be drawn at point *m*.

Ax is the axis. We drop the perpendicular *mP* (the ordinate) onto the abscissa *Ax*. Now assume that point *n* is the infinitely *closest* point on the curve beside *m*. If I drop a perpendicular *np* onto the axis, *p* must be the infinitely closest point to *P* and *np* the infinitely closest parallel line to *mP*. Now drop an infinitely small perpendicular *mR* onto *np*. If you now take the abscissa *AP...x* and the ordinate *mP...y*, then *np=mP* (or *Rp*), increased by an infinitely small increment [*nR*], or [*nR*]=*dy* (differential of *y*) and *mR* (=*Pp*)=*dx*. Since the part of the tangent *mn* is infinitely small, it coincides with the corresponding part of the curve itself. I can therefore regard *mnR* as a △(triangle), and the △*mnR* and *mTP* are similar triangles. Therefore: *dy* (=*nR*):*dx*(=*mR*)= =*y*(*mP*):*PT* (which is the subtangent of the tangent *Tn*). Thus, the subtangent $PT=y\frac{dx}{dy}$. We now have a *general differential equation* for drawing the tangent at any points on *any* curves. If I am now to operate with this equation and to determine through it the length of the subtangent PT (once I have found this, I merely need to connect the points T and m by a straight line in order to have the tangent), so I need to know the *specific character* of the curve. According to its character (parabola, ellipse, cissoid, etc.), it will have a *distinct form of general equation* for its ordinate and abscissa at any point, which one can find in algebraic geometry. Thus, if the curve mAo, e.g., is a parabola, I know that y^2 (y=the ordinate at any given point)$=ax$, where a is the parameter of the parabola and x is the abscissa corresponding to the ordinate y.

If I put this value for y into the equation $PT=\dfrac{ydx}{dy}$, I must then work out dy, i.e. to find the differential of y (which represents an infinitely small increment of y). If $y^2=ax$, I know from the differential calculus that from $d(y^2)=d(ax)$ (I have to differentiate both sides of the equation, of course), it follows that $2y\,dy=a\,dx$ (d always means differential). Thus $dx=\dfrac{2y\,dy}{a}$. If I put this value of dx into the formula $PT=\dfrac{ydx}{dy}$, I get $PT=\dfrac{2y^2\,dy}{a\,dy}=\dfrac{2y^2}{a}=$ (since $y^2=ax$) $=\dfrac{2ax}{a}=2x$. Or the subtangent of any point m on the parabola=twice the abscissa of the same point. The differential values are cancelled in the operation.

First published in: Marx and Engels, *Works*, Second Russian Edition, Vol. 31, Moscow, 1963

Printed according to the original

Published in English for the first time

1 8 6 6

119

ENGELS TO MARX

IN LONDON

Manchester, 4 January 1866[a]

Dear Moor,

£10 encl. in 2 Bank-of-England notes. How stands it with bill of exchange for LANDLORD? Tell me how much and date when due, so that I may make my dispositions.

That malicious compilation of *Social-Demokrat* garbage in the Schulze-Delitzschite pamphlet[b] had already been sent me anonymously from Berlin; it is always a good thing to have such a résumé with extracts. Schulze-Delitzsch has also announced that in the next few days he is to publish a reply to Lassalle, in which he is going to demolish him.[272]

You will already know as well that Racowiţa died of consumption, so presumably Mamsell Dönniges is once more IN THE MARKET, IF EVER SHE WAS FAIRLY OUT OF IT.

Mr Held's speech has also been sent me from Berlin. He's a real Berlin scoundrel.

Monsieur Bonaparte's progress is most decidedly that of the crab. The trouble in the army over Mexico[270] is very serious, and so is the student trouble in Paris.[269] It is very important that the Paris students should take the side of the proletariat, confused though their ideas on the subject may be. The École polytechnique will follow soon enough. It would be so splendid if the rascal lived to see his own DOWNFALL, and it now almost appears that he might. It is getting more and more rotten for Bismarck every day, too, and, if those scoundrels in Cologne had not got him out of the soup, it would probably already have been all up with him now.[237]

---

[a] The original has: 1865. - [b] [E. Richter,] *Die Geschichte der social-demokratischen Partei in Deutschland seit dem Tode Ferdinand Lassalle's.*

I am agog for the next parliament, the disintegration of the old parties must surely proceed apace now. JOHN BRIGHT IS EVIDENTLY BIDDING FOR OFFICE—it is true, I have not yet read the speech he gave yesterday.[a]

Have you read Tyndall's 'HEAT CONSIDERED AS A MODE OF MOTION'? If not, you should do so. A great deal of work has been done in this field, and the matter appears to be assuming a rational shape; the atom theory is being taken to such extremes that it must soon fall apart.

Please don't forget to send me *The Workman's Advocate* and *The Free Press*.

Regards and best wishes to your family for the New Year.

Your
F. E.

First published abridged in *Der Briefwechsel zwischen F. Engels und K. Marx*, Bd. 3, Stuttgart, 1913 and in full in *MEGA*, Abt. III, Bd. 3, Berlin, 1930

Printed according to the original

Published in English for the first time

120

MARX TO ENGELS[33]

IN MANCHESTER

[London,] 5 JANUARY 1866

DEAR FRED,

In the greatest of haste.

Best thanks for the £10.

The bill of exchange falls due on 18 February and is for £48. I wanted the LANDLORD to draw it only for the 2 terms that were due and not for the third one as well, which is not due until the end of January. But he insisted.

A plot has been hatched against the *INTERNATIONAL ASSOCIATION*, in which connection I need your co-operation. Further details later. For the moment, suffice to say: Mr Le Lubez and Vésinier (the

---

[a] Engels is referring to J. Bright's speech on the Parliamentary Reform delivered at the meeting in Rochdale on 3 January 1866, *The Times*, No. 25386, 4 January 1866.

latter well aware that an INQUIRY into his past is in progress; he is in Brussels again) have a French branch here [273] (IN FACT an opposition branch); Longuet, the editor of *Rive gauche*, also belongs to it, and it is tied up with all that pack of Proudhonists in Brussels. Vésinier began by publishing a long screed against us in the *Echo de Verviers*, OF COURSE ANONYMOUSLY.[274] Then, in the *same* paper which is putting out the SLANDERS against our Association (among other things, falsely calls Tolain and Fribourg Bonapartists, too), the London BRANCH published a programme, a draft of future statutes, which *they*, the Faithful, are going to put to the Congress.[275]

The real crux of the controversy is the *Polish question*. The fellows have all attached themselves to the Muscovitist line pursued by Proudhon and Herzen. I shall therefore send you the earlier articles by the oracles in the *Tribune du Peuple* against Poland and you must do a refutation, either for our papers in Geneva (the 'German' one[a]) or for *The Workman's Advocate*.[276] The Russian gentlemen have acquired some bran-new allies in the Proudhonised section of 'Jeune France'.[b]

Your
K. M.

First published in *Der Briefwechsel zwischen F. Engels und K. Marx*, Bd. 3, Stuttgart, 1913

Printed according to the original

Published in English in full for the first time

121

MARX TO JOHANN PHILIPP BECKER [33]

IN GENEVA[c]

London, [about 13 January 1866]
1 Modena Villas, Maitland Park,
Haverstock Hill, N. W.

My dear friend Becker,

If you are vexed with me, you have 'every right' and at the same time 'no right' to be so. (You know from Heinzen that I am a 'sophist'.) Apart from having some 1,200 pages of manuscript[d]

---

[a] *Der Vorbote* - [b] 'Young France' - [c] The letter bears the stamp: International Working Men's Association / Central Council / London. - [d] of *Capital*

to copy and my publisher[a] grumbling at me for a long time now, and apart from the fearful waste of time which the Central Committee, the STANDING COMMITTEE[21] and the Committee of Directors of *The Workman's Advocate* commit me to in this Babylon, I have had the most exceptional aggravations and difficulties in my *'private circumstances'* which obliged me to leave London for a while[249] and are still unresolved, etc., etc.

You will see from the enclosed note, which I received *today* (or rather my wife did), that a parcel, which I sent to you ABOUT *14 days ago*, has been most commendably confiscated by the French police. It contained chiefly *'Manifestoes of the Communist Party'.*[b] Also a note from me briefly answering your questions and telling you that *Bender* agreed that I should publish your appeal in *English* in *The Workman's Advocate*, ditto a report on activity in Switzerland, etc.[277]

The reason why we decided not to publish any official report on the conference[246]—apart from lack of money and the fact that the *Rules* oblige us to present a general report to the Congress, such *double emploi*[c] thus to be avoided—was basically that to initiate the public in the situation, especially the very 'fragmentary' nature of the conference, would do us more harm than good and provide our opponents with a useful weapon. We knew that two members of the Central Committee, Le Lubez and Vésinier, were just waiting to seize this opportunity. Events have confirmed this. Firstly, Vésinier's denunciation of the Central Committee and the conference in *L'Écho de Verviers*.[274] Directly following that, in the same paper, came Le Lubez' declaration of principles and draft of statutes[275] that he hoped to impose on the Association in the name of the French branch he had founded in London as a counterweight to ourselves.[273] This plot has meanwhile been frustrated. The branch has deserted its founder. Its two best men, Longuet (editor of the *Rive gauche*) and Crespelle, have joined the Central Committee. The latter has resolved that Vésinier must either substantiate his slanders or be expelled.

I cannot send you any articles *pro nunc.*[d] I have *not an hour to spare*. Engels, however, will do so, as soon as he has seen the first number[e] and knows where and how. *Liebknecht* will as well, from Leipzig. I will ditto write to Dr Kugelmann in Hanover about it. Ditto to *Stumpf* in Mainz.

No. 1 of *Dupleix*'s paper[f] is weak. Jung has written to him about it.

---

[a] Otto Meissner - [b] by K. Marx and F. Engels - [c] double work - [d] for now - [e] of *Der Vorbote* - [f] *Journal de l'Association Internationale des Travailleurs*

Liebknecht is living at 2 Gerichtsweg, Leipzig (*address J. Miller*[a]). In one way the movement here has progressed well, but badly in another respect. The Reform League we founded has held a mass MEETING for universal suffrage, bigger than I ever saw here in London.[267] All the speakers were working men. *The Times* itself was shocked and published 2 leading articles about the 'ugly' incident.[b] The obverse side is that this movement is demanding far too much of our best working-class forces.

The Workman's Advocate is weak. It will improve now that *Eccarius* is editor. But there are enormous difficulties in raising the money for it.

I have received a letter from Berlin, signed by Vogt,[c] Metzner and other workers, in which they give a perceptive and critical assessment of the present state of the workers' movement in Germany. The only uncritical thing about it is their demand that I should come to Berlin and take the matter in hand. Surely they must know that the Prussian government has 'forbidden' me to settle in Prussia.[d]

Before I hear from you *by what way* I can let you have the 'Manifestoes', I am going to send one experimentally *via Mainz*. You may be able to make use of some things in it for your paper.

The best thing the German sections can do is for the time being to register in Geneva and keep in continuous contact with you. As soon as some such arrangement is made, let me know, so that at last I can announce at least some progress in Germany *here*.[278]

I am sending this letter under cover to Dupleix, on account of the 'French confiscation'. The Empire seems to me to be tottering. *D'abord*,[e] the business with Mexico and the UNITED STATES.[270] Then the mutiny of 3 French regiments.[279] Then the student unrest.[269] Bonaparte's losing his head, as manifested in his row with England about the renewal of the 'extradition treaty'[280] and his banning of the lickspittling *'Indépendance belge'*. Finally, the *trade crisis*, which will be greatly hastened by the present English, resp. European, overimporting to the UNITED STATES.

Best greetings from wife and children.

Your
K. Marx

First published in: Marx and Engels, *Works*, First Russian Edition, Vol. XXV, Moscow, 1934

Printed according to the original

Published in English in full for the first time

---

[a] conspiratorial pseudonym of Wilhelm Liebknecht - [b] *The Times,* Nos. 25367 and 25368, 13 and 14 December 1865. - [c] August Vogt - [d] See this volume, p. 201. - [e] Firstly

122

MARX TO ENGELS[33]

IN MANCHESTER

[London,] 15 January 1866[a]

DEAR FRED,

Laura quite forgot to send you the *Tribunes*[b] which I had put out ready a week ago. She is today making amends for her negligence. Ditto a *Workman's Advocate*.

I am enclosing with this letter:

1. Communication from the publisher in Vienna.[c] (You must send this back.)[281]

2. Dr Kugelmann.

3. Meyer[d] from Berlin. (I have only written back to these people today. Time is so very short.)[282]

In the meantime, we have crushed the wretched plot hatched by Vésinier in Belgium[274] and by Le Lubez in London. The editor of the *Rive gauche* and friend of Rogeard, Longuet, also Mr Crespelle—the two most intelligent members of the branch founded by Le Lubez[273]—have joined our Central Committee. His branch has declared itself against him, for us. The CENTRAL COMMITTEE HAS SUMMONED VÉSINIER 'TO SUBSTANTIATE HIS ACCUSATIONS OR TO BE EXPELLED'. The fellow reproaches us in the *Echo de Verviers* among other things for:

'Il' (le comité) 'a été chargé d'un des plus grands intérêts de l'humanité et il abandonne de gaieté de coeur le but sublime pour dégénérer *en comité des nationalités à la remorque du bonapartisme.*'[e]

And this degeneration was in fact made manifest in us by our statement in favour of Poland, against Russia.[283]

'Cédant à des influences fâcheuses'[f] (the idiot imagines the Polish § of the programme originated from the PARIS DELEGATES, whereas the latter sought in every possible way to get rid of it as 'inopportune'), 'il a inscrit dans le programme du Congrès de Genève des questions en dehors du but de l'association et contraires au droit, à la justice, à la liberté, à la fraternité, à la solidarité des peuples et des

---

[a] The original has: 1865. - [b] *La Tribune du Peuple* containing a series of articles by H. Denis, entitled 'La question polonaise et la démocratie'. - [c] Arnold Hilberg - [d] Sigfrid Meyer - [e] 'They' (the Committee) 'were charged with one of mankind's greatest concerns but are frivolously abandoning their lofty goal in order to degenerate *into a committee of nationalities in tow to Bonapartism.*' - [f] 'Succumbing to pernicious influences'

races, telles que celles: "D'anéantir l'influence russe en Europe etc.", et cela juste au moment où les serfs russes et polonais viennent d'être émancipés par la Russie, tandis que les nobles et les prêtres polonais ont toujours refusé d'accorder la liberté aux leurs. On conviendra au moins que le moment est mal choisi. Avant d'approuver *ces articles,* les membres anglais du comité auraient bien dû se demander s'il ne serait pas aussi urgent de mettre un terme aux progrès effrayants du paupérisme anglais, de la prostitution des ouvrières, et de la misère des ouvriers de la Grande Bretagne, de la famine et du dépeuplement de l'Irlande etc.! Quant au membre allemand du comité, qu'il nous dise aussi si l'influence de la politique de M. de Bismarck n'aurait pas aussi besoin d'être anéantie en Europe; la Prusse et l'Autriche ne sont-elles pas copartageantes de la Pologne et solidaires du crime de la Russie contre cette nation malheureuse? Et quant aux prétendus délégués de Paris, sont-ils bien venus de flétrir l'influence russe, alors que les soldats de Bonaparte occupent Rome qu'ils ont bombardée, massacrant les défenseurs de la république mexicaine après avoir détruit la république française? Que l'on compare les fautes et les crimes commis par les gouvernements, et l'on sera convaincu qu'il ne faut mettre aucun peuple au ban de l'humanité pour les forfaits de ses oppresseurs, que le devoir du comité central était de proclamer la solidarité, la fraternité entre tous les peuples, *et non d'en mettre un seul d'entre eux au ban de l'Europe.'* ᵃ

He then appended this lie:

'Cette faute énorme a déjà eu de fatales conséquences: les Polonais ont demandé en masse à faire partie du Comité, et sous peu ils seront en immense majorité.' ᵇ (CAPTAIN Bobczyński is the *only one* who is on it—Holtorp doesn't count

---

ᵃ 'they included in the programme for the Geneva Congress questions not concerning the goal of the Association and contrary to law, justice, liberty, fraternity and the solidarity of peoples and races, such as: "the elimination of Russian influence in Europe etc."; and this they did at the very moment when the Russian and Polish serfs had just been emancipated by Russia, whereas the Polish nobility and priests have always refused to grant freedom to their own. It will at least be agreed that the moment was ill-chosen. Before approving *these articles,* the English members of the committee should have really asked themselves if it was not a matter of equal urgency to put an end to the frightening increase in English pauperism, in the prostitution of working women and the misery of working men in Great Britain, in famine and depopulation in Ireland, etc.! As for the German members of the committee, let them also tell us whether the influence of Mr Bismarck's policy in Europe does not equally merit elimination; do not Prussia and Austria have an equal share in the partitioning of Poland, are they not equally responsible for Russia's crime against that unfortunate nation? As for the self-styled delegates from Paris, does it come well from them to condemn the influence of Russia, when Bonaparte's soldiers are occupying Rome, which they have bombarded, are massacring the defenders of the Mexican republic, having already destroyed the French republic? If one compares the misdeeds and crimes committed by governments, one is persuaded that no people should be put beyond the pale of humanity for the infamies of its oppressors, and that it was the duty of the Central Committee to proclaim solidarity and fraternity among all peoples, *and not to put one of them alone beyond the pale of Europe.'* - ᵇ 'This enormous error has already had dire consequences: the Poles have asked to join the Committee *en masse* and before long they will represent the overwhelming majority.'

and is himself conspiring with Le Lubez.) 'Déjà ils ne se font pas faute de dire qu'ils se serviront de *l'Association* pour aider au rétablissement de leur nationalité, sans s'occuper de la question de l'émancipation des travailleurs.'[a]

The Poles—they had just sent a deputation to see us—burst out laughing when these PASSAGES were read out. We are commemorating their revolution on 23 January.[284]

You will be amused by WISEACRE Denis' *concluding prayer to Proudhon*.[285] This SENSATIONAL WRITER has done great harm with his little bit of learning and with his Lassalle-like trumpeting of scholarship, of which he had no conception, with his spurious critical superiority over the SOCIALIST SECTARIANS.

Le Lubez is of no account. Fox rightly calls him 'Le père enfantin',[b] but Vésinier is just the fellow for the Russians. Of little merit as a writer, as his *Vie du Nouveau César* and his other pamphlets attacking Bonaparte show. But with talent, great RHETORICAL POWER, much energy and above all unscrupulous through and through.

Salut.

Your

K. M.

First published abridged in *Der Briefwech-sel zwischen F. Engels und K. Marx*, Bd. 3, Stuttgart, 1913 and in full in *MEGA*, Abt. III, Bd. 3, Berlin, 1930

Printed according to the original

Published in English in full for the first time

123

MARX TO WILHELM LIEBKNECHT[1]

IN LEIPZIG[c]

[London,] 15 January 1866

Dear LIBRARY,[d]

Happy New Year!

You must excuse my silence, ditto the brevity of these lines of mine. You will not believe how BOTHERED I am for time.

---

[a] Already they do not shrink from saying that they will make use of *the Association* to help to restore their nationhood, without concerning themselves with the question of the emancipation of the workers.' - [b] 'Le père enfantin' ('The childish father')—a pun on 'Père Enfantin' ('Father Enfantin'). An allusion to Le Lubez' efforts to imitate the chief representative of the Saint-Simonian school, Barthélemy Prosper Enfantin. - [c] The letter bears the stamp: International Working Men's Association / Central Council / London - [d] nickname for Wilhelm Liebknecht

Indisposition, for ever recurring periodically, all manner of unfortunate *mischances, demands made on me* by the INTERNATIONAL ASSOCIATION, etc., have confiscated every free moment I have for writing out the fair copy of my manuscript.[a] I hope to be able to take Volume I of it to the publisher[b] for printing myself in March. (The whole thing, the two volumes, will, however, appear *simultaneously.*[233] This *is good.*)

So, this very much by way of summary.

Today I am sending you by post the 2 latest issues of *The Workman's Advocate,* of which Eccarius is now editor.[c] If, as I hope, you send any *articles* for it, please do so to me (political, social, as you will).

I also enclose CARDS OF MEMBERSHIP for you. I have paid for them. You can therefore give them to whomever you like, and have only to inscribe the name and after the £, put 0, but after the 0s., 1d.

The conditions, GENERALLY, are these: *a society as such* that wishes to join has an *Association collective membership Card,* for which 5s. per year is to be paid. But, if all the members join *individually,* they have to take out cards of the kind I am sending you. This is advantageous for workers. The cards serve as a passport abroad, and their *confrères*[d] in London, Paris, Brussels, Lyons, Geneva, etc., will get jobs for them.

The Association has made great progress. It already has 1 official English paper, *The Workman's Advocate,* a Brussels one, *La Tribune du Peuple,* a French one in Geneva, *Journal de l'Association Internationale des Travailleurs, Section de la Suisse Romande,* and a German one in Geneva, *Der Vorbote,* which will be appearing in a few days. *Address: 6 rue du Môle, Genf, J. P. Becker,* in case you want to write to the old man occasionally (as I hope you will).

I am now hoping you will soon make it possible for me to announce the foundation of a Leipzig section and enable me to present correspondence. (*In English.* It can then be used in *The Workman's Advocate* as well.) The number is not important, although THE MORE, THE BETTER.

If people want to join *en masse,* as a society, you will see that the *total price* of 5s., which they have to pay annually, is *nothing.*

J. P. Becker writes to me[e]:

'Sections are going to be formed in Leipzig, Gotha, Stuttgart and Nuremberg; shall we register them here for the time being, until there is a large number and a Central Committee has been formed in Germany?'[278]

---

[a] *Capital* - [b] Otto Meissner - [c] See this volume, p. 224. - [d] colleagues - [e] J. Ph. Becker to Karl Marx, 18 December 1865

I have replied *in the affirmative*.[a] However, since there can be several branches in one town, you and your people can establish links direct with us.

I have had a second letter from the Berliners.[b] I am at last writing to them today.[282] Ditto to Dr Kugelmann.

Salut.

Your
K. M.

I will let you know next time what questions are to be dealt with at the Geneva Congress at the end of May.[286]

First published in: Marx and Engels, *Works*, First Russian Edition, Vol. XXIX, Moscow, 1946

Printed according to the original

124

MARX TO LUDWIG KUGELMANN[65]

IN HANOVER

London, 15 January 1866
1 Modena Villas, Maitland Park,
Haverstock Hill

Dear Friend,

A happy New Year and best thanks for your kind letter.

You must excuse the brevity of these lines on account of my being excessively busy at present. I'll write more fully next time.

I am enclosing two cards[287] and will let you know in my next letter which questions are to be dealt with at the public congress in Geneva at the end of May.[286]

Our Association has made great progress. It already has 3 official organs, one in London, *The Workman's Advocate*, one in Brussels, *La Tribune du Peuple*, one put out by the French section in Switzerland, *Journal de l'Association Internationale des Travailleurs, Section de la Suisse Romande* (Geneva), and in a few days time a journal is to be put out by the German-Swiss section, *Der Vorbote*,

---

[a] See this volume, p. 215. - [b] August Vogt, Sigfrid Meyer and Theodor Metzner

under the editorship of *J. P. Becker.* (Address: 6 rue du Môle, Genf, J. P. Becker, in case you wanted to send him an occasional article, political or social).

We have succeeded in attracting into the movement the only really big workers' organisation, the English 'TRADE UNIONS', which previously concerned themselves *exclusively* with the wage question. With their help, the English society we founded to achieve UNIVERSAL SUFFRAGE[a] (half of its Central Committee consists of members—working men—of our Central Committee) held a giant MEETING a few weeks ago, at which only working men spoke.[267] You can tell what effect it had from the fact that the LEADERS of two successive issues of *The Times* were concerned with this MEETING.[b]

As regards my work,[c] I am now busy 12 hours a day writing out the fair copy. I am thinking of taking the manuscript of the first volume to Hamburg myself in March and using the opportunity to see you.

I was much amused by the antics of Justus von Möser's successor.[d] How wretched a man of talent must be who seeks and finds satisfaction in trivialities of that kind![e]

As regards Bürgers, he is doubtless well-meaning, but weak. It is not much over a year ago that he declared at a public MEETING in Cologne (it appeared in print in the Cologne papers) that Schulze-Delitzsch had 'solved' the social question once and for all and that only *personal friendship for me* had induced him (Bürgers) to stray onto the tangled paths of communism! After such *public statements*, could I regard him as other than a 'renegade'?

Your most sincere friend
K. Marx

First published abridged in *Die Neue Zeit,* Bd. 2, Nr. 1, Stuttgart, 1901-1902 and in full in *Pisma Marksa k Kugelmanu* (Letters of Marx to Kugelmann), Moscow-Leningrad, 1928

Printed according to the original

---

[a] the Reform League - [b] *The Times,* Nos. 25367 and 25368, 13 and 14 December 1865. - [c] *Capital* - [d] Johannes von Miquel - [e] See this volume, pp. 207-08.

125

MARX TO SIGFRID MEYER

IN BERLIN

[London,] 24 January 1866

Dear Friend,

At the same time as I sent the cards to you, I wrote a detailed letter to Mr Vogt.[a] I thought I was being very clever in using two different addresses. The only error I may possibly have committed is to have put No. 6 instead of 16 in Vogt's address.[288]

I should therefore be grateful if you would enquire at the Post Office and inform me of the results. Since I wrote to you,[282] a fresh carbuncle has developed in a spot that is very painful when I sit, so that after my daily labour of fair-copying my manuscript[b] for the publisher,[c] I am extraordinarily exhausted.

Your
K. M.

First published in: Marx and Engels, *Works*, First Russian Edition, Vol. XXV, Moscow, 1934

Printed according to the original

Published in English for the first time

126

ENGELS TO MARX

IN LONDON

Manchester, 26 January 1866

Dear Moor,

What is holding me up is that I have no material and hardly any recollection either about the way in which the emancipation of the serfs was finally carried out in Russia, what land the peasant received, who paid for it, what his present *de facto* relation is to

---

[a] August Vogt - [b] *Capital* - [c] Otto Meissner

the landowner, etc., etc. I have undoubtedly seen the earlier *plans* of the nobility and the emperor,[a] but not the definitive implementation. Have you any material on it[b]?

Your
F. E.

N.B. I shall not refer *directly* to the article in the 1864 *Tribune*,[c] *cela serait lui faire trop d'honneur.*[d]

First published in *Der Briefwechsel zwischen F. Engels und K. Marx*, Bd. 3, Stuttgart, 1913

Printed according to the original

Published in English for the first time

<hr>

127

MARX TO ENGELS[33]

IN MANCHESTER

[London,] 10 February 1866

Dear Fritz,

It was a close shave this time. My family did not know how *sérieux* the *cas*[e] was. If the matter recurs in that form three or four times more, I shall be a dead man. I am marvellously wasted away and still damned weak, not in the mind but about my loins and in my legs. The doctors are quite right to think that *excessive work at night* has been the chief cause of this relapse. But I cannot tell these gentlemen the reasons that *force* this extravagance on me—nor would it serve any purpose to do so. At this moment, I have all kinds of little progeny about my person, which is painful but no longer in the least dangerous.

What was most loathsome to me was the interruption in my work,[f] which had been going splendidly since January 1st, when I got over my liver complaint. There was no question of '*sitting*', of

<hr>

a Alexander II - b See this volume, pp. 212-13. - c H. Denis, 'La question polonaise et la démocratie', *La Tribune du Peuple*, Nos. 41-43, 45, 46; 5, 26 March, 17 April, 29 May, 30 June 1864. - d that would be doing it too great an honour - e serious the case - f on *Capital*

lying down, I was able to forge ahead, even if only for short periods of the day. I could make no progress with the really theoretical part. My brain was not up to that. I therefore elaborated the section on the 'Working-Day' from the historical point of view, which was not part of my original plan. What I have now 'inserted' supplements your book[a] (*sketchily*) up to 1865 (and I say so in a note[289]) and fully justifies the discrepancy between your estimation of the future and what will actually happen. Therefore, as soon as my book appears, it is necessary to have the second edition of your book, which will be easy in the circumstances. I shall provide the necessary theory. Regarding the additional historical supplement, which you should give as an appendix to your book, *all the material*, excepting the 'FACTORY REPORTS',[b] the 'Children's Employment Commission Reports' and the 'Board of Health Reports',[c] is utter trash and scientifically unusable. Your energy being undiminished by carbuncles, you will easily cope with this material within 3 months.

As far as the *Russians* are concerned, I have *no* material. As soon as my condition permits, I shall go to the Museum[d] about it and look around for it among the Poles. There's been a great crisis with *The Workman's Advocate*. which will appear tomorrow as *The Commonwealth,* a transformation pushed through by the bourgeois element, for which *my* absence from the COUNCIL was to blame. From my sickbed I have, nevertheless, managed to baulk the plot by means of written threats, with the effect that *Eccarius* has been made editor instead of a gentleman from *The Nonconformist,* and an EDITORIAL SUPERVISION COMMITTEE has been appointed which will meet weekly. It consists of myself, Fox, Howell, Weston and Miall (the PUBLISHER-EDITOR of *The Nonconformist* and our PUBLISHER NOW), 4 atheists against one 'PROTESTANT'.[290] Poor Eccarius now needs *your* article[e] *urgently* (there being a whole mass of intrigues and I unable to help; my book requires all my writing time).

Your wine is having a miraculous effect on me. While my illness was in full bloom I had to buy bad PORTWINE—it being the only wine suitable for an acute carbuncle condition.

Apropos. As I see from one of the latest 'FACTORY REPORTS', John Watts has published a pamphlet 'ON MACHINERY.'[f] Ask him, on my behalf, to send me a copy.

---

[a] F. Engels, *The Condition of the Working-Class in England.* - [b] *Reports of the Inspectors of Factories to Her Majesty's Principal Secretary of State for the Home Department.* - [c] *Public Health. Reports of the Medical Officer of the Privy Council.* - [d] the British Museum Library - [e] F. Engels, 'What Have the Working Classes to Do with Poland?' - [f] J. Watts, *Trade Societies and Strikes.... Machinery....*

I am going to write a few lines to Wilhelm[a] cursing him for his spinelessness. The collapse of the *Social-Demokrat* and of all the Lassallean trash is, of course, the very thing we want.[291]

Lyons (the workers there) have sent £8 to the INTERNATIONAL COUNCIL.

Salut.

Your

Moor

First published in *Der Briefwechsel zwischen F. Engels und K. Marx*, Bd. 3, Stuttgart, 1913

Printed according to the original

Published in English in full for the first time

128

ENGELS TO MARX[26]

IN LONDON[b]

Manchester, 10 February 1866

Dear Moor,

I have just spoken to Gumpert here and discussed your condition with him. He is firmly of the opinion you should try arsenic. He has used it in one case of carbuncles and one of very virulent furunculosis, and achieved a complete cure in approx. 3 months. He is now giving it to three ladies, so far with the greatest of success; they are positively thriving on it. FOWLER'S SOLUTION is what he is giving, I believe it is 3 drops 3 times a day (I am not quite so sure about that any more), but altogether the patient takes *about 1 grain of arsenic a day.* In view of the specific effect that arsenic has with all skin diseases, there is every prospect of it being effective with you, too. He thinks iron would only have a symptomatic and hence strengthening effect. And with arsenic there is no special diet to be observed at all, *just living well.*

You really must at last do something sensible now to shake off this carbuncle nonsense, even if the book[c] is delayed by another 3

---

[a] Wilhelm Liebknecht - [b] The letter bears the stamp: Albert Club / Manchester. - [c] *Capital*

months. The thing is really becoming far too serious, and if, as you say yourself, your brain is not UP TO THE MARK for the theoretical part, then do give it a bit of a rest from the more elevated theory. Give over working at night for a while and lead a rather more regular life. When you are yourself again, come up here for a fortnight or so, so that you have a bit of a change, and bring enough papers along with you for you to be able to do a spot of work here—if you like. Incidentally, the 60 sheets will make 2 thick volumes.[233] Can you not so arrange things that the first volume at least is sent for printing first and the second one a few months later? This would keep both publisher[a] and public happy and yet no time will have been lost *realiter.*[b]

You must also bear in mind that as things stand now, the situation on the Continent may change rapidly. In Prussia things are moving with marvellous rapidity. Bismarck is pressing hard for a crisis. First the decision by the Supreme Tribunal,[292] and then now the threat of an authentic interpretation of the constitution by the King.[c] The philistines' last illusion about peaceful historical development has gone to the devil. The first plausible pretext, perhaps no more than a serious complication over Schleswig-Holstein even, may be the spark that sets it off, once the troops are concentrated on the frontier; although I myself hardly believe that anything will happen without a more general cause, but the possibility is there. What would be gained in these circumstances by having perhaps a few chapters at the end of your book completed, and not even the first volume can be printed, if events take us by surprise? Something may happen any day in France, too, in Austria the attempted reconciliation with Hungary can only lead to sharper division.[293]

Q.E.D.: get yourself back on your feet and *ad hoc*[d] give the arsenic a try.

Your
F. E.

Kind regards to Madame[e] and the YOUNG LADIES.

First published in *Der Briefwechsel zwischen F. Engels und K. Marx*, Bd. 3, Stuttgart, 1913

Printed according to the original

Published in English in full for the first time

---

[a] Otto Meissner - [b] in actual fact - [c] William I - [d] to that end - [e] Jenny Marx

129

MARX TO ENGELS[101]

IN MANCHESTER

[London,] 13 February 1866

DEAR FRED,

Tell or write to Gumpert to send me the prescription with instructions for use. As I have confidence in him, he owes it to the best of 'Political Economy'[a] if nothing else to ignore professional etiquette and treat me from Manchester.

I was laid up again yesterday with a vicious cur of a carbuncle erupting on left loin. If I had enough money, that is, more>-0, for my family, and if my book were ready, I would care not a fig whether I was thrown on the charnel heap today or tomorrow, alias perished. But things being as they are, that cannot be contemplated just yet.

As far as this 'damned' book is concerned, the position now is: it was *ready* at the end of December.[227] The treatise on ground rent alone, the penultimate chapter, is in its present form almost long enough to be a book in itself.[294] I have been going to the Museum[b] in the day-time and writing at night. I had to plough through the new agricultural chemistry in Germany, in particular Liebig and Schönbein, which is more important for this matter than all the economists put together, as well as the enormous amount of material that the French have produced since I last dealt with this point. I concluded my theoretical investigation of ground rent 2 years ago. And a great deal had been achieved, especially in the period since then, fully confirming my theory incidentally. And the opening up of Japan[295] (by and large I normally never read travel-books if I am not professionally obliged to) was also important here. So here was the 'SHIFTING SYSTEM', as it was applied by those curs of English manufacturers to *one and the same* persons in 1848-50, being applied by me to myself.[296]

Although ready, the manuscript, which in its present form is gigantic, is not fit for publishing for anyone but myself, not even for you.

I began the business of copying out and *polishing the style* on the dot of January first, and it all went ahead swimmingly, as I

---

[a] *Capital* - [b] the British Museum Library

naturally enjoy licking the infant clean after long birth-pangs. But then the carbuncle intervened again, so that I have since been unable to make any more progress but only to fill out with more facts those sections which were, according to the plan, already finished.

Otherwise, I agree with you and shall get the first volume to Meissner as soon as it is ready.[a] But in order to complete it, I must at least be able to *sit*.

Please do not forget to write to Watts,[b] as I have now reached my chapter on machinery.[297]

Could you not dash off an article on Prussia for *The Commonwealth*, under the rubric *Berlin*? Bear in mind how important it is for us to have a firm footing in London. The articles on Poland[c] can take their time. But with the German papers, which are at your disposal, it would be fun for you to write about Prussia. My influence here depends partly on people seeing at last that I do not stand entirely alone.

I am less bothered by political affairs (not *qua*[d] individual but on account of the book) than by the *economic* situation, which is pointing more and more ominously to a crisis.

Salut.

Your
K. M.

Greetings to your 'Irish' lady-friend.[e] The Irish ladies, notabene Roses O'Donovan, etc., have thanked us for the appeal in our paper and for Fox's articles.[298]

First published in *Der Briefwechsel zwischen F. Engels und K. Marx*, Bd. 3, Stuttgart, 1913

Printed according to the original

Published in English in full for the first time

---

a See this volume, p. 226. - b ibid., p. 224. - c F. Engels, 'What Have the Working Classes to Do with Poland?' - d as - e Lizzy Burns

130

MARX TO ENGELS

IN MANCHESTER

[London,] 14 February 1866

Dear FRED,

Most sincere thanks for the first half of the £50 note.

In respect of the 'Viennese',[a] I wrote him LONG SINCE that he should write to you. I told him I was agreeable to anything, except that I did not know UNDER PRESENT CIRCUMSTANCES if I would be capable of supplying a contribution for the first issue.[281]

That cur of a carbuncle is working away, but I hope to be rid of it in a few days.

Things are really aboil in Prussia. Yet the patience of our friends is great. If Bismarck sends them home, everything will now result in banqueting and Kappel-Klassenmann.[224] On the other hand, if the Chamber sits for long, the outcome may be nasty.[299]

Salut.

Your

K. M.

First published in *Der Briefwechsel zwischen F. Engels und K. Marx*, Bd. 3, Stuttgart, 1913

Printed according to the original

Published in English for the first time

131

MARX TO FRIEDRICH LESSNER[300]

IN LONDON

[London,] 14 February 1866

Dear Lessner,

You will see what the matter is from the enclosed letter from Freiligrath. Please do what you can.

Salut.

Your

K. M.

---

[a] Arnold Hilberg

I cannot find Freiligrath's letter. His wife will give you the details about Ulmer's situation. His wife has died, and he has no money to bury her. Our Society[a] must therefore do something at once. You must send the money to Freiligrath.

First published in: Marx and Engels, *Works*, First Russian Edition, Vol. XXV, Moscow, 1934

Printed according to the original

Published in English for the first time

132

ENGELS TO MARX

IN LONDON

Manchester, 19 February 1866

Dear Moor,

Had encl. £10 note for you in my pocket, but could not get to speak to you on your own yesterday.[301] I hope that today's expiry date for the bill of exchange passed uneventfully and that the trifling deficit from the full amount occasioned no unpleasantness.

I have forgotten everything—'Klein Zaches'[b] that I put on top of a row of upright books in the book-case at the foot of the sofa in your room, the 'FACTORY REPORT'[c] and *The Commonwealth*. Please send me a copy of the latter for me to read Fox's article.[d]

How is the upper carbuncle, and the one down on your thigh? I have not yet been able to see Gumpert.

Your
F. E.

Sincere regards to the LADIES and especially little Tussy[e] from her chimpanzee.

First published in *Der Briefwechsel zwischen F. Engels und K. Marx*, Bd. 3, Stuttgart, 1913

Printed according to the original

Published in English for the first time

---

[a] The German Workers' Educational Society in London - [b] E. T. A. Hoffmann, *Klein-Zaches, genannt Zinnober*. - [c] *Reports of the Inspectors of Factories to Her Majesty's Principal Secretary of State for the Home Department.* - [d] P. Fox, 'The Irish Question', *The Commonwealth*, Nos. 153 and 154, 10 and 17 February 1866. - [e] Eleanor Marx

133

MARX TO ENGELS[6]

IN MANCHESTER

[London,] 20 February 1866

Dear FRED,

You can imagine how opportunely the £10 came. I had been served with two threats of distraint, for £6 "0" 9d. for the bloody municipal TAXES, and for 1sh. 16d. for the QUEEN'S TAXES. And I had until Friday to pay.

As regards the carbuncles, the position is:

Concerning the *upper one,* from my long practical experience I was able to tell you that it really needed *lancing.* Today (Tuesday), after receiving your letter, I took a sharp razor, a RELICT OF DEAR LUPUS, and *lanced the cur myself.* (I cannot abide doctors meddling with my private parts or in their vicinity. Furthermore, I have Allen's testimony THAT I AM ONE OF THE BEST SUBJECTS TO BE OPERATED UPON. I always recognise *what has to be done.*) The *sang brûlé,*[a] AS MRS LORMIER SAYS, spurted, or rather leapt, right up into the air, and I now consider this carbuncle buried, although IT STILL WANTS SOME NURSING.

As far as the *lower* cur is concerned, it is becoming malignant and is *beyond* my control and kept me from sleeping the whole night through. If this diabolical business advances, I shall have to send for Allen, of course, as, owing to the *locus* of the cur, I am unable TO WATCH AND CURE it myself. And in general it is clear that ON THE WHOLE I know more about carbuncular complaints than most doctors.

And by the by, I still hold to the view that I *suggested* to Gumpert during my last STAY in Manchester: that is, that the itching and scratching between my testis and posterior over the past $2^{1}/_{2}$ years and the consequent *peeling of the skin* have been more aggravating to my constitution than anything else. The business started 6 months before the first monster carbuncle which I had on my back, and it has persisted *ever since.*

My dear BOY, in all these circumstances one appreciates MORE THAN EVER the good fortune of a friendship such as exists between

---

[a] bad blood

ourselves. You should know for your part that there is *no* relationship I value so highly.

I will send you 'Zaches' and 'FACTORY REPORTS'[a] tomorrow. You will understand, MY DEAR FELLOW, that in a work such as mine,[b] there are bound to be many SHORTCOMINGS in the detail. But the *composition*, the structure, is a triumph of German scholarship, which an individual German may confess to, since it is IN NO WAY **his** merit but rather belongs to the *nation*. Which is all the more gratifying, as it is otherwise the SILLIEST NATION under the sun!

The fact, which Liebig had 'denounced' and which prompted Schönbein's investigations, was this:

The *upper* layers of the soil always contain more ammonia than the *deeper* ones, instead of containing less of it as they would have to do if they had lost it through cultivation. The *fact* was recognised by every chemist. Only the cause was *unknown*.

Hitherto, decay was considered to be the sole source of ammonia. All chemists (including Liebig) denied that the nitrogen in the air could serve as a nutrient for plants.

Schönbein proved (by experiment) that any flame burning in the air converts a certain quantity of the nitrogen in the air into ammonium nitrate, that every process of decomposition gives rise to both nitric acid and ammonia, that the mere evaporation of water is the means causing the formation of both plant nutrients.

Finally, Liebig's 'jubilation' at this discovery:

'The combustion of a pound of coal or wood restores to the air not merely the elements needed to reproduce this pound of wood or, under certain conditions, coal, but the process of combustion *in itself* (note the Hegelian category) 'transforms a certain quantity of nitrogen in the air into a nutrient indispensable for the production of bread and meat.'[c]

I FEEL PROUD OF THE GERMANS. IT IS OUR DUTY TO EMANCIPATE THIS 'DEEP' PEOPLE.

Your
K. M.

First published in: Marx and Engels, *Works*, Second Russian Edition, Vol. 31, Moscow, 1963

Printed according to the original

---

[a] E. T. A. Hoffmann, *Klein-Zaches, gennant Zinnober*; *Reports of the Inspectors of Factories...* - [b] *Capital* - [c] J. Liebig, *Die Chemie in ihrer Anwendung auf Agricultur und Physiologie*, pp. 77-78.

134

ENGELS TO MARX[302]

IN LONDON

Manchester, 22 February 1866

Dear Moor,

Thanks for 'Klein Zaches',[a] etc., which I take as evidence that you have received the £10.

I have just come from Gumpert, whom I did not see until this evening on account of my influenza and having missed him several times. He considers that you *should start the arsenic at once*. Whatever happens it can do you no harm, but only good. He dismisses Allen's comment that it does not agree with you as rubbish. He also considers treatment with poultices to be nonsense; it only encourages *inflammation of the skin*, which is precisely what needs to be suppressed, while it does not encourage suppuration. Ice-packs would be much better, but as long as you are in Allen's hands, these could only be applied if he prescribed them, of course. But above all, sea air, to restore your strength. A spot on the south coast would be preferable, it is true, as in this season the weather there is better than up here, but if you would rather be near Gumpert, there are places enough on the coast here WITHIN AN HOUR'S RIDE FROM MANCHESTER.

You can see I have got Gumpert to change his attitude, so that he is now pressing you to take arsenic at once, even though Allen is still treating you externally, whereas before, for reasons of etiquette, he would not hear of it. But do me a favour now and take the arsenic, and come up here just as soon as your condition permits, so that you do at last get better. With this constant procrastination you are just ruining yourself; no one can withstand such a chronic succession of carbuncles for long, apart from the fact that eventually you may get one that becomes so acute as to be the end of you. And where will your book[b] and your family be then?

You know that I am prepared to do what is in my power, and, in this extreme case, more even than I ought to risk in other circumstances. But you must be sensible, too, and do me and your family the one favour of *getting yourself cured*. What would become

---

[a] E. T. A. Hoffmann, *Klein-Zaches, genannt Zinnober.* - [b] *Capital*

of the whole movement if anything were to happen to you, and the way you are proceeding, that will be the *inevitable* outcome. I really shall not have any peace day or night until I have got you over this business, and every day that passes without my hearing anything from you, I worry and imagine you are worse again.

Nota bene. You should never again let things come to such a pass that a carbuncle which actually ought to be lanced, is not lanced. That is extremely dangerous.

Kindest regards to the LADIES.

Your
F. E.

First published in *Der Briefwechsel zwischen F. Engels und K. Marx*, Bd. 3, Stuttgart, 1913   Printed according to the original

135

MARX TO ENGELS

IN MANCHESTER

[London,] 2 March 1866

DEAR FRED,

The thing will soon be all over now. I think that by tomorrow or the day after at the latest I shall not merely be able to rise from my bed, but to go out, and that with this last malignant cur the series of carbuncles is finished, FOR THIS SEASON. I also feel much better again GENERALLY. This last attack was atrocious. It did not merely put paid to any work, but to any reading, too, EXCEPT Walter Scott.

I found the arsenic not at all unpleasant to begin with (when the taste of the CINNAMON predominated). Now I am beginning to find its specific flavour most repugnant. Otherwise, I believe it was helpful. I took it 3 TIMES A DAY from the outset.

How are things with your contributions for *The Commonwealth*? [a]
And with John Watts 'ON MACHINERY'? [b]

---

[a] F. Engels, 'What Have the Working Classes to Do with Poland?' - [b] See this volume, pp. 224, 228.

The sofa to which I have been confined for 9 days now is in my study, but right by the window, so that at certain times of day, e. g. as at this moment, I can enjoy a most refreshing breeze.

You have no further cause for anxiety now, but AS FAR AS ACTUAL OUTBREAKS ARE CONCERNED you can regard the business as terminated. *Salut.*

Your
K. M.

Little Tussy[a] 'SENDS HER BEST COMPLIMENTS TO HER CHIMP'.

First published in *Der Briefwechsel zwischen F. Engels und K. Marx*, Bd. 3, Stuttgart, 1913

Printed according to the original

Published in English for the first time

136

ENGELS TO MARX

IN LONDON

Manchester, 5 March 1866

Dear Moor,

Gumpert is *décidément*[b] of the opinion that, just as soon as your condition allows, you should go to the seaside for at least 4 weeks and in any case have a change of air. Now what do you think of that? Would you prefer to go to a seaside resort near here (Lytham, or Blackpool or New Brighton perhaps) or on the south coast? Make your MIND up about it, and if the former, then come up here. I shall raise the money for the purpose and, as I promised you, a bit more as well. These constantly recurring carbuncles have really just got to stop, or you will be unable either to work or to do anything else. So, you must reach a decision.

You yourself disrupted my contributions for *The Commonwealth*[c] by asking for something on Prussia as well as on the Polish business.[d] As a result, the one was interrupted and the other not completed in time either. I was suddenly collared to CANVASS for the money for the Schiller Institute[28] which I told you about, and that kept me off it every evening last week, and I have to go out again now.[e] I expect to have got that behind me in a fortnight but, at all events, to dispatch an article on Poland this week.

---

a Eleanor Marx - b decidedly - c F. Engels, 'What Have the Working Classes to Do with Poland?'- d See this volume, p. 228. - e See present edition, Vol. 20, pp. 402-04.

Fine revelations from Jamaica. And what an embarrassment they are to *The Times*, as well as Russell's resignation. The paper is going DOWN very rapidly.[303]

If possible, you must read the statement by the Cologne-Minden directors about their shady deal. They say that insofar as they are party to it, it is *in law* just a *private arrangement*; as soon as the King[a] ratifies it, *he* will have to sort out the constitutional side. In other words, the bourgeoisie in Cologne themselves do not want to have a constitution.[304]

Kind regards to the LADIES.

Your

F. E.

First published in *Der Briefwechsel zwischen F. Engels und K. Marx*, Bd. 3, Stuttgart, 1913

Printed according to the original

Published in English for the first time

137

MARX TO ENGELS

IN MANCHESTER

[London,] 6 March 1866

Dear FRED,

As it seems decided I am to go away, I think it is best to go to Margate. The air is particularly good there. Besides, not far from London in case anything were to happen. And although the last carbuncle has also disappeared, the wound has not healed up yet, so lengthy train journey would be awkward for me.

Now what ought I to do 'AT LARGE'?—according to Gumpert's prescriptions?

I am going out into the open air again for the first time today. *Salut.*

Your

K. M.

First published in *Der Briefwechsel zwischen F. Engels und K. Marx*, Bd. 3, Stuttgart, 1913

Printed according to the original

Published in English for the first time

---

[a] William I

138

ENGELS TO MARX

IN LONDON

[Manchester, about 10 March 1866]

Confidential!

Excerpt from a letter to Freiligrath,[305] who asked me for information on some commercial philistine and, at the same time, expressed his regret at your illness and wished you well:

'Marx needs to rest from working at night and from worry, as well as sea-air and good living. That will put him back on his feet all right. Such troubles are spared to plump bourgeois like Blind. Instead, the poor man has the misfortune that for all the levers and thumbscrews he applies, nobody speaks of him other than Blind himself. Such fellows have their carbuncles on the insides of their skulls. But enough of the "deliberate liar".

'How are you actually doing now? I hear the bank in London[a] has closed down. A good thing too, for you, in the long run, the liaison with Fazy and Co. could have compromised you later in some unforeseen way.[212] I am sure you will soon pick up a decent position again.'

In haste.

Your

F. E.

First published in *Der Briefwechsel zwischen F. Engels und K. Marx*, Bd. 3, Stuttgart, 1913

Printed according to the original

Published in English for the first time

139

MARX TO ENGELS[33]

IN MANCHESTER

[London,] 10 March 1866

Dear Fred,

Did you receive the lines I wrote last Tuesday?[b] I need to know in order to ascertain whether my letters are being tampered with. It was addressed to Mrs Burns.

---

[a] a branch of the Bank of Switzerland - [b] See this volume, p. 236.

If I am to go to the seaside at all, it will have to be now, as I do not wish to waste any time. I told you in my last letter that in that case I wanted to go to *Margate*, and the requisite steps must be attended to now. I also asked you in my little letter what Gumpert has in mind by the 'cure'? Continuing with the arsenic, etc., or what?

Everything is at sixes and sevens on the 'INTERNATIONAL COUNCIL' and the 'newspaper board',[a] and a great desire is being manifested to rebel against the absent 'tyrant',[b] but at the same time to wreck the whole shop as well.[c] My wound (from the last carbuncle) has healed up sufficiently (and so far no new one has appeared) for me to go out into company next Monday and Tuesday; but, at the same time, I can still scarcely endure those late meetings in some corner of Fleet Street,[306] and what is even worse, I am still in a state of such nervous irritation that I could hardly contain the storms within 'the bounds of pure reason',[d] but would more probably explode with excessive violence, which would be pointless.

When shall we finally see Polish article I?[e]

Your

K. M.

First published abridged in *Der Briefwech-sel zwischen F. Engels und K. Marx*, Bd. 3, Stuttgart, 1913 and in full in *MEGA*, Abt. III, Bd. 3, Berlin, 1930

Printed according to the original

Published in English in full for the first time

140

MARX TO ENGELS

IN MANCHESTER[f]

[London,] 15 March 1866

My dear Frederic,

The bearer of these lines is citizen Orsini, the brother of the immortal martyr,[g] and a member of our association. He leaves

---

a *The Commonwealth* - b i.e. Marx - c See this volume, pp. 249-51. - d Presumably an ironical allusion to Kant's *Kritik der reinen Vernunft*. - e in the series of articles 'What Have the Working Classes to Do with Poland?' - f The letter bears the stamp: International Working Men's Association / Central Council / London. - g Felice Orsini

England for the United States, whence he will return in some months. Your advice on commercial matters may, perhaps, prove useful to him. At all events, you will be delighted to make his personal acquaintance.

Yours truly
K. Marx

Mr *Frederic Engels*, 7 Southgate, St Mary's, Manchester.

PS. I know that Bradlaugh is an honest man and occupies a respectable position in the city as solicitor.

First published, in German, in *Der Brief-wechsel zwischen F. Engels und K. Marx*, Bd. 3, Stuttgart, 1913 and in the language of the original, English, in *MEGA*, Abt. III, Bd. 3, Berlin, 1930

Reproduced from the original

141

MARX TO ENGELS

IN MANCHESTER

Margate [16 March 1866]
5 Lansell's Place

Dear Fred,

I arrived here yesterday evening.[307] I have been dashing about all day today (after taking a warm sea-bathe) and have only just returned to my lodgings (right by the sea) in order to send you my address before the post-office closes. You will get more detailed news tomorrow. Your first Polish article[a] will appear not this week, but next. The air here is wonderful.

Salut.

Your
K. M.

First published in *Der Briefwechsel zwischen F. Engels und K. Marx*, Bd. 3, Stuttgart, 1913

Printed according to the original

Published in English for the first time

---

[a] F. Engels, 'What Have the Working Classes to Do with Poland?'

142

MARX TO HIS DAUGHTER JENNY

IN LONDON

Margate, 16th March, 1866
5 Lansell's Place

My dear Child,

I arrived here yesterday evening, $^3/_4$ past seven. According to your instructions I left my luggage behind me in the cloakroom and was then landed by the omnibus at a small inn called the 'King's Arms'. Having ordered a rump steak, and being shown to the coffee room, which was rather dimly illuminated, I took rather fright (you know my anxious temper) at a lean, long, stiff sort of man, midway between parson and commis-voyageur, solitarily and motionlessly seated before the chimney. From the vagueness of his glanceless eye, I thought him a blind man. I was confirmed in that notion by some long, scarf-like, narrow white thing spread over his legs, with regular holes in it. I fancied it to be paper outcut by the blind man to serve as a catchpenny from the frequenters of the inn. When my supper arrived the man began somewhat to wave, quietly took off his boots and warmed his elephantine feet at the fire. What with this agreeable spectacle, and his supposed blindness, and what with a rump steak, which seemed, in its natural state, to have belonged to a deceased cow, I passed the first Margate evening anything but comfortably. But, in compensation, the bedroom was snug, the bed clean and elastic and the sleep sound. When at the breakfast table, who should step in but the man of the evening. He turned out to be deaf and not blind. What had so much vexed me—I mean the thing on his knees—was a pocket handkerchief of singular fashion, with a greyish ground interspersed by black eyes which I had mistaken for holes. Feeling shy of the man, I settled my bill as soon as possible and, after some erratic course, hit upon my present lodging, in front of the sea, a large sitting room and a bedroom, 10/- per week. When striking my bargain the additional clause was agreed upon that, on your arrival, you will get your bedroom *for nothing*.

The first thing I did was to take a warm sea-bathe. It was delicious, so is the air here. It is a wonderful air.

As to boarding houses, they are about empty now, and, as I understood the librarian, hardly yet prepared for the reception of guests. As to dining-rooms, there was some difficulty to get at a proper one, but by the by this obstacle will be overcome.

And now, with my best compliments to all, by-bye.

Yours

Mohr

I have already walked five hours to-day.

First published, in Russian, in *Voin-stvuyushchy materialist*, Book 4, 1925 and in the language of the original, English, in *The Socialist Review* (London), No. 44, September 1929

Reproduced from the original

143

MARX TO ANTOINETTE PHILIPS

IN SALT-BOMMEL

Margate, 18 March 1866
5 Lansell's Place

My dear Child,

From the address you will see that I have been banished, by my medical adviser, to this seaside place, which, at this time of the year, is quite solitary. Margate lives only upon the Londoners, who regularly inundate it at the bathing season. During the other months it vegetates only. For my own part right glad I am to have got rid of all company, even that of my books. I have taken a private lodging which fronts the sea. In an inn or Hotel one might have been exposed to the danger of falling in with a stray traveller, or being pestered by local politics, vestry interests, and neighbourly gossip. As it is, 'I care for nobody, and nobody cares for me'.[a] But the air is wonderfully pure and reinvigorating, and you have here at the same time sea air and mountain air. I have become myself a sort of walking stick, running up and down the

---

[a] from the English folk-song 'The Miller of the Dee'

whole day, and keeping my mind in that state of nothingness which Buddhaism considers the climax of human bliss. Of course, you have not forgotten the pretty little diction: 'When the devil was sick, the devil a monk would be; when the devil was well, the devil a monk was he.'

Withdrawing a little from the seaside, and roaming over the adjacent agricultural districts, you are painfully reminded of 'civilisation', because from all sides you are startled by large boards, with governmental proclamations on them, headed: *Cattle Disease.* The ruling English oligarchs were never suspected to care one farthing for 'der Menschheit ganzes Weh',[a] but as to cows and oxen, they feel deeply. At the opening of Parliament, the horned cattle gentlemen of both houses, commoners and lords, made a wild rush at government. All their talk sounded like a herd of cows' lowing, translated into English. And they were not like honest king Wiswamitra, 'der kämpfte und büsste für die Kuh Sabalah'.[b] On the contrary. They seized the opportunity to '*battre monnaie*'[c] out of the cows' ailings at the expense of the people.[308] By the by, the East sends us always nice things—Religion, Etiquette, and the Plague in all forms.

I am very glad to hear of Waaràtje's[d] winding up adventure. Verily, verily, I tell thee, my sweet little cousin, I always felt deep sympathy for the man, and always hoped that one day or other he should fix his melting heart in the right direction, and not persevere performing the nasty part in the children's tale: 'The Beast and the Beauty'.[e] I'm sure he will make a good husband. Is his inamorata a 'Bommelerin' or an importation?

A few days before leaving London, I made the acquaintance of Mr Orsini, a very fine fellow, the brother of the Orsini who was sent to the grave for sending Bonaparte to Italy.[309] He has now left England for the U. States, in commercial matters, but during the few days of our acquaintance, he did me good service. Although an intimate friend of Mazzini's, he is far from sharing

---

[a] 'all misery of mankind'. Paraphrase of a passage from Schiller's poem 'Das Eleusische Fest': 'doch der Menschheit Angst und Wehen / Fühlet mein gequältes Herz' (yet the pains and woes of humans / ever fill my tortured heart) - [b] 'who wrangled and suffered for the cow Sabalah'—an episode from the epic poem *Ramayana*; used by Heine in *Buch der Lieder*, 'Die Heimkehr' (Marx gives a free rendering of the words from Heine's poem; see this volume, p. 245). - [c] 'coin money' - [d] *Waaràtje* ('really', 'indeed')—the word always used by student Petrus from Hildebrand's novel *Camera obscura*. Marx presumably refers in this letter to pastor Roodhuizen who later became Antoinette's husband. - [e] 'La Belle et la Bête', a tale by Jeanne Marie Le Prince de Beaumont.

the antiquated antisocialist and theocratical views of Mazzini. Now, during my forced and prolonged absence from the Council of the International Association, Mazzini had been busy in stirring a sort of revolt against my leadership. 'Leadership' is never a pleasant thing, nor a thing I ambition. I have always before my mind your father's[a] saying in regard to Thorbecke that 'der Eselstreiber den Eseln immer verhasst ist'.[b] But having once fairly embarked in an enterprise which I consider of import, I certainly, 'anxious' man as I am, do not like to give way. Mazzini, a most decided hater of freethinking and socialism, watched the progress of our society with great jealousy. His first attempt of making a tool of it and fastening upon it a programme and declaration of principles of his hatching, I had baffled.[c] His influence, before that time very great with the London working class, had sunk to zero. He waxed wroth, when he saw that we had founded the English *Reform League*[155] and a weekly paper, *The Commonwealth*, to which the most advanced men of London contribute, and of which I shall send you a copy after my return to London. His anger increased, when the editors of the *Rive gauche* (the journal of *la jeune France*,[d] directed by Rogeard, author of the *Propos de Labienus*,[310] Longuet, etc.) joined us, and when he became aware of the spread of our society on the Continent. He improved my absence, to intrigue with some English workingmen, raise their jealousies against 'German' influence, and even sent his bully, a certain Major Wolff (a German by birth) to the Council there to lodge his complaints and more or less directly to denounce me. He wanted to be acknowledged as 'the leader (I suppose *par la grace de dieu*[e]) of the continental democratical movement'. In so doing, he acted so far quite sincerely, as he utterly abhors my principles which, in his eyes, embody the most damnable 'materialism'. This whole scene was enacted behind my back, and after they had made sure that my malady would not allow me to be present. The English wavered, but, although still very weak, I rushed to the following *séance*, Mr Orsini accompanying me. On my interpellation, he declared them that Mazzini had lost his influence even in Italy and was, from his antecedents and prejudices, quite disabled from understanding the new movement.[311] All the Foreign secretaries declared for me, and, if you, our Dutch secretary,[312] had been present, I hope you would have also cast your vote for your humble servant and admirer. As it was, I carried a complete

---

[a] Lion Philips - [b] 'the ass-driver is always hateful to the ass' - [c] See this volume, pp. 16-18. - [d] young France - [e] by the grace of God

victory over this redoubtable adversary.[313] I think that Mazzini has now had enough of me and will make *bonne mine à mauvais jeu.*[a]

I hope to receive a few lines from you. Don't forget that I am quite an insulated hermit.

Your most sincere friend

Bloch[b]

First published in the language of the original, English, in the *International Review of Social History,* Vol. I, Part 1, Assen, 1956

Reproduced from the text of the journal

144

MARX TO LAURA MARX

IN LONDON

Margate, 20 March 1866
5 Lansell's Place

My dear Cacadou,[c]

Very good news indeed! I prefer Mrs Grach to the mother of all the Gracchi.[314] I am right glad that I have taken my lodgings in a private House, and not in an Inn or Hotel where one could hardly escape being pestered with local politics, vestry scandals, and neighbourly gossip. But still I cannot sing with the miller of the Dee, that I care for nobody and nobody cares for me.[d] For there is my landlady, who is deaf like a post, and her daughter, who is afflicted with chronic hoarseness, but they are very nice people, attentive, and not intruding. As to myself, I have turned into a perambulating stick, running about the greatest part of the day, airing myself, going to bed at 10 o'clock, reading nothing, writing less, and altogether working up my mind to that state of nothingness which Buddhaism considers the element of human bliss. However, with all that, I shall not turn out, on Thursday,[e] that paragon of beauty which worthy By Bye,[f] in his phantastic

---

[a] a good face on a bad business - [b] Presumably this is Marx's nickname, or may be the signature he chose to be incognito in Margate. - [c] Laura's jocular nickname - [d] from the English folk-song 'The Miller of the Dee' - [e] 22 March, when Marx intended to go to London to attend a soirée arranged by his daughters (see this volume, pp. 249-50). - [f] Marx's daughter Jenny

mood, seems to expect. The toothache on the right side of the
face has not yet altogether disappeared, and the same side is
afflicted with an inflammation of the eye. Not that there is much
to be seen of it, but that eye has taken to the vicious habit of
shedding tears on its own account, without the least regard to the
feelings of his master. But for this state of things, I should have
my photogramme already taken, since you get here 12 *cartes de
visite* for 3 s. 6 d. and 48 *cartes* for 10 sh. Mummelchen[a] will
oblige me by pacing her steps to Mr Hall and ordering him to
prepare a solution of zink (he will know the composition of the
drug) for my eye the which I expect to find ready on my arrival at
London. This bad eye interferes with my nightrest. Otherwise, I
am turning [over] a new leaf.

Withdrawing somewhat from the seaside, and roaming over the
adjacent rustic district, you are painfully reminded of '*civilisation*'
by large boards, staring at you everywhere, headed 'Cattle
Disease', and placarded over with a government proclamation, the
result of the wild rush which the horned cattle gentry, lords and
commoners, made at the government, on the opening of
Parliament.[308]

> Oh, oh King Wiswamitra
> What fool of an oxen art thou,
> That thou so much wrangle'st and suffer'st
> And all that for a cow.[b]

But if honest Wiswamitra, like a true Indian, tormented himself
for the salvation of the cow Sabala, those English gentry, in the
true style of modern martyrs, bleed the people to compensate
themselves for their cows' ailings. The horn plague upon them!
The horn, the horn, as discreet By Bye rings it lustily.

On Sunday, I made up my mind to walk *per pedes*[c] to
Canterbury. Unhappily, I only formed this grand resolution, after
having already measured for two hours the length and breadth of
the piers and so forth. So I had already expended too much
physical power, when I set out for the archbishop's seat or see, as
you like. And from here to Canterbury are fully 16 miles. From

---

[a] Marx's wife Jenny - [b] Heinrich Heine, 'Den König Wiswamitra' (from *Buch der
Lieder*, 'Die Heimkehr'). Marx quotes an English translation of the second stanza of the
poem, which in the German original reads as follows:

> O, König Wiswamitra
> O, welch ein Ochs bist du,
> Dass du so viel kämpfest und büssest
> Und alles für eine Kuh!

[c] on foot

Canterbury I returned to Margate by rail, but I had overworked myself, and could not sleep during the whole night. Limbs and loins were not tired, but the plants of my feet turned out tender hearted rogues. As to Canterbury, you know, of course, all about it, and more than I can boast, from your Eves, the trusted source of knowledge for all English Eves. (One cannot help, in your company, bad punning. But mark, Thackeray did worse, by playing upon Eves and Ewes.) Happily, I was too tired, and it was too late, to look out for the celebrated cathedral. Canterbury is an old, ugly, medieval sort of town, not mended by large modern English barracks at the one, and a dismal dry Railway Station at the other end of the oldish thing. There is no trace of that poetry about it, which you find in continental towns of the same age. The swaggering of the private soldiers and the officers in the streets, reminded me somewhat of Vaterland.[a] In the inn, where I was scantily purveyed with some slices of cold beef, I caught the newest scandal. Captain Le Merchant, it seems, had been taken up by the police on Saturday night, for systematically knocking at the doors of all the most respectable citizens. And a summons will be taken out against the Captain because of this innocent pastime. And the redoubtable Captain will have to bend down his diminished head before aldermanic majesty. This is my whole packet of 'Canterbury Tales'.[b]

And now, Cacadou, pay my compliments to Elly[c] to whom I shall write one of those days, and whose little letter was very welcome. As to Möhmchen,[d] she will hear of me by the by.

That damned boy Lafargue pesters me with his Proudhonism, and will not rest, it seems, until I have administered to him a sound cudgelling of his Creole pate.

My good wishes to all.

Your master

Has Orsini still received the letter I sent him?[111]

First published, in German, in *Die Neue Zeit*, Bd. 1, Nr. 2, 1907-1908 and in the language of the original, English, in *Annali*, an. 1, Milano, 1958

Reproduced from the original

---

[a] Fatherland - [b] An allusion to Chaucer's *Canterbury Tales*. - [c] Eleanor Marx - [d] Marx's wife Jenny

145

ENGELS TO HERMANN ENGELS

IN BARMEN

Manchester, 22 March 1866

Dear Hermann,

Your document is with the LAWYER. Unfortunately, he was out today when I called, so I can't tell you whether he has already sent it to Liverpool, nor what progress has been made with the relevant fair copies. But I shall call again one day soon to prod him.

I am writing to you today about the statement of my account which you sent to me and which had to wait until I had a quiet day to look through, as your entries for the last half year of 1864 have been done quite differently from ours. I therefore had to go through all the stuff again from the beginning and have at last sorted it out. The items coincide with the exception of the remittances which, according to your letter of 20 July 1864, were credited direct to my account with F. Engels & Co., so I shall presumably find these items in my statement of account with F. Engels & Co. These items are:

		Remittance via Apolda £	2.	2.	2
1864, 30 June	{» Munich	»	1.	2.	—
	{» Rieslingen	»	8.	19.	6
» 3 July	» London tot.	»	287.	3.	3

I find that, according to your statements of account I am actually losing money in respect of the transferred balances debited to me here. The exact calculation of the difference for the 18 months amounts to £ 1. 14. 9, and in future I shall therefore take the liberty of sending you a statement every 6 months for I naturally have no alternative but to accept the statements of the firm here. For my convenience, I am still keeping your account here separate as well.

Please be so good as to send me a summary statement of my account with F. Engels & Co. *as soon as possible*, so that I can make up my private account-book. And from *mid-year* 1864, of course, as I have had no statement for this account from you since then at all—as far as I am aware. (If you didn't make up the account in mid-year 1864, then from the *beginning of 1864*.)

Business has got better again since last September; we have been fully occupied since then, at present even excessively so, and are setting up new DT-machines. Prices have improved too, and in the last half-year of 1865 we have even made enough to cover my costs from June 1864 onwards, with a little left over for myself as well; in the first year of my PARTNERSHIP we didn't make a brass farthing, you know, even without writing anything off for machinery. We must be doing splendid business now, but if cotton should drop below 18d. for MIDDLING ORLEANS owing to the greater supply, we shall lose everything again. However, I'm not expecting that to happen; I think good American cotton will, by and large, hold at approx. 19d., while Surat may admittedly fall a lot. Moreover, I think we are not getting more cotton than we need and will, by and large, stay at approx. 19d. for MIDDLING ORLEANS until about the autumn, when there may perhaps be some more speculating, which will force prices up.

I shall be writing to Mother[a] in a day or two, as soon as I can manage it; I received her letter last Monday and was glad to learn she is well again now. My kindest regards to her and all our brothers and sisters from

Your
Friedrich

Apropos. As you know, the capital credited to me here amounted to a little over £13,000 as far back as 30 June 1864, and since I am under no obligation to have more than £ 12,000 in the business, there is no need for you to provide cover for purchases through us; or I could send you some remittances, especially as approx. another £ 300 is due in interest at the end of June. I can also make payments to Funke on your account if you so wish; in this way, you can draw approx. £ 1,500 up to 30 June, or at once. Only please do not draw bills on us, since Gottfried[b] objects, he thinks people might regard it as improper practice, the name of the firms being one and the same.

Anton[c] already has 4-5 patents now. There is no stopping him, every other day a new patent of his is announced in the press.

First published in *Deutsche Revue*, Jg. 46, Bd. II, 1921

Printed according to the original

Published in English for the first time

---

[a] Elisabeth Engels - [b] Gottfried Ermen - [c] Anton Ermen

Karl Marx with his daughter Jenny.
End of March 1866, Margate

146

MARX TO ENGELS[33]

IN MANCHESTER

Margate, 24 March 1866
5 Lansell's Place

Dear FRED,

The belated arrival of this letter will tell you how 'professionally' I am applying my time here. I am reading nothing, am writing nothing. The mere fact of having to take the arsenic three times a day obliges one to arrange one's time for meals and for strolling by the sea and over the adjacent HILLS in such a way that one finds 'no time' for anything else. And in the evening one is too tired to do anything other than sleep. The weather is, by and large, rather raw, and in particular there is often an east wind blowing here, which is SOMEWHAT CHILLING, but one soon becomes accustomed to that, too. You can tell how much I am restored from the fact that last Sunday I marched *per pedes*[a] to Canterbury (17 miles from here) in less than 4 hours. As regards company here, it does not exist, of course. I can sing with the MILLER OF THE DEE: 'I CARE FOR NOBODY AND NOBODY CARES FOR ME.'[b]

The day before yesterday[c] I had to go to London in the evening to attend a 'soirée' of my daughters. My uncle[d] had sent them £ 5 at Christmas, which was, however, 'borrowed' from them for GENERAL PURPOSES and which they only got back when your money arrived. They arranged their annual 'PARTY' with it and so bombarded me with letters that I 'made' for London, as Mr Nothjung used to say. But I returned to my hermitage here the very next morning (i. e., yesterday).

Before setting off for Margate (which I did on Wednesday, 14 March[e]), I had to attend the consecutive evening meetings, on 12 and 13 March, firstly of the SHAREHOLDERS of *The Commonwealth*[290] and secondly, on the 13th, of the CENTRAL COUNCIL, although still in a thoroughly wretched condition at the time.

On the former occasion Mr Cremer had set everything up for Eccarius to be given his marching orders, which would probably

---

[a] on foot - [b] from the English folk-song 'The Miller of the Dee' - [c] 22 March - [d] Lion Philips - [e] Presumably this is not correct, for Marx arrived at Margate on Thursday, 15 March (see this volume, p. 239).

have happened if I had not appeared. So, the meeting only achieved the 'voluntary' resignation of Mr Cremer from the editorial board. How the matter turned out later, I do not know, since the whole thing was only SETTLED 'provisionally' for one week, and the general SHAREHOLDERS-MEETING was deferred to 19 March. But it will probably mean *beati possidentes*[a] here too, and as a result of that meeting Eccarius was, to begin with, the *possidens.*[b]

The intrigue on the CENTRAL COUNCIL was closely bound up with the RIVALRIES and JEALOUSIES concerning the journal (Mr Howell wished to be EDITOR-IN-CHIEF and Mr Cremer ditto). Mr Le Lubez had used this to agitate against GERMAN INFLUENCE, and at the meeting of 6 March a beautifully and quietly prepared scene took place. To wit, Major Wolff suddenly appeared and made a solemn speech in his own name and in Mazzini's and in that of the ITALIAN SOCIETY[20] against the reply to Vésinier's attacks, which Jung had sent to the *Echo de Verviers* in the name of the CENTRAL COUNCIL.[274] He made a very violent attack on Jung and (*impliciter*[c]) myself. Odger, Howell, Cremer, and others gave vent to their longstanding Mazzinism. Le Lubez fed the flames and, AT ALL EVENTS, a resolution was passed which included what amounted to an *amende honorable*[d] for Mazzini, Wolff, etc. It was a serious matter, as you can see. (Of the FOREIGNERS, there were only A FEW PRESENT, and none of them voted.) It would really be a neat trick of Mazzini's to let me bring the Association so far and then to appropriate it for himself. He demanded that the English should recognise him as leader of the continental democrats, as though it was for the English gentlemen to appoint leaders for *us*!

On Saturday (10 March) the FOREIGN SECRETARIES of the Association gathered at my house to hold a council of war (Dupont, Jung, Longuet, Lafargue, Bobczyński). It was resolved that, whatever happened, I was to attend the COUNCIL on Tuesday (13th) and *protest* against the PROCEEDINGS in the name of *all* the FOREIGN SECRETARIES. The PROCEEDINGS were irregular, you see, as Wolff is no longer a MEMBER OF THE COUNCIL, therefore no resolution on a matter in which he was personally implicated ought to be passed in his presence. Furthermore, I was to explain Mazzini's position vis-à-vis both our Association and the CONTINENTAL WORKINGMEN'S PARTIES, etc. Finally, the French were to bring Cesare Orsini (who is BY THE BY a personal friend of Mazzini) along to give EVIDENCE on Mazzini, Wolff and the STATE OF 'SOCIALISM' in Italy.

---

[a] blessed are they who have possession (Horace, *Odes*, IV, IX, 45) - [b] the man in possession - [c] by implication - [d] apology

The affair went off better than I had ever expected[313]; though the English element was unfortunately not well represented (on account of the bloody Reform League[155]). I gave that Lubez a thorough dressing down. In any case, it has been made clear to the English (in fact only a minority is meant here, too) that the whole CONTINENTAL ELEMENT stands behind me as one man and that here it is by no means, as Mr Lubez had insinuated, a case of GERMAN INFLUENCE. Lubez had sought to put it to them that as LEADER of the ENGLISH ELEMENT on the COUNCIL, I was holding DOWN the other CONTINENTAL ELEMENTS; the English gentlemen are, on the contrary, now persuaded that by means of the CONTINENTAL ELEMENT I have got *them* entirely under my thumb, should they kick over the traces. More about that next time.

Before coming here, I did, of course, pay off the most pressing DEBTS at home, as otherwise I should not have had a moment's peace of mind. If you can send me a little bit more at the end of this month, I would appreciate it. Meanwhile, the power of attorney from the Cape[a] will be here at last, and thus something will at least be flowing into the coffers, even if it is not very much.

MY COMPLIMENTS TO MRS LIZZY.[b]

Your
K. M.

First published in *Der Briefwechsel zwischen F. Engels und K. Marx*, Bd. 3, Stuttgart, 1913

Printed according to the original

Published in English in full for the first time

147

ENGELS TO MARX

IN MARGATE

Manchester, 27 March 1866

Dear Moor,

I had just made up my mind to write you a letter of congratulations on what I inferred from your silence to be your

---

[a] from Johann Carl Juta (Marx presumably refers to the power of attorney for receiving his share of legacy at the death of his aunt, Esther Kosel; see this volume, p. 194) - [b] Lizzy Burns

conscientious abstinence from work, when your letter arrived. It reassured me not a little, as I was beginning to suspect that another carbuncle might be the reason for your obstinate silence. You must keep taking plenty of exercise and continue visiting the archbishop in Canterbury *per pedes*,[a] that is the sure way to eradicate it once and for all. In this case, and in others, too, the most important thing is to endure the boredom of the seaside for long enough; if you can, you should stay there for the whole of April, so that the trouble can be completely cured.

Old Hill has just come and interrupted me. So I must break off for today. The £10 encl.

E/T 96963, Manchester, 20 January 1865.

Your
F. Engels

First published in *Der Briefwechsel zwischen F. Engels und K. Marx*, Bd. 3, Stuttgart, 1913

Printed according to the original

Published in English for the first time

148

MARX TO ENGELS [33]

IN MANCHESTER

Margate, 2 April 1866
5 Lansell's Place

Dear FRED,

D'abord,[b] the £10 received with kindest thanks.

In my absence there has been a *changement de décoration*,[c] or rather, *de direction* on *The Commonwealth* which will be realised next week.[290] *Odger*, EDITOR; *Fox*, SUBEDITOR; the 'SON OF TOIL'[d] contracted to supply an article a week for 10s.; *Cremer* OUT OF PLACE; has also tendered his resignation as GENERAL SECRETARY of the 'INTERNATIONAL ASSOCIATION'. Taken as a whole, I have no objection to the CHANGE. Eccarius could hardly have (or at least ought not to have) imagined that he would be allowed to retain nominal control

---

[a] on foot - [b] Firstly - [c] change of decor - [d] pen-name for Johann Georg Eccarius

from the moment the paper established itself. I warned him to no avail. It was a 'political' error on my part to have given way to his entreaties and proposed him by letter for his now defunct job. If I had not been ill, he would have knocked on the door in vain. I knew in advance that I would find the affair coming home to roost. Avoidance of any appearance of pursuing personal interests or abusing personal influence for clandestine purposes, and good understanding with the English must, of course, be more important to us than satisfying Eccarius' more or less justified ambition.

People of a dry disposition like Eccarius also have a certain dry egoism, which easily leads them astray. When the Reform League decided on the big meeting in St Martin's Hall, [267] the League's Council nominated him as one of the public speakers. The fellows in Potter's clique objected to him as a foreigner. I warned him expressly not to accept his 'brief'. However, he thought he had got over all his troubles and flattered himself with the important part in the metropolitan movement. And he was a dead failure. The poor fellow has, of course, lived a life of disappointments, and the honorary positions the English spontaneously allowed him, as Vice-President of the 'International', etc., deceived him to the point where he now believed he could suddenly make up for the whole of his past life. If he had followed me, operated slowly, maintained a modest posture, everything would be in the best of order. If I even went so far as to muddy myself for his sake, despite his lack of discipline and his wilful behaviour, I was moved to do so particularly by the consideration that he has always worked with us and never reaped the fruits of it. But one always makes blunders if one allows oneself to be influenced by suchlike considerations.

As regards the newspaper itself,[a] the danger—arising from lack of funds—lies in the growing encroachments and dominance of the *Nonconformist* clique.[b]

The accursed traditional nature of all English movements is manifesting itself again in the reform-movement. The same 'instalments' which but a few weeks ago were rejected with the utmost indignation by the people's party—they had even refused Bright's ultimatum of household suffrage—are now treated as a prize worthy to be fought for. And why? Because the Tories are screaming blue murder.[315] These fellows lack the mettle of the old Chartists.

---

[a] *The Commonwealth* - [b] See this volume, p. 224.

What do you think of the Austro-Prussian troubles [316]? I see no continental papers at all. However, it is at least clear to me that Russia is behind the Prussians and that the Austrians, who know this, are *nolens volens*ª consoling themselves with French support. A pretty game these heads of state are playing! It is the eternal dilemma the German philistine confronts us with at every turn. For Bonaparte, real CIVIL WAR IN GERMANY would be a true GODSEND.

Admittedly, there is still always the possibility that one fine day the affair will simply end with the worthy Bismarck's dismissal. But since Düppel,[27] 'William the Conqueror'ᵇ believes his 'glorious armies' are invincible, and a second Olmützᶜ must appear to be a risk even to him, in view of the INTERNAL CONFLICT.[317]

The weather has been very bad here for several days, as if it had been made especially to order for the COCKNEYS who have invaded this place for the Easter holiday.

For how long must I take the arsenic?

MY COMPLIMENTS TO MRS BURNS.

Your
K. M.

My friend Kaub has written to me from Paris that a certain M. Rebour has found a means to separate water into hydrogen and oxygen, using a method which would entail the expenditure of 2 sous per day FOR A FIRE TO MELT IRON WITH. He is, however, keeping the matter secret for the time being still, as on a previous occasion a discovery had been stolen from him and patented in London. *Qui vivra verra.*ᵈ You know how often we have both dreamed of a cheap way of making fire from water.

First published in *Der Briefwechsel zwischen F. Engels und K. Marx,* Bd. 3, Stuttgart, 1913

Printed according to the original

Published in English in full for the first time

ª willy-nilly - ᵇ William I (an ironical comparison with the Norman William who conquered England in 1066) - ᶜ Czech name: Olomouc - ᵈ Time will tell.

149

ENGELS TO MARX

IN MARGATE

Manchester, 2 April 1866

Dear Moor,

I hope you have received the £10 which I sent to you in Margate. I was in Wales over the holiday and have at last got round to writing to you today.

Orsini called on me, but unfortunately I could do nothing for him; I have no connections of any kind in New York any more, and it is OUT OF THE QUESTION to find anyone here to run the guano DODGE with him and advance the funds for it. He is a very nice fellow.

Polish article No. 3^a will be done tomorrow evening, if nothing interferes. I shall send it direct to Eccarius, CARE OF EDITOR OF *The Commonwealth*. Unfortunately, the proof-reading is so abysmal, and it's about time that they stopped reprinting the LEADERS from *The Nonconformist* every week. It really is sheer impudence on Miall's part to pass the newspaper off so openly as a mere appendix of *The Nonconformist.*

What do you say to Bismarck? It almost looks now as if he is pushing for war and is thereby offering Louis Bonaparte a splendid opportunity to acquire a piece of the left bank of the Rhine without any effort and thus set himself up *à vie.*^b Even though all those who bear any responsibility for this war—if it comes to that—deserve hanging, and I would with equal impartiality gladly extend that to the Austrians as well, yet I would most of all like to see the Prussians soundly thrashed. Then there are 2 possibilities: 1. the Austrians will dictate the peace in Berlin within a fortnight, and direct intervention from abroad will thereby be avoided, but at the same time the present regime in Berlin will be made impossible, and there will be another movement which will disavow the specific nature of the Prussian regime right from the outset; or 2. there will be a sudden change in Berlin before the Austrians arrive, in which case the new movement will also get under way.

My opinion of the military situation is that the two armies are more or less evenly matched, and that the battles will prove very

---

^a F. Engels, 'What Have the Working Classes to Do with Poland?' - ^b for life

bloody. In any case, however, Benedek is a better general than Prince Frederick Charles, and unless Francis Joseph assists Benedek or Frederick Charles has some very good and influential staff officers, I believe the Prussians are in for a drubbing. Alone the braggery after Düppel [27] indicates that another Jena is possible. [203]

If the first battle ends in a decisive defeat for the Prussians, there will be nothing to stop the Austrians advancing on Berlin. If Prussia wins, she has not the power to launch and sustain an offensive to Vienna across the Danube, let alone to Pest and beyond. Austria is quite capable of imposing a peace on Prussia SINGLE-HANDED, although Prussia cannot do so on Austria. Every Prussian success would thus be an encouragement to Bonaparte to intervene. Furthermore, both the German swine will now already be seeking to outbid each other with offers of German territory to the third, French, swine.

Your
F. E.

First published in *Der Briefwechsel zwischen F. Engels und K. Marx*, Bd. 3, Stuttgart, 1913

Printed according to the original

Published in English for the first time

150

ENGELS TO MARX

IN MARGATE

Manchester, 6 April 1866

Dear Moor,

That the Russians are behind the Prussians at once struck me as very probable, too. The mere fact that the Austrian paper guilder is almost at par again and will thus have to be disturbed again, aroused suspicion, but the simultaneous Cuza affair [318] even more so, and *ce cher* [a] Bismarck would not have put out all his efforts if he did not have the Russians behind him. It is possible that things are so far committed already that neither Bismarck nor that old

---

[a] that dear

jackass William have a say in the matter any more and that it depends entirely on the whim of the St Petersburgers whether there shall be war or peace. How clumsily this Bismarck is acting, incidentally. It is too absurd how he tries to represent the poor Austrians as the attacking party. Even more splendid, however, is the fact that the fellow is seriously thinking of convening a German parliament *on 1 June* to reform the federal constitution. This is to be a remedy against the smaller states: he—*lui* Bismarck[a]—is appealing to the people instead of to the governments. That even called forth universal derisive laughter from the German philistines.[316]

After the upheaval that has occurred on *The Commonwealth*,[b] by the way, I was no longer able to get the said articles[c] to the editors on time, as they would have had to take the roundabout route via Margate, so I am sending them to you for the next number. I found the relevant data on the emancipation of the Russian serfs in an article by Mazade, *Revue des II Mondes*.[d]

And how is your health now? You haven't had any further carbuncles or small furuncles? And how are you otherwise, are you building yourself up? Are you still visiting old '*Cantuar*'[e] *per pedes*[f]? The arsenic must be taken for at least 3 months, and will not do you the slightest harm anyway.

Otherwise, there is nothing new here except for a foul east wind and clouds of dust.

How much longer are you thinking of staying in Margate? At least until the end of this month, I hope?

Reform movement—general admission of general indolence. What a tiny INSTALMENT![315]

Your
F. E.

First published in *Der Briefwechsel zwischen F. Engels und K. Marx*, Bd. 3, Stuttgart, 1913

Printed according to the original

Published in English for the first time

---

[a] Bismarck of all people - [b] See this volume, pp. 252-54. - [c] F. Engels, 'What Have the Working Classes to Do with Poland?' - [d] 'La Russie sous l'empereur Alexandre II.—La société et le gouvernement russes depuis l'insurrection polonaise', *Revue des deux Mondes*, Vol. 62, 15 March 1866. - [e] the Archbishop of Canterbury - [f] on foot (see this volume, p. 249).

151

MARX TO ENGELS [33]

IN MANCHESTER

Margate, 6 April 1866
5 Lansell's Place

DEAR FRED,

I have been greatly restored here, and not the smallest sign of a return of the atrocious carbuncles. The spot where the last and most malignant one was still feels a little tender. Perhaps it healed too quickly and an atom of pus is still lurking beneath the healed skin. However, if that were so, the warm sea bathes and the rough towel that I dry myself with would no doubt have dissipated the foul matter; and indeed in the last two days this vestige of the wound seems to be disappearing altogether. The only drawback is a recurrence here of rheumatic pains in my right shoulder, which is seriously disturbing my sleep. I have now been here for nearly 4 weeks and have lived for my health's sake alone. It is time to put a stop to that soon.

Our letters crossed, so that you have answered mine. You do not mention the possibility of Italy creating a diversion for Prussia's benefit.

There can be no shadow of doubt that Russia is behind the Prussians, although she is allowing Mr Bonaparte to act as arbiter on the stage. One must not lose sight of the fact (to use a Hegelian turn of phrase) that the DANUBIAN MINE [318] WAS SPRUNG at the very moment that Bismarck made his démarche. [316]

Even granted, which is probable, that the Prussian curs withdraw with their tails between their legs, it remains clear, and must become clear even to the German philistines, that *unless there is a revolution* in Germany, the Hohenzollern and Habsburg curs will throw our country back for another 50-100 years by civil (dynastic) war.

I must tell you frankly that the 'INTERNATIONAL' is in a sorry state, particularly since the impatience of the French has led to the congress being fixed for the *end of May*. [286]

THE FACT IS THIS, that the English LEADERS in London, now that we have given them a platform (to which must be added the inability of any Englishman to do two things at once), are very *cool* within our MOVEMENT proper. My absence for almost 3 months has done *untold harm.* **What is to be done?** In France, Belgium, Switzerland (and here and there in Germany, and even sporadically in America) the Association has made great and sustained progress. In England, the reform movement, which we brought into being, has almost KILLED us. That would be of no consequence, if the Geneva Congress had not been announced for the end of May, and if the Parisians, for whom this movement is *the sole possibility,* had not, through their own paper *Le Congrès,* made it almost impossible to prorogue the congress.[319] The English would soon see the rottenness of the REFORM MOVEMENT, as it now is. After my return the threat of flirtation with the Potter-clique, etc., would soon put everything back on the right lines. But THERE IS NO TIME. For the English even the FAILURE of the congress is a trifle. But for us? *A fiasco of European dimensions!!* I really do see scarcely a way out. The English have neglected to do anything which might give the congress any kind of respectable form. *Que faire!*[a] Do you think I *should go to Paris* to put to the people there how *impossible* the congress now is? Answer soon. The only possible way out I can see is by agreement with the Parisians. On the other hand, I know that their position itself is at stake if the congress does not take place. *Que faire!* Mr *Vésinier* has *challenged* our Parisians. They are to go to Belgium to shoot it out with him. *L'imbécile.* As TO Orsini, I knew that there was nothing you could do. But I could not refuse him the introduction to you.[b]

Your

K. M.

First published in *Der Briefwechsel zwischen F. Engels und K. Marx,* Bd. 3, Stuttgart, 1913

Printed according to the original

Published in English in full for the first time

152

ENGELS TO HERMANN ENGELS

IN BARMEN

Manchester, 6 April 1866

Dear Hermann,

Best thanks for your statement of account for 27 March, which appears to be in order by and large. The only thing is, it is hard to

---

[a] What is to be done? - [b] See this volume, p. 255.

check the interest if it is not given in detail as in other statements, and one just has to take the 'interest-account' at its word. But then, on 31 December 1865, you credit me with the transfer of 2,112,21.8 talers from Ermen & Engels, Barmen, whilst according to E. & E., Barmen's statement, the same transfer amounts to £316.18.2 and à $^6/_{20}$ makes 2,169.1.8 talers. I can make no sense of that.

It is rather awkward that you make up your accounts on 31 December, whereas we do so on 30 June. I shall therefore only send you a statement once, on 31 December, which will thus never coincide with yours, but in the end it will make no odds.

To keep our entries clear, I would be glad if you would enter all *business items* from E. & E. under E. & E., Barmen, and all *private items* under F. Engels & Co.

I passed the information on the agent Brown straight on to Fr. Boelling; Karth wrote to us about a different matter.

I do *not* advise you to obtain your SEWINGS through us as a rule, G. Ermen will always try to palm off his yarn from Pendlebury on you, and that would surely not always be in your interest. Besides, he would at once claim payment of 2% commission from you as the business expands. But if you can make use of his yarn (and why not, since we can use it?), you had best apply to us. I am today posting you a sample of No. 16, of which he has 120 BALES [at] 10 pounds, 7 LEAS in stock, and would take 2 [s.] $^1/_2$ d. per No. 16, perhaps even less. You can also obtain the same yarn from the broker F. A. Schmits. Fine Nos. and COPS, on the other hand, in which G. Ermen has no interest we can always supply you with.

How much does the hock cost? That is what really matters. And how much of it is there? You should have sent 3 dozen bottles straightaway, instead of 3.

I shall ask around about the PONIES. Good, strong COBS, however, are at the moment much sought after here, and expensive, and bargains—a good pair in one lot—not easily come by.

You don't think there'll be war either? It would be a terrible business if it came to that, and there is no telling where it would end. Recently, when the affair first started, I dreamed that I had got mixed up with an enormously large army somewhere on the Mosel. They were volunteers of some description, all manner of fellows dashing about full of self-importance, and now and again someone would shout, 'We're surrounded!'—at which they all took to their heels. At length, I found my way into the headquarters and encountered Peter and Gottfried Ermen there as GENERALS *en chef,* and Anton[a] as chief-of-staff. Now I asked him a few questions, but received such bizarre replies that I finally asked him whether he did actually have maps of the area where he was? At which he looked down at me from a great height and said, 'Maps? We do everything here much better without maps.' When I tried to explain to him that he really could not manage without maps, nor even find quarters for his men, etc., he answered, 'If absolutely necessary, we do have some maps', and, with a look of triumph, he pulled a map of a quite different area, the other side of Aachen and Maastricht, out of his pocket. Don't imagine I have just made this up as a bad joke, that is literally how it happened.

Kindest regards to Mother[b]—I'll write to her one of these days—and to all our brothers and sisters.

Your
Friedrich

First published abridged in the *Deutsche Revue,* Jg. 46, Bd. II, 1921 and in full in: Marx and Engels, *Works,* First Russian Edition, Vol. XXV, Moscow, 1934

Printed according to the original

Published in English for the first time

153

MARX TO WILHELM LIEBKNECHT

IN LEIPZIG

Margate, 6 April 1866
5 Lansell's Place

My dear Miller,[c]

You see from the address that I have been banished to the seaside by my medical adviser.[307]

After having received your last letter, and some letters on the part of our Berlin friends,[d] my sickness assumed a really dangerous character. For some time it was very doubtful whether or not that decomposition of the blood, under which I labour, should get the better of me. It was only towards the middle of March that I was bodily enabled to remove myself to this place. I

---

[a] Anton Ermen - [b] Elisabeth Engels - [c] Liebknecht's conspiratorial pseudonym - [d] August Vogt, Sigfrid Meyer and Theodor Metzner

am now restored, and shall very soon return to London. But again a quarter of a year has been lost!

Write me immediately under my London address.

After my return, I shall regularly send you *The Commonwealth* (under which altered title *The Workman's Advocate* is now published).[290] It is only since a few weeks that it has been registered for Transmission for abroad. Eccarius is no longer the editor, but only a contributor. It was to be foreseen, that so soon as the paper should get some sort of standing, a Foreigner would not be allowed to retain the nominal leadership.[a]

Write me

1) about the state of 'our' movement in Germany,
2) about the state of German politics.

Yours truly
K. M.

My best compliments to Madame.[b]

First published in: Marx and Engels, *Works,* First Russian Edition, Vol. XXIX, Moscow, 1946 and in the language of the original, English, in: *Wilhelm Liebknecht. Briefwechsel mit Karl Marx und Friedrich Engels,* The Hague, 1963

Reproduced from the original

154

MARX TO LUDWIG KUGELMANN[65]

IN HANOVER

Margate, 6 April 1866
5 Lansell's Place

Dear Friend,

I shall return to London from here the day after tomorrow. My doctor banished me to this seaside place, where I am indeed *much recovered.* But another two months and more—February, March and half of April have thus been entirely lost to me again, and the completion of my book[c] put back once more! It is enough to drive one out of one's mind.

---

[a] See this volume, pp. 252-53. - [b] Ernestine Liebknecht - [c] *Capital*

I was suffering from CARBUNCLES, not furuncles. It was a dangerous business this time. You are, of course, right that 'dietetic' sins lay behind it. I am too accustomed to working at night, studying by day and writing by night. That, together with all manner of worries, private and public, and—whenever I am immersed in work—neglect of regular diet, exercise, etc., is quite enough to upset the blood.

I received Mr Menke's contribution of 10 talers for the 'International' with your letter.[a] I have not got the addresses of my French friends in Paris here. However, if Mr Menke approaches my friend K. Kaub (33, Rue des trois Couronnes du Temple), the latter can introduce him to V. Schily (German) and Tolain, Fribourg, etc., the people on the Paris Committee.

The news from Germany is rather depressing.[316] Prussia is being egged on by Russia (and Bonaparte), Austria by the latter (following on rather reluctantly, in self-defence). Will our philistines at last realise that, unless there is a revolution to remove the Habsburgs and Hohenzollerns (it being superfluous to mention the lesser dung-beetles), another Thirty Years' War[320] and another partition of Germany are ultimately inevitable!

A movement on the part of the Italians might help Prussia. But just considering Austria and Prussia on their own, the latter would almost certainly be at a disadvantage, for all their bragging about Düppel.[27] At all events, Benedek is a better General than Prince Frederick Charles. Austria might well impose a peace on Prussia SINGLE-HANDED, but Prussia cannot do so on Austria. Any Prussian success would be an encouragement to Bonaparte to interfere.

Bismarck may perhaps have already drawn in his horns again as I write these lines to you. But that, too, would only delay the conflict. Such a delay is probable in my opinion.

This turmoil in Germany is an extraordinary piece of luck for Bonaparte. His position is completely undermined. But war would give him a new lease of life.

Write to me soon, and in particular about the situation in Germany.

Yours

K. M.

First published abridged in *Die Neue Zeit*, Bd. 2, Nr. 2, Stuttgart, 1901-1902 and in full in *Pisma Marksa k Kugelmanu* (Letters of Marx to Kugelmann), Moscow-Leningrad, 1928   Printed according to the original

---

[a] of 30 March 1866

155

ENGELS TO MARX

IN MARGATE

Manchester, 10 April 1866

Dear Moor,

To all appearances, the Russians *want* war, their purpose seeming to be restoration of Poland under Russian rule and possibly annexation of Moldavia. The *Kölnische Zeitung*, which is, of course, in mortal fear of war, has sent J. von Wickede, its military man, to Bohemia, to inspect what is claimed to be Austria's state of armament. The fellow arrives—on 3 April, that is 14 days after Bismarck's note[316]—and everywhere finds things on a profoundly pacific footing, except that some *Bohemian* regiments have been transferred to their western districts, so that they can put themselves on a war footing more quickly. No soldiers recalled from leave, no fortress armed. Nothing.[a] The whole disgraceful affair thus *deliberately provoked by Bismarck.*

Furthermore: the Russians are concentrating troops on the Austrian and on the *Prussian* frontier with Poland, and the soldiers are saying quite openly that those who are positioned on the Prussian frontier will shortly occupy *Posen* as soon as the Prussian troops take the field against the Austrians. Apart from the fact that the Russians would thereby secure the rest of Prussian Poland for themselves immediately, their mission will also be to suppress any revolutionary movements in Berlin. However, that would in all probability be a miscalculation and, at any rate, disqualify the Hohenzollerns for the future.

Finally, today's LEADER in *The Times* which comes down stupidly, mendaciously, woodenly but decisively on Prussia's side and represents Austria as the attacking party. That was written to order.[b]

In view of all this, war seems to me certain; the situation within Germany also makes it inevitable, following the new Austrian note appealing to the Confederation, as well as Monsieur Bismarck's proposal regarding a German parliament[321]—what a dunderhead the fellow must be to believe that that would assist him even in the

---

[a] Engels refers to the report 'Die Lage, Köln, 7. April', *Kölnische Zeitung*, 8 April 1866. - [b] *The Times*, No. 25468, 10 April 1866, leader.

very slightest! The Austrian note seems to be based on the assumption that the storm will break after all. Otherwise they would at least have left the back-door open to facilitate the Prussians' retreat through Bismarck's resignation. But the moment that they appeal to the Confederation, that's an end to it; another ministry in Prussia would not submit to a Confederation majority either.

Bonaparte will probably keep quiet, at least for the time being; Bismarck has already offered him Saarbrücken, etc., and, if need be, he would also make him a present of the Bavarian Palatinate. If he sees the Russians committed on the Prussian side, he won't risk anything rash.

If the storm really does break, for the first time in history the course of events will depend on the attitude taken by Berlin. If the Berliners hit out at the right time, things may turn out well—but who can rely on *them*?

As regards the congress of the International, I don't properly see how you can hope to avoid it.[a] Nor do I see how a further postponement would improve things much. *Après tout,*[b] any demonstration of that kind would in a certain sense—at least as far as we ourselves are concerned—always be a fiasco. But in full view of Europe? I believe that could still be avoided even now. After all, the Germans with their polyglot capacities would have the whole thing under their control, and it is precisely the Germans who are on our side. Whether the congress *decides* anything useful is a secondary matter, as long as all scandal can be avoided; and that surely will now be the case. General resolutions of a theoretical kind or referring to international support for strikes, etc., can surely be passed without any danger. Nevertheless, you must know that better than I, I cannot really judge of it from here. Meanwhile, I would definitely not go to Paris about it. You have no one to protect you, and the police will have no qualms about striking—emissary from a public workers' association with distinctly revolutionary tendencies, which can easily be used to conceal other clandestine matters— *cela suffit.*[c] The whole business is just not worth the risk.

You would do much better to stay in Margate until the last scar is no longer in the slightest degree susceptible, and do plenty of walking in the fresh air. Who knows how soon you will once more have need of a stout constitution. The atmosphere is highly electric, and we shall perhaps soon be in the midst of the storm

---

[a] See this volume, pp. 258-59. - [b] After all - [c] that will suffice

again; that will no doubt also help resolve the difficulty with the congress.

I shall be letting you have a bit of money as soon as I can. I shall also try and see Gumpert and ask him about terminating the sea-cure and what you should do afterwards about the arsenic.

Your

F. E.

First published in *Der Briefwechsel zwischen F. Engels und K. Marx*, Bd. 3, Stuttgart, 1913

Printed according to the original

Published in English for the first time

156

ENGELS TO MARX [101]

IN MARGATE

[Manchester,] 13 April 1866

Dear Moor,

As I do not exactly know whether you are in Margate at the moment, I am today sending your wife

E/R 13430, Manchester, 21 January 1865 £10

E/P 43331, Manchester, 20 January 1865 £10-£20

and am telling her that I have informed you of it.

So, Bismarck has executed his *suffrage universel coup*,[321] even though without his Lassalle. It would appear that, after some show of reluctance, the German bourgeois will go along with it, for Bonapartism really is the true religion of the modern bourgeoisie. It is becoming increasingly clear to me that the bourgeoisie does not possess the qualities required to rule directly itself, and that therefore, unless there is an oligarchy as here in England capable of taking over, for good pay, the management of state and society in the interest of the bourgeoisie, a Bonapartist semi-dictatorship is the normal form; it promotes the great material interests of the bourgeoisie even against the bourgeoisie, but allows it no share in the government itself. Conversely, this dictatorship itself is in turn compelled unwillingly to adopt these material interests of the bourgeoisie. So, now we have Monsieur Bismarck adopting the programme of the National Association.[152] Its execution is admittedly quite another matter, but Bismarck will scarcely be baulked by the German bourgeois. A German, who has just returned from there, reports that he has already encountered many who have nibbled at this bait; according to Reuter (*vide*[a] below), the people in Karlsruhe have approved of the matter, and the *Kölnische Zeitung*'s unbounded embarrassment over the affair is a clear indication of a forthcoming change of course.

That Bismarck has direct agreements with the Russians, however, is once more proved firstly by the fact that not only *The Times* but *Reuter*, too, is beginning to lie on Prussia's behalf, in complete contrast to their usual custom. There is a method in the mistranslations with which the telegrams are now infested more than ever. Until a short while ago, *against* Prussia. Now against Austria. Reuter telegraphs: Austria would only go along with the plan if *all* the Austrian provinces (that is, including the *non-German* ones) were represented.[b] In the German original it merely says: conditional upon the regions of Austria being represented, too.—Further: according to the *Bromberger Zeitung* and the *Ostsee-Zeitung* (the latter is a Russian organ), the Russians are continuing to gather more troops in the south-western provinces, from the Kingdom of Poland[322] to the Prut, doing so very slowly and unobtrusively; the soldiers are *all* expecting to move with Prussia against Austria, and those on the Warta repeat that their role is to occupy Posen so that the Prussians there can march away.

The Russians can, incidentally, leave Schleswig-Holstein to the Prussians for the time being, as the Peace of Vienna and the annexation have, after all, saved the main issue for them: the Treaty of London and thereby the succession in *Denmark*.[323] If they have the Sound,[c] what does Kiel signify to them?

At all events, your best course is to stay in Margate until you no longer feel *anything at all* in the affected part, and you are in general convinced of a marked turn for the better.

Write soon.

Your
F. E.

First published in *Der Briefwechsel zwischen F. Engels und K. Marx*, Bd. 3, Stuttgart, 1913

Printed according to the original

Published in English in full for the first time

---

[a] see - [b] 'Austria and Prussia. Berlin, April 10', *The Times*, No. 25469, 11 April 1866 (Reuter's telegram reporting on Austria's reaction to Bismarck's proposition for the assembly of a German parliament for the reorganisation of the German Confederation). - [c] Danish name: Øresund

11*

157

MARX TO ENGELS [324]

IN MANCHESTER

[London,] 23 April 1866

Dear FRED,

You will have had little difficulty in explaining my long silence as arising from the mental condition that is generated by more than 2 weeks of incessant toothache and rheumatism. However, a turning-point appears to have been reached today.

As the pain of the rheumatism, which was particularly acute at night, greatly interfered with my sleep and my whole domestic routine—as a consequence of which I was several times attacked by vomiting—I thought it wise to stop, or suspend, the arsenic. But I shall continue with it again now (if a turning-point has really been reached). Nor is there the slightest sign of any furuncular or carbuncular bother, and I have not the slightest doubt that once I am over these INCIDENTS, which are connected more with the weather, I shall be fully restored. But indeed it is high time as I have already lost so much time.

With the 'INTERNATIONAL' the situation is as follows: since my return [307] discipline has by and large been re-established. The successful intervention of the 'INTERNATIONAL' in the tailors' strike (by means of letters from the secretaries for France, Belgium, etc.) has also created a sensation among the TRADES UNIONS here. [325] With respect to the Geneva Congress, I have resolved to do all that I can here to promote its success, but not to attend it in person. I thereby evade all personal responsibility for its conduct. [a]

As far as *The Commonwealth* is concerned, the ENCROACHMENTS of Miall *et* Co. would be more tolerable if they were at least founded on the pretext of financial assistance really worthy of mention. But the fellows are exceedingly liberal with good advice and petty criticisms, and exceedingly parsimonious with CASH, so that the existence of the paper is assured only from one week to the next. Its readership is spreading week by week, but a PENNY PAPER, be it ever so successful, needs to be funded for at least a year ahead. To make it SELF-SUPPORTING in a shorter space of time is QUITE OUT OF THE QUESTION. If the paper is for the moment no worse than it is,

---

[a] See this volume, pp. 325-27.

then that is thanks to Fox alone, who has to fight a continuing battle.

For the present, they do not seem to be coming to blows in the Fatherland after all. Prussian braggadocio is slow indeed to draw the sword! Whatever the outcome, we shall have the pleasure of a Prussian disgrace before both a domestic and foreign audience. For all that, it still seems uncertain whether war might not break out one fine morning. The Russians want war (although they have indeed already gained and are continuing to gain much merely from the bickering and bellicose threats in Germany), and for Bonaparte it would be a GODSEND. At all events, Mr Bismarck has set 'the movement' going again in Germany.

The phase of the Civil War [11] over, only now have the UNITED STATES really entered the revolutionary phase, and the European WISEACRES who believe in the omnipotence of Mr Johnson will soon be disappointed.

In England, the Tories and Palmerstonian Whigs really deserve thanks for frustrating Russell's quiet SETTLEMENT. [326] At one of the latest sittings, Mr Gladstone himself, expressed his 'melancholy' conviction that now, quite contrary to his benevolent expectations, a 'long series of struggles' was imminent.

What do you say to the '8th' sage of the world—*Mill*? [a]

Best regards to Mrs Lizzy. [b]

Tout à vous [c]

K. M.

First published in *Der Briefwechsel zwischen F. Engels und K. Marx*, Bd. 3, Stuttgart, 1913

Printed according to the original

Published in English in full for the first time

158

ENGELS TO MARX [26]

IN LONDON

Manchester, 1 May 1866

Dear Moor,

I hope you are happily over your rheumatism and faceache and are once more sitting diligently over the *book*. [d] How is it coming

---

[a] Marx presumably refers to J. S. Mill's speech in Parliament of 17 April 1866 in which he urged the duty of paying off the national debt before Britain's coal supplies exhausted. See *The Times*, No. 25475, 18 April 1866. - [b] Lizzy Burns - [c] Entirely yours - [d] *Capital*

on, and when will the first volume be ready? By the by, you must go on with the arsenic, it should be taken for at least 3 months and is quite unconnected with the rheumatism, etc. The liver troubles may have been a factor contributing to the carbuncles, by disturbing the digestion or blood-formation, and, for that very reason, you will also have to go on taking several hours continuous exercise regularly each day and keep off working at night, so that everything can return to normal. Where the tendency to hyperaemia of the liver has established itself in such a classic and systematic form as in your case, it does not, of course, just vanish again all at once.

It's good that you have no more worries about the congress and the INTERNATIONAL ASSOCIATION. Apropos, a shipload of *57 German tailors* has been imported to Edinburgh TO PUT DOWN A STRIKE and 2 more loads are expected. Probably from Hamburg. Can you not discover the details in Edinburgh and put a stop to this, too?[327]

Bismarck *wants* war *à tout prix*,[a] and after he failed in Bohemia, he seems likely to succeed in Italy.[328] I hope that, if he pulls it off, the Berliners will hit out. If they proclaim a republic there, the whole of Europe can be overturned in 14 days. But, but, will they? How do our connections there stand?

Have you seen how little Louis Blanc, as a good *démocrate impérial*, is now declaring in the *Temps* that, if Prussia absorbs the smaller German states, France must have *at least* the left bank of the Rhine.[b] There's a real revolutionary for you.

In order to incite my ancient rage somewhat, in the last few days I have been reading the book by Röckel, the 49er imprisoned in Dresden, about his treatment in gaol.[c] These infamies perpetrated by the Saxons exceed everything that I have ever come across. There will be a harsh reckoning to be had with a large number of villains. Such brutality was quite unknown in the old days *before* '48, and the Prussian fortresses of that time seem like paradise in comparison.

These Adullamites really are tremendous jackasses to put up such resistance to this *pauvre*[d] REFORM BILL, the most conservative thing that has ever been done here.[326] However, *quem deus vult perdere*,[e] etc.

I already sent my third article on Poland[f] to *The Commonwealth* 3 weeks ago and asked for it to be returned if it should be too late

---

[a] at any price - [b] L. Blanc, 'Lettres de Londres', *Le Temps*, No. 1815, 23 April 1866. - [c] A. Röckel, *Sachsens Erhebung und das Zuchthaus zu Waldheim.* - [d] poor - [e] *quem deus vult perdere, prius dementat*: whom God wishes to destroy, he first makes mad - [f] F. Engels, 'What Have the Working Classes to Do with Poland?'

for *that* week. I then received a reply from Fox a week later that it could not appear until the *forthcoming* issue, returning the article at the same time. Sent it off again on Wednesday, but too late. You were still in Margate at that time. I will send the following Nos. to you again if time does not make immediate, direct submission necessary.

Kind regards to your wife and the girls.

Your

F. E.

First published in *Der Briefwechsel zwischen F. Engels und K. Marx*, Bd. 3, Stuttgart, 1913

Printed according to the original

Published in English in full for the first time

159

MARX TO WILHELM LIEBKNECHT

IN LEIPZIG[a]

[London,] 4 May 1866

My dear Friend,

As I am at this moment, after so long an interruption of work,[b] very busily engaged in making up for lost time, you will excuse me for writing this time only a few lines.

I shall send you to-day the last number of *The Commonwealth*. The financial position of the paper is such that it struggles from week to week and is altogether disabled from paying one farthing for Foreign Correspondence. Its circulation is increasing, but you know that a penny paper wants at least 20,000 subscribers, and cannot even then make the two ends meet without a goodly number of advertisements. *The Commonwealth* is of too recent an origin to come up to those requisites.

The Congress at Geneva has been postponed for the 3d of September next.[286] The society is rapidly spreading, particularly in France. Italian societies have also recently joined.[c] The propagan-

---

[a] The letter bears the stamp: International Working Men's Association / Central Council / London. - [b] on *Capital* - [c] See this volume, p. 47.

da in London has taken a new start, principally due to the circumstance that the successful strikes of the London tailors and wireworkers were due to our intervention which prevented the import of workingmen from France, Switzerland, Belgium, which had been contemplated by the masters. This proof of its immediate practical importance has struck the practical English mind.[329]

For the same purpose you find, on the last page of this letter, an 'avis'[a] to the German tailors which I call upon you to have inserted in such German papers as you have access to.[327] At the same time you will oblige me by sending me a copy or two of some papers in which the 'avis' will have been inserted, telling me at the same time the names of all other papers that should have reprinted it. Kugelmann might also be useful for this purpose.

My best compliments to Mrs. Liebknecht.[b] I feel exceedingly thankful for her friendly interest in my welfare.

Yours fraternally

A. Williams[c]

First published in: Marx and Engels, *Works*, First Russian Edition, Vol. XXIX, Moscow, 1946 and in the language of the original, English, in: *Wilhelm Liebknecht. Briefwechsel mit Karl Marx und Friedrich Engels*, The Hague, 1963

Reproduced from the original

160

ENGELS TO MARX

IN LONDON

Manchester, 9 May 1866

Dear Moor,

I am becoming concerned at your silence, I almost fear your health is not what it should be. You have not got carbuncles again?

What is this strange business of Cohen the blind,[d] who cannot hit the tall Bismarck with five shots and gets himself arrested by

---

[a] 'warning'. Marx means his article 'A Warning'. - [b] Ernestine Liebknecht - [c] Marx's conspiratorial pseudonym - [d] Engels makes a pun here: the German word *blind* means without sight, blind; *Blind*—the name of Cohen's stepfather.

him into the bargain. He could have done Bismarck no greater favour.[330]

IT STRIKES ME that the Prussians are 14 days behind the Austrians with their mobilisation and cannot attack before the end of this inst. If the Austrians take advantage of this, they may win a big battle and be in Berlin before the Prussians have concentrated.

Your

F. E.

First published in *Der Briefwechsel zwischen F. Engels und K. Marx,* Bd. 3, Stuttgart, 1913

Printed according to the original

Published in English for the first time

161

MARX TO ENGELS

IN MANCHESTER

[London,] 10 May 1866

Dear FRED,

No CARBUNCLES WHATEVER! But the accursed rheumatism and toothache have tormented me cruelly, until the former at last seems to be yielding to embrocation with pure alcohol. I must tell you candidly as well that my mind still feels somewhat *weak* and my capacity for work is only returning *very gradually.* Perhaps that can be attributed to the interruption in the arsenic treatment, which I started again after your last letter.

Cohen[330] was a very good lad (although not particularly gifted) for whom I have a special regard as he was an old friend of my Musch.[a] Freiligrath naturally dashed straight to Blind yesterday and came to us from him. I was not at home. Freiligrath's chief lament was the bad name Blind was giving him and others (nominal contributors to the *Eidgenosse,*[b] whose symbol is a hand holding a dagger with the motto *'haec manus tyrannis',*[c] etc.). He

---

[a] Marx's deceased son Edgar - [b] *Der deutsche Eidgenosse* - [c] *'manus haec inimica tyrannis'*—'this hand is hostile to tyrants' (an expression from *The Life and Memoirs of Algernon Sidney*)

said he had not visited him for 9 months and that the affair was not even 'excusable'. In short, he was in fact only upset about the possible impression the affair might make on the London philistines. By the by, our trickster from Baden duped him nicely again. He played the broken man and gave his friend Freiligrath no inkling that in the first throes of grief he had the presence of mind to exploit the tragic incident for some good advertising for himself and family in the various London papers. Always an eye to business. His wife[a] is naturally inconsolable, and the funny thing about the affair is that Blind has by his idiotic regicidal blether sacrificed not his own son, but old Cohen's Isaac,[b] on the altar of freedom.

In consequence of their sad experiences in 1859[331] the Austrians are in the accursed situation of being scarcely capable of grasping the favourable moment, and although they have been forcibly presented with the *initiative*, they cannot seize it, or at least they will hesitate greatly before doing so. Of course, European 'public opinion' benefits them not a tittle and requires something silly of them. These same liberal jackasses, who are now generally admitting that Austria is the challenged party and that there is a systematic conspiracy against her, would tomorrow (the English lords included) scream with one voice if Austria were to strike the first blow and did not wait quietly for her enemies to give the signal.

Repugnant though Bonaparte is to me, his coup in Auxerre did uncommonly amuse me.[332] That old jackass Thiers and the *chiens savants*[c] of the Corps législatif,[4] who applauded him, fancied they would be allowed to play with Louis-Philippism unpunished! *Les imbéciles!*

The Russians as always are playing their part to a T. Having encouraged their worthy Prussians, they enter on the scene as men of peace and arbiters of Europe, but were, at the same time, canny enough to inform Mr Bonaparte that Poland could not, of course, be on the agenda at any congress, in short, that Russia was entitled to meddle in European, but not Europe in Russian affairs.

Following upon the importation of German and Danish tailors to Edinburgh, we have 1. sent a German and a Dane[d] (both tailors themselves) to Edinburgh, and they have already put an end to the understanding between importers and imported; 2. I have put out a warning in the name of the International Association to the

---

[a] Friederike Blind - [b] An allusion to the Biblical legend about Abraham who sacrificed his son Isaac (Genesis 22:9). - [c] scholarly dogs - [d] Albert F. Haufe and N. P. Hansen

German tailors in Germany.[a] The affair has been extraordinarily useful to us in London.[327]

A very disagreeable matter for me was the necessity of paying a lump sum of £25 for school fees. This money, for 3 quarters, could no longer be put off as Jenny and Laura are leaving the school, the latter taking no lessons at all, and the former only one music lesson a week now *outside* school. (Baumer has resigned from the school, you know.)

The Commonwealth is rapidly going from strength to strength and would certainly be PAYING within the space of a year. But it is probable that we shall soon have to suspend it for lack of money.

Salut.

Your
K. M.

First published in *Der Briefwechsel zwischen F. Engels und K. Marx*, Bd. 3, Stuttgart, 1913

Printed according to the original

Published in English for the first time

162

ENGELS TO MARX

IN LONDON

Manchester, 16 May 1866

Dear Moor,

The Freiligrath affair is very amusing and very gratifying. That's what comes of him attaching himself to the respectable people among the émigrés and renouncing the 'party'. As regards Blind, the fitting cry in respect of his: *manus haec inimica tyrranis*[b] should be that children ought not to play with guns. It is incidentally quite clear from the affair that Bismarck wears an armoured shirt.[330] The shots must all have hit him, the last 3 are admitted to have been direct hits, and as the revolver was so designed that it could not be fired in contact with the target, there is just no other possibility. They make these things very fine and

---

[a] K. Marx, 'A Warning' - [b] this hand is hostile to tyrants (see this volume, p. 273)

yet strong nowadays. His friend Bonaparte will no doubt have supplied him with one and recommended it to him.

Monsieur Bismarck has obviously been gravely disappointed in the smaller states, *hinc*[a] the threat of an imperial constitution and Bennigsen. There must also have been some financial mishaps. But can one conceive of anything more comical than that the same William, who as top general in the year 1849 bore the imperial constitution to its grave, now wants to resuscitate it, or rather has to. Bismarck as restorer of the 'German fundamental rights',[333] it's too funny. Things are not looking quite as they should in the militia and in the reserves, who have been recalled, either; in Görlitz there was a serious fracas amongst them, soldiers of the line had to be called out and then withdraw because the fellows were not willing to tolerate intervention of that kind. If these people are kept hanging around under arms for another 3-4 weeks, there is no knowing what they might do. And since neither Prussia nor Italy is ready to attack, they will presumably have to stick there until the end of May at least.

This much is certain: Monsieur Bismarck has ridden into a morass with which neither he nor any of the present regime can cope. If things are settled peaceably, he will have burnt up the available funds and therefore he will no longer be able to help himself, and if there is war, he will have to *Acheronta movere,*[b] who will certainly consume him. In these circumstances, even a direct victory of the Chamber-burghers will be revolutionary in character and is bound to lead to other things.

For all that, I still cannot think that in the middle of the 19th century North and South Germany will come to blows with each other, just because Bismarck would have it so in the interests of the Russians and Bonaparte. However, if the storm does break, it may go ill with the Prussians. This time, the Austrians seem to be intent on going to the limit of their strength, and, even if their big talk of 900,000 men is nonsense, it is still possible that they may take the field in Saxony with substantial numerical superiority. Against Austria, Prussia cannot draw on the Rhenish and Westphalian corps at all, and only on part of the Saxon. There remain the other six army corps, which will scarcely be able to muster 240,000 men to face the enemy. If, as is suggested, the Austrians initially remain on the defensive in Italy, they will only need 150,000 men there, and can perfectly well send 300-350,000 men against Prussia—unless the Russians compel them to keep a

---

a hence - b call the powers of the underworld to his aid (Virgil, *Aeneid,* VII, 312).

strong force in Galicia. The deciding battle could then be fought by 180,000 Prussians against 240-280,000 Austrians and would almost infallibly be another Jena [203] and lead directly to Berlin. But it is difficult to speculate about this, as the Austrians' troops are always much stronger on paper, and they tell a lot of lies, at present in particular.

Unfortunately, Monsieur Charles[a] is behind with the ledger, which has my account in it, so that at the moment I cannot even properly ascertain how I stand, and as the financial year ends in 6 weeks and I then must have a certain amount of capital in the business, I shall have to make my dispositions accordingly. As soon as I can, I shall add up my worldly assets and send you some money, if it is at all possible. But, at all events, you can count on my letting you have a £50 early in July immediately after the accounts for the financial year have been made up.

The *Kreuz-Zeitung*[b] makes delightful reading, advocating as it does universal suffrage, Bonapartism, Victor Emmanuel, etc. The dirt *those* fellows are now being obliged to eat is abundant.

Kindest regards to your wife and the girls.

Your
F. E.

First published in *Der Briefwechsel zwischen F. Engels und K. Marx*, Bd. 3, Stuttgart, 1913

Printed according to the original

Published in English for the first time

163

MARX TO ENGELS [33]

IN MANCHESTER

[London,] 17 May 1866

Dear Fred,

How are the *articles on Poland*[c] progressing? The paper[d] may or may not hold out, you must give as much as you can. The Poles

---

a Charles Roesgen - b *Neue Preussische Zeitung* - c F. Engels, 'What Have the Working Classes to Do with Poland?' - d *The Commonwealth*

here are waiting for the next article and BOTHER ME with enquiries.[334] The articles have created a stir in other respects, too. Having earlier praised them, *Foxikins* launched a DIATRIBE the day before yesterday in the Central Council against the passage in which you ascribe the partitioning to the corruption of the Polish aristocracy. Amongst other things, he singled out the Germans for attack, for having ruined the Poles in particular through the Saxon dynasty, etc. I replied to him in brief.[335]

It is true that for all their big talk the Prussians are inclined to draw in their horns, and Bismarck is meeting strong opposition from Burp,[a] too. But a retreat is scarcely possible in Italy, and that may have repercussions on Prussia again. What Izzy[b] is missing by being so dead! Bismarck would have had him playing a part now. Bismarck is surely cursing us (and thinking us Austrian agents) for spoiling his easy game with the workers.

From the beginning of this week my work[c] has at last been advancing again. If you can send me some *vino*, please do so, as the sudden abstinence may do harm.

Mr Mazzini gave himself no rest until he had founded an 'INTERNATIONAL REPUBLICAN COMMITTEE' in opposition to us. On it are jackass Holtorp, Langiewicz, Ledru, Kinkel, Blind, I believe also—Bolleter! Our Association is gaining ground daily. Only in Germany nothing can be done, on account of jackass Liebknecht (GOOD FELLOW AS HE IS!).

The present crisis appears to me to be merely a premature, specifically financial crisis. It could only become important if the business in the UNITED STATES goes rotten, and there would scarcely be time for that now. What effect is it having on you COTTONLORDS? And what effect has the fall in cotton prices had?

Salut.

Your
K. M.

First published in *Der Briefwechsel zwischen F. Engels und K. Marx*, Bd. 3, Stuttgart, 1913

Printed according to the original

Published in English in full for the first time

---

[a] William I - [b] Ferdinand Lassalle - [c] on *Capital*

164

ENGELS TO MARX

IN LONDON

[Manchester,] 25 May 1866
Mornington Street

Dear Moor,

The PANIC has, at all events, come much too soon and may possibly spoil a good solid crisis for us which would otherwise have occurred in 1867 or 1868. If we had not simultaneously chanced to have the big fall in cotton, we would barely have been affected by it here. The collapse of the LIMITED LIABILITY and FINANCING swindles had after all been long foreseen and hardly affected our TRADE at all. But the colossal losses on cotton which occurred simultaneously threaten to make it a grave matter here, so many houses here and in Liverpool are entangled in it through their branches in Bombay, etc., and as it occurred at the same time as the MONEY PANIC and the 10% bank-rate, it may be very grave for those who are holding much cotton. Here at least the business is far from over yet.

If the Austrians are canny enough not to attack, that will surely put the cat among the pigeons in the Prussian army. The fellows have never been as rebellious as they are in the present mobilisation. Unfortunately, one only learns the tiniest part of what is happening, but even that is enough to prove that a war of attack is impossible with this army. Once these lads are concentrated in large numbers, and begin to count themselves and discover that $^3/_4$ of the army is of one mind, and if they then have to hang around under arms for 3-4 weeks during the congress, things will inevitably lead to a crisis, and one fine morning obedience will be refused. Something is bound to spark it off; and with an army like that, once *one* battalion starts, it will spread like wildfire. But even if an open outbreak were to be avoided, it is certain that *this* army, with its MORALE as it is, and commanded by the old William, with Frederick Charles and the Crown Prince[a] under him commanding the wings, would at once be beaten beyond salvation by the furious Austrians under Benedek, who will have none of the Archdukes, nor any interference in the

---

[a] Frederick William

appointment of his staff, and has 300-360,000 men under him. The old jackass[a] knows that, too, and I am convinced that he will withdraw as soon as ever he can, precisely because of the mood in his armies. What I said in my pamphlet[b] last year about the character of the *mobilised* Prussian army, has been fully confirmed.

Delightful is the embarrassment of the National Association-ites[152] since Bismarck has plagiarised their programme; those fellows will now have to oppose their own Great-Prussia phrases, exactly as the *Kreuz-Zeitung*[c] did with its own feudal phrases.

The London correspondent of *The Manchester Guardian* reports that in this solemn performance of state[336] Louis Bonaparte has made the following conditions the price for his approval: Sardinia from Italy, Luxemburg, Saarlouis and Saarbrücken from Prussia (Landau is the only thing he has forgotten)—and that is the minimum.[d]

I shall see if I can complete my article on Poland[334] tomorrow. To be quite frank, it is a sacrifice for me to provide that jackass Miall with contributions when one is for ever being explicitly reminded that the editors do not accept responsibility for the section from contributors, whilst they obviously do so for the asininities printed elsewhere in the paper.[337] If I had known beforehand how our pieces were going to be treated in a paper[e] which is after all supposed to be our own—or at least to belong to the workers' party, and that we were merely going to be thus tolerated in it, and we are supposed to be grateful, as it were, into the bargain,—I would not have written a single line. But you were sick at the time, and I didn't want to do anything that might disturb your convalescence. But I was vexed by it nonetheless. All the same, one has said 'A' and must see that one also says 'B'.

Kindest regards.

Your
F. E.

First published in *Der Briefwechsel zwischen F. Engels und K. Marx*, Bd. 3, Stuttgart, 1913

Printed according to the original

Published in English for the first time

---

[a] William I - [b] F. Engels, *The Prussian Military Question and the German Workers' Party*. - [c] *Neue Preussische Zeitung* - [d] 'From our London correspondent', *The Manchester Guardian*, No. 6165, 22 May 1866. - [e] *The Commonwealth*

165

MARX TO ENGELS [103]

IN MANCHESTER

[London,] 7 June 1866

Dear Fred,

I am in a most awkward situation: pawning has now reached its Thule [a] and I am being most furiously dunned as well. Regarding my physical condition, there has fortunately been no recurrence of anything carbuncular. However, I was obliged to go to Allen about my liver throuble, since Gumpert is not here and this thing cannot be treated from a distance. I have still nearly a whole BOTTLE of arsenic left, but have not taken it for several weeks now, as it is incompatible with my present style of life.

Were you among the victims of the CONSOLIDATED BANK? Dr Rode was here the day before yesterday and maliciously reported that Dronke has suffered serious losses owing to the Barnett CRASH. [338]

So, there will be war after all, unless a miracle occurs. The Prussians will pay dearly for their bragging, and, whatever happens, the idyll in Germany is over. The Proudhonist clique among the students in Paris (*Courrier français*) is preaching peace, declaring war out of date and nationalities nonsense, and attacking Bismarck and Garibaldi, etc. [339] As polemic against chauvinism, their activities are useful and understandable. But as faithful followers of Proudhon (my very good friends here, Lafargue and Longuet, are also among that number) who believe that the whole of Europe must and will sit quietly on its arse until the French monsieurs have abolished '*la misère et l'ignorance*', [b] under which latter they themselves are labouring in inverse proportion to their squawking about '*science sociale*', they are grotesque. In their articles about the PRESENT AGRICULTURAL CRISIS in France, their 'knowledge' quite takes one's breath away. [c]

The Russians, who are for ever playing at the old game of playing off the jackasses of Europe against each other, and being PARTNER at one moment of A, and at the next of B, have of late indisputably PUSHED ON the Austrians, 1. because Prussia has not yet

---

[a] limit; usually *ultima Thule*—extreme limit (Virgil, *Georgics*, I, 30) - [b] poverty and ignorance - [c] Ch. Longuet, 'La question agricole, et le libre échange', *La Rive gauche*, No. 15, 15 April 1866.

made the appropriate concession over Oldenburg, 2. in order to tie the Austrians' hands in Galicia, and 3. no doubt also because Mr Alexander II, like Alexander I (in his last years), is in such a conservatively morose mood on account of the attempt on his life[340] that his diplomatic gentlemen at least require some 'conservative' excuses, and an alliance with Austria is conservative. Come the OPPORTUNE MOMENT, and they will show the BACKSIDE of the coin.

The official tone adopted by the 'BLOOD AND IRON'-Prussians[341] shows how very anxious they are. They are now even doing obeisance to the French Revolution of 1789! They are complaining about Austrian tetchiness!

The best thing in the lousy debate here in Parliament was the register of sins that Disraeli laid at the unfortunate Clarendon's door.[342]

Salut.

Your
K. M.

Italian enthusiasm will no doubt get its bucket of cold water. Even its melodrama, in keeping with the national character, by the way, would be tolerable, if right underneath it all[328] they were not setting their hopes on Badinguet.[a] I cannot forget my Izzy.[b] If he were still alive now, what a scandal he would create!

First published in *Der Briefwechsel zwischen F. Engels und K. Marx*, Bd. 3, Stuttgart, 1913

Printed according to the original

Published in English in full for the first time

166

MARX TO ENGELS[33]

IN MANCHESTER

[London,] 9 June 1866

DEAR FRED,

Many thanks for the £10.

Whatever the pressure from events, my work[c] has been progressing poorly owing to purely physical factors ever since my

---

[a] nickname of Napoleon III (the name of a bricklayer in whose clothes Napoleon fled from prison in 1846) - [b] Ferdinand Lassalle - [c] on *Capital*

return from Margate.[307] I have been so low over the last few weeks that I have not been able even to attend the INTERNATIONAL ASSOCIATION any more. I had Gumpert's prescription (for my liver) made up for me yesterday, as Allen's stuff was of no use at all to me. Furthermore, I have had a tooth pulled, to put an end to the toothache, and probably a second one will have to go, too.

If your wine-cellar permits (that is, if you are not thereby obliged to buy in more), I should appreciate it if you would send me some, as I am now forbidden beer altogether.

The verses await your 'commentary'. They are nothing in my hands.

This evening I am compelled to go to the meeting of the 'DIRECTORS AND FRIENDS' of *The Commonwealth*.[290] The thing is on its last legs. Apart from the acute financial difficulties, there are internal political ones as well. Since that jackass of a Bradford MANUFACTURER, Mr Kell (who has given £50, his brother ditto, and hints of more to come), has Miall entirely under his thumb, Dr Bridges, Professor Beesly, Harrison (the COMTEISTS) have threatened not merely to resign but also to make a public statement about their resignation.

I am tired of the business and shall propose to the people this evening that they should *sell* their bankrupt institution to Kell *et* Co. and put an end to the farce of A BRADFORD MANUFACTURER directing a London 'workers' organ'. If they do not agree, I shall, at all events, announce my withdrawal. The paper cannot survive for much longer on its own resources, is therefore dependent on advances of bourgeois money, and thereby loses its own character. I have shown great patience in this matter, because I always hoped that the workers themselves would make sufficient efforts to continue the undertaking on their own; and, for another thing, I did not want to be a wet blanket.

Mr Gottfried Kinkel has been appointed to a chair in Zurich.

Since the sounds of war started up, the 'Saxon' workers have been flocking to join the 'INTERNATIONAL ASSOCIATION'.

Salut.

Your
K. M.

COMPLIMENTS TO MRS LIZZY.[a]

Apropos. Lafargue tells me that the whole new French school of microscopical physiologists, with Robin at their head, is pronounc-

---

[a] Lizzy Burns

ing against Pasteur, Huxley, etc., and in favour of *generatio aequivoca*.[a] He is going to inform me of some new writings on the subject.

First published in *Der Briefwechsel zwischen F. Engels und K. Marx*, Bd. 3, Stuttgart, 1913

Printed according to the original

Published in English in full for the first time

167

ENGELS TO MARX

IN LONDON

Manchester, 11 June 1866

Dear Moor,

The crate of Bordeaux will be sent off to you this evening. It is very good wine from Borkheim. I should have sent it to you before, but the lads here have dilly-dallied over it, partly from overwork. I had written out the address for them long since. I hope that it and regular exercise will do you good. What do you say to coming up here for a week, say, end of this inst. would suit me, and then you could take the money straight back with you early in July? At the same time, you could for once have a thorough consultation with Gumpert.

We have so far just escaped the spate of bank-failures unscathed. Dronke told me himself that he was in for a bit with Barnett, but more because he had had to change his banker; he had £3,000 credit there—however, he was also a shareholder, and that's where he will lose. Eichhoff also has had the honour of seeing his banker fail, and has come a cropper to the tune of £16. He is not losing any sleep over it; if he cannot pay a bill that's due, he just lets it be.

Mr G. Kinkel has been putting it around every year that he has been offered the chair in Zurich—so, does that mean the people of Zurich are in fact really going to have to believe it at last?

In Germany it looks more like revolution every day. In Berlin and Barmen menacing crowds of laid-off workers are roaming the

---

[a] spontaneous generation

streets. G. Ermen, who came back on Friday, told me that he happened to engage in discussion about the war with some Prussian lieutenant on the Rhine Bridge at Coblenz, and the man had been very doubtful about the issue of the affair, admitted that both the men and the leadership of the Austrians were better than the Prussians', and when G. Ermen asked, 'What would happen if the Prussians were whacked?' he answered, 'Then we'll have a revolution.' Another philistine told me that he had heard from a reliable source in Cologne that the militia companies are being dispersed among the line, and that the militia regiments are being topped up with line; the order has apparently been given out. In any case, the army must be in such a state that a victory can only be expected if the Austrians move across the frontier *first*, and this time they seem to be flatly refusing to do so. But, for that same reason, the Prussians don't want to move either. This state of affairs may drag on for another week, until the situation is so tense that it breaks.

There is a delightful historical irony being enacted through Bismarck's person. At the same moment that he utters liberal phrases he is forced to perform absolutist actions. In one and the same breath he will proclaim the German imperial constitution and suspend the Prussian constitution (the ordinances are already prepared).[321] Good idea to try and play the Bonaparte against the bourgeoisie with the Junkers behind one instead of the peasants!

The militia will be just as much of a danger to the Prussians in this war as the Poles were in 1806,[343] who also comprised over $^1/_3$ of the army and threw the whole show into disorder before the battle. Only instead of disbanding, the militia will rebel after the defeat.

The whole left bank of the Rhine has been denuded of troops, there are only 2 militia regiments stationed in Luxemburg, and they say the fortress is already being secretly evacuated; in Saarlouis there is merely a militia battalion that is not yet up to strength. Von der Heydt is to arrange the Saarbrücken coal-mine and State Railway deal via Oppenheim to raise money, and the Westphalian State Railway is to be sold to the Bergisch-Märkische Railway. The bonds for its *Cologne-Minden shares*[237] have been advanced to the state by the Bank of Prussia, which was the sole purpose of the affair. In all this the Berlin bankers are all working hand in glove with the government.

I think that in a fortnight the storm will break in Prussia. If this opportunity passes without being used, and if the people allow that to happen, we can then calmly pack up our revolutionary paraphernalia and devote ourselves to pure theory.

Stieber is chief of police in the field, is organising the 'Blind conspiracy' and has, to this end, sent our friend Greif to London again. Can we not arrange for him to be given a good hiding? Kindest regards.

Your
F. E.

First published abridged in *Der Briefwechsel zwischen F. Engels und K. Marx*, Bd. 3, Stuttgart, 1913 and in full in *MEGA*, Abt. III, Bd. 3, Berlin, 1930

Printed according to the original

Published in English for the first time

168

MARX TO ENGELS [344]

IN MANCHESTER

[London,] 20 June 1866

Dear Fred,

This damned weather is having a particularly evil effect *sur mon physique*[a]; and this is the reason why I did not acknowledge the 'wine' earlier, nor write to you otherwise. There is no chance of coming to Manchester, as I cannot leave the house in my present state; besides, I have to be here for the 'International', where my French friends have already used my absence once in these trying circumstances to execute some tomfoolery in the name of the Association.[313]

As regards newspapers here, in my view the best thing to do, if nothing comes of the Manchester business, is to send a proper military article to *The Times*, to which you can present yourself as the English correspondent of the Darmstadt *Militär-Zeitung*.[b] No need for any political considerations, as one London paper is just as bad as any other, and what matters is to obtain the widest publicity.[345]

---

[a] on my constitution - [b] *Allgemeine Militär-Zeitung*

You must now keep me 'critically' *au courant des affaires* in ITALY and GERMANY.

There was a debate at yesterday's meeting of the INTERNATIONAL COUNCIL about the present war. It was announced beforehand and our ROOM was very full. Even the Italian gentlemen had honoured us with their presence again. The discussion WAS WOUND UP, as could have been foreseen, with the 'QUESTION OF NATIONALITY' in general and the attitude we should adopt to it. This *sujet* adjourned until next Tuesday.[346]

The French, very strongly represented, GAVE VENT to their cordial dislike for the Italians.

The representatives of '*jeune France*'[a] (*non-workers*), by the way, trotted out their view that any nationality and even nations are '*des préjugés surannés*'.[b] Proudhonised Stirnerianism. Everything to be broken down into small '*groupes*' or '*communes*', which in turn form an 'association', but not a state. Furthermore, this 'individualisation' of mankind and the '*mutualisme*'[347] it entails are to proceed by bringing history to a halt in every other country and the whole world waits until the French are ready to carry out a social revolution. Then they will demonstrate the experiment to us, and the rest of the world, being bowled over by the force of their example, will do the same. Just what Fourier expected from his *phalanstère modèle*. *D'ailleurs*,[c] everyone who clutters up the 'social' question with the 'superstitions' of the Old World is a 'reactionary'.

The English laughed heartily when I began my SPEECH with the observation that our friend Lafargue, and others, who had abolished nationalities, had addressed us in '*French*', i.e., in a language which $^9/_{10}$ of the audience did not understand. I went on to suggest that by his denial of nationalities he seemed quite unconsciously to imply their absorption by the model French nation.

For the rest, the position is difficult now because one must equally oppose the silly Italianism of the English, on the one hand, and the mistaken polemic against it of the French, on the other, and above all prevent any demonstration which would involve our Association in a one-sided course.

Salut.

Your

K. M.

First published in *Der Briefwechsel zwischen F. Engels und K. Marx*, Bd. 3, Stuttgart, 1913

Printed according to the original

---

[a] young France - [b] outdated prejudices - [c] Besides

169

ENGELS TO MARX

IN LONDON

[Manchester,] 4 July 1866

Dear Moor,

The other half of the note enclosed. Unfortunately, your telegram reached me *after 12 o'clock*,[46] so that I could not make use of the first post.

What do you say to the Prussians? Their initial successes were exploited with enormous vigour, and, if it had not been for this intensity, Benedek would probably have quietly withdrawn to Olmütz,[a] but he was obviously forced to come to battle yesterday, and there could be no doubt about the issue after what had befallen. To determine the outcome of such a decisive battle in 8 hours is quite unprecedented; in other circumstances, it would have lasted 2 days.[348] But the needle-gun is a merciless weapon, and then these fellows really do fight with a verve that I have never before observed in such peace-time troops. For the defender, the attacker's need to take positions by storm compensates for his superiority in weapons, and here too the Prussians appear to have accomplished a great deal. Benedek, with his deep 'plan', turns out to have been not merely a jackass but a dullard as well. How splendidly he could, with sufficient men, have caught those fellows in the mountains!

At all events, Bismarck will now try to set up his Imperial Germany, and that should include Bohemia, which he hopes to take from the Austrians and thereby establish a link between Silesia and Bavaria. In the treaty with Italy, he did after all stipulate '*un territoire autrichien équivalent à la Vénéti*'.[b][328]

Berlin is again acting with the vileness for which it is famed and yesterday even went so far as to elect a whole load of ministers. What will those camels of men of Progress[99] say now?

The farce up in the North-West is delightful and will probably soon be no less so in the South, too.

The only safeguard against the betrayal that Bismarck has plotted with Bonaparte is the quite unexpected magnitude of the

---

[a] Czech name: Olomouc - [b] 'Austrian territory equivalent to Venetia'

victories. He will now find it difficult to cede much, and the Belgians will probably have to pay part of the price.[349]
Kindest regards to the LADIES.

Your
F. E.

First published in *Der Briefwechsel zwischen F. Engels und K. Marx,* Bd. 3, Stuttgart, 1913

Printed according to the original

Published in English for the first time

170

MARX TO ENGELS[101]

IN MANCHESTER

[London,] 7 July 1866

DEAR FRED,

D'abord[a] my heartfelt thanks for the Californian consignment. Yet, I was unable to pay the LANDLORD, who is again owed for two quarters. I had to allow priority to part-payments to the fellows who are dunning me every hour of the day.

As regards my state of health, first of all, I have *had my nose properly to the grindstone* again over the past two weeks, and hope that by the end of August, if I preserve this degree of health, I shall have finished the first volume,[b] which I am having published by itself. It is true that I am obliged to continue with Gumpert's liver-medicine every day, as I would otherwise be laid low at once. Question: is the *arsenic* (*put aside* for many weeks now) compatible with it? I am asking because for 4 days now another carbuncle has been appearing above my right collar-bone. I owe more to the Bordeaux than to any medicine. I am incidentally only working in the day-time, as a sporadic attempt to work at night (once or twice) immediately had very unfortunate consequences.

Before passing to general matters, can you translate '*PUT STRETCHES UPON THE MULE*' into German for me, and tell me what '*PICKS*' in weaving are called in German? What is a '*FLYER*' on the mule?

The workers' demonstrations in London are fabulous compared with anything seen in England since 1849, and they are solely the

---

[a] First of all - [b] of *Capital*

work of the '*INTERNATIONAL*'. MR Lucraft, F.I., the captain in Trafalgar Square, is ONE OF OUR COUNCIL.[350] This shows the difference between *acting* behind the scenes whilst retiring in public, and the democrats' habit of puffing themselves up in public and *doing nothing*.

The *Commonwealth* is about to expire.[290] Fox is leaving it next week. Apropos. Stumpf has written to me from Mainz that among the workers the demand for your book '*The Condition*, etc.'[a] is growing daily and that you must certainly bring out the second edition, if only for party reasons. At the same time, his personal experiences lead him to believe that immediately after the war[345] 'the labour question' in Germany will come noticeably to the fore.

Freiligrath has put out a melancholy-lyrical little turd on the fratricidal war, which his daughter Kate has englished in today's *Athenaeum*.[b]

Beside a great Prussian defeat, which perhaps (oh but those Berliners!) might have led to a revolution, there could have been no better outcome than their stupendous victory. Thiers had been so successful in denouncing Bonaparte's policy of helping to 'make' Prussia (for beside the English, your Frenchman in fact really *hates* only the Prussians), that Boustrapa[76] had to amend the constitution he had imposed on the French and '*abolish*' discussion of the address *par ordre du*[c] *Moniteur*. (I am enclosing J. Favre's speech on Mexico and Glais-Bizoin's bad witticisms for you, so that you can see what Boustrapa's position was before the outbreak of war.)[351] Mr Bonaparte was counting on victory and defeat swinging back and forth between Prussians and Austrians, so that eventually he would be able to step in between the exhausted combatants like Jupiter Scapin.[d] The Prussians' success really puts his regime in France in dire peril (it is his second great miscalculation since the American Civil War) if he does not manage to dictate the terms of peace. On the other hand, the same success (we are not back in 1815 now) makes it impossible, almost impossible, for the Prussian dynasty to accept terms other than those which Austria *must* reject, not to mention the fact that handsome William,[e] alias Alexander the Great, cannot possibly cede German territory to France. The Prussians' decision will depend on the 'nephew' in St Petersburg.[f] It is impossible to say

---

[a] F. Engels, *The Condition of the Working-Class in England*. - [b] F. Freiligrath, 'Westphalian Summer Song', *The Athenaeum*, No. 2019, 7 July 1866. - [c] by order of the - [d] Scapin—a character from Molière's *Les fourberies de Scapin*. - [e] William I - [f] Alexander II

what he will do, as that would require one to be in possession of the material in the Russian State Chancellory. But I, for my part, cannot understand how the Russians, who are furthermore offended that the Austrians refused their help, can permit Austria to get her breath back and miss this favourable moment for their Turco-Danubian manoeuvres. Mr Victor Emmanuel is also in a pretty pickle. Venice now belongs to Bonaparte. If he accepts it from him as a present, that will be the end for his dynasty. On the other hand, *what* can he do against France, and *where* can *he* now attack Austria?[352]

But what do you say to our *Foxikins*, who dashed breathlessly into our house the day before yesterday, exclaiming: 'Bonaparte has *saved* Germany!' This view is shared by Beesly, Harrison, etc., and the whole COMTEIST clique. Write to me soon, as pen and ink have to serve in place of oral communication in this EVENTFUL PERIOD.

My best compliments to MRS Lizzy.[a]

Little Jenny would like to know how your 'Africans' are doing?[353]

Salut.

Your
K.M.

Naturally, Bonaparte does not want war now, until he has introduced the NEEDLE-GUN or an equivalent. A *YANKEE*[b] has offered the war ministry here a rifle which, so I am assured by a REFUGEE Prussian officer (Wilke), is as superior to the needle-gun as the latter is to 'OLD BESS',[354] by virtue of its extreme simplicity of design, non-susceptibility to heating, reduced need for cleaning, and cheapness. Is there any sphere in which our theory that the *organisation* of labour is determined *by the means of production* is more dazzlingly vindicated than in the industry for human slaughter? It really would be worth your while to write something on the subject (I have not the necessary knowledge for it) which I would include as an appendix to my book[c] under your name. Give the matter some thought. If you do it, however, it must be done *pour le premier volume,*[d] in which I am dealing *ex professo*[e] with this topic. You will appreciate what great pleasure it would give me if you were also to appear in my principal work (previously I have only produced trifles) as a direct collaborator, and not just in quotation!

---

[a] Lizzy Burns - [b] Jacob Snider - [c] *Capital* - [d] for the first volume - [e] in particular

I am studying Comte on the side just now, as the English and French are making such a fuss of the fellow. What seduces them about him is his encyclopaedic quality, *la synthèse*. But that is pitiful when compared with Hegel (although Comte is superior to him as a mathematician and physicist by profession, i.e., superior in the detail, though even here Hegel is infinitely greater as a whole). And this shitty positivism came out in 1832!

First published in *Der Briefwechsel zwischen F. Engels und K. Marx*, Bd. 3, Stuttgart, 1913

Printed according to the original

Published in English in full for the first time

171

ENGELS TO MARX

IN LONDON

Manchester, 9 July[a] 1866

Dear Moor,

History, i.e., world history, is becoming ever more ironical. What could be more splendid than that Bonaparte should be thus mocked in practice by his pupil Bismarck, who, backwoods junker as he is, has suddenly outgrown his master and all at once gives the whole world a tangible demonstration of how very much this *arbitre de l'Europe* exists ON SUFFERANCE. And then this Bismarck himself, who, in order to be able to govern to all appearances feudally and absolutely for a few months at home, is pursuing the policy of the bourgeoisie WITH A VENGEANCE abroad, preparing the ground for the bourgeoisie to rule and striking along paths where progress is only possible by liberal, even revolutionary means, and, in so doing, making his own backwoods junkers be daily at variance with their own principles. The presenters of the ceremonial shield to Francis Bomba[b] are in alliance with Garibaldi, and the advocates of Thrones by the grace of God go swallowing up whole countries in spite of Victor Emmanuel![355] Never has there been anything quite so splendid as the *Kreuz-Zeitung*[c] in

___

[a] The original has: June. - [b] Francis II of Naples and Sicily, son of Ferdinand II nicknamed King Bomba for the bombardment of Messina in September 1848. - [c] *Neue Preussische Zeitung*

these last 4 weeks, and the historico-feudal party, which cost the genius of Frederick William IV of blessed memory so much toil and trouble to found, is now choking on the filth which it is being forced to gobble up at its own leader's command.

The simple fact is: Prussia has 500,000 needle-guns and the rest of the world not even 500. It is not possible to equip an army with breech-loaders in under 2, 3 or perhaps 5 years. Until then Prussia will be dux. Do you think Bismarck will not make use of such a moment? Certainly he will. Bonaparte will take very good care not to pick a quarrel, and as for the Russians, it is true they are setting up a most furious howl in the *Journal de St.-Pétersbourg*,[a] but militarily they are now less to be feared than ever. I have no doubt at all that this sudden enormous growth of Prussia's might will drive Bonaparte and the Russians together, and that their first endeavour will be to prevent each and every increase in Prussia's might. But they will take care to hold back from war; as for France, if she were to intervene actively, that would assuredly be the best way to drive the South Germans properly into the arms of the Prussians and consign the civil war to oblivion.[356] And as for the Russians, Monsieur Bismarck is the man to threaten them with a new Polish insurrection, and they know that the fellow is unscrupulous enough for that. In general, Bismarck is only too well aware of his power and also knows that it can only maintain its present magnitude for a few years, and I believe he will exploit it to the very last drop. Moreover, Bonaparte can always be bought off with Belgium in the end, and only just before the war Goltz, Bonaparte and the Crown Prince of Holland[b] 'considered the possibility' of dividing Belgium between France and Holland, which would then cede Luxemburg to France.[349] I believe the war is not over yet by a long chalk, and there is much that can still happen.

The Russians really do seem to have realigned themselves towards Austria some time ago now, and this tremendous success of the Prussians will make it impossible for them to go back on it in any way. The more so since Austria will now be ready to receive Bosnia or Walachia in exchange for Venice, with Russia then taking Moldavia.

You see, by the by, how right I was in my appraisal of the Prussian army when I repeatedly said there was far more to it than people were wont to admit. After these successes and after

---

a 'Nouvelles de L'Extérieur', *Journal de Saint-Pétersbourg*, No. 140, 23 June (5 July) 1866. - b William, Prince of Orange

the absolutely brilliant performance of the troops, they will be so much more self-confident and, at the same time, more experienced at war that they could take the field against the French tomorrow, even if the latter had breech-loaders, and the French bayonet, at all events, has had its day, like the Spanish pike in its time. When breech-loading becomes general, the cavalry will come into its own again.

I must make a proper report to Jenny about the Africans,[353] as I have been meaning to for a long time now.

Many regards.

Your
F. E.

First published in *Der Briefwechsel zwischen F. Engels und K. Marx*, Bd. 3, Stuttgart, 1913

Printed according to the original

Published in English for the first time

172

ENGELS TO MARX

IN LONDON

Manchester, 12 July 1866

Dear Moor,

I have written about your history to Gumpert, who is in Wales; as I do not know his address, the letter will first have to go to his home here, hence certainly some delay. As soon as I have a reply, I'll write to you, but meanwhile I should advise you to take arsenic *at once* and put off everything else, so as to stop the damned carbuncle. Put an end to *this* abomination at any cost.

Bonaparte's little plan and his intervention are in part probably a consequence of an earlier agreement with Bismarck, but certainly also—the new Confederation of the Rhine, etc.—are threats in his direction. But how the fellow can be so stupid as to make *this* plan public is beyond my comprehension[357]: as with Schapper—that he could be *so* stupid, etc.—It will assuredly drive the whole of South Germany into the arms of the Prussians and even the old philistines at the Exchange here are quite beside themselves about it. One old man from Frankfurt told me: it's worth more to the Prussians than a reinforcement of 100,000 men.

You see how the stupid South Germans are letting themselves be picked off one by one without even taking the trouble to close ranks.[356] It'll soon be the old, old story, we've been betrayed, we'll be led like lambs to the slaughter![a] 1849 all over again. I feel sorry for the fellows, they're good soldiers. Only now does one understand how the French were able to score such successes against the 'Empire', but *not* how the Empire was able to hold out for so long against a concentrated monarchy like France.[358]

I will try and produce the stuff about the mass-murder-industry for you.[b]

Many regards.

Your
F. E.

First published in *Der Briefwechsel zwischen F. Engels und K. Marx*, Bd. 3, Stuttgart, 1913

Printed according to the original

Published in English for the first time

173

MARX TO ENGELS

IN MANCHESTER

[London,] 21 July[c] 1866

DEAR FRED,

The carbuncle has fortunately departed again of its own accord. But in the present heat my LIVER has been and still is scourging me sorely. For all that, my work[d] is progressing well and will continue to do so if my present condition lasts. It is, of course, embarrassing for me to have to pester you again already, but as you will gather from the enclosed note (which you must return to me) there is *periculum in mora*.[e] I have with difficulty obtained an

---

[a] Engels uses the South-German dialect here: 'Man will uns uf die Schlachtbank fihre!' - [b] See this volume, p. 291. - [c] The original has: January. - [d] on the first volume of *Capital* - [e] danger in delay (Livy, *The History of Rome*, Vol. XXXVIII, Chap. 25)

extension until next Tuesday. From your last communication I am in doubt as to whether you are in Manchester. Nor have I received any more copies of *The Manchester Guardian*. Or has nothing else of yours appeared in it?[345]

One must refrain from passing any judgment on the present circumstances, pending news either of a ceasefire or of a decisive battle at Vienna. At any rate, the course of events has demonstrated the extraordinary decay of the Austrian system.

For the moment, these English of ours are, as always, paying homage to success. The great Arnold Ruge, too, has made his *pronunciamento* for Prussia 14 days ago, as the great Kinkel did earlier still. If the Prussians continue victorious to the end, what a throng of place-seekers and fatherland-rescuers will surge towards Frankfurt!

At all events, the *'homme prestige'*,[a] 'Jupiter Scapin',[b] GROTESQUE PROVIDENCE OF EUROPE is shaken and even overshadowed by Bismarck. That is some consolation.

The VTH REPORT of the CHILDREN'S EMPLOYMENT COMMISSION appeared here a few days ago. It concludes the *enquête*[c] into the manufactories, and only a supplement has yet to appear concerning the 'ORGANISED GANGS' of women and children, who are sporadically used in agriculture. There could have been no more dreadful blow to the optimism of the bourgeoisie since 1850 than from these 5 BLUE BOOKS. Furthermore, the VIIIth REPORT of the BOARD OF HEALTH[d] was brought out a few days ago, which contains in particular a very detailed *enquête* of the living conditions of the proletariat.[359]

Salut.

Your
K. M.

First published in *Der Briefwechsel zwischen F. Engels und K. Marx*, Bd. 3, Stuttgart, 1913

Printed according to the original

Published in English for the first time

---

[a] 'man of prestige' - [b] Scapin—a character from Molière's *Les fourberies de Scapin* (here Napoleon III is meant) - [c] enquiry - [d] *Eighth Report of the Medical Officer of the Privy Council.*

Frederick Engels. 1860s. Manchester

174

ENGELS TO MARX [101]

IN LONDON

Manchester, 25 July 1866

Dear Moor,

I think you will now have received the notes all right; in a moment of distraction I must have put in, in their stead, the piece of paper on which I had noted the Nos. The notes themselves I had slipped inside the cover of my writing-case, which is where I found them when I had recovered from the initial shock of your telegram.[46] I hope they still arrived in time.

The business in Germany now seems fairly straightforward to me. From the moment of Bismarck's so colossal success in using the Prussian army to put the bourgeois plan for Little Germany into effect,[360] developments in Germany have moved so decisively in that direction that we shall have to accept the *fait accompli* just like everybody else, WE MAY LIKE IT OR NOT. As regards the *national* aspect of the question, at all events, Bismarck will set up a Little German Empire of the dimensions envisaged by the bourgeoisie, i. e., including South-West Germany, the phrases about the Main boundary and the OPTIONAL SOUTH GERMAN SEPARATE CONFEDERACY, at any rate, only being intended for the French[357]; meanwhile the Prussians are marching on Stuttgart. Incidentally, before very long, the German provinces of Austria will join this Empire too, since Austria is certain to go Hungarian now,[293] and the Germans will become the 3rd nation in the Empire—lower even than the Slavs.

Politice[a] Bismarck will be forced to rely on the bourgeoisie, whom he needs against the Imperial Princes. Perhaps not at this moment, as his prestige and the army are still sufficient. But simply to ensure that parliament will grant the necessary conditions for central power, he will have to give something to the bourgeoisie, and the natural course of events will constantly compel him or his successors to appeal to the bourgeoisie again; so that, even if Bismarck perhaps gives the bourgeoisie no more than he absolutely *has to* now, he will, nevertheless, be driven increasingly in a bourgeois direction.

---

[a] Politically

The good aspect to the affair is that it simplifies the situation and makes revolution easier by putting an end to the brawling among the smaller capitals and, at all events, hastens developments. A German parliament is after all quite a different thing from a Prussian Chamber. All the little states will be drawn into the movement, there will be an end to the worst localised tendencies, and the parties will at last become truly national instead of merely local.

The chief disadvantage—and it is a very substantial one—is the inevitable swamping of Germany by Prussianism. Also the temporary exclusion of German Austria, a consequence of which will be an immediate advance of the Slav cause in Bohemia, Moravia and Carinthia. Unfortunately, *nothing* can be done to prevent *either.*

In my view, therefore, we can do nothing whatsoever but simply accept the fact, without approving of it, and use, as far as we can, the increased opportunities which are, at all events, bound to arise now, to organise and unite the German proletariat *nationally.*

I did not need Stumpf's letter to tell me that BROTHER Liebknecht would launch himself into fanatical support of the Austrian cause, it was absolutely inevitable.[361] Incidentally, there was no mistaking his furious despatches from Leipzig in the *Neue Frankfurter Zeitung.* This *N. F. Zeitung,* with its Blind-ish regicidal tendencies, went so far as to reproach the Prussians for their disgraceful treatment of '*His Highness the Elector of Hesse*'[a] and was beside itself with enthusiasm for the poor blind Guelph.[b]

Nothing more of mine in the *Guardian.*[345]

Your
F. E.

Best wishes to the LADIES.

First published in *Der Briefwechsel zwischen F. Engels und K. Marx,* Bd. 3, Stuttgart, 1913

Printed according to the original

Published in English in full for the first time

---

[a] Ludwig III - [b] George V of Hanover

175

MARX TO ENGELS[101]

IN MANCHESTER

[London,] 27 July[a] 1866

Dear Fred,

Best thanks for the £10. They came in the nick of time.

I have not written to Stumpf, precisely because he asked for a line of 'conduct', and my view was that he would do best not to 'conduct' himself at all until events took a decisive turn.[361] That was a view which I RATHER thought advisable not to put to him in writing. Mainz is at present still encircled, so far as I know, so postal communication is also presumably interrupted. Did you write to Stumpf?

The comedy in Frankfurt makes up somewhat for the exhalation of the victors. Lord, lord, they howled, 25 million! And his worship the mayor[b] goes and hangs himself![362] And the Prussians, for their part, officially declare that Frankfurt will have to fork out because its papers have 'insulted' His Majesty William the Conqueror.[c] Since his government post in Brünn is only temporary, Stieber will eventually become mayor of the Frankfurter-on-Mainers, whom by the way I have always thought the most insufferable scoundrels. And Edgar Bauer will be imposed on them as Censor-in-Chief. But as regards the Eschenheimer Gasse,[363] Privy Counsellor Duncker would—except that he is, of course, ruling in Kassel.

I am entirely at one with you that we must take the mess as it is. It is, nevertheless, pleasant to be far off at this youthful time of love's first dawning.[d] The arrogance of the Prussians and the foolishness of handsome William,[e] who believes that nothing has changed since his dream of victory, except that he is now a great potentate, etc., will have their effect soon enough. The Austrians now find themselves where the Slav fanatics from Prague wanted them in 1848.[364] However, for the moment their loss of Venice, their enforced concentration of strength is in no way to the Russians' advantage. Being a Pan-Slavic empire themselves, they

---

[a] The original has: August.- [b] Karl Fellner - [c] William I of Prussia (an ironical comparison with the Norman William who conquered England in 1066) - [d] F. Schiller, *Das Lied von der Glocke.* - [e] William I

will be all the more antagonistic to the Muscovites. In view of the extraordinary decline of the Habsburgs, it is certainly to be feared that BY and BY they will allow the Russians to tempt them into a combined attack on Turkey.

For the workers, of course, everything that centralises the bourgeoisie is to their advantage. At all events, even if peace is concluded tomorrow, it will be even more provisional than that of Villafranca and Zurich was.[365] As soon as the 'arms reform' has been completed by the various parties, it will be back to 'bashing', as Schapper calls it. At all events, Bonaparte has suffered a setback, too, although the setting up of military kingdoms on all sides right and left fits the Plon-Plonist[93] scheme 'de la démocratie générale'.[a]

The government has almost caused a mutiny here. Your Englishman first needs a revolutionary education, of course, for which two weeks would suffice if Sir Richard Mayne had absolute powers of command. In actual fact, it all hung on one point. If the RAILINGS had been used—and it almost came to that—for offence and defence against the police, and some score of the latter killed, the military would have had to 'step in', instead of merely parading. And then things would have got quite jolly. This much is certain: that these stiff-necked John Bulls, whose sconces appear made to measure for the constables' BLUDGEONS, will accomplish nothing without a really bloody clash with those in power.

A touching scene, that, between that old jackass Beales and the equally asinine old Walpole, and then the intervention of the thin-voiced, INTRUSIVE, self-important Holyoake, who through 'love of the truth' is constantly finding his way into *The Times*—nothing but peace and dissoluteness.[366] Meanwhile, whilst these riff-raff are patting each other on the back and belick-spittling each other, that cur Knox, the police magistrate of Marylebone, is sending people down in a summary fashion, which shows what would happen if London were Jamaica.[252]

Disraeli has made a fine fool of himself, firstly by his pathetic remark in the Lower House,[b] 'he did not know whether he still had a house', and then by the strong military occupation of that same house, although, thirdly, the MOB (instructed beforehand by the REFORM LEAGUE people) deliberately left the house of Mr 'Vivian Grey'[c] UNTOUCHED. The house lost not a hair from its head. For which Elcho's window-panes had to suffer the more. I had

---

a 'of universal democracy' - b on 24 July 1866 - c an ironic reference to Disraeli, the author of a novel under the same title

dropped the HINT to Gremer and other MANAGERS that it might be appropriate to pay a visit to the *'Times' Newspaper.* As they did not immediately 'take' the HINT, or did not want to, I did not press it.

The cholera is paying us (I mean the Londoners) its respects with the utmost gravity, and Dr Hunter's report, in the VIIIth REPORT of the HEALTH BOARD[a] on the 'HOUSING of the POOR', which appeared last week,[359] is presumably intended to serve Madam Cholera as a DIRECTORY of addresses calling for preferential visitation.

MY BEST COMPLIMENTS TO MRS Lizzy.[b]

Your
K. M.

First published in *Der Briefwechsel zwischen F. Engels und K. Marx*, Bd. 3, Stuttgart, 1913

Printed according to the original

Published in English in full for the first time

176

ENGELS TO MARX

IN LONDON

Manchester, 6 August 1866

Dear Moor,

The humour in your last letter leads me to conclude that your liver must be much better, although you do not say anything about it yourself. As regards the Frankfurters,[362] you should have just heard the wailing and gnashing of teeth by the ones here, of whom we have a whole legion here and who got the most frightful letters from their brothers, etc. On this occasion the Prussian lieutenant did, of course, conduct himself with all the charm for which he is renowned, but it was to be expected from the beginning that these gentlemen would be MORE FRIGHTENED THAN HURT. In the rest of South Germany, where the Frankfurters are not especially popular either and where they are reproached for running with the hare and hunting with the hounds, there was

---

[a] *Eighth Report of the Medical Officer of the Privy Council.* - [b] Lizzy Burns

positive pleasure that it was they who were treated so roughly. I have seen such letters myself.

So, Bismarck won in the end, and Wilhelmchen[a] has issued a form of words to conciliate his Highnesses, Noble Lords and Faithful Followers, simultaneously affirming, however, that if they refuse him money again, the spending of money without approval will unfortunately be 'unavoidable' again. I still do not see how the conflict can thereby be resolved, even with this Chamber. Then there is a German, or RATHER North German parliament as well, about whose possible position or at least powers Mr Eulenburg has resolutely refused to give any information whatsoever—there are splendid prospects for a dust-up before long. Bismarck himself will surely seek to avoid a dispute, he is not that stupid, but that old brute of a Hohenzollern is bound to embroil himself, and then he will be amazed at the intelligence of his bayonets.[367]

That we shall soon be back to bashing is clear enough. I believe things will come to a head with the French. Bonaparte is shrewd enough to want to avoid this as long as at all possible, but the mass of Frenchmen, in particular the bourgeoisie, with their distaste for any strengthening of Germany, really is too short-sighted and fanatical to be denied the *expansion de la France qui ne peut avoir lieu que du côté de l'Allemagne,*[b] and war against Prussia is also popular with the peasants and more stupid workers; therefore there is no telling how soon the storm will break.

Wehner, who has just returned from Hanover, tells me that the Prussian officers have already made themselves thoroughly hated there, too, likewise the bureaucrats and police.

I shall probably not spend long in Germany this year either. What with the exhalation of the victors in the North and the Republicans bawling out their enthusiasm for the Elector of Hesse[c] in the South, where ought one to go? I shall attempt to go into the Harz by a roundabout route, there are fortunately no garrisons there.

The *Kölnische Zeitung* is now screaming with much frothing at the mouth for the exclusion of South Germany. This is the catchword put out by Bismarck to facilitate Bonaparte's retreat, and the *Kölnische* is storming in this direction with such insane fervour that one sees through the whole nonsense immediately. No paper has yet behaved quite so vilely as this one. Having been most vociferously shouting for peace, it leapt into the contrary

---

[a] William I - [b] Expansion of France which can only occur in the direction of Germany - [c] Ludwig III

stance as soon as it saw that Bismarck with his cry of 'Austria wants war! Up and at 'em!' was not to be put off the scent, and ever since it has been Bismarck's best friend, at least in good will if not in finesse. It is his lap-dog in the press.

If the new breech-loading gun the American showed to the government here is the Snider-Enfield, it is not up to much. It was most probably another one you were referring to.[a] Incidentally, a more rapid rate of fire than that already achieved by the needle-gun is of little consequence, as in practice the difference is virtually reduced to zero; on the other hand, greater precision and accuracy of aim are now becoming increasingly important. I am just re-reading Griesheim's tactics[b]—how outdated almost all of it already is now!

Kindest regards to the LADIES.

Your
F. E.

First published in *Der Briefwechsel zwischen F. Engels und K. Marx*, Bd. 3, Stuttgart, 1913

Printed according to the original

Published in English for the first time

177

MARX TO ENGELS[368]

IN MANCHESTER

[London,] 7 August 1866

Dear FRED,

You inferred correctly from my last letter that my state of health has improved, although it fluctuates from one day to the next. Meanwhile, the feeling of being fit to work again DOES MUCH FOR A MAN. Unfortunately, I am constantly interrupted by SOCIAL TROUBLES and lose a lot of time. Thus, for example, the butcher has suspended meat supplies today, and by Saturday even my stock of paper will be used up.

Since yesterday Laura is half promised to Monsieur Lafargue, my medical Creole. She treats him like the others, but the

___
[a] See this volume, p. 291. - [b] G. von Griesheim, *Vorlesungen über die Taktik.*

outbursts of feeling these Creoles are subject to, a slight fear that the *jeune homme*[a] (he is 25) might do away with himself, etc., some fondness for him, undemonstrative as always with Laura (he is a good-looking, intelligent, energetic lad of athletic build), have more or less led to a semi-compromise. The boy attached himself to me first of all, but soon transferred the ATTRACTION from the old man to his daughter. His economic circumstances are middling, as he is the only child of a former planter-family.[b] He is *rayé de l'université de Paris pour deux ans*,[c] on account of the *congrès à* Liège,[269] but intends to sit his examination at Strasbourg. In my judgment, he has an outstanding gift for medicine, in which he is, however, infinitely more sceptical than our friend Gumpert. Scepticism in medical matters appears to be the order of the day with both professors and students in Paris. E. g., Magendie, who declares all therapeutics, in their present STATE, to be fraudulent. As always, this scepticism not only does not exclude CROTCHETS, but embraces them. E. g., Lafargue believes in alcohol and electricity as the chief cures. Fortunately, he is having a good adviser in Professor Carrère, a refugee (*hautes mathématiques*,[d] physics and chemistry), and will be able to acquire much practical experience in the London hospitals. I have managed to get him admitted there through the good offices of a third party.

A very important work which I shall send on to you (but on condition that you send it back, as it is not my property) as soon as I have made the necessary notes, is: '*P. Trémaux, Origine et Transformations de l'Homme et des autres Êtres, Paris 1865.*' In spite of all the shortcomings that I have noted, it represents a *very significant* advance over Darwin. The two chief theses are: *croisements*[e] do not produce, as is commonly thought, variety, but, on the contrary, a unity typical of the *espèces*.[f] The physical features of the earth, on the other hand, *differentiate* (they are the chief, though not the only basis). Progress, which Darwin regards as purely accidental, is essential here on the basis of the stages of the earth's development, *dégénérescence*,[g] which Darwin cannot explain, is straightforward here; ditto the rapid extinction of merely transitional forms, compared with the slow development of the type of the *espèce*, so that the gaps in palaeontology, which Darwin finds disturbing, are necessary here. Ditto the fixity of the *espèce*, once established, which is explained as a necessary law

---

[a] young man - [b] the family of François Lafargue - [c] sent down from the University of Paris for two years - [d] higher mathematics - [e] crossings - [f] species - [g] degeneration

(apart from individual, etc., variations). Here hybridisation, which raises problems for Darwin, on the contrary supports the system, as it is shown that an *espèce* is in fact first established as soon as *croisement* with others ceases to produce offspring or to be possible, etc.

In its historical and political applications far more significant and pregnant than Darwin. For certain questions, such as nationality, etc., only here has a basis in nature been found. E.g., he corrects the Pole Duchiński, whose version of the geological differences between Russia and the Western Slav lands he does incidentally confirm, by saying not that the Russians are Tartars rather than Slavs, etc.,[a] as the latter believes, but that on the surface-formation predominant in Russia the Slav has been tartarised and mongolised; likewise (he spent a long time in Africa) he shows that the common negro type is only a degeneration of a far higher one.

'Hors des grandes lois de la nature, les projets des hommes ne sont que calamités, témoins les efforts des czars pour faire du peuple polonais des Moscovites. [...] Même nature, mêmes facultés, renaîtront sur un même sol. L'œuvre de destruction ne saurait toujours durer, l'œuvre de reconstitution est éternelle... Les races slaves et lithuaniennes ont avec les Moscovites, leur véritable limite dans la grande ligne géologique qui existe au nord des bassins du Niémen et du Dnièper... Au sud de cette grande ligne: les aptitudes et les types propres à cette région sont et demeureront toujours différents de ceux de la Russie.'[b] [P. Trémaux, *Origine et transformations de l'homme...*, pp. 402, 420, 421.]

Salut.

Your
K. M.

First published in *Der Briefwechsel zwischen F. Engels und K. Marx*, Bd. 3, Stuttgart, 1913

Printed according to the original

---

[a] See this volume, pp. 163-64. - [b] 'If not comprehended by the great laws of nature, man's undertakings are but calamities, witness the efforts of the Czars to make Muscovites of the Polish people. [...] The same soil will give rise to the same character and the same qualities. A work of destruction cannot last forever, but a work of reconstitution is everlasting... The true frontier of the Slav and Lithuanian races with the Muscovites is represented by the great geological line which lies to the north of the basins of the Niemen and the Dnieper... To the south of that great line, the talents and the types fitted to that region are and will always remain different from those of Russia.'

178

ENGELS TO MARX

Manchester, 10 August 1866

Dear Moor,

I don't know whether I should offer full, semi- or no congratulations at all on Laura's semi-engagement. But whatever quantity of congratulations may be admissible, it affects their quality not a wit, and I therefore congratulate with all my heart.

About how much does the Trémaux book[a] cost? If it is not excessively dear on account of illustrations or anything, I'll get it myself, and then you won't need to send it to me.

To allay your butcher's wrath and replenish your stock of paper, I am enclosing J/F 65865 and 66, 2 £5 notes totalling £10, dated Manchester, 30 January 1865. I wish that I could set aside more than £200 a year for you, but unfortunately I cannot. If all goes well, it is true that I shall probably be able to provide another £50, but cotton is falling again now, and Bonaparte's note concerning the 1814 frontiers[369] is alarming the philistine, and that affects the accounts.

That note of Bonaparte's seems to indicate that a HITCH has cropped up between him and Bismarck. Otherwise, his demand would surely not have been so discourteous and unexpected, nor would it have been made at such a very inopportune moment for Bismarck. Bismarck undoubtedly stands to lose nothing by complying with it, but how can he do so now? What will his victorious army say to it? And the German parliament, and the Chambers, and the South Germans? And the old jackass,[b] who will now look as idiotically beatific as my black and white dog Dido when he's eaten his belly full, and who has said, not an inch of German soil, etc.?

The note was a great folly on Bonaparte's part, but the howling of the opposition and probably of the army, too, will presumably have forced him to precipitate the matter. It may turn out to be exceedingly dangerous for him. Either Bismarck enables a concession to be made, and then he will be forced to start a war with Bonaparte at the earliest opportunity in order to take his

---

[a] P. Trémaux, *Origine et transformations de l'homme et des autres êtres.* - [b] William I

revenge; or else he may not give way, and then there will be war even sooner. In either case, Bonaparte runs the risk of fighting a war he does not want and without the appropriate diplomatic preparation, without any sure allies, for the publicly avowed purpose of conquest. Incidentally, Bismarck told the Hanoverian minister Platen several years ago that he would put Germany under the Prussian helmet and then lead it against the French in order to 'forge it into one'.[370]

Circulars are circulating here for a 'Kinkel-fête', put round by Leppoc, 'a great poet and a great man', on the occasion of Gottfried-the-Pious' departure for Zurich. I have said I am willing to take part in it for the sum of one farthing.

With kindest regards to your wife and the girls.

Your

F. E.

First published abridged in *Der Briefwechsel zwischen F. Engels und K. Marx*, Bd. 3, Stuttgart, 1913 and in full in *MEGA*, Abt. III, Bd. 3, Berlin, 1930

Printed according to the original

Published in English for the first time

179

MARX TO PAUL LAFARGUE[371]

IN LONDON

London, 13 August 1866

My dear Lafargue,

Allow me to make the following observations:

1. If you wish to continue your relations with my daughter,[a] you will have to give up your present manner of 'courting'. You know full well that no engagement has been entered into, that as yet everything is undecided. And even if she were formally betrothed to you, you should not forget that this is a matter of long duration. The practice of excessive intimacy is especially inappropriate since the two lovers will be living at the same place for a necessarily prolonged period of severe testing and purgatory. I

---

[a] Laura Marx

have observed with alarm how your conduct has altered from one day to the next within the geological period of one single week. To my mind, true love expresses itself in reticence, modesty and even the shyness of the lover towards the object of his veneration, and certainly not in giving free rein to one's passion and in premature demonstrations of familiarity. If you should urge your Creole temperament in your defence, it is my duty to interpose my sound reason between your temperament and my daughter. If in her presence you are incapable of loving in a manner in keeping with the London latitude, you will have to resign yourself to loving her from a distance. I am sure you will take the hint.

2. Before your relationship with Laura is finally settled, I must have proper clarification of your financial position. My daughter believes that I am conversant with your affairs. She is mistaken. I did not raise this question because I believed it was incumbent upon you to take the initiative. You know that I have sacrificed my whole fortune to the revolutionary struggle. I do not regret it. Quite the contrary. If I had to begin my life over again, I would do the same. I would not marry, however. As far as it lies within my power, I wish to save my daughter from the reefs on which her mother's life was wrecked. Had it not been for my direct intervention (a weakness on my part) and the influence that my friendship for you exerted on my daughter's conduct, this affair would never have progressed to its present point; for this reason I bear a heavy personal responsibility. As far as your immediate situation is concerned, the information which has come my way, although I did not seek it, is by no means reassuring. But let's not deal with that now. Regarding your position in general, I know that you are still a student, that your career in France has been half ruined by the events at Liège,[269] that you still lack an indispensable tool for your acclimatisation in England, the language, and that your prospects are at best entirely problematic. Observation has persuaded me that you are not very industrious by nature, despite spasmodic feverish activity and good intentions. In these circumstances, you will need external support if you are to set out in life with my daughter. I know nothing of your family. Although they may enjoy a comfortable living, that does not in itself mean that they would be disposed to make sacrifices for you. I do not even know with what favour they regard your proposed alliance. I repeat that I must have positive clarification on all these matters. Moreover, as an avowed realist, you cannot, of course, expect that I should behave as an idealist in respect of my daughter's future. Such a positive person as yourself, who would

abolish poetry, will not wish to make poetry to the detriment of my child.

3. To preclude any misinterpretation of this letter, I would like to state that—were you in a position to enter into matrimony today—it would not come about. My daughter would refuse. I myself should object. You must have achieved something in life before thinking of marriage, and a long period of testing is required of you and of Laura.

4. I would like this letter to remain confidential between ourselves. I await your reply.

Yours very truly
Karl Marx

First published in: Marx and Engels, *Works,* Second Russian Edition, Vol. 31, Moscow, 1963

Printed according to the original

Translated from the French

Published in English in full for the first time

180

MARX TO ENGELS[26]

IN MANCHESTER

[London,] 13 *août*[a] 1866

Dear Fred,

Lenchen[b] reached the post-office too late on Saturday to send off my note gratefully acknowledging receipt of the £10.

You must forgive me if I do *not* write a letter today. I have the most pressing business on my back. I wrote a long letter in French to Lafargue today, telling him that I must have *des renseignements positifs*[c] from his family concerning his economic circumstances before the affair can proceed or an ARRANGEMENT can be arrived at.[d] A letter that he passed to me yesterday from a famous French doctor[e] in Paris speaks well of him.

The title of the book: '*P. Trémaux: Origine et Transformations de l'Homme et des autres Êtres*. Première Partie. *Paris* (Librairie de

---

a August - b Helene Demuth - c positive information - d See this volume, pp. 307-09. - e Jules Antoine Moilin

L. Hachette) *1865.*' Part Two has not yet appeared. No *planches.*[a]
The man's geological MAPS are in his other works.

Snippet from Liebknecht enclosed. I shall be sending you his
newspapers,[b] too, but they are not worth a pinch of snuff.[372]
Salut.

Your
K. M.

I shall also be getting the chief work by the above-mentioned
Parisian *médecin*[c] and will let you have it as soon as I have read it
myself.

First published in *Der Briefwechsel zwischen F. Engels und K. Marx*, Bd. 3, Stuttgart, 1913

Printed according to the original

Published in English in full for the first time

181

MARX TO ENGELS[373]

IN MANCHESTER

London, 23 August 1866

DEAR FRED,

Just a few lines today. The Lafargue affair has been arranged
inasmuch as his old man[d] has written to me from Bordeaux,
requesting the title of *promesso sposo*[e] for his son and offering a
very favourable economic settlement. Furthermore, it is accepted
that Lafargue *jeune*[f] first has to qualify as a doctor in London and
then in Paris before thinking of marriage. SO FAR THE THING IS SETTLED.
But I also informed our Creole yesterday that if he cannot calm
himself DOWN to English manners, Laura will show him the door
without more ado. He must be absolutely clear about this or
nothing will come of the affair. He has a heart of gold but is an
enfant gâté[g] and too much a child of nature.

---

[a] plates - [b] *Mitteldeutsche Volkszeitung* - [c] doctor. J. A. Moilin (le docteur Tony),
Leçons de médecine physiologique. - [d] François Lafargue - [e] fiancé - [f] junior - [g] spoilt
child

Laura declares that before she will formally let herself become betrothed, she must have your CONSENT.

I am threatened with new carbuncles here and there, but they keep disappearing again; they do, however, oblige me to keep my hours of work very much WITHIN LIMITS.

Kindest regards to Lizzy.[a]

Salut.

Your
K. M.

First published in *Der Briefwechsel zwischen F. Engels und K. Marx*, Bd. 3, Stuttgart, 1913

Printed according to the original

182

MARX TO LUDWIG KIGELMANN[65]

IN HANOVER

London, 23 August 1866

My dear Friend,

You must justifiably be angered by my prolonged silence, despite your sundry friendly communications.

However, you will have to excuse me, on account of the extraordinary circumstances in which I find myself.

In consequence of my long illness, my economic situation has reached a point of crisis. I have accumulated debts, which are a crushing mental burden and make me incapable of any activity other than the work in which I am immersed. If I do not succeed in taking out a loan of at least 1,000 talers at an interest of say 5%, I can really see no way out. And despite the numerous letters of acknowledgement I receive from Germany, I do not know where to turn. I can only accept aid from personal friends, nothing public. You will understand that in such conditions letter-writing becomes difficult.

I have not yet succeeded in re-establishing my former lucrative links with America.[374] They are so taken up with their own

---

[a] Lizzy Burns

movement there that they regard any expenditure on European reports as *faux frais de production.*[a] I could help them by emigrating myself. But I consider it my duty to remain in Europe and complete the work on which I have been engaged for so many years.[b]

As regards that work itself, I do not think I shall be able to deliver the manuscript of the first volume (it has now grown to 3 volumes[227]) to Hamburg before October. I can only work productively for a very few hours per day without immediately feeling the effects physically, and for my family's sake I suppose I must, however unwillingly, resolve to observe the hygienic limits until I am fully recovered. My work is furthermore often interrupted by the impingement of adverse external circumstances.

Although I am devoting much time to the preparations for the congress in Geneva,[375] I cannot go myself, nor do I wish to, because my work cannot be subjected to prolonged interruption. I consider that what I am doing through this work is far more important for the working class than anything I might be able to do personally at any *congrès quelconque.*[c]

I regard the international situation in Europe as only temporary. As regards Germany in particular, we must take things as we find them,[376] i.e., promote the interests of revolution in a manner appropriate to the changed conditions. As to PRUSSIA, it is now more important than ever TO WATCH AND TO DENOUNCE her RELATIONS TO RUSSIA.

Your very sincere friend

K. Marx

First published in *Die Neue Zeit*, Bd. 2, Nr. 2, Stuttgart, 1901-1902

Printed according to the original

183

ENGELS TO EMIL ENGELS

IN ENGELSKIRCHEN

Manchester, 23 August 1866

Dear Emil,

In great haste, just to ask you to send the Funke document not to me but to

---

[a] unnecessary costs - [b] *Capital* - [c] congress whatsoever

Hall & Janison, SOLICITORS,
Manchester,
as soon as it is signed.

I am leaving for Germany tomorrow,[377] you see.

Kind regards to everyone. I am thinking of coming to Engelskirchen after Marie Blank's wedding.

Your
Friedrich

First published in: Marx and Engels, *Works*, First Russian Edition, Vol. XXV, Moscow, 1934

Printed according to the original

Published in English for the first time

184

MARX TO LAURA MARX

IN HASTINGS

[London,] 28 August 1866

My dear Cacadou,[a]

I have received your letter, but not unopened, since it had to pass through the fingered hands of the Emperor.[b]

It was always my opinion that to give the last finishing stroke to your 'heducation' some sort of boarding school training was still wanted. It will do you a great deal of good.

Il hidalgo della figura trista[c] left me at the corner of his house. His heart having been considerably shaken before, he seemed to bear his separation *from me* with a rather heroic indifference.

My best wishes to ±∞∓.[d]

I enclose 5 l., the remainder to be sent in the second week.

Yours humbly
Old One

---

[a] Laura's jocular nickname - [b] Marx's daughter, Jenny, who acted as his secretary - [c] the knight of the woeful character (Don Quixote); here Marx means Paul Lafargue - [d] Eleanor Marx

Mama will start upon her own expedition to-morrow or after-to-morrow.[378] A great push was wanted to set her amoving.

First published in the language of the original, English, in *Annali*, an. 1, Milano, 1958

Reproduced from the original

185

MARX TO JOHANN PHILIPP BECKER [1]

IN GENEVA [a]

[London,] 31 August 1866

Dear Becker,

It is absolutely imperative that *Jung* be made President of the congress,[375]

1. because he speaks the 3 languages, English, French, and German.

2. Jung *truly represents* the CENTRAL COUNCIL, Odger (who furthermore only knows his mother-tongue) was *not* elected by the CENTRAL COUNCIL; we elected 4 delegates, with Jung at the head; Odger was only to go if he could raise the money himself (guaranteed by us, of course). He has done *nothing* for the Association.

3. Cremer and Odger have hatched a very mean plot to prevent Jung and Eccarius leaving on the very last day.

4. *Odger* wishes to be elected *President of the congress* as a means of impressing the English and imposing himself as President of the CENTRAL COUNCIL for next year, against the *wish of the great majority of the COUNCIL.*

5. Cremer and Odger have both *betrayed* us in the Reform League, where they came to a *compromise with the bourgeoisie* against our wishes.[315]

6. Mr Cremer has *morally debased* himself completely. All his efforts are now aimed at securing a '*paid*' post for himself, so that he need not work. *In no circumstances must* he therefore be elected *as General Secretary* by the congress. (The only paid post.) They

---

[a] The letter bears the stamp: International Working Men's Association / Central Council / London.

must elect *Fox*, on the pretext, which is incidentally true, that the General Secretary must know *more than one language.*

9.[a] The *President of the* CENTRAL COUNCIL must **not** be elected *by the* congress but here *in London,* as a figure of *merely local importance.*

10. At the election of the *President for the congress,* you must say at the outset that an *international congress* can only be presided over by a man who can speak the various languages, simply to save time, etc.

11. Convey this to Dupleix.

12. I should be glad if you would get Eccarius to translate the instructions[b] which I wrote in the name of the CENTRAL COMMITTEE for the London delegates into German beforehand.

Regards and handshake.

Your
Karl Marx

First published in: Marx and Engels, *Works*, First Russian Edition, Vol. XXV, Moscow, 1934   Printed according to the original

186

MARX TO ELEANOR MARX

IN HASTINGS

[London,] 5 September 1866

My beloved master ±∞∓.

I bow to the earth before your immensity, whatever part you may condescend to act, that of the infinitely small or the infinitely grand.   .

Your letters have enchanted us, and we were really bursting out with laughter on reading that fine passage in which you describe the spontaneous explosion produced by the exhibition spinster.

I am belaboured by a gorilla offspring[c] who can hardly spend the separation from a velvet mouse he has put his mind upon.[d] If he knew her, as well as I do, he would, of course, be still more

---

[a] Marx omitted points 7 and 8 here. - [b] K. Marx, 'Instructions for the Delegates of the Provisional General Council. The Different Questions'. - [c] Paul Lafargue - [d] Laura Marx

Calypso, *qui ne pouvait se consoler du départ d'Ulysse*.[a] She may be a Calypso, but he is not an Ulysses, with all that. A spoonzy fellow rather. However, he deserves some praise at my hands. He has worked hard (from 1 o'clock p.m. to 9) in translating the instructions[b] I had to draw up for the Geneva Congress delegates.[375] He has worked not less hard as a tailor at certain gymnastic apparatus you are to use. Last, not least, he affects great attention to the scientific gabble I affect to treat him with, although he and myself are far away from the scene of the mental entertainment.

The day before yesterday the Lormiers were here and the Negrillo,[c] too. Old Lormier, on the pretext of having to communicate him some gymnastic trick, told him '*secretly*' and discreetly, of course, he must stop that fountain of saliva which, while smoking, he is in the habit of inundating the chimney with. When both returned from the kitchen, where the secret communication was taking place, our poor Negrillo looked rather downcast, and behaved like a 'good boy'.

In fact, I liked the boy, at the same time, I think, rather jealous of his encroachments upon my old 'geheimsecretar'.[d]

Don't forget to write me *immediately* what you have to pay *per week*.

The damned weather! I hope it will still mend.

Address of Memeliten[e]: 'Mrs Goodbun, Rose and Crown, Dover.'

Adio, my dear child. Many kisses to you and to the immortal Cacadou,

$$\text{Yours } \frac{0}{\infty}$$

You don't want to write to Mama, as she probably leaves Dover on Friday for another watering-place.

First published, in Russian, in *Voin-stvuyushchy materialist*, Book 4, 1925 and in the language of the original, English, in *The Socialist Review* (London), No. 44, September 1929

Reproduced from the original

---

[a] who could not be consoled after Ulysses' departure - [b] K. Marx, 'Instructions for the Delegates of the Provisional General Council. The Different Questions'. - [c] Paul Lafargue - [d] 'secret secretary', i.e., Laura Marx - [e] Marx's wife

187

MARX TO LAURA MARX

IN HASTINGS

[London, about 8 September 1866]

My dearest Cacadou,[a]

You must excuse if I write those few lines only. We want the inclosed Post Office Order for £3 to leave with the first Post, that is before 11 o'clock a.m. You will oblige me by writing us with what train you will leave Hastings next week, and *when* you will arrive here?

Poor child, your toothache would have been spared to you, if my advice had been followed and my own 'dentist' resorted to.

Your last letter has given much pleasure (the toothache news excepted) because we saw from it with what calm energy our Cacadou knows how to act.

Tell Quoquo[b] that mischief is brewing. The Emperor[c] fancies to be neglected by *his* subjects and feels rather sore.

Yours truly
Old One

First published in: Marx and Engels, *Works*, Second Russian Edition, Vol. 31, Moscow, 1963

Reproduced from the original

Published in English for the first time

188

MARX TO ENGELS[33]

IN MANCHESTER

[London,] 26 September 1866

DEAR FRED,

Receipt enclosed for Moore (I only got the receipt from Dell yesterday).[379]

Mr *Sawyer*, the LANDLORD, has also written me letter that the 3 quarters (£46) are due on 2 October. I have not received a FARTHING from Holland yet and so cannot count on that.

---

[a] Laura's jocular nickname - [b] Eleanor Marx - [c] Jenny, Marx's daughter

By way of demonstration against the French monsieurs—who wanted to exclude everyone except *'travailleurs manuels'*,[a] in the first instance from membership of the INTERNATIONAL ASSOCIATION, or at least from eligibility for election as delegate to the congress— the English yesterday proposed *me* as *President of the* CENTRAL COUNCIL. I declared that under *no* circumstances could I accept such a thing, and proposed *Odger* in my turn, who was then in fact re-elected, although some people voted for me despite my declaration. Dupont, incidentally, has given me the key to the Tolain and Fribourg operation. They want to stand as *workers'* candidates for the Corps législatif[4] in 1869, on the 'principle' that *only workers* can represent the workers. That is why it was exceedingly important for these gentlemen to get this principle proclaimed through the Congress.[380]

At yesterday's meeting of the CENTRAL COUNCIL there were all manner of dramatic scenes. E.g., Mr Cremer fell to earth with a bump when Fox was appointed General Secretary in his stead. He controlled his fury only with great difficulty. Another scene when Mr Le Lubez had to be officially informed of his expulsion from the CENTRAL COUNCIL *par décret*[b] of the congress. He gave vent to the turmoil in his breast in an hour-long speech, in which he spat fire and brimstone at the Parisians, represented himself in terms of astonishing self-esteem and mumbled all manner of dubious things about intrigues whereby the nationalities who were well-disposed towards him (Belgium and Italy) were prevented from attending the congress. Finally, he demanded a vote of confidence from the Central Council[381]—and this will be discussed next Tuesday.

Salut.

Your
K. M.

First published in *Der Briefwechsel zwischen F. Engels und K. Marx*, Bd. 3, Stuttgart, 1913

Printed according to the original

Published in English in full for the first time

---

[a] manual workers - [b] by decree

189

MARX TO ENGELS

IN MANCHESTER

[London,] 1 October 1866

Dear Engels,

I do not know whether I told you last time I wrote that there is a *bill of exchange* (no longer in the LANDLORD's hands) outstanding against me for the rent. Sawyer had written that the bill was due on the 2nd inst., i.e., tomorrow. I called on him yesterday, as by my reckoning the thing could not be due until 3 October, as I had drawn the bill on 1 July for 3 MONTHS, so that 3 days sight must be added. And it turned out I was right. The amount is £46 (3 QUARTERS), and I have been *sans sou*[a] for many weeks, since the SMALL SUMS, which were still obtainable via pawnbrokers, dried up.

As I am furthermore now HARD PRESSED from the daily 'supplies' which have once more accumulated in recent months and in present circumstances (Lafargue) must avoid any *éclat*[b] more than ever, I would leave for the Continent at once to see what I can arrange there 'personally'. However, I must defer that until my manuscript[c] is completed, so that I can take it with me and am not subjected to fresh interruption.

You must forgive me for constantly BOTHERing and plaguing you with my private morass. I had put too much reliance on having the money from Holland.

Your

K. Marx

What do you think of Moilin?[d]

First published in *Der Briefwechsel zwischen F. Engels und K. Marx*, Bd. 3, Stuttgart, 1913

Printed according to the original

Published in English for the first time

---

[a] penniless - [b] scandal - [c] of the first volume of *Capital* - [d] See this volume, p. 310.

190

ENGELS TO MARX

IN LONDON

Manchester, 2 October 1866

Dear Moor,

You did not tell me that you had signed a bill for £46, which was why I sent you half notes for only £40 yesterday; the missing halves follow today, as well as a further five-pound-note I/F 98815, Manchester, 30 January 1865.

Our cashier has not got a second five-pound-note, and it's too late for a POST OFFICE order, so I cannot include the remaining SOVEREIGN; but you will no doubt surmount *that* difficulty.

Regarding Moilin[a] and Trémaux,[b] I will write at greater length in the next few days; I have not quite finished reading the latter yet, but I have come to the conclusion that there is nothing to his whole theory because he knows nothing of geology, and is incapable of even the most common-or-garden literary-historical critique. That stuff about the NIGGER Santa Maria and the whites turning into Negroes is enough to make one die of laughing.[382] Especially the idea that the traditions of the Senegal NIGGERS necessarily deserve credence, *just because these fellows cannot write!* In addition, it is another pretty notion of his to ascribe the differences between a Basque, a Frenchman, a Breton, and an Alsatian to the surface-structure, which is, of course, also to blame for the people speaking four different languages.

Perhaps the man will demonstrate in the 2nd volume how he explains that we Rhinelanders on our Devonian transitional massif (which has not been covered again by the sea since long before the coal was formed) did not become idiots and NIGGERS ages ago, or else he will assert that we are really NIGGERS.

The book is utterly worthless, pure theorising in defiance of all the facts, and for each piece of evidence it cites it should itself first provide evidence in turn.

---

[a] J. A. Moilin (le docteur Tony), *Leçons de médecine physiologique* (see this volume, pp. 309-10, 319). - [b] P. Trémaux, *Origine et transformations de l'homme...* (ibid., pp. 304-05, 309-10).

Kindest regards to the LADIES.

Your

F. E.

First published in *Der Briefwechsel zwischen F. Engels und K. Marx*, Bd. 3, Stuttgart, 1913

Printed according to the original

Published in English for the first time

191

MARX TO ENGELS [243]

IN MANCHESTER

[London,] 3 October 1866

Dear Engels,

The enclosed bill will give you some idea of what adventures I have had today and yesterday. It was not yesterday that it became due, as Sawyer had said. This delay of one day would have been welcome in other circumstances, but in present circumstances it was exceedingly unfortunate. When your letter arrived yesterday, I went straight to our baker, Whithers, as there was nothing left to pawn, and borrowed £1 from him. But when the bill arrived this morning, it was for £48-1-5d. and not, as I had thought, £46. It was my own fault, of course, for not noting the amount. I had thought Sawyer would have deducted the PROPRIETOR TAX which I had paid and which was not deducted from the previous bill (by law it falls on him). That was not the case. (He will therefore have to deduct the whole lot for next quarter.) Hence my mistake over the £46. The bill was presented this morning at 9 o'clock sharp, and I discovered to my horror that I was £2-1-5d. short. *Que faire?*[a] I asked the presenter of the bill to wait (at our house), as I had to go and change some money. I had no alternative but to return to the good baker, who pulled a very long face, as I am deep in the red on account of his supplying of provisions. However, he performed.

---

[a] What was to be done?

Ad vocem[a] *Trémaux*[b]: your verdict 'that there is nothing to his whole *theory* because *he* knows nothing of geology, and is incapable of even the most common-or-garden literary-historical critique'[c] recurs *almost word for word* in Cuvier's 'Discours sur les Révolutions du Globe' in his attack on the doctrine of the *variabilité des espèces*,[d] in which he makes fun of German nature-worshippers, among others, who *formulated* Darwin's basic idea in its entirety, however far they were from being able to *prove* it. However, that did not prevent Cuvier, who was a great geologist and for a naturalist also an exceptional literary-historical critic, from being wrong, and the people who formulated the new idea, from being right. Trémaux's basic idea about the *influence of the soil* (although he does not, of course, attach any value to historical modifications of this influence, and I myself would include amongst these historical modifications the chemical alteration in the surface soil brought about by agriculture, etc., as well as the varying influence which, with varying modes of production, such things as coalfields, etc., have) is, in my opinion, an idea which needs only to be *formulated* to acquire permanent scientific status, and that quite independently of the way Trémaux presents it.

Salut.

Your
K. Marx

First published in *Der Briefwechsel zwischen F. Engels und K. Marx*, Bd. 3, Stuttgart, 1913

Printed according to the original

Published in English in full for the first time

192

ENGELS TO MARX

IN LONDON

Manchester, 5 October 1866

Dear Moor,

I am tickled by your naivety in having bills outstanding against you without knowing the amount; however, it's lucky the

---

[a] As regards - [b] P. Trémaux, *Origine et transformations de l'homme...* - [c] See this volume, pp. 320-21. - [d] mutability of species

difference was no bigger and the good baker was at hand. So that you can repay the sum in question to that excellent man at once and thus preserve your credit, I am enclosing £5 I/F 59667, Manchester, 30 January 1865, for you, and am also returning the bill now settled.

Ad vocem[a] Trémaux. When I wrote to you, I had admittedly only read a third of the book, and that was certainly the worst part (at the beginning). The second third, the critique of the schools, is far better; the third, the conclusions, very bad again. The man deserves credit for having emphasised the effect of the 'soil' on the evolution of races and logically of species as well more than had previously been done, and secondly for having worked out more accurate (though, in my view, still very one-sided) views on the effects of crossing than his predecessors. In *one* respect, Darwin is also right in his views on the effect crossing has *in producing change*, as Trémaux incidentally tacitly acknowledges, in that, when it suits him to do so, he also treats crossing as a means of change, even if ultimately as one that cancels itself out. Similarly, Darwin and others have never failed to appreciate the effect of the soil, and if they did not especially emphasise it, this was because they had no notion of *how* the soil exerts an influence—other than that fertility has a favourable and infertility an unfavourable effect. And Trémaux is little the wiser about that either. The hypothesis that, as a general rule, the soil favours the development of higher species to the extent that it belongs to more recent formations, sounds exceedingly plausible and may or may not be correct; however, when I see the ridiculous evidence with which Trémaux seeks to substantiate it, of which $^9/_{10}$ is based on erroneous or distorted facts and the remaining $^1/_{10}$ proves nothing, I cannot but extend the profound suspicions I have of the author of the hypothesis to the hypothesis itself. But when he then goes on to declare that the effect of the soil's greater or lesser age, modified by crossing, is the *sole* cause of change in organic species or races, I see absolutely no reason to go along with the man thus far, on the contrary, I see numerous objections to so doing.

You say that Cuvier also criticised the German natural philosophers for their ignorance of geology when they proclaimed the mutability of species, and yet they were proved right.[b] At that time, however, the question had nothing to do with geology; but if someone puts forward a theory of the mutability of species based on *geology alone* and makes such geological howlers in it,

---

[a] As regards - [b] See previous letter (p. 322).

falsifies the geology of whole countries (e.g., Italy and even France) and takes the rest of his examples from countries of whose geology we are as good as totally ignorant (Africa, Central Asia, etc.), then that is altogether a different matter. With regard to the ethnological examples in particular, the ones that concern countries and peoples which are generally known are almost without exception erroneous, either in their geological premisses or in the conclusions drawn from them—and he completely ignores the many contrary examples, e.g., the alluvial plains in Central Siberia, the enormous alluvial basin of the River Amazon, all the alluvial land southward from La Plata almost to the southern tip of America (east of the Cordilleras).

That the geological structure of the soil is closely related to the 'soil' in which everything grows is an old idea, likewise that this soil which is able to support vegetation influences the flora and fauna that subsist on it. It is also true that this influence has as yet been scarcely examined at all. But it is a colossal leap from there to Trémaux's theory. At all events, he deserves credit for having emphasised this previously neglected aspect, and, as I said, the hypothesis that the soil *encourages* evolution in proportion to its greater or lesser geological age, may be correct *within certain limits* (or again it may not), but all the further conclusions he draws I consider to be either totally mistaken or incredibly one-sided and exaggerated.

I was very interested by Moilin's book,[a] particularly for the results the French have obtained by vivisection; it is the only way to ascertain the functions of certain nerves and the effects of interfering with them; these fellows appear to have taken the art of animal-torture to a very high level of perfection; and I can very well understand the hypocritical fury of the English against vivisection; these experiments no doubt came as a most unpleasant surprise to many of the comatose gentlemen here and overturned many of their speculations. Whether there is anything new in the theory of inflammations, I am in no position to judge (I intend giving the book to Gumpert); this whole new French school does, however, appear to have a certain free-and-easy character, making big claims and being rather less scrupulous with evidence. As regards medicines, it contains nothing that any competent German doctor does not also know and accept; Moilin just forgets that 1. one is often obliged to choose the lesser evil, medicine, in order to get rid of the greater, namely, a symptom which in itself

---

[a] J. A. Moilin (le docteur Tony), *Leçons de médecine physiologique.*

represents a direct danger, in exactly the same way that by surgery one destroys tissues where there is no alternative, and 2. that one does have to stick to the medicines for as long as one has nothing better. As soon as Moilin can cure syphilis with his electricity, mercury will soon vanish, but scarcely until then. Incidentally, no one can go on telling me that only the Germans can 'construct' systems, THE FRENCH BEAT THEM HOLLOW AT THAT.

Kindest regards.

Your
F. E.

First published in *Der Briefwechsel zwischen F. Engels und K. Marx*, Bd. 3, Stuttgart, 1913

Printed according to the original

Published in English for the first time

193

MARX TO LUDWIG KUGELMANN [65]

IN HANOVER

London, 9 October[a] 1866
1 Modena Villas, Maitland Park,
Haverstock Hill

Dear Friend,

I hope I must not conclude from your lengthy silence that my last letter[b] has in any way offended you. The case should be quite the reverse. Any person, who is in desperate straits, sometimes feels the need to ventilate his feelings. But he only does so to people in whom he has a special and exceptional confidence. I do assure you that my domestic troubles disquiet me far more for being an obstacle to the completion of my work[c] than for any personal or family reasons. I could dispose of the whole problem tomorrow if I were prepared to take up a practical trade tomorrow, instead of working for the cause. And I equally hope that you are not embarrassed by the fact that *you* can do nothing to alleviate my plight. That would indeed be the most unreasonable of reasons.

---

[a] The original has: November. - [b] See this volume, pp. 311-12. - [c] *Capital*

And now to some more general matters.

I was profoundly apprehensive about the first congress in Geneva.[375] By and large, however, it went off better than I expected. We had not in the least anticipated the effect it would have in France, England and America. I was unable to attend, nor did I wish to, but I did write the programme for the London delegates.[a] I deliberately confined it to points which allow direct agreement and combination of efforts by the workers and give direct sustenance and impetus to the requirements of the class struggle and the organisation of the workers into a class. The Parisian gentlemen had their heads stuffed full of the most vacuous Proudhonist clichés. They prattle incessantly about science and know nothing. They spurn all *revolutionary* action, i.e. arising from the class struggle itself, every concentrated social movement, and therefore also that which can be achieved by *political means* (e.g., such as limitation of the working day *by law*). Beneath the *cloak of freedom* and anti-governmentalism or anti-authoritarian individualism these gentlemen, who for 16 years now have so quietly endured the most wretched despotism, and are still enduring it, are in actuality preaching vulgar bourgeois economics, only in the guise of Proudhonist idealism! Proudhon has done enormous harm. His pseudo-critique and his pseudo-confrontation with the Utopians (he himself is no more than a philistine Utopian, whereas the Utopias of such as Fourier, Owen, etc., contain the presentiment and visionary expression of a new world) seized hold of and corrupted first the '*jeunesse brillante*',[b] the students, then the workers, especially those in Paris, who as workers in luxury trades are, without realising it, themselves deeply implicated in the garbage of the past. Ignorantly vain, arrogant, compulsively talkative, rhetorically inflated, they were on the verge of spoiling everything, as they flocked to the congress in numbers quite out of proportion to the number of their members. In my REPORT I shall give them a discreet rap over the knuckles.

I was exceedingly pleased at the American workers' congress, which took place at the same time in Baltimore. The watchword there was organisation for the struggle against capital, and, remarkably enough, most of the demands I had put up for Geneva were put up there, too, by the correct instinct of the workers.[383]

---

[a] K. Marx, 'Instructions for the Delegates of the Provisional General Council. The Different Questions'. - [b] brilliant youth

The reform movement here, which was called into being by our Central Council (*quorum magna pars fui*[a]), has now assumed enormous and irresistible dimensions.[155] I have always kept behind the scenes and have not further concerned myself with the matter since it has been under way.

Your
K. Marx

Apropos. The *Workman*[b] is a philistine paper, and has nothing to do with us. *The Commonwealth* belongs to our people, but has for the moment transformed itself purely into a mouthpiece for Reform (partly for economic and partly for political reasons).

I have recently read Dr *T. Moilin: 'Leçons de Médecine Physiologique'*, which came out in Paris in 1865. A lot of fanciful ideas in it and too much 'construing'. But a lot of criticism of traditional therapeutics, too. I would be glad if you would read the book and let me have your opinion in detail. I would also recommend to you *Trémaux: 'De l'origine de tous les êtres*, etc.' Although written in a slovenly way, full of geological howlers and seriously deficient in literary-historical criticism, it represents—WITH ALL THAT AND ALL THAT—an advance over Darwin.[c]

First published in *Die Neue Zeit*, Bd. 2, Nr. 2, Stuttgart, 1901-1902   Printed according to the original

194

MARX TO LUDWIG KUGELMANN[65]

IN HANOVER

London, Saturday, 13 October 1866

Dear Friend,

Since I wish to reply to you at once and your letter has arrived just before the Post closes (and no post goes from here tomorrow, Sunday), I shall summarise the quintessence of my INTERCEPTED LETTER[384] in a few words. (This confiscation of letters is certainly

---

[a] in which I played an important part (Virgil, *Aeneid*, II, 6) - [b] *The Working Man* - [c] See this volume, pp. 304-05.

not at all pleasant, as I have not the slightest desire to make Mr Bismarck a confidant to my *private affairs*. If, on the other hand, he wishes to know my views on *his* policies, he can approach me direct, and I am sure I shall not mince my words.)

My economic situation has deteriorated so much following my prolonged illness and the many expenses it entailed that I am faced with a financial crisis in the *immediate* future, something which, quite apart from its direct effects on myself and family, would also be ruinous for me politically, especially here in London, where one must keep up *appearances*. What I wanted to find out from you was this: do you know anyone, or a few people (under *no circumstances* must the affair become *public*), who could advance me about 1,000 talers at an interest rate of 5 or 6% for at least 2 years? I am now paying 20-50% interest for the small sums I am borrowing, but for all that I can no longer keep the creditors at bay, with the result that the old firm is about to come crashing down about my ears.

Since my penultimate letter to you[a] I have suffered another series of relapses and have consequently only been able to pursue my theoretical work very intermittently. (The practical work for the International Association goes on as ever, and there is a lot of it, as I am in fact having to run the whole Association myself.) I shall be sending the first sheets[b] to Meissner next month, and will continue to do so until I go to Hamburg with the remainder myself. At all events, I shall take that opportunity to call on you.

My circumstances (endless interruptions, both physical and social) oblige me to publish *Volume One* first, not both volumes together, as I had originally intended. And there will now probably be 3 volumes.

The whole work is thus divided into the following parts:
Book I. The Process of Production of Capital.
Book II. The Process of Circulation of Capital.
Book III. Structure of the Process as a Whole.
Book IV. On the History of the Theory.
The first volume will include the first 2 books.

The 3rd book will, I believe, fill the second volume, the 4th the 3rd.[227]

It was, in my opinion, necessary to begin again *ab ovo*[c] in the first book, i. e., to summarise the book of mine published by Duncker[d] in *one* chapter on commodities and money.[385] I judged

---

[a] See this volume, pp. 311-12. - [b] of the first volume of *Capital* - [c] from the beginning - [d] K. Marx, *A Contribution to the Critique of Political Economy.*

The British Museum

this to be necessary, not merely for the sake of completeness, but because even intelligent people did not properly understand the question, in other words, there must have been defects in the first presentation, especially in the *analysis of commodities.* Lassalle, e. g., in his *Kapital und Arbeit,*[a] in which he claims to give the 'Intellectual quintessence' of my argument, makes serious blunders, which is incidentally something to which he is always prone with his very carefree manner of appropriating my works. It is comical how he even copies my literary-historical 'errors', because, you see, I sometimes quote from memory, without checking things. I have not yet finally made up my mind whether to pass a few remarks in the foreword about Lassalle's plagiarising. The impudence of his disciples towards me would at all events justify it.[105]

The London COUNCIL of the ENGLISH TRADE-UNIONS (its secretary is our President, Odger) is deliberating at the present moment as to whether it should declare itself to be the BRITISH SECTION OF THE INTERNATIONAL ASSOCIATION. If it does so, the control of the working class here will IN A CERTAIN SENSE pass into our hands, and we shall be able to give the movement a good 'PUSH ON'.[18]

Salut.

Your

K. Marx

First published abridged in *Die Neue Zeit,* Bd. 2, Nr. 2, Stuttgart, 1901-1902 and in full in *Pisma Marksa k Kugelmanu* (Letters of Marx to Kugelmann), Moscow-Leningrad, 1928

Printed according to the original

195

MARX TO LUDWIG KUGELMANN[65]

IN HANOVER

[London,] 25 October 1866

Dear Friend,

These few lines *immediately,*

1. to *thank* you for your efforts;
2. to acknowledge receipt of your last letter and of the preceding ones;

---

[a] F. Lassalle, *Herr Bastiat-Schulze von Delitzsch der ökonomische Julian, oder: Capital und Arbeit,* Ch. 3.

3. you misunderstand how things stand between myself and *Engels.* He is my closest friend. I keep no *secrets* from him. If it had not been for him, I would long ago have been obliged to start a 'trade'. In *no* circumstances, therefore, would I wish any third person to intercede with him on my account. There are also, of course, certain limits to what he *can* do.[386]

4. Dr Jacobi,[a] so I am informed by workers, has become quite a good citizen and should not therefore be importuned in any way with my private affairs.

I shall have to see what I can do, but I do see that you have tried everything that was within your power, and therefore entreat you to consider *this* matter as settled.

I am *not* writing for *The Commonwealth.*

Your
K. M.

Miquel *et* Co. will have a long time to wait before they become Prussian ministers.[b]

First published in *Die Neue Zeit,* Bd. 2,   Printed according to the original
Nr. 3, Stuttgart, 1901-1902

196

MARX TO ENGELS[6]

IN MANCHESTER

[London,] 8 November 1866

Dear Engels,

It will not have escaped you that I have not written. I thought you had been informed of the receipt of the £5, as Laura had taken charge of the matter, but, as emerged later, she forgot to do so. I have, furthermore, been in such desperate straits that I was prevented from writing. You know that the £10 which you sent me before your departure[377] were only for payment of taxes and the subsequent £50 for rent. I have thus been completely broke for months. The so-called legacy[c] proved to be divided between at

---

[a] Abraham Jacobi - [b] See also Marx's letter to Engels of 7 May 1867 (this volume, p. 373). - [c] See this volume, p. 194.

least 20 people, so that the share that fell to me at the beginning of the summer was—80 talers! My attempts to drum up money in Germany or Holland have all come to nothing. The only thing that still makes us think of the pawnshop (and my wife has pawned so many possessions that she herself can scarcely go out) is the interest it asks for. I thus had to go round London begging small loans left and right, as in our worst refugee days—and that from a limited number of people who are themselves impecunious—to make even the most essential cash purchases. On the other hand, I am being threatened by tradesmen, some of whom have withdrawn their credit and threatened to take me to court. This state of affairs was all the more critical in that Lafargue (until his departure for Bordeaux a few days ago) was constantly in the house and the REAL STATE OF THINGS had to be anxiously concealed from him. Not merely has my work[a] been frequently interrupted by all this, but by trying to make up at night for the time lost during the day, I have acquired a fine carbuncle near my PENIS. I know you have done everything in your power, and more. But recourse of some kind must be found. Would it not be possible to take up a LOAN or some such transaction?

Salut.

Your
K. M.

First published abridged in *Der Briefwech-sel zwischen F. Engels und K. Marx*, Bd. 3, Stuttgart, 1913 and in full in *MEGA*, Abt. III, Bd. 3, Berlin, 1930

Printed according to the original

197

MARX TO ENGELS

IN MANCHESTER

[London,] 10 November 1866

Dear Engels,

My best thanks for coming to my aid so quickly and ditto for the port wine. I know your own circumstances exactly, and that makes it doubly painful for me thus to put PRESSURE on you. You know, we

---

[a] on *Capital*

really must put an end to this business once and for all, but that will not be possible until I can go to the Continent and act there in person.

Next week the first BATCH *of the manuscript*^a *will go off to Meissner at last.* This summer and autumn it was really not the theory which caused the delay, but my physical and civil condition. It is just 3 years ago now that the first carbuncle was lanced. Since then I have had only short periods of respite from it, and as Gumpert will confirm, of *all* types of work, theory is the most unsuitable if one has this devil's brew in one's blood.

As regards the present fellow, it will be cured in the space of ABOUT 14 days. I now know exactly how it has to be treated and I have therefore started taking the arsenic again.

In great haste.

Your
K. Marx

First published in *Der Briefwechsel zwischen F. Engels und K. Marx,* Bd. 3, Stuttgart, 1913

Printed according to the original

Published in English for the first time

198

ENGELS TO MARX

IN LONDON

[Manchester,] 11 November 1866
86 Mornington St.

Dear Moor,

Many thanks for *The Free Press.* Can you send me the *August* and *September* issues? I have not received them.

Encl. the 2nd halves of the £30. I would have liked to send you more, but I really cannot. I'll see what I can do next month, and on 31 December we shall be doing our accounts again; if they turn out well, no doubt we shall be able to manage a bit more.

The news that the manuscript^a has gone off is a load off my mind. So, a *commencement d'exécution*^b at last, as the *Code pénal* has

---

^a of the first volume of *Capital* - ^b commencement of proceedings

it.[387] To that end I shall drink a special glass to your particular health. The book has greatly contributed to wrecking your health; once you have got it off your back, you'll be quite a different fellow again.

I hope that Birch despatched the port yesterday, but I am none too sure of it; at all events, however, it is sure to arrive by Monday evening or Tuesday morning.

Prussians will be Prussians. As a reward for voting for the indemnity, Twesten and Frenzel are arraigned for speeches made in the Chamber.[388] Such stupidity is quite incomprehensible, but it is a point of principle. The burghers[a] of Frankfurt are still furious, they are now playing the part of Poles, going about in mourning and wearing cravats with the city colours of Frankfurt.[362] A Prussian lieutenant entered a Sachsenhausen tavern and found all the seats taken. Someone got up in one corner and left, at which his neighbour drew the lieutenant's attention to the empty chair, but he said thank you very much, he did not like to sit on a warm chair. Oh, said the other, you have no need to worry about that, our bums are all freezing since the Prussians have been here.

I have heard the most marvellous stories here from eyewitnesses about the Imperial warfare.[b] Such things are unprecedented. E.g., the Nassauers were ordered to bridge the Main at Höchst. Having failed once on account of a *storm* (a storm on the Main!), they found upon their 2nd attempt that they had *too few pontoons* and could only bridge the Main *half-way*. They therefore wrote to Darmstadt, asking for the loan of a few pontoons, which did eventually arrive then, and thus the bridge over the horrendous stream was completed. Then the Nassauers immediately received orders to march south. They left the bridge standing, without a guard, merely leaving it to the care of an old boatman to see that it did not drift away down the Main. A few days later, the Prussians arrived, took possession of the completed bridge, fortified it and marched across!

Your
F. E.

First published in *Der Briefwechsel zwischen F. Engels und K. Marx*, Bd. 3, Stuttgart, 1913

Printed according to the original

Published in English for the first time

---

[a] Engels uses the South-German dialect here: 'Borjer'. - [b] Engels refers to the Austrian Empire and its allies in the Austro-Prussian war of 1866.

199

MARX TO FRANÇOIS LAFARGUE[389]

IN BORDEAUX

London, 12 November 1866

My dear Mr Lafargue,

I hope our friend *il amoroso*[a] has apologised to you on my behalf for my inexcusable silence. On the one hand, I have been plagued by constantly recurring illness, on the other, I have been so taken up by a very lengthy work[b] that I have neglected my correspondence with my closest friends. If I did not count you among that category, I should never have dared so to offend against propriety.

My sincere thanks for the wine. Being myself from a wine-growing region, and former owner of a vineyard,[390] I know a good wine when I come across one. I even incline somewhat to old Luther's view that a man who does not love wine will never be good for anything. (There are exceptions to every rule.) But one cannot, for example, deny that the political movement in England has been spurred on by the commercial treaty with France and the import of French wines.[391] That is one of the good things that Louis Bonaparte was capable of doing, whereas poor Louis Philippe was so intimidated by the manufacturers in the North that he did not dare enter into commercial treaties with England. It is only to be regretted that regimes such as the Napoleonic one, which are founded on the weariness and impotence of the two antagonistic classes of society, buy some material progress at the expense of general demoralisation. Fortunately, the mass of working men cannot be demoralised. Manual labour is the great antidote for all the ills of society.

You will have been just as delighted by the defeat of President Johnson in the latest elections as I was.[392] The workers in the North have at last fully understood that white labour will never be emancipated so long as black labour is still stigmatised.

On Saturday evening Citizen Dupont brought me a letter addressed to Paul[c] by the secretary of the College of Surgeons. He required some papers which were neither in the possession of my daughter[d] (except for his *baccalauréat* diploma) nor of the person

---

[a] the lovelorn gentleman (Paul Lafargue) - [b] *Capital* - [c] Paul Lafargue - [d] Laura Marx

who has charge of your son's effects. You will therefore have to send us these documents *at once.*

Please be so good as to tell your son that he will greatly oblige me by desisting from propaganda in Paris. This is a *dangerous* time. The best thing he can do in Paris is to use his time to profit by his association with Dr Moilin. It will do him no harm to spare his polemical strength. The more he holds himself in check, the better he will be as a fighter when the right moment comes.

My daughter asks me to request you to be so kind as to send with Paul some photograms of Madame Lafargue and of yourself.

All my family joins me in greetings to the Lafargue family.

Yours ever

Karl Marx

First published in the language of the original, French, in *Annali*, an. 1, Milano, 1958

Printed according to the original

Translated from the French

200

MARX TO PAUL LAFARGUE

IN LONDON

[London,] 7 December 1866

My dear Lafargue,

I am so taken up by a piece of work[a] which must be completed by Monday that I am unable to reply to you at once. Meanwhile, if I have offended you by my brusque monologue, I beg your pardon. One should not lose one's temper even when one is in the right.

Greetings.

Karl Marx

First published in: Marx and Engels, *Works,* Second Russian Edition, Vol. 31, Moscow, 1963

Printed according to the original

Translated from the French

Published in English for the first time

---

[a] on the first volume of *Capital*

201

MARX TO ENGELS

IN MANCHESTER

[London,] 8 December 1866

Dear Fred,

Meissner has not begun printing yet,[a] as he wanted to finish off some other things first. I am expecting a letter from him next Monday. All in all, I found the delay by no means disagreeable, as I have only been rid of that vile carbuncle for a few days, and, moreover, my creditors are badgering me in a truly edifying manner. I only regret that private persons CAN not FILE THEIR BILLS FOR THE BANKRUPTCY COURT with the same propriety as men of business.

A while ago, *Kladderadatsch* printed a swipe at the *Brimstone Gang* in large type, in a bad lampoon on Collins' *The Woman in White*. The author of this garbage is that miserable Bettziech, and I should not be surprised if the order had emanated from Kinkel or Hatzfeldt. Nor have I any doubt that the old bag was the cause of Liebknecht's arrest.[393]

The Prussian swine are acting precisely as we should wish them to. There will be no progress until heads roll.

Salut.

Your
K. M.

First published in *Der Briefwechsel zwischen F. Engels und K. Marx*, Bd. 3, Stuttgart, 1913

Printed according to the original

Published in English for the first time

202

ENGELS TO MARX

IN LONDON

Manchester, 14 December 1866

Dear Moor,

You just would not believe how overrun I am at present by all manner of folk. Young men recommended by customers, seeking

---

[a] the first volume of *Capital*

positions here; agents, or such as would like to be so; then this week my most likeable nephew Blank[a] as well, who has established himself in London—and so it goes on continuously, and you will realise how difficult it is thereby to find the time to write. Then, from time to time, I also get someone arriving on the doorstep like the writer of the enclosed letter[394] and putting a pistol to my breast. When I read the letter, I knew at once who had sent this sterling fellow to plague me—it was good old Dr Rode, as the said sterling fellow indeed confirmed when he came up to my office. This shameless Rode is taking some weird liberties in my regard. First, he makes the silliest kind of trouble between myself and Klings after the latter called here,[b] and then he even goes so far as to send people like that to plague me, referring them to me as cashier for the whole émigré community. If the fellow attempts anything else of that kind with me, he may be sure of a warm response. Why cannot he leave me be, I do not know him at all?

The Prussian swine are certainly behaving quite splendidly. I would indeed not have imagined them to be quite so stupid, but it is really impossible to imagine them stupid enough. That is all to the good. Things are on the move again now, and the revolution will come all the sooner for it, and this time heads are bound to roll, as you yourself say.

They are locking up the office, and I must close, too. Enclosed two five-pound-notes:

I/S 38969 and I/S 62239, Manchester, 26 January 1866.

That is as much as I can risk sending until I know how I stand, and I cannot check on it until the books are made up.

Kindest regards to your wife and children.

Your
F. E.

First published in *Der Briefwechsel zwischen F. Engels und K. Marx*, Bd. 3, Stuttgart, 1913

Printed according to the original

Published in English for the first time

---

[a] Emil Blank - [b] See this volume, p. 152.

203

MARX TO ENGELS

IN MANCHESTER

[London,] 17 December 1866

DEAR FRED,

THANKS FOR THE £10.

As far as Rode is concerned, he is obsessed with political connections and his own self-importance. As you are finding this obsession a nuisance—and JUSTLY SO—you should write to him at the first opportunity saying that you have not the honour of his acquaintance and requesting him to desist from such LIBERTIES.

The *Revue des deux Mondes* and the *Revue Contemporaine* had two detailed articles on the 'INTERNATIONAL', which treat it and its congress as one of the most significant events of the century.[a] The like also in *The Fortnightly Review*, in consequence.[b] Meanwhile, we are in practice paralysed BY WANT OF FUNDS and even OF MEN, with all the English being totally absorbed by the REFORM MOVEMENT. The French government is (*heureusement*[c]) beginning to treat us as enemies.[395] One of our more dubious ACQUISITIONS was the joining (AT New York) of HEAD CENTRE[396] Stephens.

Was not the Pope's[d] address to the French OFFICERS capital? Only an Italian priest could thus, before the whole of Europe, deliver Bonaparte a kick in the form of a BLESSING.[397]

It is highly characteristic of the *status rerum*[e] that neither Bonaparte nor William the Conqueror[f] are quite right in the top DEPARTMENT. The latter believes that God Almighty has entrusted him with a special mission, and the former has been TURNED SO TOPSY-TURVY by Mexico[270] and Bismarck that he sometimes appears positively demented.

And do you not think that there will be peace for another year yet at least (apart from ACCIDENTS, of course, such as the death of Bonaparte, etc.)? The fellows all need time for the CONVERSION and PRODUCTION OF ARMS, do they not?

Not a word from Mr *Meissner* yet. I presume that now, at the

---

[a] L. Reybaud, 'L'économie politique des ouvriers', *Revue des deux Mondes*, Vol. 66, 1 November 1866; J. E. Alaux, 'Une forme nouvelle du socialisme. Le Congrès ouvrier de Genève', *Revue contemporaine*, Vol. 53, 15 October 1866. - [b] Marx refers to an editorial published in *The Fortnightly Review*, No. 37, December 1866. - [c] fortunately - [d] Pius IX - [e] state of affairs - [f] An ironic reference to William I of Prussia

year's end, he finds the pressure of business very great. The contract does give me surety in the event of any evasive manoeuvres. In the second, emended and *definitive* version, the contract contains NO STIPULATION WHATEVER AS TO THE TERM FOR WHICH THE MANUSCRIPT [a] IS TO BE READY. But if there is no answer by tomorrow, I shall write again.

As you enjoy credit with *quelconque*[b] bookseller and I CAN not SPEND a FARTHING on books at the moment, you would be doing me a great favour if you could *get as quickly as possible* for me: '*J. E. Th. Rogers: A History of Agriculture*'. I must have a look at the book and have left a gap in one chapter for the purpose.[398] Although it has already been out for a long time, it is not yet in the library. Nor at Mudie's, so I am assured by Eccarius, for whom *The Commonwealth* took out a subscription there.

Salut.

Your
K. M.

First published in *Der Briefwechsel zwischen F. Engels und K. Marx*, Bd. 3, Stuttgart, 1913

Printed according to the original

Published in English for the first time

204

ENGELS TO MARX [399]

IN LONDON

Manchester, 21 December 1866

Dear Moor,

I also think that the leaders in Western Europe will do their utmost to preserve the peace next year and until everyone is equipped with breech-loaders. However, whether the Russians will not consider this very time opportune for cutting Austria down to size with Bismarck's help, for annexing Galicia and dividing Turkey up into a multitude of small Slav states, is another question. Moreover, it could happen that in France, too, war will become a necessity—for the sake of this military reorganisation, because without a war good old Boustrapa[76] will

[a] of the first volume of *Capital* (see this volume, pp. 174-75) - [b] some

not be able to get it accepted. The last war[a] has placed the fellow in a curious dilemma: either he lets everything stand as it is, in which case he will no longer be a MATCH for Prussia, or else he carries the matter out, which will be disastrous for him, first because of his tremendous unpopularity, and second because he is completely *debonapartising* the army. From the moment that some kind of military service for all is introduced in France, the praetorian system[400] will cease of its own accord and the 25-30% of RE-ENLISTED FELLOWS, who now serve in the French army, will disappear for the most part. However, as there will still be substitution,[401] this time Mr Bonaparte will find himself in the comical predicament of needing the support of the *bourgeoisie* to oppose the *peasantry.* But the course of history really is quite impudently ruthless in dealing with this noble fellow, and he must be forgiven if he loses faith in the ways of God and the World. I hope he, like me, reads his Horace for recreation: *justum ac tenacem propositi virum,*[b] etc. Old Horace reminds me in places of Heine, who learnt a great deal from him and was *au fond*[c] *politice*[d] no less common a cur. Remember how the sterling fellow challenged the *vultus instantis tyranni*[e] and licked Augustus' boots. And the old goat is quite charming in other respects, too.

I will get the book[f] for you next week if I can.

It is very pleasing about the articles in the *Revue des deux Mondes* and *Fortnightly,* although I have not yet been able to read them.[g] *Revue contemporaine*[h] does not exist here.

Wehner, who was recently in Germany, tells the following anecdote, which was told by Bennigsen (of the National Association[152]) himself: when Bennigsen had his meeting with Bismarck before the war, the latter expounded his whole National-Associationist German policy to him, whereupon Bennigsen enquired how it was that Bismarck was choosing the difficult path of war in order to carry it out, instead of simply 'relying on the support of the people', as the liberal cry has it. Bismarck stared at him for a few moments and then said: Could *you* jump a ditch with a rheumatic nag? He also brought back the news that the unhappy Crown Prince,[i] who used to put on such liberal airs, has

---

[a] the Austro-Prussian war - [b] a just man, firm of purpose (Horace, *Odes,* III, iii, 1) - [c] basically - [d] in respect of politics - [e] the tyrant's threatening countenance (Horace, *Odes,* III, iii, 3) - [f] J. E. Th. Rogers, *A History of Agriculture* (see previous letter) - [g] L. Reybaud, 'L'économie politique des ouvriers', *Revue des deux Mondes,* Vol. 66, 1 November 1866; the leading article in *The Fortnightly Review,* No. 37, December 1866. - [h] See this volume, p. 338. - [i] Frederick William

become even more crazed than the old man[a] since the war, which is one good thing at least.

I enclose another two five-pound-notes, so that you shall not be quite without money over the holidays:

M/W 34768, London, 12 October 1866,

I/S 49080, Manchester, 26 January 1866, in the not entirely unfounded expectation that the accounts will indemnify me for it at the end of the year.

Many regards to the LADIES.

Your
F. E.

First published abridged in *Der Briefwech-sel zwischen F. Engels und K. Marx*, Bd. 3, Stuttgart, 1913 and in full in *MEGA*, Abt. III, Bd. 3, Berlin, 1930

Printed according to the original

Published in English in full for the first time

205

MARX TO ENGELS[33]

IN MANCHESTER

[London,] 31 December 1866

DEAR FRED,

Happy New Year! Ditto for Madame Lizzy[b]! May the devil take Russians, Prussians, Bonaparte and the BRITISH JURYMAN in the coming year!

Apropos. The French government had confiscated papers and documents intended for us which were being brought across the frontier by French MEMBERS after the Geneva Congress, and attached them for the police archives. We claimed the things back through Lord Stanley, FOREIGN MINISTER, as 'BRITISH PROPERTY'. And in fact POOR Bonaparte had to surrender everything to us via the FOREIGN OFFICE.[402] Is that not priceless! He has been outwitted but himself does not know how.

I received some very sad news today—my uncle[c] has died, he was an excellent man. However, he made a good death, quick,

---

[a] William I - [b] Lizzy Burns - [c] Lion Philips

surrounded by all his children, fully conscious and dispensing subtle Voltairean irony over the priest.

The whole family sends you New Year greetings.

Salut.

Your
K. M.

First published in *Der Briefwechsel zwischen F. Engels und K. Marx*, Bd. 3, Stuttgart, 1913

Printed according to the original

Published in English in full for the first time

1867

206

MARX TO ENGELS [26]

IN MANCHESTER

[London,] 19 January 1867

Dear Engels,

After a long silence, for which he pleaded overwork, Meissner has written that my plan 'is unacceptable to him'.

1. He wants to have the 2 volumes[a] ready at the same time[233];

2. not to print piecemeal, as he wants to have one proof-sheet done per day and only to leave the final correction (revision) to me.

I replied *ad* 2 that it is a matter of indifference to me, as he can shortly have the whole manuscript of Volume I. If he commences printing later but prints by so much faster, it will be all the same in the end. However, in the case of a book with so much annotation in various languages, he should reflect whether the manner of correcting he is wanting is feasible without the text being gravely marred by printing errors. *Ad* 1, it is an impossibility without the whole job being greatly delayed, nor is anything of the kind agreed in our contract. I explicated the various reasons to him, but have as yet had no reply.[111]

Aside from the delay, a yet greater obstacle to my committing myself to the 2nd volume is the fact that, when the first one has appeared, I shall have to make a pause for my health's sake; and I shall in any case have to travel to the Continent to ascertain whether I can in any way sort out my financial circumstances. These are becoming worse day by day, and there is a danger of everything coming crashing about our heads. The baker alone is owed £20, and there is the very devil with butcher, GROCER, TAXES, etc. To crown it all, I recently received a letter from a Mr Burton in Torquay, informing me he has bought the house from Sawyer, and he is dunning me 1. for the outstanding rent for the last

---

[a] of *Capital*

QUARTER, 2. as my lease expires in March, requesting me to state if I wish to take the house subsequently, either for a longer LEASE or annually. I did not reply immediately. Whereupon I received a second letter yesterday, saying I must explain myself, as otherwise his 'AGENT' would have to take steps to find another tenant. So IN A FIX.

As for my physical condition, it has been better for some weeks, a few small carbuncles on my left loin, but not significant. Only dreadful insomnia, which makes me very RESTLESS, although the chief cause is probably mental.

THANKS for the Rogers.[a] A lot of material in it. Regarding the STRIKE question, or at least the Manchester WEAVERS' DISPUTE, I should be obliged to you if you would write me an exact account of the STATE OF AFFAIRS, as I can still include it.[b]

Politics frozen up, too cold even for the Russian bear. I am tickled by the Prussians' black, white and red flag![403]

Best wishes to MRS Lizzy.[c]

What does Gumpert have to say about Moilin[d]?

Your

K. M.

First published in *Der Briefwechsel zwischen F. Engels und K. Marx*, Bd. 3, Stuttgart, 1913

Printed according to the original

Published in English in full for the first time

207

ENGELS TO MARX

IN LONDON

Manchester, 29 January 1867

Dear Moor,

I have been so overrun by philistines this morning that I did not manage to despatch the second half of the note by first post, but am doing so herewith.

I expect Meissner will accept your opinion. At all events it is obvious that after the first volume[e] you must have a 6 week rest,

---

[a] See this volume, pp. 339 and 340. - [b] in the first volume of *Capital* - [c] Lizzy Burns - [d] J. A. Moilin (le docteur Tony), *Leçons de médecine physiologique* (see this volume, pp. 324-25). - [e] of *Capital* (see this volume, p. 343).

and also see how you can put money in your purse on the
Continent. I think it will be all right if you take him the rest of the
manuscript yourself.

The position regarding WORKINGMEN AND MANUFACTURERS is as
follows: India, China, Levant, etc., grossly oversupplied, in
consequence of which CALICOS have been almost unsaleable for the
last 6 months. In some districts feeble attempts by the MANUFACTUR-
ERS to organise SHORT TIME ensued. Being only sporadic, all of these
collapsed. Meanwhile, the manufacturers go and send *consignments*
of their goods, unsaleable here, to India and China, etc., thereby
aggravating the GLUT. They then discover that this does not agree
with them either, and they finally propose the HANDS should take a
5% REDUCTION OF WAGES. Whereupon counterproposal from the HANDS
to work just 4 days a week. *Refus*[a] of the MASTERS—AGITATION. In the
last fortnight, finally, a situation has gradually been reached, and
most recently become general, where SHORT TIME at 4 days a week
has been introduced everywhere in the weaving mills and in the
spinning mills that spin for them, in some cases *with* and in some
cases *without* the 5% reduction in wages. The workers therefore
were right in theory and were proved right in practice, too.[404]

The scoundrel Bismarck has splendidly gulled the scoundrel
Bonaparte over the Peace of Prague, exactly as Bonaparte gulled
the Austrians at Villafranca about the expelled Italian princes *qui
rentreront dans leurs états*[b]—but without recourse to foreign
troops.[365] Bismarck is thus saying: the South German states *auront
une existence internationale indépendante,*[c] but only for so long as
they *themselves wish*; from the moment that they *wish* to join with
us, they shall be entirely free to do so, otherwise after all they
would be not indépendants![405] Poor Bonaparte has never been a
member of a student fraternity at a German university, nor has he
ever practised the art of interpretation at one of their beer-
conventions, and is consequently no match for the Hon. Bismarck.
In Hanover they are most frightfully vexed at the Prussians,[355]
and not just the city itself but even more so amongst the
peasantry—they are flocking to the queen[d] and putting all their
assets at her disposal.

There is much ludicrous sentimentality therein, mixed with
hatred for the military and the police; the very same people, e. g.,
are themselves saying that the administration is much improved,
etc., but the Prussians' talent for inspiring hatred for themselves

---

[a] Rejection - [b] who *will return* to their states - [c] will have an *independent* international existence - [d] Marie of Hanover

has once again proved itself here, too. I have this from 2 people who were there a short while ago and are themselves annexationists and Hanoverians.

If I can manage it, I'll come down and see you for a few days at the end of this week or next, i. e., from Friday to Sunday evening. Providing it does not freeze again.

Kindest regards to the LADIES.

Your

F. E.

First published in *Der Briefwechsel zwischen F. Engels und K. Marx*, Bd. 3, Stuttgart, 1913

Printed according to the original

Published in English for the first time

208

MARX TO LUDWIG KUGELMANN [65]

IN HANOVER

[London,] 18 February 1867

Dear Kugelmann,

Will you see to it that the following reply[a] is placed in the *Zeitung für Norddeutschland*, and, if they refuse it, in another Hanoverian paper? It is a matter of some importance to me as I really am intending to travel to Germany in a few weeks' time. The whole notice reeks of Stieber.[406]

In the next few days I shall send you the official report of the congress in Geneva, which is now appearing *in instalments* in English and French in a paper here.[407] *The Commonwealth* is entirely given over to the REFORM MOVEMENT. Its editorship is in very bad hands. For the present we have reasons for letting it go as it is, although as shareholders we are entitled to intervene.

Our Association has recently had all manner of bother with Mr Bonaparte.[402] More next time. Kindly inform me what Liebknecht is doing and where he is hiding.

Yours

K. M.

First published in *Die Neue Zeit*, Bd. 2, Nr. 3, Stuttgart, 1901-1902

Printed according to the original

---

a K. Marx, 'A Correction'.

209

MARX TO ENGELS

IN MANCHESTER

[London,] 21 February 1867

Dear Engels,

I have been putting off writing from one day to the next, but I am hard pressed now. A GROCER is sending the bailiffs in on Saturday (the day after tomorrow) if I do not pay him at least £5.

I have had some additional expenses, firstly £2 for champagne (a small bottle), it having been prescribed for Laura's health, and secondly ditto for gymnastics lessons I had to send her to again on doctor's advice, with payment in advance.

The work[a] will soon be complete, and would have been so today if I had been subject to less harassment of late.

You will detect Stieber's hand in the enclosed cutting sent me by Dr Kugelmann (and which comes most amiss in view of my intended journey).[406]

Your
K. M.

First published abridged in *Der Briefwechsel zwischen F. Engels und K. Marx*, Bd. 3, Stuttgart, 1913 and in full in *MEGA*, Abt. III, Bd. 3, Berlin, 1930

Printed according to the original

Published in English for the first time

210

MARX TO ENGELS[399]

IN MANCHESTER

[London,] 25 February 1867

DEAR FRED,

BEST THANKS FOR £20.

Letter from Dr Kugelmann enclosed.[406]

At this moment, I can only write you these few lines as the LANDLORD'S AGENT is here and I have to act the part of Mercadet in

---

[a] the first volume of *Capital*

Balzac's comedy[a] for his benefit. Apropos Balzac, I advise you to read *Le Chef-d'Œuvre Inconnu* and *Melmoth réconcilié*. They are two little *chefs d'œuvres*, full of the most delightful irony.
Salut.

Your
K. M.

First published in *Der Briefwechsel zwischen F. Engels und K. Marx*, Bd. 3, Stuttgart, 1913

Printed according to the original

Published in English in full for the first time

211

ENGELS TO MARX[26]

IN LONDON

Manchester, 13 March 1867

Dear Moor,

The reason I have not written to you is in part that all manner of things have prevented me, but in part also it was deliberate, as I wanted to let the date pass when 'the book'[b] was due to be completed, and now I hope that it is ready. So, when will you be going to see Mr Meissner? When you do, I will give you an authorisation to collect the fee for my last pamphlet.[c]

Apropos the latter, by now the Lassallean gentlemen will have had time enough to convince themselves how right I was about the effect of universal suffrage and the power it would give the aristocracy in the countryside.[d] The Lassallean gentlemen *failed* to get *2 men* through; the two Saxon workers' candidates[e] who did get through are very dubious and appear to be rather of Wuttke's ilk. As a whole, incidentally, the elections did show that in Germany they are not remotely susceptible to the kinds of pressure that can be applied to them in France, and that is already to the good.[408] I am also convinced that the more bureaucratic meddling there is, the worse each fresh election in Germany will

---

[a] *Le faiseur* - [b] the first volume of *Capital* - [c] F. Engels, *The Prussian Military Question and the German Workers' Party* - [d] See present edition, Vol. 20, pp. 74-75. - [e] A. Bebel and R. Schraps

turn out for the government, and that 15 years of government-controlled elections such as we have had in France are impossible in our country.

But what a fine lot we have in the noble House,[409] to be sure! They may pull a wry face but they won't offer much protest as they are bartering away the few lousy safeguards still contained in the Prussian constitution for the indirect annexation of the 6 million people in the little states, who have *de facto* already been annexed and mediatised without any constitution at all.[376] *Au fond*,[a] it is quite immaterial what nonsense the fellows contrive; with the philistines in their present mood of Bismarckolatry, they represent bourgeois public opinion and will only do what the latter wants. The worthy burgher seems determined to avoid any further 'conflict'. The movement—both at home, where it is now bestirring itself once more, and in Europe—will soon enough leave all this ordure behind and turn to the real issues of the day.

Scoundrel Schweitzer offered himself for election here, there and everywhere, but got nowhere. I have been sent 2 pamphlets about him from Barmen, of which one enclosed and the other, shorter one, to follow; I do not have it with me. The enclosed obviously bears the mark of the Hatzfeldt lot.

Stieber is again creating in the *Volks-Zeitung* over Eichhoff's pieces in the *Hermann,* Koller is also mentioned. See *Hermann.*[410]

The moderate result of universal suffrage in Germany has, in any case, contributed to the sudden popularity of HOUSEHOLD SUFFRAGE in official circles here. It would be splendid if HOUSEHOLD SUFFRAGE got through as a result, there would soon be a good many changes here and the movement would get going.

TRADE HERE is still stagnant to an exceeding degree. India and China have been swamped by the consignments from the manufacturers, 20,000 people are on STRIKE in Stockport, SHORT TIME is spreading and, if this does not change soon, in May we shall have a superb crisis of overproduction. That can only benefit the *radical* reform movement.

The Diplomatic Review is excellent this time.[b] Provided old D. Urquhart gets hold of FACTS, he is ALL RIGHT; but Beust's curious manoeuvres had already aroused my suspicions. Notwithstanding the fact that the Saxons (*vide*[c] Mr von Seebach in the Crimean War[411]) have always been in cahoots with the Russians, notwithstanding the fact that Beust sent that ostentatiously rude despatch

---

[a] At bottom - [b] D. Urquhart, 'Fall of Austria, and Its Consequences to the World', *The Diplomatic Review*, Vol. XV, No. 3, 6 March 1867. - [c] see

to the Russians during the Danish war,[9] I do, nevertheless, find it difficult to decide whether the Russians have *actually bought* the fellow or whether they have got him gratis and without being aware of it. It almost seems to me that the boundless vanity of that little Saxon shit suffices to explain the whole affair — the Russians naturally KNOW HOW TO IMPROVE THE OCCASION.

As an exercise in vulgar democracy, I have recently...[a]

First published in *Der Briefwechsel zwischen F. Engels und K. Marx*, Bd. 3, Stuttgart, 1913

Printed according to the original

Published in English in full for the first time

212

MARX TO ENGELS[33]

IN MANCHESTER

[London,] 2 April[b] 1867

Dear Engels,

I had resolved not to write to you until I could announce completion of the book,[c] which is now the case. Nor did I wish to bore you by explaining the further delay, viz., carbuncles on my posterior and near the PENIS, the final traces of which are now fading but which made it extremely painful for me to adopt a sitting (hence writing) posture. I am *not* taking *arsenic* because it dulls my mind too much and I needed to keep my wits about me at least at those times when writing was possible.

Next week I shall have to take the manuscript to Hamburg myself.[412] I did not like the tone of Mr Meissner's last letter. Added to which, I received the enclosed scrawl from Borkheim yesterday. I have every reason to believe that the 'continental friend' is Mr Privy Councillor Bucher.[413] Borkheim had written him a letter, you know, which he read out to me, about his arrangements for travelling to Silesia, which he wishes to visit on family business. Bucher replied directly. I therefore scent a plot behind these *canards* and will have to put the knife to Meissner's

---

[a] The end of this letter is missing. - [b] The original has: 27 March. - [c] the first volume of *Capital*

breast myself. Otherwise, the fellow would be in a position to hold back my manuscript (some 25 closely printed proof-sheets by my reckoning) and, at the same time, *not* have it *printed* on the pretext that he was 'awaiting' the second volume.[233]

I must now *d'abord*[a] reclaim my clothes and timepiece from their abode at the pawnbroker's. I can also hardly leave my family in their present situation, they being *sans sou*[b] and the creditors becoming more brazen each day. Finally, before I forget, all the money that I could afford to spend on Laura's champagne-treatment has gone the way of all flesh. She now needs red wine, of better quality than I can command. *Voilà la situation.*[c]

Our 'INTERNATIONAL.' has just celebrated a great victory. We were providing financial support from the LONDON TRADE-UNIONS for the Paris bronze WORKERS, who were out on STRIKE. As soon as the masters learnt of that, they gave in.[414] The affair has created a deal of commotion in the French papers, and we are now an established force in France.

It appears to me there must have been collusion between Bismarck and Bonaparte over the Luxemburg affair. It is possible, though improbable, that the former either cannot or will not keep his word.[415] That the *Russians* have been meddling in German affairs is crystal clear from:

1. the treaty between *Württemberg* and Prussia, which was already concluded on 13 August before all the others;

2. Bismarck's demeanour in respect of the Poles.[416]

The Russians are more active than ever. They are setting the stage for trouble between France and Germany. Austria is pretty well paralysed in herself. Our English gentlemen are about to be led a fine song and dance in the UNITED STATES.

Salut.

Your
K. M.

First published abridged in *Der Briefwech-sel zwischen F. Engels und K. Marx*, Bd. 3, Stuttgart, 1913 and in full in *MEGA*, Abt. III, Bd. 3, Berlin, 1930

Printed according to the original

Published in English in full for the first time

---

a first of all - b penniless - c That is the situation.

213

ENGELS TO MARX [26]

IN LONDON

Manchester, 4 April 1867

Dear Moor,

Hurrah! There was no holding back that exclamation when at last I read in black and white that the 1st volume [a] *is* complete and that you intend taking it to Hamburg at once. So that you shall not be short of the *nervus rerum*,[b] I am sending you enclosed the halves of seven five-pound-notes, £35 in toto, and will despatch the other halves immediately I receive the usual telegram. Do not let the scrawl from Bucher [413]—it is *undoubtedly* from him—worry you, it is just Prussian police gossip and the scandal-mongering of men of letters, of the same ilk as that recent stuff about the Polish trip.[406] I enclose a note for you to give to Meissner, so that you can also collect my fee.[c]

There is no longer even a shadow of doubt about the alliance between Bismarck and the Russians. However, the Russians have never yet had to pay so high a price for their Prussian alliance, they have had to sacrifice their whole traditional policy in Germany and, if this time they were to imagine, as is their wont, that it is only 'for the moment', they may well be making the very deuce of a blunder. For all the shouting about the Empire, etc., German unity already seems on the point of outgrowing Bismarck and all those Prussians. They will have to press on all the harder in the Orient—the Russians, that is—, the present favourable conjuncture will surely not endure long. But how great does the financial need have to be and how sluggish must the industrial progress be, *s'il y'en a*,[d] in Russia, if those fellows are still without a railway to Odessa and Bessarabia, 11 years after the Crimean War, when it would now be worth two armies to them! And so I also believe that the storm will break this year, if everything goes well for the Russians.

The Luxemburg affair [415] appears to be taking the same course as with Saarlouis and Landau.[369] Bismarck undoubtedly offered to sell it in 1866, but Louis [e] really does seem to have held back at

---

[a] of *Capital* - [b] sinew of things - [c] for *The Prussian Military Question and the German Workers' Party* (see this volume, p. 348) - [d] if there is any - [e] Napoleon III

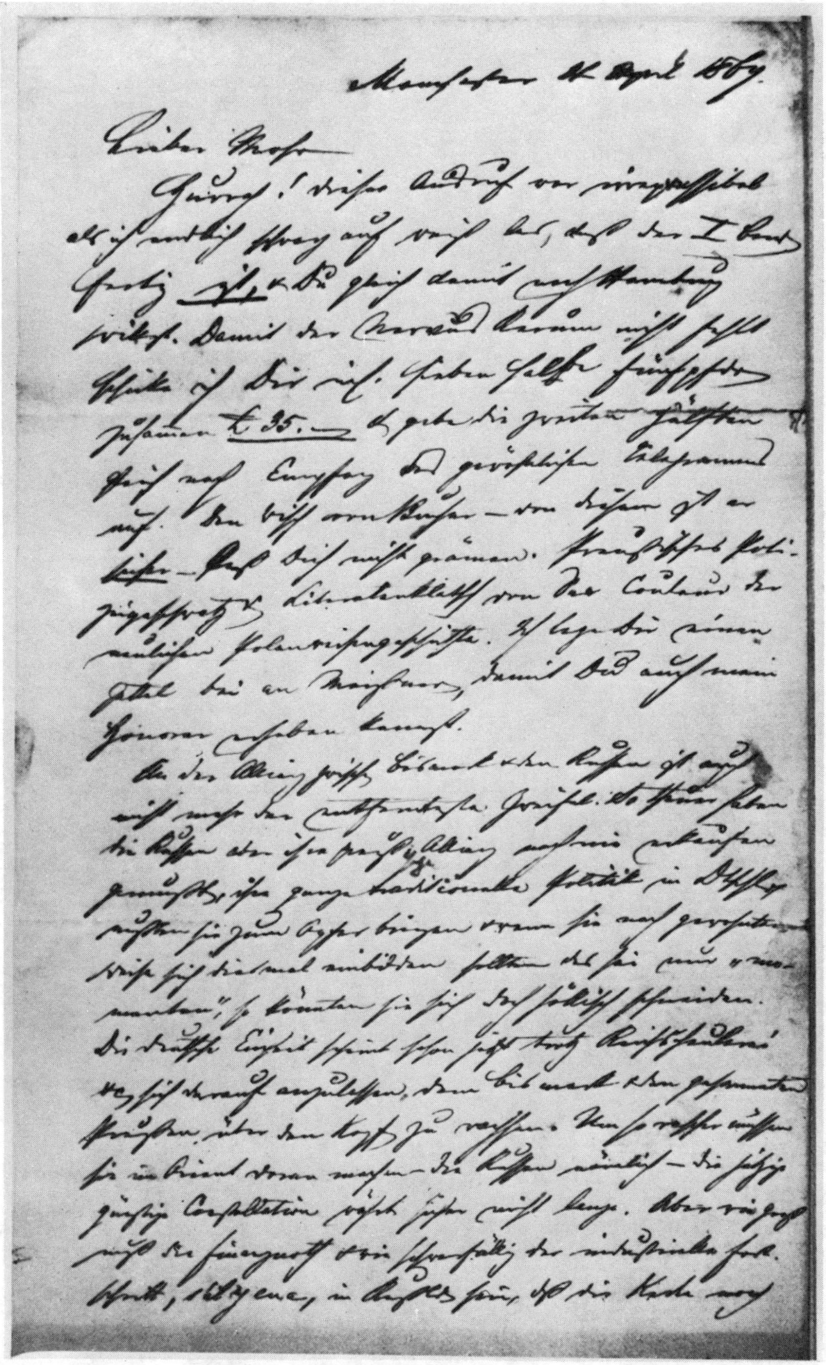

First page of Engels' letter to Marx of 4 April 1867

that time in the hope that he would later get far more *as a present.* I have *positive knowledge* that the Prussian Ambassador Bernstorff told the Hanseatic ditto (Geffcken) in London a few days ago that he had received a despatch to the effect that Prussia was not going to give way over the Luxemburg question under any circumstances. This is the same despatch that *The Owl* refers to as requesting Britain to make representations at The Hague, which are then said to have succeeded in making Holland withdraw from the deal. The point is that in the present situation Bismarck cannot remotely allow the French to annex German territory without making all his achievements appear ridiculous. What is more, that old jackass William[a] has gone and pronounced the words 'not a *single* German village' and is personally committed. It is, however, as yet by no means certain that the deal may not still come to fruition after all; the *Kölnische Zeitung* is screaming quite hysterically that we really cannot start a war over Luxemburg and that we *have* no right to it at all; Luxemburg, they say, should no longer be counted part of Germany, etc., so they have never behaved quite so despicably.

Bismarck may not be Faust, but he does have his *Wagener.*[b] The way in which the poor devil translates his Lord and Master into Wagnerese makes you die of laughing. Bismarck recently employed another of his horse-metaphors, and not wanting to be outdone in this either, Wagener ended a speech by trumpeting: Gentlemen, it is time for us to stop riding our hobby-horses and *to mount that noble thoroughbred mare Germania!*[c] *Montez Mademoiselle,*[d] the Parisians used to say during the Terror.[417]

I hope that your carbuncles are more or less mended now and that the journey will help get rid of them entirely. You *must* put an end to this nonsense this summer.

Many regards to the LADIES and Lafargue.

Your
F. E.

First published in *Der Briefwechsel zwischen F. Engels und K. Marx*, Bd. 3, Stuttgart, 1913

Printed according to the original

Published in English in full for the first time

---

[a] William I - [b] Hermann Wagener. Here and below Engels makes a pun on Wagner, a character from Goethe's *Faust* (a young scholar imitating Faust in every respect). - [c] *Der Social-Demokrat*, No. 38, 27 March 1867. - [d] Mount the guillotine (during the French Revolution the people nicknamed the guillotine 'Mademoiselle').

214

MARX TO ENGELS[6]

IN MANCHESTER

Hamburg, 13 April 1867

Dear FRED,

I arrived here at 12 o'clock noon yesterday. The boat left London on Wednesday[a] at 8 o'clock in the morning.[412] In which fact you see the whole history of the voyage. The most fearful weather and gales. Having been confined for so long, I felt as voraciously fit as 500 hogs.[b] However, with ALL that riff-raff being sea-sick and falling about to left and right of us, it would all have become *ennuyant*[c] in time, if a certain NUCLEUS had not held firm. It was a very 'mixed' nucleus, VIZ., a German ship's captain, who bore a marked resemblance to yourself in his face, but a small fellow, he also had a good deal of your humour and the same good-natured frivolous twinkling of the eyes; a London cattle-dealer, a true John Bull, BOVINE IN EVERY RESPECT; a German clockmaker from London, a nice fellow; a German from Texas; and, the real protagonist, a German who had been roaming around Eastern Peru for 15 years, an area that has only recently been geographically charted, where, amongst other things, human flesh is still consumed in no mean quantity. An eccentric, energetic and high-spirited fellow. He had a most valuable collection of stone axes with him, etc., which merited being discovered in the 'caves'. One female personage as hanger-on (the other ladies were all SEASICK and vomiting in the ladies CABIN), a toothless old hag with a refined Hanoverian accent, daughter of some primeval Hanoverian minister, von Baer or suchlike, she has now long been an improver of men, pietistic, concerned to raise the condition of the working class, acquainted with Jules Simon, full of spiritual radiance, with which she bored our BOVINE FRIEND to death. WELL! On Thursday evening, when the storm was at its worst, with all the tables and chairs adance, we were boozing *en petit comité*,[d] with that old hag of a woman lying on a couch, from which the movement of the ship—to divert her a trifle—occasionally tipped her onto the floor in the middle of the cabin. What was keeping this beautiful creature so spellbound in these inimical circumstances?

---

[a] 10 April - [b] Cf. J. W. Goethe, *Faust*, Part I, Scene 5. - [c] boring - [d] in a small group

Why did she not withdraw to the ladies' chamber? Our savage German was regaling us with an enthusiastic account of the sexual depravities of savages. *Voilà le charme*[a] for this delicate, pure, refined lady. One example: he was received in an Indian hut where the woman was giving birth that very day. The afterbirth is roasted and—supreme expression of hospitality—he is obliged to partake of the SWEETBREAD!

I called on Meissner immediately upon our arrival. Clerk tells me he won't be back before 3 o'clock (afternoon). I left my card and invited Mr Meissner to dine with me. He came but he had someone with him and wanted me to accompany him as his wife was expecting him. I declined but agreed that he should call on me at 7 o'clock in the evening. He mentioned *en passant* that Strohn was probably still in Hamburg. I therefore called on Strohn's brother.[b] Our man had left for Paris THE VERY SAME MORNING. So, Meissner came round in the evening. A pleasant fellow, despite something Saxon about him, as his name suggests. After a brief parley, everything ALL RIGHT. Manuscript taken straight to his publishing house, where it was put in a SAFE. Printing will start IN A FEW DAYS and proceed apace. We then drank together, and he expressed his great 'delight' at making my esteemed acquaintance. He now wants that the book should appear *in 3 volumes.* In particular he is opposed to my compressing the final book (*the historico-literary part*) as I had intended. He said that from the publishing point of view and with the 'dull' mass of readers in mind, this was the part by which he was setting most store. I told him that, as far as that was concerned, I was his to command.[418]

AT ALL EVENTS, in Meissner *we* have someone entirely at our disposal; he has great contempt for the whole pack of vulgar scribblers. I thought it prudent to delay presenting your LITTLE BILL.[c] Always keep the pleasantest surprises till last.

And now *adio*, OLD BOY.

Your

K. Marx

BEST COMPLIMENTS TO MRS BURNS!

First published abridged in *Der Briefwechsel zwischen F. Engels und K. Marx*, Bd. 3, Stuttgart, 1913 and in full in *MEGA*, Abt. III, Bd. 3, Berlin, 1930

Printed according to the original

---

[a] That was the attraction - [b] Eugen Strohn - [c] Marx refers to the fee for Engels' pamphlet *The Prussian Military Question and the German Workers' Party* (see this volume, p. 352).

215

MARX TO LUDWIG KUGELMANN

IN HANOVER

[Telegram]

[Hamburg, 16 April 1867]

Dr L. Kugelmann
Hanover

I arrive this evening about nine.

Marx

First published in: Marx and Engels, *Works*, Second Russian Edition, Vol. 31, Moscow, 1963

Printed according to the photocopy of the telegram

Published in English for the first time

216

MARX TO JOHANN PHILIPP BECKER[419]

IN GENEVA

Hanover, 17 April 1867

Dear Friend,

I left London by STEAMER last Wednesday[a] and after a tempestuous crossing reached Hamburg on Friday afternoon to deliver the manuscript of the first volume to Mr Meissner there. Printing has already started at the beginning of this week, so that the first volume will appear at the end of May. The whole work will appear in 3 volumes.[418] The title is *Capital. A Critique of Political Economy.* The first volume comprises the *First Book*: 'The *Process of Production of Capital'*. It is without question the most terrible MISSILE that has yet been hurled at the heads of the bourgeoisie (landowners included). It is important now that you draw attention to the forthcoming publication in the press, i.e., in the papers to which you have access.

---

[a] 10 April

If you send the next issue of the *Vorbote* as a sample to *Otto Meissner, Hamburg*, he may be of assistance in the distribution of your paper, too.

I must finish now (*more later*) as Dr Kugelmann, who sends his best compliments, intends to acquaint me with the splendours of Hanover.

Tout à toi[a]
K. Marx

First published in: *Marx Festnummer zum 40. Todestage*, Wien, 1923

Printed according to the original

Published in English in full for the first time

217

MARX TO ENGELS[101]

IN MANCHESTER

Hanover, 24 April 1867

Dear FRED,

I have been here as Dr Kugelmann's guest for a week now. I was obliged to stay in Hamburg or right near Hamburg on account of the printing.[b] Things stand as follows. Meissner wants to have the whole undertaking complete in 4-5 weeks, but cannot get the printing done in Hamburg, both because there are not enough printers, and because the proof-readers are insufficiently learned. He is therefore having the printing done at Otto Wigand's (or RATHER his son's,[c] as that puffed-up old cur only has a nominal share in the business now). He sent the manuscript to Leipzig a week ago. He now wants to *have me to hand* to check the first 2 proof-sheets and *at the same time to decide* whether it is **'possible'** to print quickly *with a single proof-reading on my part*. In this case, the whole undertaking would be complete in 4-5 weeks. However, Easter week is now holding it up. Wigand Jr wrote to Meissner that he cannot start until the end of *this* week. At Kugelmann's pressing invitation, I therefore came here (which also

---

[a] Entirely yours - [b] of the first volume of *Capital* - [c] Hugo Wigand

has economic advantages) for the interim. Before I say anything about 'local' affairs, I must not forget to tell you: Meissner would appreciate it, and asks me to pass on the request to you, if you would write a *warning concerning Russia*, for the benefit of the Germans and the French simultaneously. If you do undertake it, he wishes it done quickly. He would, however, prefer you to write *at some length* rather than more briefly, as small pamphlets do not sell well. You could discuss conditions when you send him the manuscript, as he says the two of you would not fall out over the matter. You could write with 'no holds barred', as Meissner considers that there is no need whatever to be concerned about considerations.

Regarding Hanover, then.

Kugelmann is a doctor of great eminence in his special field, which is gynaecology. He is in correspondence with Virchow and the other authorities (including one Meyer in Berlin) and formerly with von Siebold in Göttingen and with Semmelweis in Vienna, before he went mad. Whenever there is a difficult case in this field over here, he is always brought in as consultant. As an instance of the professional jealousy and stupidity of the locals, he told me he had initially been blackballed, i.e., not admitted to the doctors' association here, because 'gynaecology' is a 'cesspit of immorality'. Kugelmann is very talented technically, too. He has invented a mass of new instruments in this field.

Kugelmann is secondly a fanatical supporter (and for my taste excessively Westphalian in his admiration) of our ideas and the two of us personally. He sometimes bores me with his enthusiasm, which is at odds with the detachment he displays as a doctor. But he *understands*, and he is a really *excellent man*, unaffected by qualms, capable of making sacrifices, and, most important of all, *convinced*. He has a charming little wife and an 8-year old daughter who is positively sweet.[a] He has in his possession a far better collection of our works than the two of us together. I even came across *The Holy Family* again here, which he presented to me and of which he will be sending you a copy. I was pleasantly surprised to find that we have no need to feel ashamed of the piece, although the Feuerbach cult now makes a most comical impression upon one. The ordinary people, and in the capital, Hanover, even the bourgeoisie, are extremely *hostile to the Prussians* (ditto in *Electoral Hesse*) and miss no opportunity of expressing their sentiments. They openly proclaim their longing—

---

[a] Gertruda and Franziska Kugelmann

Karl Marx. End of April 1867. Hanover

for the French. If one remarks to them that this is unpatriotic, they say, 'The Prussians did just the same thing. When they marched through here, they were boasting, the officers first and foremost among them, that the French would come to their aid—if need be.' Wehner's father is much respected here and is considered a Guelph.[420] Bismarck sent one of his satraps, the advocate Warnebold, to see me yesterday (keep this *under your hat*). He wishes to 'make use of me and my great talents in the interests of the German people'. Von Benningsen will be paying 'meah'[a] his respects tomorrow.

The standing the two of us enjoy in Germany, particularly among the 'educated' officials, is of an altogether different order from what we imagined. Thus, e.g., the director of the statistical bureau here, Merkel, visited me and told me, he had been studying questions of money for years to no avail, and I had immediately clarified the matter once and for all. 'Your Dioscurus Engels,' he told me, 'was recently acknowledged by my colleague Engel before the royal family in Berlin.' These are trifling things, but they are important for us. We have more influence on these officials than on the louts.

I was also invited to attend the society of 'Europeans', as they call the anti-Prussian, North-Germanic members of the National Association[152] here. What jackasses!

I also received an invitation from the head (head-in-chief, as Stieber calls it[421]) of the railway here. I went along, he provided some good herb wine, his wife was 'delaighted', and as I was leaving, he thanked me 'for doing him such an honour'.

I have a debt of honour—£ 10—to settle with Mr Wheeler, a member of our Council[b] and MANAGER of the EMPIRE INSURANCE CORPORATION. You would oblige me greatly if you would send him the money on my behalf: '*G. Wheeler,* Esq., 27 Gresham Street, *E.C. Private*' (London). I am also very much afraid that my family in London may be 'in profundis'.[c] This grieves me the more particularly because poor good little Jenny's birthday is May 1st. I have cast out nets with a view to making a monetary haul. With what success remains to be seen.

My health is extraordinarily improved. No trace of the old complaint. What is more, in good spirits, despite all adversity, and no liver trouble.

---

[a] In the original the South-German dialect here: 'mür'. - [b] General Council of the International Working Men's Association - [c] in dire straits

Do please write me a few lines *by return* (address: Dr Kugelmann, Hanover). *Salut* to Mrs Burns.

Your
Moor

Freiligrath is making a fool of himself by his public beggary in Germany.[422] Meissner tells me he has disappeared without trace in North Germany.

First published abridged in *Der Briefwech-sel zwischen F. Engels und K. Marx*, Bd. 3, Stuttgart, 1913 and in full in *MEGA*, Abt. III, Bd. 3, Berlin, 1930

Printed according to the original

Published in English in full for the first time

218

ENGELS TO MARX [101]

IN HANOVER

Manchester, 27 April 1867

Dear Moor,

I have received both your letters, the second yesterday afternoon, and would have replied to your first long before, if I had known where to. Firstly, BUSINESS. I am sending £10 to your wife, who wrote to me this morning, and likewise the other £10 to Wheeler at the beginning of next month. This will give you some peace of mind in that regard, and, from what you write, the future also looks rosier at last. I always had the feeling that that damn book,[a] which you have been carrying for so long, was at the bottom of all your misfortune, and you would and could never extricate yourself until you had got it off your back. Forever resisting completion, it was driving you physically, mentally and financially into the ground, and I can very well understand that, having shaken off that nightmare, you now feel quite a new man, especially as, once you have got back into it again, the world doesn't seem so gloomy a place as it did before. Especially when you have such a capital publisher as Meissner appears to be. Incidentally, a quick printing will only be possible, I fear, if you can remain in the vicinity throughout, i.e., on the continent;

---

[a] *Capital*

Holland would also be near enough for the purpose. I do not believe the Leipzig proof-readers will have enough learning for your approach. Meissner also got Wigand to print my pamphlet,[a] and the things those wretches corrected into it! I am convinced that the book will create a real stir from the moment it appears, but it will be very necessary to help the enthusiasm of the scientifically-inclined burghers and officials on to its feet and not to despise petty stratagems. There is much that can be done to that end from Hanover *after publication,* and you could also enlist to advantage the support of *amicus*[b] Siebel, who is at the moment *en route* back from Madeira via England, in the best of spirits, as he says. This will be necessary vis-à-vis the vulgar scribbling fraternity, of whose deep-seated hatred for us we have proof enough. Furthermore, thick, scholarly works are always slow to make their mark without such assistance, but with it they act like 'wildfire'—*confer*[c] Heraclitus the Dark,[d] etc.[423] On this occasion, however, we must be all the more assiduous in ensuring this is done, as *money* is also at stake. Meissner will then be happy to take the collected essays, which would mean more money and further literary success. The pieces from the *Neue Rheinische Zeitung,* the '18th Brumaire',[e] etc., will make an enormous impression on the philistines just now, and once we have gained a little more ground on that basis, all manner of other lucrative possibilities will soon present themselves, too. I am exceedingly gratified by this whole turn of events, firstly, for its own sake, secondly, for your sake in particular and your wife's, and, thirdly, because it really is time things looked up. In 2 years my CONTRACT with that swine Gottfried[f] expires, and the way things are going here, neither of us will really be wishing to extend it; it is even not impossible that our ways may part even earlier. If that should be so, I shall have to *leave* COMMERCE *entirely,* for to start up a business of my own at this late stage would mean 5-6 years of the most fearful drudgery with nothing worth speaking of to show for it, and then another 5-6 years of drudgery to reap the benefits of the first 5 years. But that would be the end of me. There is nothing I long for so much as for release from this vile COMMERCE, which is completely demoralising me with all the time it is wasting. For as long as I am in it, I am good for nothing else, especially since I have become principal it has been much aggravated on account of the greater

---

[a] F. Engels, *The Prussian Military Question and the German Workers' Party.* - [b] friend - [c] compare - [d] F. Lassalle, *Die Philosophie Herakleitos des Dunklen von Ephesos.* - [e] K. Marx, *The Eighteenth Brumaire of Louis Bonaparte.* - [f] Gottfried Ermen

responsibility. If it were not for the increased remuneration, I really would rather be a clerk again. At all events, in a few years my life as a businessman will come to an end, and then my income will be very, very much reduced, and the question of what we can do then has always been in my mind. However, if things go as they are now beginning to, we shall be able to make provision for that all right, too, even if no revolution intervenes and puts an end to all financial schemes. If that does not happen, I have a plan up my sleeve to have a fling for my deliverance and write a light-hearted book entitled: *Woes and Joys of the English Bourgeoisie.*

I cannot go along with Meissner's suggestion.[a] *A few sheets* could be quickly knocked together, but something longer, 6 *à* 10 sheets, would require more work and be *too late* for the war now brewing.[415] One really cannot just knock together rubbish in the manner of Vogt's *Studien.*[b] Furthermore, the stuff would be looked upon more or less as a party manifesto, and for that we would have to discuss the matter first. However, I have had an anti-Russian piece in mind for some time, and, if events provide me with an excuse, I shall start on it without more ado and write to Meissner. The only thing I am still in two minds about is whether I should make the 'nationality principle'[424] or the 'Eastern Question' the chief theme.

I had expected that Bismarck would come knocking at your door, although not his haste.[c] It is characteristic of the fellow's mentality and outlook that he judges everybody by his own standards. The bourgeoisie may well admire the great men of today, it sees itself reflected in them. All the qualities to which Bonaparte and Bismarck owe their successes are the qualities of businessman: the pursuit of a specific purpose by a policy of wait-and-see and experimentation, until they hit the right moment, the diplomacy of always leaving the back door open, negotiating and haggling, swallowing insults if it is in one's interest, the attitude of *'ne soyons pas larrons',*[d] in short, the businessman in all things. In his own way, Gottfried Ermen is as great a statesman as Bismarck, and, if one follows the tricks of these great men, one is constantly reminded of the Manchester Exchange. Bismarck thinks, if I only continue knocking at Marx's door, I am bound to hit upon the right moment eventually, and then we shall do a deal together after all. Gottfried Ermen to a tee.

---

[a] See this volume, pp. 359-60. - [b] C. Vogt, *Studien zur gegenwärtigen Lage Europas* (for Marx's criticism of this work see present edition, Vol. 17). - [c] See this volume, p. 361. - [d] let us not be robbers

I would not have expected the Prussians to be *so* hated there. But how do you reconcile that with the election results? Those jackasses from the National Association [152] did get half their men through, and in Electoral Hesse all but one.

Vogt has got a life-size portrait of himself in the *Gartenlaube*.ª He has become a proper porker in the last few years, and looks fine.

In the *Demokratische Studien*, which recently came my way, Simon of Trier has quite naively copied out whole pages from *Po and Rhine*,ᵇ without suspecting from what poisoned source he was drawing!ᶜ Similarly, in 'Preussen in Waffen', the lieutenant who writes the military articles in *Unsere Zeit* has borrowed at length from my pamphlet,ᵈ likewise without giving his sources, of course.

Rüstow will stop at nothing to become a Prussian general, as though that could be as easily done as with Garibaldi. In his abysmal and slipshod book on the war,ᵉ he *grovels in optima forma*ᶠ before William the Conqueror and the Prince.ᵍ *That's why* he is moving to Berlin.

I saw Ernest Jones the other day, he has had enquiries from 4 places about standing for election under the new Bɪʟʟ [425]—from Manchester as well. Has not a good word to say for the workers here ᴀɴᴅ ʙᴀᴄᴋs ᴛʜᴇ ᴘʀᴜssɪᴀɴs ᴀᴛ ᴀɴʏ ᴏᴅᴅs ᴀɢᴀɪɴsᴛ ᴛʜᴇ Fʀᴇɴᴄʜ. I hope this wretched war passes over, I cannot see that any good can come of it. A French revolution saddled in advance with the obligation to go a-conquering would be very nasty; it almost seems as though Bonaparte would be satisfied with the tiniest tit-bit, but whether the Lord of Hosts will permit handsome William to grant him even that tit-bit, time alone will show.

My kindest regards to Dr Kugelmann, although we are not acquainted, and my thanks to him for *The Holy Family*.ʰ

Your
F. E.

First published abridged in *Der Briefwech-sel zwischen F. Engels und K. Marx*, Bd. 3, Stuttgart, 1913 and in full in *MEGA*, Abt. III, Bd. 3, Berlin, 1930

Printed according to the original

Published in English in full for the first time

ª *Die Gartenlaube*, No. 10, 1867. - ᵇ F. Engels, *Po and Rhine*. - ᶜ L. Simon, 'Deutschland und seine beiden Grossmächte', *Demokratische Studien*, 1860. - ᵈ F. Engels, *The Prussian Military Question and the German Workers' Party*. - ᵉ W. Rüstow, *Der Krieg von 1866 in Deutschland und Italien*. - ᶠ in top form - ᵍ William I of Prussia (an ironical comparison with the Norman William, who conquered England in 1066) and Frederick Charles - ʰ by K. Marx and F. Engels; see this volume, p. 360.

219

MARX TO SIGFRID MEYER[426]

IN NEW YORK

Hanover, 30 April 1867

Dear Friend,

You must think very badly of me, and all the more so when I tell you that your letters did not merely give me *great pleasure* but were a **real comfort** to me since they reached me at a time of great affliction. The knowledge that a capable man, *à la hauteur des principes*,[a] has been won for our party, is some compensation to me for the worst. Your letters were furthermore full of such warm friendship for me personally, and you will appreciate that I who am engaged in a most bitter struggle with the (official) world can least afford to underestimate such things.

Why then did I not answer you? Because I was the whole time at death's door. I thus had to make use of **every** moment when I was capable of work to complete my book,[b] to which I have sacrificed my health, happiness, and family. I hope this explanation suffices. I laugh at the so-called 'practical' men and their wisdom. If one wanted to be an ox, one could, of course, turn one's back on the sufferings of humanity and look after one's own hide. But I should really have thought myself *unpractical* if I had pegged out without finally completing my book, at least in manuscript.

The first volume of the book will be published by *Otto Meissner* in Hamburg in a few weeks. The title of the work is: '*Capital. A Critique of Political Economy*'. I travelled to Germany to bring over the manuscript, and I am spending a few days with a friend in Hanover[c] on my way back to London.[412]

Volume I comprises the '*Process of Production of Capital*'. As well as setting out the general theory, I examine in great detail the conditions of the English—agricultural and industrial—proletariat *over the last 20 years*, ditto the condition of *Ireland*, basing myself on *official* sources that have never previously been used. You will immediately realise that all this serves me solely as an *argumentum ad hominem*.[d]

---

[a] of high principles - [b] the first volume of *Capital* - [c] Ludwig Kugelmann - [d] evidence against the adversary

I hope that a year from now the whole work will have appeared. *Volume II* contains the continuation and conclusion of the theory, *Volume III the history of political economy from the middle of the 17th century.*[418]

As to the 'International Working Men's Association', it has become a power to be reckoned with in England, France, Switzerland, and Belgium. You should form as many branches as possible in America. CONTRIBUTION PER MEMBER 1 PENNY (ABOUT 1 silver groschen) per year. However, every branch gives what it can. Congress in Lausanne this year, 3 September. Every branch can send one representative. Do write to me about this matter, about how you are faring in America and about conditions in general. If you do not write, I shall take it as showing that you have not yet absolved me.

With warmest greetings

Your
Karl Marx

First published abridged in *Die Neue Zeit,* Bd. 2, Nr. 33, 1906-1907 and in full in: Marx and Engels, *Works,* First Russian Edition, Vol. XXV, Moscow, 1934

Printed according to the original

220

MARX TO LUDWIG BÜCHNER[427]

IN DARMSTADT

Hanover, 1 May 1867
(*c/o Dr Kugelmann*)

Dear Sir,

Although we are entirely unacquainted, I am taking the liberty of addressing a personal letter to you, on a personal, although at the same time scientific, matter; and I hope you will excuse my so doing on account of the confidence you inspire in me as a man of science and of the party.

I have come to Germany to deliver the first volume of my work *'Capital. A Critique of Political Economy'* to my publisher, Mr Otto Meissner in Hamburg. I have to stay here a few days longer to see if it will be possible for the printing to be done as quickly as Mr Meissner intends, VIZ., whether the proof-readers are sufficiently learned for such a mode of operation.

The reason I am writing to you personally is this: I should like to have the thing published in French as well, in Paris, after its publication in Germany. I cannot go there myself, at least not without risk, as I have been expelled from France, first under Louis Philippe and a second time under Louis Bonaparte (*Président*),[428] and finally I have been ceaselessly attacking Mr Louis during my exile in London. I cannot therefore go personally to seek out a translator. I know that your work on 'Stoff und Kraft'[a] has appeared in French, and therefore suppose that you can put me in touch, directly or indirectly, with a suitable person. As I have to prepare the second volume for printing this summer and the concluding third volume[418] next winter, I do not have the time to attend to the French version of the book[429] myself.

I consider it to be of the greatest importance to emancipate the French from the erroneous views under which Proudhon with his idealised petty bourgeoisie has buried them. At the recent congress in Geneva,[375] ditto in the links that I have with the Paris branch as a member of the General Council of the International Working Men's Association, I am constantly confronted with Proudhonism's most repugnant consequences.

As I do not know for how long I shall be staying here, I should be obliged to you for an early answer. If I, for my part, can be of any service to you in London, I shall do so with the greatest pleasure.

Yours most respectfully

Karl Marx

First published in: Marx and Engels, *Works*, First Russian Edition, Vol. XXV, Moscow, 1934

Printed according to the original

---

[a] L. Büchner, *Kraft und Stoff. Empirisch-naturphilosophische Studien* (the French edition, *Force et matière*, appeared in 1863).

221

MARX TO HIS DAUGHTER JENNY

IN LONDON

Hanover, 5 May 1867

My dear Child,

Your letter gave me the greatest pleasure. It is written in the true Imperial style.[a] I hope to find you plump and fresh like a May rose.

The enclosed photograph was to be sent to you for your birthday, but was not ready. It is backed by the photograph of Mme Tenge (by-the-by, the aunt of the Baer's girl, of whom Edgar[b] told us so much), who, however, is not so beautiful in reality as her shadow indicates. But she is a really noble nature, of a peculiar suavity, frankness and simplicity of character. Nothing of 'falsche Bildung'.[c] She speaks English, French and Italian (she is of Italian descent) perfectly. Although a great musician, she does not kill one with *Kunstgeschwäts*,[d] which, on the contrary, she abhors. She is an atheist and inclines to Socialism, although rather little informed on that point. What distinguishes her above all is a spontaneous kindness and the absence of all pretensions. I feel sure you would in no time become very intimate friends. Mrs Kugelmann is also a nice little woman.

To-day, on my birthday, I receive the first 'Bogen'[e] for revision. I fear the book will become rather a little too big. In consequence of the Easter week business, the printing did not commence before 29th April, Meissner growing very wild at this suspense. Meanwhile, time has not been lost. Preliminary notices have been published almost in all German papers. Kugelmann has very many connections, which were all put into motion.

Your birthday[f] was solemnly celebrated here.

Except part of the bourgeoisie, lawyers and such ones, there reigns here at Hanover a fanatical hatred of the Prussians, which much amuses me.

I was very glad to hear of your Polish surprise. If the things have no mercantile value, they have a historical one.[430]

The delay of war is exclusively due to the Derby Cabinet. As

---

[a] An allusion to Jenny's jocular nickname: 'the Emperor'. - [b] Edgar von Westphalen - [c] sham education - [d] chatter about art - [e] sheet (of the first volume of *Capital*) - [f] 1 May

long as it remains at the head of England, Russia will not ₁sound the war signal—a phrase, by-the-by, which is conceived in the true colletian style.

I cannot exactly state the day of my return. I have still to receive letters from different sides. I shall return directly from here via Hamburg (there to have another interview with my publisher[a]) to London.

I had, very soon after my arrival here, written to Liebknecht.[111] He has answered. His wife[b] cannot be saved. She is approaching the catastrophe. She sends her compliments to you all and was cheered up by your letters.

Hegel's photograph will be looked after. It is not to be had at Hanover. As to his 'Philos. of Hist.', I shall try to find it at London.

I consider that Cacadou[c] might have written some lines long since, but excuse her with her equestrian studies.

And now, with my best wishes to all, *adio*, my dear 'Joe'.[d]

> Your
> Old One

I add ₐa few lines for Tussy.[e]

First published, in Russian, in *Voin-stvuyushchy materialist*, Book 4, 1925 and in the language of the original, English, in *The Socialist Review* (London), No. 44, September 1929   Reproduced from the original

222

MARX TO ENGELS[26]

IN MANCHESTER

Hanover, 7 May 1867

Dear FRED,

D'abord,[f] best thanks for your intervention in the most pressing *casus delicti*,[g] as well as for your very detailed letter.

---

[a] Otto Meissner - [b] Ernestine Liebknecht - [c] Laura's jocular nickname - [d] a character from Louisa May Alcott's *Little Women* - [e] Eleanor Marx (these lines have not been found) - [f] First of all - [g] difficult case

First, BUSINESS. That damned Wigand did not start printing[a] until 29 April, so that I received the first sheet for correction the day before yesterday, on my birthday. *Post tot pericula!*[b] The misprints were relatively insignificant. It's impossible to wait here until the printing is completed. In the first instance, I fear that the book will prove much fatter than I had originally calculated. Second, I am not getting the manuscript back, so that for many quotations, especially those involving figures or Greek, I need to have my home manuscript to hand, nor can I impose on Dr Kugelmann's hospitality for too long. Finally, Meissner is demanding the 2nd volume by the end of the autumn at the latest. I shall therefore have to get my nose to the grindstone as soon as possible, as a lot of new material relating especially to the chapters on credit and landed property has become available since the manuscript was composed. The third volume must be completed during the winter, so that I shall have shaken off the whole *opus* by next spring.[418] The business of writing, of course, is quite different once the proofs for what has already been done start coming in *à fur et mesure*,[c] and under PRESSURE from the publisher.

Meanwhile, my time here has not been wasted. Letters have been written to all and sundry, and preliminary notices have appeared in most German papers.

I hope and confidently believe that in the space of a year I shall be made, in the sense that I shall be able to fundamentally rectify my financial affairs and at last stand on my own feet again. Without you, I would never have been able to bring the work to a conclusion, and I can assure you it always weighed like a nightmare on my conscience that you were allowing your fine energies to be squandered and to rust in commerce, chiefly for my sake, and, INTO THE BARGAIN, that you had to share all my *petites misères*[d] as well. On the other hand, I cannot conceal from myself that I still have a year OF TRIAL ahead of me. I have taken a step on which a great deal depends, viz., on which it depends whether several £100 will be made available to me from the only quarter where that is possible. There is a tolerable prospect of a positive outcome, but I shall remain uncertain for ABOUT 6 weeks. I shall not have definite confirmation until then. What I am most afraid of—apart from the uncertainty—is my return to London, which will be necessary in 6-8 days. My debts there are considerable, and

---

[a] the first volume of *Capital* - [b] After so many perils! (Paraphrase of an expression from Virgil's *Aeneid*, I, 204: *post tot discrimina rerum*—after so many setbacks.) - [c] gradually - [d] little miseries

the Manichaeans[431] are 'urgently' awaiting my return. And then the torments of family life, the domestic conflicts, the constant harassment, instead of settling down to work refreshed and free of care.

Dr Kugelmann and his wife[a] are being exceptionally kind to me and anticipate my every need. They are splendid people. They really leave me no time to explore 'the gloomy paths of my inner self'. Apropos, the Bismarck affair must be kept absolutely secret.[b] I promised to tell no one, not even Kugelmann, about it. Nor have I done so. I did, however, of course make the *reservatio mentalis* to except yourself.

You express surprise that the National-Liberals[432] (or, as Kugelmann calls them, *the Europeans*) did so well in the elections,[c] when the Prussians are so hated here. The matter is very simple. They did badly in all the larger towns, in smaller places they owed their victories to their organisation, which has existed ever since Gotha.[433] These fellows do, on the whole, show how important party organisation is. That is the position in Hanover. In Electoral Hesse, there is no limit to the influence of Prussian intimidation, backed up by the shouting of the members of the National Association.[152] The Prussians meanwhile are operating quite in the Persian manner here. It is true that they cannot transplant the population to their Eastern provinces, but they are doing so with their officials, right down to the RAILWAY conductors, and for the officers. Even those poor devils of postmen are having to move to Pomerania. In the meantime, trains full of Hessians, Hanoverians, etc., are to be seen on the railway every day *en route* to Bremen, emigrating to the United States. Not since dear old Germany came into existence has it sent such a motley crowd of people from all parts across the Atlantic. One is trying to avoid his taxes, another, his military service, a third the political situation, and all of them the hegemony of the sword and the gathering storm of war.

I am greatly diverted by the (pro-Prussian) bourgeoisie here. They want war, but *immédiatement*.[d] Business, they say, can stand the uncertainty no longer, and where the devil are the taxes to come from if business stagnates for much longer? Incidentally, you would scarcely conceive the burden that the last war and taxation have imposed upon the rural populace in Prussia. Here in the vicinity of Prussian Westphalia, e.g., truly Irish conditions prevail.

By THE BY a few days ago the director of the joint-stock foundry

---

[a] Gertruda Kugelmann - [b] See this volume, p. 361. - [c] to the North German Parliament (see this volume, p. 365) - [d] immediately

here (manufacturing chiefly water and gas pipes) conducted me round the works. On the whole, it is very well organised and utilises much quite modern equipment. But, on the other hand, there is still a good deal of turning by hand (detail work), where the English and Scots are using automatic machinery. The same director took me into the Hermann's-column workshop. The thing is as long in the making as Germany itself. Hermann's head is so colossal that you'd seem like a child beside it, and it has a fine look of honest stupidity, and Mr Arminius was above all a diplomat. His air of worthy Westphalian simplicity served but as a mask for a most subtle mind. As chance would have it, I had renewed my acquaintance with Mr Arminius, shortly before my departure from London, in the Grimm edition of historical sources[a] with which you are familiar.

I am sure you will recall J. Meyer (at Bielefeld), who refused to print our manuscript on Stirner, etc.,[b] and sent the youth Kriege to annoy us?[434] A few months ago he threw himself out of the window in Warsaw, whither his business affairs had taken him, and broke his neck, if you please.

Our friend Miquel, who declared himself prepared to sacrifice freedom so readily for the sake of unity, is believed to be job-hunting. In my view, *le brave homme*[c] has miscalculated. Had he not hurled himself so fanatically and unconditionally at Bismarck's feet, he would have been able to pick up a generous gratuity. But now! What need is there for that? He has made himself so hated by his performance in the North German Parliament[435] that he is chained to the Prussians like one convict to the next. And the Prussians, as you know, do not like to make 'useless' and superfluous *dépenses*.[d] Recently, the Bismarckite newspaper, the *Norddeutsche Allgemeine*, produced by that scoundrel Brass published a very witty article[e] about the National-Associationites, pleading inability to emulate even the *de mortuis nil nisi bene*.[f] It sent Bismarck's North-German-Confederationite, National-Associationite minions packing with some artistic kicks delivered *con amore*.[g]

As far as the war is concerned, I am entirely of your opinion. *At the present moment*, it can only do harm. If it could be delayed, even

---

[a] *Die geschichtsschreiber der deutschen Vorzeit*, Vol. 1, *Die Urzeit* (Jacob Grimm took part in publishing this series of historical documents). - [b] K. Marx and F. Engels, *The German Ideology*. - [c] the good man - [d] expenditure - [e] 'Politischer Tagesbericht. 25. April 1867', *Norddeutsche Allgemeine Zeitung*, No. 97, 26 April 1867. - [f] motto, [speak] only good of the dead (Diogenes Laertius, *De vitis philosophorum*, I, 3, 70) - [g] with love

just for a year, that would be worth its weight in gold to us. In the first place, Bonaparte and William the Conqueror[a] would necessarily be made to look foolish. The opposition is reviving in Prussia (its only press organ just now is *Die Zukunft* in Berlin, founded by Jacobi[b]), and events may occur in France. Business is becoming more and more stagnant, and it will then be impossible to cover up the suffering there on the Continent with empty phrases, whether they be of teutonic or gallic provenance.

In my view, we owe the postponement of war *exclusively* to the Derby ministry. It is anti-Russian, and Russia dares not give the signal until she is sure of Britain. Gladstone, THE PHRASEMONGER (entirely under the influence of LADY Palmerston, Shaftesbury, and LORD Cowper), and Bright, not forgetting Russell, would gladly provide her with the guarantees that Britain was disposed as required. Derby had to be removed in 1859, too, in order to stage the Great Drama in Italy.[c] In the North German Parliament Bismarck was obliged to throw down the gauntlet to the Poles in the most brutal manner[416] and thus declare his total subservience to the Tsar[d].

In the Prussian army there prevails deep distrust of the Russians amongst the better officers, as I learnt personally from Captain von Bölzig here (Guards Regiment, raised in the Cadet Corps, loyal to the Prussian monarchy, but a nice fellow). 'Bismarck's conduct in North Schleswig is incomprehensible to me. Only the Russians,' this he said quite unprompted, 'have any interest in maintaining tension between ourselves and Denmark.' He went on to call Frederick William IV a 'shady cavalier', who had turned Germany into Russia's lackey for $1/2$ century. The Russian officers were 'shitty fellows', the army good for nothing, except for the Guards Regiments, Austria alone was capable of matching the Russian army, etc. I also put a good many more ideas into his head about the Muscovites.

And now *adio*. Kindest regards to MRS Lizzy.[e]

Tout à vous.[f]

Your

Moor

First published abridged in *Der Briefwechsel zwischen F. Engels und K. Marx*, Bd. 3, Stuttgart, 1913 and in full in *MEGA*, Abt. III, Bd. 3, Berlin, 1930

Printed according to the original

Published in English in full for the first time

---

[a] An ironic reference to William I of Prussia. - [b] Johann Jacobi - [c] the war of France and Piedmont against Austria - [d] Alexander II [e] Lizzy Burns - [f] Entirely yours.

223

MARX TO LAURA MARX

IN LONDON

Hanover, 13 May 1867

My pretty little Cacadou,[a]

My best thanks for your letter, and that of the worthy Quoquo.[b]

You complain that I had given no signs of life, but on reviewing the question you will find that, on the whole, I have given weekly signals. Moreover, you know that I am not of a very 'demonstrative' character, of rather retiring habitudes, a slow writer, a clumsy sort of man or, as Quoquo has it, an anxious man.

I shall leave Hanover the day after to-morrow, and probably leave Hamburg by first steamer for London. Yet, you must not expect me to settle the day and the hour. I have still some business to transact with my publisher.[c] At all events, this is the last week of my continental stay.[412]

I am very glad that my photogramm has met with such good reception. The shadow is at all events less troublesome than the original.

As to Mrs Tenge, I wonder that you ask me how she looks, whether she is pretty? I have sent Jenny her photogramm, hidden behind my own. How could it have been lost? Now, to answer your questions, she is 33 years of age, mother of 5 children, rather interesting than pretty, and certainly no professional wit. But she is a superior woman. As to 'flirting', he would be rather a bold man who were to try it. As to 'admiration', I owe it, and there may, perhaps, have been on her side, some overestimation of your most humble and 'modest' master. You know, if no one is a prophet on his own dunghill (speaking symbolically), people are easily overvalued by strangers who, *legen sie nicht aus, so legen sie doch unter*,[d] and find what they were resolved upon to find in a fellah. She has left Hanover Thursday last.

Eight days since, the weather was still frosty and rainy. Now summer has at once burst into full bloom. On the whole, the weather, since my departure, was here as bad and changeable as it used to be in London. Only, and this is a great thing, the air is thinner.

---

[a] Laura's jocular nickname - [b] Eleanor Marx - [c] Otto Meissner - [d] if they do not interpret something in their own way, so they attribute it (a play on the German verbs *auslegen* and *unterlegen*).

These continentals have an easier life of it than we on the other side of the Northern sea. With 2,000 Thalers (300£) you can live here most comfortably. For inst., there exist here different gardens (à la Cremourn,[436] but 'respectable', and where all sort of people meet), much more artistically arranged than any in London, good music being played every evening, etc., where you can subscribe for self and family—for the whole year—at the price of 2 Thalers, 6 sh.! This is only a specimen of the cheap life the Philister indulge in at this place. Young people amuse themselves more freely and at almost no expense, comparatively speaking. There is of course one great drawback—the atmosphere is pregnant with dullness. The standard of existence is too small. It is a lot of *pygmées* amongst whom you want no very high frame to feel like Gulliver amidst the Lilliputians.

There arrive this morning rather 'excited' letters from Berlin. It seems that a collision between the workmen and the *Pickelhauben*[a] is apprehended. I do not expect much for the present, but there is something brewing. The working class, in the greater centres of Germany, are commencing to assume a more decided and threatening attitude. One fine morning there will be a nice dance!

And now my dear little birdseye, Cacadou, secretary, cook, equestrian, poet, *auf Wiedersehn.*[b] *Viele Grüsse, an*[c] Möhmchen, Quoquo and Queque, Helen,[d] and, last not least, our 'mutual friend'.[e]

Adio.

Your master
Old Nick[f]

Enclosed Hegel,[g] presented by Kugelmann to Mons. Lafargue.

First published, in German, in *Die Neue Zeit*, Bd. 1, Nr. 2, 1907-1908 and in the language of the original, English, in *Annali*, an. 1, Milano, 1958

Reproduced from the original

---

[a] policemen - [b] good-bye - [c] Many greetings to - [d] Marx's wife—Jenny, his daughters Eleanor and Jenny, and Helene Demuth - [e] Paul Lafargue - [f] Marx's family nickname - [g] See this volume, p. 370.

224

MARX TO ENGELS

IN MANCHESTER

Manchester [about 22 May 1867]
86 Mornington St.

Dear FRED,

Arrived in London Sunday.[a] Got here today.[437] But:

Notice: with me one H. Meyer from St Louis, whom I am about to collect from the railway REFRESHMENT ROOM, where I deposited him, and I am going to deposit him here in the NEIGHBOURHOOD, *Star.*

He was Weydemeyer's last *compagnon* at his death and took his wife (Weydemeyer's wife), who was also *mourante,*[b] away from St Louis to friends and gave her support. Came to me with a recommendation from Jacobi[c] (New York).

This Meyer, who is travelling to Germany, *came to England solely to visit us both.* He arrived yesterday. I was not at home. My wife told him that I would be travelling to Manchester today to visit you.

These HINTS will be sufficient to explain to you how it comes about that he accompanied me on the journey here. He will only be staying here 2 days. AT FIRST I was vexed. But for Weydemeyer's sake! This Meyer is a fine, active fellow. However, COOKS slowly and somewhat boring.

Salut.

Your
Moor

First published in *Der Briefwechsel zwischen F. Engels und K. Marx*, Bd. 3, Stuttgart, 1913

Printed according to the original

Published in English for the first time

---

[a] 19 May - [b] dying (Louise Weydemeyer) - [c] Abraham Jacobi

225

MARX TO ENGELS

IN MANCHESTER

[London,] 3 JUNE 1867

DEAR FRED,

The reason why sheets 10 and 11 are not being sent to you, indeed why no more proofs[a] at all, you will discover from the enclosed note from Wigand. On the other hand, you will receive the first 5 pulls that have been sent to me. You can keep them ABOUT 8-10 days, but then you must let me know exactly *which points* in the exposition of the *form of value* you think should be specially popularised for the philistines in the supplement.[438]

Fenians ordered.[439] Other commissions will be executed BY AND BY.

See the *Hermann* of last week. It is now the private herald of Mr Freiligrath, who is reporting on the PROGRESS OF THE SUBSCRIPTION here each week via Juch.[422] Little Jenny says that if her father ever did such a thing, she would publicly proclaim him her non-father. Whereupon Lafargue asked her: *Mais qu'est-ce que votre mère dirait là-dessus?*[b] The noble poet[c] is incidentally sly enough to declare already that he will *have* to remain in London on account of his resp. part in the Shakespeare translation. Ferdinand and Ida,[d] Ida and Ferdinand, A WELL-ASSORTED COUPLE, THOSE TWO!

Apropos. When Gumpert asked me which hospital Lafargue was at, I said St Thomas's. I was, however, mistaken. He is at *Bartholomew's* Hospital and asks for the ERROR to be corrected.

Please do not forget to supply a photogramm of yourself and Lupus.

MY BEST COMPLIMENTS TO MRS Lizzy,[e] Moore and Chlormayer.[f] *Salut.*

Your
K. M.

I was exceedingly pleased to read in the Paris correspondence of *The Times* that the Parisians chanted their support for the Poles to

---

[a] of the first volume of *Capital* - [b] But what would your mother say to that? - [c] Ferdinand Freiligrath - [d] Ferdinand Freiligrath's wife - [e] Lizzy Burns - [f] The name given by Marx in joke to Carl Schorlemmer, a chemist by profession.

Alexander's *face,* etc.[440] Mr Proudhon and his little doctrinaire clique are not the FRENCH PEOPLE.

First published abridged in *Der Briefwech-sel zwischen F. Engels und K. Marx,* Bd. 3, Stuttgart, 1913 and in full in *MEGA,* Abt. III, Bd. 3, Berlin, 1930

Printed according to the original

Published in English for the first time

226

MARX TO LUDWIG KUGELMANN[65]

IN HANOVER

London, 10 June 1867

Dear Friend,

The delay attending this letter will expose me to the more or less 'well-founded suspicion' of being a 'bad fellow'. The sole extenuating circumstance I can plead is that I have only been 'resident' in London for the last few days. In the interval I was visiting Engels in Manchester.[437] But I am sure you and your dear wife[a] now know me sufficiently to realise that epistolary negligence is the rule with me. Nevertheless, my thoughts were with you every day. I count my stay in Hanover among the most splendid and refreshing oases in life's desert.[412]

My stay in Hamburg was uneventful, except that, despite all precautions, I made the acquaintance of Mr Wilhelm Marr. In respect of his personal manner, he is Lassalle translated to Christianity, but there is naturally far less to him. Mr Niemann was also performing in the few days I spent there. However, I had been too spoiled by the society in Hanover to wish to attend a theatrical performance in less good company. Mr Niemann thus escaped me.

Apropos. Meissner is willing to print the medical pamphlet you are planning. You need only send him the manuscript and mention my name. Regarding the precise conditions, you will have to negotiate the rest with him yourself.

The crossing from Hamburg to London was by and large fair, if one discounts somewhat raw weather on the first day. A few hours

---

[a] Gertruda Kugelmann

before we reached London, a young German lady, who had already caught my attention by her military bearing, announced that she intended travelling from London to Weston supra Mare the same evening[a] and did not know how she should set about it with all her considerable luggage. The casus was all the more problematical as helping hands are hard to come by in England on the Sabbath. I got her to show me the name of the railway station to which she was to proceed in London. Friends had written it down on a card. It was the NORTH WESTERN STATION, which was on my way as well. I therefore chivalrously offered to set the young lady down there. Agreed. On further reflection, however, it occurred to me that Weston supra Mare lay to the south-west, whereas the STATION which I was to pass and which had been written down for the young lady was north-west. I consulted the SEA-CAPTAIN. Correct: it appeared she should be deposited in a quite different part of London from my own. However, I was now committed and had to assume *bonne mine à mauvais jeu*.[b] We arrived at 2 o'clock in the afternoon.. I took *la donna errante*[c] to her STATION, where I learned that her train did not leave until 8 o'clock in the evening. So, I WAS IN FOR IT, and had 6 hours to kill with Mademoiselle, walking in Hyde Park, sitting in ICE-SHOPS, etc. It emerged that her name was Elisabeth von Puttkamer, *a niece of Bismarck's*, as whose guest she had just spent several weeks in Berlin. She had the whole army list by heart, this family providing our 'gallant regiments' with stout hearts and true in super-abundance. She was a cheerful, educated girl, but aristocratic and black and white[d] to her finger-tips. She was not a little astonished when she learned that she had fallen into '*red*' hands. I reassured her, however, that our encounter would pass 'without bloodshed' and saw her depart *saine et sauve*[e] for her destination. Just think what fodder that would provide for Blind or other vulgar democrats—my CONSPIRACY WITH Bismarck!

Today I despatched the 14th corrected proof-sheet.[f] I received the majority of them while staying with Engels, who is exceedingly pleased with them and, except for sheets 2 and 3, finds them written in a manner *very* easy to understand. I was reassured by his verdict, as I am always very dissatisfied with my things when I see them printed, especially at first sight.

Please convey my special thanks to your dear wife once more for her warm and friendly welcome to me; I am sending her the photogramm of my 2nd daughter Laura, as the other photo-

---

[a] 19 May - [b] put a brave face on it - [c] the wandering lady - [d] the Prussian colours - [e] safe and sound - [f] of the first volume of *Capital*

gramms have all gone and new ones will have to be made. Engels is ditto having fresh copies made of his own and Wolff's[a] photo-gramms. He was greatly amused by your missives.

My best compliments to 'little madam'[b] Eleanor is at school, otherwise she would write to her.

AND NOW, *Adio!*

Your
Karl Marx

First published abridged in *Die Neue Zeit,* Bd. 2, Nr. 3, Stuttgart, 1901-1902 and in full in *Pisma Marksa k Kugelmanu* (Letters of Marx to Kugelmann), Moscow-Leningrad, 1928   Printed according to the original

227

ENGELS TO MARX [101]

IN LONDON

Manchester, 16 June 1867

Dear Moor,

I have been so distracted by all manner of bother with Monsieur Gottfried[c] and other suchlike affairs and disturbances for the past week that I seldom had the leisure to study the form of value. Otherwise, I would have sent the sheets[d] back to you long ago. Sheet 2 in particular has the marks of your carbuncles rather firmly stamped upon it, but there is not much that can be done about it now and I think you should not deal with it any further in the supplement, as your philistine really is not accustomed to this kind of abstract thinking and will certainly not torment himself for the sake of the form of value. At most, you could provide rather more extensive historical evidence for the conclusions you have here reached dialectically, you could, so to speak, apply the test of history, although you have already made the most essential points in that respect; but you have so much material that you can surely still write quite a good excursus on it, which will by historical

---

[a] Wilhelm Wolff - [b] Franziska Kugelmann - [c] Gottfried Ermen - [d] of the first volume of *Capital*

means demonstrate to the philistine the need for the development of money and the process by which this takes place.

It was a serious mistake not to have made the development of these rather abstract arguments clearer by means of a larger number of short sections with their own headings. You ought to have treated this part in the manner of Hegel's Encyclopaedia,[a] with short paragraphs, each dialectical transition emphasised by means of a special heading and, as far as possible, all the excurses or merely illustrative material printed in special type. The thing would have looked somewhat like a school text-book, but a very large class of readers would have found it considerably easier to understand. The *populus*, even the scholars, just are no longer at all accustomed to this way of thinking, and one has to make it as easy for them as one possibly can.

Compared with your earlier presentation (Duncker),[b] the dialectic of the argument has been greatly sharpened, but with regard to the actual exposition there are a number of things I like better in the first version. It is a great pity that the carbuncles have left their mark on the important second sheet in particular. However, there is nothing to be done about it now, and those who are capable of thinking dialectically will understand it, nevertheless. The other sheets are very good, and I was delighted by them. I hope you will soon be able to send me another five or six sheets (and could you please enclose sheet 5 again so that I can pick up the thread properly); the sheets I have been reading one by one here will make a much better impression when read together.

I've discovered a few more misprints. I would only list as errata those which really distort the sense.

I called on Gumpert yesterday. *Pauvre garçon!*[c] He is deteriorating with each day that passes. It was impossible to arouse his interest in anything scientific or even political. Town gossip and nothing more than town gossip. And yet he cannot understand why people don't call on him more often.

Have read Hofmann.[d] For all its faults, the latest chemical theory does represent a great advance on the old atomistic theory. The molecule as the smallest part of matter *capable of independent existence* is a perfectly rational category, a 'nodal point',[441] as Hegel calls it, in the infinite progression of subdivisions, which does not terminate it, but marks a qualitative change. The atom—formerly

---

[a] G. W. F. Hegel, *Encyclopädie der philosophischen Wissenschaften im Grundrisse.* -
[b] K. Marx, *A Contribution to the Critique of Political Economy.* - [c] Poor fellow! -
[d] A. W. Hofmann, *Einleitung in die moderne Chemie.*

represented as the limit of divisibility—is now but a *state*, although Monsieur Hofmann himself is forever relapsing into the old idea that indivisible atoms really exist. For the rest, the advances in chemistry that this book records are truly enormous, and Schorlemmer says that this revolution is still going on day by day, so that new upheavals can be expected daily.

Best regards to your wife, the girls and the electrician.[a]

Your
F. E.

Am sending back 5 sheets today.

<table>
<tr>
<td>First published in Der Briefwechsel zwischen F. Engels und K. Marx, Bd. 3, Stuttgart, 1913</td>
<td>Printed according to the original

Published in English in full for the first time</td>
</tr>
</table>

228

MARX TO ENGELS [101]

IN MANCHESTER

[London,] 22 June 1867

Dear Fred,

Herewith 4 more sheets[b] enclosed for you which reached me yesterday. The fellows have left a number of misprints that I corrected perfectly legibly. One error we corrected in ourselves was 'Childrens' Employment Commission', Childrens'. For *Children* is nominative *pluralis,* genitive mark is'. I saw it at once when I had another look at the Blue Books[359] myself.

King has written to say that the *Fenians*[439] are *not yet out.* They are postponing it for as long as possible and as near to the close of the session as possible.

I hope you are satisfied with the 4 sheets. That you have been satisfied with it so far is more important to me than anything the rest of the world may say of it. At all events, I hope the bourgeoisie will remember my carbuncles until their dying day. Here is a fresh

---

[a] Paul Lafargue (an allusion to his inclination to use electricity in medicine) - [b] of the first volume of *Capital*

sample of what swine they are! You know that the CHILDREN'S
EMPLOYMENT COMMISSION has been at work for 5 years now. When its
first report appeared in 1863, the industries it exposed were at
once 'called to order'. At the beginning of this session the Tory
ministry introduced a BILL *per* Walpole, THE WEEPING WILLOW, accepting
all the Commission's proposals, though on a very reduced scale.
The fellows who were to be called to order, among them the big
metal manufacturers, and especially the vampires of 'domestic
industry', maintained a cowardly silence. Now they are presenting a
petition to Parliament and demanding—a *New Enquiry*! The old
one, they say, was biassed! They are counting on the Reform
Bill [425] taking up the public's entire attention, so that the thing
would be cosily and PRIVATELY smuggled through, at the very time
that the TRADE UNIONS are having a rough passage. [442] The worst
things about the *REPORTS* are *the fellows' own statements.* They are
well aware that a new enquiry means *one thing* only, and that is
precisely 'what we bourgeois want'—a new 5-year lease for
exploitation. Fortunately, my position in the 'INTERNATIONAL' enables
me to frustrate those curs' little game. It is a matter of the utmost
importance. What is at stake is the *abolition of torture* for
$1^{1}/_{2}$ million people, not including the ADULT MALE WORKINGMEN! [443]

With regard to the development of the *form of value,* I have both
followed and *not* followed your advice, thus striking a dialectical
attitude in this matter, too. That is to say, 1. I have written an
appendix in which I set out *the same subject* again as simply and as
much in the manner of a school text-book as possible, and 2. I
have divided each successive proposition into paras. etc., *each with
its own heading,* as you advised. In the *Preface* I then tell the
'*non-dialectical*' reader to skip page x-y and instead read the
appendix. [438] It is not only the philistines that I have in mind here,
but young people, etc., who are thirsting for knowledge. Anyway,
the issue is crucial for the whole book. The economists have
hitherto overlooked the very simple fact that the equation *20 yards
of linen = 1 coat* is but the primitive form of *20 yards of linen = £2,*
and thus that the *simplest form of a commodity,* in which its value is
not yet expressed in its relation to all other commodities but only
as something *differentiated* from its own natural form, embodies the
whole secret of the money form and thereby, *in nuce,*[a] *of all bourgeois
forms of the product of labour.* In my first presentation (Duncker),[b] I
avoided the difficulty of the development by not actually analysing

---

[a] in embryo - [b] K. Marx, *A Contribution to the Critique of Political Economy.*

the᾽ *way value is expressed* until it appears as its developed form, as expressed in money.

You are quite right about Hofmann.[a] Incidentally, you will see from the conclusion to my Chapter III, where I outline the transformation of the master of a trade into a capitalist—as a result of purely *quantitative* changes—that *in the text* there I quote Hegel's discovery of the *law of the transformation of a merely quantitative change into a qualitative one* as being attested by history and natural science alike. In the *note* to the text (I was as it happened attending Hofmann's lectures at that time) I mention the *molecular theory*, but not Hofmann, who has discovered *nothing* in the matter except contributing general *direction*; instead I do mention Laurent, Gerhardt and *Wurtz*, the latter being *the real man*.[444] Your letter struck a faint chord in my memory, and I therefore looked up my manuscript.

Printing has proceeded slowly in the last two weeks (only 4 sheets), probably on account of Whitsun. But Mr O. Wigand will have to make up for this lost time. Apropos. *Your* book[b] is still available. The Workers' Association[c] has ordered and been sent 2 NEW COPIES from O. Wigand. (2nd impression 1848.[445])

Now for private matters.

My children are obliged to invite some other girls for dancing on 2 July, as they have been unable to invite anyone for the whole of this year, to respond to invitations, and are therefore about TO LOSE CASTE. So, hard-pressed though I am at the moment, I had to agree to it and am counting on you for the wine (claret and Rhenish), i.e. on your supplying me with it in the course of next week.

Secondly, as 'misfortunes' never come singly, Lina[d] has announced her arrival for next week. My wife will then have to return to her the £5 which she owes her, and you will understand that after fending off the first wave of creditors, I cannot AFFORD that.

I am in fact exceedingly vexed with the people who have promised me money but have not sent word (so far, at least). They have a personal interest in me. That I do know. They also know that I cannot continue my work unless I have a modicum of peace and quiet. And yet they have sent no word!

Our 'noble' poet Freiligrath really is going to collect a tidy sum.[422] For they say that going begging to the rich Germans in

---

[a] A. W. Hofmann, *Einleitung in die moderne Chemie* (see this volume, pp. 382-83). - [b] F. Engels, *The Condition of the Working-Class in England*. - [c] the German Workers' Educational Society in London - [d] Caroline Schöler

South America and—China! and the West Indies! is most lucrative, as these fellows regard it as *national duty*! Meanwhile, the Freiligraths are continuing to live in *relatively* grand style, constantly entertaining and constantly visiting. That is one reason why the German merchants in London are so unforthcoming. Fat as he is, he is said (so I am told by my wife, who called on them) to look very nerve-wracked and unwell and depressed. But Ida[a] is positively blooming and has never been in better spirits in her life.

Kindest regards to Mrs Lizzy.[b]

Your
K. M.

Honoris causa[c] you must procure *Madame Gumpert's* photogramm for me.

First published abridged in *Der Briefwechsel zwischen F. Engels und K. Marx*, Bd. 3, Stuttgart, 1913 and in full in *MEGA*, Abt. III, Bd. 3, Berlin, 1930

Printed according to the original

Published in English in full for the first time

229

ENGELS TO MARX [419]

IN LONDON

Manchester, 24 June 1867

Dear Moor,

Sheets[d] up to and incl. 12 received with thanks, though have not yet read beyond No. 8. Thus far, the chapters on the transformation of money into capital and the production of surplus-value[446] are the best, as far as presentation and content are concerned. Yesterday I did a rough translation of them for Moore, who understood them correctly and was most astonished that conclusions could be arrived at so simply. At the same time, I have solved the question of *who* should translate your book into English: Moore himself. He has enough German now to read Heine fairly fluently and will soon work his way into your style (except for the form of value

---

[a] Ida Freiligrath - [b] Lizzy Burns - [c] Honour requires that - [d] of the first volume of *Capital*

and the terminology, where I shall have to give him considerable assistance). It is, of course, understood that the whole task will be performed under my immediate supervision. As soon as you have a publisher, who *nota bene* will *pay* him something for his work, he is quite ready to do it. The fellow is diligent and reliable, and, at the same time, has as much prior understanding of the theory as one can expect of an Englishman. I have told him that you would rewrite the analysis of commodities and the section on money in English yourself. For the rest, however, we also need a *terminology* (English) now to translate the Hegelian expressions, and you might be giving some thought to the matter in the meantime, as it is not easy, but there is no way round it.

I have quite lost track of how many sheets have now in fact been type-set—it must surely be half the book by now, mustn't it? I am looking forward to the embarrassment of the economists when they reach the two above-mentioned passages. The development of the form of value is, of course, the quintessence of all the bourgeois trash, but the revolutionary consequences are not yet fully evident, and people can more easily get round these abstractions and confine themselves to clichés. But an end is put to that here, the issue is so crystal clear that I do not see what they can say to it.

I hope you will succeed in tripping up our bourgeois gentlemen with their new Enquiry.[442] Just a few days ago, I heard one of the iron-founders and engineering manufacturers bemoaning the impending danger. Meanwhile, it is very good that the Commission has permanently frustrated the Sheffield star-chamber organisation.[447] It was precisely this local terrorism and its great success that deterred the fellows from joining the great national movement, and confirmed them in their parochialism. The cries of horror emanating from the bourgeoisie are comical. As though our bourgeois gentlemen had not had their own star-chambers, their VIGILANCE COMMITTEES in Australia and California, etc., which acted in exactly the same fashion, but claimed far more victims.

I shall be sending you the wine, and another £10 before the end of this month. I would have preferred it if you had set a later date than 2 July for your PARTY. You will understand that I cannot draw £100 on the very *first* day of the financial year without exciting considerable comment, and I shall have to prevent the people in the office wondering too much about what I may be up to with such a sum all at once.

Regarding the molecular theory, Schorlemmer tells me that Gerhardt and Kekulé are the chief figures involved, and that

Wurtz has only popularised and elaborated it.[a] He is going to send you a book setting out the historical development of the subject.

Are there not old pre-Baconian, pre-Lockeian philosophical writings in English, in which we might be able to find material for the terminology? I have a feeling that something of that kind exists. And how about English attempts at reproducing Hegel?

Kindest regards to your wife and the girls.

Your
F. E.

First published in *Der Briefwechsel zwischen F. Engels und K. Marx*, Bd. 3, Stuttgart, 1913

Printed according to the original

Published in English in full for the first time

230

ENGELS TO MARX[448]

IN LONDON

Manchester, 26 June 1867

Dear Moor,

'Pursuant to mine faithfully of yesterday', two half five-pound-notes enclosed, whose 2nd halves will follow by 1st post early tomorrow morning and thus be in your possession tomorrow evening.

With regard to the production of surplus-value, another point: the manufacturer, and with him the vulgar economist, will immediately interject: if the capitalist only pays the worker the price of 6 hours for his 12 hours' labour, no surplus-value can be produced, since in that case each hour of the factory worker's labour counts only$=1/2$ an hour's labour,$=$the amount which has been paid for, and only that value can be embodied in the value of the labour product. Whereupon there will follow the usual formula by way of example: so much for raw materials, so much for wear and tear, so much for wages (wages *actually paid* per hour's actual product), etc. Atrociously superficial though this argument may be, however much it may equate exchange-value

---

[a] See this volume, pp. 382-83 and 385.

with price, and value of labour with labour-wage, and absurd though its premiss may be that if for one hour's labour only half an hour is paid, then only $^1/_2$ hour's worth goes into the value, I do, nevertheless, find it surprising that you have not already taken it into account, for you will **most certainly** be immediately confronted with this objection, and it is better to anticipate it. Perhaps you return to it in the following sheets.

You must supply me with an address in London to which I can have the £100 sent next week. I am thinking of taking Lizzie[a] via Grimsby to Hamburg, Schleswig, Copenhagen, etc., one week from now, and will probably be away for 4 weeks.[449] I shall therefore have to get our cashier to send the money there on Thursday or Friday, for which purpose I need a *neutral* address, if possible *commercial*. You must therefore consider whom you would prefer for this purpose, and let me know at once.

When I have sent Lizzie back to Grimsby from Hamburg, I shall also go on to visit Meissner and Kugelmann, and then travel to the Rhine.

Kindest regards.

Your

F. E.

First published in *Der Briefwechsel zwischen F. Engels und K. Marx*, Bd. 3, Stuttgart, 1913

Printed according to the original

Published in English in full for the first time

231

MARX TO ENGELS[448]

IN MANCHESTER

[London,] 27 June[b] 1867

Dear FRED,

The 2 half £5-notes received with kindest thanks. With respect to the address, use *Borkheim*. He knows my situation, though with as much concealment as I consider necessary in his regard. I would even like him to know that you are lending me money. But

---

a Lizzie Burns - b The original has: July.

you must write and tell me *when* the money is to be sent to him. I do not see why I should involve yet a 3rd philistine.

The *Fenians* should be delivered to you today.[439]

I was so very pleased by your lines of yesterday, and that requires no further elaboration from me.

Sheet 20[a] was the latest to reach me. It will probably run to 40 or 42 sheets in all. I've *not* as yet received *any corrected proofs* after the ones already sent you. On your departure send me back those which are in your possession.

Regarding the objection that you mentioned the philistines and vulgar economists will infallibly raise (they forget, of course, that, if they reckon *paid labour* as *wages,* they are reckoning *unpaid* labour as *profit,* etc.), it amounts, in scientific terms, to the following question:

How is the *value* of the commodity *transformed* into its *price of production,* in which

1. the *whole of the labour appears paid for* in the form of *wages;*

2. the surplus-labour, however, or the surplus-value, assumes the form of an *addition to the price,* and goes by the name of interest, profit, etc., *over and above* the *cost-price* (=price of the constant part of capital+wages).

Answering this question presupposes:

I. That the *transformation* of, for example, the *value of a day's labour-power* into *wages or the price of a day's labour* has been explained. This is done in *Chapter V* of this volume.[450]

II. That the *transformation of surplus-value* into *profit,* and of *profit into average profit,* etc., has been explained. This presupposes that the *process of the circulation of capital* has been previously explained, since the turnover of capital, etc., plays a part here. This matter cannot therefore be treated prior to the 3rd book (*Volume II* is to contain books 2 and 3).[418] Here it will be shown how the philistines' and vulgar economists' *manner of conceiving things* arises, namely, because the only thing that is ever reflected in their minds is the immediate *form of appearance* of relations, and not their *inner connection.* Incidentally, if the latter were the case, we would surely have no need of *science* at all.

Now if I wished to *refute* all such objections *in advance,* I should spoil the whole dialectical method of exposition. On the contrary, the good thing about this method is that it is constantly *setting traps* for those fellows which will provoke them into an untimely display of their idiocy.

---

[a] of the first volume of *Capital*

By the by, Para. 3: '*The Rate of Surplus Value*', which was the last one you had in your possession, is immediately followed by the Para.: '*The Working Day*' (struggle for the reduction of working time), whose argument demonstrates *ad oculos*[a] to what extent those bourgeois gentlemen comprehend the source and nature of their profit *in practice*. This is also shown in the *Senior* CASE, where your bourgeois assures us that his whole profit and interest derive from the *last unpaid hour of labour.*[451]

Kindest regards to MRS Lizzy.[b]

Your

K. M.

You must stop over for a few days here on your journey home.[449]

Apropos. I judged it in every way imprudent to take Mr *Meissner* into my confidence regarding my private circumstances.

First published in *MEGA*, Abt. III, Bd. 3, Berlin, 1930

Printed according to the original

Published in English in full for the first time

232

MARX TO ENGELS[419]

IN MANCHESTER

[London,] 27 June 1867

DEAR FRED,

The children send you their best thanks.

I have written to Meissner today that the 'Leipzig' method cannot continue in this fashion.[111] I've had *nothing* since Monday. The proofs[c] have been reaching me most irregularly throughout, so that I am for ever being interrupted in other work and am for ever kept quite pointlessly on tenterhooks. Having perhaps received 1 sheet in a whole week, *on Saturday evening* I at last get a successor which is too late for me to send off. I have written to

---

[a] vividly - [b] Lizzy Burns - [c] of the first volume of *Capital*

Meissner that Wigand must send a *minimum* of 3 sheets *on certain agreed days*, but that he is always welcome to send *more* at ANY TIME.

If I get 13th and 14th sheets of the corrected copy in time, you shall have them on Sunday. I would have liked you to see my dressing-down of Senior and my introduction to the analysis of the *working day*[451] before your departure.[449] Incidentally, the section on the 'Working Day' occupies 5 printed sheets, which do, of course, contain predominantly factual material. To show you how closely I have followed your advice in my treatment of the appendix,[a] I'll now copy out for you the divisions, sections, headings, etc., of same appendix.[438]

Appendix to Chapter I, 1

The Form of Value

I. Simple Form of Value

§ 1. *The two poles of the expression of value: relative form and equivalent form of value.*

 a. Inseparability of the two forms.

 b. Polarity of the two forms.

 c. Relative value and equivalent, both being but forms of value.

§ 2. *The relative form of value.*

 a. The relation of equality.

 b. Value-relations.

 c. Qualitative content of the relative form of value implied in value-relations.

 d. Quantitative determination of the relative form of value implied in value-relations.

 e. The relative form of value considered as a whole.

§ 3. *The equivalent form.*

 a. The form of direct exchangeability.

 b. Quantitative determination not contained in the equivalent form.

 c. The peculiarities of the equivalent form.

 α. First peculiarity: use-value becomes the form of appearance of its opposite, value.

 β. Second peculiarity: concrete labour becomes the form of appearance of its opposite, abstract human labour.

---

[a] See this volume, p. 381.

γ. *Third peculiarity: private labour takes the form of its opposite, namely, labour in its directly social form.*

δ. *Fourth peculiarity: the fetishism of the commodity-form more striking in the equivalent form than in the relative value-form.*

§ 4. *The form of value or independent manifestation of value = exchange value.*

§ 5. *Simple form of value of the commodity = simple manifestation of the contradictions it contains within itself between use-value and value.*

§ 6. *Simple form of value of the commodity = simple form of an object as commodity.*

§ 7. *Relationship between commodity-form and money-form.*

§ 8. *Simple relative form of value and individual equivalent form.*

§ 9. *Transition of the simple into the expanded form of value.*

II. Total or Expanded Form of Value

§ 1. *The endless series of relative expressions of value.*

§ 2. *Sequential determination implied in the expanded relative form of value.*

§ 3. *Defects of the expanded relative form of value.*

§ 4. *Expanded relative form of value and specific equivalent form.*

§ 5. *Transition to the general form of value.*

III. The General Form of Value

§ 1. *Altered character of the relative form of value.*

§ 2. *Altered character of the equivalent form.*

§ 3. *Concurrent development of relative form of value and equivalent form.*

§ 4. *Development of the polarity between relative form of value and equivalent form.*

§ 5. *Transition from the general form of value to the money-form.*

IV. The Money-Form

(The following on the money-form is simply for the sake of continuity—perhaps barely half a page.)

§ 1. *How the transition from the general form of value to the money-form differs from the previous transitions in the development.*

§ 2. *Transformation of the relative form of value into the price form.*

§ 3. *The simple form of commodity is the secret of the money-form.*
You may sprinkle sand on this!

Your

K. Moro

Don't forget to drop a line to Borkheim before you depart, so that no 'misunderstanding' is possible.[a]

Regarding the *English translation*,[b] I am trying to track down a fellow in London who will *pay decently*, so that both Moro[c] as translator and I as author get our due. If I am successful, Mrs Lizzy[d] shall also receive *her* share (you must IN THAT CASE allow me that pleasure—but the bird is not yet in the hand) in the form of a London DRESS. I have some expectations, as Mssrs Harrison *et* Co. are most desirous to study the book *in English*.[229] Eccarius has, of course, told them that he is A HUMBLE pupil OF MINE—(*his* critique of Mill has impressed them hugely, they having previously been believers in Mill[e])—and that the Prophet Himself is JUST NOW having the quintessence of all wisdom published, that is printed, in Germany.

I am quite sickened by the REPORT on the FENIANS.[439] These swine boast of their *English* humanity in *not* treating political prisoners *worse* than murderers, street-thieves, forgers and pederasts! And this O'Donovan Rossa, what 'A QUEER FELLOW', because as a FELONY-CONVICT he refused to grovel before his worst enemies! A QUEER FELLOW INDEED! Incidentally, would even the Prussians have been capable of acting in a more bureaucratic fashion than these emissaries of the WEEPING WILLOW,[f] that Knox (read ox) and Pollock (BULL-DOG), who naturally accept the evidence given by the SUBORDINATE 'WARDER' as unimpeachable. But if you don't believe the WARDERS, you have the word of—Wermuth, the chief of police!

Mrs O'Donovan Rossa has written the 'INTERNATIONAL' A VERY FLATTERING AND VERY GRACEFUL LETTER[g] on her departure for America.

The fury of that Bismarck-oracle, the *Norddeutsche*,[h] at Stanley's and Derby's statements about the Luxemburg TREATY has quite cured my nausea.[452] That jackass Brass calls it an innovation! Palmerston has LAID DOWN once and for all the principle that COMMON TREATIES impose only the *right* and not by any means *the duty* of intervention FOR ANY STATE. And if that were not so, whatever BECAME of the OBLIGATIONS which *England* assumed at the Congress of

---

a See this volume, pp. 386-87 and 389-90. - b of the first volume of *Capital* (see this volume, pp. 386-87) - c Samuel Moore - d Lizzy Burns - e J. G. Eccarius, 'A Working Man's Refutation of some Points of Political Economy endorsed and advocated by John Stuart Mill', *The Commonwealth*, Nos. 192-195, 198, 200, 203, 204, 206-211, November 1866-March 1867. - f Walpole - g See this volume, p. 228. - h *Norddeutsche Allgemeine Zeitung*, Nos. 139 and 146, 18 and 26 June 1867: 'Politischer Tagesbericht'.

Vienna with regard to *Poland,* in respect of both Prussia and Russia, and France ditto?

First published in *Der Briefwechsel zwischen F. Engels und K. Marx* Bd. 3, Stuttgart, 1913

Printed according to the original

Published in English in full for the first time

233

MARX TO LUDWIG KUGELMANN [65]

IN HANOVER

London, 13 July 1867

Dear Friend,

THANKS FOR HEGEL AND the young madam! [a]

I shall now briefly answer all the points you raised.

Engels is in Denmark at present and will be paying you a visit one day in the course of this month. [449] *Ad vocem* [b] *the same*: you recall you told me that Menke (or whatever the man in your *statistical* office in Hanover is called) made some very appreciative remarks about the work of mine [c] that was published by Duncker. For Engels' ears I have *twisted* this, to the effect that Menke expressed his great appreciation *to me* of Engels' 'Condition of the Working Class'. [d] *The reason for this pia fraus* [e] (and I have perpetrated various *fraudes* [f] with the same object in view): to *spur* Engels *on* to write and publish the second volume, concerning the period from 1845 to the present. I have at last *succeeded* in this to the extent that he has promised to get down to it. So, if *by chance* conversation should turn to the statistician, *do not let the cat out of the bag.*

Nothing is fixed for *my wife's journey,* nor can it be, it having been overtaken by another event, the proposed departure of my 3 daughters for Bordeaux, to visit Lafargue senior. [g]

I do *not* advise you to go to *Paris.* It is impossible to study anything in the midst of that Babylon of things and among that

---

[a] for the portrait of Hegel and the photograph of Kugelmann's daughter, Franziska - [b] Concerning - [c] K. Marx, *A Contribution to the Critique of Political Economy.* - [d] F. Engels, *The Condition of the Working-Class in England.* - [e] white lie - [f] deceits - [g] François Lafargue

throng of people, unless one stays there for at least 6 weeks, which is *very expensive.*

My book[a] comprises ABOUT 50 sheets. You see how I had miscalculated AS TO ITS EXTENT. A few days ago I sent the *Appendix,* entitled *The Form of Value, Appendix to Chapter I, 1,* to Leipzig. You know who was the *author of this plan,* and I herewith offer him my thanks for his SUGGESTION.[438]

You will excuse me if I terminate these lines here. Another proof-sheet has just come.

With my best compliments to your wife and the young madam.[b]

Yours

K. Marx

With my next letter I shall send *membership cards*[c] for MRS Kugelmann and MRS Tenge. One lady, MRS Law, has been promoted to membership of our Central Council.

Best thanks from Eleanor for the STAMPS. The photograms will follow.

First published slightly abridged in *Die Neue Zeit*, Bd. 2, Stuttgart, Nr. 3, 1901-1902 and in full in *Pisma Marksa k Kugelmannu* (Letters of Marx to Kugelmann), Moscow-Leningrad, 1928

Printed according to the original

234

MARX TO ENGELS

IN HANOVER [449]

[London,] 20 July 1867

Dear Engels,

I am writing these lines in haste, in the hope that they may still find you in Hanover. *C'est une chose brûlante.*[d] Old Lafargue[e] has invited my 3 daughters to Bordeaux (they depart tomorrow with the *secrétaire*[f]), whence they will go with him and his wife to a

---

[a] the first volume of *Capital* - [b] Gertruda and Franziska Kugelmann - [c] of the International Working Men's Association - [d] It is a matter of urgency. - [e] François Lafargue - [f] Paul Lafargue (he was Corresponding Secretary for Spain on the General Council)

seaside resort. It was all the harder for me to refuse as the state of health of all 3 girls made this invitation a real blessing. But propriety required that the *secrétaire de l'Espagne* should not be allowed to pay the expenses of the journey. The latter (return) approximately £30, which I thus had to disburse to him. Furthermore, their watches, dresses, etc., had to be reclaimed from the pawnshop. In this way, the £45 which I had in reserve for the rent on 3 August (*bill drawn on myself*) melted into thin air.

I can now think of no other recourse than writing to you. If the letter catches you, please write to me at once *with enclosure to Borkheim* asking him to advance me the money.

While you are in Germany you must read: 'Zwölf Streiter der Revolution von Gustav Struve und Gustav Rasch'. Under the heading of the 'fighting revolutionary' Freiligrath, you will find a fresh instance of this fine fellow's treachery towards us.[a]

Your
K. M.

First published abridged in *Der Briefwechsel zwischen F. Engels und K. Marx*, Bd. 3, Stuttgart, 1913 and in full in *MEGA*, Abt. III, Bd. 3, Berlin, 1930

Printed according to the original

Published in English for the first time

235

MARX TO FERDINAND FREILIGRATH [6]

IN LONDON

[Copy]

[London,] 20 July 1867

Dear Freiligrath,

I am not a regular reader of German literary trash, but I cannot prevent friends in Germany from occasionally sending me excerpts containing personal references to me. Thus, yesterday I received all the passages referring to myself in a publication by a certain Rasch entitled 'Zwölf Streiter der Revolution'. I should be obliged to you for an explanation of the following[b]:

---

[a] See next letter. - [b] G. Struve and G. Rasch, *Zwölf Streiter der Revolution*, p. 61.

'Freiligrath had, etc., broken off relations with Marx entirely; *a quite unpardonable action on Marx's part*, about which I wish to say no more here, had been the last straw. It can only be explained as due to the obnoxious character of a man like Marx. I was so indignant about it that one day I asked Freiligrath for *details*, but he tactfully passed over it.'[453]

Your

K. M.

First published in: Marx and Engels, *Works*, First Russian Edition, Vol. XXV, Moscow, 1934

Printed according to Marx's notebook

236

MARX TO ENGELS

IN MANCHESTER

[London,] 10 August 1867

Dear Fred,

Enclosed charming letter from Dronke in Manchester, received today. He has taken about a fortnight to give me the good advice to 'sell' wine and coffee to cover the cost of transport!

By the by, the little Frenchman was here again today and threatened to write to Old Lafargue.[a] All I could do was to appease him with the promise that he would have his money on Tuesday morning.

Parcel of *Courrier français* along with 2 *Diplomatic Reviews* now due will be despatched on Monday.

Salut.

Your

K. M.

First published in *Der Briefwechsel zwischen F. Engels und K. Marx*, Bd. 3, Stuttgart, 1913

Printed according to the original

Published in English for the first time

---

[a] François Lafargue

237

ENGELS TO MARX

IN LONDON

Manchester, 11 August 1867

Dear Moor,

Enclosed a five-pound-note which I fortunately obtained yesterday and which will now satisfy your FRENCHMAN. Also Dronke's letter. So, the little man has got himself properly into the mire with his petty speculations. I fear that, if he is to shake off his obligations in respect of the Barnedi shares, he will have to go through the BANKRUPTCY COURT. It is very hard for the little fellow, firstly the court-case over the insurance business, and now these blows. However, I assume he will still have his agency, and with its help and with speculation a little less heated, he may soon restore his fortunes.

I have cursorily read through as far as sheet 32[a] and will give you my comments on it in due course; the numerous examples in this section, on cursory first reading, somewhat obscure its coherence. But there are some very fine things in it, and both capital and its sycophants will be eternally grateful to you.

On my journey back here[449] I had the added pleasure of a rifle-bullet shattering the window and flying through the carriage not 12 inches from my chest: some VOLUNTEER probably wished to demonstrate yet again that he ought not to be entrusted with a firearm. It is the strangest RAILWAY ACCIDENT I have ever encountered.

Lizzie[b] also had a rather bad return journey, she says she will never go by sea again.

Kindest regards to your wife.

Your
F. E.

First published in *Der Briefwechsel zwischen F. Engels und K. Marx*, Bd. 3, Stuttgart, 1913

Printed according to the original

Published in English for the first time

---

[a] of the first volume of *Capital* - [b] Lizzie Burns

238

MARX TO ENGELS

IN MANCHESTER

[London,] 14 August 1867

Dear FREDERICK,

As you will see from the enclosed, I am threatened with distraint if I do not pay the taxes (amounting to £11-9s.) next Friday. I have an additional £1-15s. interest to pay to the pawnshop at the end of this week, or the things will lapse. I did not tell you of all these abominations before, as I had previously been attempting—vainly, I'm afraid—to rustle up the money in London.

With the huge sums that you have sent me this year, there would be no such PRESSURE, if it had not been for over £200 in previous debts. If I am to straighten out my affairs and not to PRESSURE you so dreadfully, it is imperative that I raise a loan somewhere else, even if another journey to the Continent is required for the purpose. But I cannot lift a finger until the printing is complete.[a] I received the 48th sheet today. So this week the whole vile business will be over.

Salut.

Your
K. M.

First published in *Der Briefwechsel zwischen F. Engels und K. Marx*, Bd. 3, Stuttgart, 1913

Printed according to the original

Published in English for the first time

---

[a] of the first volume of *Capital*

239

MARX TO LONDON BOOKSELLER[a]

[London,] 14 August 1867
1 Modena Villas, Maitland Park,
Haverstock Hill

Dear Sir,

Will you send me,

The 2 reports on the *Orissa famine*[b];

'*The Hours of Labour Regulation Act*',[c] as soon as it is printed, and ditto:

'*The Artisans' and Labourers' Dwelling Bill*'.

Yours truly
Karl Marx

First published in: Marx and Engels, *Works*, First Russian Edition, Vol. XXV, Moscow, 1934

Reproduced from the original

Published in the language of the original, English, for the first time

240

ENGELS TO MARX

IN LONDON

Manchester, 15 August 1867

Dear Moor,

Encl. 3 £5-notes I/V 65551⎫ Manchester
" " " 65113⎬ 29 January 1866
" " " 44954⎭

and the tax-slip returned. In *these* circumstances, it is *essential* that my return be kept a secret from Borkheim,[449] so that I do not

---

[a] This presumably refers to P. St. King. - [b] Marx refers to *East India (Bengal and Orissa Famine). Papers and Correspondence relative to the Famine in Bengal and Orissa, including the Report of the Famine Commission and the Minutes of the Lieutenant Governor of Bengal and the Governor General of India... Ordered, by the House of Commons, to be printed, 31 May 1867; East India (Madras and Orissa Famine). Return to an Address of the Honourable House of Commons, dated 4 July 1867. Ordered, by the House of Commons, to be printed, 30 July 1867.* - [c] *An Act for Regulating the Hours of Labour for Children, Young Persons, and Women employed in Workshops..., 21 August 1867.*

need to pay him until as late as possible in *September*, otherwise I shall be completely stuck, since you will understand that I too have a mass of payments to make here, especially in the new half-year. Furthermore, consequent upon the fall in the price of yarns, we are having to enter the stock in the accounts at approx. £2,500 less than by the prices which applied at the time of my departure. Which is not very pleasant either!

When do you wish to have some of the sheets[a] returned? Schorlemmer asked me to pass them on to him a few at a time, as I finished with them, but that naturally depends on you. I have now read the thing through to the end (cursorily) and definitely think that the second volume is also *indispensable*, and the sooner you finish it, the better.[418] I am now looking through the whole thing again, i.e., the more theoretical aspects. The fellows will be astonished to see with what consummate ease the most difficult points, such as Ricardo's theory of profit, are dealt the *coup de grâce* here 'in this way'.

Kindest regards to your wife.

Your
F. E.

Lupus was born in Tarnau[b] on 21 June 1809, died 9 May 1864.[c]

First published in *Der Briefwechsel zwischen F. Engels und K. Marx*, Bd. 3, Stuttgart, 1913

Printed according to the original

Published in English for the first time

241

MARX TO ENGELS[118]

IN MANCHESTER

[London,] *16 August 1867, 2.0.a.m.*

DEAR FRED,

Have just finished correcting the *last sheet* (49th) of the book.[a] The appendix— *Form of Value—in small print*, takes up $1\frac{1}{4}$ sheets.[438]

---

[a] of the first volume of *Capital* - [b] Polish name: Tarnów - [c] Marx wanted to know this because he meant to dedicate the first volume of his *Capital* to Wilhelm Wolff (Lupus).

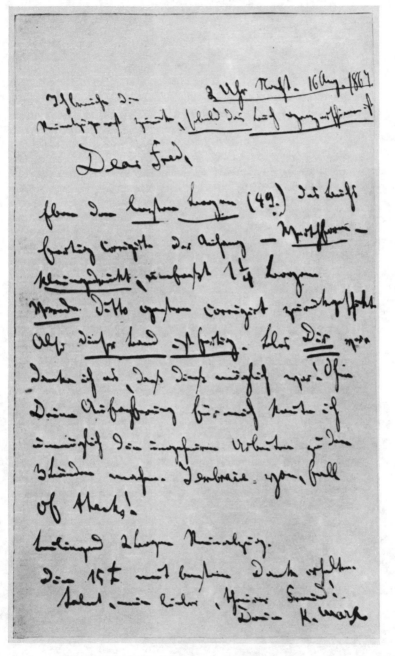

Marx's letter to Engels of 16 August 1867

Preface ditto returned corrected yesterday. So, *this volume is finished.* I owe it to **you** alone that it was possible! Without your self-sacrifice for me I could not possibly have managed the immense labour demanded by the 3 volumes.[418] I EMBRACE YOU, FULL OF THANKS!

Enclosed 2 sheets of corrected proofs.

The £15 received with best thanks.

Salut, my dear, valued friend.

Your
K. Marx

I do not need to have the corrected proofs back *until the book is completely out.*

First published in *Der Briefwechsel zwischen F. Engels und K. Marx*, Bd. 3, Stuttgart, 1913

Printed according to the original

242

ENGELS TO MARX[419]

IN LONDON

Manchester, 23 August 1867

Dear Moor,

I have now worked through as far as sheet 36ª approx., and I congratulate you on the comprehensive way in which the most complex economic problems are elucidated simply and almost sensuously merely by arranging them suitably and by placing them in the right context. Likewise, in respect of subject-matter, on the quite splendid exposition of the relationship between labour and capital—for the first time here in its full context and complete. I was also greatly diverted to see how you have worked your way into the language of technology, which must surely have given you much trouble and on which account I had various MISGIVINGS. I have corrected several SLIPS OF THE PEN in pencil in the margin, and also ventured to make a few conjectures. But how could you leave the

---

ª of the first volume of *Capital*

outward structure of the book in its present form! The 4th chapter is almost 200 pages long and only has 4 sub-sections, indicated by four headings in ordinary print, which it is hardly possible to refer back to. Furthermore, the train of thought is constantly interrupted by illustrations, and the point to be illustrated is *never* summarised after the illustration, so that one is for ever plunging straight from the illustration of *one* point into the exposition of another point. It is dreadfully tiring, and confusing, too, if one is not all attention. It would have been highly desirable here to have subdivided the text more frequently and to have made the most important sections stand out more,[454] and this must emphatically be done for the English version. In this exposition (especially of cooperation and manufacture) there are indeed several points that are not yet quite clear to me, where I cannot work out which facts lie behind the argument that is expressed solely in general terms. To judge by the *outward* form of the exposition, this 4th chapter also appears to be the most hurriedly written and the least carefully revised. However, all that is of no import, the main thing is that our economists are not given a weak point anywhere through which they can shoot holes; I am indeed curious to hear what these gentlemen will say, they have not been left even the smallest opening. Roscher and his ilk will not be unduly perturbed, but for the people here in England who do not write for 3-year-olds, it is a different matter altogether.

I very much look forward to your sending me some more sheets as soon as you can, I particularly want to read the section on accumulation in its context.[455]

Give your wife my best wishes. When are the girls coming back?[a]

Your
F. E.

First published in *Der Briefwechsel zwischen F. Engels und K. Marx*, Bd. 3, Stuttgart, 1913

Printed according to the original

Published in English in full for the first time

---

[a] See this volume, pp. 396-97.

243

MARX TO ENGELS[101]

IN MANCHESTER

[London,] 24 August 1867

DEAR FRED,

I have received no further corrected proofs[a] since the 2 last that I sent you. I am exceedingly vexed with Meissner. He has obviously *held back* what Wigand has sent him in order to send *everything at once*—and save 4d. postage!

The same Meissner wrote me last week that he is printing a certain part of my preface specially (and he has indeed made the *right choice*) to send to the German newspapers. I wrote asking him to send me COPIES of it at once. I reckoned that *you* would translate the thing into *English* (I shall then give it to *The Bee-Hive*, which is taken by Mill, Beesly, Harrison, etc.), and Lafargue with Laura's help into French for the *Courrier français*, finally I wanted to send ONE COPY to my correspondent in America.[456] To save the 4d., Meissner has sent *nothing*. He will be sending it all together. But *a great deal of time* is lost in the process!

The best points in my book are: 1. (this is fundamental to *all* understanding of the FACTS) the *two-fold character of labour* according to whether it is expressed in use-value or exchange-value, which is brought out in the very *First* Chapter; 2. the treatment of *surplus-value regardless of its particular* forms as profit, interest, ground rent, etc. This will be made clear in the second volume especially.[418] The treatment of the particular forms in classical political economy, where they are for ever being jumbled up together with the general form, is an *olla potrida*.[b]

Please *enter* your *desiderata*,[c] critical remarks, QUERIES, etc., on the corrected proofs. This is very important for me, as I am reckoning on a 2nd edition sooner or later.[454] As regards CHAPTER IV, it was a hard job finding *things themselves*, i.e., their *interconnection*.[d] But with that once behind me, along came one BLUE BOOK[359] after another just as I was composing the final *version*, and I was delighted to find my theoretical conclusions fully confirmed by the

---

[a] of the first volume of *Capital* - [b] hotchpotch - [c] recommendations - [d] See previous letter.

FACTS. Finally, it was written to the accompaniment of CARBUNCLES and daily dunning by creditors!

For the conclusion to the 2nd book (*Process of Circulation*), which I am writing *now*,[457] I am again obliged to seek your advice on one point, as I did many years ago.

Fixed capital only has to be replaced *in natura*[a] after, say, 10 years. In the meantime, its value returns partially and *gradatim*,[b] as the goods that it has produced are sold. This PROGRESSIVE RETURN of the fixed capital is only required for its replacement (aside from REPAIRS and the like) when it becomes defunct in its material form, e.g., as a machine. *Prior to that*, however, these SUCCESSIVE RETURNS are in the capitalist's possession.

Many years ago I wrote to you that it seemed to me that in this manner an *accumulation fund* was being built up, since *in the intervening period* the capitalist was of course *using* the returned money, before *replacing* the *capital fixe* with it. You disagreed with this SOMEWHAT SUPERFICIALLY in a letter.[458] I *later* found that MacCulloch describes this SINKING FUND as an *accumulation fund*.[c] Being convinced that no idea of MacCulloch's could ever be right, I let the matter drop. His *apologetic* purpose here has already been refuted by the Malthusians, but *they, too, admit the* FACT.

Now, as a manufacturer, you must know what you do with the RETURNS on *capital fixe before* the time it has to be replaced *in natura*. And you must answer this point for me (without theorising, *in purely practical terms*).

Salut.

Your
K. M.

(*Salut* TO MRS Lizzy[d]!)

The children are still at Royan, near Bordeaux.

First published in *Der Briefwechsel zwischen F. Engels und K. Marx*, Bd. 3, Stuttgart, 1913

Printed according to the original

Published in English in full for the first time

---

[a] in kind - [b] piecemeal - [c] J. R. McCulloch, *The Principles of Political Economy*, Edinburgh, 1825, pp. 181-82. - [d] Lizzy Burns

244

ENGELS TO MARX[419]

IN LONDON

Manchester, 26 August 1867

Dear Moor,

On the question of the replacement-fund, full details with accompanying calculations tomorrow. You see, I must ask some other manufacturers whether our practice is the customary one or an exception. The question is whether, with an original outlay of £1,000 on machinery, where £100 is written off in the 1st year, the rule is to write off 10% of the £1,000 in the 2nd year, or of £900, etc. We do the latter, and understandably the matter goes on thereby in *infinitum*,[a] at least in theory. This complicates the arithmetic considerably. But, otherwise, there is no doubt that the manufacturer is *using* the replacement-fund *on average* for $4\frac{1}{2}$ years before the machinery is worn out, or at least has it at his disposal. However, this is included in the calculations, by way of what one might call a certain guarantee against moral wear and tear, or alternatively the manufacturer says: the assumption that in 10 years the machinery will be completely worn out is only approximately correct, i.e., it presupposes that I receive the money for the replacement-fund in 10 annual instalments from the outset. At all events, you shall have the calculations; regarding the economic *significance* of the matter, I am none too clear about it, I do not see how the manufacturer is supposed to be able to cheat the other partners in the surplus-value, that is, the ultimate consumers, by thus falsely representing the position—in the long run. *Nota bene*, as a rule, machinery is depreciated at $7\frac{1}{2}\%$, which assumes a useful life of approximately 13 years.

Moore sends you his photograph, enclosed, and reminds you that you promised him yours, which he is very eager to have.

The chapter on accumulation is quite splendid.[455]

Your

F. E.

First published in *Der Briefwechsel zwischen F. Engels und K. Marx*, Bd. 3, Stuttgart, 1913

Printed according to the original

Published in English in full for the first time

---

[a] indefinitely

245

ENGELS TO MARX [459]

IN LONDON

Manchester, 27 August 1867

Dear Moor,

Enclosed two schedules for machinery, which will make the matter fully clear to you. The rule is that part of the original sum is written off each year, usually $7^1/_2\%$, but to simplify the calculation I have kept to 10%, which is not excessive for many machines either. Thus, e.g.,

1860 1 Jan. Purchases	£	1,000
1861 1 Jan. Written off 10%	"	100
	£	900
New purchase	"	200
	£	1,100
1862 1 Jan. Written off 10% £1,200 (£1,000+£200)	"	120
	£	980
New purchase	"	200
	£	1,180
1863 1 Jan. Written off 10% £1,000+£200+£200 etc.	"	140
	£	1,040 [a]

In schedule No. 1 I am now assuming that the manufacturer puts his [money] out *at interest* for writing-off purposes; on the day when he has to replace the old machinery with new, he has not £1,000 but £1,252-11s. Schedule No. 2 assumes that he puts the money straight into new machinery, each year. As is shown in the last column giving the value of the total purchases as it stands on the last day of the 10 years, it is true that the *value* of his machinery then does not exceed £1,000 (and he cannot have more, as he has, after all, only invested the *value* of what has been worn out, and the *total* **value** of the machinery cannot thus grow by the process), but he has extended his factory from year to year, and as an average over the 11 years he has employed machinery which cost £1,449 in investment, in other words, he has produced and earned substantially more than with the original £1,000. Let us assume he is a spinner and every £ represents one spindle together with the roving-frame; in that case, he has on average

---

[a] The original has: £1,020.

spun with 1,449 spindles instead of 1,000, and, after the original spindles have ended their useful lives, he begins the new period on 1 January 1866 with 1,357 spindles that he has purchased in the meantime,to which is added a further 236 from the writing off as per 1865, which makes 1,593 spindles. The money advanced for writing off has thus enabled him to *increase* his machinery by 60% and without putting a FARTHING of his *actual profit* into the new investment.

Repairs have been disregarded in both schedules. At 10% write-off, the machine should cover its own repair costs, i.e., the latter should be included. Nor do they affect the issue, as they are either included in the 10%, or else they prolong the useful life of the machine in proportion, which amounts to the same thing.

I hope schedule No. 2 will be sufficiently clear to you; if not, just write, I have a copy of it here.

In haste.

Your

F. E.

I. The manufacturer invests the renewal-fund at 5% interest

1856 on Jan. 1 machinery purchased for			£ 1,000		
1857 Jan.	1 10% written off for wear and tear			£	100
1858 "	1 10% " " " "	£ 100			
	Interest on £100	" 5		"	105
				£	205
1859 "	1 Interest on £205	£ 10-5s.			
	10% written off	" 100		"	110-5s.
				£	315-5s.
1860 "	1 Interest on £315-5s.	£ 15-15s.			
	10% written off	" 100		"	115-15s.
				£	431
1861 "	1 Interest on £431	£ 21-11s.			
	10% written off	" 100		"	121-11s.
				£	552-11s.
1862 "	1 Interest on £552-11s.	£ 27-13s.			
	10% written off	" 100		£	127-13s.
				£	680-4s.
1863 "	1 Interest on £680-4s.	£ 34			
	10% written off	" 100		"	134
				£	814-4s.

1864   "   1 Interest on £814-4s. .... £ 40-14s.
              10% written off .... " 100   " 140-14s.
                                                                                                  _____
                                                                                                  £ 954-18s.
1865   "   1 Interest on £954-18s. .... £ 42-15s.
              10% written off .... " 100   £ 142-15s.
                                                                                                  _____
                                                                                                  £ 1,097-13s.
1866   "   1 Interest on £1,097-13s. .... £ 54-18s.
              10% written off .... " 100   " 154-18s.
                                                                                                  _____
        Total after 10 years .... £1,252-11s.
        or on January 1, 1866: instead of the £1,000 in worn-out
        machinery, £1,252-11s. in ready cash.

II. The renewal-fund is reinvested in machinery each year

			reinvestment	wear and tear %	value on Jan. 1, 1866
1856	on Jan. 1 machinery purchased		£ 1,000	100%	£ -
1857	Jan. 1 10% written off and reinvested		£ 100	90%	£ 10
1858	Jan. 1 10% write-off	£ 1,000 £ 100 " 100 " 10	" 110	80%	" 22
		£ 210			
1859	Jan. 1 10% write-off	£ 1,000 £ 100 " 210 " 21	" 121	70%	" 36
		£ 331			
1860	Jan. 1 10% write-off	£ 1,000 £ 100 " 331 " 33	" 133	60%	" 53
		£ 464			
1861	Jan. 1 10% write-off	£ 1,000 £ 100 " 464 " 46	£ 146	50%	" 73
		£ 610			
1862	Jan. 1 10% write-off	£ 1,000 £ 100 " 610 " 61	" 161	40%	" 97
		£ 771			
1863	Jan. 1 10% write-off	£ 1,000 £ 100 " 771 " 77	" 177	30%	" 124
		£ 948			

1864	Jan. 1	10% write-off	£ 1,000 £ 100				
			" 948 " 95	" 195	20%	£ 156	
			£ 1,143				
1865	Jan. 1	10% write-off	£ 1,000 £ 100				
			" 1,143 " 114	" 214	10%	" 193	
			£ 1,357				
1866	Jan. 1	10% write-off	£ 1,000 £ 100				
			" 1,357 " 136	" 236	0%	" 236	

Nominal value of the new machinery   £ 1,593

Real value of the new machinery .... £ 1,000

@ £1 per spindle he has employed:

1856 .... 1,000 spindles	Brought forward .... 9,486 spindles
1857 .... 1,100 "	1863 .... 1,948 "
1858 .... 1,210 "	1864 .... 2,143 "
1859 .... 1,331 "	1865 .... 2,357 "
1860 .... 1,464 "	In 11 years .... 15,934 spindles
1861 .... 1,610 "	
1862 .... 1,771 "	On average 1,449 spindles

Brings forward   9,486 spindles
and begins 1866 with
1,357
236

1,593 spindles.

First published in *Der Briefwechsel zwischen F. Engels und K. Marx*, Bd. 3, Stuttgart, 1913

Printed according to the original

246

MARX TO AUGUSTE VERMOREL[67]

IN PARIS

London, 27 August 1867
1 Modena Villas, Maitland Park,
Haverstock Hill

Citizen,

Two things astonish me in your newspaper,[a] for whose character, courage, good will and talent I have respect.

---

[a] *Le Courrier français*

1. You are turning your paper into an echo for *Russian lies* (and Greek, the Greeks having been taken in by the Russians) about the so-called revolution in Crete.[460] May I be permitted to send you an *English extract* on the true state of affairs in Candia.[a]

2. You reproduced the *canards* (of *Russian* origin) concerning the initiative North America is to take against the Turks. You ought to know that the President of the United States does not have the power to declare war. The Senate alone can decide. If President Johnson, *who is a dirty tool of the* SLAVEHOLDERS, although you are so naive as to make him out to be a second Washington,[b] seeks to win a little popularity by entangling foreign-policy affairs and BY SWAGGERING ABROAD, the YANKEES are neither children nor French. The mere fact that he has taken the *initiative* amid all this tentative exploration suffices to nullify any serious effect it may have.

You must excuse my taking the liberty of writing to you thus. We are both pursuing the same aim, the emancipation of the proletariat. This entitles us to be frank with one another.

I would ask you *not to publish* these lines. I am addressing them to you privately and as a friend.

Greetings and fraternity,

Karl Marx
Member of the General Council
of the International Working
Men's Association

I am most astonished at your plaudits for the Peace League.[461] It is no less (I refer to the Peace Congress) than cowardice in action. One must either protest in Berlin and Paris, or else—if one is too cowardly to do that—at least not deceive the public with ambiguous, ineffectual and declamatory pronouncements.[c]

First published in: Marx and Engels, *Works,* First Russian Edition, Vol. XXV, Moscow, 1934

Printed according to the original checked with the rough copy of the letter

Translated from the French

Published in English in full for the first time

---

[a] Grete - [b] The rough copy has: If President Johnson, who is a mere *tool in the hands of the former* SLAVEHOLDERS (although you make him out a hero *à la* Washington)... - [c] See this volume, p. 420.

247

MARX TO SIGFRID MEYER

IN NEW YORK

London, 27 August 1867
1 Modena Villas, Maitland Park,
Haverstock Hill

Dear Meyer,

Excerpt enclosed from the preface to the first volume of my book,[a] which is being published next week. Try to place it as far as you can in German-American papers and, where feasible, in English-American papers as well. Be so kind as to send me *a copy,* where it appears, since this is important for my publisher.[b]

Ad vocem Weber.[c] His father[d] is a fool, *exilé* from Baden, clockmaker. The boy with whose presence you are blessed there is a scoundrel. The Hatzfeldt woman picked him for the assassination of Lassalle's KILLER.[e] He took the money and followed his intended victim as far as Augsburg or thereabouts. Then he funked it. He then absconded with the Hatzfeldt money from Germany to America (trying to squeeze yet more from the old woman by threats).

His worthy father and his brother,[f] living here, said in the (German) Communist Society[g] here that **I** *denounced* the good lad *to the German police.* That was how they explained his exit and cheating of Countess Hatzfeldt. I went along to the Society, denounced the scoundrels, and Weber jun. was chucked out in disgrace.

Now you know the facts of the matter.
Salut.

Your
K. Marx

First published in: Marx and Engels, *Works,* First Russian Edition, Vol. XXV, Moscow, 1934

Printed according to the original

Published in English for the first time

---

[a] *Capital* - [b] Otto Meissner - [c] Regarding (Wilhelm) Weber - [d] Joseph Valentin Weber - [e] Janko von Racowiţa - [f] Louis Weber - [g] the German Workers' Educational Society in London

248

MARX TO ENGELS [33]

IN MANCHESTER

[London,] 31 August 1867

Dear FRED,

Received both your letters with the calculations. THANKS.

I have got to pay £4 between 2 shitty *épiciers*[a] by *next Tuesday* (3 September), and that's only a part of what I owe them both. I have the feeling these fellows are pressing harder this year than ever.

The children are returning a week on Sunday (morning).[b] I wish they had stayed away longer. They were enjoying themselves over there. But Lafargue has to get back to his school. (It always vexes him if I ask: *N'allez-vous pas à votre école?*[c])

For the congress at Lausanne (INTERNATIONAL)[462] from here: Eccarius, Lessner, Dupont. Also, the president of the Coventry RIBBON WEAVERS[d] and A. Walton, Esq. (from Wales). Eccarius has safely received the contribution about the congress for *The Times*—having previously made enquiry of the latter.

Judging from all the news from Paris, Bonaparte's position there is looking very shaky.

Salut.

Your

K. M.

First published abridged in *Der Briefwechsel zwischen F. Engels und K. Marx*, Bd. 3, Stuttgart, 1913 and in full in *MEGA*, Abt. III, Bd. 3, Berlin, 1930

Printed according to the original

Published in English in full for the first time

---

a shop-keepers - b See this volume, pp. 396-97. - c Are you not going to your school? - d Daniel Swan

249

ENGELS TO MARX[419]

IN LONDON

Manchester, 1 September 1867

Dear Moor,

I have just received payment for a very long-standing bad debt of £5 which will put me in a position to send you that sum tomorrow as soon as I have cashed the CHEQUE. Otherwise, I should have been in something of a fix, what with the repayment of the £45 to Borkheim now due. What about Borkheim, is he back? I am now able and therefore wish to settle up.

The 8 sheets[a] received with thanks. The theoretical side is quite splendid, as is the exposition of the history of expropriation. But the piece you have inserted on Ireland was done in the most fearful haste, and the material is not properly knocked into shape at all. On first reading often positively incomprehensible. Further comments as soon as I have considered the stuff more closely. The *résumé* on the expropriation of the expropriators is most brilliant and will create quite an effect.[463]

It is fortunate that almost all of the book is 'enacted' in England, so to speak; otherwise para. 100 of the Prussian Penal Code would be operable: 'Whosoever ... shall incite the subjects of the State to hatred or contempt of each other',[b] etc.—and confiscation would ensue. Bismarck seems to be needing to stage a little demonstration against the workers anyway. In Erfurt or thereabouts a Lassallean poet, printer and publisher[464] have been arraigned for high treason, and in Elberfeld they have even confiscated a scrawl by the noble Schweitzer.[c] So, it is possible that the book would be prohibited in Prussia, but, anyway, that would not have any effect in present conditions.

Your
F. E.

First published in *Der Briefwechsel zwischen F. Engels und K. Marx*, Bd. 3, Stuttgart, 1913

Printed according to the original

Published in English in full for the first time

---

[a] of the first volume of *Capital* - [b] *Strafgesetzbuch für die Preussischen Staaten.* Vom 14. April 1851. - [c] J. B. Schweitzer, *Der Kapitalgewinn und der Arbeitslohn.*

250

ENGELS TO MARX [10]

IN LONDON

Manchester, 2 September 1867

Dear Moor,

The £5 banknote enclosed. You will have received the booklet 'Transactions' [of the] R[oyal] Society.[465] Can you send me the July and August *Free Presses*, as promised?

Things appear to have taken a very sharp turn in Paris; every day all the papers are following Girardin's example in recalling 1829 and 1847,[466] and the Lille speech, full of resignation, appears to prove that there is nothing to be done in South Germany and Austria *precisely now* when he[a] needs it, obviously solely in consequence of the sorry state of the latter. 'And hence' it is only 'weak governments' which incline to use foreign conflicts as a means of avoiding internal difficulties.[467] Then, the constantly reiterated allusions to '*mon fils*'[b] do not appear to imply any very significant confidence in the longevity of the '*père*' *quem nuptiae demonstrant*[c] either. You must press ahead with the second volume,[418] things may soon start to happen.

On Saturday I saw a Californian newspaper, which suggested the 8 hours-movement must have had an enormous impact amongst the building trades there. The masters are forming a 10-hours-association to oppose it and are setting up a considerable wailing. Contracts for $1\frac{1}{2}$ million dollars are said to have been withdrawn as a result of the 8 hours business.[468]

Gumpert is back and says that in Electoral Hesse the rage at the Prussians is as furious as in Hanover, though less demonstrative. The moment the military were to leave, every 'Prussian' would be slaughtered. Amongst other things the Prussians have confiscated the officers' widows and pension fund in Kassel which derived from *compulsory contributions from the officers*. He found things even hotter in Hanover than I did.

Kugelmann also wanted to attend the Lausanne Congress,[462] i.e., as a spectator, perhaps it would be a good thing to inform Eccarius of this. He will probably encounter Schorlemmer, who left yesterday (via Grimsby), at the Naturalists' Congress in Frankfurt.

---

[a] Napoleon III - [b] 'my son' (Eugène Bonaparte) - [c] father, who became so by marriage

Moore is travelling to Thuringia in approx. 3 weeks, to learn German for 6 weeks; I have sent him off there so that he may get off the TRACK of the BRITISH TOURISTS.

Kindest regards.

Your
F. E.

First published in *Der Briefwechsel zwischen F. Engels und K. Marx*, Bd. 3, Stuttgart, 1913

Printed according to the original

Published in English in full for the first time

251

MARX TO ENGELS [33]

IN MANCHESTER

[London,] 4 September 1867

DEAR FRED,

The £5 received with thanks.

Borkheim wrote to me a few days ago from Berne and sent me 'for comment if you would be so kind' the *brouillon*[a] for the speech, which he is intending to give at the PEACE CONGRESS in Geneva.[469] He also wanted your assistance. I wrote to him, as we had agreed, that you had not yet returned. You can, however, send the money to his associate *Schyler*, 65 Fenchurch Street. But it is £50, not 45. When I looked, I found that the bill was on £48, and Borkheim then told me that he could probably give me the full sum of £50. I did not tell you of this before, as I was expecting the money I had been promised any day, and then wanted to pay the £50 myself.

Enclosed:

1. the last sheets of the proofs.[b]
2. 2 *Diplomatic Reviews* and 1 number of *Courrier français*.

Regarding the final sheets, they have put the *Addendum to the Notes* in *large* print, and the *Appendix on the Form of Value* in *small* print, *despite my instructions*.[470] They probably did this so that the book should be neither over nor under 50 sheets in length. In my

---

[a] draft - [b] of the first volume of *Capital*

opinion, Meissner has made a serious blunder in increasing the purchase-price from 3 talers to 3 talers 10 silver groschen. It is, however, possible as well that he has subsequently received so many more firm orders that this was commercially the correct thing to do.

A word of explanation concerning the article in the *Courrier français* (which you must *send back* to me after you have read it through): '*Les Conditions de la Paix*'[a]:

You know that on the GENERAL COUNCIL I expressed my opposition to our joining the peace-at-any-price party.[b] My speech lasted ABOUT ¹/₂ HOUR. As minute-secretary, Eccarius reported on it in *The Bee-Hive*, giving only a few sentences of what I said. The reprint in the *Courrier* even omits the sentences about the necessity for armies vis-à-vis Russia and about the *cowardice* of these fellows.[471] The affair has, nevertheless, created quite a stir. The jackasses from the PEACE CONGRESS, whose agent in London is M. de Colleville, completely *changed* their original programme and even smuggled into the new one, which is much more democratic, the words 'THE HARMONIZING OF ECONOMIC INTERESTS WITH LIBERTY', which could mean almost anything, including just FREETRADE. They have been bombarding me with letters and even had the impertinence to send me the enclosed scrap of paper with the new programme. Their impertinence consists in nominating me as a 'MEMBER OF THE GENEVA, ETC., CONGRESS' in the address. The *Courrier*, which was their most vociferous advocate in Paris, is deserting them, as you will see. The same *Courrier* has changed its policy in respect of Russia, following a private letter that I wrote to Vermorel ABOUT a fortnight ago[c] (we are not acquainted).

The main point was that these fine gentlemen from the peace congress, Victor Hugo, Garibaldi, L. Blanc, etc., had kept themselves supremely aloof from our INTERNATIONAL ASSOCIATION. I have now obliged them to acknowledge us as a real force.

From *Naples* I have received the first 2 numbers of a paper *Libertà e Giustizia*. In No. I they declare themselves to be *our organ*. I have passed it to Eccarius to place before the congress.[462] No. II, which I shall send you, contains a very good attack on *Mazzini*.[d] I suspect that Bakunin has a hand in it.

With regard to the confiscation and prohibition of my book,[e] there is a world of difference between prohibiting electoral

---

[a] by L. Dubois. See *Le Courrier français*, No. 77, 2 September 1867. - [b] i.e., the League of Peace and Freedom - [c] See this volume, pp. 413-14. - [d] 'La questione romana', *Libertà e Giustizia*, No. 2, 24 August 1867. - [e] See this volume, p. 417.

pamphlets and a book of 50 sheets which has such an air of erudition and even contains notes in Greek. Admittedly, that might be of little avail if I had chosen 12 administrative districts in Prussia instead of 12 COUNTIES in England to describe the conditions of the agricultural workers. I also feel that Mr Bismarck will think twice about the matter before provoking me into attacking his regime in London and Paris.

What conditions are like in Prussia, incidentally, is shown by the following statement by O. *Hübner*, Director of the *Central Statistical Archive*, in a message to his electors:

'The people are already overburdened. Apart from the armament factories, almost every trade is depressed, hundreds of hungry men are applying for the humblest positions, in the cities the number of empty dwellings and of citizens, who cannot afford to pay rent, is growing, a whole host of estates and houses are being subjected to compulsory auction, the poor-houses are being besieged *by our maimed victors* and by the unemployed, everywhere there is a lack of confidence in the present and the future, and the budgets of the poorest are beset by the realisation *that they are already paying more for the services of the state than they are worth.*'

In Berlin, neither the government nor the National-Liberal Party[432] has got a single candidate through.[a] But just what utter blockheads those men of Progress[99] are who now form the extreme left, is shown amongst other things by the following extract from their 'most radical' organ, the *Zukunft*:

'The whole English nation is permeated by a *snobbery which treats all alike* and to which all personal industry is anathema. [...] It is *this same snobbery* which is for ever urging *reduction of working hours* and prohibits *overtime* on account of the UNIONS!'[b]

Would you credit it! Even now the Parisian press is truly a giant compared with the German press!

Your

K. Marx

First published in *Der Briefwechsel zwischen F. Engels und K. Marx*, Bd. 3, Stuttgart, 1913

Printed according to the original

Published in English in full for the first time

---

[a] at the elections to the North German Reichstag (end of August-beginning of September 1867) - [b] 'Englische Briefe', *Die Zukunft*, No. 199 (supplement), 27 August 1867.

252

MARX TO ENGELS

IN MANCHESTER

In haste

[London,] 7 September 1867

DEAR FRED,

1 letter from Lessner enclosed. I already had the *Gazettes de Lausanne.*[472] *The Times* has cut Eccarius quite disgracefully.[473] I am, at the same time, sending you NEWEST *Diplomatic Review* and copies of the *Courrier français*, which I must always have *back.* The *Courrier français* has made nonsense of the short notice I sent it about Hübner[a] by putting '*tomber sous le marteau des démolisseurs*'[b] instead of *tomber sous la subhastation*[c] (which is an expression from the *Code Napoléon*).
Adio.

Your
K. Marx

First published in *Der Briefwechsel zwischen F. Engels und K. Marx*, Bd. 3, Stuttgart, 1913

Printed according to the original

Published in English for the first time

253

ENGELS TO MARX

IN LONDON

[Manchester, 9 September 1867]

Dear Moor,

I intended writing yesterday and today but COMMERCE prevented me from doing so. The *Courriers* returned enclosed. Vermorel is a fine one with his talk of the influence of the French at the congress and their *caractère sérieux* and them *not making any speeches.*[474] POOR ECCARIUS!

---

[a] *Le Courrier français*, No. 81, 6 September 1867. - [b] fall beneath the hammer of the demolishers - [c] be subjected to compulsory auction (see this volume, p. 421)

I must congratulate you on your appendix on the form of value.[438] In this form, it is BROUGHT HOME TO THE MOST REBELLIOUS UNDERSTANDING. Likewise with regard to the preface. But who did the appalling, ungrammatical translation in *The Bee-Hive*?[456] Why was it not sent to me, saying what you wanted? I am afraid it will harm your reputation with Beesly, etc., who will think you did it yourself.

Apropos, what shores does the '*trans*atlantic Ocean' wash, exactly?

More tomorrow.

Your

F. E.

First published in *Der Briefwechsel zwischen F. Engels und K. Marx*, Bd. 3, Stuttgart, 1913

Printed according to the original

Published in English for the first time

254

MARX TO ENGELS [101]

IN MANCHESTER

[London,] 11 September 1867

DEAR FRED,

Regarding the '*trans*atlantic Ocean', it is a matter for the final corrector to put right such *lapsus pennae*.[a] I see that the *Zukunft* has reprinted this splendid 'flow' along with the greater part of the preface.[b]

The translation in *The Bee-Hive*[c] is by Eccarius. I believe that most of the errors stem not from him, but, because of his bad hand-writing, from *The Bee-Hive*'s CORRECTORS. I would naturally have preferred you to do the translation. However, as Eccarius offered his services *de prime abord*,[d] and is now on the staff of *The Bee-Hive*, that was not feasible.

I shall personally deliver the coup de grâce to those Proudhonist jackasses at the next congress in Brussels. I have DIPLOMATICALLY

---

[a] slips of the pen - [b] to the first volume of *Capital* (*Die Zukunft*, No. 206, 4 September 1867) - [c] of a part of the preface to the first volume of *Capital* (*The Bee-Hive Newspaper*, No. 308, 7 September 1867) - [d] initially

MANAGED the whole affair and did not want to COME OUT *personally* before my book appears and our Association is firmly rooted. By the by, I shall give them a caning in the OFFICIAL REPORT of the GENERAL COUNCIL (despite all their efforts, the Parisian wind-bags were unable to prevent our re-election[475]).

MEANWHILE our Association has made great progress. The wretched *Star*, which wanted to ignore us entirely, announced in its leading article yesterday that we are more important than the PEACE CONGRESS.[461] Schulze-Delitzsch could not prevent his '*Workers' Association*' in Berlin from joining us.[476] Those wretches from among the English TRADE UNIONISTS, who think we are too 'extreme', are coming flocking. Besides the *Courrier français,* there have been reports on our congress in Girardin's *Liberté, Siècle, Mode, Gazette de France*, etc. *Les choses marchent.*[a] And when the next revolution comes, and that will perhaps be sooner than might appear, *we* (i.e., you and I) will have this mighty ENGINE *at our disposal*. COMPARE WITH THIS THE RESULTS OF MAZZINI'S, ETC., OPERATIONS SINCE 30 YEARS! And with no money to boot! And with the intrigues of the Proudhonists in Paris, Mazzini in Italy and the jealous Odger, Cremer, Potter in London, with the Schulze-Delitzsch and the Lassalleans in Germany! We can be well satisfied!

My children arrived back safe and in good spirits with Lafargue yesterday.[b] He has brought an enormous crystal goblet (holds $1^1/_2$ POTS) back with him for you. He appears to be impressed with your 'transatlantic Ocean'.

In these days, Lafargue would like to visit you for 3 days at this time before his lectures begin again. The most awkward thing about it is that he is demanding (of course, not being IN THE SECRET OF MY MONEY-AFFAIRS) that I should accompany him, and I have not yet found a satisfactory excuse for turning down this tour, which I just cannot manage.

I am exceedingly vexed with Meissner. He has wasted weeks in bringing out the book. Why?

Salut.

Your

K. M.

2nd letter from Lessner enclosed.[477]

Apropos. Our plump poet's[c] begging-campaign, which, *vide*[d] the latest *Hermann,*[e] is not proceeding quite as desired, has had one

---

[a] Things are going ahead. - [b] See this volume, pp. 396-97. - [c] Ferdinand Freiligrath - [d] see - [e] *Hermann,* 7 September 1867.

good result.[422] Kätchen of the sturdy calves[a] is to get married.
Notice of betrothal to A CERTAIN Kröker (a most poetic name) in the
Zukunft![b]

First published abridged in *Der Briefwech-
sel zwischen F. Engels und K. Marx*, Bd. 3,
Stuttgart, 1913 and in full in *MEGA*,
Abt. III, Bd. 3, Berlin, 1930

Printed according to the original

Published in English in full for the
first time

255

ENGELS TO MARX[419]

IN LONDON

Manchester, 11 September 1867

Dear Moor,

The congress really does appear to have been swept away in the
French tide this time, the number of Proudhonist resolutions is
really far too large.[462] It is good that it will be coming to Belgium
next time, by then it will perhaps be possible to do something in
North Germany as well, and then, with the help of the English, to
dam up the flood. Meanwhile, whatever they resolve there is more
or less just wasted breath as long as the CENTRAL COUNCIL remains in
London. Once again *notre cher*[c] Philipp Becker appears to have
committed some of his unpremeditated blunders, for which one
must forgive the old agitator when he has no one to guide him.[478]

That Eccarius wrote the reports in *The Times* must be kept
secret.[473] In view of the manner in which the editors have trimmed
his story, it could do him enormous harm. The next time that he
reports to the paper, he will have to consider more carefully to
what extent his humour can be exploited by the bourgeois editors
to cast RIDICULE on the whole business and not just on the few
crapauds.[d]

Since you are in contact with Vermorel, can you not moderate
the fellow's asininities with regard to Germany? It is really too
much if the jackass is demanding that *Bonaparte* should become

---

[a] Käthe Freiligrath - [b] *Die Zukunft*, No. 208 (supplement), 6 September 1867. -
[c] our dear - [d] toads; philistines (here Engels refers to the French Proudhonists,
delegates to the Lausanne Congress)

liberal, bourgeois liberal, and then start a war to liberate Germany from the tyranny of Bismarck![a] These *crapauds*, who will have to handle Germany with great delicacy even *if* they do make a revolution, believe that but a slight turn toward liberalism would enable them to revert to their old roles. I regard it as most important, particularly in the event of a revolution, that these gentlemen should become accustomed to treating us *d'égal à égal*.[b] According to them, Bismarckism in Germany is an inherent characteristic of Germany, which they must destroy by intervening, but their own Bonapartism is a mere accident and could be terminated just by a change of ministers and transformed into its opposite.

The great Schweitzer has been happily elected with the assistance of the pietists[55] of Elberfeld and Barmen, and will now have the opportunity to bowdlerise various points from your book[c] in the 'Reichstag'. You may wager your life that he will do so. However, it can only do good and will afford us much entertainment; once the book is out, only good can come of such things.

Apropos of Barmen, I am reminded of Siebel. The poor devil is dreadfully sick again and is once more having to leave Barmen, though I do not know whereto; it is possible he will not live out the winter. He must be very bad, so I cannot count on him raising any cry for your book in the newspapers. He has written me a very DESPONDING letter.

The TRADES OUTRAGE COMMISSION's[442] conclusions here are entirely farcical and are no different from those reached 7 years ago. If they do not produce anything better, they might as well pack their bags. Just imagine seeing BRICKMAKING AND BRICKLAYING treated as the chief industries of Manchester!

The defects which have become apparent in the tests carried out on the Chassepot rifle here are the very ones which had already been discovered in Berlin and which Bölzig told me of in Hanover. At that time, I thought that they had *deliberately* allowed faulty specimens to fall into the hands of the Prussians, but now it rather looks as though there is something in it, in which case the rifle is not half as good as the Prussians' needle-gun.

Meissner's people in Leipzig appear to be taking an inordinately long time to send the book out. Still no notices anywhere. Do you think I should attack the thing from the bourgeois point of view,

---

[a] A. Vermorel, 'La prochaine campagne de la Prusse', *Le Courrier français*, No. 84, 9 September 1867. - [b] as equals - [c] the first volume of *Capital*

to get things under way? Meissner or Siebel would surely get that accepted by a paper.[479] As for it being prohibited,[a] I don't believe it myself, but one can never swear that the zeal of some government official will not get the better of him, and once a case has been brought, you could rely on your friend Lippe.

Kindest regards to your wife and the girls, who I presume are back now.[b]

The *Diplomatic Reviews* received with thanks.

Your
F. E.

First published abridged in *Der Briefwechsel zwischen F. Engels und K. Marx*, Bd. 3, Stuttgart, 1913 and in full in *MEGA*, Abt. III, Bd. 3, Berlin, 1930

Printed according to the original

Published in English in full for the first time

256

MARX TO ENGELS[33]

IN MANCHESTER

[London,] 12 September 1867

Dear FRED,

Meissner's procrastination bodes most ill. He could have disposed of many COPIES[c] at the congress in Lausanne.[462] And the book would have been discussed there as a real event. Such stupidity is beyond my comprehension. Next Saturday it will be *4 weeks* since I sent the last corrections to Leipzig.[d]

Your plan to attack the book *from the bourgeois point of view* is *the best tactic*. However—once the thing is out—I consider it better to have this done through Siebel or Rittershaus, rather than Meissner. There is no need to let even the best publishers see through one's game. On the other hand, you must write a few instructions to *Kugelmann*, who is back, concerning the positive aspects he should emphasise. Otherwise, he will do something *foolish*, enthusiasm alone being insufficient in this case. Naturally, you will feel less inhibited about doing this than I.

---

[a] See this volume, pp. 417 and 420-21. - [b] Ibid, pp. 396-97 and 424. - [c] of the first volume of *Capital* - [d] See this volume, pp. 402, 405.

I am entirely of your mind *quoad*[a] Eccarius.[b] A worker is lacking in diplomatic finesse, especially one with the critical bluntness of Eccarius. He writes to *The Times* as though he were writing for the *Neue Rheinische Zeitungs-Revue*.[c] However, no harm has been done. Here in London they are saying that the INTERNATIONAL ASSOCIATION, etc., must be strong indeed for *The Times* to report so expressly on it. Eccarius' SNEERS are taken to be *Times* SNEERS.[473]

It was the wretched *French Swiss*, who, being very strongly represented, gave the French wind-bags from Paris so much scope. Old Becker was responsible for the most serious BLUNDER.[478] He first disrupted the agenda we had planned, so as to spring *his freedom resolution*. This then provided the Parisians with the opportunity to let themselves go.

But none of that signifies. The main thing is that the congress was held, not what happened there. *On se moquera bien*[d] of the Paris WISEACRES in our GENERAL REPORT. To the latter's great dismay, a resolution was adopted that *those who do not pay* (and the Parisians have not paid a farthing) cannot send delegates in future. The aim must be to send 20 English and 30 Germans to Brussels next time.[475] As TO THE BELGIANS THEMSELVES, they can only send 1 MAN per 500, so there will not be very many of them. They are furthermore RATHER REBELLIOUS towards the Parisians.

Nota bene: the worst thing is, we have not a single man in Paris who could make contact with the workers' sections which are *hostile* to the Proudhonists (and they form the majority!). If Dupont were to spend a few weeks in Paris, everything would be in order, but the police have him under close surveyance.

In due course I shall write privately to Vermorel and knock those absurd notions about German politics out of him.[e] I shall have to proceed *gradatim*[f] and therefore deliberately began with the UNITED STATES, RUSSIA and TURKEY, because this is 'neutral' ground between Germans and French.[g]

Laura and Lafargue are just now translating part of the preface for the *Courrier français*.[456]

Salut.

Your
K. M.

First published in *Der Briefwechsel zwischen F. Engels und K. Marx*, Bd. 3, Stuttgart, 1913

Printed according to the original

Published in English in full for the first time

---

a concerning - b See this volume, p. 425. - c *Neue Rheinische Zeitung. Politisch-ökonomische Revue* - d We shall make fun - e See this volume, pp. 425-26. - f gradually - g See this volume, pp. 413-14.

257

MARX TO ENGELS

IN MANCHESTER

[London,] 12 September 1867

Dear Fred,

I am sending this 2nd letter, because Eccarius' LETTER has just arrived.[480]

Apropos. What Eccarius could not have known: L. Blanc has absented himself from the Geneva Congress,[a] because '*my*' people would be playing tricks there; Jules Favre, because the 'class question'[b] (as a SUPPORTER of Cavaignac in the June days,[481] his CONSCIENCE is, of course, not CLEAN) has been adopted by the *Courrier français*, along London lines.

Your
K. M.

First published in *Der Briefwechsel zwischen F. Engels und K. Marx*, Bd. 3, Stuttgart, 1913

Printed according to the original

Published in English for the first time

258

ENGELS TO MARX

IN LONDON

Manchester, 12 September 1867

Dear Moor,

You have *not* enclosed letter No. 2 from Lessner.[477] If Lafargue does come, I would much appreciate it if you came too,[c] as I do not rightly know how to entertain our comrade during my business hours. If possible, you should come straight away tomorrow, or at least on the morning of the day after, so that we can be together on Saturday and Sunday, and I can also more

---

[a] of the League of Peace and Freedom - [b] See this volume, p. 420. - [c] ibid., p. 424.

easily take some French leave on Monday. But write or telegraph beforehand, so that I can arrange lodging (telegraph the office, except Saturday after 11.0.a.m. and Sunday).

£5 enclosed to help with money-matters; apart from the cost of travelling here, you can leave it at home for your wife.

Here, too, the press is treating the International much more decently than before. *All* the newspapers here have carried some part of the proceedings,[a] the *Examiner & Times*[b] had a philistinishly benevolent LEADER.

Would it not be appropriate also to report on the meetings of the CENTRAL COUNCIL in the German newspapers? e.g., the *Zukunft*; Wilhelmchen[c] might perhaps find somewhere else, too. Where actually is the noble fellow now?

The Lassalleans are beset by a fresh shindig again. Dr Reincke in Hagen and Schweitzer are AT DAGGERS DRAWN. Reincke went along with the party-of-Progress clique[99]—Bürgers and E. Richter—to ensure his election in Hagen, Düsseldorf and Solingen, but failed in the two latter.

We really must try to establish a direct link with the workers in Germany again, that is what we most lack, otherwise everything is buoyant enough.

I read of the betrothal of *Käthe*,[d] as she calls herself, in the *Kölnische Zeitung*.

You will have to give me a verbal account of the congress telegrams from Germany.

The *Courriers*[e] returned herewith. Apropos of the vote in Schleswig, it is splendid how those jackasses declared: *avons une carte devant nous*,[f] which shows Holstein within Schleswig (or vice versa)! Likewise, they first have the *Federal troops* and then the *Dutch* (instead of the Luxemburgers themselves) marching into Luxemburg. And it is they who want to abolish IGNORANCE!

Your
F. E.

First published in *Der Briefwechsel zwischen F. Engels und K. Marx*, Bd. 3, Stuttgart, 1913

Printed according to the original

Published in English for the first time

---

[a] of the Lausanne Congress - [b] *The Manchester Daily Examiner & Times* - [c] Wilhelm Liebknecht - [d] Freiligrath's daughter (see this volume, p. 425) - [e] *Le Courrier français*, Nos. 85 and 86, 10 and 11 September 1867. - [f] we have *a map before us*

259

MARX TO ENGELS[482]

IN MANCHESTER

[Telegram]

London, 13 September 1867

From Karl Marx, 1 Modena Villas, Maitland Park. *To* Fred Engels, Southgate, St. Mary's.

Will start from Euston station 4.15 p.m.

First published in the language of the original, English, in *MEGA*, Abt. III, Bd. 3, Berlin, 1930

Reproduced from the photocopy of the telegram

260

ENGELS TO LAURA MARX

IN LONDON

Manchester, 23 September 1867

Dear Löhrchen,

I have received your delightful letter, and as soon as the books arrived I despatched the various copies[a] to their resp. recipients—those to Imandt and Strohn sent securely packed by BOOK POST, but the one intended for me, for which my best thanks to Moor, straight to the binders.

You will be interested to learn that a week ago last Saturday I already showed Lafargue[482] the battlefield where the great Fenian liberation battle was enacted the previous Wednesday.[483] We were actually within ten paces of the railway arch; however, he will scarcely recollect it.

So that you may see what man, and cotton-man in particular, is capable of, I am sending you enclosed the latest abomination of this kind in the form of a cotton sheen-wig. These GUYS are now being made and sold in colossal quantities.

Your friend Library[b] has been successfully elected at Schneeberg in Saxony to the great North German Reichstag

---

[a] of the first volume of *Capital* - [b] Wilhelm Liebknecht

against Count zur Lippe, and will no doubt soon be making a great maiden speech.[484] THE RIGHT MAN IN THE RIGHT PLACE.

With hearty greetings to the whole family, most sincerely

Your

F. Engels

First published in: Marx and Engels, *Works*, Second Russian Edition, Vol. 31, Moscow, 1963

Printed according to the original

Published in English for the first time

261

MARX TO ENGELS [33]

IN MANCHESTER

[London,] 4 October 1867 [a]

DEAR FRED,

Since my return from Manchester [482] almost until now, I have had a feverish cold. I caught the COLD in the course of the railway *malheur.*[b]

As there are many things about which I wish to write to you, ON PUBLIC AND PRIVATE AFFAIRS, in this letter, I shall start with the *book*,[c] so that I do not forget it. You would have spent long indeed searching in Table C for the decrease in the cultivation of green crops (p. 695). Mr Wigand has printed C instead of B (p. 690), which tells us, under the heading '*Green Crops*', that from 1861-65 107,984 acres were put out of cultivation.[485] Indeed you will observe from the schedule of misprints on p. 784 that Mr Wigand has wilfully *abbreviated* it from p. 292 onwards in order to accommodate it on the last page. The section concerning Ireland was certainly written very hastily, but for a second edition it could be put in order with but a few formal alterations. The most important thing is the FACTS, which are not known even in England.[463]

I have heard nothing from Meissner. Schabelitz (Basle) told Borkheim he has requested 5 *copies for sale or return* on the

---

[a] The original has '1859' corrected by Engels: '!! 1867', with the note *Voilá bien, le père Marx!* (There you are, Father Marx!). - [b] misfortunes - [c] the first volume of *Capital*

strength of 5 copies which he ordered for cash payment, but Meissner replied he did not have enough to send him so many for sale or return. However, this may merely be a diplomatic manoeuvre on Meissner's part. I see from the enclosed note from Liebknecht (who BY THE BY has done us proud with his first intervention in the Reichstag, *vide*[a] the *Zukunft* No. 229 of 1 October[486]) that Meissner is not *always* so punctilious. It was agreed that he should send 1 copy to Liebknecht and 1 copy to Dr Weiss for the editors (*Zukunft*).

Professor Beesly has now returned home, and I shall be hearing from him before very long. *Quant à*[b] Siebel, I should also like to know whether he has received the copies, 1 for himself and 1 for Rittershaus? and how the latter has requited it?

Ad vocem[c] *Vogt*: you will find some news about Vogt in the enclosed letter from Kugelmann.[487] After Kugelmann had departed[d] and the gang thought Borkheim had likewise gone, a final meeting of the Germans took place, at which Borkheim suddenly appeared and witnessed the following occurrence. Mr Goegg handed a slip of paper to the Vice-President, Büchner, in which he declared that the Bonapartist rumours, etc., regarding Vogt were false, and offered a *testimonium virtutis*[e] for the man, whom he claimed to have known for 20 years. He demanded that Büchner *sign* this note, i.e., *certify* that it had been communicated to him. Büchner naturally did so. Whereupon LITTLE Beust jumps up, states in writing that Goegg is only expressing a private opinion which is by no means shared in Switzerland, etc., etc. Ditto demands certification of his *protest* by Büchner, which the latter supplies. Vogt's manoeuvre was thus frustrated. To what depths that fellow has descended!

Another INCIDENT at the Peace Congress! Ludwig Simon approaches Goegg: 'Why have you not moved my name nearer to the top of the list of speakers! Why is Borkheim given the floor before me?' *Goegg*: 'Those fellows— the proletarians—had 4 of the German vice-presidents. To bring in *our man Grün* and get Borkheim to give up his place, we had to make this concession to him, etc.!' Hardly were the words out of that beau's[f] mouth than he looks round and to his horror sees Eccarius grinning behind his back.

Ad vocem Stumpf: Maybe Stumpf understands me, but I do not understand Stumpf. Perhaps you will be more fortunate and be

---

[a] see - [b] As regards - [c] Regarding - [d] from the inaugural congress of the League of Peace and Freedom - [e] certificate of virtue - [f] The German word used by Marx here is *Geck*, a pun on *Goegg*.

able to 'delineate the scientific process of pauperisation' and ditto 'the correct conclusion' from the 'evidence' which he keeps in his pocket and does not divulge. His letter enclosed.[488]

Ad vocem Dronke: Borkheim spoke to a man in Paris who has a precise acquaintance with all Dronke's affairs and described him as a '*voleur*'[a] The copper company had served notice on Dronke a year ago. It now has a firm in Glasgow as its associate and therefore has no more need of an English agency. Dronke, *dicitur*,[b] has been guilty of much 'embezzlement' in the past year and has made himself the object of an 'embarrassing' investigation. I hope the affair will be hushed up.

Ad vocem Collet: what follows is by way of explanation for the enclosed *curiosa*: Collet's little girl (whom you have met) and her even younger brother were visiting us a few days ago. The boy had a boxing match with Lafargue, who eventually pinned him to the floor in a humiliating position. Then says the boy, 'REMEMBER HOW YOU GOT ON AT WATERLOO!' Hence this comical correspondence, with the girl denouncing the lad to the old man.

Collet has withdrawn from *The Diplomatic Review*, although his name still figures on the paper this time. I immediately noticed the change of editor, as I was only sent 1 COPY. You shall have it as soon as I am finished with it. It is a thoroughly foolish number. Garibaldi is described as 'a common bandit, atheist, FOOL, etc.', M. Dupanloup, the *évêque*[c] of Orleans, by contrast, as the great man of the age.[d] Will David[e] yet become a Catholic one day perhaps? The Peace Congress in Geneva was, of course, a fabrication of the Russians, which is why they sent along their 'WELL WORN OUT AGENT Bakounine'. I have the impression that *The Diplomatic Review* is on its last legs.

Ad vocem INTERNATIONAL ASSOCIATION. At my suggestion, the office of president has been abolished, after Odger had already been proposed for re-election.[489]—Fox, who has missed no opportunity to exhibit his profound hatred for Eccarius since the latter's return,[f] gave notice for the next meeting (Tuesday) that he would ask the COUNCIL to consider *censuring Eccarius* for his '*Times*' articles.[473] To Fox's great surprise I thereupon gave ditto notice that I would interpellate Fox next Tuesday about a '*SECRET LETTER*' that he had written to Becker[g] requesting him 'TO DO ALL IN HIS POWER TO REMOVE THE SEAT OF THE CENTRAL COUNCIL FROM LONDON'.[490] Fox, who is

---

a thief - b it is said - c bishop - d 'Events of the Month', *The Diplomatic Review*, 2 October 1867. - e David Urquhart - f from the Lausanne Congress of the International - g Johann Philipp Becker

altogether composed of CAPRICES and CROTCHETS, imagines that he must found an '*opposition party*' on the COUNCIL against the '*German dictatorship*', as he calls it. He will be astonished at his success in this LINE!

Ad vocem Borkheim: *d'abord*,[a] the following FACTS. Borkheim spoke (or rather read from his manuscript) for over 20 minutes, whereas only 10 were permitted by the rules.[469] Naturally, like Garibaldi and Edgar Quinet, he too felt he could afford to take liberties. Secondly, he mounted the rostrum in a state of extreme excitement, and, as Eccarius says, 'did not let himself get a word in edgeways'. Nobody understood him. All that people heard were the few catchwords about Schulze-Delitzsch, at which Vogt jumped up and clenched both his fists, and about the Cossacks.[b] That was fortunate indeed. His speech was thought to be significant because it was *not* understood. He therefore plays some part, both in *The Times*[491] and in the *French press*. But now comes the DRAWBACK. The fool wishes to have his speech printed in German, English, Russian and in the *French original*. I now have the latter in front of me.[c] He sent it to me so that Lafargue could look through it. With the exception of the few catchwords, which I whispered into his ear, it is not merely a *tasteless* hotchpotch, but often pure balderdash. And his French! E.g.,

'Sans stultification il serait impossible de discuter, s'il faudrait d'abord faire enlever la femelle Isabelle, faire sauter le mâle Bismarck ou faire s'évanouir l'agile hermaphrodite Beust. Il y a de grands orateurs, de profonds penseurs français, membres de cette union, mais fûssent-ils tous des Mirabeaux achevés et des Descartes consommés, les têtes allemandes seraient trop carrées pour le trouver rond, qu'il fût d'abord et avant tout le gouvernement français, l'abolition duquel introniserait l'ère de la paix internationale.'[d]

Assez![e]

How little he suspected the quality of 'his French' is clear from the note he jotted in the margin of the manuscript he sent me:

'Please ask Mr Lafargue to look quickly through it and correct *any* (!) bad French in the margin!'

---

[a] firstly - [b] *Le Courrier français,* No. 88, 13 September 1867. - [c] S. Borkheim, *Ma perle devant le congrès de Genève.* - [d] 'It would be impossible, without descending to the level of idiocy, to discuss whether the first task should be to arrange for the female Isabella to be abducted, for the male Bismarck to be overthrown, or for the nimble hermaphrodite Beust to evaporate. Among the French members of this Association there are some great orators and some profound thinkers, but were they all accomplished Mirabeaux and consummate Descartes, the Germans would be too squareheaded to accept roundly that it would be first and foremost the French government whose destruction would inaugurate the era of international peace.' - [e] Enough!

I was, OF COURSE, OBLIGED to tell him that Lafargue would have to see him, as he could not proceed to make the 'deletions' (to begin with, Lafargue wants to delete the whole of THE FIRST HALF) and 'amendments' in his absence. He is therefore coming to see me *this evening*. Lafargue additionally showed me *French commis voyageur*^a SLANG in almost every sentence. E.g., '*parlons rondement!*'^b

PRIVATE AFFAIRS: I have talked to Borkheim about the possibility of finding me a LOAN of at least £100 in London. He says yes, he is willing to be 1 guarantor if you will be the other. But he would, after all, need to hear from yourself about the matter first. The situation is simply that I can neither complete Volume II,[418] nor find the time for the intrigues required for the English edition,[229] nor even remain in England, if I do not manage to pacify the Manichaeans[431] for SOME WEEKS AT LEAST. If the English transaction succeeds, and if they proceed in such a manner in Germany— which does not seem difficult to me—that a 2nd impression[454] soon becomes necessary, the crisis will have been overcome.

This damned year has been made even worse by Lafargue staying with me until now, Laura is to marry in the spring, etc. *Salut.*

Your
K. M.

First published abridged in *Der Briefwechsel zwischen F. Engels und K. Marx*, Bd. 3, Stuttgart, 1913 and in full in *MEGA*, Abt. III, Bd. 3, Berlin, 1930

Printed according to the original

Published in English in full for the first time

262

ENGELS TO MARX^c

IN LONDON

Manchester, 8 October 1867
7 Southgate

Dear Moor,

Detailed letter tomorrow. Just the letters returned enclosed and the *one* question: will Borkheim be writing to me about the LOAN or

---

^a commercial traveller - ^b let us not beat about the bush - ^c The letter is written on the blank of the Ermen & Engels firm in Manchester.

is he expecting *me* to write to him?[a] I shall send the newspapers back to you tomorrow.

Meissner will no doubt have sent the copies[b] to Weiss and Liebknecht through a bookshop, where they would not arrive until *about 1 October* in Berlin, about the time when the other copies arrived there and came into the shops. The *Kölnische* and *Augsburger Zeitung* only carried the notice a few days ago.[c]

Your
F. E.

First published in *Der Briefwechsel zwischen F. Engels und K. Marx*, Bd. 3, Stuttgart, 1913

Printed according to the original

Published in English for the first time

263

MARX TO ENGELS[33]

IN MANCHESTER

[London,] 9 October 1867

DEAR FRED,

Borkheim is expecting a letter from you first that you are willing to be co-guarantor.[d]

Poor Lafargue is in the final throes today, putting Borkheim's *preface* into decent French (insofar as that is possible!). The latter has baptised his opus: '*Ma perle* devant le Congrès de Genève'.[469] Curious how the itch for literary fame can make a FOOL of an otherwise quite intelligent *garçon*[e]!

So, yesterday, Fox was to decapitate Eccarius.[f] The former took more than 1 hour to speak his indictment. He had most maliciously assembled the worst passages and displayed all the arts of an Old Bailey[g] barrister, also continually attacking me. In my riposte I dealt him such telling blows that in his final REPLY he quite lost his composure and self-control. Everyone joined in the

---

[a] See previous letter. - [b] of the first volume of *Capital* - [c] *Allgemeine Zeitung*, No. 273, 30 September 1867. - [d] See previous letter. - [e] fellow - [f] A reference to the meeting of the General Council of the International on 8 October 1867 (see this volume, pp. 434-35). - [g] Old Bailey—Central Criminal Court in London

discussion. The outcome: my MOTION (or amendment RATHER) 'to proceed to the order of the day' was accepted by an enormous majority. Nevertheless, Eccarius got a regular dressing down in the course of the debate.

You must read the piece 'Le troisième larron' I have marked in the *Courrier*[a] that you will get at the same time (splendid that the French are already *sans gêne*[b] calling *their* Bonaparte one of the *larrons*[c]).[492] As soon as I have the numbers back from Lormier, I shall send the interesting COMMUNICATIONS about the MEXICAN affair.[270]

Salut.

Your

K. M.

Apropos. Strohn spent the day here yesterday. He fancies you meant to slight him on his last visit to Manchester, with your remark, 'Yes, in Bradford the *commis voyageur*[d] still counts for something.' I tried to drive this nonsense out of his mind.—He says Dronke had procured the British *associé* for the copper company himself. He had probably demanded to be indemnified for it, and no doubt he had based himself on spurious but legally defensible claims when appropriating or laying his hands on a portion of the copper passing through his hands. He did not believe that Dronke had unwarrantedly *frisé*[e] the *code pénal* directly. *Tant mieux*[f]

<table>
<tr><td>

First published abridged in *Der Briefwechsel zwischen F. Engels und K. Marx*, Bd. 3, Stuttgart, 1913 and in full in *MEGA*, Abt. III, Bd. 3, Berlin, 1930

</td><td>

Printed according to the original

Published in English in full for the first time

</td></tr>
</table>

264

MARX TO ENGELS [302]

IN MANCHESTER

[London,] 10 October 1867

DEAR FRED,

You will see from the enclosed letter from Kugelmann that the time for ACTION has now come.[493] You are better placed to write to

---

[a] *Le Courrier français* - [b] without inhibition - [c] thiefs - [d] commercial traveller - [e] infringed - [f] So much the better.

him about my book^a than I am. He must, at the same time, avoid divagations and not send us the things for correction, but *after* they have appeared. You must impress on him that 'making a commotion' is what matters most, far more than how it is done or being thorough.

Nothing in the enclosed note from Meissner. How can he expect reviews before his own publisher's notices have appeared?

Salut.

Your

K. M.

<table>
<tr><td>First published in Der Briefwechsel zwischen F. Engels und K. Marx, Bd. 3, Stuttgart, 1913</td><td>Printed according to the original</td></tr>
</table>

265

ENGELS TO MARX

IN LONDON

Manchester, 11 October 1867

Dear Moor,

Kindest thanks for the letters and newspapers, which I shall send back in a few days.

I am writing to Borkheim that I will gladly take on the guarantee with him, provided he can so arrange the matter that everything proceeds secretly and that, e.g., no references are required of me—as I am contractually forbidden to become SURETY, and my relations with Monsieur Gottfried^b are such that he would seize upon *any* occasion TO PUT ME IN THE WRONG BEFORE A COURT OF ARBITRATION. So long as he cannot do that, I am prepared to give him my solemn assurance that I will be co-liable for the £100, and await further proposals. Or would Freiligrath, e.g., be sufficient reference for me? The point is that the business would have to be concluded entirely behind the backs of all my commercial connections. *Enfin nous verrons.*^c

---

^a the first volume of *Capital* - ^b Gottfried Ermen - ^c Well, we shall see.

Tomorrow afternoon I shall put something together for Kugelmann; if we are to wait until *he* has read the book[a] through, we shall not get far. I shall write to Siebel, too. I do not know what you have in mind with the Freiligrath-bard Rittershaus, *I* do not know the fellow at all, and as far as I know, he is definitely not one of our people.

There was much else about which I wished to write you, but then along comes that damned old Jew Leibel Choras, whom you know, and detains me for over an hour. Then another fellow immediately following. For a week now I have been overrun with clients, 2 more this morning. Yet another expected tomorrow morning. On top of that, endless bother with Gottfried, it is enough to drive one mad.

So till tomorrow.

Your
F. E.

First published in *Der Briefwechsel zwischen F. Engels und K. Marx*, Bd. 3, Stuttgart, 1913

Printed according to the original

Published in English for the first time

266

MARX TO LUDWIG KUGELMANN[65]

IN HANOVER

[London,] 11 October 1867

Dear Kugelmann,

D'abord,[b] best thanks for your two letters.[c] You would give me great pleasure if *you were to write as often as your time allows.* But you must not expect an *exactly equal response*, as my time is in any case scarcely sufficient now for the multifarious correspondence which I am obliged to conduct with a variety of parties.

First, before turning to the subject of my book,[d] a preliminary word or a wordy preliminary. I fear that *Borkheim* is, *malgré lui,*[e] on the point of doing me a very bad turn. He is publishing his

---

[a] the first volume of *Capital* - [b] Firstly - [c] of 29 September and 8 October 1867 (see this volume, pp. 433 and 438) - [d] the first volume of *Capital* - [e] despite himself

'Geneva speech'[a] in 4 languages, French, German, English, and Russian.[469] He has, furthermore, provided it with a baroque and tasteless preface, overladen with quotations. Between ourselves— and in the interests of the party—I must tell you the plain truth. Borkheim is a capable man and even an *homme d'esprit*.[b] But when he takes up the pen, beware! All tact and taste leave him. Nor has he the necessary education. He is like those savages who imagine that they are enhancing their appearance by tattooing their faces with all possible gaudy colours. Banality and sensationalism always get the better of him. Almost his every phrase instinctively dons cap and bells. If he were not so vain through and through, I could have prevented the publication and made it clear to him that it was his good fortune that people *had not understood* him in Geneva except for a few good POINTS from his SPEECH. On the other hand, I owe him a debt of gratitude for the part he played in the Vogt affair,[494] and he is a personal friend of mine. There are in his speech, etc., a number of phrases in which he *has fatuously garbled*[c] certain views of mine. My enemies (Vogt has already hinted in the *Neue Zürcher-Zeitung* that *I* am the secret author of the speech[d]) will now have the greatest fun in making me responsible for Mr *Borkheim*, his follies and eccentricities, instead of attacking my *book*. If anything of that kind should occur, you will have to use Warnebold, etc., to place some short articles in the newspapers to which you have access, to expose these tactics and, without insulting Borkheim in any way, nevertheless to state quite plainly that only ill intention or an exceedingly uncritical mind could identify things that are so disparate. The baroque and confused manner in which our views are reflected in Borkheim's mind (from the moment he ceases to speak and starts to write), will naturally offer the vile PRESS-GANG the most welcome excuse for an offensive and might even indirectly serve to harm my book.

However, if, as I scarcely dare to hope, since Borkheim is meticulously despatching his progeny to all the newspapers, the press says nothing about it, you must do *absolutely nothing* to break this *solemn silence*.

If Borkheim were not a personal friend, I should publicly disown him. You will understand my *fausse position*[e] and at the

---

[a] S. Borkheim, *Ma perle devant le congrès de Genève.* - [b] a man of some wit - [c] The original has: *verkladderadatscht*—from *Kladderadatsch*, a German satirical weekly. - [d] in his note on the congress of the League of Peace and Freedom in Geneva, see *Neue Zürcher-Zeitung*, No. 254, 13 September 1867. - [e] false position

same time my vexation. Here one is presenting to the public a
work that has cost much trouble to write (and perhaps no work of
this kind has ever been written in more difficult circumstances),
with the purpose of giving the greatest possible lift to the party
and of disarming even ill-disposed critics by the very method of its
exposition, and at that same moment a member of the party clad
in cap, bells and motley insists on standing next to one in the
market-place and provokes a barrage of rotten apples and eggs,
which may hit one in the head even as a party member!

Your manoeuvres against Vogt in Geneva have greatly *satisfait*[a]
me.[487] I am glad you like my book.

Concerning your questions:

Ernest Jones had to speak as a party man to *Irish men* in
Ireland, in other words, since the big landownership there is
identical with *English proprietorship of Ireland,* he had to speak
against the big landownership. You must never look for any
matters of principle in HUSTINGS SPEECHES by English politicians, but
only for what is *immediately* expedient.

Peonage is the advancing of money against future labour. The
consequences of these advances are the same as with ordinary
usury. The worker does not merely remain in debt throughout his
life, thus performing forced labour for his creditor, but the
relationship is inherited by the family and the next generation,
who thus actually *belong* to the creditor.[495]

The completion of my second volume[418] depends chiefly on the
success of the first. This I require in order to find a publisher in
England, and, *without the latter,* my material circumstances will
remain so difficult and disruptive that I shall be able to find
neither time nor peace for speedy completion. Naturally, these are
things which I do *not* wish Mr Meissner to know. It thus now
depends on how skilful and active my party friends in Germany
are, whether the second volume takes a long or a short time to
appear. Considered criticism—whether from friend or foe—can
only be expected to appear gradually, as one needs time to read
and digest such a compendious and, in parts, difficult work. But
its immediate success will not be decided by considered criticism,
but, to put it bluntly, by making a noise and beating the drum,
which compels even the adversaries to speak. To begin with, it is
less important *what* is said than that *something* should be said.
Above all, no time must be lost!

I have sent your last letter to Engels for him to send you the

---

[a] gratified

necessary suggestions. He can write about my book better than I can myself.

My kindest compliments to your dear wife.[a] One of these days I shall send her a recipe for reading the book.[b]

Yours
K. M.

Please keep me *au fait*[c] with all developments in Germany respecting Volume I.

Paul *Stumpf* (*Mainz*) has written me a letter[d] in which he calls Borkheim's speech '*my*' speech, and as at present I have *no time* to write to Stumpf, you would oblige me by writing to him yourself to tell him the true situation and to advise *silence* when Borkheim's pamphlet appears. *Entre nous*[e] Stumpf tends to put his foot in it himself whenever he takes up the pen.

First published in *Die Neue Zeit*, Bd. 2, Nr. 3, Stuttgart, 1901-1902   Printed according to the original

267

ENGELS TO LUDWIG KUGELMANN

IN HANOVER

Manchester, 12 October 1867

Dear Kugelmann,

Marx sent me your letter of the 8th,[493] believing I would be better able to give you the right ideas for a review of his book[f] than he could himself. To save trouble, I have just set out what are, in my opinion, the most suitable ideas for the *populus*[g] in two complete articles which will probably be appropriate for almost any bourgeois paper[496]; they may, however, be of use to you until you have worked your way through the 50 sheets' yourself, for writing both long and short articles for other publications. The

---

[a] Gertruda Kugelmann - [b] See this volume, p. 490. - [c] informed - [d] of 29 September 1867 (see this volume, p. 434) - [e] Between ourselves - [f] the first volume of *Capital* - [g] public

main thing is not *what* and *how* but *that* the book be discussed, and that the Fauchers, Michaelis, Roschers and Raus *forced* to express an opinion on it. In as many papers as possible, political and other, wherever it can be done. Long and short notices, provided they come thick and fast. We must make it impossible for these gentlemen to pursue their policy of total silence, which they would dearly love to try, and indeed *as quickly as possible.* Make sure you always send a copy of what is printed to Marx, so that we, and Meissner, too, are informed of events.

Liebknecht is giving a pretty good account of himself in the Berlin cattle-shed.[a] He is consistently voting *against everything* and also made a good maiden speech—immediately interrupted by Zeus Cronion Simson. And what's more, his motion [486] was the only sensible one.

I hope all has been well with you since my departure.[449] I have been back here for 2 months now, sitting at my office desk and frittering good time away with this lousy COMMERCE. You will have heard about our little Fenian *coup de main*[b] here. The affair was splendidly organised and executed; but the ringleaders were caught unfortunately.[497]

With best greetings.

Yours

F. Engels

Marx expressly asks that all the articles should be placed there immediately and that you should only send them to him *after* publication.[c]

First published in: Marx and Engels, *Works*, First Russian Edition, Vol. XXV, Moscow, 1934

Printed according to the original

Published in English for the first time

---

[a] A reference to the North German Reichstag. - [b] surprise attack - [c] This sentence was written by Engels in the margin.

268

ENGELS TO MARX [26]

IN LONDON

Manchester, 13 October 1867

Dear Moor,

I have written Kugelmann two articles about the book from different points of view and sent them to him [496]; I think they are such as almost any newspaper can take, and he can do others from them. That should help him a bit.

I shall be writing to Siebel tomorrow, I must first know where the fellow is and how his health is. [498]

Borkheim written to. [131]

Liebknecht is doing very well; he has retained sufficient from us to realise that the only correct policy consists in *voting against everything without exception.* This he has faithfully done so far. If you should be writing to him again these days, you can draw his attention to the following: the final article of the law on freedom of movement reads: this law shall not apply to the Aliens' Police. [499] With the consequence that what one gains as a North German citizen, one loses again as an 'alien'. It would have a great effect here if Liebknecht were to propose: the Aliens' Police be *abolished.* Only on the Continent does such an absurdity exist; the proposition would have a great effect. In fact, it would in general strengthen his position to suggest he chaff the bourgeois members with the fact that *he,* the communist, is obliged to champion their own interests despite *their opposition.* Liebknecht's speech was much better in the *Kölnische Zeitung,* by the way, than in the *Zukunft.* [486]

I was very pleased to read the things about Vogt.[a] For all his manoeuvres, your attack[b] has put paid to him entirely, and only the liberal bourgeoisie still considers him the German Véron.

All that *Stumpf*[c] is asking for is that you supply him with theoretical and factual material to explain how it comes about that the petty bourgeois gradually yields to the proletarian. And you know that as well as I do, but you just want to get out of the work. Of course, good old Stumpf thinks that one page of a letter would suffice—for *him* to learn how to handle the question. That, however, I would doubt.

---

[a] See this volume, p. 433. - [b] K. Marx, *Herr Vogt.* - [c] See this volume, pp. 433-34.

Dronke.[a] Borkheim is just as much of a scandalmonger as the little fellow himself,[b] and if the 2 of them say anything about each other, it will be SIX OF ONE AND HALF A DOZEN OF THE OTHER. Dronke still has enough *jus*[c] in his little head to take care to avoid direct CRIMINAL PROSECUTION, within the periods prescribed by present extradition treaties.[500] You know, by the way, how in COMMERCE even the most blatantly criminal affairs can be taken care of simply as civil law cases. But the little fellow has certainly been too clever by half and much too greedy.

Strohn is the same curious old fellow as ever. Fancy him applying a remark to himself the moment that *I* make it, when he has made it countless times himself![d]

I cannot wait to see Borkheim's '*Pearl*'.[e] In the matter of literary vanity, the fellow is pure 'Yid'.

Gumpert has a cousin staying here, ex-Electoral-Hessian, now Prussian lieutenant. The fellow enlisted with the Prussians, full of high expectations, but found the old pack-drill in full flower once again. Gymnastics, etc., performed by *commands*, parading, ramrod marching order, etc. Some of it may be exaggerated, but there is no doubt that the latest successes[f] have also lent a certain sanction to military display. The exaggeration derives from the disagreeable impression, which the newly recruited officers have already received, that 9 out of every 10 of them will never reach the rank of staff-officer. And the fellow is just looking for an opportunity to extricate himself.

Kindest regards to your wife, the girls and Lafargue.

Your
F. E.

First published abridged in *Der Briefwechsel zwischen F. Engels und K. Marx*, Bd. 3, Stuttgart, 1913 and in full in *MEGA*, Abt. III, Bd. 3, Berlin, 1930

Printed according to the original

Published in English in full for the first time

---

[a] See this volume p. 434. - [b] Ernst Dronke - [c] juridical knowledge - [d] See this volume, p. 438. - [e] S. Borkheim, *Ma perle devant le congrès de Genève*. - [f] i.e., Prussian victories in the Austro-Prussian war of 1866

269

MARX TO ENGELS

IN MANCHESTER

[London,] 14 October 1867

Dear FRED,

You will see from the enclosed letter No. II from Juch that, although Achilles[a] is dead, Beta is still alive. Juch's letter was probably provoked by the fact that Beta speaks well of Kinkel but not Freiligrath, and that Beta's article also contains some malicious remarks directed at Juch. When Freiligrath and Juch form an alliance, they are incapable of producing even a bad joke. For which reason I am to be incited to action, being 'thoroughly venomous', as Beta calls me in that vile scrawl of an article he wrote: 'Die Deutschen in London', which begins with the Norman Conquest and ends with that oily Jew Bender as the sole epitome of mankind in England.

This is about the 6th time now that Mr Juch has offered me his stale columns[b] for the purpose of 'self-glorification', for him a well proven tactic which he has used, successfully of course, with Blind, Kinkel, Freiligrath, and Heintzmann. I wrote him a few lines only.[111] And *not* to Mr. Freiligrath's *liking* either. I told him *privatim* of what happened at Beta's *How do you do?* editorial office when I went there in the company of Ziegenhainer, Freiligrath, and our W. Wolff.[501] So as to give him one bad joke for his trouble, I told him that I would not allow Kinkel the credit for being more than the α and ω to this Beta.

Typical of Juch: he sends me Payne's people's calendar[502] which contains the *corpus delicti* (like all such abominations in Germany, *Gartenlaube*, etc., this calendar has 250,000 subscribers), along with the inevitable invoice for 11d., which I immediately enclosed with my reply. Though admittedly he was once more on the threshold of the BANKRUPTCY COURT and has with great difficulty SETTLED with his creditors for monthly payments of 2s. 6d. in the £.

How shall I answer the enclosed from Nahmer?[503]

Has Borkheim sent you the *Courrier français* with the translation of my preface[c]? I am asking because POOR Lafargue is on tenterhooks for 'your verdict'—every day. The Belgian *Liberté*

---

[a] Ferdinand Lassalle - [b] in the *Hermann* - [c] to the first volume of *Capital*

arrived today, having ditto printed the *préface*, with very 'fulsome' PREAMBLE,[456] in which it reminds the Belgian government of my EXPULSION.[236]

I had already replied to Liebknecht,[111] but had to write to him again today because I only today received the 2 ACTS relating to the TRADE UNIONS COMMISSION.[504] Your tips[a] attached to my letter.

Salut. COMPLIMENTS TO MRS BURNS.

Your

Moro

First published slightly abridged in *Der Briefwechsel zwischen F. Engels und K. Marx*, Bd. 3, Stuttgart, 1913 and in full in *MEGA*, Abt. III, Bd. 3, Berlin, 1930

Printed according to the original

Published in English for the first time

270

ENGELS TO MARX

IN LONDON

Manchester, 15 October 1867

Dear Moor,

In the greatest of haste, just this:

Borkheim wants me to allow a bill to be drawn on myself, which more than anything else I am not permitted to do. I have written to him [131] that I will give him a guarantee for the £150 (having at the same time increased the amount) and am prepared to give *him privatim* any SECURITY that it will be paid ANY TIME after 1 August 1868, and asked him whether in these circumstances he can raise the money.[b] He has said nothing further about the LOAN. Perhaps it would be best if you saw him, as he is going away at the end of the week and will not be back for a fortnight.

Your

F. E.

First published in *Der Briefwechsel zwischen F. Engels und K. Marx*, Bd. 3, Stuttgart, 1913

Printed according to the original

Published in English for the first time

---

[a] See this volume, p. 445. - [b] Ibid., pp. 436, 437 and 439.

271

MARX TO LUDWIG KUGELMANN [65]

IN HANOVER

[London,] 15 October 1867

Dear Kugelmann,

You must *not* write to Borkheim. It would be pointless in any case as the work[a] has already been announced in the *Buchhändlerbörsenblatt*[b] and is being already published by Schabelitz. Moreover, Borkheim himself is now in Bordeaux: such a letter from you could have no effect whatsoever except to make an *enemy* of Borkheim for me.[505]

Ce qui est fait, est fait.[c] Never mind! It was just that, my mind being in a turmoil from working all night, I at first exaggerated the gravity of the *événement*.[d] And indeed, *je suis puni par où j'ai péché!*[e] You see I was amused *au premier abord*[f] by the thought of the scandal that our friend would create amongst the respectable philistines of Geneva. Of course, I did not foresee the *fruits it would bear in the book trade.* I should, moreover, have reflected that, in working out his plan, Borkheim would *naturally* overstep the bounds of prudence which I suggested to him in my letter.[469] The only policy we can pursue now is *silence,* for as long as our opponents do not speak; as soon as they speak and attempt to hold me responsible, we must make *bad jokes* about their being obliged to burden me with Borkheim's pranks in order *not* to have to reply to my book.[g] Borkheim ought furthermore to be treated *indulgently* in that event, for after all, except for his literary vanity, he is a capable and well-meaning man, and good as an *homme d'action*,[h] as long as his sense of devilry does not get the better of him.

You will probably already have received Engels' recipes.[496] I am in correspondence with Liebknecht and Becker.[i]

By the 'success of the book', I only meant that *it should sell quickly,* on account of the effect this will have back in England.

The *Courrier français* (at present the Paris daily which creates the biggest stir) and the *Liberté* in Brussels have published a

---

[a] S. Borkheim, *Ma perle devant le congrès de Genève.* - [b] *Börsenblatt für den Deutschen Buchhandel,* No. 230, 3 October 1867. - [c] What is done, is done. - [d] event - [e] I am punished for my sins! - [f] initially - [g] the first volume of *Capital* - [h] man of action - [i] Johann Philipp Becker

French translation of my preface along with COMPLIMENTARY PREAM-BLES.[456]

One Nahmer in New York has offered his services as English translator over there.[503] *Quod non.*[a]

I am very pleased with Liebknecht's performance in Berlin.[486] I sent him over some instructions from here.

Poor Becker has reached such a pass that he is on the verge of abandoning politics and writing altogether.[506] How one regrets not being able to help in such circumstances!

My compliments to your dear wife and my little friend,[b] for whose portrait I have not yet thanked you.

Yours

K. M.

First published in *Die Neue Zeit,* Bd. 2,   Printed according to the original
Nr. 3, Stuttgart, 1901-1902

272

ENGELS TO MARX[26]

IN LONDON

Manchester, 18 October 1867

Dear Moor,

I have written to Borkheim that I cannot accept in any circumstances and that now that I have guaranteed him the amount, it all depends on *his* sources of credit, as mine are tied up.[c]

The letters returned enclosed. Liebknecht appears to have been SICK, or else he could surely have said something about the combination law. PERHAPS IT IS BETTER SO. Schweitzer has shown himself to be a vain jackass and phrasemonger. He's finished now.[507]

I was much amused by the Beta correspondence.[d]

The *Courrier français*[e] has arrived, but I have no time whatsoever to form an opinion of it today.

---

[a] Impossible. - [b] Gertruda and Franziska Kugelmann - [c] See this volume, p. 448. - [d] Ibid., p. 447. - [e] No. 308 of 6 October 1867 containing a French translation of part of Marx's preface to the first volume of *Capital.*

I could write another 4-5 articles about your book[a] from various points of view, but don't know where to place them. Goodness knows where Siebel is! Maybe in Algiers or in Palermo! But I hope to have an answer from him soon. If I could have them copied in London, so that my handwriting would not be recognised, it might after all be wisest to send them to Meissner.

Kindest regards to all.

Your
F. E.

First published in *Der Briefwechsel zwischen F. Engels und K. Marx,* Bd. 3, Stuttgart, 1913

Printed according to the original

Published in English in full for the first time

273

ENGELS TO HERMANN MEYER[10]

IN LIVERPOOL

Manchester, 18 October 1867

Dear Meyer,

I received your telegram this morning and can't say how sorry I am that I am unable to go to Liverpool this evening. My *associé*[b] and our chief clerk[c] are both away tomorrow, and so I have to be here to sign cheques and keep an eye on everything myself. Moreover, we close at 1 o'clock here on Saturdays, and as you yourself are not arriving in Liverpool until about 11 o'clock this evening and the *Russia* sails at 12 o'clock, you will see for yourself that there is nothing to be done.

Please write your address and Mrs Weydemeyer's on the enclosed piece of paper and then hand in the envelope at the hotel for posting. Please convey my hearty greetings to Mrs Weydemeyer and tell her I would have written her a few lines long ago if I had known her address.

I hope you will be able to bring Marx's book[a] to the attention of the German-American press and of the workers. With the

---

[a] the first volume of *Capital* - [b] Gottfried Ermen - [c] Charles Roesgen

8-hour-agitation that is in progress in America now,[468] this book with its chapter on the *working day* will come at just the right time for you over there, and, in other respects too, it is likely to clarify people's minds on a variety of issues. The future of the party in America will be greatly beholden to you for any step you can take in that direction.

Please pass on my best greetings to Jacobi[a] in New York as well. Have a safe journey!

Yours most sincerely
Friedrich Engels

First published in: Marx and Engels, *Works*, First Russian Edition, Vol. XXV, Moscow, 1934

Printed according to the original

Published in English in full for the first time

274

MARX TO ENGELS[243]

IN MANCHESTER

London, 19 October 1867

DEAR FRED,

As regards *Borkheim*, I told him: what Engels wrote is final and is not subject to '*negotiation*'. He (today he left for Bordeaux) let himself be ruled by me to the extent of paying out £40 to me and promising TO FIND THE REST by 10 November without further prevarication if you were *unable*, etc. But as a businessman and a Jew he had to make just one more attempt!

Incidentally, Borkheim has just had a hugely gratifying experience. Schabelitz put an exceedingly bombastic notice of Borkheim's '*Perle*'[b] in the *Buchhändlerbörsenblatt*,[c] in which Borkheim is featured as Peter the Hermit *vis-à-vis Russia*. WELL! The *Moscow Newspaper*[d] has *printed* this (in translation) as a curiosity, and he thus had the pleasure of seeing himself and his name in print *in Russian*! He showed me a copy and interpreted it for me.

---

[a] Abraham Jacobi - [b] S. Borkheim, *Ma perle devant le congrès de Genève*. - [c] *Börsenblatt für den Deutschen Buchhandel*, No. 230, 3 October 1867. - [d] Московскія вѣдомости, No. 210, 28 September 1867.

Lafargue was put to a deal of trouble translating Borkheim's French at least passably into French.[a] I had to give him some assistance, of course, especially for the quotations from Kant, Fichte and Hegel, which Borkheim probably did not quite understand even in German. But he has these gentlemen in his library.

I am glad the matter is thus SETTLED. In recent weeks I have found it perfectly impossible to write for more than maybe 2 hours. Apart from the incursions FROM WITHOUT, there are all the aggravations of home life, which I always find especially nerve-racking. I have been suffering from insomnia again and had the pleasure of seeing 2 small carbuncles blossom near the *membrum*. Fortunately, they have faded away. My sickness always originates in the mind. While on the subject of the *membrum*, may I commend the following lines to you *for Moore* from the French satirist of the 16th century, *Mathurin Régnier*. Well-read though I am in this field, I do not think that *chaude pisse* has ever been more poetically described:

> Mon cas, qui se lève et se hausse,
> Bave d'une estrange façon;
> Belle, vous fournites la sausse,
> Lors que je fournis le poisson.
>
> Las! si ce membre eut l'arrogance
> De fouiller trop les lieux sacrés,
> Qu'on lui pardonne son offence,
> Car il pleure assez ses péchés.[b]

And this by the same poet is not bad either:

> *Fluxion D'Amour*
>
> L'amour est une affection
> Qui, par les yeux, dans le cœur entre,

---

[a] See this volume, pp. 435-36.

[b] My will, which riseth up in pride,
Doth spout most curiously;
The sauce, my love, thou didst provide,
The fish it was from me.

Ah, did that member overween
To delve the sacred place?
Pray pardon him his grievous sin,
He weepeth his disgrace.

M. Régnier, *Stances.*

Et, par la forme de fluxion,
S'écoule par le bas du ventre.[a]

Finally:

Lizette tuée par Régnier

Lizette, à qui l'on faisait tort,
Vint à Régnier tout éplorée,
Je te pry: Donne-moi la mort,
Que j'ai tant de fois désirée!
Lui, ne la refusant en rien,
Tire son... vous m'entendez bien;
Et dedans le ventre la frappe.
Elle, voulant finir ses jours,
Lui dit: Mon cœur, pousse toujours,
De crainte que je n'en réchappe.
Régnier, las de la servir,
Craignant une seconde plainte,
Lui dit: Hastez-vous de mourir,
Car mon poignard n'a plus de pointe.[b]

2 Freiligrath snippets enclosed.[508]
Enclosed *2 Courrier français* and *1 Liberté.* There is no need for
you to send back these journals. But do keep them! I have not

---

[a] *Love's Fluxion*

Our love is an affection
That by our eyes attains the heart,
Then takes the form of fluxion
And issues through the nether part.

M. Régnier, *Épigrammes,* X.

[b] *Lizette slain by Régnier*

Lizette, beset by slander's breath,
To Régnier came with tearful eyes:
My friend, I pray thee, give me death,
Therein my only yearning lies.
He, ever eager to obey,
Unsheaths his ... what more need I say?
And at her belly lunges low.
She, hoping that he her would kill,
Tells him, my heart it yearneth still,
I fear I shall my fate forego,
But Régnier, weary of his pledge,
Fearing a second suppliant cry,
Tells her, oh haste thee now and die,
For this my sword has lost his edge.

M. Régnier, *Épigrammes,* XV.

read the nonsense in the *Courrier* on the *Art Militaire*, but I did read Proudhon on the *generatio aequivoca*[a]! I suspect that *l'un vaut l'autre*.[b]

H. Meyer was here the day before yesterday *en route* for America. Perhaps he called on you, too.

Let me have your recipes[c] for the German newspapers. I will have them copied out and find the most suitable PLACEMENTS. They will even find *double emploi*,[d] at least in part, as Meyer was also asking for something of the kind for over there and will put them to good use. As soon as this has been done in Germany— *and that is the most important thing*, for success *here* depends largely on what happens there—you must write a critique for *The Fortnightly Review*.[509] Beesly will get it in. This is a necessary prerequisite TO CATCH A PUBLISHER IN LONDON. The paper is secretly (so secretly that not a soul notices it) of Comteist persuasion, but wishes to provide an outlet for *every* point of view. If your critique arouses Mr Lewes' (the Goethe man, and unfortunately semi-Comteist, too) interest in the book (Lewes is secretly also CO-PROPRIETOR of the *Review*), it will be easy to find a publisher. And even without that, a publisher will in any case be easier to find then. The latest number contains a truly pitiful article by Thornton, in which he reproduces MALTHUSIANISM (in which the real MONGERS do *not* believe) in the most commonplace and trivial form.[e]

What our party lacks is money, as the enclosed letters from Eccarius and Becker once more painfully demonstrate.[510] But for this deficiency, we should always be, despite great and irreplaceable losses, today as in 1848, *les plus forts*.[f]

Regards to Mrs Lizzy.[g]

Your
K. M.

First published abridged in *Der Briefwechsel zwischen F. Engels und K. Marx*, Bd. 3, Stuttgart, 1913 and in full in *MEGA*, Abt. III, Bd. 3, Berlin, 1930

Printed according to the original

Published in English in full for the first time

---

[a] spontaneous generation - [b] the one is as bad as the other. A reference to L. Nougués, 'L'Art militaire et le progrès' (*Le Courrier français*, Nos. 123 and 125, 18 and 20 October 1867) and to P. J. Proudhon, 'Lettres inédites de P.-J. Proudhon sur les générations spontanées' (ibid., Nos. 121, 123 and 124, 16, 18 and 19 October 1867). - [c] reviews of the first volume of *Capital* (see this volume, p. 451) - [d] double utilisation - [e] W. T. Thornton, 'Stray Chapters from a Forthcoming Work on Labour', *The Fortnightly Review*, Vol. II, No. 10, 1 October 1867. - [f] the greatest force - [g] Lizzy Burns

275

ENGELS TO MARX

IN LONDON

Manchester, 22 October 1867

Dear Moor,

The letters from Becker and Eccarius returned enclosed.[a] The lack of money is, of course, a great misfortune for the party, and a yet greater one for those poor devils.

Siebel has written to me from Honnef on the Rhine that he is coming here at the beginning of November to embark at Liverpool again for Madeira. He says I should send him the articles[b] *by return*; this evening I shall set to work to knock a few into shape for him. What I am writing for the *German* press is, of course, all *dressed up in disguise*; I shall have to write differently for America, since one can take greater liberties there.

Sam Moore has written from Eisenach; he seems to be making considerable progress with his German.

I am greatly amused by Liebknecht. It is truly fortunate that he is still thoroughly infected with the South-German-Federalist nonsense and can consequently attack Bismarckism with great SINGLENESS OF PURPOSE and with undaunted moral indignation. A somewhat more critical and more dialectical outlook would only sow confusion in his mind and lead him astray. He has obviously taken Lupus in the Frankfurt Parliament[511] as his model and has properly earned his call to order by describing the Reichstag as the fig-leaf of naked absolutism. You will have seen that he has inserted a paragraph for the protection of factory children in the combination law.[512]

The Party of Progress[99] has rejected the Commission of Inquiry as not being within the competence of the Reichstag.[504] The *Confederation is*, however, competent to deal with all matters of trade and industry, only the *Reichstag* cannot appoint a commission, although it can indeed request the Federal authority to do so.

In the interest debate Bismarck has rejected the idea of granting the mortgage banks state assistance, saying that if it is a question of state support, this could only be approved for the *workers'*

---

[a] See this volume, p. 455. - [b] on the first volume of *Capital*

associations at most. So, the scoundrel still thinks he can dupe the workers.

Victor Emmanuel appears to be playing a most risky game. For all that, the Roman fracas is not yet over.[513] The air is becoming more electric every day, and I should not be at all surprised if the storm were to break right next spring.

Best regards to your wife, the girls and Doctor Eisenbart.[a]

Your
F. E.

I'm glad the Borkheim business is straight now. Under no circumstances can I give Gottfried Ermen a pretext *just now* to terminate his contract with me on the grounds of direct breach of contract. I hope the money drives away your carbuncles; don't forget to take plenty of exercise in the open air.

I shall be glad to do the thing for *The Fortnightly Review*.[509] But you must let me know about how much space I am allowed for it. I presume you will prefer me to summarise, so as briefly to give the main points of the book[b]—origin of capital—surplus-value— working day—revision of Ricardo's laws, etc., etc., after all I really cannot criticise the thing. I should also like to know approximately when the thing must be complete. It is too late for the 1 November number, so for the 1 December number it will have to be.

First published abridged in *Der Briefwech-sel zwischen F. Engels und K. Marx*, Bd. 3, Stuttgart, 1913 and in full in *MEGA*, Abt. III, Bd. 3, Berlin, 1930

Printed according to the original

Published in English for the first time

276

ENGELS TO MARX

IN LONDON

Dear Moor,   Manchester, 1 November 1867

What is the matter? Why have I not heard from you at all? Ever since your last letter I have been in constant fear that you have the

---

[a] Paul Lafargue (Engels jocularly calls Lafargue by the name of a wandering German physician, which became synonymous with a quack) - [b] the first volume of *Capital*

carbuncles again. Have you heard any more from across the water? From Kugelmann or Meissner concerning articles on your book[a]? I am getting no news of any kind and, in the circumstances, there is damn little I can do.

Just how far Dizzy[b] has contrived not merely to DISH the Whigs but to disorganise the Tories, too, was demonstrated to me the day before yesterday in a conversation with two of that ilk. They were agreed:

1. that the Irish Church and thus the Established Church in England, too, should fall forthwith,

2. that the LAWS OF PRIMOGENITURE AND ENTAIL[514] are no longer tenable,

3. that when the Queen[c] dies, a revolution will probably soon follow here.

Your
F. E.

First published in *Der Briefwechsel zwischen F. Engels und K. Marx,* Bd. 3, Stuttgart, 1913

Printed according to the original

Published in English for the first time

277

MARX TO ENGELS[101]

IN MANCHESTER

[London,] 2 November 1867

DEAR FRED,

Although none of my recent CARBUNCLES has fully developed, fresh ones are forever appearing; they always disappear again, BUT FRET ME. And then my old insomnia. But it has been better for ABOUT the last 3 DAYS. The silence about my book[a] makes me FIDGETY. I have had no news of any kind. What good fellows the Germans are! *Their* achievements in the service of the English, French and even the Italians in this field would indeed entitle them to ignore me and my affairs. Our people over there do not have the knack

---

[a] the first volume of *Capital* - [b] Benjamin Disraeli - [c] Victoria

of agitation. Meanwhile, we must do as the Russians do—wait. Patience is the core of Russian diplomacy and of their successes. But the likes of us, who only live once, may well never live to see the day.

Letter enclosed from the German communist association.[515] Well meant. But strangely loutish in style.

Enclosed letter from Maughan, man of private means, old Owenite, very decent fellow. These people are obviously intending to emancipate the FREETHINK movement from the PROFESSIONAL AGITATORS Bradlaugh, etc. I very politely declined.[516] On the one hand, it is true that I would thereby have had the chance, which I am wanting so much, of becoming acquainted with all manner of people who are to a greater or lesser extent, directly or indirectly, connected with the English press. On the other hand, I have not the time, nor do I think it right that I should figure on the LEADING COMMITTEE of any English sect.

A certain Auberon Herbert,[a] brother of the EARL OF CARNARVON and COUSIN to Stepney (who is member of our CENTRAL COUNCIL) and much dabbling in socialism (I.E., CO-OPERATIVE DODGES, etc.), has asked Stepney to arrange a rendezvous with me. As I first want to have sight of the man and smell him over, I have made an appointment to see him next Tuesday at the Cleveland Hall, where we hold our meetings. This 'channel' (Vogt)[517] may perhaps prove useful for reaching publishers.

Apropos. SUBSCRIPTIONS for the INTERNATIONAL: now have to be renewed. As soon as Moore is back send your SUBSCRIPTIONS to me per POST OFFICE ORDER (Charing Cross), but drawn on our TREASURER: *Robert Shaw,* 62 Hall Place, Hall Park, London W. It would be desirable for Schorlemmer to send his at the same time as you, even if only A FEW SHILLINGS. Is he back yet? When shall I be getting his Chemistry[b]?

I don't know whether you are familiar with the course of the Italian affair,[513] fragments of which have *accidentellement*[c] found their way into the English and German press in the form of extracts from Russian and other papers. It is easy to lose track of such threads.

At the time of the Luxemburg affair[415] Mr Bonaparte came to an agreement (informal) with Victor Emmanuel, by which the latter was given the right to annex the remaining Papal States

---

[a] The original has: Egerton Herbert.- [b] H. E. Roscoe, *Kurzes Lehrbuch der Chemie nach den neuesten Ansichten der Wissenschaft. Deutsche Ausgabe, unter Mitwirkung des Verfassers bearbeitet von Carl Schorlemmer.* - [c] by chance

except Rome, in exchange for offensive alliance against Prussia in the event of war.[518] But when the Prussian hornets' nest[376] turned into good will to all men, Mr Bonaparte began to regret the thing and with his usual cunning attempted to betray Emmanuel and make advances to Austria. As we all know, nothing came of it in Salzburg either,[519] and so for a while the witches' cauldron that is Europe appeared not to seethe. Meanwhile the Russian gentlemen, who had as usual procured a copy of the agreement, thought the moment had come to inform Mr Bismarck of it, who, in his turn, had the Prussian envoy[a] lay it before the Pope.[b] Whereupon, at the Pope's instigation, the pamphlet written by Bishop Dupanloup of Orleans.[520] On the other side, Garibaldi set on by Emmanuel. Subsequently: Rattazzi dismissed as an enemy of Prussia and Bonapartist. Hence the present *imbroglio*.[c] That scoundrel Bonaparte is now up to his eyes in the mire. War, not just with Italy, but Prussia and Russia, and in a cause which in France enjoys the most fanatical hatred of Paris, etc., hated in England, etc.—or yet another retreat! The fellow attempted to save himself by appealing to Europe, a *European Congress*. But Prussia and England have already sent him their reply, that, having made his bed, he must now lie on it. The fellow does not know what year it is. He is no longer secret general to Russia and Europe.

If retreat, then with present corn-prices, business in crisis and disaffection in France revolution is possible ONE FINE MORNING.

One good thing about our Bismarck—although he is the chief instrument of Russian intrigues—is that he is pushing things towards crisis in France. However, in respect of our German philistines, their entire past has shown that unity can only be imposed on them by the grace of God and the sabre.

The Fenian trial in Manchester exactly as was to be expected.[497] You will have seen what a scandal 'our people' have caused in the REFORM LEAGUE. I sought by every means at my disposal to incite the English workers to demonstrate in favour of FENIANISM.[521]

Salut.

Your

K. M.

I once believed the separation of Ireland from England to be impossible. I now regard it as inevitable, although FEDERATION may follow upon separation. The way the English are proceeding is

---

[a] Karl Georg von Usedom - [b] Pius IX - [c] confusion

shown by the AGRICULTURAL STATISTICS for this year, which appeared a few days ago. Over and above that the manner of the EVICTION. The Irish VICEROY, Lord Abicorn[a] (the name is *something like* that), has 'CLEARED' his ESTATE in the last few weeks by forcibly driving thousands from their homes. Among them, well-to-do tenant-farmers, their IMPROVEMENTS and capital investments being thus confiscated! In no other European country has foreign rule assumed this form of direct expropriation of the natives. The Russians confiscate only for political reasons; the Prussians in West Prussia buy out.

First published in *Der Briefwechsel zwischen F. Engels und K. Marx*, Bd. 3, Stuttgart, 1913

Printed according to the original

Published in English in full for the first time

278

ENGELS TO MARX[522]

IN LONDON

Manchester, 5 November 1867

Dear Moor,

Enclosed placed in the *Elberfelder Zeitung* by Siebel.[b] It is such a pity that the poor devil, who will probably be arriving here tomorrow, will have to leave straight away, he would probably have arranged a few more things. However, I will see what else he can do, perhaps something will be possible nonetheless.

Notre ami[c] Kugelmann appears to have miscalculated in respect of the Hanoverian newspapers, too—at least, to my utter astonishment I discovered one of the articles[d] sent him, and the *tamest* of them at that, shortened and mutilated to boot, in the *Zukunft!*[e] We hardly needed *amicum*[f] for that, and at all events I would have written differently for *that* paper. But I was writing for the national-liberal papers he had boasted about.

---

[a] James Hamilton Abercorn - [b] F. Engels, 'Review of Volume One of *Capital* for the *Elberfelder Zeitung*'. - [c] Our friend - [d] on the first volume of *Capital* - [e] F. Engels, 'Review of Volume One of *Capital* for the *Zukunft*. - [f] this friend

We must adopt a different approach. Have you Liebknecht's
present address, or alternatively his old one in Leipzig? If you let
me have it, I will spur him on a bit. I now realise that I shall have
to write all the articles myself (Eccarius could probably also do
one); the people on the Continent are finding the book is still
lying too heavily on the stomach, and, if we are to wait until they
have digested it, the opportunity will have been missed. I shall
write to Kugelmann again, too,[a] asking him at least what he has
done with the other article and whether he can place any more.[523]
You must write to Meissner and ask whether *he* can place any if
they are sent to him, and where. In addition, I shall write to Klein
in Cologne about the *Rheinische Zeitung*, and offer an article if
need be. It is a dreadful handicap not being on the spot oneself. If
we were in Germany, we should already have created a stir in all
the papers, and have managed to get the book *denounced*, which is
always the best thing.

Louis[b] in Paris does not know which way to turn. What a mess
he has got himself into! Either another retreat or war on behalf of
the Pope.[c] I can hardly believe that he has really served the
Italians an ultimatum to evacuate Roman territory, no more than I
can believe that he can let things rest with Moustier's churlish
note.[524] In either case, he is *foutu*.[d] The present mood in Paris was
shown at the *cimetière* Montmartre.[525] Things may begin to happen
any day now, and I hardly believe that the great man will celebrate
another 2 December,[e] or at least it will probably be for the last
time. He is in such a bad way that even the philistines here only
treat him as a common adventurer now.

If the storm does break, however, the revolution will everywhere
be faced with a quite different situation from 1848. After last year,
the disorganisation of that time will be out of the question in
Germany, and even if an immediate violent uprising in Berlin has
little chance, the impact of events would provoke clashes there,
too, which would inevitably end in the downfall of the present
regime. Monsieur Bismarck would very soon lose command of the
situation. And then this time England would be dragged in
straightaway and ABOVE ALL the social question would at once
become the burning issue throughout Europe.

Yesterday Blackburn showed the depths to which the English
judges have sunk when he asked the witness Beck (who had first
sworn to *William* Martin, but said afterwards that it was *John* M.):

---

[a] See this volume, pp. 467-69. - [b] Napoleon III - [c] Pius IX - [d] done for - [e] the
anniversary of the Bonapartist coup d'état of 2 December 1851

THEN YOU SWORE TO WILLIAM, AND YOU *MEANT* TO SWEAR TO JOHN? The whole prosecution will, I believe, crumble increasingly with each new BATCH of accused, the amount of perjury to get the £200 reward is quite incredible.[497]

Can you tell me where I can find more details about Lord Abercorn's EVICTIONS?[a]

Louis in Paris would once more have to mind bombs and bullets. The Italians are not to be trifled with.

I shall return the *Courriers*[b] to you tomorrow if I can.

Kindest regards to your wife, the girls and the lovelorn cobbler.[c]

Your
F. E.

First published in *Der Briefwechsel zwischen F. Engels und K. Marx*, Bd. 3, Stuttgart, 1913

Printed according to the original

Published in English in full for the first time

279

MARX TO ENGELS[522]

IN MANCHESTER

[London,] 7 November 1867

DEAR FRED,

My *remerciments*[d] for the *Elberfelder*.[e]

Liebknecht's old address: '11, Braustrasse, Leipzig.' By the way, perhaps *safer* to forward it through Kugelmann, who is in contact with a friend of Liebknecht's in Leipzig.

I forgot to tell you in my letter of Saturday[f] 1 sheet maximum for the *Fortnightly*.[g] [509] If longer than half a sheet, it should be set out as FIRST NOTICE, SECOND NOTICE.

As regards Meissner, it appears to me to be undiplomatic to let him see into our cards too much. What he can do from his own resources, he does anyway. It would be important—and for the present more important than the English article—to send a more

---

[a] See this volume, pp. 461. - [b] *Le Courrier français* - [c] Paul Lafargue - [d] thanks - [e] F. Engels, 'Review of Volume One of *Capital* for the *Elberfelder Zeitung*'. - [f] 2 November (see this volume, pp. 458-61) - [g] *The Fortnightly Review*

detailed report (perhaps broken down into several articles) to the Austrian *Internationale Revue* (*Arnold Hilberg's* publishing house, 4, Kolowrat-Ring, Vienna). As Arnold Hilberg lists you and me as his contributors (and through me has asked us both for contributions), there are no obstacles here. It is in fact the sole German 'Review' which is open to us.

The only weekly paper here in London which has a certain impartiality and is much concerned with things German, such as German philology, natural science, Hegel, etc., is a—*Catholic paper, The Chronicle.* It is obviously their tendency to show that they are more learned than their Protestant rivals. I sent them ONE COPY ᵃ at the end of last week with A SHORT LETTER TO THE PURPOSE, saying that my book does not share their opinions, but that the 'scholarly' nature of their paper suggests THAT 'SOME NOTICE WILL BE TAKEN OF THIS FIRST ATTEMPT AT APPLYING THE *DIALECTIC METHOD* TO POLITICAL ECONOMY'.[111] *Nous verrons!* ᵇ There is a great desire prevailing at present in the more refined circles (I am referring, of course, to the INTELLECTUAL portion of the latter) to become acquainted with the dialectical method. And perhaps that is after all the easiest way to get at the English.

The most interesting thing in the enclosed *Diplomatic Review* is the excerpts from the new book by Prokesch.ᶜ

Detailed description of Abercorn's EVICTIONS appeared ABOUT a fortnight ago in the (Dublin) *Irishman.*ᵈ I may manage to get again the copy which was only lent me for 24 hours.

At the MEETING ᵉ presided over by Colonel Dickson and at which Bradlaugh delivered a lecture on Ireland, our OLD Weston, SECONDED BY Fox and Cremer, put forward a RESOLUTION in support of the FENIANS, which was passed unanimously. Last Tuesday ditto, during Acland's lecture on the REFORM BILL, Cleveland Hall (right above us, we were meeting downstairs in the COFFEE ROOM, which is in the basement), tempestuous demonstration in favour of the FENIANS. The business is boiling up in the intelligent section of the WORKING CLASS here.

How very characteristic of the diplomatic farce being enacted in Europe at present, that at the same time as Bonaparte is intervening in Italy, France, Italy and Prussia are jointly, and most

---

ᵃ of the first volume of *Capital* - ᵇ We shall see! - ᶜ 'Conference held on August the 27th, 1822, at Constantinople. From the Work of Baron Prokesch', *The Diplomatic Review,* 2 October 1867 (excerpts from the book by A. Prokesch-Osten, *Geschichte des Abfalls der Griechen vom Türkischen Reiche im Jahre 1821*). - ᵈ See this volume, pp. 461 and 463. - ᵉ In this paragraph Marx refers to the meetings of the Reform League branches.

obediently at Russia's behest, delivering a threatening note to the Porte.[526]

Salut.

Your
K. M.

Old Urquhart with his Catholicism, etc., GROWS MORE AND MORE DISGUSTING.

On lit dans un registre d'une inquisition d'Italie cet aveu d'une religieuse; elle disait innocement à la Madonne: 'Degrâce, sainte Vierge, donne moi quelqu'un avec qui je puisse pécher.'[a] However, the Russians are *plus forts*[b] in this, too. A case is reported of a fellow in the best of health who emerged dead after only 24 hours in a Russian nunnery. The nuns had ridden him to death. Of course, in their case *le directeur des consciences n'entre pas tous les jours*[c]!

<table>
<tr>
<td>First published abridged in Der Briefwechsel zwischen F. Engels und K. Marx, Bd. 3, Stuttgart, 1913 and in full in MEGA, Abt. III, Bd. 3, Berlin, 1930</td>
<td>Printed according to the original

Published in English in full for the first time</td>
</tr>
</table>

280

ENGELS TO MARX

IN LONDON

Manchester, 8 November 1867

Dear Moor,

In great haste:

Siebel will be here tomorrow or in Liverpool, where I shall see him. He can place another 3 articles,[d] which I have prepared at once and which we shall then despatch with all speed. If I had known that it would be so long before he came, he should have received them in Barmen long ago.

---

[a] The following confession from a nun is to be found in an inquisition record in Italy, who innocently prayed to the madonna: 'I beg of you, Holy Virgin, send me someone with whom I may sin.' - [b] stronger - [c] the Father Confessor *does not come in every day* - [d] on the first volume of *Capital*

The idea about the *Internationale Revue* had already occurred to me, too, and shall be attended to. Likewise with *The Fortnightly Review*, as soon as acceptance is assured.[509] For the moment, however, I believe it is most important to create a rumpus in the German daily press, *pour forcer la main à ces gueux d'économistes*.[a]

The DOWNBREAK of the police in the trial here has been more rapid and more complete than I had expected. But there is probably even better to come. OLD Blackburn also appears to be changing his tune, today he complimented Ernest Jones most fulsomely on his speech.[497]

Have you read Bismarck's instructions to Usedom (in the *Augsburger Abendzeitung*,[b] denied, of course[518])? The fellow is making no bones about exposing the Italians' intrigues with Bonaparte; one has to grant him that he is capable of the most undiplomatic manners if it suits him. (*Kölnische Zeitung* of Wednesday has reprinted it.) This stance of Bismarck's also explains the Italians' retreat and their present grovelling.

Concerning the true nature of the inspections, checks and interferences of the Prussian bureaucracy: my brother writes that the manufacturers want to set up an association on the Rhine and in the Ruhr, like the ones here, to have their boilers periodically examined by competent engineers, and he goes on to say of the government control:

'Here at our place, a District Architect inspects 7 boilers in half an hour (!!) and goes home quite satisfied, in another factory a similar official *took 2 hours for 35 boilers*!! If anyone is so foolish as to imagine he can sleep soundly after such an inspection, he is, of course, deceived. It would be a real blessing if this nonsense were done away with and replaced by some sensible practical arrangement. At one inspection, *I first* explained the boiler with all its fittings to the District Architect, *then* I carried out *his* instructions as well and *finally wrote the report for the government* for him.'

There are the Prussians for you! Portrayed by themselves.

First published in *Der Briefwechsel zwischen F. Engels und K. Marx*, Bd. 3, Stuttgart, 1913

Printed according to the original

Published in English for the first time

---

[a] to force the hand of these miserable economists - [b] *Augsburger Abendzeitung*, No. 303, 4 November 1867.

281

ENGELS TO LUDWIG KUGELMANN[522]

IN HANOVER

Manchester, 8 and 20 November 1867

Dear Kugelmann,

Since my last letter[a] neither Marx nor I have heard anything from you, and I can scarce believe that you are so deeply ensconced in some *anteflexio uteri* as to be entirely incommunicado. I have, moreover, a letter to send to Liebknecht, and Marx advises me to forward it to you, as we do not have the exact address and do not know whether he is in Berlin or Leipzig; I am therefore enclosing it.[131]

The German press is still observing complete silence in respect of *Capital*, and it really is of the greatest importance that something should be said. I have discovered that one of the articles[b] I sent you is in the *Zukunft*; I am sorry I did not know that it might eventually be destined for that paper; one could probably have taken greater liberties there. However, it does not matter. The main thing is that the book should be discussed over and over again, in any way whatsoever. And as Marx is not a free agent in the matter, and is furthermore as bashful as a young girl, it is up to the rest of us to see to it. Please be so kind therefore and let me know what success you have so far had in the matter, and which papers you think you may still be able to use. In the words of our old friend Jesus Christ, we must be innocent as doves and wise as serpents.[c] The good old vulgar economists at least have enough intelligence to treat the book with respect and to take good care not to talk of it if they are not obliged to. And that is what we must *compel* them to do. If the book is being discussed in 15-20 newspapers at once—never mind whether favourably or not, whether in articles, regular features or unsolicited pieces in the correspondence section—even if merely as a phenomenon of some significance that merits attention, then the whole crowd of them will start yapping away, too, of their own accord, and the Fauchers, Michaelis, Roschers, and Max Wirths will then *have to* do the same. We have a moral obligation to

---

[a] See this volume, pp. 443-44. - [b] F. Engels, 'Review of Volume One of *Capital* for the *Zukunft*. - [c] Matthew 10:16

damned well get these articles into the papers, and *as near simultaneously as possible*, especially the European ones, and that includes the reactionary ones. In the latter, we might point out that the vulgarian gentlemen make a deal of noise in parliaments and economic gatherings, but now, when they are confronted with *the consequences* of their own science, they prefer to keep their mouths shut. And so forth. If you think my assistance would be desirable, let me know which paper you wish to have something for—in the service of the party I am always on call. The letter to Liebknecht concerns the same business, and you will therefore oblige me exceedingly by *ensuring* it reaches its destination.

The Roman affair[513] has again been an absolute boon to us. The noble Bonaparte appears to me to be gargling his last gasp, and when this episode comes to an end in France, with the position in England becoming more revolutionary every day, and with revolution in Italy inescapable—, then this must surely also spell the end of the reign of the 'Europeans'[a] in Germany. Rapid progress is being made here in England with the formation of a really revolutionary party, and revolutionary conditions are developing hand in hand with it. With his REFORMBILL,[425] Disraeli has thrown the Tories into confusion and routed the Whigs, although all he has done is to render it impossible to continue dilly-dallying as before. This REFORMBILL will either prove to be nothing at all (and this is now impossible, there is too much momentum behind it), or it will infallibly and immediately bring in its train BILLS of an altogether different character, which will go much farther. The next steps, which will have to be taken forthwith, are the allotting of representatives in proportion to population and the secret ballot, and that will be the end of the old scheme of things here. The capital thing about Disraeli is that his hatred for the COUNTRY GENTLEMEN in his own party and his hatred of the Whigs have set things going on a course which can no longer be halted. You will be astonished, and the German philistines who think England is finished will be even more astonished, at what will happen here once the REFORMBILL is in force. The Irish are also doing their bit to keep things properly on the boil, and every day the London proletarians are more openly declaring their support for the Fenians,[257] in other words, and this is without precedent here and really splendid, for a movement that firstly advocates the use of force and secondly is anti-English.

Have you heeded my medical advice and taken to horseback?

---

[a] See this volume, pp. 361 and 372.

Since my return [449] I have again found the beneficial effects of riding amply demonstrated, and you will see how quickly all your complaints and reservations about drink disappear thanks to an hour's riding daily. As a gynaecologist, you owe it to science, for after all gynaecology is intimately connected with riding or being ridden, and a gynaecologist must therefore be in every sense the master of his mount.

Schorlemmer kept an eye open for you at the congress of naturalists in Frankfurt but maintains you were not there.

So, dear friend, let us hear from you soon. The photograph of Lupus has been ordered and will be ready as soon as the fine weather comes, unfortunately we do not have much daylight here in winter. Please convey my best compliments to your wife,[a] despite our being unacquainted, and best regards from

Yours

F. E.

Address: Ermen & Engels, Manchester FOR F. E.

20 November. Since I wrote the above, Marx has communicated to me your letter to him,[b] and I am sorry to see from it that we can hardly count on further press-notices in your locality. Might it not be possible, perhaps through third persons, to get *attacks* on the book, either from a bourgeois or a reactionary point of view, into some of the papers? This seems to me to be one means of publicity, and there would be no difficulty in producing the articles. And then: what about scientific journals, or purely literary or semi-literary ones?

Respecting the *Rheinische Zeitung,* I am writing to Cologne in case there has still been no progress.[523]

Büchner ought to be able to get things into the papers as well; you can refer him to me for the articles if necessary. Give him no peace.

I have still not received the photographs, but they are sure to come one of these days.

Once more, in all friendship

Yours

F. E.

First published in: Marx and Engels, *Works,* First Russian Edition, Vol. XXV, Moscow, 1934

Printed according to the original

Published in English in full for the first time

---

a Gertruda Kugelmann - b of 6 November 1867

282

MARX TO ENGELS[527]

IN MANCHESTER

[London,] 9 November 1867

Dear Fred,

Enclosed from Kugelmann.
Salut.

Your
Moor

[Postscript from Laura Marx in English]

Dear Engels,

As Mohr's Secretary I am really rather ashamed to send off a letter of this kind.

Yours sincerely
Kakadou[a]

First published in *MEGA*, Abt. III,
Bd. 3, Berlin, 1930

Printed according to the original

Published in English for the first time

283

ENGELS TO MARX

IN LONDON

Manchester, 10 November 1867

Dear Moor,

What touching gaucheness in dear old Kugelmann's letter! And what discernment of character in respect of that Warnebold! The fellow extracts all his secrets from him, and all the while he is a Prussian spy! You *must* tell Kugelmann the truth about that cur—at least sufficiently to stop the Prussians learning every detail

---

[a] Laura's jocular nickname

of our activities.[528] The cur is abusing your confidences, which absolves you from any obligation toward him.

I saw Siebel yesterday in Liverpool. I fear the poor devil's days are numbered. Since I last saw him, his desease has advanced considerably, his health broke down in Barmen, he has had 3 successive attacks of pleurisy and is coughing very violently (he calls them coughing-spasms, and they recur periodically), however he has lately regained some of his health and strength at Honnef on the Rhine. Unfortunately, I could only speak to him alone for a short while, there were always several relatives there apart from his wife. Despite that, we settled the most important things.

D'abord[a]: Siebel has up to the present moment *neither received a copy*[b] *nor even seen one, although he wrote to Meissner* asking to be sent one by post immediately on publication. Mr Rittershaus, however, who has not lifted a finger, has received one, and Siebel thought you had not sent him one at all, but had done so to Rittershaus, which may have piqued him. I naturally explained the true position to him, but a few lines from you to him, which you can enclose in a letter to me, really are called for. But you must now take Meissner to task forthwith for this negligence. This affair has cost us 20 short notices which Siebel would immediately have had in all the papers, but could not because he did not have the book. Furthermore, I must have a copy here *by 22 November at the latest* to send to Siebel in Madeira, where he will make up for lost time as far as he can. But really what can one say to such a slapdash approach? And these are the Germans who are demanding self-government and CANNOT LOOK AFTER THEIR OWN BUSINESS!

Of the 3 articles I took with me, we sent off 2 to the *Frankfurter Börsenzeitung*[c] and to the *Düsseldorfer Zeitung*[529] forthwith—the latter will do Mr Heinrich Bürgers good, with his circumspect scruples: my article[d]—a very simple report, which makes no judgments and was composed for a *national-liberal* newspaper—is too dubious for that brute![523] Siebel took the 3rd with him, it will probably go to the *Barmer Zeitung*.[530] Notices will also appear in all kinds of illustrated and other papers, as soon as Siebel himself has the book. Furthermore, the *Weser-Zeitung* will receive an article *a tempo*[e] from him for its literary section, and one on the book, and will be faced only with the choice of taking both or neither. (Siebel is using the literary section articles as a bait for editors, they are desperate for them, and he often lets them pocket the fee

---

a Firstly - b of the first volume of *Capital* - c *Frankfurter Zeitung und Handelsblatt* - d F. Engels, 'Review of Volume One of *Capital* for the *Rheinische Zeitung*'. - e in time

themselves.) Other ideas will occur to him as soon as he has the book.

Ad vocem^a Freiligrath: that worthy's debts amounted to approx. £6,000, £4,000 with the Swiss Bank advanced for shares in the Mansfield Co. which are now worthless, and the rest debts of honour. The *Comité*[422] has settled these debts at 5% dividend, a few of them at 10%. Freiligrath has thus gone bankrupt *in optima forma*.^b The collection will amount to approx. 30,000 talers. Freiligrath is said to have lied to the *Comité* through and through, concealed his debts and pretended his wife knew nothing of it and must not be allowed to know anything of it either, so that eventually they were very rude to him; even on the day when he knew that a letter was to arrive from London to say that the debts of honour totalled £2,000, he was still saying they were only £1,500, etc. In short, his conduct has been disgraceful and cowardly. I said I was quite convinced that dear old Ida^c knew all about it, to which he replied: how was it then possible for her to give *fêtes*^d last summer in Barmen? Just imagine, Ida goes a-begging and at the same time holds *fêtes* for the people she is begging from with the money that has not yet been given!

I am surprised Tussy^e has not yet sent me a receipt for my contribution to the Freiligrath funeral-fund. THAT IS NOT BUSINESSLIKE.

Your
F. E.

First published abridged in *Der Briefwechsel zwischen F. Engels and K. Marx*, Bd. 3, Stuttgart, 1913 and in full in *MEGA*, Abt. III, Bd. 3, Berlin, 1930

Printed according to the original

Published in English for the first time

284

MARX TO CARL SIEBEL[531]

IN MADEIRA

London, 10 November 1867

Dear Siebel,

For the time being I am sending you this personal copy of mine.^f At the same time I wrote to Meissner, the deuce take him! I

---

^a Regarding - ^b in the best of form - ^c Ida Freiligrath - ^d parties - ^e Eleanor Marx - ^f the first volume of *Capital*

had actually instructed him to send you the *first* copy to appear in Germany. I hope that Madeira will do you good.

Karl Marx

First published in: Marx and Engels, *Works*, First Russian Edition, Vol. XXV, Moscow, 1934

Printed according to the text of Volume XXV of the First Russian Edition

Translated from the Russian

Published in English for the first time

285

MARX TO ENGELS

IN MANCHESTER

[London,] 14 November 1867

DEAR FRED,

A letter from Russia enclosed and one from Solingen.[532] I believe the Russo-German[a] must be the same man that Meyer[b] told us about.

Kugelmann has sent me a copy of the *Deutsche Volkszeitung* (Hanover) containing a short notice of my book[c] written by himself. In it, Kugelmann has imitated one of your articles,[d] and by no means happily. As this paper is democratic, he could have gone into the content more. Among other things, he has me arrive 'at the' admittedly 'astonishing conclusion that all capital is derived *from unpaid labour power*'. Among the 'German authorities on political economy' whose 'verdict' he seeks, Mr 'Faucher' (fortunately printed as 'Taucher') appears at the *head* of the list and Roscher at the end.

Your 'revelations' in respect of Freiligrath have created a great sensation here at home.

At this moment, Bonaparte has need of a riot or a secret society in Paris if he is to extricate himself from his predicament. For the time being, he is treating the *Ligue de la Paix*[e][461] as such. However,

---

[a] Joseph Dietzgen - [b] Sigfrid Meyer - [c] the first volume of *Capital* (*Deutsche Volkszeitung*, 10 November 1867) - [d] F. Engels, 'Review of Volume One of *Capital* for the *Zukunft*'. - [e] League of Peace

that jackass Pyat is JUST NOW preparing the necessary *corpus delicti* for him from here.

I am being plagued by a carbunculum on the right side of my back.

Salut.

Your

K. M.

First published in *Der Briefwechsel zwischen F. Engels und K. Marx*, Bd. 3, Stuttgart, 1913

Printed according to the original

Published in English for the first time

286

ENGELS TO MARX [522]

IN LONDON

Manchester, 24 November 1867

Dear Moor,

The letters returned enclosed.

So, yesterday morning, and by Mr Colcraft's hand, the Tories have really performed the ultimate act of separation between England and Ireland. The *only thing* the Fenians still lacked were martyrs. Derby and G. Hardy have now provided them with these. It was the execution of those 3 [a] which will transform the liberation of Kelly and Deasy into an act of heroism, such as will now be sung at the cradle of every Irish child in Ireland, England and America. The Irish women will see to that as surely as did the Polish womenfolk.

The only time that anyone has, to my knowledge, been executed for anything similar in a civilised state was the case of John Brown at Harpers ferry.[533] The Fenians could not wish for a better precedent. And yet even the SOUTHERNERS had the decency to treat J. Brown as a *rebel*, whereas here no effort is spared to convert an act of political violence into a common crime.

Everybody knows that while he was leading his band of ruffians at Boulogne, Louis Napoleon shot the duty-officer dead.[534] He

---

[a] the Fenians Michael Larkin, William Allen and Michael O'Brien

thus *did* what Allen is supposed to have done but did *not do*. For which the English government hangs Allen, while the English queen[a] kisses Louis Napoleon's cheek and the English aristocracy and bourgeoisie his backside.

The latter point should be made in the press.

Your

F. E.

First published in *Der Briefwechsel zwischen F. Engels und K. Marx*, Bd. 3, Stuttgart, 1913

Printed according to the original

Published in English in full for the first time

287

ENGELS TO MARX

IN LONDON

Manchester, 26 November 1867

Dear Moor,

I have not received the promised letter *in quo tua res agebatur*.[b] Meissner's proposal to send out new notices with excerpts from the reviews was what I had in mind to suggest to you as soon as Siebel's articles (i.e. the ones I gave him[c]) appear. The excerpt from the *Zukunft* is quite good,[535] but a few more would be even better; he should send you the whole caboodle, and you can then prepare a notice from it. Or if you do not wish to, then he can send it to *me* and I will do it. I was most struck by the fact that the first notice *took up precisely the same space* as the one for my little pamphlet,[d] and it had not a word of commentary with it.[536]

If the matter does not turn out differently soon, then *I* shall have to write—with your consent OF COURSE—to Meissner and offer him articles written by *myself* for newspapers to be specified by him. I am sure that could not compromise you.

I have just managed to convey Meissner's excuses to Siebel[131] before the post office closed. They are admittedly persuasive,

---

a Victoria - b in which your business was dealt with (see next letter) - c F. Engels, 'Review of Volume One of *Capital* for the *Elberfelder Zeitung*' and 'Review of Volume One of *Capital* for the *Düsseldorfer Zeitung*'. - d F. Engels, *The Prussian Military Question and the German Workers' Party*.

Siebel was at the time AT A VERY LOW EBB and only recovered in Honnef.

You will have received my letter of Sunday with the returned letters.[a] The tanner[b] returned enclosed, *autodidactum integrum*,[c] which does not, however, mean that other nations are incapable of bringing forth such a tanner. Philosophy, which in Jakob Böhme's day was just a shoemaker, is making progress when it assumes the shape of a tanner.

How is the carbuncle? I do not like its location, I hope Lafargue has lanced it for you. A stop really must be put to this business.

Has Borkheim paid you the money? He has not written a word to me, although I am guarantor.[d]

Your
F. E.

First published in *Der Briefwechsel zwischen F. Engels und K. Marx*, Bd. 3, Stuttgart, 1913

Printed according to the original

Published in English for the first time

288

MARX TO ENGELS

IN MANCHESTER

[London,] 27 November 1867

Dear Engels,

With regard to my private business (I intended writing to you on Saturday[e] but was prevented on that and on the following days by people consulting me from every side about the FENIAN AFFAIRS,[497] etc., in short, they were confiscating my time), Mr Borkheim—despite the best of intentions, I am sure—has throughout this month kept me suspended between frying pan and fire. You will see from his latest letter, of yesterday, that we are again faced with a new, indefinite delay. The worst part of it all is that he had *positively* promised me he would pay out the whole sum on the

---

[a] See this volume, p. 474. - [b] Joseph Dietzgen - [c] entirely self-educated - [d] See this volume, pp. 436, 437, etc. - [e] 23 November

10th of this month (at the latest), and I had made my dispositions with the creditors accordingly. The amount he has actually paid since he returned is £5. So, you will realise what TROUBLE I find myself in. The state of my health has greatly worsened, and there has been virtually no question of working. I am furthermore expecting summonses any day, and we no longer know which way to turn from one day to the next.

With regard to *Meissner*, my view is that we should let him have a free hand with his notice, as everything else would mean further delay. Thimm told Borkheim that Meissner had requested all the booksellers to send any still unsold copies[a] back to him (or to his agent in Leipzig). I have also heard from York, the Workers' Society[b] bookseller, that it is at the moment *very difficult* to obtain copies from Meissner. To me this indicates no more than 1. that the STOCK in Meissner's hands is very small, 2. that he wants to know how much of the STOCK *not in his hands* is really sold, 3. he wants to force his business 'friends' to hold as much as possible at their own expense. I shall write to Meissner that should he need notices or reviews for certain newspapers or journals (and he must tell me *which*), he can obtain them from friends such as yourself, etc. Must keep me informed.

Dr Contzen, private lecturer in political economy at Leipzig, PARTISAN and pupil of Roscher and friend of Liebknecht, has asked me through the latter for a copy with the promise of a detailed review. You will see that this has already been attended to through Meissner. Contzen is a good opening.

Liebknecht has sent me 50 of his PAMPHLETS[c] (of which I am sending you one today) for sale here, 3d. each. Lessner is seeing what can be done in the Workers' Society.

The extract from Liebknecht's SPEECH at the Berlin Workers' Society[476] on the deferment of the 'social question' which he has published as an appendix admittedly gives some grounds for Kugelmann's censure.[537] As Liebknecht is asking you, among other things, to contribute to the little paper he is planning,[538] you can give him a few hints *privatim* about how to combine political opposition with social agitation.

Letters from Liebknecht and Kugelmann enclosed.

Salut.

Your
K. M.

---

[a] of the first volume of *Capital* - [b] German Workers' Educational Society in London - [c] W. Liebknecht, *Was ich im Berliner 'Reichstag' sagte.*

What is the position regarding Mr Schorlemmer's Chemistry[a] which I was to receive?

First published in *Der Briefwechsel zwischen F. Engels und K. Marx*, Bd. 3, Stuttgart, 1913

Printed according to the original

Published in English for the first time

289

MARX TO ENGELS

IN MANCHESTER

London, 28 November 1867

Dear Fred,

I see that I did not enclose the 2 letters from Borkheim for you. But it is not really necessary. Yesterday we had the 'discussion' he desired. He has reverted to the idea (which I suggested to him 2 months ago) of a loan from the 'Atlas' Life Assurance Company, whose secretary is a friend of his. I completed the papers yesterday at his house. You only figure as a REFERENCE on them. £150 (of which Borkheim would receive £45), repayable on 1 September.

I no longer have any faith in the success of Borkheim's operations. *I have no doubt about his good will.*

Have you received his '*Pearl*'? (French and German so far[b]).

Important letter from Schily enclosed. Please send it back *by return*; give your opinion at the same time. Whatever happens I shall not permit Moses[c] to derive 'profit' from my work[d] without profiting to some extent from it myself.[539]

I am having to be diplomatic about Fenianism. I cannot keep entirely silent, but under no circumstances do I want the fellows, when criticising my book, to confine themselves to the statement that I am a demagogue.

I am *sending* you Borkheim's *Gentz* (important for the article on

---

[a] H. E. Roscoe, *Kurzes Lehrbuch der Chemie... Deutsche Ausgabe, unter Mitwirkung des Verfassers bearbeitet von Carl Schorlemmer*. - [b] S. Borkheim, *Ma perle devant le congrès de Genève* (German edition: *Meine Perle vor dem Genfer Congress*). - [c] Moses Hess - [d] the first volume of *Capital*

Russia)[a] without his knowledge. Please return it to me as soon as you have finished.

I now have a rash of furuncles more or less all over, and am glad of it. It puts paid to the carbuncle malady.

Salut.

Your
Moro

* My compliments to Mrs Burns. Jenny goes in black since the Manchester execution,[497] and wears her Polish cross on a *green* ribbon.*[430]

First published in *Der Briefwechsel zwischen F. Engels und K. Marx*, Bd. 3, Stuttgart, 1913

Printed according to the original

Published in English for the first time

290

ENGELS TO MARX

IN LONDON

Manchester, 28 November 1867

Dear Moor,

Enclosed for your immediate relief £30 in 3 notes à 10, O/U 56068 to 70, Manchester, 9 January 1867. The letter from Borkheim was not enclosed. I have also received a letter from Kugelmann[b] which I enclose and wish to have returned, I have to answer him.

Liebknecht would have done better to leave his pamphlet unprinted.[c] His speeches appear better in the *Kölnische Zeitung* than in this form, and the stuff at the end indeed shows just how pig-headedly he is stuck in his errors.[537] It is true I have already told him a thing or two by letter, but now that he is starting up another little paper, he must be told some more home truths[538];

---

[a] F. von Gentz, *Vertrauliche Bemerkungen über den Stand und die nächste Zukunft der russisch-türkischen Angelegenheiten.* - [b] of 25 November 1867 - [c] W. Liebknecht, *Was ich im Berliner 'Reichstag' sagte.'*

we could do Bismarck no greater favour than to let ourselves be lumped together with the Austrians and South German Federalists, Ultramontanes and dispossessed princes. I am awaiting a letter from him daily and will then write to him about that, too.

How goes it with your health?

Your
F. E.

More tomorrow.

The Englishman in Kugelmann's letter is Moore, who has greatly improved his German and is now sweating away assiduously at *Capital*. Schorlemmer's book[a] is still not out yet!!

First published abridged in *Der Briefwechsel zwischen F. Engels und K. Marx*, Bd. 3, Stuttgart, 1913 and in full in *MEGA*, Abt. III, Bd. 3, Berlin, 1930

Printed according to the original

Published in English for the first time

291

ENGELS TO HERMANN ENGELS

IN BARMEN

Manchester, 28 November 1867

Dear Hermann,

Forgive me for leaving your two letters unanswered for so long. Many things were to blame for this, but above all the fact that yarns were certain not to go up for the time being and—with no demand from you at the moment—there was thus no danger in delay.

The SEWINGS we normally send out bleached and dyed in the finer nos., are doubled by us from the same COPS which we also send to you. (36/45 Taylor, finer No. Knowles.) But we can have these COPS doubled by a DOUBLER for you here, and the SEWINGS would at today's prices then cost

---

[a] H. E. Roscoe, *Kurzes Lehrbuch der Chemie... Deutsche Ausgabe, unter Mitwirkung des Verfassers bearbeitet von Carl Schorlemmer*.

No.:	36	40	50	60	70	80
	19d.	19 $^1/_2$d.	2/1	2/7	2/11	3/3

For DIAMOND 2d., however, we use a yarn that has been doubled on the DOUBLING FRAME but is more loosely spun; at today's prices that costs us

No.:	36	40	50	60	70	80
	18d.	18 $^1/_2$d.	20d.	2/1	2/3	2/5

I am enclosing a sample of the latter in No. 60, but you also had some of this last spring, bale No. 319, delivery note 9 April, so you can compare whether you need this cheaper product or whether you must have the more expensive yarns with real SEWING TWIST.

We are all expecting a drop in prices here in view of the exceptionally good American harvest. MIDDLING was selling at 6$^1/_2$ FREE ON BOARD in New Orleans. However, the spinning business is very much in the doldrums just now, and so when things first pick up again yarn might well remain stable, even if there is a fall in cotton. The fine nos. will hold their own best, the ORDINARY fine DOUBLES being already cheaper than in 1860 (16d. as against 18d. for 60/RFOLD). The prices I gave you overleaf are approximately the same as those at the end of 1859 and the beginning of 1860, the *more expensive* 60s being then at 2s. 5d., the 40s at 19d., and the cheaper 60s was anything a little more expensive then. I cannot make an exact comparison as we were not using the same threads in those days.

Otherwise everything is pretty much as usual here. From time to time, a bit of a tussle, now with Anton, now with Gottfried,[a] ensures that our old love never fades.

I am wishing myself many happy returns of my birthday today from all of you, and send you all my very best wishes. I shall be answering mother's[b] letter one day soon.[131]

Your
Friedrich

First published in: Marx and Engels, *Works*, First Russian Edition, Vol. XXV, Moscow, 1934

Printed according to the original

Published in English for the first time

---

[a] Anton and Gottfried Ermen - [b] Elisabeth Engels'

292

MARX TO ENGELS

IN MANCHESTER

[London,] 29 November 1867

DEAR FRED,

BEST THANKS FOR THE £30.

Letter from Kugelmann returned enclosed. We must watch out that he doesn't commit any stupidities in his enthusiasm. Such as with Miquel, for example.[528]

As regards the paper of the *United States of Europe*[a]—and the contributions I have been asked for from Geneva—it is the purest nonsense. Mr K. Grün probably the editor. And the thing is in itself a FAILURE.

Salut.

Your

K. M.

Cold and disagreeable though it is, I am supposed to circumambulate the Heath,[b] etc., for a few days.

First published in *Der Briefwechsel zwischen F. Engels und K. Marx,* Bd. 3, Stuttgart, 1913

Printed according to the original

Published in English for the first time

293

MARX TO ENGELS [540]

IN MANCHESTER

[London,] 29 November 1867

You can see how deucedly forgetful I am. I have just sent the letter off without enclosing Kugelmann.

First published in: Marx and Engels, *Works,* Second Russian Edition, Vol. 31, Moscow, 1963

Printed according to the original

Published in English for the first time

---

[a] *Les États-Unis d'Europe* - [b] Hampstead Heath

294

ENGELS TO MARX[522]

IN LONDON

Manchester, 29 November 1867
7 Southgate

Dear Moor,

Schily returned enclosed.[539] Oh, Lord, have mercy upon us, here comes olle Moses[a] pissing up to us again! And he is congratulating himself that you certified he was right when he asserted that capital is accumulated labour!

I would be just the tiniest bit reticent in respect of that worthy. He will then take the bait all the more surely, and you know how little we can trust him if we have not made *quite* sure of him. In my view, for the present you could *permit him* to publish a few extracts from it[b] in the *Courrier français,* so that we may see how he proposes to handle the thing. He will naturally put his signature to these, and we shall thereby again have him to some degree qualified as a repentant sinner. *Then* you could talk about the translation of the whole book which he is envisaging; *your* right of revision always reserved; and discuss conditions as soon as a publisher has been found. What Schily says of Reclus seems important to me, as the man knows German.

You are perfectly right about the Fenians.[c] The vile deeds of the English must not allow us to forget that most of the leaders of this sect are jackasses and some of them exploiters, and that we can, under no circumstances, make ourselves responsible for the idiocies that are perpetrated in any conspiracy. That there will be some, is certain.

I need hardly tell you that black and green[d] are the prevailing colours in my house, too. The English press has again conducted itself abominably.[497] Larkin is said to have fainted, and the others[e] to have looked pale and confused. The Catholic priests who were there declare that is a lie. Larkin, they say, *stumbled* over an irregularity in the ground and all three showed great courage.

---

[a] Moses Hess (*olle*—Low German for 'old') - [b] the first volume of *Capital* - [c] See this volume, pp. 478-79. - [d] i.e., colours symbolising mourning and the struggle for the emancipation of Ireland - [e] William Allen and Michael O'Brien

The Catholic Bishop of Salford complained bitterly that Allen refused to repent of his deed, saying he had nothing to repent, and if he were free, he would do the same thing again. The Catholic priests, incidentally, were very impudent, it was stated from the pulpit in every church on Sunday that THESE THREE MEN WERE MURDERED.

You will have received my letter of yesterday with the £30.[a] As regards the life assurance,[b] I am willing to *guarantee* the sum concerned, provided that Borkheim retains the *original* in his own keeping and merely gives the secretary a *copy*, in the hope that this will facilitate matters.

I agree that the furuncles appear to mark the crisis of the previous illness.

Best regards to your wife, the girls and Lafargue.

Now that Liebknecht has got a little paper,[538] for which *we* shall be held responsible, it is very important that he does nothing stupid in respect of his German policy. I am most impatient for a letter from him.

Apropos. From 1 January the *Internationale Revue* will appear as joint successor to a journal produced by *Prutz*[c] which is to merge with it. Could put paid to our plans.[d] How do you think we should broach the matter with Hilberg? We shall have to be cunning about it.

Your
F. E.

First published in *Der Briefwechsel zwischen F. Engels und K. Marx*, Bd. 3, Stuttgart, 1913

Printed according to the original

Published in English in full for the first time

295

MARX TO ENGELS[541]

IN MANCHESTER

London, 30 November 1867

DEAR FRED,

Regarding Moses,[e] I shall follow your prescription exactly. At all events, we must make use of the man and, at the same time,

---

[a] See this volume, pp. 479, 481-82. - [b] Ibid., p. 478. - [c] *Deutsches Museum* - [d] See this volume, pp. 463-64. - [e] Moses Hess (see this volume, p. 484).

prevent him from misusing us. Regarding Hilberg, it would indeed be a good thing if we could keep a hold on this *Revue*,[a] being the only one still open to us, but how? is not yet clear to me. This morning I received a COPY of Schorlemmer[b] AND SEND HIM MY THANKS FOR IT.

If you have read the papers, you will have seen that 1. the INTERNATIONAL COUNCIL sent MEMORIAL for the FENIANS[542] to Hardy, 2. the debate on FENIANISM (a week ago last Tuesday[c]) was public and *The Times* carried a REPORT on it.[d] There were also REPORTERS there from the Dublin *Irishman* and *Nation*. I did not arrive until very late (I have been suffering from a fever for about 2 weeks, and have only got over it in the last 2 days) and had not in fact intended to speak, first on account of my uncomfortable physical condition, and second because of the delicacy of the situation. However, the CHAIRMAN Weston wanted to force me to, so I moved ADJOURNMENT, which obliged me to speak last Tuesday.[e] What I had in fact prepared for TUESDAY LAST was not a SPEECH but rather the POINTS for A SPEECH.[f] However, the IRISH REPORTERS did not come, and by the time we had finished waiting for them it was 9 o'clock, whereas the premises were only available to us until $10^1/_2$. At my suggestion, Fox had prepared a long SPEECH (because of a QUARREL on the COUNCIL he had made no appearance for 2 weeks, and furthermore sent in his RESIGNATION as MEMBER OF THE COUNCIL containing furious outbursts against Jung[543]). When the *séance*[g] opened I therefore declared that, on account of the BELATED HOUR, I would yield the floor to Fox. In fact—because the executions in Manchester had intervened—our subject 'FENIANISM' was bound up with the passions and heated emotions of the moment, which would have compelled *me* (though not the abstract *Fox*) to unleash a revolutionary thunderbolt, instead of the intended objective analysis of the situation and the movement. The Irish REPORTERS thus did me a great service by staying away and so delaying the opening of the meeting. I do not enjoy getting embroiled with people like Roberts, Stephens, and the like.

Fox's SPEECH was good, first because it was delivered by *an Englishman*, and second insofar as it dealt only with political and international ASPECTS. However, for that very reason he only skated over the surface of things. The resolution he brought forward was

---

a *Internationale Revue* - b H. E. Roscoe, *Kurzes Lehrbuch der Chemie... Deutsche Ausgabe, unter Mitwirkung des Verfassers bearbeitet von Carl Schorlemmer*. - c 19 November - d 'London Meetings', *The Times*, No. 25974, 21 November 1867. - e 26 November - f K. Marx, 'Notes for an Undelivered Speech on Ireland'. - g meeting

silly and pointless.[544] I opposed it and had it referred back to the STANDING COMMITTEE.[21]

What the English do not yet realise, is that since 1846 the economic content and hence the political purpose of English rule in Ireland as well has entered an entirely new phase, and that for that very reason FENIANISM is characterised by socialist (in the negative sense, as directed against the APPROPRIATION of the SOIL) leanings and as a LOWER ORDERS MOVEMENT. What could be more absurd than to lump together the barbarities of Elizabeth or Cromwell, who wanted to drive out the Irish by means of English colonists (in the Roman sense), and the present system, which wants to drive out the Irish by means of sheep, pigs and oxen! The system of 1801-1846 (EVICTIONS in that period were exceptional, particularly in Leinster, where the soil is especially suited to cattle-raising) with its RACKRENTS and MIDDLEMEN, collapsed in 1846. The ANTI-CORN-LAW-REPEAL, in part a consequence of or, at all events, hastened by the IRISH FAMINE,[545] took from Ireland its *monopoly* of supplying England with corn in normal times. Wool and meat became the watchword, hence CONVERSION OF TILLAGE INTO PASTURE. So from then on, SYSTEMATIC CONSOLIDATION OF FARMS. The ENCUMBERED ESTATES ACT which made LANDLORDS of a mass of former MIDDLEMEN who had grown rich, hastened the process.[546] *CLEARING OF THE ESTATES OF IRELAND!* is now the sole meaning of English rule in Ireland. The *stupid* English government in London naturally knows even nothing of this IMMENSE CHANGE since 1846. But the Irish do. From *Meagher's Proclamation* (1848)[547] down to *Hennessy's election address* (Tory and Urquhartite) (1866) the Irish have been expressing their awareness of it in the clearest and MOST FORCIBLE MANNER.

The question now is, what advice should *we* give the *English* workers? In my view, they must make *REPEAL of the UNION* (in short, the *farce of* 1783, only democratised and adapted to meet present circumstances) an article of their *pronunziamento*.[a][548] This is the only *legal* and hence the only possible form of Irish emancipation which can be adopted by an *English* party in its programme. Experience must later show, whether mere personal union between the 2 countries can continue to exist. I half believe it could if it comes about in due time.

What the Irish need is:

1. Self-government and independence from England.

2. Agrarian revolution. With the best will in the world the

---

[a] manifesto

English cannot do this for them, but they can give them the legal means to do it for themselves.

3. *Protective tariffs against England.* From 1783-1801 every branch of industry in Ireland flourished. By suppressing the protective tariffs which the Irish parliament had established, the Union destroyed all industrial life in Ireland. The little bit of linen industry is in no way a substitute. The Union of 1801 affected Irish industry exactly as did the measures for the suppression of the Irish wool industry, etc., on the part of the English parliament under Anne, George II, and others. As soon as the Irish became independent, necessity would turn them, like Canada, Australia, etc., into protectionists. Before I put forward my views at the CENTRAL COUNCIL (next Tuesday, this time fortunately *without* REPORTERS being present),[549] I would appreciate it if you would let me know your opinion in a few lines.

Salut.

Your
K. M.

Since Moves[a] is a cousin of *Hirsch*,[b] I am not surprised that he himself has a set of antlers. HE BEARS IT PROUDLY.[c]

First published abridged in *Der Briefwechsel zwischen F. Engels und K. Marx*, Bd. 3, Stuttgart, 1913 and in full in *MEGA*, Abt. III, Bd. 3, Berlin, 1930

Printed according to the original

296

MARX TO VICTOR SCHILY[419]

IN PARIS

London, 30 November 1867

Dear Schily,

I wrote to Meissner as soon as I received your letter and asked him to send you a COPY of the book[d] for Reclus.[111] I believe Reclus

---

[a] Moses Hess - [b] A pun on the name *Hirsch* which also means *stag*.- [c] Marx wrote this postscript at the top of the first page. - [d] the first volume of *Capital*

to be just the man to undertake the French translation, with German co-operation. In a translation, I would indicate certain changes to be made in several parts and, at the same time, reserve the right to carry out the final revision myself.[539]

What should be done, in the first instance, and as quickly as possible, is to bring out passages from the book in the *Courrier français.* I do not see why Hess should need to involve any third person for this. He would best do it by himself. I also think that the topic he had in mind on English factory legislation is the most suitable as an introduction. However, even that cannot be treated without a few introductory words about the *theory of value,* as Proudhon has sown total confusion in people's minds on that subject. They believe that a commodity is sold for its value if it is sold for its *prix de revient*[a] = price of the means of production which have been consumed in it, + wages (or *price* of the labour added to the means of production). They do not see that the *unpaid labour* which is contained in the commodity constitutes just as fundamental an element of value as the labour which has been paid for, and that this element of value now takes the *form of profit,* etc. They have no idea *what* wages are. Without an understanding of the nature of value, arguments about the working day, etc., in short, the factory laws, have no basis. *A few* words of introduction on this subject are thus called for.

My publisher[b] is satisfied with sales in Germany. The liberal and vulgar-economist gang is, of course, seeking to harm it as much as they can by their tried and tested method of *conspiration de silence.* But this time they will not succeed.

I am here enclosing 1 COPY of Liebknecht[c] for you. You will see from the back page that he is bringing out a little weekly paper of his own[d] in the coming weeks. I am to request contributions from you from Paris. (His address: 11 Braustrasse, *Mr Miller.*[e]) I have given him a dressing-down for the phrase about the 'social question' (in the supplement)[537] and ditto drew his attention to the fact that he should avoid uncritical stand of the South Germans in his polemic against Bismarck. What should already have perplexed him is the fact that Jakobus Venedey has become his admirer.

---

[a] prime cost - [b] Otto Meissner - [c] W. Liebknecht, *Was ich im Berliner 'Reichstag' sagte.* - [d] *Democratisches Wochenblatt* - [e] Liebknecht's conspiratorial pseudonym

Otto Meissner Publishing House in Hamburg where Marx brought
the manuscript of Volume One of *Capital* in 1867

For all that Liebknecht's bold stand in the Reichstag has done good.

The whole family send you their warmest greetings.

Your
A. Williams[a]

The movement is on the march here!

First published in: Marx and Engels, *Works*, First Russian Edition, Vol. XXV, Moscow, 1934

Printed according to the original

Published in English in full for the first time

297

MARX TO LUDWIG KUGELMANN[65]

IN HANOVER

London, 30 November 1867

Dear Kugelmann,

Ill-health alone is to blame for my not replying sooner. I have been laid low again for weeks now.

Firstly, my best thanks for your efforts. Engels has written to Liebknecht (or will be doing so). Liebknecht, incidentally, was intending (in conjunction with Götz, and others) to make a demand in the Reichstag for an *ENQUIRY into the conditions of the workers*. He wrote to me about his intention, and at his request I sent him a few relevant English Acts of Parliament.[504] The plan came to nothing because owing to the procedure there was no time left for it. On one point you are better placed to write to Liebknecht than either Engels or myself. And that is that it really is his duty to draw attention to my book[b] at *workers' meetings*. If he fails to do so, the Lassalleans will seize upon the thing and misconstrue it.

Contzen (lecturer at Leipzig, a pupil and follower of Roscher) has requested a copy of the book from me via Liebknecht and promised a detailed review of it, from his point of view, in return. Meissner thereupon sent him the book. This could be a good

---

[a] Marx's conspiratorial pseudonym - [b] the first volume of *Capital*

start.—I was pleased about the misprint 'Taucher' in place of 'Faucher'[a] in your notice.[b] Faucher is one of those 'travelling preachers' of political economy. The fellow has no place among the 'scholarly' German economists such as Roscher, Rau, Mohl, and others. It is doing him too great an honour even to mention him. And I have consequently never allowed him a role as a noun but only as a verb.[c]

Please be so kind as to tell your good wife[d] that the chapters on the 'Working Day', 'Co-operation, Division of Labour and Machinery' and finally on 'Primitive Accumulation'[550] are the most immediately readable. You will have to explain any incomprehensible terminology to her. If there are any other doubtful points, I shall be glad to help.

In France (Paris) there are the best prospects that the book will be discussed in detail (in the *Courrier français*, a Proudhonist paper unfortunately!) and even translated.[539]

As soon as I am better, I will write more. Meanwhile I hope you will write frequently. I always find it has a spurring effect on me.

Your
K. M.

[From Eleanor Marx, in English]

My dear Fränzchen,[e]

As Papa is in a hurry to send off his letter I have only time to send you my best love.

Your affectionate
Eleanor Marx

First published in *Die Neue Zeit*, Bd. 2, Nr. 4, Stuttgart, 1901-1902   Printed according to the original

---

[a] *Taucher*—literally: diver; *Faucher*—name of an economist. - [b] *Deutsche Volkszeitung*, 10 November 1867 (see this volume, p. 473). - [c] The name *Faucher* originates from the verb *fauchen* meaning 'to spit, snarl, hiss, puff, explode with anger or passion'. In Vol. I of *Capital* Marx makes a pun on the name and derives the words *vorfauchen* and *lügenfauchendsten* from it. - [d] Gertruda Kugelmann - [e] Franziska Kugelmann

298

ENGELS TO MARX

IN LONDON

Manchester, 4 December 1867

Dear Moor,

I have given the LOAN COMPANY the REFERENCE, I said, FROM CONFIDENTIAL INFORMATION I AM CONVINCED THAT MR MARX WILL BE IN A POSITION TO REPAY THE LOAN WHEN DUE.

The letters from Borkheim returned enclosed. I hope the business goes well.

I shall be sending you letters from Kugelmann and Liebknecht tomorrow or the day after. Both have some prospect of getting various things[a] placed in newspapers, though admittedly small ones, I shall be attending to it this and tomorrow evening.

As to Meissner's notice,[b] haste is not very advisable. The stuff must not appear in the papers until *after New Year*, otherwise it will get lost in the flood of notices for Christmas books.

Your
F. E.

First published in *Der Briefwechsel zwischen F. Engels und K. Marx*, Bd. 3, Stuttgart, 1913

Printed according to the original

Published in English for the first time

299

ENGELS TO MARX

IN LONDON

Manchester, 6 December 1867

Dear Moor,

Enclosed letters from Kugelmann (with enclosure), Liebknecht and Siebel, as well as three acknowledgments from Rau, Hilde-

---

[a] concerning the first volume of *Capital* - [b] See this volume, pp. 475 and 476.

18*

brand and Schulze-Delitzsch.[551] Please send back by return the ones from Kugelmann, with the enclosure, and Siebel, the post for Siebel is going off on *Monday evening,* and I also have to write to Kugelmann. What do you think of the little Swabian paper[a]? Kugelmann certainly does seem to be resorting to desperate means though.

I have written at length to Liebknecht and demanded that he should attack not only the Prussians but their opponents, too, the Austrians, Federalists, Guelphs[420] and other advocates of the smaller states. As I suspected, the fellow has become narrow-minded in exclusively South German fashion. He and Bebel have signed an address to the Viennese City Council,[b] in which Austria is hailed as the newly-arising state of freedom in the South, in contrast to the North's condition of servitude! IT'S ALL VERY WELL for him to make a few vague speeches in the Reichstag, but a little newspaper[c] is a different matter altogether, we shall be held responsible for it, and we really cannot allow ourselves to be confused with Austrians, Federalists and Guelphs.[552] I have also written to him about his stupidity in suspending social agitation.[537]

This evening I shall be sending Jenny the trial of Adelaide Macdonald, who fired a pistol at the policeman.[553] Her relationship with Allen is not clear. Allen was betrothed to another girl and was to marry on the Monday after the 'OUTRAGE'.

In haste.

Your

F. E.

LOAN ALL RIGHT, I presume?
Enquiries today about life assurance.

First published abridged in *Der Briefwech-sel zwischen F. Engels und K. Marx,* Bd. 3, Stuttgart, 1913 and in full in *MEGA,* Abt. III, Bd. 3, Berlin, 1930

Printed according to the original

Published in English for the first time

---

[a] *Der Beobachter* - [b] 'Adresse an den Wiener Gemeinderat', *Neue Preußische Zeitung,* 1 December 1867. - [c] *Demokratisches Wochenblatt*

300

MARX TO ENGELS[6]

IN MANCHESTER

[London,] 7 December 1867

DEAR FRED,

Yesterday I presented myself at the LOAN SOCIETY for BODILY examination. This is more than just a formality, for if I were to die *before* September, the society would *not* get a FARTHING back. I was afraid I would have to undress (the fate of an Englishman who was there with me). In the first place, I do not like such inocular speculation, and second precisely at this moment I still have a carbuncle on the left loin not far from the centre of propagation, as well as numerous furuncles. Fortunately, the fellow was so impressed with my chest that he didn't want to know about anything else. I shall get the money on Monday at 12 o'clock.

You *forgot* to put in the letter from *Siebel.* I am sending you back *Kugelmann,* along with enclosure. Also, a letter he has written to me, together with enclosures. The screed from Bürgers[554] to be put with the *documents.* That jackass was rightly reminded by the workers in Düsseldorf[a] that 1. in Lassalle's time he stated he 'wished to take due account of conditions', 2. he had 'lost his *illusions about the class struggle*', and 3. he had found in Schulze-Delitzsch the solution to all past and future social mysteries.[b]

As regards the little Swabian paper,[c] it would be an amusing coup if we could hoodwink Vogt's friend, the Swabian Mayer. It would be easy to contrive the thing as follows. *D'abord*[d] to begin by saying that whatever one may think of the drift of the book,[e] it is a credit to the '*German* spirit', for which reason, too, it was written by a Prussian in exile and not in Prussia; Prussia having long ceased to be a country where any scholarly initiative, especially in the political or historical or social field, is possible or is actually to be found, it now being the representative of the Russian and not of the German spirit. In respect of the book itself, a distinction has to be drawn between two things, between positive developments

---

[a] who voted against Bürgers at the elections to the North German Reichstag - [b] See this volume, pp. 220-21. - [c] *Der Beobachter* - [d] First - [e] the first volume of *Capital*

('solid' would be the second epithet) given by the author, and the tendentious conclusions he arrives at. The former are a direct addition to the sum of human knowledge, since actual economic relations are treated in an entirely new way by a materialistic ('Mayer' has a liking for this catchword, on account of Vogt) method. *Example*: 1. the development of money, 2. the way in which co-operation, division of labour, the machine system and the corresponding social combinations and relations develop 'spontaneously'.

Now as regards the *tendency* of the author, another distinction has to be drawn. When he demonstrates that present society, economically considered, is pregnant with a new, higher form, he is only showing in the social context the same gradual process of evolution that Darwin has demonstrated in natural history. The liberal doctrine of 'progress' (*c'est Mayer tout pur*[a]) embraces this idea, and it is to his credit that he himself shows there is hidden progress even where modern economic relations are accompanied by frightening direct consequences. At the same time, owing to this critical approach of his, the author has, perhaps *malgré lui*,[b] sounded the death-knell to all socialism by the book, i. e. to utopianism, for evermore.

The author's tendency to be *subjective*, on the other hand—which he was perhaps bound and obligated to assume in view of his party position and his past—i.e. the manner in which he represents to himself or to others the ultimate outcome of the present movement, of the present social process, bears absolutely no relation to its real development. If space permitted this to be more closely examined, it could perhaps be shown that its 'objective' development refutes his own 'subjective' fancies.

Whereas Mr Lassalle hurled abuse at the capitalists and flattered the backwoods Prussian squirearchy, Mr Marx, on the contrary, shows the *historical* '*necessity*' of capitalist production and severely criticises the landed aristocrat who does nought but consume. Just how little he shares the ideas of his renegade disciple Lassalle on Bismarck's vocation for ushering in an economic MILLENNIUM he has not merely shown in his previous protests against '*royal Prussian Socialism*'[c] but he openly repeats it on pp. 762, 763, where he says that the system prevailing in France and Prussia at present will subject the continent of Europe to the regime of the Russian knout, if it is not checked in good time.[555]

---

[a] that's Mayer to a tee - [b] despite himself - [c] K. Marx and F. Engels, "To the Editor of the *Social-Demokrat*.

That is my view on how to hoodwink the Swabian Mayer (who did after all print my preface[456]), and small though his beastly rag is, it is, nevertheless, the popular oracle of all the Federalists in Germany and is also read abroad.

With regard to Liebknecht, it is indeed a disgrace that with the numerous petty provincial papers he has at his command,[556] he did not *spontanément*[a] send in short notices to them—it would not have required of him any of the study which is so contrary to his nature. Mr Schweitzer et Co. understand this better, as you can see from the enclosed *Social-Demokrat*.[557] (Kugelmann sent it me.) Yesterday I sent Guido Weiss of the *Zukunft* (this just *between ourselves*) some juxtaposed texts,[b] on one side von Hofstetten's bowdlerised plagiarisms, on the other the original passages from my book. I wrote to him at the same time that this must be printed *not in my name* but as though emanating from the *Zukunft* (or, if that is not feasible, then as though from a *Zukunft*-reader in Berlin). If Weiss takes this (*and I think he will*), then not merely will the attention of the Berlin workers have been drawn to the book through the quotation of passages which are of direct interest to them, but an extremely useful polemic will have been initiated, and *Schweitzer's* plan to ignore the book and exploit its contents will have been dished. Marvellous how these fellows think they can go on with *Lassalle's* plan.[c] What could be more naive than the manner in which von Hofstetten and Citizen Geib have joined together at the general meeting of the General Association of German Workers in savaging the section I wrote on the 'working day'[558]?

Salut.

Your

K. Marx

MY COMPLIMENTS TO MRS BURNS. I have taken an extraordinary liking to Schorlemmer's compendium.[d]

First published abridged in *Der Briefwechsel zwischen F. Engels und K. Marx*, Bd. 3, Stuttgart, 1913 and in full in *MEGA*, Abt. III, Bd. 3, Berlin, 1930

Printed according to the original

---

[a] spontaneously - [b] K. Marx, 'Plagiarism'. - [c] See this volume, pp. 328-29. - [d] H. E. Roscoe, *Kurzes Lehrbuch der Chemie... Deutsche Ausgabe, unter Mitwirkung des Verfassers bearbeitet von Carl Schorlemmer*.

301

MARX TO ENGELS

IN MANCHESTER

[London,] 7 December 1867

DEAR FRED,

I see too late that I have forgotten to send you the *Social-Demokrat*.[557] I am now making amends and enclose a copy of *Courrier* which will interest you on account of the article by the American General Cluseret on Mentana and Garibaldi.[a][513] You must send the batch of *Courriers* back to me. I need the set because it is the only one which gives me a *continuous report on stocks and shares*.

Salut.

Your
Moor

First published in *Der Briefwechsel zwischen F. Engels und K. Marx*, Bd. 3, Stuttgart, 1913

Printed according to the original

Published in English for the first time

302

MARX TO LUDWIG KUGELMANN[65]

IN HANOVER

[London,] 7 December 1867

Dear Kugelmann,

If there were 6 people of your calibre in Germany, we should already have overcome the resistance of the mass of philistines and the *conspiration de silence* of the experts and the riff-raff of the press, at least to the extent that serious discussion would have begun. *Mais il faut attendre!*[b] That phrase contains the entire secret of *Russian policy*.

---

[a] [G. P.] Cluseret, 'Mentana', *Le Courrier français*, No. 173, 7 December 1867. - [b] But we shall have to wait and see!

I enclose a letter (which you will be so kind as to return to me) from a German-Russian worker[a] (tanner).[532] Engels rightly observes that the autodidactic philosophy—pursued by workers themselves—has made great progress in this tanner, when compared with the cobbler Jakob Böhme, ditto that none but the '*German*' worker is capable of such cerebral production.[b]

Borkheim asked me yesterday who wrote the article in the *Zukunft*[c] (he subscribes to the paper). He said it must originate from our side as you had sent him a copy. I said *I did not know.* N.B.! One must not let others see through one's game!

Heartiest thanks to your good wife[d] for the trouble she has taken in copying the letters. You should not exploit her so for 'surplus labour'.

As I told you, if I am not mistaken, Bucher has actually asked me himself to become *economic correspondent for the 'Königlich Preußische Staats-Zeitung.'*[e] So you see, if I *wished* to avail myself of such sources, I *could* do so without the mediation of any third party.[559]

I am suffering from the same illness as before. Nothing dangerous to it, but a nuisance.

With best compliments to your good wife and Fränzchen.[f]

Yours

K. Marx

First published abridged in *Die Neue Zeit,* Bd. 2, Nr. 4, Stuttgart, 1901-1902 and in full in *Pisma Marksa k Kugelmanu* (Letters of Marx to Kugelmann), Moscow-Leningrad, 1928

Printed according to the original

303

ENGELS TO MARX

IN LONDON

Manchester, 12 December 1867

Dear Moor,

Since Sunday I've been having a grand gala performance, with toothache, influenza, SORE THROAT, fever, and all manner of

---

[a] Joseph Dietzgen - [b] See this volume, p. 476. - [c] F. Engels, 'Review of Volume One of *Capital* for the *Zukunft*'. - [d] Gertruda Kugelmann - [e] *Königlich Preußischer Staats-Anzeiger* (see this volume, p. 202) - [f] Franziska Kugelmann

unpleasantnesses, only this morning am I fit to work again, and I will get down to the Swabian Mayer this evening, following your recipe,ª which—with some excessively rigorous detail discounted which would make the thing 3 times as long—is very nice.

Bürgers has been put *ad acta.*⁵⁵⁴ By one of the ironies of fate, the introduction to the article ᵇ sent him by Kugelmann necessarily cut him to the quick as the unsuccessful Reichstag candidate for Düsseldorf. I quite innocently mentioned in it the fact that the social-democratic party could no longer simply be ignored now that it is represented in the Reichstag, and that these gentlemen would make this book their Bible. With his customary tact, Kugelmann sends this to Heinrich. *Hinc illae lacrimae!*ᶜ I had quite forgotten the matter, and I was only reminded of it by Heinrich's anxious letter, which takes all this most seriously.

The *Zukunft* affair is very good.ᵈ Write and tell me when it appears,ᵉ as I cannot spare the time to consult *Zukunft* every day at the Schiller Institute.²⁸

Kugelmann becomes more simple-minded every day. If Bucher—why not go straight to Bismarck?⁵⁵⁹ I do not understand, or else I've forgotten, what he says in the letter of 3 December to you about a letter from Meissner enclosed for me.

Enclosed 1. 2 letters from Kugelmann to you, returned,
         2. 1 ditto   ”   ”   ” me   and 1
            from Stumpf to Kugelmann.
         3. The letter from Siebel.

Last post now. Kindest regards to the ladies and Lafargue.

Your

F. E.

First published abridged in *Der Briefwech-sel zwischen F. Engels und K. Marx*, Bd. 3, Stuttgart, 1913 and in full in *MEGA*, Abt. III, Bd. 3, Berlin, 1930

Printed according to the original

Published in English for the first time

ª See this volume, pp. 493-95. - ᵇ F. Engels, 'Review of Volume One of *Capital* for the *Rheinische Zeitung*'. - ᶜ Hence these tears! (Terence, *Andria*, Act I, Scene 1, 99). ᵈ See this volume, p. 495. - ᵉ K. Marx, 'Plagiarism'.

304

ENGELS TO LUDWIG KUGELMANN

IN HANOVER

Manchester, 12 December 1867

Dear Kugelmann,

Your zeal truly deserves my gratitude, but it appears greatly to overestimate my free time. I received your letter of 30 November on 2 December, held counsel with Marx, as there were several things in it to be considered, and would already have sent you various articles, if on Sunday I had not been visited by a toothache-influenza-sore throat with inevitable fever, which prostrated me on the sofa. Fortunately, that kind of thing takes an acute course with me, and so I am fit for work again today and will be setting my nose to the grindstone at once. But you must not imagine that one can just toss off a dozen reviews of one and the same book[a] and not merely say something different in each one but also so compose them that one cannot tell they are all by one author. One often has to pause for thought.[560]

I would advise against writing directly to Miquel. There are some things which can be achieved *verbally* with such people and which are scarcely to be risked in writing. He will surely be coming over to Hanover sometime.

The *United States of Europe*[b] was stillborn. And with Vogt's brother[c] and minion as editor—pshaw!

The Englishman who called on Brandes was our friend Moore from here, who spent 7 weeks in Eisenach for German-learning purposes; I had no idea he would be passing by, or I should have written him a few lines to give to you. He might perhaps have called on you anyway, except that he had curiously got it fixed in his head that you lived in Hamburg. He will probably undertake the English translation of Marx' book.[229]

Concerning Liebknecht's South German outburst, I have written to him that nothing is achieved by it.[552] He would have done better not to publish his speeches,[d] *in extenso*[e] their effect is lost, the *nonsense* in them obtrudes too much. I also wrote to him about his curious theory on the postponement of the social question.[537] You

---

[a] the first volume of *Capital* - [b] *Les États-Unis d'Europe* - [c] Gustav Vogt - [d] W. Liebknecht, *Was ich im Berliner 'Reichstag' sagte.* - [e] literally: at full length; figuratively: in print.

will recall, incidentally, that I was already telling you last autumn that he had become too much of an *Austrian* owing to his hatred of the Prussians.

This brief epistle just to keep you informed. The articles will follow in a few days time, and you can then at all events tell the Lieutenant-Colonel[a] that there will be a few more, and there will then be something for him to do.

In friendship

Yours

F. E.

I have just been ejected from the office, as it was closing time.

First published in: Marx and Engels, *Works*, First Russian Edition, Vol. XXV, Moscow, 1934

Printed according to the original

Published in English for the first time

305

ENGELS TO LUDWIG KUGELMANN

IN HANOVER

Manchester, 13 December 1867

Dear Kugelmann,

'Pursuant to mine humbly of yesterday'—so that you do not forget all the elements of commercial style—you will find enclosed 2 articles, one examining the *content* of the book, for the *Beobachter*,[b] and the other merely discussing points of fact, for the *Gewerbeblatt* or the *Staats-Anzeiger*.[c]

You will appreciate the difficulties which had to be overcome with the first of these when you consider that the editor of the *Beobachter* is the tedious talker from Swabia, *Karl Mayer*, from *Herr Vogt*, who will certainly never knowingly do us any favours. You realise that these articles must only be submitted in copy, but I

---

[a] Adolf Friedrich Seubert - [b] F. Engels, 'Review of Volume One of *Capital* for the *Beobachter*'. - [c] F. Engels, 'Review of Volume One of *Capital* for the *Staats-Anzeiger fur Württemberg*'.

would ask you to keep all the originals, as one never knows what they may be needed for.

I shall also be sending something for the *Merkur*,[a] but I cannot yet do so much work in the evening now as I get too excited by it and last night again e.g. I could scarce sleep for thinking of the articles. The weather, business and the vestiges of the *tic douloureux*[b] from last Sunday are keeping me from riding, and so I cannot get back to normal.

I have not read about the Siebenmark affair[561] in the *Zukunft*, I but rarely set eyes on the paper.

Farewell for today. It is 6 o'clock in the evening, closing time, and I am tired and hungry.

Yours

F. E.

First published in: Marx and Engels, *Works*, First Russian Edition, Vol. XXV, Moscow, 1934

Printed according to the original

Published in English for the first time

306

MARX TO ENGELS[562]

IN MANCHESTER

[London,] 14 December 1867

Dear Fred,

This latest Fenian exploit in Clerkenwell[563] is a great folly. The London masses, who have shown much sympathy for Ireland, will be enraged by it and driven into the arms of the government party. One cannot expect the London proletarians to let themselves be blown up for the benefit of Fenian emissaries. Secret, melodramatic conspiracies of this kind are, in general, more or less doomed to failure.

I received the money on Monday and paid Borkheim his £45 back together with £1 1s for inquiry fees.

Would you do me a favour and inquire of Ernest Jones the most appropriate way of marrying *civiliter*[c] in London, in Doctors'

---

[a] *Schwäbischer Merkur* - [b] pain in the nerve - [c] by civil ceremony

COMMONS or where, as Laura is to marry at the beginning of April. As it is not to be a church wedding, it was originally intended that the marriage should take place in Paris. That is, however, complicated. I should have to prove my identity there and, in so doing, might strike the police as being a little too familiar. On the other hand, my wife would like the civil marriage to take place, if in London, as far as possible in secret, as she wants no gossip among her English acquaintances. Please also ask Jones what the position is regarding the consent of Lafargue's parents? Whether it must previously be countersigned by the envoy (would that be the English one?) in Paris? I know that the formality is not necessary in England. It is, however, indispensable for the marriage to be valid according to *French* law as well. So, none of the formalities must be neglected in this respect.

What is the position regarding *witnesses* in England?

Nothing from the *Zukunft* yet.[a] It is a pity these papers are so small in format, especially at a time when their columns are so full of parliamentary filibustering.

Our friend Stumpf is obviously a great muddle-head.

Siebel returned enclosed. He is mistaken about Lange. The latter must 'buy' the book[b] and will surely already have bought it long ago.[564]

The *quid pro quo*[c] with Heinrich[d] is indeed most amusing.[e] *Salut.*

Your
K. Moor

First published abridged in *Der Briefwechsel zwischen F. Engels und K. Marx*, Bd. 3, Stuttgart, 1913 and in full in *MEGA*, Abt. III, Bd. 3, Berlin, 1930

Printed according to the original

Published in English in full for the first time

---

[a] See this volume, pp. 495 and 498. - [b] the first volume of *Capital* - [c] misunderstanding - [d] Bürgers - [e] See this volume, p. 498.

307

ENGELS TO MARX

IN LONDON

[Manchester,] 16 December 1867

Dear Moor,

Enclosed a letter from Liebknecht, who is another great muddle-head. Especially over the Austrian business. Because Austria stands on the *eve* of its 1789, Liebknecht *therefore* praises it as the state of freedom![552] I have not answered him yet, but will do so as soon as you send the letter back.

Have sent articles to Kugelmann 1. for the Swabian Mayer,[a] 2. for the *Gewerbeblatt*.[b] Ditto to Siebel for Mannheim.[c] Further Swabian articles to follow.

The piece[d] has appeared in the *Zukunft*. I now buy the paper SECOND HAND from the Schiller Institute[28] so that I can see it regularly.

In haste.

Your
F. E.

The marriage business is perfectly straightforward. THE MARRIAGE IS PERFORMED BEFORE THE REGISTRAR FOR THE DISTRICT, who also puts up the BANNS at his OFFICE 14 days previously. Two or more witnesses are necessary. You can find out all the details at that office. *For England* nothing else is required, but as regards validity in France, Jones cannot tell you either, so Lafargue senior will have to ask *his lawyer in Bordeaux*. I shall, incidentally, check the *code civil*.

Gumpert was married in this way. Your wife can tell her philistine neighbours that this way was chosen because Laura is protestant and Paul catholic.

First published in *Der Briefwechsel zwischen F. Engels und K. Marx*, Bd. 3, Stuttgart, 1913

Printed according to the original

Published in English for the first time

---

[a] F. Engels, 'Review of Volume One of *Capital* for the *Beobachter*'. - [b] F. Engels, 'Review of Volume One of *Capital* for the *Staats-Anzeiger für Württemberg*'. - [c] F. Engels, 'Review of Volume One of *Capital* for the *Neue Badische Landeszeitung*'. - [d] K. Marx, 'Plagiarism'.

308

MARX TO ENGELS[562]

IN MANCHESTER

London, 17 December 1867

Dear FRED,

Wilhelm[a] returned enclosed. You must be careful in your reply. The position is difficult. To pursue an entirely correct course would require a much more critical spirit and dialectical skill than our Wilhelm possesses.[552] We can only restrain him from committing really grave blunders. In general, hostility to Prussia is the pathos to which alone he owes his VERVE AND SINGLENESS OF PURPOSE. He has rightly sensed that the true bourgeoisie forms the core of the 'National Liberals',[432] which gives him the opportunity to bestow on his political antipathy the more elevated sanction of economics. *Ira facit poetam*[b] and also gives our Wilhelmchen cunning up TO A CERTAIN POINT.

The correspondent of *The Irishman* here is willing to print, if you write it in English, a critique of the book[c] about one column in length (Ireland must take the proper role in it, however) in that Dublin paper as a contribution under his own name. I shall send you a few copies of the paper and you will see what needs to be done.

The *Zukunft* has a talent for misprints[d] which is all the odder as Dr Guido Weiss does after all have the original.

I have a small but infinitely irritating carbuncle on my left buttock.

And if the noble fellow has no bum.
On what does he propose to sit?[e]

Yesterday I gave a 1 ½ hour lecture on Ireland[565] at our German Workers' Society (though a further 3 German workers' societies were represented, ABOUT 100 people in all), as 'standing' is the easiest posture for me just now.

Salut.

Your

K. M.

First published in *Der Briefwechsel zwischen F. Engels und K. Marx*, Bd. 3, Stuttgart, 1913

Printed according to the original

Published in English in full for the first time

---

[a] Liebknecht - [b] Anger makes the poet (Juvenal, *Satires*, I, 79). - [c] the first volume of *Capital* - [d] when it published Marx's article 'Plagiarism' - [e] J. W. Goethe, 'Totalität'.

309

ENGELS TO MARX[522]

IN LONDON

Manchester, 19 December 1867

Dear Moor,

OF COURSE our correspondence with Wilhelmchen[a] requires caution. As I have already told you,[b] his narrow-minded one-sided SINGLENESS OF PURPOSE was his good fortune and the secret of his effectiveness in the Reichstag. Unfortunately however that will only work once, and the publication of his speeches[c]—to say nothing of Kugelmann's letters—shows that it had gone *too far*. Now we have the little paper[d] to boot, in which his household words are recorded in black and white and are then laid at our door—then the Customs Union parliament,[566] and therewith *certainly* a disgrace for us unless Wilhelmchen is given some instruction. With his egregious talent for making blunders, much was to be expected there, and may be still. No doubt we can only protect him from the most serious blunders, but his Viennese address and his friendship with the Federalists,[e] i.e. Grün!! is already dreadful enough. I can therefore only put 2 chief considerations to him: 1. to regard the events and outcome of 1866 not *simplement* negatively, i.e. not as a reactionary, but critically (which he will admittedly find difficult), and 2. to attack Bismarck's enemies just as much as the man himself, as they are equally worthless. You observe how beautifully he has already compromised himself with Grün et Co.; what a fine triumph that would be for Bismarck if we or our people concluded an alliance with that rabble! Well, we shall just have to wait and see what transpires.

The Clerkenwell folly[563] was obviously the work of a few special fanatics; it is the misfortune of all conspiracies that they lead to such acts of folly because 'we really must do something, we really must get up to something'. Especially in America there has been a lot of BLUSTER amongst this explosive and incendiary fraternity, and then along come some individual jackasses and instigate this kind of nonsense. At the same time, these man-eaters are for the most

---

[a] Wilhelm Liebknecht - [b] See this volume, p. 456. - [c] W. Liebknecht, *Was ich im Berliner 'Reichstag' sagte*. - [d] *Demokratisches Wochenblatt* - [e] See this volume, pp. 492, 503.

part the greatest of cowards, including that man Allen who already appears to have turned QUEEN'S EVIDENCE. And then the notion that you can free Ireland by setting fire to some London tailor's shop!

Have you read the Russians' warning (*Russian Invalid*) that the alliance between France and Austria makes peace in Europe impossible because it prevents a solution to the German, Italian and Eastern questions?[a] Very nice. Bismarck and Gorchakov now appear to be about to take the offensive.

Your friend Lippe has been sacrificed to the shades of the dispossessed[b][567]—his dismissal was the price for which the National Liberals are dropping their opposition to the 25 million for the Guelphs and the house of Nassau.[c]

Best regards to the LADIES.

Your
F. E.

First published abridged in *Der Briefwechsel zwischen F. Engels und K. Marx*, Bd. 3, Stuttgart, 1913 and in full in *MEGA*, Abt. III, Bd. 3, Berlin, 1930

Printed according to the original

Published in English in full for the first time

---

[a] *Русскій инвалидъ*, No. 336, 5 December 1867, an anonymous item in the 'Unofficial Section' datelined 'St. Petersburg, 4 December'. - [b] deposed rulers - [c] George V, King of Hanover, and Adolf, Duke of Nassau

1868

310

MARX TO ENGELS[419]

IN MANCHESTER

[London,] 3 January 1868

DEAR FRED,

Happy New Year!

I have only been 'sitting up' again for 3 days after lying all bent for so long. It was a nasty attack. You can judge this by the fact that for 3 weeks—no smoking! My head is still shaky. In a few days I hope to be back in action.

I am absolutely opposed to arsenic.

Enclosed the *Beobachter*[a] (Lessner filched it for me from the *Workers' Society*[150]).

I have had no more letters from Siebel except the enclosed one to me.

Meissner can always have a try with the *Barmer*.[b] It can do no harm. When you send the cuttings to Meissner, you must refer to them only as something which has come to hand, without explaining to him 'our' activity.[568] Also draw his attention to the latest things in the *Zukunft*.[c]

I would like to know from Schorlemmer what is the latest and best book (German) on agricultural chemistry. Furthermore, what is the present state of the argument between the mineral-fertiliser people and the nitrogen-fertiliser people? (Since I last looked into the subject, all sorts of new things have appeared in Germany.) Does he know anything about the most recent Germans who have written *against* Liebig's soil-exhaustion theory? Does he know about the alluvion theory of the Munich agronomist Fraas (Professor at Munich University)?[d] For the chapter on ground

---

[a] F. Engels, 'Review of Volume One of *Capital* for the *Beobachter*'. - [b] *Barmer Zeitung* - [c] K. Marx, 'Plagiarism'. - [d] K. Fraas, *Die Natur der Landwirthschaft*.

rent[569] I shall have to be aware of the latest state of the question, at least TO SOME EXTENT. Since Schorlemmer is an expert on this subject he must be able to give information. Enclosed 2 Urquharts[a] and 1 *Courrier* (because of Cluseret's article).

THE COMPLIMENTS OF THE SEASON TO MRS Burns, Moore, AND Schorlemmer.

Your
Moor

[From Eleanor Marx, in English]

You bad boy, why haven't you answered my letters?—I suppose you and the hedgehog have been on the spree again.

Alberich,[b]
the grim dwarf

Happy New Year.

<table>
<tr><td>First published abridged in *Der Briefwechsel zwischen F. Engels und K. Marx*, Bd. 4, Stuttgart, 1913 and in full in *MEGA*, Abt. III, Bd. 4, Berlin, 1931</td><td>Printed according to the original

Published in English in full for the first time</td></tr>
</table>

311

ENGELS TO JENNY MARX

IN LONDON

Manchester, 3 January 1868

Dear Mrs Marx,

I must apologise for leaving your letter[570] unanswered for so long. But the Christmas period is the only time in the whole year when, apart from business, I am made to feel that I stand with one foot in the bourgeoisie, and here in Manchester this entails a lot of eating and drinking and upset stomach, and the obligatory ill humour and waste of time. This is now fairly well over, and I am beginning to breathe freely again.

I am really sorry that I was unable to lay my hands on a larger crate for the moment, but I had to take just what was available in the WAREHOUSE—I shall make up for this soon.

---

[a] probably two numbers of *The Diplomatic Review* - [b] Eleanor's jocular nickname. The words "the grim dwarf" are in German.

Enclosed the latest from Siebel. Do please return the *letter*, together with an earlier one sent to Moor, as soon as possible, I have to write to him on the 8th, the post goes only twice a month, and it is a great pleasure for the poor devil when he sees that people think of him. He does what he can honestly, despite his illness. The thing from the *Barmer Zeitung* is by him.[571] Moor might let me know what he thinks about the business with the *Kölnische Zeitung*; if he thinks it better that *I* should write about this to Meissner, I can do so, and, at the same time, send him the cutting from *Barmer*.

The *pater peccavi*[a] from Hoffstetten is very amusing.[572] He naturally suspects Liebknecht everywhere and nobody else.[b] In any case, we have now put paid to the attempt of these gentry to stifle, and at the same time to exploit, the book.[c]

I shall be writing to Wilhelmchen in the next few days. I have heard nothing more from Kugelmann as to how things have gone with the Swabian articles.[d]

Meissner could already put together quite a nice advertisement from the articles that have appeared up to now,[568] which would be quite in place now that the Christmas season is over. In particular, he might include those passages in which the economists are challenged to present their defence.

I hope that Moor has been freed from his carbuncle. But this is all no good, he must do something to get rid of the business once and for all. The 2nd volume[418] can only gain, also with regard to the time needed for completion, if the fight against the carbuncles is waged with full force for a period. How would it be if he were to take arsenic again?

Best greetings to Moor and the whole family, and a hearty Happy New Year from

Yours

F. E.

First published in *Der Briefwechsel zwischen F. Engels und K. Marx*, Bd. 3, Stuttgart, 1913

Printed according to the original

Published in English for the first time

---

[a] 'Father, I have sinned' (Luke 15:21) - [b] See this volume, p. 529. - [c] the first volume of *Capital* - [d] See this volume, p. 499.

312

ENGELS TO MARX

IN LONDON

Manchester, 6 January 1868

Dear Moor,

If you do not want to take arsenic, then for goodness sake do something else, for things cannot go on *like this*. Have you consulted Allen or another doctor recently? Gumpert was not at home when I called the other day, but I shall take the first opportunity to speak to him.

You did not send the *Beobachter* or the 2 Urquharts either.[a] However, today Kugelmann sent me the *Beobachter* and the Württemberg *Staats-Anzeiger*[b] (I am sending you the latter and when I get it back will send it to Meissner, if you do not send it to him direct). It's fine that these two PAPERS have risen to the bait. I shall now also prepare Kugelmann something for the *Schwäbischer Merkur*.[560]

Schorlemmer will put together the information for you from the latest annual reports. He was not acquainted with the book by Fraas.[c]

A natural scientist has appeared in Paris who calls himself *Chmoulevitch* (Schmulsohn!). This even beats Ephraim Artful.[d]

The first instalment of the Austrian official general staff report on the war of 66 first proves that Austria's military organisation was not fit for a simultaneous war with Prussia and Italy, this is followed by the naive passage: Under these circumstances it should really have been the task of state foreign policy to safeguard the state against such a war.[e]

The *Prussian* 2nd instalment[f] shows quite clearly that on the 28th, and even more on the evening of the 29th,[g] Benedek was in a position to attack the scattered columns of the Crown Prince[h] with superior force and *with almost absolute certainty* to throw *him*

---

[a] See this volume, p. 508. - [b] F. Engels' reviews of Volume One of *Capital* for the *Beobachter* and for the *Staats-Anzeiger für Württemberg*. - [c] K. Fraas, *Die Natur der Landwirthschaft*. - [d] Ferdinand Lassalle - [e] *Österreichs Kämpfe im Jahre 1866...*, Bd. I, S. 60-61. - [f] *Der Feldzug von 1866 in Deutschland...* (appeared in instalments) - [g] of June - [h] Frederick William

back into the mountains and take his guns. The jackass did not do it, and lost the campaign.

Salut.

Your
F. E.

First published abridged in *Der Briefwech-sel zwischen F. Engels und K. Marx*, Bd. 4, Stuttgart, 1913 and in full in *MEGA*, Abt. III, Bd. 4, Berlin, 1931

Printed according to the original

Published in English for the first time

313

ENGELS TO MARX[419]

IN LONDON

Manchester, 7 January 1868

Dear Moor,

Herewith returned the *Dühring*[a] and the *Beobachter.*[b] The former is highly amusing. The whole article is embarrassment and FUNK. You can see that the worthy vulgar economist is *frappé au vif*[c] and can find nothing to say except that it will only be possible to judge the first volume when the 3rd has come out,[418] that determination of value by labour time is not undisputed, and that there are people who have some modest doubts about the determination of the value of labour on the basis of its costs of production. You see that for this genus[d] you are by no means learned enough, for you have not confuted the great Macleod[e] on the decisive point. At the same time, there is the fear in every line that he may be exposed to a treatment *à la* Roscher.[f] The fellow was happy when he had finished the thing, but I am sure he carried it to the post with a heavy heart.

Kugelmann and Wilhelmchen[g] I shall return tomorrow. If there is anything in the copied letter from Lieutenant-Colonel Seubert

---

a E. Dühring, '*Marx, Das Kapital, Kritik der politischen Oekonomie*, 1. Band, Hamburg 1867', *Ergänzungsblätter zur Kenntniß der Gegenwart*, Bd. 3, Hildburg-hausen, 1867, S. 182-86. - b F. Engels, 'Review of Volume One of *Capital* for the *Beobachter*'. - c cut to the quick - d sort - e H. D. Macleod, *The Theory and Practice of Banking*.... - f Engels has in mind the critique of Roscher's views in Vol. One of *Capital*. - g Wilhelm Liebknecht

which could be useful to me for a further Swabian article,[560] please enclose it.

I could do something for Vienna too. Richter could perhaps be asked about the *Internationale Revue,* he is supposed to know the situation there.

Wilhelmchen's PAPER[a] is just too lovely—everything ready except the security bond, and so it cannot be published. Incidentally, if Wilhelm should go to Vienna then the fuss about the Austrian agent would really get going.[573]

How are things with Beesly, Lewes & Co. and the *Fortnightly Review*?[509]

Best greetings to the LADIES and the Doctor *amorosus.*[b]

Your

F. E.

First published in *Der Briefwechsel zwischen F. Engels und K. Marx,* Bd. 4, Stuttgart, 1913

Printed according to the original

Published in English in full for the first time

314

MARX TO ENGELS

IN MANCHESTER

[London,] 8 January 1868

DEAR FRED,

I have ditto received the *Staats-Anzeiger* and the *Beobachter*[c] from Kugelmann. I am returning you your *Staats-Anzeiger* today. Also the COPY Kugelmann sent me of the letter from the colonel[d] who arranged the whole thing.[560] Württemberg is now sufficiently provided. In my opinion,—with special regard to sales— *Austria* is now the most important. Notabene, if you have the patience to write more prescriptions.[e] Little Jenny, an expert in this respect, claims that you are developing great dramatic talent, or comic talent, in pursuing this action from 'different' viewpoints and in different disguises.

---

[a] *Demokratisches Wochenblatt* - [b] Paul Lafargue - [c] F. Engels' reviews of Volume One of *Capital* for the *Staats-Anzeiger für Württemberg* and for the *Beobachter*. - [d] Adolf Friedrich Seubert - [e] reviews of the first volume of *Capital*

In the next few days—I am still a trifle limp, and do not feel much like writing—but as soon as I am quite on my feet I shall give Wilhelmchen[a] a good hiding. This is because of his identification of my views with the specific views of Wilhelm.

Dühring's article[b] (he is lecturer at Berlin University) is very decent, particularly since I handled his master 'Carey' so roughly. Dühring obviously misunderstood various things. But the oddest thing is that he ranks me with Stein, because I pursue the dialectic, and Stein assembles thoughtlessly the greatest trivialities in clumsy hair-splitting, with a few Hegelian category conversions.[c]

Have you already received Borkheim's *Perle*[d]?

It appears that professional poesy is simply a mask for the driest sort of prosiness. Take, for example, the Freiligrath family. Kate travels (on her honeymoon) to Paris with Kröker, the young corn usurer. However, since this noble man has 'business' to do at the same time, he leaves her *alone* in one of the big Paris hotels for 2-3 days. Kate and the whole FAMILY find this quite in order. Kate even writes delightedly that in the hotel they call her 'mademoiselle' (after she had spent the night together with Kröker there), and that all the waiters and even the porter give her friendly 'nods'. But even more: Kröker (after this business trip to the provinces) returns from Paris immediately to London with Kate, and the whole family is delighted that the 'HONEYMOON' is to be postponed for 6 months, since business 'comes first'. After all, for a poet the HONEYMOON is only a flower of speech, and can be 'celebrated' before or after the accouchement, early or late (the facts were related by the Freiligrath boys[e] in my house). Kate even seems to have read Clauren, for she described herself—from Paris—as a 'grass widow'.

The Yankees will show John Bull what's what. What do you think of the latest rodomontades of the Russians?

Dwarf Alberich[f] was very delighted by your letter.[131] He is just off to the gymnastics school, where he is doing great things.

Salut.

Your

K. M.

First published abridged in *Der Briefwechsel zwischen F. Engels und K. Marx*, Bd. 4, Stuttgart, 1913 and in full in *MEGA*, Abt. III, Bd. 4, Berlin, 1931

Printed according to the original

Published in English for the first time

---

a Liebknecht - b E. Dühring, '*Marx, Das Kapital, Kritik der politischen Oekonomie*, 1. Band, Hamburg 1867'. - c A reference to L. Stein's *System der Staatswissenschaft* and *Die Verwaltungslehre*. - d S. Borkheim, *Ma perle devant le congrès de Genève*. - e Wolfgang and Otto - f Eleanor Marx

315

MARX TO ENGELS[574]

IN MANCHESTER

[London,] 8 January 1868

DEAR FRED,

Ad vocem[a] *Dühring.*[b] It is a great deal from this man that he gives almost positive acceptance to the section on '*primitive accumulation*'.[575] He is still young. As a follower of Carey he is in direct opposition to the FREETRADERS. Furthermore, he is a *university lecturer*, and therefore not displeased that *Professor* Roscher, who blocks the way for them all, is receiving some kicks.[c] One thing in his description struck me very strongly. That is, as long as the determination of value by labour time is itself left 'undetermined', as it is with Ricardo, it does not make people SHAKY. But as soon as it is brought exactly into connection with the working day and its variations, a very unpleasant new light dawns upon them. I believe one reason that Dühring reviewed the book at all is malice against Roscher. Indeed it is easy to scent his anxiety that he might also be 'Roscher'ed. Curiously, the fellow has not detected the three fundamentally new elements of the book:

1. that in contrast to *all* previous political economy, which *from the outset* treated the particular fragments of surplus value with their fixed forms of rent, profit and interest as already given, I begin by dealing with the general form of surplus value, in which all these elements are still undifferentiated, in solution as it were;

2. that the economists, without exception, have missed the simple fact that, if the commodity has the double character of use value and exchange value, then the labour represented in the commodity must also have a double character; thus the bare analysis of labour *sans phrase*,[d] as in Smith, Ricardo, etc., is bound to come up against the inexplicable everywhere. This is, in fact, the whole secret of the critical conception;

3. that for the first time wages are shown as the irrational outward form of a hidden relationship, and this is demonstrated exactly in both forms of wages: time wages and piece wages. (It was a help to me that similar formulae are often found in higher mathematics.)

---

a With regard to - b E. Dühring, '*Marx, Das Kapital, Kritik der politischen Oekonomie*, 1. Band, Hamburg 1867'. - c See this volume, p. 511. - d without more ado

As for Mr Dühring's modest objection to the determination of value, he will be astonished when he sees in Volume II[418] how little the determination of value counts for 'directly' in bourgeois society. Actually, *no form* of society can prevent the labour time at the disposal of society from regulating production in ONE WAY OR ANOTHER. But so long as this regulation is not effected through the direct and conscious control of society over its labour time—which is only possible under common ownership—but through the movement of commodity prices, then things will remain as you so aptly described them already in the *Deutsch-Französische Jahrbücher*.[a]

Ad vocem Vienna. I am sending you various Vienna papers (of which you must return to me the *Neues Wiener Tagblatt* which belongs to Borkheim, and keep the rest), from which you will see two things: firstly how important Vienna is at this moment as a market place, since there is new life there[576]; and secondly the way the matter should be handled there. I cannot find the address of Prof. Richter. Perhaps you have Liebknecht's letter which gives it. If not, ask him to send it to you, and then dispatch the article *direct to Richter*, but not via Liebknecht.

It seems to me that Wilhelmchen is by no means ALTOGETHER *bona fide*. He (for whom I have had to find so much time to make good his asininity in the *Allgemeine Augsburger*, etc.,[577]) has so far found *no time* even to *mention* publicly the title of my book[b] or my name. He overlooks the affair in the *Zukunft*[c] so as not to be put in the embarrassing position of sacrificing his own independent greatness. And there was also no time available to say a solitary word in the workers' paper (*Deutsche Arbeiterhalle*, Mannheim), which appears under the direct control of his friend Bebel. In short, it is certainly no fault of Wilhelmchen that my book has not been totally ignored. First, he has not read it (although to little Jenny he made fun of Richter, who thinks that he needs to understand a book before he can publicise it), and secondly, after he had read it or claimed to have read it, he has had no time, although he has time, since I got him Borkheim's SUBVENTION, to write letters twice weekly to Borkheim; although, instead of sending the shares[d] to Strohn for the money, which was transmitted to him through me and obtained by my good offices, he asks for Strohn's address, in order to play his tricks with him directly, behind my back,

---

a F. Engels, 'Outlines of a Critique of Political Economy'. - b the first volume of *Capital* in the *Allgemeine Zeitung* - c K. Marx, 'Plagiarism' (see this volume, p. 495). - d of the *Demokratisches Wochenblatt*

and swamp him with epistles as he does Borkheim. In short, Wilhelmchen wants to make himself important, and in particular the public should not be distracted from its interest in Wilhelmchen. We must now act half as if we did not notice this, but still treat him with caution. As for his call to Austria, you cannot believe him until it has happened.[a] And secondly if it should come to this, we shall not dissuade him, but IF NECESSARY, simply explain to him what I explained to him when he joined Brass's *Norddeutsche*,[b][578] that, if he should compromise himself again, he will be, if necessary, *publicly disavowed*. I told him this, in the presence of witnesses, when he moved off to Berlin at that time.

I think you can send articles direct to the enclosed *Neue Freie Presse* (Vienna). The present joint owner, Dr *Max Friedländer* (Lassalle's cousin and deadly enemy), was the person for whom I acted as a correspondent for a longish period for the old Vienna *Presse* and for the *Oder-Zeitung*.[c]

Finally, with regard to the *Internationale Revue*, Fox (who was sent to Vienna by an English paper to pay a visit and establish connections) asked me, from Vienna a few days ago, for a letter of introduction to Arnold Hilberg. I sent it to him, and at the same time told the said Hilberg in this letter that circumstances had prevented us writing, that we would do something this year, etc.[111]

Fortnightly Review. Professor *Beesly*, one of the triumviri who secretly direct this paper, has told his special friend Lafargue (whom he constantly invites to dine at his house) that he is morally certain (it completely depends upon him!) that a review[509] would be accepted. Lafargue would hand it in to him himself.

Ad vocem Pyat. In today's *Times* you will see the ADDRESS of the FRENCH DEMOCRATS about FENIANISM [257] (which appeared 4 weeks ago) and was sent in by Pyat.[d] What has happened is this. The French government has launched an investigation (particularly *visites domiciliaires*[e] at the homes of our correspondents in Paris) against the International Association as a *société illicite*.[f] Ditto probably sent to the British government letters about FENIANISM written by our Dupont.[579] Mr Pyat, who always ran down our 'Association' as non-revolutionary, Bonapartist, etc., is afraid of this TURN of things, and is swiftly seeking to give the appearance that *he* has something to do with the matter and is 'MOVING'.

---

[a] See this volume, p. 512. - [b] *Norddeutsche Allgemeine Zeitung* - [c] *Neue Oder-Zeitung* - [d] F. Pyat, 'Adresse des Démocrates Français à leur Frères d'Irlande et d'Angleterre. Paris, 2 décembre 1867', *The Times*, No. 26015, 8 January 1868 (*The French Democrats and the Fenians*). - [e] searches - [f] illegal society

Ad vocem Benedek[a]: can I have the journal for A FEW DAYS? You have now proven yourself twice a prophet, firstly a tactical prophet (in the Sevastopol affair), and secondly a strategic prophet (in the Prussian-Austrian affair).[580] But the sense of sensible men cannot predict the stupidities of which man is capable.

Ad vocem carbuncles. Consulted doctors. Nothing new. Everything which the gentlemen have to say indicates that one has to have *private means* to live in accordance with their prescriptions, instead of being a poor devil like me, poverty-stricken as a church-mouse. When you see Gumpert, you can tell him that I feel (up to THIS MOMENT that I write) a stinging prickle in my body, that is my blood. It seems to me that for this year I shall not be quite over the affair.

MY COMPLIMENTS TO MRS Burns.

Salut.

Your
Moor

First published abridged in *Der Briefwechsel zwischen F. Engels und K. Marx*, Bd. 4, Stuttgart, 1913 and in full in MEGA, Abt. III, Bd. 4, Berlin, 1931

Printed according to the original

Published in English in full for the first time

316

ENGELS TO MARX

IN LONDON

[Manchester,] 10 January 1868

Dear Moor,

I wanted to write to you at length today, but the intervention of a Serb and a Wallachian, who held me up for hours, has frustrated my plans. Moreover, yesterday I had a visit from the ex-dictator Amand Goegg, who is travelling for the ridiculous Peace League[461] and who ruined my evening. Luckily, Schorlemmer also happened by, and got the surprise of his life with this fossil of Federal Republic; he had not believed such a thing possible. The stupid oaf has become ten times more stupid through the unthinking repetition of the same phrases, and has lost all points of contact with the world of common sense (not to

---

[a] *Österreichs Kämpfe im Jahre 1866...*, Bd. 1 (see this volume, pp. 510-11).

mention actual thinking). Apart from Switzerland and the Canton of Baden, there is still nothing else in the world for people of this sort. For all that, he soon convinced himself of the truth of your first reply to his application for support: that the further apart we lived and the less we had to do with one another, the better we would get on. He admitted that in the Vogt affair[63] Blind had behaved like a *coward,* but said he was after all a worthy fellow, and even threatened to reconcile you and Blind! Vogt—no politician, but a worthy fellow, honest to the backbone, who simply scribbled away in the daytime without considering the content—if we 2 spent an hour together then we would be like brothers; he admitted him to be a Bonapartist, but not a paid one. To which I replied that *all* Bonapartists were paid, there were no unpaid ones, and if he could show me an unpaid *one,* then I would accept the *possibility* that Vogt was not paid; otherwise I would not. This astonished him, but finally he discovered one—*Ludwig Bamberger!* Incidentally, he said that Vogt had continually had a very hard time, his wife was a peasant girl from the Bernese Oberland, whom he had married *out of virtue* after he had made her a baby. Vogt, the artful dodger, appears to have pulled the wool well over this jackass's eyes. But when Schorlemmer and I explained to him that Vogt had not produced anything as a natural scientist either, you should have seen his rage: Had he not *popularised?* Was not that worth while?

I shall write something for *Vienna* as soon as it is in any way possible. Additionally for the *Fortnightly,*[509] but I would need to know first whether it could be made into a longer article, or should only be a short notice like those at the back of the *Fortnightly.* Beesly should be sounded out about this[a]; a short notice would be *almost useless* and Beesly himself would learn nothing about the book[b] from it.

I shall call Wilhelmchen[c] to account in a few days time about fulfilling the promises he made me: we shall make this little fellow get a move on. I have Richter's address.

Herewith returned Liebknecht, Kugelmann and Siebel.

Best greetings.

Your

F. E.

First published abridged in *Der Briefwech-sel zwischen F. Engels und K. Marx,* Bd. 4, Stuttgart, 1913 and in full in *MEGA,* Abt. III, Bd. 4, Berlin, 1931

Printed according to the original

Published in English for the first time

---

[a] See this volume, p. 516. - [b] the first volume of *Capital* - [c] Wilhelm Liebknecht

317

MARX TO ENGELS [101]

IN MANCHESTER

[London,] 11 January 1868

DEAR FRED,

The 'Fop'[a] was bustling around for a long time in London. He also visited Borkheim, where he produced just the same phrases as he did to you, only with better success, for he knew how to tickle the vanity of our Borkheim. But after he had squeezed out of the latter money for 10 shares, ditto assimilated various of his wines, he was not seen there again. For the understanding of his further activity in London, the following preliminary report. *Cremer*, as you know, was removed a long time since from his post as SECRETARY of the INTERNATIONAL COUNCIL, and in his anger at this he long ago resigned as MEMBER OF THE COUNCIL, and was not re-elected as such by the last congress either.[b] Mr *Odger* was re-elected. On my proposal, however, the post of president (the annual one) was abolished, and replaced by a CHAIRMAN, to be elected at each sitting.[489] Odger, annoyed by this, stays away from us on principle. WELL! Mr 'Fop' insinuates himself via Le Lubez to Odger (who introduced him to the LONDON TRADES COUNCIL [18]) and to Cremer. They appointed a London committee,[c] Beales as PRESIDENT, etc. In short, an affair *against* the INTERNATIONAL WORKING MEN'S ASSOCIATION. (At the founding MEETING Fop also introduced the noble Blind.) The fellows had the impudence to invite me to their 2nd MEETING LAST WEEK. Eccarius (in a very badly written article in the *Bee-Hive last* Saturday) denounced Fop and his consorts.[d]

I am writing to you naked and with alcohol compresses. I went out again for the first time the *day before yesterday,* to the British Museum, of course, because I cannot write yet. Then yesterday there was a new outbreak under my left breast. The alcohol treatment, which Nélaton used in Paris for even the largest carbuncles, is, *from my personal experience,* by far the speediest and pleasantest for the patient (apart from cutting or lancing, depending on the case). The misfortune is only the constant

---

[a] Amand Goegg. In German 'Geck' means a 'dandy' or 'fop'. - [b] Lausanne Congress of the International - [c] presumably the committee of the London branch of the League of Peace and Freedom - [d] J. G. Eccarius, 'The Geneva Peace Congress', *The Bee-Hive Newspaper,* No. 325, 4 January 1868.

activity, necessitated by the rapid evaporation of the alcohol.

At the museum, where I did nothing but leaf through catalogues, I also noted that *Dühring* is a great philosopher. For he has written a *Natürliche Dialektik* against Hegel's 'un-natural' one. *Hinc illae lacrimae.*[a] The gentlemen in Germany (with the exception of theological reactionaries) believe Hegel's dialectic to be a 'dead dog'.[581] Feuerbach has much on his conscience in this respect.

The French government has started a prosecution against the Paris Committee of the INTERNATIONAL WORKINGMEN'S ASSOCIATION (as *société illicite*[b]). This is very agreeable for me, since it means that the jackasses have been hindered and interrupted in their discussion of the programme they had already drawn up for the *congress of 1868.*[582] Dupont has apparently written something incautious about the Fenians[579] to his Paris correspondents that Bonaparte, who is now creeping dolefully up the arse of the British government, forwarded to Downing Street.[c]

It is characteristic that the disclosures of Prokesch-Osten, Gentz and Count Münster[d] are being printed one after the other—with the direct or indirect collaboration of the Austrian government. Urquhart, with his ignorance now becoming permanent, knows only the first one. It is also very indicative of his 'totality', that he does not know Moltke's Turkish War of 1828, etc.,[e] which would have provided him with excellent material. Incidentally, at the time when I was in Berlin (at Lassalle's)[583] Moltke was regarded as a declared Russophobe, inside the Royal Prussian frontiers, naturally.

If you should be writing to Borkheim some time, request him to let you have a look at the *two small Russian pamphlets* about which I *had told you.* I would particularly like you to look at the one about the emancipation of the serfs, so that you can let me know the quintessence.

From the enclosed *Courrier français* you will see that the French government is entering into a direct polemic with General Cluseret.

If you could send little Tussy cotton-yarn ball on the 16th of

---

[a] Hence these tears! (Terence, *Andria*, Act I, Scene 1). - [b] illegal society (see this volume, p. 517) - [c] seat of the British Cabinet - [d] A. Prokesch-Osten, *Geschichte des Abfalls der Griechen vom Türkischen Reiche im Jahre 1821 und der Gründung des Hellenischen Königreiches*; Fr. von Gentz, *Aus dem Nachlasse Friedrichs von Gentz*; G. H. Münster, *Politische Skizzen über die Lage Europas vom Wiener Congress bis zur Gegenwart (1815-1867).* - [e] H. K. B. Moltke, *Der russisch-türkische Feldzug in der europäischen Türkei 1828 und 1829.*

this month I should be very pleased. It is her birthday and THAT LITTLE HUMBUG loves all Chinese formalities.

It gives me much pleasure that the English government is persecuting *The Irishman*. This paper is IN REALITY not Fenian, but simply wants REPEAL.[584] What blockheads these John Bulls are! MY COMPLIMENTS TO MRS Lizzy.

Salut.   Your

Moor

Enclosed a portion of 'new philology' from the *Hermann.*

<table>
<tr><td>First published abridged in Der Briefwech-sel zwischen F. Engels und K. Marx, Bd. 4, Stuttgart, 1913 and in full in MEGA, Abt. III, Bd. 4, Berlin, 1931</td><td>Printed according to the original

Published in English in full for the first time</td></tr>
</table>

318

MARX TO LUDWIG KUGELMANN [65]

IN HANOVER

London, 11 January 1868

Dear Kugelmann,

D'abord[a] my best HAPPY NEW YEARS to your good wife, Fränzchen,[b] and you yourself. And then MY BEST THANKS for the Jupiter,[585] and for the activity and interest you display in making propaganda and leading the German press by the nose.[c] As our friend Weerth, who unfortunately died too early, used to sing:

> The finest thing in all the world
> Is making your enemies bellow,
> And cracking really awful jokes
> About each pompous fellow.[d]

With all respect for your medical authority, you have too low an opinion of the *English, German* and *French* doctors whom I have in turn consulted and continue to consult here, if you think they cannot distinguish anthrax (carbuncles) from FURUNCLES, particularly here in England, the land of carbuncles, which is essentially a

---

[a] First of all - [b] Gertruda and Franziska Kugelmann - [c] A reference to Kugelmann's assistance in having Engels' reviews of Volume One of *Capital* published in the bourgeois press. - [d] G. Weerth, 'Es gibt nichts Schönres auf der Welt'.

proletarian illness! And if the doctors made no distinctions, the patient like myself who knows both forms of monster could do so, for the subjective impression they make is very different, though as far as I know no doctor has yet managed to distinguish exactly between the two things *theoretically.* I have only been persecuted by this business for a few years. Earlier quite unknown to me. At the moment of writing to you, I am not yet quite restored, and not yet fit for work again. Once again many weeks lost, and not even *pour le roi de Prusse.*[a]

The criticism of Mr Dühring[b] shows mainly—fear! I would be grateful if you could get *Dühring's* book *Gegen die Verkleinerer Carey's* for me, ditto *von Thünen's Der isolirte Staat mit Bezug auf die Landwirtschaft* (or something like that) (*together with a note of the prices*). Orders like this take too long from here.

Finally, I must ask you to send me ABOUT 12 COPIES of my photogram (only that FULLFACED). ABOUT one dozen friends are pestering me for them.

Enclosed for Mrs Kugelmann the photograms of my eldest daughter Jenny and of Eleanor, who sends her best greetings to Fränzchen.

Ad vocem[c] *Liebknecht*: let him play *le petit grand homme*[d] just A LITTLE WHILE. *Tout s'arrangera pour le mieux dans le meilleur des mondes possibles.*[e]

I still have all sorts of personal *anecdota* to relate. But I shall save them for next time when the writing position no longer bothers me.

Salut.   Yours

K. Marx

One of my friends here,[f] who busies himself a lot with phrenology, stated yesterday about the photogram of your wife: very witty! So you see that phrenology is not the baseless art that Hegel thought it.[g]

First published abridged in *Die Neue Zeit,*   Printed according to the original
Bd. 2, No. 4, Stuttgart, 1901-1902 and in
full in *Pisma Marksa k Kugelmanu* (Letters
of Marx to Kugelmann), Moscow-
Leningrad, 1928

---

[a] literally: for the King of Prussia; figuratively: all for nothing. - [b] E. Dühring, '*Marx, Das Kapital, Kritik der politischen Oekonomie,* 1. Band, Hamburg 1867'. - [c] With regard to - [d] would-be great man - [e] Everything will be for the best in the best of all possible worlds (F. M. A. Voltaire, *Candide*). - [f] presumably Karl Schapper - [g] G. W. F. Hegel, *Werke,* Bd. II, *Phänomenologie des Geistes,* 2. Aufl., Bd. 2, Berlin, 1841, S. 251-71.

319

ENGELS TO MARX

IN LONDON

Manchester, 16 January 1868

Dear Moor,

I have just discovered that I have left all your letters at home in another coat-pocket (including the last letter from your chief HONOURABLE SECRETARY [a] for which I express special thanks) and so I shall have to reply from memory.

You received the *Courriers français* and also the *Wiener Tagblatt* yesterday.

I am sending you the Prussian report,[b] with special explanations. Or rather it is only necessary to look at the sketch contained therein on the positions on the evening of June 28th in order to see that Benedek had brought together 6 corps (not counting cavalry) in an area of 2 square miles, faced by the Crown Prince [c] with only the 5th Corps and 1 brigade of the 6th Corps. If, on the 29th, Benedek had attacked Steinmetz (5th Corps), the latter would have been thrown back across the mountains on to the 6th Corps, and on the 30th Benedek would have been able to attack the Guards and the 1st Corps at his leisure with at least 4 corps and throw them back, *après quoi* [d] the cautious Frederick Charles would have taken great care not to act unrestrainedly. Frederick Charles had 5 corps and would have been faced by at least 6; the order for them to retreat was, however, certain as soon as the 3 individual columns of the Crown Prince had been beaten, and thereby the campaign would have acquired a completely different character. That the Austrians would finally have been beaten, if the Prussians had shown some care, is clear from a comparison of the figures. But the Prussian rabble would have been forced to cast aside their lousy system, and it would not have been the reorganisation and Bismarck who triumphed, but the people.

Cluseret (who, of course, played the Fenian [257] in London as well) is even wilder than the Germans with his militia plan. The American war [11] —with militia on both sides—proves nothing except that the militia system demands enormous sacrifices of

---

[a] Laura Marx (see this volume, p. 583) - [b] *Der Feldzug von 1866 in Deutschland...* - [c] Frederick William - [d] after which

money and men, since the organisation only exists on paper. What would have happened to the Yankees if they had been faced, not by the Southern militia, but by a standing army of a few 100,000 men? Before the North could have organised itself this army would have been in New York and Boston and would have dictated peace with the help of the Democrats, whereupon the West could have played at secession. The fellow makes a good joke when he suggests that what really counts are good officers and the confidence of the men in the officers—two things that simply cannot be achieved with the militia system. What impresses people everywhere about the militia system is the great mass of men obtained at once, and the relative ease of training them, particularly in the face of the enemy. This last point is nothing new, old Napoleon was able to lead recruits of three months in formation to face the enemy; but this demands good cadres, and for this purpose something different from the Swiss-American militia system. When the war ended, the Yankees still had very imperfect cadres. Following the introduction of the breech-loader, the time of the pure militia is really at an end. This does not mean that [not] every rational military organisation lies somewhere in the middle between the Prussian and the Swiss—but where? This depends on the circumstances in each case. Only a society set up and *educated* communistically can come very close to the militia system, and even then asymptotically.

With regard to the Viennese papers, I am in some embarrassment[a]; I do, of course, see the *Neue Freie Presse* from time to time, but the whole area is rather too alien for me. What are your ideas on the subject, also with regard to the *Fortnightly*[509]? The business is worth the trouble of thorough consideration.

I hope you are *sitting* again, and have had no further volcanic outbreaks. Gumpert laughs at your antipathy to arsenic, says that it is just the thing to make you *sprightly* and is convinced there is no better remedy for you. But if you are flatly opposed to it, then you should take acids, and that constantly, so once again he encloses a prescription for the aqua regia prescribed before, and this you really will take.

Best wishes to your wife and the girls, ditto Lafargue.

Your
F. E.

---

[a] See this volume, pp. 512, 515.

Alberich, the strong dwarf,[a] I hereby greet most humbly on his birthday and empty a glass of beer to his health at this instant. They forgot about the COTTON at the factory so I shall only be able to send it tomorrow.

First published in *Der Briefwechsel zwischen F. Engels und K. Marx*, Bd. 4, Stuttgart, 1913

Printed according to the original

Published in English for the first time

320

ENGELS TO MARX

IN LONDON

Manchester, 23 January 1868

Dear Moor,

From the enclosed scrawl you can see what Wilhelmchen has *not* done.[586] I shall give him a fitting wigging in the next few days. A JOLLY IDEA, we should 'utilise' the position he has created for himself locally in Saxony, in fact stand up for him BODILY. His rag[b] arrived for me today, I have not yet been able to look at it.

I hope you are finally finished with that obstinate carbuncle. But you will at last realise, won't you, that simply letting this matter slide can no longer be tolerated, and that at the very least you must have daily vigorous exercise in the fresh air, and regular 'renunciation' of night work (as soon as the first is possible), in order that you should become at all capable of work again. *Like this*, the second volume will never eventuate.[418]

Enclosed are the shares for Strohn.[c]

I really don't know what to do about the Vienna articles. Apart from the *Neue Freie Presse* and *Wiener Tagblatt*, I do not know *by name* any paper in which Richter has a hand; owing to almost complete ignorance of the audience I have no idea *where* to begin, and this is the most important point. Laura writes that to *instruct* people is ALL VERY WELL, but to pick out the right point is the real

---

[a] Eleanor Marx (see this volume, pp. 520-21) - [b] *Demokratisches Wochenblatt* - [c] See this volume, pp. 515-16.

difficulty. I am just going through the whole book[a] once again to make this clear to myself, and your opinion would be welcome.

It is also a good presumption on the part of Wilhelmchen to suggest that I should explain to him and his readers once and for all, on one page of his rag, and from this book, what the difference really is between Marx and Lassalle. This presumption has suggested to me that it might be a good idea to write a popular little pamphlet *Marx and Lassalle* of about 6 sheets for the workers; in *this* space it could be managed and the positive things required for the workers could be developed. It would have to be sold dirt cheap, and the Lassalleans would immediately be forced to take up a position. But for this, time is needed.[587]

You really cannot ask me to drudge my way through Borkheim's Russian pamphlets[b]—at least not at the moment. I have a lot to do in the office and come home late, so that I cannot get down to anything before 8 o'clock and, moreover, I have to live a life of great regularity, since for some time now I have been sleeping badly and as a result am often a wreck in the morning, something which has never happened in my life before. Besides, there are sometimes unavoidable hindrances, and the *absolute* necessity of having physical exercise so as to get my sleep back to normal. Each Russian pamphlet would consume 8-14 days in view of my necessity of working myself in again, and the poor quality of the dictionaries. *Ne vaut pas la paine.*[c]

About the *Fortnightly*[509] next time. I am still ruminating about this point. Monetary matters—important as they may be for England—I shall probably only be able to touch upon fleetingly in the first article; otherwise this subject would take up the whole article. If a second could be placed, then it would still be suitable. What do you think?

Best wishes to your wife and the girls as well as Lafargue.

Your

F. E.

First published abridged in *Der Briefwechsel zwischen F. Engels und K. Marx*, Bd. 4, Stuttgart, 1913 and in full in *MEGA*, Abt. III, Bd. 4, Berlin, 1931

Printed according to the original

Published in English for the first time

---

[a] the first volume of *Capital* - [b] See this volume, p. 520. - [c] It is not worth the trouble.

321

MARX TO ENGELS[26]

IN MANCHESTER

[London,] 25 January 1868

DEAR FRED,

I went out again yesterday for the first time, and the scar will be healed in 1-2 days. Naturally I am still weak after this bad attack.

I hope that your indisposition is only the momentary outcome of the week on the spree. In any case, you must not neglect your health for my sake or for ANY BODY OR THING ELSE.

In last week's *Saturday Review* there is a note about my book.[a] I have not seen it yet, and also do not know who wrote it. Borkheim has communicated the FACT to me.

As regards *Liebknecht*, one *should no longer butter him up*. This young man very much likes to play the 'protector', as he already showed once earlier when he was in London. This is also shown by his latest letter to you.[586] He feels very important, and *au cas de besoin nous ferons notre petit bonhomme de chemin sans lui et malgré lui*.[b] What magnanimity that he has reprinted the preface, which nearly all the papers printed months ago![456] And in addition he has actually had 2 COPIES of my book sent to Contzen and the editor of the *Volks-Zeitung*! TO SHOW HIM THE COLD SHOULDER is best. Apart from this, I do not believe that he has yet read 15 pages of the book. He had not read *Herr Vogt* a whole year after it had appeared, and that was not very heavy reading. His motto is: teach but not learn.

As far as the 'Lassalleans' are concerned, I only deal with the TRADE UNIONS, COOPERATIVE SOCIETIES, etc. in Volume II.[c] I think therefore that I shall *at present* only take the initiative with regard to 'Lassalle' if a direct occasion should offer itself.

Regarding the way to deal with the Viennese, I shall write to you shortly, when my head is ALL RIGHT again.

Please return the enclosed letters from Kugelmann and Kertbény. I have not yet replied. Coppel the Great hasn't turned up yet.[588]

---

[a] A review of Volume One of *Capital* in *The Saturday Review of Politics, Literature, Science and Art*, 18 January 1868. - [b] if needs be we shall do our business without him and despite him - [c] of *Capital*

It would be beneficial in my present state if you could let me have a shipment of your more FULLFLAVOURED claret (also SOME HOCK or Moselle).

Card, the Pole, has written from Geneva and offered himself as French translator, he seems to have a book-seller in Geneva. Through my wife I have had this letter sent to Schily, so that he can use it in Paris to further the affair.[539] Card is absolutely unsuitable, except to give Moses[a] a fright.

For 2-3 weeks I shall do absolutely no work (i.e. *writing*), at the most read; and as soon as the wound is completely healed (in the meantime, I THINK ONLY FOR ONE OR TWO DAYS, the bad part rubs and itches when I walk) then I shall do a lot of walking. It would be dreadful if a 3rd monster were to erupt.

And now, *salut*, MY DEAR BOY.

Your

K. Marx

First published abridged in *Der Briefwech-sel zwischen F. Engels und K. Marx*, Bd. 4, Stuttgart, 1913 and in full in *MEGA*, Abt. III, Bd. 4, Berlin, 1931

Printed according to the original

Published in English in full for the first time

322

MARX TO LUDWIG KUGELMANN [65]

IN HANOVER

London, 30 January 1868

Dear Kugelmann,

Cut, lanced, etc., in short treated in every respect *secundum legem artis*.[b] Despite this, the business continues to break out again, so that I have been lying quite fallow for 8 weeks, with the exception of two or three days. Last Saturday I went out again for the first time; Monday a relapse. I hope that it will come to an end this week, but who can give me a guarantee against new eruptions? It is extremely vexatious. In addition, my head is very affected by the business. My friend Dr Gumpert in Manchester is urging the use of arsenic. What do you think about this?

---

[a] Moses Hess - [b] according to all the rules of the art

Your Coppel hasn't turned up yet.[588]

Kertbény is a German-Hungarian, whose real name, *entre nous*,[a] is Benkert. The German-Hungarians love to Magyarise their names. I don't know him personally. As he had a row with Vogt ABOUT 1860, I approached him for some information but received nothing of any use. (My Hungarian material comes partly from Szemere, partly from my personal experiences in London.) Later he turned to me in connection with a row he was having with Kossuth. Much as I have enquired around, I have learned nothing politically suspicious about him. He appears to be a scribbling BUSYBODY. His heresies *quant à*[b] Bonaparte may be found amongst many otherwise honest eastern barbarians. In any case, WATCH HIM. And I would consider it more diplomatic not to display any mistrust of him (for which reason I am enclosing, through you, the biographical note which he requested). 'Meanwhile,' as soon as the writing position no longer troubles me, I shall 'order' information about him elsewhere.

You guessed rightly about 'Plagiarism'. I intentionally wrote rudely and clumsily in order to make Hofstetten suspect Liebknecht, and to conceal the source.[572] This *entre nous*.

You probably know that Engels and Siebel have also had newspaper articles published about my book in the *Barmer Zeitung*,[c] *Elberfelder Zeitung*,[d] *Frankfurter Börsenzeitung*[529] and—to the distress of Heinrich Bürgers—in the *Düsseldorfer Zeitung*.[e] Siebel was the man in Barmen to whom I wished to introduce you. He is, however, now in Madeira for his health.

A week ago on Saturday *The Saturday Review*[f]—the 'BLOOD AND CULTURE' paper—included a note about my book in a review of recent German books. I came out of it relatively well, as you will see from the following passage:

* 'The author's views may be as pernicious as we conceive them to be, but there can be no question as to the plausibility of his logic, the vigour of his rhetoric, and the charm with which he invests the driest problems of political economy.' *589

' Ouff!

My best greetings to your dear wife and Fränzchen.[g] You will be receiving other photograms from here, for we have now discov-

---

[a] between ourselves - [b] regarding - [c] [C. Siebel,] '*Carl Marx: Das Kapital. Kritik der politischen Oekonomie*', *Barmer Zeitung*, No. 291, 6 December 1867. - [d] F. Engels, 'Review of Volume One of *Capital* for the *Elberfelder Zeitung*'. - [e] F. Engels, 'Review of Volume One of *Capital* for the *Düsseldorfer Zeitung*'. - [f] *The Saturday Review of Politics, Literature, Science and Art*, 18 January 1868. - [g] Gertruda and Franziska Kugelmann

ered that the WATERCOLOURS applied which look good on the first day, run into PATCHES immediately afterwards.

Write to me as often as time permits. During my indisposition, and many occasions for vexation, letters from friends are welcome. *Salut.*

Yours

K. M.

[Autobiographical Notes]⁵⁹⁰

Karl Marx, Ph. D., born Trier, 5 May 1818.

1842-43, first contributor, then *redacteur en chef*ᵃ of the *Rheinische Zeitung* (Cologne). During his editorship the government subjected the paper to double censorship; after censorship by the proper censor, the superior censor of the *Regierungspräsi-dent.*ᵇ Finally suppressed on cabinet orders. Marx leaves Germany, moves to Paris.

1844 publishes in Paris, with A. Ruge, the *Deutsch-Französische Jahrbücher,* banned in Germany.

Further *Die heilige Familie, Kritik der kritischen Kritik, gegen Bruno Bauer und Konsorten.* (Frankfurt a/M. Literarische Anstalt.)

January 1845,ᶜ expelled from France by Guizot at the instigation of the Prussian Government, Marx proceeds to Brussels, forms the German Workers' Society in Brussels in 1847,ᵈ gives lectures on political economy there,⁵⁹¹ contributor to the French *Réforme* (Paris), etc.

1847: Misère de la Philosophie. Réponse à la Philosophie de la Misère de M. Proudhon.

Ditto: *Discours sur le libre échange* and other pamphlets.

1848, with F. Engels: *Manifest der Kommunistischen Partei.* Arrested and expelled from Belgium, invited back to France on the written invitation of the provisional government. Leaves France April 1848, founds in Cologne:

Neue Rheinische Zeitung (June 1848-May 1849). Marx expelled from Prussia, after the government had vainly prosecuted him through legal channels. Twice acquitted at assizes (once press trial, the other time for incitement to rebellion). Marx's defence speeches published in *Zwei politische Prozesse,* Cologne.

1849. Final, red issue of the *Neue Rheinische Zeitung.*

ᵃ editor-in-chief - ᵇ District President - ᶜ Inaccuracy in the original: December 1844. - ᵈ Ditto: 1846

Marx moves to Paris. Expelled from there *August*[a] *1849*, was to be interned in Brittany (Morbihan), refuses this, expelled from France, moves to London, where he has resided until the present.

1850 published: *Neue Rheinische Zeitung. Politisch-ökonomische Revue* (Hamburg).

1851-52: contributor to the London Chartist paper: *The People's Paper*, Ernest Jones': *Notes to the People*, etc.

1852: Der 18. Brumaire des Louis Bonaparte, New York.

Enthüllungen über den Kommunistenprozess zu Köln, Basel. Since this edition was confiscated on the German frontier, new edition in Boston, 1853.

1853-54: Flysheets against Lord Palmerston.[592]

1859: Zur Kritik der Politischen Oekonomie, Berlin.

1860: Herr Vogt.

1851-1862[b]: regular contributor to the English-language *Tribune (New York).*[c] Contributions to *Putnam's Review* (New York)[593] and the new *Cyclopaedia Americana (New York).*

1861: after the amnesty visited Berlin; Prussian Government refused his renaturalisation.[583]

1864[d]: published by order of the Central Council of the International Working Men's Association *Address to the Working Class of Europe.*[e]

1867: Das Kapital. Kritik der politischen Ökonomie. Vol. I, Hamburg.

First published in *Pisma Marksa k Kugelmanu* (Letters of Marx to Kugelmann), Moscow-Leningrad, 1928

Printed according to the original

323

MARX TO ENGELS

IN MANCHESTER

Dear FRED,   [London,] 1 February 1868

I hope that you are not also indisposed, since you have not written to me this week, and not returned the letters of Kugelmann and Kertbény (I need them to reply).[588] Last Tuesday I went out to the Museum[f] and for a stroll. On Wednesday a new

---

[a] Ditto: September - [b] Ditto: 1851-1860. - [c] *New-York Daily Tribune* - [d] Inaccuracy in the original: 1865. - [e] K. Marx, 'Inaugural Address of the Working Men's International Association'. - [f] the British Museum Library

eruption broke out. It is smaller, and does not prevent me sitting, since it is on the upper side of my left thigh. Walking is harmful, however, because of the friction and the spreading of the inflammation. I believe this monster will die out during this week. After the numerous disappointments, I scarcely dare to hope that no more follow. The devil take this mucky business.

Enclosed a letter from Schily. According to him, things look rotten in Paris, as does everything connected with Moses.[a] Reclus does not seem to me to be the right man either.[539] There can naturally be no question of the Pole[b] in Geneva. As soon as your article for the *Fortnightly*[509] is AT HAND, Lafargue will do it into French for the *Courrier français.*

From the enclosed Viennese cuttings, which Fox sent me from Vienna, you can see how Lassalle and Delitzsch[c] are rampant there. At the same time as the rascal Bernhard Becker turned up there as a great man. He is now a 'Great-German'[d] in the Bismarck style.

If you still have a copy of your article in the *Frankfurter Börsenzeitung,*[e] send it to me.[529]

Salut.

Your

K. M.

The Freiligrath begging campaign[422] is going ahead; it has already raised over 32,000 talers.

First published in *Der Briefwechsel zwischen F. Engels und K. Marx*, Bd. 4, Stuttgart, 1913

Printed according to the original

Published in English for the first time

324

ENGELS TO MARX

IN LONDON

Manchester, 2 February 1868

Dear Moor,

The reason for my silence was that I wanted to inform you, together with the letter, of the dispatch of the wine. However, the

---

fellow who packs wine for me had an accident, and will be lying sick for at least 14 days, and so I have not been able to manage it yet; possibly I shall pack it myself tomorrow. You will receive very good 1863 claret and 1857 Rhine wine; I only have a few bottles of Moselle left, and they are in Mornington Street, where I cannot have them packed.

Then I was also chasing after *The Saturday Review* and have with great trouble got hold of the notice. If you have not seen it, I can send you a copy—not much in it, but nevertheless a good sign.[a]

At the moment, in addition to the tremendous amount of work connected with the annual accounts and that resulting from the revival in business, I must also rush around like mad as chairman of the Schiller Institute,[28] since the affair of the building fund must be decided within 14 days, and until then all the work falls on me myself. However, I shall start with the piece for the *Fortnightly*.[509] Important and interesting as the question of money is for England as well, I still think it appropriate to allow it to retreat into the background this time; it would distract attention from the main theme and demand a long explanation so that the English might understand that the subject is *simply money as such*, which he is accustomed to think of only in its entanglement with credit money, etc. What do you think?

Kertbény's idea of having your portrait in the Leipzig *Illustrirte* is *quite splendid*.[588] This sort of advertisement penetrates right into the depths of the philistine's heart. Give him everything he needs for this. The fellow can be used for other things too, is very willing, and has the need to intervene busily everywhere and in everything. Vain, but not stupid for a Hungarian. His assessment of the German-Austrians at that time was very correct.

Card, the Pole, has sent me an insoluble puzzle with his signature. Cwi...chiewicz, neither my knowledge of handwriting nor my philology suffices for the solution of it. OF COURSE, HE WOULD NEVER DO AS A TRANSLATOR, and what Schily writes[b] is *very* fishy. If Reclus alone wants 3,000-4,000 francs, and Moses[c] who wants to do the main work, also his share, and you should be paid the *droits d'auteur*,[d] where should the publisher come from?[539] And these people should be left to do the job of 'condensing' and 'Frenching' it? Moses, who would rather be capable of watering down into 20 volumes the chapter about absolute surplus value[594] than condens-

---

[a] A reference to the notice on the first volume of *Capital* published in *The Saturday Review of Politics, Literature, Science and Art*, 18 January 1868.- [b] See this volume, p. 52. - [c] Moses Hess - [d] author's rights

ing a page of it by one line? It is really your fault; if you write strictly dialectically for German science, then afterwards, when it comes to the translations, particularly the French, you fall into evil hands.

The *Frankfurter Börsenzeitung*[a] like all the rest I have sent to Meissner, from whom I have heard nothing since.[529] I wrote to him that he should make up an advertisement from the various articles.[131]

Liebknecht's rag[b] displeases me to the highest degree. Nothing but concealed South German federalism. The article on Swiss and Prussian military history has been worked up on the basis of *Grün* (K.) in *Les États-Unis d'Europe*,[595] almost every word is wrong. Furthermore there is nothing in the rag, and though he is as thick as thieves with Hanoverian particularists and South German louts, he attacks the Berlin *Zukunft* people who, the devil take it, are at least as good as that rabble. Incidentally I have only received 3 numbers.

What little trust the Prussians have in the internal peace in the new provinces[596] is shown by the new stationing and organisation of the army. For instance, 3 Hanoverian infantry and 2 cavalry regiments are stationed in Westphalia or rather Wesel, while in Hanover there are only 2 Hanoverian infantry and 3 cavalry regiments but, besides, in Westphalia 4 infantry and 2 cavalry regiments. It is true that in Schleswig-Holstein home regiments are stationed with one exception, but 2 infantry and 2 cavalry regiments from the old provinces as well. In Hesse there are indeed nominally 3 Hessian regiments of infantry, but of these the 82nd (2nd Hessian) consists of Westphalians! And the Nassauers have been sent to Hesse, the Hessians to Nassau, and parts of both with old Prussian regiments sent to Mainz. Finally Frankfurt is kept in order by Pomeranian infantry and Rhineland cavalry.

The great Borchardt seems to be approaching the target of his career. You know that for years he has transferred his priestly leanings from the beautiful Mrs Steinthal to the even more beautiful Mrs Schwabe, and that every year he has taken her to Germany to a spa because of her weakened health, and brought her back again, while her husband has to stay at home out of respect for his wife's health. So, Borchardt even took her, as Schwabe told Knowles and me one day, 'to Königsberg for the coronation'—whereupon I naturally asked: '*Whose* coronation?'

_____

a *Frankfurter Zeitung und Handelsblatt* - b *Demokratisches Wochenblatt*

Although I made fun of the cuckolded jackass for a whole half hour over the coronation, and fat Knowles was laughing aloud, the oaf noticed nothing. But now, after the priestly doctor had kept the husband apart from his sick wife for years, it suddenly emerges that the sick wife is pregnant and expects her accouchement about April. Remarkably, the high priest must have been guilty of some carelessness or foolishness sufficiently for the cuckolded jackass to suddenly see the light; he leaves his house here and moves to Berlin, sells his HUNTERS although he will still be here for the whole hunting season, resigns his club membership, and is so hostile to the high priest that when the latter manages to launch a collection for the East Prussians here and sends £700 to the *Zukunft*, the cuckolded jackass throws himself into the arms of the Prussian consul and together with him collects abour £350 for the official committee. Now there is a lot of talk about this amongst the philistines, and although the story above is only whispered about in the dark, the position of the high priest has been badly shattered, and many people dare to speak of him with disrespect. He no longer looks so jovial and elegant. I wonder how things will proceed. (Nota bene. The *names* in this story are *between you and me*.)

Best greetings to the ladies and Lafargue.

Your
F. E.

First published abridged in *Der Briefwechsel zwischen F. Engels und K. Marx*, Bd. 4, Stuttgart, 1913 and in full in *MEGA*, Abt. III, Bd. 4, Berlin, 1931

Printed according to the original

Published in English for the first time

325

MARX TO ENGELS

IN MANCHESTER

[London,] 4 February 1868

DEAR FRED,

Many thanks for the 'medicine BOTTLES'.

I still have two not quite withered buds under my left arm and on my left thigh. However, they do not bother me when walking. I feel GENERALLY better as well.

I quite agree with you that you should not go into the money theory for the time being, but only indicate that the matter has been treated in a new way.[a]

Enclosures from Vienna from Fox (please send them back to me). You see what effect your essay in the *Börsenzeitung*[b] is having.[529] It is perhaps best to leave Vienna to its own devices. It is enough that attention has been drawn there to my book.[c] The whole business is very immature. When you consider how agriculture still predominates in the Empire *en gros*, then it is comical to watch these somersaults. What prevails in Vienna is finance, and not large industry. However, as a ferment the hubbub cannot hurt.

Kugelmann has sent me *Dühring's Verkleinerer Carey's.* I was right that he only noticed me in order to annoy the others.[d] What is very conspicuous is the very coarse way in which this affected Berliner handles Mill, Roscher, etc., while he treats me with timid care. According to him, apart from Carey, List is the greatest genius of the 19th century. In another pamphlet *Kapital und Arbeit* which I saw today at the Museum,[e] he '*abuses*' Lassalle. I shall send you his book to look at one of these days.

Perhaps there will be no war this year. The fellows are all anxious about domestic conditions. However, the Russians will not neglect to provide causes of friction. They will lie fallow if they do not manage to bring Germany and France to blows.

Coppel was here on Sunday and will come again on Wednesday.[588] He is here to put the financial affairs of the King of Hanover[f] in order. He is a merry fellow. Kugelmann has forced this cousin of the Rothschilds to study my book.

There is little new for me in Schorlemmer's letter[g]. But still MY THANKS.

Salut.

                     Your

                     Moro

I can only send the newspaper cuttings tomorrow because the BOXES for BOOK-POST were closed.

First published in *Der Briefwechsel zwischen F. Engels und K. Marx*, Bd. 4, Stuttgart, 1913

Printed according to the original

Published in English for the first time

---

[a] See this volume, pp. 526 and 533. - [b] *Frankfurter Zeitung und Handelsblatt* - [c] the first volume of *Capital* - [d] E. Dühring, '*Marx, Das Kapital, Kritik der politischen Oekonomie*, 1. Band, Hamburg 1867' (see this volume, p. 514). - [e] the British Museum Library - [f] George V - [g] See this volume, pp. 507-08 and 510.

326

ENGELS TO MARX

IN LONDON

Manchester, 11 February 1868
7 Southgate

Memorandum from Engels to Mr Moor[597]

I have received your letter and that from your HONOURABLE SECRETARY[a] and return enclosed the Viennese cuttings and Meyer's letter. What a frightful tragedy at the Weydemeyers.[598] I am of the opinion that an article should be contributed to the *Debatte* (via Richter), and that one should strike while the iron is hot.[599] It will be sent this week. The '*specialist criticism*' in the *Frankfurter Börsenzeitung*[b] is extremely amusing.[529] It is significant that these Viennese literary gents, all Jews as cunning as foxes, who well know all the tricks, should regard the German press outside Austria as *bona fide*.

Dühring amuses me very much. The thrusts at Roscher, Mill, etc., were a godsend for him—but what a difference there is between the embarrassed tone of the criticism[c] and the saucy nature of the pamphlet.[d]

I do not believe either there will be war, if only because the Peace League[461] describes it as unavoidable; in any case, Sadowa[348] has made it impossible for Bonaparte to start a war against Germany without great alliances. And since *at the best* he could only get Austria (England, as always, or more than ever, would not count militarily), and would have Prussia and Russia against him, the whole business is fishy. Italy is no good either, and furthermore he mucked things up for himself there. HE IS FLOORED. Even the great Karl Schurz, ex-student General Fart,[e] has confided this to Bismarck secretly.[600]

It is nearly 7 o'clock, and I have not had dinner yet. I must go home first, so enough for today.

Your

F. E.

First published in *Der Briefwechsel zwischen F. Engels und K. Marx*, Bd. 4, Stuttgart, 1913

Printed according to the original

Published in English for the first time

---

[a] Laura Marx - [b] *Frankfurter Zeitung und Handelsblatt* - [c] E. Dühring, '*Marx, Das Kapital, Kritik der politischen Oekonomie*, 1. Band, Hamburg 1867'. - [d] E. Dühring, *Die Verkleinerer Carey's und die Krisis der Nationalökonomie*. - [e] *Furz* in German, rhyming with Schurz.

327

MARX TO ENGELS [26]

IN MANCHESTER

[London,] 15 February 1868

DEAR FRED,

Forced since yesterday to stay at home again, since the monster under my left shoulder-blade is developing viciously. It appears that this shit will never end.

From Bordeaux I have received all the papers for the marriage.[601] I am very worried about this. It should take place on 1 April, and nothing has been prepared for Laura. She cannot be sent out into the world like a beggar. I have written to Holland,[a][111] but NO ANSWER.

I am writing only these few lines since the writing position is uncomfortable for me today.

Have you received further PAPERS from the important Wilhelmchen[b]? I have heard and seen nothing of it since THE 2 FIRST NUMBERS.

Salut.

Your
K. M.

First published in *MEGA*, Abt. III, Bd. 4, Berlin, 1931

Printed according to the original

Published in English in full for the first time

328

MARX TO ENGELS

IN MANCHESTER

[London,] 20 February 1868

DEAR FRED,

At the same time as this I am sending you an interesting cutting from a Viennese paper,[c] received via Fox.

---

[a] to the Philipses - [b] *Demokratisches Wochenblatt* edited by Liebknecht - [c] *Neues Wiener Tagblatt*

Borkheim gave me a letter to him from Liebknecht, which I had to send back to him by return. From this the following excerpt: 'Tell Marx that Dr Contzen is working on a long review, and in a lecture has already mentioned the work[a] in the most laudatory terms from the *purely scientific* standpoint. And tell Marx, too, that he should get Engels to supply an article about *Capital* for our paper[b] which now circulates 1,300 copies equally-spread throughout Germany. I myself have *no time at present* for such a job.'

If you think it worth the trouble to supply something for the paper, it would be good to make the article longer this time (with extracts), even if it had to run through several numbers.[602] Borkheim will probably be sending you a reprint—if you do not have the paper—of the 'Russian refugees' which he wrote for it.[c]

Dr Contzen, BY THE BY, himself publishes (or published) an economic periodical *patrone*[d] Roscher.

Regarding health, CHANGE from day to day.

Salut.

Your
K. M.

First published in *Der Briefwechsel zwischen F. Engels und K. Marx*, Bd. 4, Stuttgart, 1913

Printed according to the original

Published in English for the first time

329

ENGELS TO MARX[302]

IN LONDON

Manchester, 20 February 1868
7 Southgate

Dear Moor,

This week you will have to regard me as completely out of action. I have such a frightful lot of work at the firm as a result of the sudden rise in cotton that I do not get out of the office from

---

[a] the first volume of *Capital* - [b] *Demokratisches Wochenblatt* - [c] S. B[orkheim], 'Russische politische Flüchtlinge in West-Europa', *Demokratisches Wochenblatt*, Nos. 5 and 6, 1 and 8 February 1868 (the end of the article was published in Nos. 17 and 20, 25 April and 16 May 1868). - [d] under the patronage of

the morning on until 7 o'clock in the evening, and do not get my dinner until 8 o'clock in the evening. You will understand what one is capable of after that. I hope that the damned carbuncle has got settled. Hearty greetings to your wife, the girls and Lafargue.

Your

F. E.

First published in *Der Briefwechsel zwischen F. Engels und K. Marx*, Bd. 4, Stuttgart, 1913

Printed according to the original

330

ENGELS TO MARX

IN LONDON

[Manchester,] 1 March 1868

Dear Moor,

The whole of last week I worked like a slave from morning till night in commerce so that I was good for nothing at all. This has now passed, I think, and this week I should get back on to the rails.

Enclosure from Meissner. His draft is naturally absolutely unusable: I shall see whether I cannot knock together something better for him. Now I am sorry that I sent him the articles, I should already have prepared something for him from them.[a]

I shall write something for Wilhelmchen[b]; verbatim extracts would be difficult, but I can spin out some main points to some extent for his public.[602] I, too, have seen only 3 numbers of the rag,[c] and these could have been edited by Gustav Struve. Since Wilhelmchen was left to his own devices his South German basic federative republicanism (how earnest[d] the man is) has broken out again in full glory. The fellow even re-prints Karl Grün.[595]

How is your carbuncle faring? Let us hope that this is finally the last.

---

[a] See this volume, p. 534. - [b] Wilhelm Liebknecht - [c] *Demokratisches Wochenblatt* - [d] *Ernscht* in the original; Engels is punning on the Saxon pronunciation of *ernst*.

Mr Goegg obstinately sends me the *Les États-Unis d'Europe* (the fellow wants me to get an agency for him, thus the devotion). Since the paper appears simultaneously and with the same contents in German and French, it would not be bad at all to announce your book[a] there and Goegg has promised to insert articles by you or me. What do you think of that?

Best greetings to your wife, the girls and Lafargue.

Your
F. E.

First published abridged in *Der Briefwechsel zwischen F. Engels und K. Marx*, Bd. 4, Stuttgart, 1913 and in full in *MEGA*, Abt. III, Bd. 4, Berlin, 1931

Printed according to the original

Published in English for the first time

331

MARX TO ENGELS

IN MANCHESTER

[London,] 4 March 1868

Dear FRED,

From the enclosed scrawl you will see that, if I do not pay £7.5.0 by the day after tomorrow, MY 'CHATTELS' SHALL BE DISTRAINED.

The carbuncle business is now reduced to a residuum under my left arm, which should soon fade.

That I write you only these few lines today is due to a HORRIBLE headache.

Make sure that Meissner does not write any nonsense on his own. If the jackass had only sent back the newspaper cuttings.[b]

Enclosed scrawl from S. Meyer, which you should please return.

Salut.

Your
K. M.

First published in *Der Briefwechsel zwischen F. Engels und K. Marx*, Bd. 4, Stuttgart, 1913

Printed according to the original

Published in English for the first time

---

[a] the first volume of *Capital* - [b] See this volume, pp. 534, 540.

332

MARX TO ENGELS [238]

IN MANCHESTER

[London,] 6 March 1868

DEAR FRED,

BEST THANKS FOR THE £10.

The copies of *Social-Demokrat* promised by Meissner have not arrived. This shows that he is not at all precise. Thus for instance the copies for Paris have not been dispatched either. There the worthy Moses[a] has prevaricated for so long[603] that the *Courrier français* has now finally announced that as the result of the many *amendes*,[b] etc., it will soon completely quit the stage.

I have not seen Eichhoff's lucubrations and anyway not the *Zukunft* for a very long time.[604] Since Eichhoff's brother[c] is a bookseller and specialises in political economy (he is the publisher of several opera of Dr Dühring), this is reason enough for Eichhoff to deliver lectures on the same subject.

My head is in a sorry state. But that should 'disappear' BY AND BY, as soon as the last traces of carbuncledom have gone.

I wrote to Holland[111] again yesterday since the matter is becoming *brûlante*.[d] Old Lafargue[e] has dealt with the necessary marriage BANNS, etc., in Bordeaux, and has sent all the papers here. He now expects that the wedding will take place here at the beginning of next month, and that the pair will go to Paris, to which he will later move. We, however, have not yet risked taking the necessary steps here for the BANNS, since my wife has not yet been able to acquire even the most essential things for Laura. For worthy Freiligrath all this went very smoothly, but then he is 'noble'.

As soon as this affair is SETTLED, it will be a great relief for the entire household, since Lafargue is as good as living with us, which perceptibly increases EXPENSES.

As far as the 'reviews' are concerned, I think that after you have supplied Liebknecht[602] you should abandon the German ones and only pursue the English. First, the echo of an English review in Germany is more powerful than vice versa, and secondly this is, after all, the only country where finally money can be made from the business.

---

[a] Moses Hess - [b] fines - [c] Albert Eichhoff - [d] urgent - [e] François Lafargue

Mr Macleod has nevertheless achieved a 2nd edition of his lousy and pedantic-scholastic book on BANKS.[a] He is a very stilted jackass who expresses every banal tautology 1. in algebraic form, and 2. constructs it geometrically. I have already given him a passing kick in the pamphlet published by Duncker.[b] His 'great' discovery is: credit *is* capital.

Salut.

Your

K. M.

First published abridged in *Der Briefwech-sel zwischen F. Engels und K. Marx,* Bd. 4, Stuttgart, 1913 and in full in *MEGA,* Abt. III, Bd. 4, Berlin, 1931

Printed according to the original

Published in English in full for the first time

333

MARX TO LUDWIG KUGELMANN [65]

IN HANOVER

London, 6 March 1868

Dear Friend,

As soon as Coppel vanished, my condition got worse again. Scarcely, I think, because of his departure. *Post* not *propter.*[c] (After all he is, in his way, quite a nice man. But that particular way is, in my present state, too healthy for me to harmonise with it very well.) This is therefore the reason for my silence, so that I did not even inform you of the receipt of Thünen.[d] There is something touching about the latter. A Mecklenburg squire (moreover, one with *German* distinction of thought), who treats his estate of Tellow as *the land* and Mecklenburg-*Schwerin* as *the town,* and who, proceeding from these premises, constructs for himself the Ricardian theory of ground rent, with the help of observation, differential calculus, practical accountancy, etc. This is estimable and at the same time ridiculous.

The curiously embarrassed tone used by Mr Dühring in his review[e] is now clear to me. Usually, you see, he is a very

---

[a] H. D. Macleod, *The Theory and Practice of Banking.* - [b] K. Marx, *A Contribution to the Critique of Political Economy.* - [c] After, not because. - [d] J. H. Thünen, *Der isolirte Staat in Beziehung auf Landwirtschaft und Nationalökonomie.* - [e] E. Dühring, '*Marx, Das Kapital, Kritik der politischen Oekonomie,* 1. Band, Hamburg 1867'.

bumptious, insolent lad, who sets himself up as a revolutionary in political economy. He has done two things. Firstly (basing himself upon Carey) he published a *Kritische Grundlegung der Nationalökonomie* (ABOUT 500 PAGES), and a new *Natürliche Dialektik* (against Hegelian dialectic). My book has buried him in both respects. He reviewed it out of hatred for Roscher, etc. Incidentally he practises deception, half intentionally and half from lack of insight. He knows full well that my method of exposition is *not* Hegelian, since I am a materialist, and Hegel an idealist. Hegel's dialectic is the basic form of all dialectic, but only *after* being stripped of its mystical form, and it is precisely this which distinguishes *my* method. *Quant à*[a] Ricardo, Mr Dühring has been vexed precisely because in my treatment the weak points do *not* exist which Carey, and 100 others before him, held up as proof against Ricardo. Consequently, he attempts, with *mauvaise foi*,[b] to burden me with Ricardo's narrow-mindedness. BUT NEVER MIND. I must be grateful to the man, since he is the first expert who has said anything at all.

In volume II[418] (which will probably never appear if my condition does not change) property in land will be one of the subjects analysed, competition only in so far as called for in the treatment of other themes.

During my indisposition (which I hope will soon cease altogether) I have not been able to write, but have gobbled up enormous masses of 'material', statistical and otherwise; this alone would have made SICK those whose stomachs are not accustomed to this type of fodder and the rapid digestion of the same.

My circumstances are very harassing, since I was unable to do any additional work which would bring in money, but must always maintain a certain appearance for the children's sake. If I didn't have to produce these 2 damned volumes (and look for an *English* publisher besides), which can be done only in London, I would move to Geneva where I could live very well with the means at my disposal. My daughter No. II[c] is getting married at the end of this month.[601]

Greetings to Fränzchen.

Yours

K. M.

First published in *Die Neue Zeit*, Bd. 2,   Printed according to the original
Nr. 6, Stuttgart, 1901-1902

---

[a] As for - [b] bad faith - [c] Laura Marx

334

ENGELS TO MARX

IN LONDON

Manchester, 10 March 1868

Dear Moor,

Do not forget to return to me the things from Meissner,[a] otherwise I cannot reply to him.

If the Dutch[b] do not write to you soon, I shall see what I can do. I suppose something can still be managed.

The storm in commerce is beginning to die down, so I can work again in the evening. What you say about the *Fortnightly* is quite right; what is published there can be used again afterwards in Germany. The matter should be undertaken as quickly as possible.[509] But you will understand it is not possible to do much in the evening when you only get your midday meal at 7.30 or 8 in the evening.

Eichhöffchen enclosed.— You will see that besides his brother[c] he also has other 'grounds' to lecture on political economy.[604]

So, the Russians have again postponed the business in Turkey.[605] As long as they have no railways, I really cannot believe that they seriously intend any serious action. Moreover, they have an awful famine in the interior.

The costs of the Bismarckian *gloire*, etc., are beginning to tell. 1864— population of Prussia 19,250,000. 1867— 19,668,000 for the old Provinces. According to the rate hitherto— 250,000 per year, it should have been 20 million. The rate has thus been reduced to *one half.* In the administrative districts of Münster, Minden, and Koblenz (inter alia) the population has actually declined. Biggest increase in Berlin and Düsseldorf administrative district.

Your
F. E.

First published abridged in *Der Briefwechsel zwischen F. Engels und K. Marx.* Bd. 4, Stuttgart, 1913 and in full in *MEGA*, Abt. III, Bd. 4, Berlin, 1931

Printed according to the original

Published in English for the first time

---

[a] See this volume, pp. 534, 540. - [b] the Philipses - [c] Albert Eichhoff

335

ENGELS TO MARX

IN LONDON

Manchester, 13 March 1868

Dear Moor,

For Meissner I still lack the letter from von Eynern. I wanted to prepare an advertisement[a] today but was disturbed.

Enclosed from Vienna.[606] Have written to Wilhelmchen[b] for information. I think I shall accept in general, but say that the matter must remain secret 'in order not to disturb my other connections in the Viennese press'.

I also sent Wilhelm two articles about your book, completely popular for workers (so that even Wilhelm will understand them).[c]

At the same time, I have coached him in his role in order to work over in the Reichstag the new code for crafts and manufactures (which also includes factory legislation).[607] This opportunity is very good in order to ADVERTISE the book, and I am convinced that this will also have a considerable effect, since even the official economists have to draw on it.

Since yesterday I have been fit for work again—on the one hand, I get back earlier in the evening, and, on the other, I have discovered that for 14 days I had been drinking beer poisoned probably with *cocculus indicus*,[d] which totally narcotised me in the evening. I CHANGED THE TAP YESTERDAY—by chance—noted the difference, and discovered the cause, which I had ascribed to digestive troubles.

HOW ABOUT CARBUNCLES?

Your
F. E.

First published abridged in *Der Briefwechsel zwischen F. Engels und K. Marx*, Bd. 4, Stuttgart, 1913 and in full in *MEGA*, Abt. III, Bd. 4, Berlin, 1931

Printed according to the original

Published in English for the first time

---

a See this volume, pp. 534, 540. - b Wilhelm Liebknecht - c F. Engels, 'Review of Volume One of *Capital* for the *Demokratisches Wochenblatt*'. - d Indian berries

336

MARX TO ENGELS [608]

IN MANCHESTER

[London,] 14 March[a] 1868

DEAR FRED,

Since the beginning of the week I have had carbuncles on my right thigh (not yet QUITE EXTINCT). Despite this—and the consequent difficult gait—I went to the Museum,[b] since this continuous being cooped up and *lying down* at home (the business has now lasted, with some intervals OF COURSE, over 4 months) would drive me mad. For all that, I am convinced that the present blossoms are only the last aftereffects. At the Museum—BY THE BY—I studied, amongst other things, the latest writings about the *Constitution of the German Mark, Villages, etc.*, by OLD Maurer[c] (the old Bavarian Privy Councillor, who already played a role as one of the regents of Greece, and was among the first to denounce the Russians, long before Urquhart). He demonstrates at length that private property in land only arose later, etc. The idiotic Westphalian squirearchical opinion (Möser,[d] etc.) that the Germans settled each by himself, and only afterwards established villages, districts, etc., is completely refuted. It is interesting just now that the *Russian* manner of re-distributing land at certain intervals (in Germany originally annually) should have persisted in some parts of Germany up to the 18th century and even the 19th. The view I put forward that the Asiatic or Indian property forms everywhere mark the beginning in Europe receives new proof here [609] (although Maurer knows nothing of it). But for the Russians there disappears the last trace OF ORIGINALITY, even in THIS LINE. What remains to them is that they still maintain forms long abandoned by their neighbours. OLD Maurer's books (from 1854 and 1856, etc.) are written with real German erudition, but, at the same time, in the more homely and readable manner which sets the southern Germans apart from the northern Germans (Maurer is from Heidelberg, but this applies even more to the Bavarians and

---

a 14 November in the original - b the British Museum Library - c Presumably a reference to G. L. Maurer's *Einleitung zur Geschichte der Mark-, Hof-, Dorf- und Stadt-Verfassung und der öffentlichen Gewalt; Geschichte der Markenverfassung in Deutschland; Geschichte der Fronhöfe, der Bauernhöfe und der Hofverfassung in Deutschland; Geschichte der Dorfverfassung in Deutschland.* - d J. Möser, *Osnabrückische Geschichte.*

Tyroleans, such as Fallmerayer, Fraas, etc.). Here and there a hat is doffed deeply—re, *non verbis*[a]—to OLD Grimm (*Rechtsalterthümer,*[b] etc.). Besides, I looked at the things by Fraas, etc., on agriculture.[c]

BY THE BY, you must send me back the Dühring,[d] and, at the same time, the page proofs of my book.[e] You will have seen from Dühring what Carey's great discovery is, namely, that in agriculture humanity proceeds from poorer to increasingly better soil. Partly because cultivation descends from the dry hills, etc., to the damp lowlands. But in particular because Mr Carey considers the most fertile soil *marshes* and so on, which first have to be *converted* into soil. And finally because the English colonisation in America began with that lousy New England which is Carey's model country: Massachusetts in particular.

THANKS for your efforts with the damned book. I cannot find Eynern's letter but *suffit*[f] to write to Meissner that you sent it to me.[g] I have received the same letter from Vienna, with a few modifications.[606] I enclose the cuttings about Lassalle sent me by Fox. Apart from the arch-blackguard B. Becker, Reusche is in Vienna; this vagabond is there for Hatzfeldt money (as our J. Ph. Becker writes to Borkheim)—the enclosed Viennese Lassalle-creature article is by him—in order to glorify Izzy as the Son of God, and the beastly old girl as the Mother of God.

From Holland[h] I have still not heard anything, and the wedding should be on April 8th (with difficulty despite Lafargue I have postponed the business that far).[601] In addition, I have on the 17th (next Tuesday) to pay ABOUT £5 for water and gas (also last SUMMONS). As for the DUTCH, it appears to me that I shall not squeeze anything out of them until I once again pounce upon them personally, without previous notice. But JUST NOW there can be no question of this.

Have you read about the scandal (Borkheim informed me of it) between Dühring and 'Privy Councillor' Wagener, with the former accusing the latter of pinching his manuscript[610] or something or other about workers' cooperation.

Salut.

Your

K. M.

---

[a] in fact, not words - [b] J. Grimm, *Deutsche Rechtsalterthümer.* - [c] Presumably a reference to K. Fraas' *Klima und Pflanzenwelt in der Zeit; Historisch-encyklopädischer Grundriß der Landwirthschaftslehre; Geschichte der Landwirthschaft; Die Natur der Landwirthschaft; Die Ackerbaukrisen und ihre Heilmittel.* - [d] E. Dühring, *Die Verkleinerer Carey's und die Krisis der Nationalökonomie.* - [e] the first volume of *Capital* - [f] it suffices - [g] See previous letter. - [h] i.e. the Philipses

From Maurer I have noted that the change in opinions about the history and development of 'Germanic' property, etc., proceeds from the *Danes* who are apparently tremendously active in all kinds of archaeology in every corner. But, although they thus give the impulse, something is always missing with them SOMEWHERE OR ELSE. They lack the proper critical instinct, and in particular the sense of proportion. I was extremely struck by the fact that Maurer, though often referring, for instance, to Africa, Mexico, etc., knows absolutely nothing about the Celts, and therefore ascribes the development of common ownership in France solely to the Germanic conquerors. 'As though,' Mr Bruno[a] would say, 'as though' we did not possess a Celtic (Welsh) book of laws from the 11th century[b] which is entirely communist, and 'as though' the French in recent years had not just excavated original settlements in Celtic form here and there. As though! But the matter is quite simple. Besides German and ancient Roman relations, OLD Maurer has only studied oriental (Greek-Turkish!) ones.

First published in *Der Briefwechsel zwischen F. Engels und K. Marx*, Bd. 4, Stuttgart, 1913

Printed according to the original

Published in English in full for the first time

337

MARX TO ENGELS [522]

IN MANCHESTER

[London,] 16 March 1868

DEAR FRED,

Enclosed a letter to Kugelmann from a young Bielefeld manufacturer.[c] I am particularly amused by his idea that I myself must have formerly been a sewing-machine EMPLOYING MANUFACTURER. If people only knew how little I know of all that stuff.

The question is also unavoidable: what now? The fellows all want recipes for miracle cures, and do not see the fairly graspable cure by fire and iron already plainly indicated.

---

[a] Bruno Bauer - [b] *Ancient Laws and Institutes of Wales.* - [c] Gustav Meyer (see this volume, p. 552)

It is strange how Dollfus (Alsace) has won such false *renommé*. This ʜᴜᴍʙᴜɢ, who ranks far beneath such Englishmen as Briggs, etc., has drafted his contracts with his workers, contracts that could only be entered into by a degenerate rabble, in such a way that they do in fact become his colony of serfs, and in fact he treats them well '*as serfs*', and exploits them as neatly as anybody else. And on this account the brute recently introduced in the Corps législatif the nasty paragraph of the Press Law about the '*vie privée qui doit être murée*'.[a][611] For here and there light had been thrown on his philanthropic juggling.

The way in which the English in Ireland are now treating political prisoners, or just suspects, or those only sentenced to ordinary prison terms (like Pigott of *The Irishman* and Sullivan of the *News*[b]) in fact exceeds anything seen on the Continent[612]— except Russia. They are curs!

Salut.

Your
K. M.

First published in *Der Briefwechsel zwischen F. Engels und K. Marx*, Bd. 4, Stuttgart, 1913

Printed according to the original

Published in English in full for the first time

338

ENGELS TO MARX

IN LONDON

Manchester, 17 March 1868

Dear Moor,

Yesterday evening the cashier rushed off before I had asked him for the £5 for your gas, etc., and I could not even borrow a note anywhere; it is now enclosed, and I hope this delay has not caused you any serious unpleasantness. Further money will follow in the next few days, as soon as I can view my own affairs more clearly. Has Lafargue furnished a house, etc., for he cannot take his wife into his ʟᴏᴅɢɪɴɢs?

---

[a] private life which should be surrounded by walls - [b] *Weekly News*

The proofs[a] and the Dühring[b] I shall send to you; I forgot to take the stuff with me this morning. In haste.

Your

F. E.

First published abridged in *Der Briefwechsel zwischen F. Engels und K. Marx*, Bd. 4, Stuttgart, 1913 and in full in *MEGA*, Abt. III, Bd. 4, Berlin, 1931

Printed according to the original

Published in English for the first time

339

MARX TO LUDWIG KUGELMANN[65]

IN HANOVER

London, 17 March 1868

Dear Friend,

Your letter[c] affected me both unpleasantly and pleasantly (you see I always move in a dialectical contradiction).

Unpleasantly, since I know your circumstances, and it would be wretched of me to accept such presents *at your family's expense*. I therefore regard these £15 as an *advance*, which I shall repay when I am able.

Pleasantly, not simply as a mark of your great friendship (and in the bustle of the world, friendship is the only personal thing that matters), but also because you have helped me over a great embarrassment in regard to the coming wedding.[601] In the past 4 months—quite apart from medicine and doctors—I have spent so much money on BLUE BOOKS,[359] Enquêtes and YANKEE REPORTS, etc., on BANKS that I really had nothing left for my daughter.[d]

You can imagine that I have often discussed moving from London to Geneva, not only with myself and my family, but also with Engels. Here I have to spend £400-500 annually. In Geneva I could live on £200. But CONSIDERED ALL IN ALL this is *impossible* for the time being. I can only complete my work[e] in London. And *only here* can I hope finally to derive a decent or at least adequate

---

[a] of the first volume of *Capital* - [b] E. Dühring, *Die Verkleinerer Carey's und die Krisis der Nationalökonomie.* - [c] of 13 March 1868 - [d] Laura Marx - [e] *Capital*

monetary profit from this work. This is why it is necessary *that I stay here* for the time being. Apart from the fact that, were I to move away from here at this critical period, the whole working-class movement, which I influence behind the scenes, would fall into very bad hands and leave the right track.

For the time being, therefore, *fate* binds me to London ALL DRAWBACKS NOTWITHSTANDING. *Quant à*[a] Coppel, you do him an injustice. Had I not been indisposed he would have amused me and such a diversion never hurts the family.

Engels and I have hitherto written nothing for Liebknecht's paper.[b] (Engels has now sent him 2 articles about my book.[c]) Eccarius is the regular London correspondent. Borkheim has written an article against Herzen et Co.[d]

Meyer's[e] letter gave me great pleasure. However, he has partly misunderstood my exposition. Otherwise he would have seen that I depict *large-scale industry* not only as the mother of the antagonism, but also as the producer of material and intellectual conditions for resolving these antagonisms, though this cannot proceed *along pleasant lines.*

With regard to the factory act—as a first condition, whereby the working class obtains ELBOW-ROOM for development and movement—I demand it *from the state,* as a *forcible law,* directed not only against the manufacturers, but also against the workers themselves. (Page 542, note 52, I indicate the resistance of women workers to a limitation of hours.) By the way, should Mr Meyer develop the same energy as Owen, he can break this resistance. That *the individual manufacturer* (apart from the extent to which he endeavours to influence legislation) can do little in the matter, I state ditto p. 243: 'But looking at things as a whole, all this does not, indeed, depend on the good or ill will of the *individual capitalist,* etc.' and ib. note 114.[613] Despite all this, the individual working person can do something, and this has been abundantly shown by such manufacturers as Fielden, Owen, etc. Their main effectiveness must naturally be of a public nature. As for the Dollfuses in Alsace, they are HUMBUGS who have managed, through their conditions of contract, to establish a comfortable and at the same time for them very profitable *serfdom-relationship* with their workers. They have been duly exposed in the Paris press, and for

---

[a] As for - [b] *Demokratisches Wochenblatt* - [c] F. Engels, 'Review of Volume One of *Capital* for the *Demokratisches Wochenblatt*'. - [d] S. B[orkheim], 'Russische politische Flüchtlinge in West-Europa', *Demokratisches Wochenblatt,* Nos. 5 and 6, 1 and 8 February 1868 (the end of the article was published in Nos. 17 and 20, 25 April and 16 May 1868). - [e] Gustav Meyer (see this volume, p. 549)

this very reason one of these Dollfuses, in the Corps législatif, recently introduced and CARRIED one of the most infamous paragraphs of the Press Law, namely that '*vie privée doit être murée*'.[a][611]

With heartiest greetings to your dear wife[b]

Yours

K. M.

Apropos: Did you see that my personal enemy Schweitzer has heaped *eulogies* on my head in 6 numbers of the *Social-Demokrat* on account of my book?[c] Very harrowing for that old harlot Hatzfeldt.

First published abridged in *Die Neue Zeit*, Bd. 2, No. 6, Stuttgart, 1901-1902 and in full in *Pisma Marksa k Kugelmanu* (Letters of Marx to Kugelmann), Moscow-Leningrad, 1928

Printed according to the original

340

MARX TO ENGELS[6]

IN MANCHESTER

[London,] 18 MARCH 1868

DEAR FRED,

The £5 received with many thanks.

Laura and Lafargue will first go to Paris (after the marriage), then rent an APARTMENT here (somewhere on the Heath,[d] if findable) and after Lafargue's final exam (he took the others at Bartholomew's Hospital[614]) will go back to France for a time, and then move off to America, where OLD Lafargue[e] has house and home.

Whence comes the word[615] higid, hid, hiwisc (*hida autem Anglice vocatur terra unius aratri culturae sufficiens*[f])? And also the German

---

[a] private life should be surrounded by walls - [b] Gertruda Kugelmann - [c] [J. B. Schweitzer,] 'Das Werk von Carl Marx', *Der Social-Demokrat*, Nos. 10-12, 14, 15 and 24; 22, 24, 26 and 31 January, 2 and 23 February 1868. - [d] Hampstead Heath - [e] François Lafargue - [f] hida is also the name in English for the land that can be cultivated sufficiently with one plough (see also this volume, pp. 560-61).

word: *wiffa* (*Qui signum, quod propter defensionem terrae*[a] that is to say, to declare the land INCLOSED, a sign instead of a real fence *ponitur, quod signum wiffam vocamus*[b]).
   Salut.

Your

K. M.

First published in *Der Briefwechsel zwischen F. Engels und K. Marx*, Bd. 4, Stuttgart, 1913   Printed according to the original

341

ENGELS TO MARX

IN LONDON

Manchester, 19 March 1868

Dear Moor,

Enclosed £40 in two twenties, which, it is to be hoped, will suffice at least for the most urgent purposes. I had not expected that Löhrchen[c] would be making a honeymoon trip to America. So the wedding is on 8 April, a Wednesday; had it been Friday, Saturday or Monday I could have got away easily.

The things from OLD Maurer are very nice[d]; it is really remarkable how much material already exists on these subjects, and how little the professors have been able to make of it.

I shall try to discover the Anglo-Saxon word,[e] but, since no Anglo-Saxon dictionary is available to me here, I shall have to make do with other sources, which are very dubious, in view of the large and peculiar stock of words in Anglo-Saxon. First of all, the correct spelling must be determined. With regard to *Wiffa*, a question: where is it found, so we might know whether it has Low German or High German sound shifts. If it is High German you should compare Graff's *Althochdeutscher Sprachschatz*, the *Bayerisches Wörterbuch* by Schmeller or the Swiss dictionary by Stalder. Does it not occur in Grimm's *Rechtsalterthümer*[f]?

---

[a] Here a sign to declare the land defended - [b] is erected, this sign we call *Wiffa* - [c] Laura Marx - [d] See this volume, pp. 547-49. - [e] Ibid., pp. 553-54. - [f] J. Grimm, *Deutsche Rechtsalterthümer*.

The accursed business with the ill-fated Schiller Institute here,[28] which Gumpert once pushed me into and then did nothing further, is finally reaching a crisis, and the matter will be decided by Wednesday. During these days I must — *étant engagé*[a] — make a great EFFORT; I shall therefore scarcely be left with time in this period to write the English article.[509] From the middle of next week onwards I shall have peace, and will press ahead without pause. Regarding this business here, there is every prospect that I — and everything depends upon me — shall bring everything to a happy conclusion despite Borchardt and various other German cliques. Since I have been involved in the business for 4 years, and victory or defeat fall on my head, I simply *must*.

Since you say nothing about carbuncles, I assume that everything is fading without further issue.

The most conscientious reader of your book[b] here is Sam Moore; he has really worked his way thoroughly through over 600 pages and is grinding indefatigably on.

Best greetings.

Your
F. E.

So, Plon-Plon, according to *The Times*,[c] should inaugurate the Russian-Prussian-French alliance. This Bonaparte seems to get into a worse position every day. The stupid Prussians are continually making arrests and searching houses in the annexed lands.[596] The proofs[d] and the Dühring[e] will be dispatched today or tomorrow.

First published abridged in *Der Briefwechsel zwischen F. Engels und K. Marx*, Bd. 4, Stuttgart, 1913 and in full in *MEGA*, Abt. III, Bd. 4, Berlin, 1931

Printed according to the original

Published in English for the first time

---

[a] since I have promised - [b] the first volume of *Capital* - [c] *The Times*, No. 26074, 17 March 1868, 'Prussia (From our own Correspondent). Berlin, March 14'. - [d] of the first volume of *Capital* - [e] E. Dühring, *Die Verkleinerer Carey's und die Krisis der Nationalökonomie*.

342

MARX TO ENGELS

IN MANCHESTER

[London,] Museum,[a] 23 MARCH 1868

IN HASTE

DEAR FRED,

I thought Laura would notify you about the £40. She claims, however, that I did not ask her to. Thus *malentendu.*[b]

During the whole of last week I had many bleeding shingles; particularly obstinate and hard to obliterate the mess under my left armpit. But GENERALLY I feel much better, IN FACT like a RECONVALESCENT and I am sure that the business is coming to an end.

At the same time, I am sending you the Schweitzer, which please return to me after use. A few lines from Meissner, in which he notifies me of his stupidity in informing Schweitzer that he should not continue with his EXTRACTS[c] until *I* have stated my views. *Quelle bêtise!*[d] I immediately attempted to redress things. Whatever secondary motives Schweitzer may have (e.g. to annoy old Hatzfeldt, etc.), one thing must be admitted. Although he makes a MISTAKE here and there, he has studied the stuff really hard, and knows where the centres of gravity lie. Such a 'base consciousness' is still preferable to the 'honest consciousness' of a Heinzen or the 'noble consciousness' of a Wilhelmchen.[e] Hegel forgot to list *idleness* as an essential element of 'noble-minded consciousness'.[f]

More *de diversis*[g] in the next letter.

Salut.

Your
K. M.

First published abridged in *Der Briefwechsel zwischen F. Engels und K. Marx*, Bd. 4, Stuttgart, 1913 and in full in *MEGA*, Abt. III, Bd. 4, Berlin, 1931

Printed according to the original

Published in English for the first time

---

[a] the British Museum Library - [b] a misunderstanding - [c] [J. B. Schweitzer,] 'Das Werk von Carl Marx', *Der Social-Demokrat,* Nos. 10-12, 14, 15 and 24; 22, 24, 26 and 31 January, 2 and 23 February 1868. - [d] What stupidity! - [e] Wilhelm Liebknecht - [f] See G. W. F. Hegel, *Phänomenologie des Geistes,* Abt. 'Die Bildung und ihr Reich der Wirklichkeit'. - [g] on various topics

343

MARX TO ENGELS[101]

IN MANCHESTER

[London,] 25 March 1868

Dear Fred,

I wanted to write to you yesterday from the Museum,[a] but I suddenly became so very unwell that I had to close the very interesting book I was reading. There was something like a black veil before my eyes. In addition, a frightful headache and chest constriction. So I crept home. The air and the light did me good, and at home I slept FOR SOME TIME. My state is such that I really should give up working and thinking entirely for SOME TIME; but that *would be hard for me, even if I had the means to loaf.*

Ad vocem[b] *Maurer*: his books are extremely significant.[c] Not only the primitive age but also the entire later development of the free imperial cities, of the estate owners possessing immunity, of public authority, and of the struggle between the free peasantry and serfdom, get an entirely new character.

The history of mankind is like palaeontology. Owing to A CERTAIN JUDICIAL BLINDNESS, even the best minds fail to see, on principle, what lies in front of their noses. Later, when the time has come, we are surprised that there are traces everywhere of what we failed to see. The first reaction to the French Revolution and the Enlightenment bound up with it was naturally to regard everything as mediaeval, romantic, and even people like Grimm are not free from this. The second reaction to it is to look beyond the Middle Ages into the primitive age of every people—and this corresponds to the socialist tendency, though these learned men have no idea that they are connected with it. And they are then surprised to find what is newest in what is oldest, and even EGALITARIANS TO A DEGREE which would have made Proudhon shudder.

And we are all very much in the clutches of this JUDICIAL BLINDNESS: right in *my own* neighbourhood, on the *Hunsrück,*[d] the old Germanic system survived until the *last few* years. I now remember my father[e] talking about it to me from *a lawyer's point of view.* Another proof: just as the geologists, even the best like

---

[a] the British Museum Library - [b] Regarding - [c] See this volume, pp. 547-49, and 554-55. - [d] mountains in the Rhine Province, Prussia - [e] Heinrich Marx

Cuvier, have expounded certain *faits*[a] in a completely distorted way, so philologists of the *force*[b] of a Grimm, *mistranslated* the simplest Latin sentences because they were under the influence of Möser, etc. (who, I remember, was enchanted that 'freedom' never existed among the Germans, but that '*Luft macht eigen*'[c]). E.g. the famous passage in Tacitus: '*arva per annos mutant, et superest ager*',[d] which means: they exchange the fields (*arva*) (by lot, hence also *sortes*[e] in all later *Leges Barbarorum*[616]), and there remains over communal land (*ager* in distinction to *arva* as *ager publicus*[f]), Grimm and others translate: they till every year new fields, and there is still (untilled) land left over![g]

In the same way the passage: '*colunt discreti ac diversi*'[h] is taken to prove that the Germans from the earliest times cultivated on individual farms like Westphalian squires. But *the very same* passage continues: '*Vicos locant non in nostrum morem, connexis et cohaerentibus aedificiis; suum quisque locum spatio circumdat*',[i] and such Germanic primitive villages, in the form described, still exist here and there in Denmark. Obviously Scandinavia must become as important for German jurisprudence and economics as for German mythology. Only by starting from there will we be able once again to decipher our past. Incidentally, even Grimm, etc., found in Caesar's writings that the Germans always settled as kinship groups, and not as individuals: '*gentibus cognationibusque, qui uno coierunt.*'[j]

But what would OLD Hegel say, were he to learn in the hereafter that the *general* [*das Allgemeine*] in German and Nordic means only the communal land, and that the *particular*, the *special* [*das Sundre, Besondere*] means only private property divided off from the communal land? Here are the logical categories coming damn well out of 'our intercourse' after all.

Very interesting is the book by Fraas (1847): *Klima und Pflanzenwelt in der Zeit, eine Geschichte beider*, namely as proving that climate and flora change in *historical* times. He is a Darwinist before Darwin, and admits even the *species* developing in historical

---

a facts - b importance - c J. Möser, *Patriotische Phantasien*, Th. 3, S. 329. 'Luft macht eigen'—part of a medieval German saying, 'Stadtluft macht frei, Landluft macht eigen', literally: 'town air brings freedom, country air brings serfdom'. In medieval times a serf who moved to a town became free. - d Tacitus, *Germania*, 26. - e lot - f communal land - g *Die Geschichtschreiber der deutschen Vorzeit*, Bd. 1. S. 661. - h they till separately and scattered - i '*They do not lay out villages* in our fashion, with *adjacent buildings one next to the other*; each *surrounds his dwelling with a free space*'. - j 'according to gentes and kinships, which settled together' (Gaius Julius Caesar, *Commentarii de bello Gallico*, Lib. VI, 22).

times. But he is at the same time agronomist. He claims that with cultivation—depending on its degree—the 'moisture' so beloved by the peasants gets lost (hence also the plants migrate from south to north), and finally steppe formation occurs. The first effect of cultivation is useful, but finally devastating through deforestation, etc. This man is both a thoroughly learned philologist (he has written books in *Greek*) and a chemist, agronomist, etc. The conclusion is that cultivation—when it proceeds in natural growth and is not *consciously controlled* (as a bourgeois he naturally does not reach this point)—leaves deserts behind it, Persia, Mesopotamia, etc., Greece. So once again an unconscious socialist tendency!

This Fraas is also interesting as a German case-study. First Dr. med., then inspector and teacher of chemistry and technology. At present head of Bavarian veterinary services, university professor, head of state agricultural experiments, etc. In his latest writings you see his advanced age, but he is still a dashing fellow. He has been around a lot in Greece, Asia Minor, Egypt! His history of agriculture is also important. He calls Fourier this 'pious and humanist socialist'.[a] On the Albanians, etc. 'every sort of shameless lechery and rape'.[b]

We must keep a close watch on the recent and very latest in agriculture. The *physical* school is pitted against the *chemical*.

Do not forget to send me back the letter of Kugelmann's manufacturer.[c]

Nothing pleases me better than to see you here.

Your

K. M.

Apropos. Edgar's[d] planter's hat has been found again, and this time you can take it to Mrs Lizzy.[e]

First published in *Der Briefwechsel zwischen F. Engels und K. Marx*, Bd. 4, Stuttgart, 1913

Printed according to the original

Published in English in full for the first time

---

[a] C. Fraas, *Geschichte der Landwirthschaft*, S. 12. - [b] K. Fraas, *Klima und Pflanzenwelt in der Zeit*, S. XVI. - [c] Gustav Meyer (see this volume, p. 549) - [d] Edgar von Westphalen - [e] Lizzy Burns

344

ENGELS TO MARX

IN LONDON

Manchester, 29 March 1868

Dear Moor,

I am afraid I shall not finish the article for the *Fortnightly*[509] by Tuesday. The damned Schiller Institute business[28] kept me breathless all the week, until I finally got things cleared up yesterday. If I had failed—and several stupidities on the part of my main adjutant put everything doubtful again—I would have been terribly discredited, made ludicrous for the whole of Manchester; TO BE 'DONE' IN BUSINESS, TO GET YOURSELF 'SOLD' is naturally here the worst thing that can happen to you. Now it is a great triumph and gives me the opportunity I wanted to withdraw with honour from official participation in the affair; anyway now enough people will be pushing themselves forward for it. I am doubly annoyed because this business has made it impossible for me to complete the article; but for this I would have had to rush it, and in this case the quality is very important.

Schorlemmer has made a very fine discovery: *the law of the boiling points* of the hydrocarbons of the series C_nH_{2n+2}, i.e. for three of the four isomeric series; of the 4th, too few have yet been described.[a]

I shall be arriving at your place on Wednesday evening at 9, possibly earlier.[617]

Where on earth can the enclosed article come from? And a letter of Bismarck's to cheer you up.

Best greetings.

Your

F. E.

I can find nothing about *Wiffa*. But in *higid, hiwisc, hida* you are confusing 2 if not 3 different words.[b]

Anglo-Saxon *hiwisce*, Old Saxon and Old High German *hiwiski*, Old Frisian *hiskthe*, Old Nordic *hyski*, New North Frisian *hiske = familia.*

---

[a] C. Schorlemmer, 'Researches on the Hydrocarbons of the Series C_nH_{2n+2}', *Proceedings of the Royal Society*, No. 94, 1867 and No. 102, 1868. - [b] See this volume, pp. 553-54.

Higid can be the participle of the Anglo-Saxon *hegjan*, this verb means TO FENCE IN.

Whether *hide*, which is still encountered locally today as a measure of land, is drawn from this, or is connected with *hide cutis*, Anglo-Saxon *hyde*, I cannot determine without an Anglo-Saxon dictionary.

First published abridged in *Der Briefwechsel zwischen F. Engels und K. Marx*, Bd. 4, Stuttgart, 1913 and in full in *MEGA*, Abt. III, Bd. 4, Berlin, 1931

Printed according to the original

Published in English for the first time

APPENDICES

1

JENNY MARX TO ENGELS

IN MANCHESTER

[London, not before 29 November 1864]

My dear Mr Engels,

Poor Moor once again has a large and very painful carbuncle. So, he has to lie down, and he finds writing very difficult. I hope that in a few days we shall be over the first eruption. It is dreadful to have that again. You would not credit how splendidly he had the bit between his teeth with the actual copying up of the book.[a] There is already a sizeable stack ready for printing. The long hours of sitting and writing until far, far into the night, and the excitement this entails, are undoubtedly responsible for the renewed outbreak of the disease. Karl hopes that the interruption will not be long. He even wants to try and write something today. Enclosed is a letter from Wilhelmchen[b] which he is sending you, likewise one to Weydemeyer which I would be glad if you would see to, since we do not have his address.[c] The price of the cards for the 'INTERNATIONAL SOCIETY' is 1s.1d. However, Moor thinks no one would try to stop GENTLEMEN giving 5-10s.

A thousand greetings to you, dear Mr Engels, from us all.

Yours
Jenny Marx

Apropos. We have at last had a few lines from our old Uncle Edgar.[d] The Berliners appear to be treating him decently. The BABY says in his letter that they gave him a 'Christmas present' of coats, trousers, waistcoats, gloves, cigars and a 'hymnbook'. The

---

[a] the first volume of *Capital* - [b] presumably Wilhelm Liebknecht's letter to Marx of 24 November 1864 - [c] See this volume, pp. 43-45. - [d] Edgar von Westphalen

doctor they consulted declared his illness to be heart-disease. Whenever the doctors do not know what to say, they make do with 'general' heart-disease. I believe his complaint has its seat rather in his lungs and mind.

First published in: Marx and Engels, *Works*, Second Russian Edition, Vol. 31, Moscow, 1963

Printed according to the original

Published in English for the first time

2

JENNY MARX TO ENGELS

IN MANCHESTER

[London, 30 March 1865]

Dear Mr Engels,

Thank you so much for your letter [131] and the newspaper cutting, which I now return. The worst thing about this dreadful business in which 'Wilhelmchen' [a] has once more involved yourself and Moor is that I have no idea where Moor is at present. [177] I have heard nothing from him and don't know whether he is in Germany or Holland. I have taken pot luck in sending all the filth from the newspapers after him. It is almost impossible to take up the cudgels in the newspapers with a creature like Becker, [b] [192] but FACTS must be corrected, on account of the credulous Straubingers. [618] The most ridiculous and most vexing part of the affair is to have people like Mr Reusche testifying that 'Lassalle also spoke of Marx with respect'. Lassalle, who copied everything from my husband, even his MISTAKES, who had been his friend and disciple for 15 years—he is cited as also having spoken of him with respect. And this gracious testimonial is being purveyed by people who only became friends of Lassalle in the last 2 years, at a time when he was already fully committed to that wrong path, which was taking him into Bismarck's camp, [98] into the ministry, like friend Bucher, or to the ultimate *retraite*, to Italy. And, of course, Lassalle should be rescued for these 'freedom-fighters' who have received their reward in his will! Yet these social riff-raff are after

_____

[a] Wilhelm Liebknecht - [b] Bernhard Becker

all only following their great agitator. Like his lord and master, incidentally, Mr Reusche is constantly misappropriating things of my husband's, forever reproducing every witticism from *Herr Vogt*, just as in that last opus he himself borrowed from Karl the 'grotesque CLOWN, who has nothing behind him but his own shadow' (a phrase aimed at Karl Blind).[a] The condescending manner in which this triumvirate deigns to allow Moor its protection, is the most vexing thing of all. Incidentally, Lassalle's respect for the aging Ph. Becker was also of recent date. As far back as August 1862 he believed him to be a paid agent, though in whose hire I do not know, and refused to have anything to do with him.[619] He likewise declared to me in one of his outbursts of shouting, when his voice always went OUT OF TUNE, that Moses[b] in Paris was a completely useless muddlehead with whom he desired no truck. I defended that Plonplonist[93] as an *honest* Confusionarius. I live from day to day in the hope that I shall have news of Carel; this uncertainty causes me more bother than all the other troubles.

We are all well here and send you our cordial greetings.

Yours

Jenny Marx

First published in *MEGA*, Abt. III, Bd. 3, Berlin, 1930

Printed according to the original

Published in English for the first time

3

KARL MARX

CONFESSION[620]

Zalt-Bommel, 1 April 1865

The Quality you like best	Simplicity
In man	Strength
In woman	Weakness
Your chief characteristic	Singleness of purpose
Your favourite occupation	Glancing at Netchen[c]

---

[a] See present edition, Vol. 20, p. 25. - [b] Moses Hess - [c] Nannette Philips. In Jenny Marx's album: 'Bookworming'.

The vice you hate most	Servility
The vice you excuse most	Gullibility
Your idea of happiness	To fight
Your idea of misery	To submit[a]
Your aversion	Martin Tupper[b]
Your hero...	Spartacus, Keppler
Your heroine..	Gretchen
The poet you like best	Aeschylus, Shakespeare, Goethe[c]
The prose writer you like best	Diderot[d]
Your favourite flower	Daphne[e]
Your favourite dish	Fish[f]
Your maxim:	*Nihil humani a me alienum puto*[g]
Your motto:	*De omnibus dubitandum*[h]

Karl Marx

First published, in the language of the original, English, in *International Review of Social History*, Vol. I, Part I, Assen, 1956

Reproduced from the original verified with the handwritten text in Jenny Marx's album

4

JENNY MARX TO JOHANN PHILIPP BECKER[621]

IN GENEVA[i]

[London, 29 January 1866]

My dear Mr Becker,

For the past week my husband has again been laid low with his former dangerous and exceedingly painful complaint. The affliction is all the more distressing for him this time since it further interrupts him in the copying out of his book[j] that he has just

---

a In the album this query and the one above remained unanswered. - b In the album: 'Martin Tupper, Violet powder'. - c In the album: 'Dante, Aeschylus, Shakespeare, Goethe'. - d In the album: 'Diderot, Lessing, Hegel, Balsac'. - e In the album there are three more queries and replies here; 'Favourite colour ... Red; Colour of eyes & heir ... Black; Names ... Jenny, Laura.' - f In the album the query 'The character in history you most dislike' is left unanswered. - g Nothing human is alien to me (Terence, *Heautontimorumenos*, I, 1, 25) - h Doubt everything - i written on a sheet of paper bearing the stamp: 'International Working Men's Association / Central Council / London' - j the first volume of *Capital*

Your favourite virtue — simplicity
..... in man — strength
.... woman — weakness
chief characteristic — singleness of purpose
Idea of happiness
...... misery
The vice you excuse — gullibility servility
..... detest — Martin Tupper, Violet powder
Aversion
Favourite occupation — bookworming
.... Poet — Fantasies for Shakespeare, Goethe.
..... Prose writer — Diderot, Lessing, Hegel, Balzac
..... Hero — Spartacus, Keppler
..... Heroine — Gretchen.
..... Flower — Daphne.
..... Colour — Red.
Colour of eyes & hair — black.
Names — Jenny, Laura
Dish — fish
The characters in history you most dislike
— Maxim — nihil humani a me alienum puto
— Motto — De omnibus dubitandum

Karl Marx

A page from the album of Jenny, Marx's daughter,
containing Marx's 'Confession'

begun. I think that this new eruption is simply and solely due to overwork and long hours without sleep at night. He is very sorry not to be able to attend the meetings of the 'International', since the very existence of *The Workman's Advocate* is at stake right now; until now it has had the greatest difficulties to contend with and *fonds* are now being offered by philistines and parsons.[230] The attempt must now be made to get a hold on the money without making any concessions in point of principle to the 'MONEY-LENDERS'.[a] The Reform question, which is of such immediate practical concern to the English, is also making great demands on the resources, the time and the interest of the workers and is greatly distracting them from other matters.[b] Karl and I were most taken by your *Vorbote*. Both its language and its serious approach are manly indeed! I am enclosing Lessner's letter about it. The agent to whom I entrusted the *Manifestos*[c] has written to say that he has managed to prevent them from falling into the hands of the French police and that he can now send them off to Geneva.[622] However, they cannot be stamped, so I must ask you to write and say what outlay they committed you to. The money can then be sent you together with that for the subscriptions for the *Vorbote*.

With respect to religion, a great movement is currently developing in stuffy old England. The top men in science, Huxley (Darwin's disciple) at the head, with Tyndall, Sir Charles Lyell, Bowring, Carpenter, etc., give very enlightened, truly free-thinking and bold lectures for the people in St. Martin's Hall (of glorious waltzing memory[623]), and, what is more, on Sunday evenings, exactly at the time when the lambs are usually grazing on the Lord's pastures; the hall has been full to bursting and the people's enthusiasm so great that, on the first evening, when I went there with the girls, 2,000 could not get into the room, which was crammed full. The clerics let this dreadful thing happen three times.—Yesterday evening the assembly was informed that no more lectures could be held until the court case brought by the clerics against the 'SUNDAY EVENINGS FOR THE PEOPLE' had been decided. The gathering emphatically expressed its indignation and more than £100 were immediately collected for fighting the case. How stupid of the clerics to interfere in such a matter. To the annoyance of this band, the evenings even closed with music. Choruses from Händel, Mozart, Beethoven, Mendelsohn and Gounod were sung and received enthusiastically by the English,

---

[a] See this volume, p. 224. - [b] ibid., p. 150. - [c] K. Marx and F. Engels, *Manifesto of the Communist Party.*

who had, until now, only been allowed to bawl out the hymn JESUS, JESUS, MEEK AND MILD or take themselves off to the GIN palace.

Karl, who is in great pain today, and my girls send you their warmest greetings, the little one[a] in particular, asking me to convey very best wishes to 'dear Becker'. And I extend my hand to you from afar.

Yours

Jenny Marx

First published abridged in *Der Vorbote*, Jg. 1, No. 2, 1866 and in full in: Marx and Engels, *Works*, Second Russian Edition, Vol. 31, Moscow, 1963

Printed according to the original

Published in English in full for the first time

5

JENNY MARX TO SIGFRID MEYER

IN BERLIN

[London, beginning of February 1866]
1 Modena Villas, Maitland Park

Dear Sir,

For the past week my husband has again been laid low with his former dangerous and painful complaint; this fresh affliction is all the more distressing for him since it further interrupts him in the copying out of his book[b] that he has just begun. He is very sorry that you did not receive his lengthy letter,[c] as he is at the present moment incapable of writing. He also fears that the letter has been seized, as it should have been returned long ago otherwise. The address was, by the way, perfectly correct, and I took the letter to the post myself along with many others and the newspapers, all of which arrived. With regard to the *Manifesto*,[d] being a historical document, he wishes it to be printed exactly as it originally appeared; the misprints are so obvious that anyone can correct them. He will be sending the 'International Address'[e] to you as soon as he can.

---

[a] Eleanor Marx - [b] the first volume of *Capital* - [c] See this volume, p. 216. - [d] K. Marx and F. Engels, *Manifesto of the Communist Party*. - [e] K. Marx, 'Inaugural Address of the Working Men's International Association'.

At the same time, he asks you to let him know your new address for further correspondence, when you have left Berlin. And could not Mr Vogt,[a] in turn, give us another address, as we do not think his present one is quite safe. When you write back, kindly address to A. Williams,[b] Esq., etc.

My husband sends you his warmest greetings.

Yours
Jenny Marx

First published in: Marx and Engels, *Works*, First Russian Edition, Vol. XXV, Moscow, 1934

Printed according to the original

Published in English for the first time

6

JENNY MARX TO LUDWIG KUGELMANN

IN HANOVER

[London,] 26 February 1866[c]
1 Modena Villas, Maitland Park

Dear Sir,

For 4 weeks now my poor husband has been laid low again with his old, very painful and dangerous complaint, and no doubt I need scarcely tell you under what great and fearful anxieties we have all been suffering during that time. Right at the beginning of January he had begun to prepare his whole book[d] for printing, and he was making wonderfully rapid progress with copying, so that the manuscript piled up most impressively. Karl felt in the best of 'SPIRITS' and was happy to be so far on at last, when a carbuncle suddenly erupted, soon to be followed by 2 others. The last one was especially bad and obstinate and furthermore was so awkwardly placed that it prevented him from walking or moving at all. This morning it has been bleeding more strongly, which has brought him some relief. Two days ago we began the arsenic cure, of which Karl expects a good effect. It is really dreadful for him

---

[a] August Vogt - [b] Marx's conspiratorial pseudonym - [c] The date is written in by Kugelmann. - [d] the first volume of *Capital*

to be interrupted again in the completion of his book, and in his delirium at night he is forever talking of the various chapters which are going round and round in his mind. This morning I brought him your letter [a] in bed. He was very pleased that you had been kind enough to write, and he asked me to thank you at once for it on his behalf. A further concern is that his presence is sorely needed at this moment, both in the debates about the forthcoming congress of the International Association [286] and in the discussions about the policy and editing of the new workers' paper which is appearing weekly here now under the title of *Commonwealth* and represents both the newly formed workers' party, [b] with all the Co-operative Societies, and the International Association. [290] His anxiety about all this has naturally done much to worsen the general state of his health. I hope that by the spring he will be sufficiently restored to be able to visit his friends in Germany. He had been very much looking forward to doing so.

Karl sends you his warmest greetings, to which, despite our not being acquainted, I add my respects.

Yours truly

Jenny Marx

First published in: Marx and Engels, *Works*, First Russian Edition, Vol. XXV, Moscow, 1934

Printed according to the original

Published in English for the first time

7

JENNY MARX TO LUDWIG KUGELMANN

IN HANOVER

[London,] 1 April 1866
1 Modena Villas, Maitland Park

Dear Sir,

I presume that the registered letter that I received from Hanover late yesterday evening is from you. [c] I cannot send it on to my husband in Margate until tomorrow, [307] unfortunately, as in

---

[a] of 23 February 1866 - [b] the Reform League (see Note 155) - [c] Probably Kugelmann's letter to Marx of 30 March 1866.

pious England all communications halt on Sundays. Since the reply may be held up by this delay, I hasten to let you know immediately today that the letter has arrived safely; but, at the same time, I would like to take this opportunity to apologise to you for my total silence. Just how indebted I am to you for the great sympathy and touching friendship you have shown my husband was really brought home to me when the young man from the CITY called to enquire on your behalf as to my husband's condition. Immediately after my last letter to you, Karl really became gravely ill; a fresh CARBUNCLE (not a furuncle) erupted, and was indeed so obstinate and so inflammatory that for almost 3 weeks my poor husband could scarcely move and was entirely confined to the sofa. Since we are all only too well aware how dangerous this complaint is, if it keeps recurring over a period of years, you can well imagine how melancholy the days and nights have been for us.

On the advice of Doctor Gumpert in Manchester, he decided to begin the arsenic cure, as well as to spend a few weeks at the seaside after the abscess had healed. He has now been in Margate, a coastal resort quite near here, for nearly 2 weeks, and it seems to us that his health has been greatly restored there. He will return next week to pick up with renewed energy the completion of that work of his[a] which has so often been interrupted.

Yesterday he sent me his photogram, and since you would perhaps appreciate a sunny picture of the man to whom you have shown so much friendship, although you do not know him personally, I am enclosing 1 COPY with this note.

With all my respects, despite our not being acquainted

Yours truly

Jenny Marx

First published in: Marx and Engels, *Works,* Second Russian Edition, Vol. 31, Moscow, 1963

Printed according to the original

Published in English for the first time

---

[a] the first volume of *Capital*

8

JENNY MARX TO ENGELS

IN MANCHESTER

[London,] Monday 1 o'clock
[24 December 1866]

My dear Mr Engels,

The HAMPER has just arrived, and the bottles have been put on parade, with the Rhenish to the fore! How can we thank you for all your friendship! The £10 which arrived on Saturday will avert the harshest storms of Christmastide and enable us to celebrate a MERRY CHRISTMAS. The wine was particularly welcome this year, as with the young FRENCHMAN[a] in the house we like to keep up APPEARANCES.

If the publisher in Hamburg[b] really can print the book[c] as fast as he says, it is certain to come out by Easter in any case. It is a pleasure to see the manuscript lying there copied out and stacked up so high. It is an enormous weight off my mind; we have enough troubles and worries left without that, especially when the girls fall in love and become engaged, and to Frenchmen and MEDICAL STUDENTS to boot! I wish I could see everything *couleur de rose*[d] as much as the others do, but the long years with their many anxieties have made me nervous, and the future often looks black to me when it all looks rosy to a more cheerful spirit. *Cela entre nous.*[e]

Once more, a thousand thanks for the hock and all its train!

Yours

Jenny Marx

First published in: Marx and Engels, *Works*, Second Russian Edition, Vol. 31, Moscow, 1963

Printed according to the original

Published in English for the first time

---

[a] Paul Lafargue - [b] Otto Meissner - [c] the first volume of *Capital* - [d] in rosy colours - [e] This between ourselves.

9

JENNY MARX TO JOHANN PHILIPP BECKER

IN GENEVA

London, [5 October 1867]
1 Modena Villas, Maitland Park

My dear Mr Becker,

I hope you have received my letter. You will doubtless be surprised at seeing a second one following so close behind the first. My husband would like Bakunin's address, and I am quite sure that you will be able to get hold of it easily in Geneva, perhaps via Herzen. He would very much like to send him his book[a] and write on other matters. Warmest greetings from us all and especially from

Yours
Jenny Marx

First published in: Marx and Engels, *Works*, First Russian Edition, Vol. XXV, Moscow, 1934

Printed according to the original

Published in English for the first time

10

JENNY MARX TO LUDWIG KUGELMANN

IN HANOVER

[London, 24 December 1867]
1 Modena Villas, Maitland Park

My dear Mr Kugelmann,

You can have no idea of the delight and surprise you occasioned us yesterday, and I really do not know how I should thank you for all your friendship and sympathy, and especially now for the latest visible sign of your regard, old Father Zeus, who now occupies the

---

[a] the first volume of *Capital*

place of the 'baby Jesus' in our household.[585] Our Christmas festivities this year are again very much overshadowed by the fact that my poor husband is once more laid low with his old complaint. There have been 2 further eruptions, one of which is of some size and in a most painful spot, obliging Karl to lie on one side. I hope we shall soon get the better of this illness, and that in the next letter you will no longer be confronted with the temporary private secretary.

Yesterday evening we were all at home together sitting downstairs, which in English houses is the kitchen area from which all 'CREATURE COMFORTS' make their way up to the higher regions, and were busy preparing the CHRISTMAS PUDDING with all due thoroughness. We were seeding raisins (a most disagreeable and sticky task), chopping up almonds and orange and lemon peel, minutely shredding suet, and with eggs and flour kneading together the oddest potpourri from the whole mishmash; when all at once there was a ring at the door, a carriage was stopped outside, mysterious footsteps were going up and down, whispering and rustling filled the house; at length a voice sounded from above: 'A great statue has arrived.' If it had been 'Fire, fire, the house is on fire', the 'FENIANS' have come, we could not have dashed upstairs in greater astonishment or confusion, and there it stood in all its colossal splendour, in its ideal purity, old *Jupiter tonans*[a] himself, unscathed, undamaged (one small edge of the *piédestal* is slightly chipped) before our staring, delighted eyes!! Meanwhile, the confusion having somewhat abated, we then read the accompanying kind words you sent via Borkheim, and after pausing in deepest gratitude to you, we at once began debating which would be the worthiest niche for the new 'dear god who is there in heaven and on Earth'.[b] We have not yet resolved this great question, and we shall make many trials before that proud head finds its place of honour.

My warmest thanks to you also for your great interest and indefatigable efforts on behalf of Karl's book.[c] It would seem that the Germans' preferred form of applause is utter and complete silence. You have given fresh heart to all the moaners.

Dear Mr Kugelmann, you can believe me when I tell you there can be few books that have been written in more difficult circumstances, and I am sure I could write a secret history of it which would tell of many, extremely many unspoken troubles and anxieties and torments. If the workers had an inkling of the

---

[a] Jupiter the Thunderer - [b] Matthew 6:9, 10 - [c] the first volume of *Capital*

sacrifices that were necessary for this work, which was written only for them and for their sakes to be completed they would perhaps show a little more interest. The Lassalleans appear to be the quickest to seize the book, so that they may fittingly bowdlerise it. However, that will do no harm.

But to conclude, I have a bone to pick with you. Why do you address me so formally, even using the title 'gracious', for me, who am such an old campaigner, such a hoary head in the movement, such an honest fellow-traveller and fellow-tramp? I would so much have liked to visit you and your dear wife and Fränzchen[a] this summer, of whom my husband cannot stop saying so many nice and good things, I would so much have liked to see Germany again after 11 years.[624] I have often been unwell in the past year, and I am sorry to say that of late I have lost much of my 'faith', my courage in facing up to life. I often found it hard to keep my spirits up. However, since my girls were embarking on a long journey—they had been invited to stay with Lafargue's parents[b] in Bordeaux—it was impossible for me to undertake my own excursion at the same time, and it is therefore now my fondest hope for next year.

Karl sends his warmest greetings to your wife and to yourself, to which the girls sincerely add their own, and I extend my hand to you and your dear wife from afar.

Yours

Jenny Marx

not gracious and not by the grace of God.

First published, in Italian, in *Movimento Operaio*, No. 2, 1955

Printed according to the original

Published in English for the first time

---

[a] Franziska Kugelmann - [b] François and Virginie Lafargue

11

JENNY MARX TO JOHANN PHILIPP BECKER

IN GENEVA

[London, after 10 January 1868]
1 Modena Villas, Maitland Park

My dear Mr Becker,

Don't be cross with me for not replying sooner to your kind last letter. Unfortunately, the reason for my silence was not a happy one. For my poor husband has once again been laid up and fettered hand and foot by his old, serious and painful complaint, which is becoming dangerous through its constant recurrence. Nothing depresses him more than to be constantly condemned to idleness once again, particularly now when there is so much to be done, the 2nd part^a is demanded and, to put it shortly, when the world begins once again to burn and blaze, though for the time being with 'Greek fire', and not with the 'Red Cock'.^b The idlers and loafers have cash in their pockets and health in their blood, and the people who belong to the new world, who have devoted their bodies and souls to it, are sick—poor and thus well and trully locked in HANDCUFFS. 'SHAME, SHAME' as the English shout at their meetings. You will not believe how often my husband thinks of you, with sincere honour and admiration. He regards your little paper^c as quite definitely the best and most effective, and every time we receive news of our native kindergarten, or rather *Gartenlaube*,^d he exclaims: 'If only the Germans had more men like old Becker!!' As temporary secretary, I have just written to Schily and sent him the letter of the man who has offered to make the translation.⁶²⁵ You see, Moses Hess has also offered himself as translator through Schily and wanted to launch some preliminary *ballons d'essais*^e in the *Courrier français*.⁵³⁹ But we have long heard and seen nothing of the two gentlemen, but, to judge by the letter I just mentioned, the matter will be a success. Because of his education in philosophy, and his orientation in the arts of dialectical leaps and balances, Hess would be preferable to many other translators who would be simply literal, but, on the other hand, our mystical Rabbi Rabbuni is often not quite reliable (not

---

^a of *Capital* - ^b symbol of revolutionary action in the Peasant War in Germany - ^c *Der Vorbote* - ^d The title of a German magazine - ^e sounding balloons

quite kosher), and often careless, so it would be wrong to reject other offers because of him. Schily will now act as *chargé d'affaires*, and see which is the right man.

Your last article on the Peace dawdlers[461] was excellent,[a] and, by God (the Good Lord always springs *nolens volens*[b] to the lips and the pen, although he has long left the place of honour in our hearts), was the best that we have seen hitherto.

'Goegg' is still roaming around here on his propaganda merry-go-round. And Borkheim could have been smarter than to give him 100 fr. travelling expenses. If the coins are itching and burning a hole in his pocket like that, he should let them fall and burn elsewhere. I think there are better things to do than supporting these apostles. Amand[c] was dealt with quite differently by Engels in Manchester. For your amusement, here is a passage about it from Engels' letter.[d]

'Moreover, yesterday I had a visit from the ex-dictator Goegg, who is travelling for the ridiculous Peace League and who ruined my evening. Luckily, Schorlemmer' (a very important chemist, one of 'our people') 'also happened by, and got the surprise of his life with this fossil of Federal Republic; he had not believed such a thing possible. The stupid oaf has become ten times more stupid through the unthinking repetition of the same phrases, and has lost all points of contact with the world of common sense (not to mention actual thinking). Apart from Switzerland and the Canton of Baden, there is still nothing else in the world for people of this sort. For all that, he soon convinced himself of the truth of my first reply to his application for support: that the further apart we lived and the less we had to do with one another, the better we would get on.—He admitted that in the Vogt affair Blind has behaved like a *coward*, but said he was after all a worthy fellow, and even threatened to reconcile you and Blind! Vogt—no politician, but a decent fellow, honest to the backbone, who simply scribbled away in the daytime without considering the content—if we 2 spent an hour together then we would be like brothers. He admitted him to be a Bonapartist, but not a paid one. To which I replied that *all* Bonapartists were paid, there were no unpaid ones, and if he could show me an unpaid *one*, then I would accept the *possibility* that Vogt was not paid; otherwise I would not. This astonished him, but finally he discovered one—*Ludwig Bamberger*! Incidentally, he said that Vogt had continually had a very hard

---

[a] [J. Ph. Becker,] 'Zur Friedens- und Freiheitsliga', *Der Vorbote*, No. 12, December 1867. - [b] willy nilly - [c] Amand Goegg - [d] See this volume, pp. 517-18.

time, his wife was a peasant girl from the Bernese Oberland, whom he had married *out of virtue*. Vogt, the artful dodger, appears to have pulled the wool well over this jackass's eyes. But when Schorlemmer and I explained to him that Vogt had not produced anything as a natural scientist either, you should have seen his rage: Had he not popularised? Was not that worth while?' Thus Engels. So Goegg left empty-handed. Now he is trying his luck in other towns. Have you seen or heard anything of Bakunin? My husband sent his book ª to him as an old Hegelian,—not a sign near or far. Has he received it? You can't really trust all those Russians. If they don't adhere to the 'Väterchen' in Russia, then they adhere to, or are kept by, '*Herzens* Väterchen',ᵇ which in the end comes to the same thing. Six of one and half a dozen of the other.

Things look good here, the English are running away from themselves in panic, and, if somebody hears a cork pop, he imagines it is Greek fire, and if John Bull sees an innocent phosphorus match he believes it is impregnated with glycerine, paraffin, nicotine and God knows what, and starts to run, and soon everybody is running, and finally the genuine CONSTABLES are running ahead of the false BOBBIES, the so-called SPECIALS, who are now keeping order in the streets with their lead batons. Ireland has taken the lead in the entire political programme, the *English* are already shouting in favour of Ireland at their MEETINGS, and it has almost become respectable to lament the 7-hundred-year *suffering* of sweet Erin ᶜ—to weep over it; and all this has been accomplished by a phosphorus match and a rope.⁶²⁶ How easy is it to frighten the gentlemen out of their wits!? The short fear of physical means has accomplished more than centuries of moral threats.ᵈ

First published in: Marx and Engels, *Works*, Second Russian Edition, Vol. 32, Moscow, 1964

Printed according to the original

Published in English for the first time

ª the first volume of *Capital* - ᵇ A play on words: *Väterchen*, father, little father, meaning here 'the Tsar', and *Herzens Väterchen*, meaning 'dear father', a reference to the name Herzen (Jenny Marx alludes to Bakunin's connections with Alexander Herzen). - ᶜ old name of Ireland - ᵈ The manuscript breaks off here.

12

LAURA MARX TO ENGELS

IN MANCHESTER

[London,] 13 January 1868

Dear Engels,

As Mohr is once more being victimised by his old enemies, the carbuncles, and is, by the arrival of the latest, made to feel very ill at ease in a sitting posture, he has asked me to write you these lines in his stead.

As regards the article for *The Fortnightly Review*,[509] I am to tell you that there is no question of a mere brief notice like the reviews of books generally found at the back of that periodical, but of an article of the length of those usually inserted.

Also I am to beg you to send back, as soon as possible, the earlier numbers of the *Courrier français*.[a]

With best regards from all of us and in the hope that the late frequent Christmas entertainments you have been 'undergoing' may not have interfered with your health, I remain, dear Engels,

Affectionately yours,

Laura Marx

First published in the language of the original, English, in: Friedrich Engels, Paul et Laura Lafargue, *Correspondance*, Tome I, Paris, 1956

Reproduced from the original

---

[a] See this volume, pp. 508, 520 and 523.

NOTES
AND
INDEXES

NOTES

[1] This letter was published in English for the first time in Karl Marx, *On the First International*. Arranged and edited, with an introduction and new translations by Saul K. Padover, New York, 1973.—3, 64, 92, 148, 191, 218, 314

[2] In his letter to Marx of 28 September 1864, Carl Klings, a former member of the Communist League (see Note 17), wrote about the situation in the General Association of German Workers after the death of its President, Ferdinand Lassalle, and about the forthcoming election of a new president. Bernhard Becker and Moses Hess were nominated candidates, and Klings asked Marx for advice.

The *General Association of German Workers*, which was founded at the congress of workers' associations in Leipzig on 23 May 1863 and included a number of former members of the Communist League, promoted the development of the German working-class movement and helped its members to overcome the ideological influence of the liberal bourgeoisie. However, Lassalle and his followers channelled the Association's activity along reformist lines limiting it to the campaign for universal suffrage; their programme contained a utopian demand for the establishment of state-subsidised producers' co-operatives, which they regarded as the basic means for solving social contradictions. The leaders of the Association supported the Prussian government in its drive for the unification of Germany 'from above', through dynastic wars.

The sectarian, nationalistic policy of the Lassallean leaders of the General Association made it difficult to draw the German proletariat into the International Working Men's Association (the First International) (see Note 5). By the beginning of the 1870s, however, the progressive-minded German workers had split away from Lassalleanism thanks to the consistent efforts of Marx, Engels and their associates. At a congress in Gotha in May 1875, the General Association of German Workers merged with the German Social-Democratic Workers' Party (Eisenachers) founded in 1869 and headed by August Bebel and Karl Liebknecht. The united party assumed the name of the Socialist Workers' Party of Germany.—3, 15, 58, 65, 75, 78, 103, 125, 135, 141, 150

[3] The proposal to accept the presidency of the General Association of German Workers was made to Marx by Wilhelm Liebknecht in his letters, written at the

beginning of September and early October 1864. Liebknecht also wrote that Bernhard Becker and Johann Baptist Schweitzer, its leaders, backed him in this request.—3

4 At the additional elections to the Corps législatif in March 1864 the Parisian workers put up their own candidate, the engraver Henri Tolain, whereas previously they voted for moderate bourgeois republicans. In the 'Manifesto of the Sixty' printed in February 1864 they explained this move by the need of the working class to have its own representatives in legislative bodies.

The *Corps législatif* was established, alongside the State Council and the Senate, under the Constitution of 4 February 1852, following the Bonaparte coup d'état of 1851. The members of the State Council and the Senate were appointed by the head of state, while the Corps législatif was an elected body, the elections being supervised by state officials and the police, so that a docile majority was always ensured. As its powers were confined to endorsing bills drawn up by the State Council, the Corps législatif was, in effect, a screen for Napoleon III's unlimited rule.—4, 15, 47, 274, 318

5 The inaugural meeting of the International Working Men's Association held in London on 28 September 1864 planned to call an international workers' congress in Belgium in a year's time to solve questions relating to the Rules and leadership of the entire organisation. At its meeting on 1 November 1864, the Central Council of the Association, elected on 28 September (known as the General Council from 1866), approved the Provisional Rules which made it incumbent upon the Council to convene the congress in Belgium. However, taking into account the ideological and organisational weakness of the national sections of the International, Marx proposed to convene a preliminary conference in London in September 1865 to discuss the programme of the future congress. The conference took place in London between 25 and 29 September 1865 (see Note 246).—4

6 This letter was published in English for the first time in *The Letters of Karl Marx*, selected and translated with explanatory notes and an introduction by Saul K. Padover, Prentice-Hall Inc., Englewood Cliffs, New Jersey, 1979.—5, 193, 231, 330, 356, 397, 493, 553

7 On 2 September 1864 Engels wrote to Marx about his intention to travel to Schleswig and Holstein annexed to Prussia (Schleswig) and Austria (Holstein) after the defeat of Denmark in the war of 1864. Engels left Manchester on 8 September and after a short stay with Marx in London (presumably on 9 September) travelled to the Continent. He returned to England in mid-October.—6, 11

8 Wilhelm Wolff (nicknamed Lupus), a friend and associate of Marx and Engels, died on 9 May 1864. In his will he named Marx and his family as principal beneficiaries of his small legacy. The legal procedure for receiving this legacy cost much trouble and energy, and Engels offered Marx his help.—6, 20, 21, 23, 29, 115, 116, 126

9 Engels is referring to the fact that the Bismarck government used the national contradictions between the duchies of Schleswig and Holstein and Denmark to promote Germany's unification under the aegis of Prussia. On 13 November 1863 the Danish Parliament adopted a new constitution which proclaimed the annexation of Schleswig to Denmark in violation of the London Protocol of 1852 (the latter stipulated that Denmark and the duchies could be linked only by personal union). This served as a pretext for Bismarck to declare war on

Denmark. Austria joined Prussia for she did not want Prussia, her main rival in Germany, to enjoy the fruits of victory alone. As a result of the Danish war (1 February-16 July 1864), a treaty was concluded in Vienna on 30 October 1864 which declared Schleswig and Holstein to be co-possessions of Austria and Prussia. After the 1866 Austro-Prussian war the two duchies were annexed to Prussia.— 7, 34, 121, 350

10 Part of this letter was published in English for the first time in Marx and Engels, *On the United States*, Progress Publishers, Moscow, 1979.— 9, 61, 418, 451

11 The *Civil War in America* broke out in April 1861. The Southern slaveholders rose against the Union and formed the Confederacy of the Southern States. The war was caused mainly by the conflict between the two social systems: the capitalist system of wage labour established in the North and the slave system dominant in the South. The Civil War, which had the nature of a bourgeois-democratic revolution, underwent two stages in its development: the period of a constitutional war for maintaining the Union and the period of a revolutionary war for the abolition of slavery. The decisive role in the defeat of the Southern slaveholders and the victory of the North in April 1865 was played by the workers, farmers and the Negroes. The causes and the nature of war in America were analysed by Marx in the articles published in the Vienna newspaper *Die Presse* (see present edition, Vol. 19).

The discontinuance of cotton imports from America as a result of the blockade of the Southern States by the Northern fleet caused a crisis in the cotton industry of several European countries. In England, for two or three years beginning in 1862, over 75 per cent of the spinners and weavers in Lancashire, Cheshire and other counties were fully or partly unemployed. Despite privation and distress, the European proletariat gave all possible support to the American fighters against slavery.— 10, 38, 61, 199, 269, 523

12 Engels has in mind the war against the Kingdom of Italy (formed in March 1861) waged by the counter-revolutionary forces under the former King of Naples, Francis II (he was dethroned in 1860 as a result of the liberation of Sicily and Southern Italy by Garibaldi). The actions of the Naples reactionaries assumed the form of brigandage.— 10, 39

13 Part of this letter was published in English for the first time in the *Labour Monthly*, No. 4, London, 1923.— 11

14 Marx means the death of Ferdinand Lassalle on 31 August 1864 after being fatally wounded in a duel with the Romanian nobleman Janko von Racowiţa.— 12

15 Lassalle spoke before the Düsseldorf assizes on 27 June 1864. His speech was first published in the *Düsseldorfer Zeitung*, Nos. 176-78 for 1864, and appeared separately under the title *Prozeß gegen den Schriftsteller Herrn Ferdinand Lassalle, verhandelt zu Düsseldorf vor der korrektionellen Appelkammer am 27. Juni 1864*, Düsseldorf, 1864.— 12, 38

16 The congress (general assembly) of the General Association of German Workers met in Düsseldorf on 27 December 1864. It elected Bernhard Becker President of the Association.— 15

17 A reference to the *Communist League*, the first German and international communist organisation of the proletariat formed under the leadership of Marx and Engels in London early in June 1847, as a result of the

reorganisation of the League of the Just (a secret association of workers and artisans that appeared in the 1830s and had communities in Germany, France, Switzerland and England). The programme and organisational principles of the Communist League were drawn up with the direct participation of Marx and Engels. The League's members took an active part in the bourgeois-democratic revolution in Germany in 1848-49. Though the defeat of the revolution dealt a blow to the League, in 1849-50 it was reorganised and continued its activities. In the summer of 1850, disagreements arose in the League between the supporters of Marx and Engels and the sectarian Willich-Schapper group which tried to impose on the League its adventurist tactics of immediately unleashing a revolution without taking into account the actual situation and the practical possibilities. The discord resulted in a split within the League. Owing to police persecutions and arrests of League members in May 1851, the activities of the Communist League as an organisation practically ceased in Germany. On 17 November 1852, on a motion by Marx, the London District announced the dissolution of the League.

The Communist League played an important historical role as the first proletarian party based on the principles of scientific communism, as a school of proletarian revolutionaries, and as the historical forerunner of the International Working Men's Association.— 15

18 Marx is referring to the *London Trades Council*, first elected at a conference of trade union delegates held in London in May 1860. It headed the London trade unions numbering many thousands of members and was influential amongst the British workers. In the first half of the 1860s the Council directed the British workers' campaign against intervention in the USA, in defence of Poland and Italy, and later for the legal status of the trade unions. The leaders of the following large trade unions played a big role in the Council: the Amalgamated Society of Carpenters and Joiners (Robert Applegarth), the Shoemakers' Society (George Odger), the Operative Bricklayers' Society (Edwin Coulson and George Howell) and the Amalgamated Engineers (William Allan).

The London Trades Council's representatives took part in establishing the International Working Men's Association (the First International) and were members of its Central (General) Council. But, while maintaining contacts with the International Association and collaborating with it, the London Council, influenced by some reformist trade unionists, refused (finally in January 1867) to officially affiliate to it as an English section.

The *Trades' Unionists Manhood Suffrage and Vote by Ballot Association* was founded in September 1864. Odger was its President, Hartwell its Secretary, and Trimlett its Treasurer. Subsequently all of them became members of the Central (General) Council of the International Working Men's Association.— 15, 154, 329, 519

19 On 26 March 1863 the London Trades Council held a meeting at St James's Hall to express the British workers' solidarity with the struggle of the North American States to abolish slavery. The participants also protested against Britain's plans for armed intervention in the US Civil War (see Note 11) on the side of the Southern States. The meeting was chaired by the bourgeois radical John Bright.

In early April 1864, Garibaldi visited England with a view to raising funds for an expedition to end Austrian domination in Venetia. The English public at large gave an enthusiastic welcome to Italy's national hero and official honours were therefore heaped on him at the beginning of his visit. However, Garibaldi's meeting with Mazzini, who lived in England as a political emigrant, and his speeches in support of the Polish insurgents angered the British ruling circles.

Garibaldi left England at the end of April.— 15, 33, 44, 45, 47

20 Marx is referring to the *Associazione di Mutuo Progresso* founded at the end of June 1864 by the Italian workers resident in London. Initially the Society numbered about 300 members and was influenced by Mazzini. Garibaldi was elected its Honorary President. In January 1865 the Society became affiliated to the International Association.— 16, 110, 140, 150, 170, 250

21 The *Sub-Committee* or *Standing Committee* was the executive body of the Central (General) Council of the International. It usually assembled once a week and drafted many of the decisions which were later adopted by the Council. The Sub-Committee evolved from a commission, elected when the International Working Men's Association was set up, to draft its programme documents. The Sub-Committee included the President of the General Council (until this office was abolished in September 1867), its General Secretary and the corresponding secretaries for the different countries. Marx took an active part in the work of the Standing Committee as Corresponding Secretary for Germany.— 16, 54, 130, 131, 172, 207, 214, 486

22 The Statutes submitted by Luigi Wolff at a meeting of the Sub-Committee on 8 October 1864 were an English translation of 'l'Atto di fratellanza delle Società operaie italiane' (Fraternal Bond Between the Italian Workmen's Associations) published in *Il Giornale delle Associazioni Operaie* on 31 July 1864 and adopted at the eleventh congress of Italian pro-Mazzini working men's associations in Naples on 27 October 1864. Attended by delegates from 57 organisations, the congress set up an association of Italian workers' societies which joined the International Working Men's Association. By submitting to the International these Statutes, written from bourgeois-democratic positions, Mazzini and his followers sought to take over the leadership of the international working-class movement.— 16, 44, 47

23 A reference to the following passage in the Provisional Rules of the Association: '...This International Association and all societies and individuals adhering to it, will acknowledge truth, justice, and morality, as the basis of their conduct towards each other, and towards all men, without regard to colour, creed, or nationality;

'They hold it the duty of a man to claim the rights of a man and a citizen, not only for himself, but for every man who does his duty. No rights without duties, no duties without rights' (see present edition, Vol. 20, p. 15).— 18, 47

24 In January 1863 an uprising against Tsarist oppression flared up in the Kingdom of Poland, the territory annexed to Russia by decision of the Vienna Congress of 1815. The uprising of 1863-64 was caused by the Poles' striving for national independence and the crisis of feudal relations within the Kingdom. The National Central Committee, which headed the uprising, put forward a programme of struggle for Poland's independence and a number of democratic agrarian demands. However, the inconsistency and indecision of the insurgent government, in particular its failure to abolish the privileges of the big landowners, drove the majority of the peasants away from the uprising. This was one of the main causes of its defeat.

In addition, serious damage to the uprising was done by the policy of its Right-wing leaders. They pinned great hopes on help from the ruling circles of

Bonapartist France and bourgeois-aristocratic England who were pursuing their own selfish interests in the Polish question.

The national liberation uprising was, by and large, crushed by the Tsarist government in the autumn of 1863, though some units of the insurgents continued the struggle until the end of 1864.—19, 38, 73, 164

25 In his articles denouncing the diplomacy of the ruling classes Marx made use of the documents which the conservative writer David Urquhart, who was in opposition to the British government, published in his periodicals *The Portfolio* and *The Free Press*. While printing his separate articles in *The Free Press*, Marx criticised Urquhart and his followers for their anti-democratic views and always emphasised the fundamental difference between his position as a proletarian revolutionary and that of the Urquhartists.—19

26 Part of this letter was published in English for the first time in Karl Marx, Friedrich Engels, *Selected Letters. The Personal Correspondence, 1844-1877*, Boston, Toronto, 1981.—19, 178, 225, 269, 309, 343, 348, 352, 370, 445, 450, 527, 538

27 The original has 'inneren Düppel', an expression first used in the meaning of 'enemy within' in a political survey published in the Bismarckian *Norddeutsche Allgemeine Zeitung* on 30 September 1864. It became widely current later.

Düppel (Dybböl)—Danish fortification in Schleswig which the Prussians captured by storm on 18 April 1864, during the war of Prussia and Austria against Denmark (see Note 9).—19, 121, 254, 256, 263

28 The *Schiller Institute*, founded in Manchester in November 1859 in connection with the centenary of Friedrich Schiller's birth, strove to be a German émigré cultural and social centre. Engels was critical of the Institute, noted for its tendency to formalism and pedantry, and he initially kept aloof from it. But when certain changes were introduced into its Rules, he became a member of its Directorate in 1864. Later, as the President of the Institute, Engels devoted much time to it and exercised a considerable influence on its activities.

In September 1868, while Engels was away from Manchester, the Institute invited Karl Vogt, who was connected with the Bonapartists and was slandering the proletarian revolutionaries, to deliver a lecture. Engels felt that his political reputation would be compromised if he remained President and so he left the Directorate. In April 1870 he was again elected a member of the Directorate of the Schiller Institute, but did not take an active part in it.—20, 49, 81, 98, 116, 127, 235, 498, 503, 533, 555, 560

29 Part of this letter was published in English for the first time in K. Marx and F. Engels, *The Civil War in the United States*, International Publishers, New York, [1937].—21, 49, 81, 84, 147, 149, 151, 154, 161, 167

30 Engels is referring to the operations of the Northerners at the final stage of the Civil War in America (see Note 11) when, during the general offensive started in May 1864, they besieged Richmond (Virginia), the capital of the Southern Confederacy and its main stronghold. The Southerners entrenched in Richmond resisted until April 1865, when the city was seized by the army of General Grant.—21, 39, 61, 82, 113, 121, 147, 153

31 Engels is referring to the nearly nine-month-long siege of Sevastopol during the Crimean war of 1853-56.—21

32 In April 1863 the British Parliament passed the *Public Works Act* in view of the reduced production and mass unemployment in the cotton districts of England. This Act provided the municipal authorities of these districts with funds to pay the

unemployed temporarily used for public works, mainly on laying the sewerage system, building roads, etc. The Relief Committees, which guarded the interests of the capitalists, were in charge of organising these works and paying the workers. The unemployed were forced to agree to hard labour for miserable pay.

The *ateliers nationaux* (national workshops) were instituted by the French Provisional Government immediately after the February revolution of 1848. By this means the government sought to discredit Louis Blanc's ideas on 'the organisation of labour' in the eyes of the workers and, at the same time, to utilise those employed in the national workshops, organised on military lines, against the revolutionary proletariat. Revolutionary ideas, however, continued to gain ground in the national workshops. The government took steps to reduce the number of workers employed in them, to send a large number off to public works in the provinces and finally to liquidate the workshops. This precipitated a proletarian uprising in Paris in June 1848. After its suppression, the Cavaignac government issued a decree on 3 July, disbanding the national workshops.—21, 117

[33] Part of this letter was published in English for the first time in Karl Marx, *On the First International*. Arranged and edited, with an introduction and new translations by Saul K. Padover, New York, 1973.—22, 53, 107, 128, 139, 157, 206, 212, 213, 216, 223, 237, 249, 252, 258, 277, 282, 317, 341, 350, 416, 419, 427, 432, 437

[34] In their letters of 11 November 1864, Schweitzer and Liebknecht invited Marx to contribute to *Der Social-Demokrat*, the prospective newspaper of the General Association of German Workers (see Note 2). In the same month, Schweitzer sent Marx and Engels the prospectus, which did not contain Lassalle's slogans. Since they had no other press organ to influence the workers' movement in Germany, they agreed to collaborate with *Der Social-Demokrat*. They also took into account the fact that Wilhelm Liebknecht was an unofficial member of its editorial board. Marx's 'Inaugural Address of the Working Men's International Association' and 'On Proudhon', and Engels' translation of the old Danish folk song 'Herr Tidmann' were printed in the newspaper. However, fully convinced that Schweitzer, the editor of the newspaper, was continuing the Lassallean policy of flirting with the government and the Junkers and trying to spread the cult of Lassalle, Marx and Engels on 23 February 1865 announced their break with the newspaper (see present edition, Vol. 20, p. 80). Wilhelm Liebknecht followed suit and refused to collaborate with the paper.—22, 102, 136

[35] Engels' letter to Schweitzer has not been found.

This letter of Engels to Marx and Marx's reply of 18 November 1864 show that Engels wrote to Schweitzer expressing his agreement to contribute to *Der Social-Demokrat* but asked Schweitzer first to let him know who the proposed contributors were.—24

[36] Engels is referring to the Kinkel-inspired campaign in the English press in defence of MacDonald, a British captain arrested in Bonn in September 1860 and brought to trial for disobeying the local authorities; and to the campaign by Kinkel, Hermann Juch and others in defence of a German tailor, Franz Müller, living in London, who was sentenced to death in the autumn of 1864 for assassinating an Englishman. Müller confessed his guilt to the priest Cappell on the gallows.

In mid-November 1864 the newspapers reported that the body of a man, presumably a German, had been found in the Thames, near London. The Dutchman Koehl was suspected.—25, 48

[37] Marx's letter, like one from Engels, to Schweitzer has not been found. Marx also wrote about collaboration with *Der Social-Demokrat* (see Note 34).—26

[38] Marx presumably means the leading article, 'Bescheidenheit—ein Ehrenkleid' (Modesty—a Festive Garment), published in the Stuttgart *Beobachter* (No. 245) on 21 October 1864. It ridiculed Karl Blind's address to the American people (on the occasion of presidential elections), which was distinguished for his excessive claims to political importance and boasting. The article was probably written by the paper's editor, Karl Mayer.—27

[39] This refers to the second congress of the *Union of German Workers' Associations* (set up in June 1863) which met in Leipzig on 23-24 October 1864. The Union at this stage was still under the influence of the liberal bourgeoisie (Schulze-Delitzsch and other members of the Party of Progress—see Note 99). The congress developed into a fierce battle between the followers of Schulze-Delitzsch and members of the General Association of German Workers (see Note 2), the latter striving to persuade the workers' educational societies into adopting the Lassallean political programme (the demand for universal suffrage). The young August Bebel was elected, among others, into the Union's leading body. Under his influence the organisation began to shake off the liberals' tutelage and acquire a proletarian class character.

Professor Huber, mentioned by Marx, was a conservative champion of co-operativism and attended the congress as a guest.—27

[40] The cotton crisis was caused by the stoppage of cotton deliveries from America because of the blockade of the slave-holding Southern States by the Northern fleet during the US Civil War of 1861-65 (see Note 11). The cotton famine in England occurred shortly before the crisis of overproduction.—27, 53, 116

[41] In a letter to Engels of 19 November 1864, Schweitzer, in reply to Engels' enquiry, named the proposed contributors to *Der Social-Demokrat*. They were: Moses Hess, Georg Herwegh, Bernhard Becker, Johann Philipp Becker, Wilhelm Liebknecht, Friedrich Wilhelm Rüstow and Johann Karl Heinrich Wuttke.—29

[42] In her letter to Marx of 21 November 1864, Countess von Hatzfeldt wrote that a pamphlet in commemoration of Lassalle was being prepared and asked Marx's advice about illustrations. The pamphlet *Ferdinand Lassalle. Dokumentarische Darstellung seine letzten Lebenstage. Von Augenzeugen und Freunden* appeared in Berlin in 1865. At first Wilhelm Liebknecht agreed to edit it, but when he learned, at the end of 1864, about Lassalle's direct association with Bismarck, he refused to take part in the work.

The Countess also asked Marx to come out in defence of Lassalle against the attacks on him by the petty-bourgeois democrat Karl Blind.—29, 44

[43] Marx's letter to Liebknecht in which Marx enquired about the contributors to *Der Social-Demokrat* has not been found. In his reply of 2 December 1864, Liebknecht wrote that Lothar Bucher and Johann Rodbertus had gone over to the side of the Prussian government.—30

[44] In this article Karl Blind, polemising with the Lassalleans, quoted Lassalle's defence speech at the Berlin assizes in March 1864.—30, 57

[45] In the pamphlet in honour of Lassalle's memory (see Note 42) Countess von Hatzfeldt intended to place, next to a photograph of Lassalle on his death bed, portraits of Janko von Racowiţa and Helene von Dönniges, who were guilty of his death, regarding this as a form of revenge on the 'assassins'. In a letter to Marx on 21 November 1864 she asked Marx for his opinion of her intention.—30, 31

[46] Marx's telegram has not been found.—31, 288, 297

[47] Wilhelm Wolff, to whom Marx dedicated the first volume of *Capital*, died in Manchester on 9 May 1864. Marx delivered a short oration at his funeral (see Marx's letter to Jenny Marx of 13 May 1864, present edition, Vol. 41).—31

[48] In his pamphlet *Herr Vogt* (a copy of which Marx sent to Lassalle and Sophie von Hatzfeldt after its publication), Marx exposed Blind's cowardly attempts to deny his authorship of the flysheet *Zur Warnung* (A Warning) (it was published in London in 1859 and reprinted in the Augsburg *Allgemeine Zeitung*), which revealed Vogt's connections with the Bonapartists. Blind's statements in the press citing false evidence of Fidelio Hollinger, the owner of a print-shop where the flysheet had been printed, and of a compositor, Johann Wiehe, gave Vogt a pretext to attribute the authorship of the flysheet to Marx and his friends.—31

[49] On 15 November 1859 Marx sent Lassalle his reply to Blind's declaration regarding Karl Vogt (see present edition, Vol. 40, p. 526), asking him to have it published in the Berlin *Volks-Zeitung*. In his reply of 20 November 1859 Lassalle recommended Marx to avoid any controversy with Blind in the press. Marx's declaration was published in the supplement to the *Allgemeine Zeitung*, No. 325, 21 November 1859 (see present edition, Vol. 17, pp. 8-9).—32

[50] Lassalle was in London in July 1862.—32, 101

[51] Marx presumably means the members of the *Deutsche Freiheit und Einheit*, an association which was founded in London about 1860 and included, besides Blind, Eduard Bronner, Karl Heinrich Schaible, Ravenstein (secretary) and Wolffsohn (cashier).—32

[52] In view of Garibaldi's forthcoming visit to England, the German refugees in London set up a Garibaldi Committee on 6 April 1864. It included Blind, Juch (publisher of the *Hermann*), Trübner, Freiligrath, Kinkel and others.

Blind met Garibaldi on the Isle of Wight on 9 April. Blind and his associates took advantage of the meeting with Italy's national hero to advertise themselves in the English press.—33

[53] The *Shakespeare Committee* was set up to mark the tercentenary of Shakespeare's birthday which was celebrated from 23 April to 3 May 1864. German men of letters were represented by Freiligrath, who recommended that Karl Blind should also be a member of the committee.—35

[54] In the spring of 1849, during an uprising in defence of the Imperial Constitution in Southern and Western Germany, a Provisional Government was formed in Baden headed by the petty-bourgeois democrat Lorenz Peter Brentano. In face of the impending intervention of Prussian troops in Baden and the Palatinate, this government, having in fact sabotaged the actions of the revolutionary masses, applied for help to France. Karl Blind was sent to Paris with this purpose. The Baden government counted on the support of the party of petty-bourgeois democrats headed by Ledru-Rollin, but by that time it had

been pushed into the background by the bourgeois 'party of Order' and the Bonapartists. This predetermined the failure of Blind's mission.—35

55 The *Low Church*—a trend in the Anglican Church which laid special emphasis on Christian morality; its following originally consisted predominantly of the bourgeoisie and the lower clergy.

Pietism—a trend in the Lutheran Church that emerged in Germany in the seventeenth century. Distinguished by extreme mysticism, it rejected rites and attached special importance to personal religious experience.—36, 426

56 Blind's address 'Ein Freundeswort an Deutschlands Arbeiter, Bürger und Bauer' was published in a number of German newspapers and as a leaflet in June 1863. In it, Blind opposed Lassalle's agitation among the workers saying that the campaign for universal suffrage did not accord with the 'main principles of German democracy'.—36

57 Part of this letter was published in English for the first time in K. Marx and F. Engels, *Letters to Americans. 1848-1895*, International Publishers, New York, 1953.—37, 43, 121

58 Engels' correspondence with Joseph Weydemeyer was interrupted by the Civil War in America, in which Weydemeyer fought on the side of the North. In a letter written at the end of October 1864, Weydemeyer told Engels about Karl Blind's attacks on Lassalle in the American press and sent him a cutting from *Die Westliche Post* with Blind's article 'Ein Republikanischer Protest'. Engels forwarded Weydemeyer's letter to Marx who quoted it in his statement 'To the Editor of the Stuttgart *Beobachter*' (see present edition, Vol. 20, p. 23).—37, 40

59 The *Carlists*—a reactionary clerico-absolutist group in Spain consisting of adherents of the pretender to the Spanish throne Don Carlos, the brother of Ferdinand VII. Relying on the military and the Catholic clergy, and also making use of the support of the backward peasants in some regions of Spain, the Carlists launched in 1833 a civil war which in fact turned into a struggle between the feudal-Catholic and liberal-bourgeois elements and led to the third bourgeois revolution (1834-43).—39

60 The *battle at Pittsburgh-Landing*, also known as the *battle of Shiloh*, took place on 6-7 April 1862 on the Tennessee River, twenty miles north of Corinth. The Northern army under General Grant inflicted a heavy blow to the Confederate troops commanded by generals Johnston and Beauregard.—40

61 *Sonderburg* (now *Sønderborg*)—the town and fortress on the Alsen Island, one of the strongpoints on the Düppel fortification line captured by Prussian troops on 18 April 1864, during the war of Prussia and Austria against Denmark (see notes 9 and 27).—40

62 *Der Beobachter*, No. 268, 17 November 1864 carried an anonymous report from Bradford, which was a reply to the criticism of Blind in the newspaper's leading article 'Bescheidenheit—ein Ehrenkleid' published on 21 October 1864 (see Note 38). The anonymous writer exaggerated Blind's role in the political life of the USA. He also attempted to dispute the reference of the leader's author to the description of Blind by Marx in his *Herr Vogt*, and to refute the pamphlet's revelations concerning Blind's cowardly attitude towards Vogt's slanderous campaign against proletarian revolutionaries (see Note 48). All this prompted Marx to write a letter to the editor of *Der Beobachter* on 28 November 1864 (see present edition, Vol. 20, pp. 23-25). At the request of Sophie von Hatzfeldt, a

friend of Ferdinand Lassalle, Marx also came out in this letter against Blind's attacks on Lassalle.—41, 42, 44, 51, 107

63 Marx is referring to the *affidavits* made by two London compositors, Wiehe and Vögele, on Blind's authorship of the flysheet *Zur Warnung* (see Note 48), which exposed Karl Vogt as a Bonapartist agent. Blind cravenly denied his participation in composing the flysheet, thus making Marx's campaign against Vogt's lies more difficult. Marx described Blind's cowardly behaviour both in *Herr Vogt* (see present edition, Vol. 17, pp. 128-31 and 318-20) and the statement 'To the Editor of the Stuttgart *Beobachter*' (Vol. 20).—41, 518

64 The *Beobachter* editor confined himself to publishing only the covering letter to Marx's statement (see present edition, Vol. 20, p. 22) and his own 'comments' on this statement.

Marx foresaw that the *Beobachter* editor might not publish his statement and sent a copy of it to Sophie von Hatzfeldt for publication in other German papers. Without notifying Marx, the Countess sent the statement to Karl Bruhn, the editor of the Lassallean *Nordstern*. He published it on 10 December 1864, with the following editorial note: 'We have got the article through second hand, and only because of this particular circumstance is it accepted for publication in the *Nordstern*.' Marx expressed his indignation at this in a letter to Sophie von Hatzfeldt on 22 December (see this volume, pp. 56-57).—43, 53, 57

65 This letter was published in English for the first time in Karl Marx, *Letters to Dr. Kugelmann*, Co-operative Publishing Society of Foreign Workers in the USSR, Moscow-Leningrad, 1934.—45, 101, 220, 262, 311, 325, 327, 329, 346, 379, 395, 440, 449, 489, 496, 521, 528, 543, 551

66 This refers to Marx's plans for the publication of his main work, *Capital*. At that time, Wilhelm Strohn, at Marx's request, conducted talks with the Hamburg publishing house of Meissner and Behre. At the end of January 1865, a preliminary agreement was reached on publishing the book in two volumes. The text of the agreement (see present edition, Vol. 20, p. 361) was sent to Marx by Meissner in his letter of 21 March 1865.—46, 78

67 Part of this letter was published in English for the first time in K. Marx, *On America and the Civil War*. Edited and translated by Saul K. Padover, New York, 1972.—46, 413

68 From 1799 to 1805 and 1814 to 1866 the Venetian Region was part of the Austrian Empire and a centre of the Italian national liberation movement against Austrian rule, of which the Bismarck government made use when preparing for a war with Austria for supremacy in Germany.—47, 54

69 The *High Church*—a trend in the Anglican Church which stressed the latter's derivation from Catholicism, maintained the traditional rituals and originally drew its following mainly from the aristocracy.—48

70 The address 'To Abraham Lincoln, President of the United States of America' (see present edition, Vol. 20) was written by Marx on the occasion of Lincoln's re-election to the presidency. The text was approved by the Sub-Committee, unanimously confirmed by the Central Council of the International Working Men's Association on 29 November 1864 and sent to President Lincoln through Adams, the American envoy to London.—49

[71] In view of the anniversary of the Polish insurrection of 1830-31, the Central Council of the International resolved, on Peter Fox's proposal, at its meeting of 29 November 1864 to issue an address to the Polish people on behalf of the British members of the Council. The latter delegated the drafting of the address to the Sub-Committee, which in its turn instructed Fox accordingly. Fox's address, however, reflected the view current among the Right-wing Polish émigrés and certain West European bourgeois democrats. It alleged that the foreign policy of the French ruling circles favoured the restoration of Poland's independence. That was why Marx and other members of the Sub-Committee and the Central Council opposed it (see Marx's letter to Engels of 10 December 1864, and Note 77).— 49, 54

[72] The London Amalgamated Union of Building Workers (George Potter, a reformist, was one of its leaders) started a campaign for a nine-hour working day in 1859. At the end of July 1859 they called a strike in response to the employers' refusal to reduce working hours. At a joint meeting on 27 July the employers declared open war on the trade unions. They refused to employ their members and on 6 August locked out over 20,000 workers. The strike ended in February 1860 with a compromise: the employers agreed to take on trade union members, while the workers were compelled to withdraw their demand for a nine-hour working day.— 50

[73] Heinrich Heine caustically derided Karl Mayer, a poet of the reactionary-Romantic Swabian school, in his *Atta Troll* (Chap. 22) and in *Deutschland. Ein Wintermärchen* (Chap. 3).— 52

[74] Hermann Becker (nicknamed Red Becker), a former Communist League member (in the 1860s he went over to the liberals), wrote to Marx on 7 December 1864 that the *Rheinische Zeitung* editors refused to print his statement against Karl Blind (see notes 62 and 64) justifying this on the grounds of their 'unwillingness' to advertise such an 'insignificant' figure as Blind.— 52, 53

[75] Marx means the famous 'march to the sea' undertaken by General Sherman's troops on 7 May 1864 through Georgia as part of the Union's new strategic plan for crushing the Confederacy. Despite heavy losses, the offensive was a success: on 2 December Sherman seized Atlanta and on 10 December he reached the sea. By cutting the Confederate territory in two, Sherman's march ensured the rout of the main Confederate forces in Virginia in the spring of 1865 and the final victory of the North in the US Civil War.— 53, 61, 113, 121

[76] *Boustrapa*—nickname for Louis Bonaparte, composed of the first syllables of the names of the places where he and his supporters staged Bonapartist *putches*: Boulogne (August 1840), Strasbourg (October 1846) and Paris (coup d'état of 2 December 1851).— 55, 182, 290, 339

[77] After a preliminary discussion in the Sub-Committee, on 6 December 1864, of the address to the Polish people drawn up by Peter Fox (see Note 71), the debate continued at the Central Council meetings on 13 and 20 December 1864 and 3 January 1865. Marx spoke twice on the subject, on 13 December and 3 January (see present edition, Vol. 20, pp. 354 and 356). Drawing on the wealth of factual material on Polish-French relations he showed, particularly in his speech on 3 January 1865, that the French ruling circles, both under absolutism and under bourgeois regimes right up to the time of Napoleon III, had always sought to exploit the Polish question in the selfish interests of the ruling classes and that their policy was not favourable to the cause of Poland's

independence, of which the sole defenders were the representatives of the revolutionary proletariat. Marx's arguments made the Central Council adopt a decision to introduce the appropriate amendments in Fox's address.—55

78 At its meeting on 8 November 1864 the Central Council decided on Marx's proposal, seconded by Hermann Jung, that any person not being able to attend the meetings cannot be a member of this Council (see present edition, Vol. 20, p. 353). The decision to abolish honorary membership in the International was adopted presumably at that time too.—55

79 This refers to Sophie von Hatzfeldt's intention to republish Marx's *The Eighteenth Brumaire of Louis Bonaparte.* It was to be printed in Switzerland. Liebknecht informed Marx of this on 2 December 1864 and asked him to send two copies of the book for the purpose. Marx objected because he was obviously afraid that the Lassalleans might use his works to propagate Lassalle's cult.

Subsequently, Liebknecht, independently of Hatzfeldt, attempted to come to terms with the Swiss publisher, but in vain. The second edition of *The Eighteenth Brumaire* appeared only in 1869, in Germany.—57, 139, 165

80 Marx seems to be referring to the advertisement about his and Engels' contribution to *Der Social-Demokrat,* published in the specimen issue of the newspaper (No. 1) on 15 December 1864 (see also notes 34 and 35).—58

81 The reference is presumably to Wilhelm Liebknecht's letter to Marx of 20 December 1864. It clearly shows that Marx asked Liebknecht to do his utmost to get the General Association of German Workers to join the International Working Men's Association. In this way Marx hoped to encourage this workers' organisation to abandon its Lassallean reformist programme and tactics and take the path of genuinely proletarian, revolutionary struggle.—58

82 The congress (general assembly) of the General Association of German Workers which opened in Düsseldorf on 27 December 1864 did not discuss the affiliation of this organisation to the International Working Men's Association.—58

83 The English original of this letter is published here for the first time. The letter was first published in a German translation in Marx/Engels, *Werke,* Bd. 31, Berlin, 1965, and in an English retranslation in Karl Marx, *On the First International.* Arranged and edited, with an introduction and new translations by Saul K. Padover, New York, 1973.—60

84 Marx stayed with Engels in Manchester approximately from 7 to 14 January 1865.—60, 62, 66

85 At its meeting of 29 December 1864, the Central Council decided to invite the bourgeois radicals Beesly, Beales and Harrison to a soirée to be held on 16 January 1865 to celebrate the founding of the International Working Men's Association. This decision was recorded in the Minutes of that meeting. The report of the meeting was not published, and Cremer, when sending the report of the next meeting, of 3 January 1865, to the newspapers, included the above-mentioned decision in it and recorded it for a second time in the Minute Book. Moreover, on his own initiative, Cremer inserted in the decision Grossmith's name who, as a Central Council member, did not have to be specially invited. As is evident from Jung's reply letter to Marx of 11 January, Marx's protest against the inclusion of Grossmith's name was read out at the Central Council meeting of 10 January; Cremer admitted his mistake, and

Grossmith's name was deleted from the Minutes of the meeting of 3 January.— 61

86 Engels is probably referring to the operations by the Confederate army under General Lee in northern Virginia in the spring and summer of 1863. One of its corps was commanded by Longstreet. Successful counter-attacks on the part of the Confederates led to their victory at Chancellorsville on 2-4 May 1863. Lee's troops began to invade the territory beyond the Potomac and marched to Washington. But in the Battle of Gettysburg on 1-3 July, Lee's army sustained heavy losses and was compelled to retreat beyond the Potomac.

General Hood, who succeeded Johnston as commander of the Confederate troops, undertook two major counter-attacks on 20 and 22 July 1864 against General Sherman's army, concentrated at the time to the north and east of Atlanta (see Note 75). The attempt to throw back Sherman's troops failed and Hood's army retreated, taking cover in Atlanta.— 61

87 Military operations confirmed Engels' prognosis. The city of Charleston (South Carolina) on the Atlantic coast of the USA was captured by the Northerners on 17 February 1865.— 61

88 The first three issues of Der Social-Demokrat were specimens. On 4 January 1865, No. 4 appeared, the first regular issue for the subscribers. When it was confiscated by the police, Marx congratulated Schweitzer, the editor, on the occasion and emphasised that an open break with Bismarck's ministry was necessary (see K. Marx, 'Statement Regarding the Causes of the Breach with the Social-Demokrat', present edition, Vol. 20).— 63

89 Bloomer costume or Bloomer—female costume of short skirt and trousers introduced in the 1850s by the American dress reformer, Amelia Jenks Bloomer (1818-1894).

Davenport tricks were practised by the Davenport brothers, two American circus artists, in the 1860s.— 64

90 Marx is referring to 'Botschaft des Präsidenten', a message by Bernhard Becker, President of the General Association of German Workers, to the delegates of the general assembly of the Association that opened on 27 December 1864 in Düsseldorf (see notes 16 and 82). It was published in Der Social-Demokrat, No. 3, 30 December 1864 and contained a hint that the Association could not establish close ties with the International because that would allegedly damage its organisation and did not promise to be of any practical value.— 65

91 In his report from Paris, dated 10 January 1865 and published in Der Social-Demokrat on 13 January, Moses Hess misrepresented the efforts of the Central Council of the International Association to draw French workers into its ranks. He alleged that the Council was essentially unscrupulous in selecting its representatives in Paris and accused Tolain and certain other French members of the International of having ties with the Bonapartists (see Marx's letter to Engels of 25 January 1865). Hess repeated this accusation in his report from Paris printed in the newspaper on 1 February, following which Marx and Engels wrote a statement to Der Social-Demokrat refuting this false accusation (see present edition, Vol. 20, p. 36).— 65

92 The letter was published in English for the first time (without the postscripts) in Karl Marx, On the First International. Arranged and edited, with an introduction and new translations by Saul K. Padover, New York, 1973.— 65

93 The name *Plon-Plonists* is derived from Plon-Plon, the nickname of Prince Napoleon Joseph Bonaparte, Napoleon III's cousin, whose residence was the Palais Royal while Napoleon III resided in the Tuiliers.

Joseph Bonaparte headed a group of Bonapartists who sought to divert the people's attention from the struggle against the regime of the Second Empire by means of social demagogy and sham opposition to the government's policy.— 66, 76, 208, 300, 567

94 Marx's letter to Paris, presumably addressed to Victor Schily, has not been found.— 66

95 Marx is referring to the discussion of the conflict in the Paris Section by the Central Council on 24 January 1865.

The Paris Section of the International Association was founded at the end of 1864 by the Proudhonistically-minded workers, Henri Tolain and Charles Limousin who took part in the inaugural meeting of 28 September 1864 at St Martin's Hall. Besides Tolain's group, a French lawyer and bourgeois republican, Henri Lefort, who also participated in organising the 28 September meeting, likewise claimed to be representative of French workers. Soon it became evident that Lefort was in touch with the Council's Corresponding Secretary for France, Le Lubez, and with the French petty-bourgeois refugees in England who strove to bring their influence on the International Working Men's Association. The bourgeois republicans accused Tolain of being in contact with the Bonapartists (in particular with Prince Joseph Bonaparte). The accusation was published by Moses Hess in *Der Social-Demokrat*. In reply to Marx's enquiry sent to Schily and Schweitzer, the former answered on 19 January 1865 that Tolain's libellous accusation had originated with the people close to *L'Association*, the journal of co-operative societies, of which Lefort was an editor. Schily also promised to send additional information.

The conflict in the Paris Section was repeatedly discussed in the Sub-Committee and the Central Council in February and March 1865. Marx sought to protect the section from attacks by bourgeois republicans and, at the same time, to find ways of overcoming the influence of Proudhonist utopian ideas on the French workers.— 66, 80, 108, 115, 118, 130

96 Sections of the International Associations began to be set up in Switzerland immediately after the press reports about the inaugural meeting at St Martin's Hall. On 11 October 1864, a group of Geneva workers headed by François Dupleix, a bookbinder, formed a provisional committee to establish contacts with the workers of other countries. At the Central Council meeting on 24 January 1865 the news about the Geneva workers' intention to affiliate to the International was met with approval. Hermann Jung, the Corresponding Secretary for Switzerland, sent Dupleix the Rules of the International Working Men's Association; he also advised the Swiss workers, in the name of the Central Council, to set up a Central Committee for the whole of Switzerland.

The above-mentioned soirée to celebrate the founding of the International Working Men's Association was arranged on 16 January 1865 at Cambridge Hall, London.— 66

97 This reference is to the *British National League for the Independence of Poland* founded in London on 28 July 1863. Its establishment was preceded by a meeting at St James's Hall on 22 July arranged to express solidarity with the participants in the Polish insurrection (see Note 24). The meeting, which was one of the harbingers in the founding of the International, was attended by British trade unionists and representatives of the international democratic

movement, as well as by a French workers' delegation from Paris. The meeting resolved to send a delegation to the Foreign Secretary, John Russell, to hand in a protest against the British government's double-faced policy towards the Polish insurgents. Russell refused to receive the delegation, and a second meeting was called on 28 July 1863, this time at the premises of *The Bee-Hive Newspaper*, at which the League was founded. Radical Edmond Beales was elected president and John R. Taylor—honorary secretary.

By the *Polish society here* Marx means the revolutionary democrats from among the Polish émigrés in London grouped round the representative of the National Central Committee of Poland that stood at the head of the 1863-64 uprising. At the Central Council's meeting on 10 January 1865, also attended by representatives of the National League and the National Central Committee of Poland, a resolution was passed which emphasised that 'this Association pledges itself to assist by all means in its power the commemoration of the glorious, though unsuccessful, Revolution of 1863'.

The 'meeting for the Poles' mentioned by Marx took place on 1 March 1865 (see Note 168).—66, 86, 109

98 Wilhelm Liebknecht wrote to Marx before 20 January 1865 that he had learned of Ferdinand Lassalle's agreement with Bismarck's government: he promised support from the General Association of German Workers over the annexation of Schleswig-Holstein by Prussia if it introduced universal suffrage. Marx and Engels regarded this political 'bequest' by Lassalle as betrayal of the proletariat's interests. The Lassalle-Bismarck correspondence published in 1928 fully confirmed Liebknecht's information.—66, 69, 71, 75, 102, 124, 566

99 A reference to the members of the *Party of Progress* formed in June 1861 (the most eminent figures were Waldeck, Virchow, Schulze-Delitzsch, Forchenbeck and Hoverbeck). The party's slogans were the unification of Germany under the aegis of Prussia, the convocation of an all-German Parliament, and the formation of a strong liberal Ministry responsible to the Chamber of Deputies. Fearing a popular revolution, the Party of Progress gave no support to the basic democratic demands—universal suffrage and freedoms of the press, association and assembly. In 1866 the party split, and its Right wing founded the National Liberal Party, which capitulated to the Bismarck government.—67, 69, 71, 75, 84, 90, 96, 97, 104, 111, 150, 176, 288, 421, 430, 456

100 The *constitutional conflict* in Prussia arose in February 1860 over the refusal of the bourgeois majority of the Lower Chamber of the Prussian Provincial Diet to confirm the army reorganisation project proposed by War Minister von Roon. However, the government soon managed to secure allocations from the Provincial Diet to 'maintain the army ready for action', which in fact meant the beginning of the planned reorganisation. When, in March 1862, the liberal majority of the Chamber refused to endorse military expenses and demanded a Ministry responsible to the Provincial Diet, the government dissolved the Diet and announced new elections. The Bismarck Ministry was formed at the end of September 1862. In October it again dissolved the Provincial Diet and began to carry out the military reform without the sanction of the Diet. The conflict was settled only in 1866 when, after Prussia's victory over Austria, the Prussian bourgeoisie capitulated to Bismarck.—68, 82, 84

101 Part of this letter was published in English for the first time in Karl Marx and Friedrich Engels, *Correspondence. 1846-1895.* A Selection with Commentary and Notes, Martin Lawrence Ltd., London [1934].—68, 72, 77, 79, 94, 135, 159, 172, 227, 266, 289, 297, 299, 359, 362, 381, 383, 407, 423, 458, 519, 557

102 Engels' letter to the editors of *Der Social-Demokrat* in which he asked them to send him projects for the reorganisation of the Prussian army has not been found.—69

103 Part of this letter was published in English for the first time in Marx and Engels, *Selected Correspondence*, Foreign Languages Publishing House, Moscow, 1955.—70, 281

104 By Hess' 'expulsion from Brussels' Marx means his departure from Belgium's capital in March 1846 due to the aggravated ideological struggle between the Brussels Communist Correspondence Committee, headed by Marx and Engels, and the representatives of petty-bourgeois 'true socialism' of which Hess was one of the spokesmen.

By the 'ejection from Cologne' Marx means Hess' forced departure from Rhenish Prussia in the spring of 1848, when Marx and Engels thwarted the attempt of Hess and his followers to take over from the proletarian revolutionaries the initiative in starting a revolutionary democratic newspaper in Cologne.—70

105 Marx realised this intention in a footnote to the Preface to the first German edition (1867) of Volume One of *Capital* (see present edition, Vol. 35).—71, 329

106 Neither letters nor written statements by Marx to the editor of *Der Social-Demokrat* have been found.—71

107 A reference to the workers' right to organise trade unions and to go on strike. In January 1865 the Prussian Provincial Diet debated the right of association in connection with the workers' opposition to the trade regulations then in force. Two members of the Party of Progress, Schulze-Delitzsch and Faucher, used the occasion to have the articles restraining capitalism repealed. They proposed to revoke Article 181, which forbade employers to resort to lockouts, and also demagogically demanded the cancellation of Article 182 concerning the punishment of workers for incitement to strike. The workers in turn wanted the repeal of Article 183 which made them obtain police permission to form associations, and of Article 184 banning strikes.

On 14 February 1865 the Prussian Provincial Diet annulled Articles 181 and 182 and left the workers' demand for freedom of association unsatisfied.—71

108 The decree of the Constituent Assembly of 14 June 1791 declared strikes to be a 'crime against freedom and the declaration of the rights of man' and the formation of workers' associations was liable to a fine of 500 livres and deprivation of political rights for a year. Le Chapellier made a report on this subject. The Chapellier Law was in force in France (as regards prohibition of strikes) till 1864, while the freedom of activity for the trade unions was not legalised until 1884.—71

109 The *Ten Hours' Bill*, the struggle for which had been waged for many years, was passed by Parliament in 1847, against a background of sharply intensified contradictions between the landed aristocracy and the industrial bourgeoisie, generated by the repeal of the Corn Laws in 1846. In revenge on the industrial bourgeoisie, some Tory MPs supported the Bill. Its provisions applied only to women and children. Nevertheless, many manufacturers evaded it in practice.—71

110 In his letter to Marx of 30 January 1865, Wilhelm Strohn wrote that he had seen the Hamburg publisher Otto Meissner who agreed to publish Marx's

Capital on share principles. Meissner wanted to have the manuscript for study (see also Note 66). Strohn also wrote that Meissner had received, through a certain Siebold, offers from Arnold Ruge and Karl Blind concerning the publication of periodicals, and that Ferdinand Freiligrath had promised to contribute to Blind's republican newspaper.—72

111 This letter by Marx has not been found.—73, 75, 101, 107, 108, 118, 149, 194, 246, 343, 370, 391, 447, 448, 464, 487, 516, 538, 542

112 On 28 January 1865, on Lincoln's instructions the American Envoy Adams handed over the President's reply to the address of the Central Council of the International (see Note 70). This reply, in the form of Adams' letter, was published in *The Times*, No. 25101, on 6 February 1865, under the title 'Mr. Lincoln and the International Working Men's Association'.—73, 80, 86, 161

113 The *Emancipation Society* was founded in London in November 1862 by English bourgeois radicals. It supported the London Trades Council (see Note 18) in its campaign against Britain's interference in the US Civil War (1861-65) on the side of the South (see Note 11). Among its leading figures were Edmond Beales, Edward Beesly and John Stuart Mill.—73, 74, 86

114 The *Literary Society of the Friends of Poland* was founded in Paris in April 1832 by the aristocratic-monarchist Polish émigrés under Adam Czartoryski. Its London branch was set up in the same year with the help of English aristocrats from among the Whig Party.—73

115 At the Central Council meeting of 31 January 1865 a letter was read from Léon Fontaine, a member of the Belgian democratic Universal Federation. In his letter dated 29 January, Fontaine wrote that the Federation had decided to join the International Association and intended to translate the Association's documents into French. As it turned out later, Fontaine had no connections with the workers and did not take any further steps to establish a section of the International. The first section in Belgium was set up on 17 July 1865 with the direct participation of the Belgian socialist César de Paepe.—73

116 This refers to the participation of Central Council members in a preliminary conference of electoral reform supporters scheduled for 6 February 1865. At this conference, a group of bourgeois radicals set up a provisional committee to convoke a meeting in support of manhood suffrage in London on 23 February. Marx attached great importance to the campaign for the democratisation of Britain's political system. He therefore thought it possible to co-operate with the bourgeois radicals but on conditions that would ensure a genuinely democratic reform as well as an independent and leading role for the International Working Men's Association in the reform campaign.

At its meeting on 31 January 1865, the Central Council elected a deputation to the reform conference. Besides Eccarius and Le Lubez, it included Carter, Odger, Whitlock, Cremer, Wheeler and Dell.—74

117 Marx's letter to Jones has not been found. As can be seen from Jones' reply of 10 February 1865, Marx outlined a plan for drawing the masses of English workers into a reform campaign under the leadership of the Central Council of the International, and substantiated its platform (the demand for manhood suffrage, etc.). In his letter Jones expressed his agreement with the platform, emphasising, in particular, the need to oppose the moderate position of the Manchester liberal bourgeoisie on this question.—74, 91

118 This letter was published in English for the first time in Karl Marx and Friedrich Engels, *Correspondence. 1846-1895.* A Selection with Commentary and Notes. Martin Lawrence Ltd., London [1934].—75, 86, 88, 402

119 On 1 February 1865 Carl Siebel wrote to Marx that he had met Carl Klings after the general assembly of the Lassallean General Association of German Workers in Düsseldorf at the end of December 1864. Therefore Marx's recommendation to Klings, sent through Siebel, that the general assembly should propose the Association's affiliation to the International, reached him too late (see Note 82).—75, 78

120 The cutting from the *Rheinische Zeitung* enclosed in Siebel's letter to Marx of 1 February 1865 has not been found. Siebel assumed that the leading article was written by Hermann Becker (Red Becker). Judging by Liebknecht's letter to Marx of 16 February, the author contrasted the revolutionary position of Marx and Engels who supported the democrats against the government with that of the Lassalleans who supported the government against the democrats.— 75, 80

121 Marx's letter to Schweitzer with a proposal that the latter should stand up to Bismarck in *Der Social-Demokrat* has not been found. It is quite possible that Marx wrote about this in the final version of his letter to Schweitzer of 16 January 1865. The draft of this undiscovered letter is published on pp. 64-65 of this volume.—75, 95

122 *Der Social-Demokrat,* No. 16 for 1 February 1865, published an item 'Paris, 28. Januar. Internationale Arbeiter-Association.—Geldkrisis' (signed *H*). It repeated the libel that the French members of the International (Henri Tolain and Charles Limousin) were in contact with the Bonapartists (see Note 91).— 75

123 The coup d'état in Prussia in November-December 1848 resulted in the dissolution of the National Assembly (convened in Berlin in May 1848 to draw up a constitution). The constitution imposed ('granted') by the King introduced a two-chamber system; the First Chamber was transformed by age and property qualifications into a privileged 'chamber of the nobility'. According to the electoral law of 6 December 1848, the right to vote in the two-stage elections to the Second Chamber was granted only to the so-called independent Prussians. In April 1849 Frederick William IV dissolved this Chamber and promulgated a new electoral law on 30 May which established a three-class election system based on high property qualifications and unequal representation of the various strata of the population.—76

124 *Road books* (Wanderbücher) were issued in Prussia to journeymen artisans under the law introduced in 1831. They recorded their places of residence and contained an assessment of their trustworthiness.—77

125 Marx attached to this letter his rough copy of a statement to the editor of *Der Social-Demokrat* (see present edition, Vol. 20, p. 36) with a protest against the publication of the report by Hess, who libellously accused the French members of the International (see Note 91). The criticism by Marx and Engels compelled the editors to change the newspaper's tone to some extent. Issue No. 21 of 12 February 1865 carried an item by Hess in which he withdrew his accusations. For that reason Marx and Engels did not insist on the publication of their statement. However, they decided to stop contributing to the

newspaper for the time being. Marx and Engels announced their final break with *Der Social-Demokrat* on 23 February 1865 (see this volume, p. 97).—79, 95

126 Marx forwarded to Engels Wilhelm Liebknecht's letter of 4 February 1865 in which Liebknecht treated collaboration on *Der Social-Demokrat* as a compromise with the Lassalleans. He also described his material hardships and asked Marx to find a place for him as a schoolmaster in northern England or Scotland. Marx's postscript to this letter to Engels (originally written at the end of Liebknecht's letter) was published in previous editions as a separate letter.—80, 81

127 On 8 February 1865, War Minister Roon spoke in the Chamber of Deputies about his Bill on changes in and addenda to the Prussian law on military service. These changes signified minor concessions to the opposition bourgeois majority in the Chamber and did not resolve the constitutional conflict (see Note 100).—83

128 Marx supported Lefort's appointment as the International's literary defender in Paris because he had gathered from Schily's letter of 5 February 1865 that the conflict in the Paris Section (see Note 95) had been resolved. He hoped this would help to draw French workers active in the co-operative movement into the International and also to utilise the journal *L'Association* for propagating the International's ideas.

When translating the Provisional Rules of the Association into French, at the end of 1864, the Proudhonist leaders of the Paris Section distorted the text in some places. In particular, in the third paragraph of the Preamble to the Rules ('That the economical emancipation of the working classes is therefore the great end to which every political movement ought to be subordinate as a means'), the words 'as a means' were omitted.—85

129 On Marx's advice Engels formulated this passage in his pamphlet in such a way that it could not have been interpreted as the author's agreement with Lassalle's slogans. He also incorporated the suggestion Marx made below on changing the description of the position of the German bourgeoisie during the 1848-49 revolution in Germany (see present edition, Vol. 20, pp. 69 and 57).—87

130 On 27 March 1849 the Frankfurt National Assembly, elected in April-May 1848 to draw up an all-German Constitution, adopted a law introducing direct universal suffrage. The law was published by the Imperial Regent, Archduke John, in an official government edition on 12 April 1849. Since, however, the King of Prussia and other German princes had rejected the Imperial Constitution drawn by the National Assembly, the law was not put into effect.—87

131 This letter by Engels has not been found.—88, 99, 174, 445, 448, 467, 475, 481, 513, 534, 566

132 The *Tory Chartists* or *Tory philanthropists*—representatives of a trend among England's conservative politicians and writers in the 1830s-50s, including the Young England group, whose members (Disraeli and Ferrand among them) founded a separate group in the House of Commons in 1841. Voicing the discontent of the landed aristocracy at the growing economic and political power of the bourgeoisie, the Tory philanthropists criticised the capitalist system and supported the half-hearted measures for improving the condition of the workers. However, they adopted a hostile attitude to the independent revolutionary working-class movement.—88

133 Marx forwarded Engels a letter from Johann Baptist Schweitzer of 11 February 1865. It was written in reply to the statement by Marx and Engels concerning Hess' insinuations against the French members of the International. In his letter Schweitzer promised to publish immediately an item by Hess admitting his assertions to be erroneous (see Note 125). Below Marx drew Engels' attention to this item.—89

134 Neither the original of Marx's letter to Johann Baptist Schweitzer of 13 February 1865 nor the copy of it which Marx retained has survived. However, a large fragment from it is quoted in Marx's letter to Engels of 18 February (see this volume, pp. 95-96). In this volume, this fragment is not published separately but within the above-mentioned letter to Engels.—89, 95, 108

135 On 11 February 1865 the Minister of Commerce, Count Itzenplitz, read out a government statement in the Prussian Chamber of Deputies during the debate on the right of combination (see Note 107). In an attempt to maintain the ban on the formation of workers' associations, the government demagogically alleged that freedom of association could not improve the workers' condition and proposed instead to help in setting up workers' co-operatives.—90

136 The *Rules Governing Servants* (Gesindeordnung)—the feudal rules and regulations that existed in Prussian provinces in the 18th and early 19th centuries and sanctioned the big landowners' arbitrary treatment of servants and agricultural labourers, including corporal punishment.—90, 96, 104

137 The *Order of the Swan*, a German mediaeval religious order of knights, was founded in Brandenburg in 1443 and disintegrated during the Reformation. In 1843 Frederick William IV of Prussia made an abortive attempt to restore this Order, hoping that its philanthropic activity would enhance the prestige of the Prussian monarchy which, he claimed, had a social mission.—90

138 The campaign for the right of combination was launched by the Berlin printers in early 1865 under the influence of Wilhelm Liebknecht's propaganda. When the leaders of the Lassallean General Association of German Workers realised that the campaign was widely supported by the workers, they decided to join it too, despite Lassalle, who held that associations were of no use for the workers. On 1 February 1865, *Der Social-Demokrat* published Bernhard Becker's instructions for the General Association's representatives with a proposal that, at their meetings, the workers should adopt resolution demanding the abolition of articles 183 and 184 of trade regulations (see Note 107) that prohibited associations and strikes.—90

139 Marx is referring to Eccarius' articles in *Der Social-Demokrat*. Eccarius continued to contribute to the paper for some time after Marx had actually ceased co-operating with it (see Note 125). His last article was printed in *Der Social-Demokrat* on 31 March 1865.—91

140 At a meeting of the Central Council of the International held on 14 February 1865, Marx read out Ernest Jones' letter to him of 10 February, which was a reply to Marx's letter of 1 February (Marx's letter is not extant) and written with a view to being read at the Council. Jones agreed with Marx's plan for drawing the broad mass of British workers into the electoral reform movement.—91

141 Marx forwarded to Engels a letter from a Cologne worker, G. Matzeratt, to Friedrich Lessner dated 8 January 1865. Matzeratt wrote about the disagree-

ments between Bernhard Becker and Carl Klings in the General Association of German Workers. On behalf of a group of the Association's members, he asked Lessner to inquire about Marx's opinion and help them to clarify the matter. As can be seen from Engels' letter to Marx of 7 February 1865, Becker gained the upper hand over Klings (see this volume, p. 82).—94

[142] During the debate on the right of combination in the Prussian Chamber of Deputies (see Note 107), Hermann Heinrich Becker, a deputy from Dortmund, moved a proposal, on 11 February 1865, that the right of combination be extended to the agricultural labourers as well. He also proposed to abolish the law of 24 April 1854 on the punishment of servants and day labourers for the violation of their duties.—94

[143] This refers to Liebknecht's withdrawal from the editorial board of *Der Social-Demokrat*, of which Liebknecht informed Marx in a letter dated 16-17 February 1865.—94, 108

[144] The passage in Schweitzer's letter of 15 February 1865 to Marx, written in reply to Marx's letter of 13 February, reads as follows: 'If you wish to enlighten me, as in your last letter, on theoretical questions, I would gratefully accept such instruction on your part. But as regards the practical questions of immediate tactics I beg you to consider that in order to assess these things one must be in the centre of the movement. You are therefore doing us an injustice if you express your dissatisfaction with our tactics anywhere and anyhow. You should only do this if you were absolutely familiar with conditions.'—95

[145] Marx is referring to the third article in Schweitzer's series *Das Ministerium Bismarck*. It was published in *Der Social-Demokrat*, No. 23, 17 February 1865, i.e. after Marx's demand for a stop to the flirtation with Bismarck. In these articles Schweitzer supported Bismarck's policy of unifying Germany under the supremacy of Prussia and approved of the Prussian government's demagogical attempts to show that it favoured a solution to the labour question.—95, 104

[146] A reference to the 'liberal' course announced by Prince William of Prussia (King of Prussia from 1861) when he became Regent in October 1858. He made the Manteuffel Ministry resign and called the moderate liberals to power. The bourgeois press dubbed this the position of the 'New Era'. It was, in fact, solely intended to strengthen the position of the Prussian monarchy and the Junkers. This soon became clear to the representatives of the liberal opposition whose hopes had been deceived and who refused to approve the government project of a military reform. The constitutional conflict (see Note 100) that ensued and Bismarck's advance to power in September 1862 put an end to the 'New Era'.—96, 103

[147] Marx refers to the journal of German petty-bourgeois democrats, *Der deutsche Eidgenosse*, published in London and Hamburg from 1865 to 1867. Among its editors were Karl Blind, Ludwig Büchner, Ferdinand Freiligrath, Ludwig Feuerbach and Ernst Haug.—97

[148] Marx enclosed in this letter to Engels some scraps of paper, in an unknown hand, about the unseemly behaviour of people from the élite of the Second Empire.—99

[149] The full text of the letter has not been found. This excerpt has been preserved in Marx's Notebook for 1865; it is also quoted by Marx in a letter to Engels of 25 February 1865 (see this volume, pp. 107-08).—101

150 At the beginning of February 1865 Marx made a speech at the celebration of the 25th anniversary of the German Workers' Educational Society in London (see present edition, Vol. 20, p. 360). He criticised the views of the Lassalleans, in particular their dogma about the assistance by the existing state to workers' co-operative societies. The report on the celebration meeting was drawn up by Eccarius and published in *Der Social-Demokrat*, No. 24, 19 February 1865. The content of Marx's speech was presented by Eccarius inaccurately. He ascribed to Marx the idea that joint action by the proletariat and the bourgeoisie against the feudal monarchy was impossible.

The *German Workers' Educational Society in London* was founded in February 1840 by Karl Schapper, Joseph Moll and other members of the League of the Just. After the foundation of the Communist League (see Note 17), the latter's local communities played the leading role in the Society. In 1847 and 1849-50, Marx and Engels took an active part in its work, but on 17 September 1850 Marx, Engels and a number of their followers withdrew because the Willich-Schapper sectarian-adventurist group had increased their influence in the Society. In the late 1850s, Marx and Engels resumed their work in the Educational Society. During the activity of the International Working Men's Association the Society (Lessner was one of its leaders) was its German Section in London. The Educational Society in London existed until 1918, when it was closed down by the British government.— 101, 106, 107, 507

151 In his letter to Marx of 19 February 1865, Ludwig Kugelmann enclosed a letter from Miquel, a former member of the Communist League, dated 22 December 1864. Miquel alleged in it that Marx's work *A Contribution to the Critique of Political Economy* 'contains little of what is actually new' and that its conclusions were not applicable to Germany's social and political conditions. At the same time, Miquel tried to justify his desertion to the liberal camp.— 102, 107, 112

152 The *National Association* (Deutscher National-Verein) was a party of the German liberal bourgeoisie which advocated the unification of Germany (without Austria) in a centralised state under the supremacy of the Prussian monarchy. Its inaugural meeting was held in Frankfurt am Main in September 1859. The National Association was dissolved in November 1867, after the Austro-Prussian war of 1866 and the establishment of the North German Confederation.— 102, 163, 204, 207, 266, 280, 340, 361, 365, 372

153 On 20 March 1848, King Frederick William IV of Prussia declared that he was ready, for the salvation of Germany's unity and freedom, to 'assume the leadership of the whole nation'. Hence the phrase 'Prussian leadership' ('preussische Spitze'), which won currency as a euphemism for Prussia's efforts to unite the country under its supremacy.— 103

154 In connection with the enthronement of King William I of Prussia an amnesty was granted in Prussia on 12 January 1861 guaranteeing, in words, all political refugees unimpeded return to the country. In the spring of 1861, during his stay in Berlin, Marx submitted an application to the Prussian government requesting the restoration of his Prussian citizenship. His request was rejected by the Prussian authorities on the grounds that in 1845 Marx had surrendered his status as a Prussian of his 'own free will' and 'therefore' could be regarded 'as a foreigner' (see present edition, Vol. 19, pp. 339-58).— 105, 201

155 On 23 February 1865 a public meeting was held in St Martin's Hall, London. On the initiative and with the direct participation of the Central Council of the International Association, the meeting passed a decision to found a *Reform*

League as a centre of the mass electoral reform movement. The League's leading bodies—the Council and the Executive Committee—included the Central Council members of the International, mainly British trade union leaders. The programme of the movement was drafted under the influence of Marx who was advocating the independent position of the British working class in the reform campaign. Unlike the bourgeois parties, which confined their demand to household suffrage, the Reform League, on Marx's insistence, advanced the demand for manhood suffrage. The League had branches in all big industrial cities and in provinces. However, the vacillations of the bourgeois radical leaders, who became afraid of the movement's mass character, and the conciliation of the trade union leaders prevented the League from following the line charted by the Central Council of the International. The British bourgeoisie succeeded in splitting the movement, and a moderate reform was carried out in 1867 which granted franchise only to the petty bourgeoisie and the upper layers of the working class.— 105, 108, 130, 150, 243, 251, 327, 574

156 The *Combination Law of 11 March 1850* in force in Prussia banned all societies that established contacts with other organisations abroad. Hence, this law prevented the setting up of societies in Germany connected with the International Association and the affiliation to it of those already existing. Therefore, as far back as February 1865 Marx proposed to accept the form of individual membership in Germany that would allow to evade the existing laws, and that proved to be a rather flexible means of drawing the advanced German workers into the ranks of the International.— 105

157 This refers to the leading article in *Der Social-Demokrat*, No. 25, 22 February 1865, which was reprinted from the *Norddeutsche Allgemeine Zeitung* of 19 February 1865.— 106

158 Thanks to Liebknecht and Siebel, Marx and Engels' statement about their break with *Der Social-Demokrat* (see this volume, p. 97) was published in many German newspapers, among them *Barmer Zeitung* and *Elberfelder Zeitung* (No. 60) on 26 February 1865; *Düsseldorfer Zeitung* (No. 59) on 28 February; *Rheinische Zeitung* (No. 60), *Berliner Reform* (No. 51), *Neue Frankfurter Zeitung* (No. 60), *Breslauer Zeitung* (No. 102), *Staatsbürger-Zeitung* (No. 60) on 1 March, and later in several other papers.

The above-mentioned letters of Marx to Schweitzer and Liebknecht about the said statement have not been found.— 108

159 It is clear from Schily's letter to Marx of 25 February 1865, and the 'Private Instruction to Schily' extant in Marx's notebook (see present edition, Vol. 20, p. 83), that Marx's instructions were aimed at finding such a way of settling the conflict in the Paris organisation of the International Association that would strengthen the position of the Paris Section's Administration and help draw into the International those workers who were still under the influence of bourgeois republicans (participants in the co-operative movement, and so on).— 108, 127

160 The 'Resolutions of the Central Council on the Conflict in the Paris Section', adopted on 7 March 1865 (see present edition, Vol. 20, pp. 82-83), acknowledged as erroneous the view typical of the Proudhonists, in particular the Administration of the Paris Section of the International, that only a worker can be an official in a workers' organisation. This Proudhonist view was ultimately rejected by the Geneva Congress of the International held in September 1866 (see Note 380).— 109

161 Participation in the solidarity meeting with the Polish national liberation movement, called to mark the first anniversary of the Polish insurrection of 1863-64, was discussed by the Central Council on 21 February 1865. The following resolution was adopted unanimously: 'That the Central Council of the International Working Men's Association lend their unreserved support to the commemorative meeting for Poland on March 1st at St Martin's Hall, and they invite the attendance thereat of their friends.'— 109

162 On 24 February 1865, *The Morning Star* printed a notice, 'German Democracy', obviously written by Karl Blind, about the forthcoming publication of the journal *Der deutsche Eidgenosse* (see Note 147).— 110

163 Engels' notice announcing the publication of his pamphlet *The Prussian Military Question and the German Workers' Party* (see present edition, Vol. 20, p. 81) was printed anonymously in a number of German papers with the help of Carl Siebel, Johann Klein and Wilhelm Liebknecht (Engels' letters to Klein and Liebknecht requesting to publish the notice have not been found). The notice was published anonymously in *Berliner Reform* (No. 53), *Düsseldorfer Zeitung* (No. 62), *Elberfelder Zeitung* (No. 62) and *Rheinische Zeitung* (No. 62) on 3 March 1865; *Oberrheinische Courier* (No. 56) on 7 March, and others. Moreover, on 9 March the *Rheinische Zeitung* carried a special article 'Für die Arbeiterpartei' about Engels' pamphlet containing long passages from it.— 111, 112

164 Engels is referring to the silence of the German press over his anonymously published pamphlets *Po and Rhine* (1859) and *Savoy, Nice and the Rhine* (1860) (see present edition, Vol. 16).— 111

165 Since Marx and Engels' statement was published in many German newspapers (see Note 158), Schweitzer was compelled to print it in *Der Social-Demokrat* too (it appeared there only on 3 March 1865 in issue No. 29).— 113

166 This refers to Schweitzer's article published in *Der Social-Demokrat*, No. 29, 3 March 1865, in the section 'Politische Theil'. It said that the German Social-Democrats who were not members of the General Association of German Workers did not belong to the Social-Democratic Party. By this attack on Marx, Engels and their close associates in Germany, the editors of *Der Social-Demokrat* sought to weaken the impression of Marx and Engels' statement on their breach with the newspaper. See also Engels' letter to Joseph Weydemeyer of 10 March 1865 (this volume, pp. 124-25).— 114, 116, 125

167 Marx succeeded in having items about Engels' *The Prussian Military Question and the German Workers' Party* published in the German-language newspapers in London. On 17 March 1865 such an item appeared in the *Londoner Anzeiger*, and on 18 March the *Hermann* published, also anonymously, Marx's review of the pamphlet (see present edition, Vol. 20, pp. 85-86).

Marx's letter to Ludwig Kugelmann, mentioned above, concerning the popularisation of Engels' pamphlet has not been found.— 114

168 The meeting to mark the anniversary of the Polish insurrection of 1863-64 was held in St Martin's Hall, London, on 1 March 1865. It was initiated by the British National League for the Independence of Poland (see Note 97), and the Central Council of the International contributed much to preparing and conducting it (see Note 161). The British bourgeois press, the London liberal *Daily News* included, covered the speeches Beales, Leverson and other bourgeois radicals made at the meeting, but passed over in silence a resolution

submitted on behalf of the International and the speeches of Peter Fox and
Georg Eccarius, the Central Council members. A full report of the meeting
appeared in *The Bee-Hive Newspaper* (No. 177) on 4 March 1865, and Marx
used it when writing his notice entitled 'A Correction' and intended for the
Zurich *Der weiße Adler*, which reproduced a garbled report from the British
newspapers (see present edition, Vol. 20, pp. 97-98).—114, 130, 143

169 The reference is to the manuscript of *The Great Men of the Exile* written by
Marx and Engels (see present edition, Vol. 11, pp. 227-326). At the end of
June 1852, Marx passed on the manuscript to the Hungarian émigré Bangya
who offered to have it published in Germany. Later, it turned out that Bangya
was a police spy and had handed over the manuscript to the Prussian police.
The actions of Bangya, who managed to win Marx's confidence for a time,
were unmasked by Marx in his article 'Hirsch's Confessions', written in April
1853 and published in American newspapers (see present edition, Vol. 12,
pp. 40-43).

Marx also exposed Bangya as a spy and an *agent provocateur* in *Herr Vogt*,
published in 1860 (see present edition, Vol. 17, pp. 219—20).—118, 176, 191

170 The Prussian authorities managed to suppress the *Neue Rheinische Zeitung*,
published by Marx and Engels during the 1848-49 revolution in Germany, by
means of repressive measures against its editors. On 16 May 1849, its
editor-in-chief Marx, who had just returned from his trip to Northern
Germany, was ordered to leave Prussia within 24 hours on the pretext that he
was a foreigner who had no Prussian citizenship and had violated the rights of
hospitality. Ernst Dronke and Georg Weerth, members of the editorial board,
were deported for the same reasons, while Engels was prosecuted for
participating in an uprising in Elberfeld, Rhine Province. The last issue of the
Neue Rheinische Zeitung, printed in red ink, appeared on 19 May 1849.—118

171 The *People's Bank* (Crédit au travail) was founded in Paris in 1863 by the
petty-bourgeois socialist Jean Pierre Béluze to grant credits to producer and
consumer co-operative societies and draw workers' savings to promote the
co-operative movement. It existed until 1868.—119

172 The first issue of *Der deutsche Eidgenosse,* of 15 March 1865, published Karl
Blind's address to all friends inviting them to contribute to the journal, as well
as Gustav Struve's article, 'Die "Teig-Gesichter" in Deutschland', and Gustav
Rasch's 'Ein Immortellenkranz auf das Grab eines Märtyrers (Max Dortu)'.

On the title page of the journal an emblem consisting of a hand with dagger
was printed with the inscription in Latin: 'Manus haec inimica tyrannies' ('This
hand is the Enemy of Tyrants').—119

173 In its issue No. 31 of 8 March 1865, *Der Social-Demokrat* published the
statement by Georg Herwegh and Friedrich Wilhelm Rüstow of their refusal,
following Marx and Engels, to contribute to this newspaper. Commenting on the
statement, Schweitzer distorted Marx's and Engels' attitude to Lassalle and
falsified the reasons for their withdrawal from the editorial board of *Der
Social-Demokrat.* To prove that Marx and Engels were allegedly inconsistent and
their actions unjustified, Schweitzer quoted Karl Blind's article published in the
Neue Frankfurter Zeitung, No. 64, 5 March 1865.— 120, 126, 129

174 In a letter to Engels, dated 20 January 1865, Joseph Weydemeyer gave a short
description of the preceding events in the Civil War in America (see Note 11),

in particular the Red River expedition by Northern troops in 1864, undertaken with a view to entrenching themselves in Texas. General Banks, who headed the expedition, marched from New Orleans and intended to join forces at Shreveport with General Steel who set out from Arkansas. However, Banks' troops were suddenly attacked by the Southerners in the Texas woods and were forced to retreat.— 121

175 *Missunde*—a Danish stronghold captured by Prussian troops on 2 February 1864, during the Danish war (see Note 9).— 121

176 This refers to the military operations between the allied Anglo-Spanish-Portuguese troops under Wellington and those of Napoleonic France on the Peninsula in 1808-14, and to the Crimean war, 1853-56, between Britain, France, Turkey and later Piedmont, on the one hand, and Tsarist Russia, on the other.

The *battle of Alma* took place during the Crimean war, on 20 September 1854. It was the first battle after the Allies' landing at Eupatoria in the Crimea on 14 September. The defeat and withdrawal of the Russian troops opened up the way to Sevastopol for the Allies.— 122

177 Marx stayed with his relatives, the Philipses, at Zalt-Bommel (Holland) from 19 March to 8 April 1865.— 128, 133, 139, 566

178 In his comments on the statement of Herwegh and Rüstow, Schweitzer quoted Blind's article (see Note 173) mentioning the following passage from Marx's private letter of condolence to Sophie von Hatzfeldt, written on 12 September 1864 on the occasion of Lassalle's death: 'He died young, at a time of triumph, as an Achilles' (see present edition, Vol. 41, p. 563). These words taken from the letter, without Marx's knowledge and consent, were published in *Der Social-Demokrat*, No. 1, 15 December 1864, over his signature and were used to extol Lassalle. In due time Marx lodged a protest against this breach of ethics on Schweitzer's part.— 129

179 Marx realised his intention by writing, on 15 March 1865, the 'Statement Regarding the Causes of the Breach with the *Social-Demokrat*'. It was published in the *Berliner Reform* (No. 67) on 19 March 1865 (see present edition, Vol. 20, pp. 87-90).— 129

180 Marx enclosed in his letter the text of the Central Council's resolutions on the conflict in the Paris Section (see Note 95) written by him and approved by the Council on 7 March 1865, and the text of the private instruction to Schily who was appointed a special representative of the Central Council in the Paris Administration (see present edition, Vol. 20, pp. 82-83).— 130

181 On 11 March 1865, in Radleys Hotel, London, there was a conference of the workers' delegation elected at the meeting in St. Martin's Hall (see Note 155) and representatives of the radical and liberal bourgeoisie. This conference, sponsored by participants in the electoral reform movement, was a step in founding the Reform League. About 20 trade union delegates, among them members of the Central Council of the International, and as many bourgeois representatives, including four MPs, attended the conference. John Bright, leader of the Free Traders, advocated household suffrage. The demand for manhood suffrage was rejected by the bourgeois delegates, and no agreement on joint action was reached.

Marx's letter to Jones mentioned above has not been found.— 130

[182] In its issue No. 299 of 4 March 1865, the *Nordstern*, published by Karl Bruhn, carried two leading articles in which the editors came out against any compromise with the government and described people of Schweitzer's type as intriguers.— 130

[183] This refers to the resolutions on the conflict in the Paris Section (see Note 95) adopted by the Central Council of the International on 7 March 1865.

No letter from Marx to Cremer has been found, nor has the letter to Schily of 13 March 1865, which he wanted to send.— 131

[184] On 12 March 1865 Jung wrote to tell Marx that the Central Council had instructed him to draw up a summary of the conflict in the Paris Section for the information of the International's members in France, and asked Marx to help him in the matter. On 18 March Marx met Jung and handed him his written remarks on the latter's document. (For Marx's comments, entitled 'Memorandum to Hermann Jung about the Conflict in the Paris Section', see present edition, Vol. 20, pp. 331-36.)— 132

[185] The *Berliner Reform* of 3 March, the *Rheinische Zeitung* of 4 March 1865 and other German papers published a report on Marx's and Engels' break with *Der Social-Demokrat* which Wilhelm Liebknecht made on 28 February in the Berlin Printers' Association that declared its adhesion to the International. The printers approved of Marx and Engels' statement of 23 February and Liebknecht's refusal to contribute to *Der Social-Demokrat.*— 134

[186] On 11 March 1865, the *Nordstern* (No. 300) published a protest by Georg Herwegh, Friedrich Wilhelm Rüstow and Friedrich Reusche. It was against a report in *Der Social-Demokrat*, of 26 February 1865, which said that Lassalle was flirting with the Prussian monarchy. The authors of the protest asserted that Lassalle did not show any special respect for the King of Prussia and that the report's allegations were unfounded.— 134

[187] In early March 1865 Carl Siebel forwarded to Engels a letter he received from the then editor of the *Düsseldorfer Zeitung*, Dresemann. The latter invited Marx and Engels to contribute to the *Sphinx*, a newspaper which Friedrich Albert Lange intended to found in Duisburg.— 136

[188] Marx criticised the Ricardian 'law of population' in the first volume of *Capital* (see the English edition published in 1887 under Engels' editorship: Part VII, Chapter XXV, Section 3, and the present edition, Vol. 35).— 137

[189] Malthus' plagiarisms in his *An Essay on the Principle of Population, as It Affects the Future Improvement of Society, with Remarks on the Speculations of Mr. Godwin, M. Condorcet, and other Writers* are mentioned by Marx in the first volume of *Capital* (see the English edition published in 1887 under Engels' editorship: Part VII, Chapter XXV, Section 1, and the present edition, Vol. 35).— 137

[190] The words '*Caveant consules ne quid respublica detrimenti capiat*' ('Let the consuls beware lest the Republic suffer harm') used to be addressed by the Roman Senate to the consuls in time of danger for the state; the meaning was that they were empowered to appoint a dictator.— 137

[191] Schulze-Delitzsch, a German bourgeois economist and a leader of the Party of Progress, supported small savings banks and loan offices, and consumer and producer co-operatives based on the workers' own means, with the aim of diverting workers from the revolutionary struggle against capital. Schulze-Delitzsch advocated harmony of capitalists' and workers' interests, asserting that

co-operatives could help improve workers' conditions under capitalism and save small producers and artisans from ruin.—138

192 Bernhard Becker, President of the General Association of German Workers, made a speech at a meeting of the Association's Hamburg Section on 22 March 1865 in which he slandered the International Working Men's Association and also Marx, Engels and Liebknecht. Marx rebuffed Becker in an article 'The "President of Mankind"', published in the *Rheinische Zeitung*, No. 102 (second supplement), 12 April and the *Berliner Reform*, No. 88 (supplement), 13 April 1865 (see present edition, Vol. 20, pp. 92-96). On 27 March, Becker was denounced by Liebknecht at a meeting of the Association's Berlin Section when it discussed the question of the presidency. On 1 April 1865 the *Nordstern* (No. 303) printed statements by Rüstow and Herwegh against the attacks made by Becker on Countess Hatzfeldt.

In view of the growing discontent among the rank-and-file members of the General Association with Becker as President, the Berlin Section resolved to expel him. Many other sections followed suit. In June 1865 Becker was compelled provisionally to delegate his presidential powers to his deputy Fritzsche and completely renounced them in November.—139, 140, 566

193 Lefort's statement about his withdrawal from the International was published in *L'Association*, No. 6, April 1865.—140

194 At the Central Council meeting of 28 March 1865 the General Secretary, William Cremer, spoke on behalf of the Council's deputation (Eccarius, Weston, Jung, Fox, and others). He reported on the results of their meeting with the delegates of the National Shoemakers' Union and its adoption of the following resolution: 'That we cordially agree with the principles of the International Association as represented so eloquently by the deputation from that body and pledge ourselves to join them for the furtherance of those principles and endeavour to spread their liberal and glorious ideas among our constituents.'—140

195 In his letters to Engels, dated 10 January and 1 April 1865, Sigismund Borkheim wrote that Adolph Kolatschek, an Austrian journalist, intended to resume publication of the *Stimmen der Zeit* and invited Marx and Engels to contribute to it. Kolatschek's intention did not materialise.—141

196 The notice entitled 'A Correction' was published with slight changes in *Der weiße Adler*, No. 48, 22 April 1865 over Jung's signature (see present edition, Vol. 20, pp. 97-98).—143

197 This letter has reached us as a draft in Marx's notebook for 1865. The notebook also reproduced the text attached to the letter of the Central Council official resolution of 11 April 1865, signed by Odger, the President, and Cremer, the General Secretary of the Council, appointing Marx Corresponding Secretary for Belgium *pro tem* instead of Le Lubez who abandoned this post. The following postscript was entered in the notebook: 'Letter sent on Monday, 17 April 1865.'—144

198 In his article 'Falsche Freunde und offene Feinde', published in the *Nordstern*, No. 304, on 8 April 1865, Friedrich Reusche defended Georg Herwegh, Friedrich Rüstow and Johann Philipp Becker whom Bernhard Becker called 'false friends' for their refusal to co-operate on *Der Social-Demokrat* (see Note 173). Written in a melodramatic tone, the article refers to the oath given by the above-mentioned men to the dying Lassalle to bring his cause to a finish,

and calls Bernhard Becker, Schweitzer and their followers 'venal mercenaries and tools of reaction'.

By mentioning Willich's apple-tree Engels means the oath which Willich and his volunteer corps gave under an apple-tree during the Baden-Palatinate uprising in 1849; better die on German soil than go back into exile. However, as a result of the insurgents' defeat, Willich's corps was compelled to cross the Swiss frontier. Engels described this episode in his letter to Marx of 23 November 1853 which Marx included in his pamphlet *The Knight of the Noble Consciousness* (see present edition, Vol. 12, pp. 489-93).— 147

199 The coopting of Pierre Vinçard, a working-class journalist and veteran of the 1848 revolution, for the Paris Administration (which already included Fribourg, Limousin and Tolain) was meant to make the French members of the International familiar with the revolutionary and socialist traditions of the French working-class movement of the 1840s. However, Vinçard did not accept the appointment for personal reasons, about which he informed Dupont, the Corresponding Secretary of the Central Council for France, in a letter of 30 April 1865.— 149

200 On Friedrich Lessner's proposition, the German Workers' Educational Society in London (see Note 150) at its meeting on 22 March 1865 broke with the Lassalleans.

At the general meeting of the Society and its branches, Teutonia and Eintracht, called on 5 April 1865 to discuss the behaviour of Bernhard Becker, President of the General Association of German Workers, and the editorial board of *Der Social-Demokrat*, Louis Weber tried to defend the Lassallean leaders. He wanted to pass a resolution declaring the political position of some Party officials to be their personal affair that should not be discussed by members of the Society. Weber's proposition was turned down by the meeting. The report of this meeting was given in *Der Social-Demokrat*, No. 50, 21 April 1865, in a distorted way.

Teutonia—an educational society of German workers who lived in the southern districts of London, a branch of the German Workers' Educational Society. Together with the latter, it joined the International Working Men's Association in January 1865. The leaders of the Teutonia were A. Klinker and Klinke.— 150, 174

201 This refers to the 'Address of Germans to the American Nation' written on the occasion of the assassination of US President, Abraham Lincoln, on 14 April 1865 and published in *The Times*, No. 25171, 28 April 1865.— 151

202 Engels is referring to the report from Solingen, published in the *Nordstern*, No. 307, 29 April 1865, on the meeting of the Solingen section of the General Association of German Workers. The section was in opposition to Bernhard Becker, President of the Association. Its members formed a community of their own and dissociated themselves from those sections which continued to recognise Becker's leadership. In opposition to *Der Social-Demokrat* edited by Schweitzer, they declared the *Nordstern* the official organ of the Association. In September 1865 the Solingen community constituted itself as a section of the International in Germany.— 152

203 At the *battle of Jena* (14 October 1806) the French army, commanded by Napoleon, routed the Prussian army, thus forcing Prussia to surrender.— 153, 256, 277

204 According to a report from Cologne published in the *Nordstern*, No. 308, 6 May 1865, the growing opposition to Bernhard Becker, President of the General Association of German Workers, compelled him to raise the question of confidence at the meeting of the Association's local branches in Cologne. The majority of the meeting walked out, and of the remaining 24 members only 15 voted for Becker.— 154

205 The Central Council of the International failed to acquire most of *The Bee-Hive Newspaper* shares through lack of funds and because at the decisive moment, in May 1865, its members were distracted by the campaign for electoral reform in England. On the eve of the shareholders' general meeting, Council members Odger, Cremer, and Howell left for Manchester to attend a conference of reformers, which allowed Potter to retain the majority of votes in his favour.— 155, 169, 173

206 US President Abraham Lincoln was assassinated by John Wilkes Booth, an agent of Southern planters and New York bankers. Andrew Johnson became President. On 2 May 1865 the Central Council of the International took a decision to draw up an address to the American people. At the Council meeting of 9 May Marx read out the 'Address from the Working Men's International Association to President Johnson' which he had written. The Address was passed to President Johnson through Adams, the American envoy to England (see present edition, Vol. 20, pp. 99-100).— 155

207 After Marx, Engels, Liebknecht, Herwegh, Rüstow and Johann Philipp Becker refused to collaborate with *Der Social-Demokrat*, Moses Hess continued to work on it, and when the *Rheinische Zeitung* printed a notice about Hess' refusal to contribute to the newspaper, he denied it.— 156, 158

208 In its issue No. 58 (the literary section) of 10 May 1865, *Der Social-Demokrat* reprinted from the *Allgemeine Zeitung* (of 29 April 1865, supplement) a commentary on Wuttke's *Städtebuch des Landes Posen*. In this book Wuttke tried to prove that the Germans had an inherent right to the Polish lands.— 156

209 In his report from Paris published in the supplement to issue No. 57 of *Der Social-Demokrat* of 7 May 1865, Moses Hess again slandered the French members of the International (see notes 95 and 122).— 157

210 The national Reform Conference, sponsored by the liberal National Reform Union, was held in Manchester on 15 and 16 May 1865. Most of its delegates were representatives of the bourgeoisie. They refused to include the demand for universal manhood suffrage in the conference's resolutions as proposed by the International's Central Council member Cremer, who was supported by Ernest Jones and some delegates of the Reform League (see Note 155). Edmond Beales, President of the Reform League, and other radicals adopted an indecisive attitude to the nature of the reform. As a result, the conference carried a moderate resolution to extend the franchise to householders and house tenants who paid poor-rates. The report of the Manchester Conference was published in *The Bee-Hive Newspaper*, No. 188, 20 May 1865.— 158

211 Early in May 1865 the House of Commons turned down Baines' moderately liberal Bill which envisaged the reduction of the electoral qualification in the cities from £10 to £6. This reflected the sentiments of the British bourgeoisie which was scared by the scope of the reform movement among the workers. On 2 May 1865 the Executive Committee of the Reform League addressed a

manifesto to the British workers, calling on them to take part in the campaign for manhood suffrage.— 158

212 At the elections to the Geneva Cantonal Council in August 1864 the radical James Fazy, who headed the canton's government in 1846-53 and 1855-61, suffered a crushing defeat because of the exposure of his financial machinations as President of the Banque Générale Suisse. After the elections Fazy's followers made an armed attack on some of those who voted against him. When Swiss government troops arrived in Geneva, Fazy had to flee to France.— 158, 185, 237

213 A reference to the correspondence between Le Lubez, the Corresponding Secretary of the Central Council of the International for France, and Henri Lefort, the International's correspondent in Neufchâteau, during the conflict in the Paris Section of the International (see Note 95). Le Lubez tried to set Lefort against the Central Council and the Paris Administration.— 158

214 From May to August 1865 the Central Council of the International discussed economic questions raised by John Weston. Apart from the speech made at the special Council meeting of 20 May 1865 whose minutes have not survived, Marx delivered a report on the subject at the Council meetings on 20 and 27 June, known as 'Wages, Price and Profit'. This report was not printed in the lifetimes of Marx and Engels. It was first prepared for the press by Marx's daughter, Eleanor, and published with Edward Aveling's preface, as a pamphlet in London in 1898 under the title *Value, Price and Profit*. In the present edition of the *Collected Works* of Marx and Engels it is printed under this title (see Vol. 20, pp. 101-49).— 160, 162

215 A German translation of Marx's 'Address from the Working Men's International Association to President Johnson' (see Note 206) was published in *Chicago, Sonntags-Zeitung*, 4 June 1865.— 161

216 A reference to the statements made by a number of branches of the General Association of German Workers against Bernhard Becker and published in the *Nordstern*, No. 313, 24 June 1865 (see Note 192).— 161, 176

217 The first Congress of the International Working Men's Association scheduled for 1865 in Brussels was held between 3 and 8 September 1866 in Geneva. The decision to postpone the Congress was taken by the Central Council on 25 July 1865 on Marx's insistence. He considered that the local organisations of the International were not yet strong enough in ideological and organisational terms and suggested that a preliminary conference be held in London in September 1865.

Official reasons for postponing the congress were set out in the 'Report of the Sub-Committee on the Questions of a Congress and Conference' drawn up by the Central Council's decision of 13 June 1865 and approved by the Council on 25 July (see present edition, Vol. 20, pp. 375-77).— 163, 171, 174, 179

218 In a letter written at the end of May-early June 1865, Liebknecht asked Marx whether he knew Dr Kugelmann from Hanover and supposed that Kugelmann was a friend of Pieper's and adhered to 'communism'.

In the 1850s, while in exile in London, Pieper was a friend of Marx and Engels. From 1859 he lived in Bremen and late in February 1864 he visited Marx in London.— 165

219 Liebknecht's letter to Marx of 13 May 1865 contained a postscript from Paul Stumpf from Mainz who visited Berlin at the time. Stumpf wrote to Marx that

he had sent him a letter ten days ago through Bruhn from Hamburg, in which he asked Marx for his opinion on the disagreements between the *Nordstern* and *Der Social-Demokrat,* on the situation in the General Association of German Workers and the position of its President, Bernhard Becker. Stumpf also asked Marx about his latest works and those of Engels and whether he had received the letter.— 165

220 Marx here speaks ironically about the assertions in Liebknecht's letters that the International was widely supported in Germany.— 165

221 This refers to Countess Sophie von Hatzfeldt's lawsuit and to Ferdinand Lassalle's mother who challenged Lassalle's will.— 165

222 The *Permissive Bill* empowered parishes to grant licences for the sale of alcoholic beverages. From 1864 to 1877 it was repeatedly introduced in the British Parliament.— 168

223 In the 1850s Windmill Street, Soho, was the seat of the German Workers' Educational Society in London (see Note 150).— 168

224 A banquet of the opposition liberal majority of the Chamber of Deputies, organised by the Rhineland men of Progress (see Note 99) headed by the Town Councillor Classen-Kappelmann, was scheduled for 22-23 July 1865, in Cologne. On 17 July the Bismarck government forbade the banquet. Despite numerous protests on the part of the workers in the various towns of Germany against this arbitrary measure, most opposition members did not dare to show open resistance. Only some 80 delegates out of the 250 invited arrived in Cologne. The banquet's organiser, Classen-Kappelmann, fearing arrest, left for Belgium. Since the hall where the banquet was to take place had been closed by the police, the deputies tried to hold the banquet in the Zoological Gardens, but were driven out of it by soldiers and policemen.— 169, 182, 185, 229

225 The reference is to a series of banquets in favour of electoral reform that took place in France from July 1847 to January 1848 and became a prelude to the February bourgeois-democratic revolution of 1848.— 169

226 Marx wrote this letter to Léon Fontaine after he had become acquainted with the state of affairs in Belgium from the letter of Charles Limousin, a French member of the International who visited Belgium, to Eugène Dupont, the Central Council's Corresponding Secretary for France, the letter being dated 6 July 1865. In the summer of 1865, a group of Brussels workers discontent with Fontaine's inertness decided to set up a section of the International in Belgium. However, they met with Fontaine's resistance: he demanded that he should be acknowledged as the only representative of the Central Council of the International. On 17 July a Belgian Section was organised with the active participation of César De Paepe. It elected a provisional committee which established direct contacts with Marx and the Central Council.

Marx's letter to Léon Fontaine has been preserved as a draft in Marx's notebook for 1865.

The letter was first published in English in Karl Marx, *On the First International.* Arranged and edited, with an introduction and new translations by Saul K. Padover, New York, 1973.— 170

227 After the publication of Part One of *A Contribution to the Critique of Political Economy* in 1859, Marx wrote a voluminous economic manuscript in 1861-63 which is a second, after the manuscript of 1857-58, detailed rough version of his future *Capital.* By 1863, Marx had finally decided to publish his work in

four books: the first three books—theoretical, and the fourth—historical-literary. Having completed the 1861-63 manuscript, in August 1863 Marx began preparing his *Capital* for the press.

In the course of this work he wrote a third preparatory version of *Capital*—the Economic Manuscript of 1863-65 consisting of three theoretical books (the outline of the fourth book, *Theories of Surplus Value*, was in the 1861-63 manuscript). Subsequently, having finished them, Marx again returned to the first book. On Engels' advice he decided to publish it before the others were ready. Marx gave the finishing touches to it in 1866 and most of 1867. The first German edition of the first book—Volume One of *Capital*—appeared in September 1867. As agreed with Otto Meissner, a Hamburg publisher, the second and third books, devoted to the analysis of the process of circulation of capital and the forms of capitalist production as a whole, were to be published as Volume Two of *Capital*, and the fourth book, on the 'history of economic theories', as the concluding volume, Volume Three, of *Capital*.

However, during his lifetime Marx did not manage to prepare the last books of *Capital* for the press. It was Engels who after Marx's death did this and published his manuscripts of the second and third books, as Volume Two (1885) and Volume Three (1894) of *Capital*. Engels also intended to publish the above-mentioned manuscript of the fourth book, as Volume Four of *Capital*, but did not materialise this intention during his lifetime. In the present edition of the *Collected Works* of Marx and Engels, this book is included in the Economic Manuscript of 1861-63 (vols 30-34), while the first three volumes of *Capital* published in vols 35-37.— 173, 227, 312

228 By Jacob Grimm's method Marx means the method Jacob and his brother Wilhelm used in compiling their German Dictionary. It was published in instalments, beginning in 1832; each was prepared independently from one another.— 173

229 The English translation of Volume One of *Capital* by Samuel Moore and Edward Aveling, edited by Engels, was published after Marx's death, in 1887. Eleanor Marx-Aveling took an active part in preparing this edition.— 173, 394, 436, 499

230 At the end of July 1865 John Bredford Leno, the proprietor of *The Miner and Workman's Advocate* published in London from 1863, proposed placing this weekly at the service of the Central Council of the International. The proposal met with approval by the Council members. They discussed the matter at the meetings of 8 and 15 August 1865, in the absence of Marx who was busy with his *Capital*. However, Eccarius informed him in detail about this in a letter dated 16 August 1865.

On 22 August an inaugural meeting was held of shareholders of the joint-stock company for financing the workers' paper, which was called the Industrial Newspaper Company. The meeting, which Marx attended, approved the address to the working men of Great Britain and Ireland and the Company's Prospectus (both published in the present edition, Vol. 20). On 25 September 1865 the London Conference of the International declared the newspaper, which in September assumed the name of *The Workman's Advocate*, an official organ of the International. At the beginning of November 1865 the paper became the full property of the Industrial Newspaper Company. Marx was a member of the Company's Board and remained on it until June 1866. However, the growing influence of reformist elements in the paper's Editorial Board and the vacillation and conciliatory policy of the trade union leaders on the Company's Board did not allow Marx and his followers to prevent the transformation of this working-class paper into an organ supporting the bourgeoisie.—173, 201, 206, 571

231 Marx is referring to a campaign of preparations for the Anglo-French industrial exhibition timed for the fiftieth anniversary of the peace treaty between Britain and France (1815) which was to open on 8 August 1865. At its meeting on 30 May 1865 the Central Council of the International censured this attempt to divert the workers from the political struggle and diminish the influence of the International.—174

232 An aliens act was passed in Belgium as early as 1835 and was renewed every three years. Despite widespread protests by the Belgian press and the public, this law was renewed for the tenth time at the end of June 1865.—174

233 The reference is to the terms of the 1865 agreement between Marx and the Hamburg publisher Otto Meissner on which Marx's *Capital* was to be printed. The text of the agreement was sent to Marx by Meissner in his letter of 21 March 1865 (see Note 66). The date of the agreement was not indicated. As preliminarily agreed, the whole of *Capital* was to be printed simultaneously in two volumes, each not exceeding the agreed number of printed sheets (about 50). In 1867 Meissner agreed to change the terms: to print the entire work in three volumes, publishing them at different time and enlarging the size of each volume (see Marx's letter to Engels of 13 April 1865, this volume, p. 357). Meissner left it to Marx's discretion to decide how the manuscript was to be delivered to him: by instalments or as a whole. Marx could avail himself of the agreement only in two years, when he finished his work on Volume One of *Capital*.—175, 219, 226, 343, 351

234 Influenced by Sophie von Hatzfeldt, Carl Schilling published the pamphlet *Die Ausstossung des Präsidenten Bernhard Becker aus dem Allgemeinen Deutschen Arbeiter-Verein und der 'Social-Demokrat'* (Berlin, 1865). It was a report of the meeting of the Berlin branch of the General Association of German Workers held on 27 and 30 March 1865. Liebknecht spoke at the meeting in defence of Marx against Becker's slanders. The report contained distortions which Wilhelm Liebknecht and other followers of Marx, Theodor Metzner and August Vogt, refuted in a statement of 22 June 1865 published in the *Volks-Zeitung*, No. 145, 24 June 1865 and in other newspapers.—176, 180, 191

235 In a letter to Marx, dated 15 July 1865, Liebknecht wrote that the local Printers' Association and the Berlin Journeymen's Association had organised a demonstration in his honour. The latter had invited him as an honorary guest to its annual celebration in the countryside. In connection with this, Liebknecht wrote to Marx that he thought all local worthwhile elements from among the working class were ready to follow him, as well as Marx himself and Engels.—176

236 During their stay in Brussels Marx, Engels and other members of the Communist League were persecuted by the Belgian government. Early in March 1848 Marx received a royal order deporting him from Belgium; he and his wife were immediately arrested by the Brussels police. Engels, too, was detained and evicted across the French frontier in early October 1848 (he had come to Belgium in order to hide from the Prussian authorities).—179, 448

622 Notes

237 On 18 July 1865 an agreement was concluded between the Bismarck government and the Board of the Cologne-Minden Railway Joint-Stock Company. It granted the Company's Board the right to buy up its shares which until then belonged to the government alone. This deal placed a considerable sum of money at the disposal of the Bismarck government. The agreement was to be ratified by the Prussian Provincial Diet, but on 28 August the shareholders' general meeting unanimously approved it without the Diet's ratification.— 179, 182, 211, 285

238 Part of this letter was published in English for the first time in K. Marx, *On History and People*, McGraw-Hill Book Company, New York, 1977.— 180, 542

239 On 4 August 1865 Siebold wrote to tell Marx that there was a Workers' Association in Copenhagen led by an MP, C. V. Rimestad. He advised him to establish ties with the association but warned that Rimestad was a Bonapartist. At the same time Siebold made it clear that he regretted Marx's quarrel with Karl Blind.— 180, 182

240 *Rotten Row*—a broad pathway in Hyde Park, London, fashionable for riding.— 181

241 Engels made a trip to Germany, Switzerland and Italy at the end of August and mid-September 1865.— 182, 183, 190, 192

242 Returning to Siebold's letter to Marx, Engels criticises his proposal to establish contacts with the Copenhagen Workers' Association (see Note 239). This Association was under the influence of the Danish liberal party (Eider-Danes) which advanced the slogan 'Denmark up to the Eider'. The Eider-Danes demanded that the Duchy of Schleswig, populated mainly by Germans and separated from other German regions by the Eider river, should be united with Denmark. Schleswig and Holstein were at the time when the letter was written under the joint rule of Prussia and Austria (see Note 9).— 183

243 Part of this letter was published in English for the first time in *The Letters of Karl Marx*, selected and translated with explanatory notes and an introduction by Saul K. Padover, Prentice-Hall Inc., Englewood Cliffs, New Jersey, 1979.— 183, 321, 452

244 *Apsides*—the points in the orbit of a planet or comet at which it is nearest to (perihelion) or farthest from (aphelion) the sun.— 185

245 In the third book of *Capital* Marx analysed the parliamentary reports on banking for 1857-58 and criticised the theories of money and capital contained in them.— 186

246 The *London Conference of the International Working Men's Association* was held from 25 to 29 September 1865. It was convened on Marx's insistence, for he considered that the Association's sections were not yet strong enough to succeed in holding a general congress in 1865 as stipulated by the Provisional Rules. The conference was attended by Central Council members and by delegates from the principal branches in France, Switzerland and Belgium. Wilhelm Liebknecht could not come to the conference, and Germany was represented by Karl Marx as the Corresponding Secretary of the Central Council for the country and Johann Philipp Becker who had credentials from the Solingen branch of the General Association of German Workers which was in opposition to the latter's Lassallean leadership.

The conference heard the Central Council's report, its financial statement, and also delegates' reports on the situation in individual sections. The main point discussed was the agenda and the procedure for convening the forthcoming congress. It was decided to hold it in Geneva in May 1866 (later the Central Council postponed it until early September 1866). Though the Proudhonists demanded that the Polish question should be struck off the agenda of the Congress and that the right of any member of the Association to participate in it be recognised, the conference retained in the agenda the point of the restoration of Poland's independence and recognised only elected delegates as competent members of the Congress. Other proposals of the Council concerning the programme of the Congress were also approved.

The London Conference of 1865 which was prepared and conducted under Marx's guidance played an important part in the formation and organisational shaping of the International.— 189, 201, 214

[247] On 15 September 1865 Liebknecht wrote to Marx that he could not go to the London Conference of the International because of urgent matters and the removal of his family to Leipzig, but promised him to send a report on the working-class movement in Germany. This report was sent to Marx on 23 September but Marx did not read it out at the conference because, he believed, it said too much about his personal services (see Marx's letter to Liebknecht of 21 November 1865, this volume, pp. 201-03).— 190

[248] The *Nordstern* of 19 August 1865 published Moses Hess' article 'Eine Warnung' ('A Warning') in which he opposed the idea of reorganising the General Association of German Workers under the leadership of Johann Philipp Becker. In his Paris correspondence 'Der Kongress der "Internationalen Arbeiter-Association" vertagt' published in *Der Social-Demokrat*, No. 130, of 30 August, Hess described the leaders of the International Association as 'some demagogues sitting at a safe distance from the firing line'.— 190

[249] Marx stayed with Engels in Manchester from 20 October to early November 1865.— 193, 196, 201, 208, 214

[250] On 16 July 1865 Marx's aunt Esther Kosel, who lived in Frankfurt am Main, died intestate. Along with other close relatives Marx was entitled to receive part of her legacy. Dr Salomon Fuld, a Frankfurt lawyer, was in charge of this matter.— 194

[251] The enclosed letter, dated 13 November 1865, was from Theodor Metzner, Sigfrid Meyer and August Vogt, members of the Berlin branch of the General Association of German Workers. During Wilhelm Liebknecht's stay in Berlin all three came into close contact with him which they continued to maintain after his expulsion from Berlin. In their letter the Berlin workers who gravitated towards the International informed Marx about the working-class movement in Germany and the split in the General Association and asked Marx to come to Berlin to lead it.— 196, 197, 198, 201

[252] The mass Negro uprising in Jamaica, the British colony in the West Indies, took place in October 1865. It was caused by the severe exploitation of the Negroes by the colonists, though slavery had been abolished on the island in 1833. The uprising was brutally suppressed by the Governor of Jamaica, General Eyre. The atrocities perpetrated by Eyre caused public outrage in Britain, and the British government was compelled to dismiss him from his post.— 197, 199, 205, 300

²⁵³ Part of this letter was published in English for the first time in K. Marx and
F. Engels, *On Colonialism*, Foreign Languages Publishing House, Moscow,
1955.—198, 204

²⁵⁴ Marx alludes to the Prussian authorities' refusal to have his Prussian citizenship
restored despite the amnesty granted to political refugees on 12 January 1861
(see Note 154).—198

²⁵⁵ The French delegates' report on the London Conference of the International
Working Men's Association held in 1865 (see Note 246) was published in
L'Opinion national, 8 October, *L'Avenir national*, 12 October, *Le Siècle*, 14
October 1865 and in other French newspapers.—199

²⁵⁶ *The Workman's Advocate*, No. 141, of 18 November 1865 printed Peter Fox's
report of the Central Council meeting of 14 November 1865 (see *The General
Council of the First International. 1864-1866. The London Conference 1865.
Minutes*, Progress Publishers, Moscow, 1961, pp. 138-41). At this meeting the
Corresponding Secretary for France, Eugène Dupont, read out the preface to
the French delegates' report of the London Conference published in *Le Siècle*
on 14 October 1865. The author of the preface was Henri Martin, a French
historian and member of the International. He highly appreciated the activities
of the International, its first conference and the programme of the future
congress, in particular its Point 9 demanding the 'reconstruction of Poland
upon a democratic and socialist basis'. The French Proudhonists Henri Tolain
and Ernest Fribourg opposed this point at the conference and after it, for they
advocated the proletariat's abstention from political activity.—199, 202

²⁵⁷ The mass eviction of the Irish from land and their emigration, caused by the
transfer from small peasant renting to large-scale pasturing, led to the growing
national liberation struggle in Ireland. As a result, the Fenian movement
developed there in the 1850s and 1860s.
    The *Fenians* were Irish revolutionaries who named themselves after the
'Féne'—a name of the ancient population of Ireland. Their first organisations
appeared in the 1850s in the USA among the Irish immigrants and later in
Ireland itself. The secret Irish Revolutionary Brotherhood, as the organisation
was known in the early 1860s, aimed at establishing an independent Irish
republic by means of an armed uprising. The Fenians, who expressed the
interests of the Irish peasantry (see Marx's letter to Engels of 30 November
1867), came chiefly from the urban petty bourgeoisie and intelligentsia and
believed in conspiracy tactics. The British government attempted to suppress
the Fenian movement by severe police reprisals. In September 1865 it arrested
a number of Fenian leaders, among them Thomas Clarke Luby, John O'Leary,
Jeremiah O'Donovan Rossa and other editors of the banned newspaper *The
Irish People*. They were sentenced to long terms of imprisonment (O'Donovan
Rossa for life). The Central Council of the International organised a campaign
in defence of the condemned prisoners.—199, 468, 516, 523

²⁵⁸ The data mentioned in the letter were given by Marx in Chapter III of the
first edition of Volume One of *Capital*, He specified these data in the second
German edition of the volume.—199

²⁵⁹ Included in this letter, the text of the programme of the Geneva Congress was
drawn up by Marx and approved by the London Conference of the
International (see Note 246). It was first published in G. Jaeck, *Die
Internationale*, Leipzig, 1904.

This letter was first published in English in full in Karl Marx, *On the First International* Arranged and edited, with an introduction and new translations by Saul K. Padover, New York, 1973.—200

[260] A detailed report on the London Conference of the International Working Men's Association, entitled 'Great International Conference of Working Men', was published in *The Workman's Advocate*, No. 134, 30 September 1865.—200

[261] Marx is referring to Liebknecht's 'Report on the Working-Class Movement in Germany' drawn up for the London Conference of the International (see Note 247). The manuscript of the report preserved among Marx's papers was published in English for the first time in *The General Council of the First International. 1864-1866. The London Conference 1865. Minutes*, Progress Publishers, Moscow, 1961, pp. 251-60.—201

[262] In a letter to Marx written in mid-November 1865 Liebknecht told him that a certain Quenstedt from Berlin intended to write to Marx and help him publish reviews of *Capital* in scientific journals.—202

[263] In a letter to Marx of 8 October 1865 Lothar Bucher invited him to contribute to the official organ of the Prussian government. Marx's reply letter to Bucher has not been discovered. Later, in 1878, Marx wrote a special item, 'Herr Bucher', concerning this offer, and gave a rebuff to this agent of Bismarck's in another article, 'Reply to Bucher's "Declaration"' (see present edition, Vol. 24).—202

[264] Kugelmann could not answer Marx's letter of 23 February 1865 (see this volume, pp. 101-05) until 20 December (see Marx's reply of 15 January 1866 in this volume, pp. 220-21).—203, 207

[265] On 25 November 1865 César De Paepe read a letter from Marx at a meeting of the Brussels Section of the International Association. (The Institute of Marxism-Leninism does not have the original of this letter at its disposal.) The Minutes of this meeting recorded only that part of the letter which enumerated the points of the programme of the Geneva Congress drawn up by Marx and approved by the London Conference of the International (see Note 246). The differences from the similar text cited by Marx in his letter to Jung of 20 November (see this volume, p. 200) are possibly due to the inaccuracies in the record of the above-mentioned Minutes.—203

[266] On 24 November 1865 Schweitzer was sentenced to one year's imprisonment for the political articles in *Der Social-Demokrat* However, in May 1866 he was temporarily released for health reasons and amnestied after the Austro-Prussian war of 1866.—205

[267] The mass meeting was held by the Reform League (see Note 155) in London, in St Martin's Hall, on 12 December 1865.
The committee for preparing the meeting consisted of the following members of the Central Council of the International: George Odger, John B. Leno, John Longmaid, William Dell, William Stainsby, George Howell and Robert Hartwell. The majority of those present at the meeting were workers and trade union members. The meeting adopted a resolution demanding manhood suffrage.—207, 215, 221, 253

268 *Der Vorbote*—an official monthly of the German sections of the International Working Men's Association—began to appear in Geneva from January 1866 under the editorship of Johann Philipp Becker. On the whole, this monthly pursued the policy of the Central (General) Council of the International. It published documents of the International, reports on its congresses and information about the activities of its sections in different countries. *Der Vorbote* was widely circulated in Switzerland and Germany, while in Austria and Hungary it was distributed illegally. Also among its readers were German workers living in London, Paris, New York, Chicago and other cities. The journal ceased publication in December 1871.—207

269 In December 1865 and January 1866 France was the scene of student disorders. They were caused by the decision of the Paris Academy Council to expel students who took part in the International Students' Congress held in Liège (Belgium) at the end of October 1865. The congress was attended by students from many European countries, the most numerous delegation being from France (Paul Lafargue, Charles Longuet, Charles Victor Jaclard, and others). Most speakers at the congress expressed the revolutionary students' protest against the regime of the Second Empire.—208, 211, 215, 304, 308

270 In December 1861 France started an armed intervention in Mexico, jointly with Britain and Spain, to overthrow the progressive government of Benito Juárez and turn the Mexican republic into a colony of European powers. The invaders also intended to use Mexican territory as a spring-board for intervening in the US Civil War on the side of the slaveholding Southern States. In the summer of 1863 the French occupied the city of Mexico (Britain and Spain recalled their troops in April 1862 because of contradictions with France) and declared Mexico an empire with Napoleon III's henchman, the Archduke of Austria Maximilian, at its head. However, the Mexican people put up a stubborn resistance to the French colonialists and inflicted a heavy defeat on them. In March 1867 they were compelled to withdraw.—208, 211, 215, 338, 438

271 This is presumably an extract appended to one of Marx's letters to Engels written at the end of 1865 or beginning of 1866.—208

272 The Augsburg *Allgemeine Zeitung*, No. 1, of 1 January 1866 printed Schulze-Delitzsch's announcement about the publication of his new work, *Die Abschaffung des geschäftlichen Risico durch Herrn Lassalle. Ein neues Capitel zum Deutschen Arbeiterkatechismus.* Written in reply to Lassalle's *Herr Bastiat-Schulze von Delitzsch, der ökonomische Julian, oder: Capital und Arbeit*, it soon after appeared in Berlin.—211

273 The *French Section (branch) in London* was founded in the autumn of 1865. Besides proletarian members like Eugène Dupont, Hermann Jung, Paul Lafargue and others, it included petty-bourgeois refugees like Victor Le Lubez and, later, Félix Pyat. On 7 July 1868 the General Council of the International adopted a resolution, on Marx's proposal, condemning the provocative behaviour of Félix Pyat (see present edition, Vol. 21, p. 7). After this a split occurred in the section: the proletarian elements left it and it actually lost ties with the International.—213, 214, 216

274 On 16 and 18 December 1865 the Belgian democratic newspaper *L'Echo de Verviers*, Nos. 293 and 294, published an anonymous article which slandered the Central Council's activities and the work of the London Conference of the International held in 1865 (see Note 246). Its author was the French petty-bourgeois republican Pierre Vésinier, a refugee in Belgium and the

spokesman for petty-bourgeois elements in the French Section in London who opposed Marx and the Central Council.

Vésinier's article was discussed in the Central Council on 26 December 1865 and on 2 and 9 January 1866. On the instructions of the Council, Vésinier's slanderous attacks were refuted by Hermann Jung, who with Marx's help wrote a letter to *L'Echo de Verviers*. By the Council's decision of 6 February 1866 the letter was sent to the editor (see present edition, Vol. 20, pp. 392-400).—213, 214, 216, 250

275 The draft of the new statutes drawn up by Le Lubez was published in *L'Echo de Verviers*, No. 301, on 27 December 1865. This draft expressed the federalist views of some petty-bourgeois democrats, members of the French Section in London, and nullified the leading role of the Central Council by turning it into a mere representative body with purely technical informative and statistical functions.—213, 214

276 Marx is referring to a series of articles against Poland by Proudhonist Hector Denis published in the Belgian newspaper *La Tribune du Peuple* in March-June 1864 under the heading *La question polonaise et la démocratie*.

At Marx's request, between the end of January and early April 1866 Engels wrote a series of articles, entitled *What Have the Working Classes to Do with Poland?*, in which he substantiated the International's stand on the nationalities question and criticised the Proudhonists' national nihilism and the Bonapartists' profiteering by the so-called principle of nationalities (see present edition, Vol. 20, pp. 152-61).—213

277 Marx refers to Johann Philipp Becker's address, 'Rundschreiben der deutschen Abtheilung des Zentral Komites der Internationalen Arbeiterassociation für die Schweiz an die Arbeiter', issued in Geneva in November 1865. In it Becker urged the workers to join the International and wrote about the forthcoming publication of its German (*Der Vorbote*) and French (*Journal de l'Association Internationale des Travailleurs*) press organs.

An English translation of some passages from this address was published in *The Workman's Advocate*, No. 145, 16 December 1865.

A report of the International's activities in Switzerland was printed in issue No. 1 of *Der Vorbote* in January 1866 under the heading 'Entwicklungsgang unserer Association'.

The note to Becker mentioned by Marx has not been found.—214

278 From November 1865 the Central Committee of the German sections in Switzerland, headed by Johann Philipp Becker, served as the organising centre for sections uniting the German workers not only in Switzerland but also in Germany, Austria and in other countries where German refugee workers lived.—215, 219

279 On 27 October 1865 in Port-au-Prince in Martinique (the French colony in the West Indies) three Zouave regiments refused to obey the French command to join the intervention in Mexico.—215

280 In 1865 the French government attempted to make the British government extend the Franco-British extradition treaty of 1843 (see Note 500) to persons guilty of political crimes.—215

281 On 2 January 1866, Austrian journalist Arnold Hilberg from Vienna wrote to Marx inviting him to contribute to the planned journal *Internationale Revue*. Marx's reply to him has not been found, but from Hilberg's next letter to

Marx, of 18 January, it is clear that Marx agreed (see also Marx's letter to Engels of 14 February in this volume, p. 229). However, his work in the International and on *Capital* presumably prevented Marx from materialising his intention.—216, 229

282 Marx's letter to Sigfrid Meyer of 15 January 1866 has not been found. It was written in reply to one from Theodor Metzner, Sigfrid Meyer and August Vogt (see Note 251).—216, 220, 222

283 This refers to Point 9 on the agenda of the London Conference of the International in 1865 which reads as follows: 'The Muscovite invasion of Europe, and the re-establishment of an integral and independent Poland' (see *The General Council of the First International. 1864-1866. The London Conference 1865. Minutes*, Progress Publishers, Moscow, 1961, p. 305).—216

284 The meeting to commemorate the third anniversary of the Polish insurrection of 1863-64 (see Note 24) was held in St. Martin's Hall, London, on 22 January 1866 and was presided over by a Polish democrat, Ludwik Oborski. As reported by *Głos Wolny*, the organ of the democratic wing of Polish emigrants, the meeting was sponsored by the International Working Men's Association and the Polish emigrants. It unanimously adopted Fox's resolution, which was supported by Marx, expressing solidarity of the workers and democrats of Britain and other European countries with the Polish national liberation struggle.

The report of the meeting was published in *The Workman's Advocate*, No. 151, 27 January, *Głos Wolny*, No. 93, 31 January, and *The Bee-Hive Newspaper*, No. 225, 3 February 1866.—218

285 Marx presumably refers to *L'Anti-Proudhon*, a book by Denis (de Chateaugiron), that appeared in Rennes in 1860. From the Catholic standpoint Denis polemises over Proudhon's views set forth in his three-volume work *De la Justice dans le Révolution et dans l'Église*, Paris, 1858.—218

286 The London Conference of the International Association (see Note 246) decided to hold the first congress of the International in Geneva in May 1866. Later, however, the Central Council found it necessary to postpone the congress. All sections of the International agreed with this decision, except for the Paris Section whose Proudhonist leaders wanted to hold the congress as soon as possible because they calculated to impose their programme and principles on it. The congress met on 3-8 September 1866.—220, 258, 271, 574

287 In his letter to Marx of 20 December 1865 Ludwig Kugelmann asked him to send two membership cards of the International Association for himself and Theodor Heinrich Menke, and enclosed two talers for the purpose.—220

288 Marx's letter addressed to August Vogt, and presumably also meant for Sigfrid Meyer and Theodor Metzner, has not been found.—222

289 See this note by Marx in the English edition of Volume One of *Capital* published in London, under Engels' editorship, in 1887 (Part III, Chapter X, Section 2, p. 223).

In the first German edition of Volume One of *Capital* (1867), the section 'The Working Day' was part of Chapter III while in the second and subsequent German editions it made up Chapter VIII of Part III. In the English edition of 1887 it is Chapter X in Part III (see present edition, Vol. 35).—224

290 *The Workman's Advocate* (see Note 230) was renamed *The Commonwealth* on 10 February 1866. Despite the reorganisation the newspaper remained the official organ of the International Working Men's Association. It continued to publish reports of the Central Council meetings and other documents of the International. Marx remained on the Board of the Industrial Newspaper Company which owned the paper until 9 June 1866. Thanks to his efforts Eccarius, who became the editor of *The Workman's Advocate* not long before, retained his post. However, the reformist leaders of trade unions managed to paralyse the influence of Marx's supporters. In April 1866 George Odger was appointed its editor-in-chief. In issue No. 183, 8 September 1866, the newspaper declared itself to be the organ of the Reform League (see Note 155) and in fact fell under the influence of the radical bourgeoisie. It ceased publication on 20 July 1867.—224, 249, 252, 262, 283, 290, 574

291 In his letter of 18 January 1866 to Marx Wilhelm Liebknecht wrote that J. B. von Hofstetten, an editor of *Der Social-Demokrat,* had made one more attempt to persuade Marx, Engels and himself to contribute to the newspaper and use it for propagating the ideas of the International.—225

292 On 29 January 1866 the Prussian Supreme Tribunal adopted a decision to institute court proceedings against Karl Twesten and Frenzel, members of the Chamber of Deputies, for their Chamber speeches delivered in 1865 in which they criticised the government press.

This decision was adopted despite the fact that the courts of first and second instance rejected the prosecutor's demand to apply this measure to the said deputies. The Chamber of Deputies of the Prussian Provincial Diet found the Supreme Tribunal's decision contradictory to the Prussian Constitution and to the principle of the inviolability of deputies, and turned it down. Nevertheless, Twesten's case was referred to the Berlin City Court, but in May 1866 Twesten was acquitted.—226

293 Engels refers to the negotiations between the Austrian ruling circles and the Hungarian moderate bourgeois-landlord opposition headed by Ferencz Deák on the reorganisation of the Habsburg Empire's state structure. In the spring of 1867 an Austro-Hungarian agreement was concluded under which the Austrian Empire turned into the dual state of Austria-Hungary.

This compromise between the ruling classes of the two countries aimed at suppressing the national liberation movement of the other peoples in the Empire, above all the Slavs. The concessions made to the Hungarians were also due to Austria's defeat in the Austro-Prussian war of 1866.—226, 297

294 Marx set forth the theory of ground rent in Chapter VI of the manuscript of Book III of *Capital.* In the third volume of *Capital* published by Engels it is given as Part VI: 'Transformation of Surplus-Profit into Ground Rent' (see present edition, Vol. 37).—227

295 Marx presumably meant H. Mahon's *Aus dem Bericht an den Minister für die landwirtschaftlichen Angelegenheiten in Berlin über die japanische Landwirtschaft.* This work was published as a supplement to J. Liebig's *Die Chemie in ihrer Anwendung auf Agricultur und Physiologie,* Braunschweig, 1862. Marx's notebook of excerpts for 1865, which he probably filled in while working on his *Economic Manuscript of 1863-65,* contains synopses of these two works.

When developing the theory of ground rent Marx used, besides the above-mentioned work by Liebig, the following books: L. de Lavergne, *The Rural Economy of England, Scotland and Ireland.* Translated from the French,

Edinburgh and London, 1855; and L'Mounier, *De l'agriculture en France, d'apres les documents officiels, avec des remarques par Rubichon*, Tomes 1-2, Paris, 1846.— 227

296 The *shifting system* or *Relay system* was used by the British manufacturers to circumvent the laws limiting the working hours of children and juveniles. Under this system the children and juveniles, after several hours' work, were moved the same day to another workshop or factory in order to deceive the factory inspectors. As a result, their entire working day was often even longer than before the adoption of the ten hours act (see present edition, Vol. 35).— 227

297 The reference is to Section IV of Chapter IV of the first edition of Volume One of Marx's *Capital*. In the second and subsequent editions it is given as Chapter XIII: 'Machinery and Industry'. In the English edition of 1887 edited by Engels it is Chapter XV in Part IV (see present edition, Vol. 35).— 228

298 By decision of the Central Council of the International, *The Workman's Advocate* (No. 148) of 6 January 1866 reprinted from *The Cork Daily Herald* an appeal by the wives of the Irish revolutionaries O'Donovan Rossa and Luby to collect funds for the imprisoned Fenians (see Note 257). It was entitled 'The State Prisoners. An Appeal to the Women of Ireland'.

At the Central Council meeting of 16 January 1866 Marx announced that Fox had received a letter from Mrs O'Donovan Rossa thanking him for the reprint of the appeal and for his articles published in *The Workman's Advocate* on 14, 21 and 28 October 1865: 'The British Coup d'État in Ireland' (No. 136), 'The Influence of Irish National Feeling upon the Relations between Great Britain and the United States' (No. 137), and 'The Irish Difficulty. Continued' (No. 138).— 228

299 During the Prussian Provincial Diet's session in January and February 1866, the Party-of-Progress majority in the Chamber of Deputies opposed the Bismarck government on many issues. For instance, the Chamber voted down the decision of the Supreme Tribunal on the prosecution of the deputies Karl Twesten and Frenzel (see Note 292), opposed the annexation of the duchy of Lauenburg by Prussia without the approval of both Chambers and denounced the prohibition of the banquet in Cologne (see Note 224). The Chamber's commissions opposed the increase of the military budget for 1866 and the agreement between the government and the Cologne-Minden Railway Joint-Stock Company (see Note 237).

Following these actions, the Prussian government ordered that the session be closed down ahead of time on 23 February 1866 and on 9 May 1866 it disbanded the Provisional Diet.— 229

300 Marx's letter bears a mark in Lessner's hand: 'von Karl Marx F. Lessner London January 1901'.— 229

301 Engels stayed at Marx's house in London from 14 to 18 February 1866.— 230

302 This letter was published in English for the first time in Karl Marx, Friedrich Engels, *Selected Letters. The Personal Correspondence, 1844-1877*, Boston, Toronto, 1981.— 233, 438, 539

303 A reference to the publication of the findings of the Parliamentary commission investigating the atrocities committed by the British army in suppressing the Negro rebellion in Jamaica (see Note 252). The commission condemned these actions. Initially supporting the colonialists, *The Times* later on had to heed

public opinion: on 3 and 5 March 1866 (Nos. 25436 and 25437) it published editorials and reports in which the brutalities committed 'by persons wearing the English uniform' were denounced.

The news of Russell's resignation turned to be premature. The Russell government resigned in June 1866, following the failure of Gladstone's Reform Bill (see Note 315).—236

304 The agreement between the Bismarck government and the Board of the Cologne-Minden Railway Joint-Stock Company (see Note 237) was discussed by a Commission of the Prussian Chamber of Deputies on 21 February 1866 and declared to be 'unconstitutional and invalid'. Due to its dissolution ahead of time (see Note 299), the Chamber was unable to consider the issue. Soon after that a statement appeared allegedly issued by the Board, which cancelled the agreement. On 28 February 1866, however, the Board officially denounced this as a rumour.—236

305 The full text of Engels' letter to Freiligrath cited below has not been found. Like the letter to Marx, it may have been written on about 10 March 1866 as a reply to Freiligrath's letter to Engels of 8 March 1866. In his letter Freiligrath expressed his anxiety about Marx's health, undermined by systematic night work, and wrote that a long rest in the countryside would restore his strength.—237

306 The Central (General) Council's meetings took place in the premises at 18 Bouverie Street, Fleet Street, from January 1866 to 25 June 1867.—238

307 From 15 March to approximately 10 April 1866 Marx stayed in Margate where he took treatment and had a rest.—239, 261, 268, 283, 574

308 The reference is to the heated debates, which started on 6 February 1866 at the British Parliament session over the bill on compensation to the cattle-owners in the event of epizootic disease. The debates ended on 20 February with the adoption of the corresponding Act.—242, 245

309 The Italian patriot Felice Orsini was executed in March 1858 for organising an attempt on Napoleon III's life. After Orsini's arrest, the leadership of the *Carbonari,* a secret revolutionary society, which Louis Bonaparte joined in 1831 when in Italy, sent him letters reminding him of his oath, which he had broken, to struggle for Italy's liberation. After Orsini's execution, it passed an official death sentence on Napoleon III.—242

310 A. Rogeard, *Les propos de Labienus*—a pamphlet published in 1865; it criticised Napoleon III's empire under the guise of Julius Caesar's dictatorship in Rome.—243

311 At the Central Council meeting of 13 March 1866, Cesare Orsini refuted Luigi Wolff's statement made at the Council meeting of 6 March that there were no Socialists in Italy in the French sense of the word; he also noted Mazzini's reactionary attitude towards science.—243

312 A member of the Dutch Section of the International, Antoinette Philips in her letters gave an extensive account of the events in Holland, which is why Marx jokingly calls her his Dutch secretary.—243

313 Marx and many of his supporters were unable to attend the Central Council meeting of 6 March 1866. Taking advantage of this, Le Lubez and L. Wolff, supported by the English trade unionists Odger, Howell, Cremer and others, had a resolution passed on the response by the Central Council to a slanderous

article by Vésinier published in *L'Echo de Verviers* (see Note 274). The resolution stated that the Central Council withdrew on everything that had been said with regard to 'an eminent writer of the Latin race', i.e. Mazzini, and his followers. By this the refutation of Vésinier's statement that Mazzini was the author of the International's programme documents, specifically the Rules, was disavowed. As a result of the stand taken by Marx and his supporters, the resolution was withdrawn at the meeting of 13 March. Thus the claims of the petty-bourgeois elements to the leadership in the International were rebuffed. (For details of this episode see Marx's letter to Engels of 24 March 1866, this volume, pp. 249-50).—244, 251, 286

314 A pun on the similarity of the names Grach and Gracchi—the name of the ancient Roman reformers. Marx's wife Jenny deposited 1,300 talers with Grach, a banker in Trier, who went bankrupt and concealed the fact from the depositors. At the request of Grach's wife, who promised to return the money after she had received an inheritance, Jenny Marx refrained from pursuing the matter in the courts (see Marx's letter to Engels of 8 March 1855, present edition, Vol. 39, p. 526). In Marx's subsequent letters, however, there is no indication whether the banker's wife paid the debt or not. Marx may be referring here to reassuring news about this matter.—244

315 From the beginning of 1866, the Electoral Reform Movement in Britain came under the influence of moderate bourgeois elements; the reformist trade union leaders (Odger, Cremer and others) showed themselves increasingly willing to make concessions to them. Thus, at the National Conference held by the Reform League on 28 February-1 March 1866 in St Martin's Hall, London, they opposed the Central Council delegation (Fox, Carter, Jung, Lessner and others), which supported manhood suffrage, and announced that they would be quite satisfied with household suffrage as an immediate aim.

On 12 March 1866 the Russell-Gladstone liberal government submitted to the House of Commons a Reform Bill providing for lower property qualifications for the electors (£10 in the counties and £7 in the towns). This would have meant a certain numerical increase of electors and included the wealthier strata of the working class as well. Under the influence of the bourgeois radicals and conciliatory-minded trade union leaders, the Reform League's Council supported, at its meetings of 16 and 20 March 1866, this extremely moderate bill of Gladstone which, however, was strongly opposed by the Tories and some Liberals and rejected by the Commons.—253, 257, 314

316 In the spring of 1866 the conflict between Prussia and Austria sharpened over their joint possession of the duchies of Schleswig and Holstein. The Bismarck government regarded Austria as its main rival in the struggle for hegemony in Germany and sought for a *casus belli*. With this aim in view it accused Austria, which ruled Holstein, of encouraging the anti-Prussian movement there. Austria rejected Prussia's accusations and on 16 March 1866 sent a circular dispatch to several member states of the German Confederation (a union of German states founded by the Vienna Congress in 1815) asking for their mediation in the conflict or military assistance against Prussia. Prussia in its turn also sought the support of the German Confederation. In its circular dispatch of 24 March 1866 to the German states, the Prussian government proposed a reform of the political and military institutions of the German Confederation. Bismarck demagogically proposed that this reform be carried out through a German parliament elected on the basis of universal suffrage.—254, 257, 258, 263, 264

[317] A meeting between the Prime Minister of Prussia, Manteuffel, and the Austrian Prime Minister, Schwarzenberg, took place in *Olmütz* (Olomouc) on 29 November 1850. Under the pressure of the Russian Emperor Nicholas I, Prussia had to give up her claims to take part in suppressing the uprising in the Electorate of Hesse in favour of Austria and in general, to abstain from attempts to establish her hegemony in Germany.—254

[318] A reference to Alexander Cuza's abdication in February 1866. Cuza was Hospodar of Moldavia and Wallachia, which united in 1862 into the single Romanian state. The coup d'état was approved of by Russia and France, and was supported by Prussia. The boyar-bourgeois coalition, which was dissatisfied with the progressive reforms introduced by Cuza, invited Prince Charles Hohenzollern-Sigmarinen, a relative of the Prussian King, to the throne in March 1866. The new hospodar soon began to pursue a policy of subjecting Romania to the economic and political interests of Germany.—256, 258

[319] A reference to the pamphlet *Congrès ouvrier. Association Internationale des Travailleurs* published by the Paris Section of the International early in 1866. It contained a French translation of the International's Provisional Rules, with some passages distorted by the Proudhonists; an appeal of the Paris Section to the members of the International Association which had first been published in the summer of 1865 and which included the Section's programme for the congress initially intended to be held in Brussels; the French delegation's report about the London Conference of 1865; the programme for the Geneva Congress of 1866, which had been approved by the London Conference, and other material.—259

[320] The *Thirty Years' War, 1618-48*—a European war, in which the Pope, the Spanish and Austrian Habsburgs and the German Catholic princes rallied under the banner of Catholicism and fought against Protestant countries: Bohemia, Denmark, Sweden, the Republic of the Netherlands, and a number of German states. The rulers of Catholic France, rivals of the Habsburgs, supported the Protestant camp.—263

[321] A reference to the circular dispatch of 16 March 1866 sent by the Austrian government (see Note 316).

On 9 April 1866, the Prussian government submitted to the Federal Diet a proposal that an all-German parliament be convened through universal suffrage in order to decide the question of reforming the German Confederation.—264, 266, 285

[322] The *Kingdom of Poland*—the Polish territory annexed to the Russian Empire in accordance with the decision of the Vienna Congress of 1815.—267

[323] The *Vienna Treaty*, which concluded the war of 1864 waged by Prussia and Austria against Denmark (see Note 9), confirmed a number of previous treaties and conventions on Denmark, Schleswig and Holstein, in particular the clauses of the London Protocol of May 1852 on the Danish succession. In the Protocol, the Emperor of Russia was named as one of the lawful claimants to the Danish throne (being a descendant of Charles Peter Ulrich, Duke of Holstein-Gottorp, who reigned in Russia as Peter III). The claimants waived their rights in favour of Duke Christian of Glücksburg, who was named heir to King Frederick VII. This created a precedent for the claims of the Russian Emperor to the Danish throne in the event of the extinction of the Glücksburg dynasty.—267

[324] An excerpt from this letter was first published in English in K. Marx and F. Engels, *The Civil War in France*, London, 1937.—268

[325] In March 1866, London tailors demanded a wage increase. A number of owners of large tailors' shops responded with a lock-out. On 27 March, all London tailors went on strike. The Executive Committee of the Journeymen Tailors' Protective Association, which had been formed at the national conference of British tailors held in Manchester on 12-17 March 1866, appealed to all tailors in Britain to support the strike. At its meeting of 27 March 1866, the Central Council of the International decided to instruct the Continental corresponding secretaries to call upon the tailors on the Continent not to go to Britain, where the employers were going to use them as strike-breakers. The Central Council's support of the strike played an important part in the victory of the London tailors in April 1866 and added to the popularity and prestige of the International Working Men's Association among the British working class. On 17 April, the Tailors' Protective Association joined the International.—268

[326] This is a reference to the resistance with which Russell-Gladstone Reform Bill (see Note 315) was met by the Conservatives and some Liberals. Marx calls the Right-wing Liberals, who were once headed by Lord Palmerston, Palmerstonian Whigs. In 1866, they were nicknamed the Adullamites by John Bright as an allusion to the biblical legend about David's persecution by King Saul and his refuge in the cave of Adullam. The nickname became a synonym for dissatisfaction with everything and was used to condemn the Right-wing Liberals for their opposition to the Reform Bill.—269, 270

[327] On 26 March 1866, Edinburgh tailors went on strike. With a view to preventing the importation into Scotland of German and Danish tailors to be used as strike-breakers, German tailors living in London formed a committee headed by Lessner and Haufe, and decided to act jointly with the Central Council of the International. At Marx's request, Lessner and Haufe sent him on 3 May details about the events in Edinburgh for use in a report for the Central Council. On 4 May, Marx wrote and sent Liebknecht, on behalf of the Central Council, a short article, entitled 'A Warning', which was published in several German papers (see present edition, Vol. 20). At the same time a leaflet written by Lessner and Haufe was issued in London. They appealed to the German workers in London to raise funds and support the strikers. Moreover, the Central Council sent Haufe and Hansen to Edinburgh to wreck the employers' plans. The Central Council's efforts contributed to the success of the strike, and promoted the International's influence in Britain.—270, 272, 275

[328] A reference to the steps taken by Bismarck to find allies in the war with Austria that he was preparing. On 8 April 1866, Prussia and Italy signed a secret treaty under which they were to join in a war against Austria until Italy received Venetia and Prussia equivalent territories in Germany.—270, 282, 288

[329] On the *London tailors' strike* see Note 325.

On 23 April 1866, the London wire-workers went on strike, demanding a 10 per cent wage increase. The same day, the strike committee sent out letters to all towns in England, Scotland and Ireland requesting the wire-workers there not to take jobs in London during the strike. With the help of the Central Council of the International, similar letters were sent to France and Germany. At the Central Council meeting of 24 April 1866, B. Patis, a member of the

London Association of Wire-Workers, thanked the Council for its help to the strikers and promised that the wire-workers would join the International.—272

330 On 7 May 1866, Ferdinand Cohen, a student and Karl Blind's stepson, made an unsuccessful attempt to assassinate Bismarck. He was arrested and committed suicide in prison.—273, 275

331 A reference to Austria's defeat by France and Piedmont in the Austro-Franco-Italian war of 1859.—274

332 In preparing a war against Austria, Bismarck's government sought for France's benevolent neutrality. On 6 May 1866, the Emperor Napoleon III made a speech at an agricultural festival in Auxerre, in which he said that, like the majority of the French nation, he felt an aversion for the treaties of 1815, which certain parties would like to make the only foundation of France's foreign policy (see *The Times*, No. 25492, 8 May 1866). This statement, which was a response to a critical speech made by Louis Adolphe Thiers in the Corps législatif, implied the demand that the clauses of the Vienna treaties concerning France's eastern borders be revised. In Prussia, it was regarded as an encouragement for Bismarck's intention to reorganise the German Confederation which had been formed on the basis of the decisions of the Vienna Congress of 1815.—274

333 On Bismarck's intended reform of the German Confederation, see Note 316.
The *Fundamental Rights of the German People* (Die Grundrechte des deutschen Volkes), approved by the Frankfurt National Assembly late in 1848, formulated, like the *Déclaration des droits de l'homme et du citoyen*, the basic bourgeois freedoms; they were incorporated into the Imperial Constitution of 1849, which was worked out by the National Assembly, but rejected by the King of Prussia and other German sovereigns (see Note 130). The main points of the Fundamental Rights were included in the constitutions of some German states, but were later on either deleted from them, or revised and curtailed on the basis of the decision of the Federal Diet of 23 August 1851.—276

334 Engels' series of articles, 'What Have the Working Classes to Do with Poland?', was never finished. This may have been because of the increasing influence of the radical bourgeois on the editorial board of *The Commonwealth*, where it was being published.—278, 280

335 At the Central Council meeting of 8 May 1866, Peter Fox announced that, at the next meeting, he would speak against a passage in Engels' third article ('The Doctrine of Nationality Applied to Poland') from the series 'What Have the Working Classes to Do with Poland?' (present edition, Vol. 20). Judging by this letter of Marx's, Fox made a speech at the Central Council meeting of 15 May 1866; however, there are no records, in the minutes of this meeting, either of Fox's speech or of Marx's reply.—278

336 Marx uses the term *Haupt- und Staatsaktionen* ('principal and spectacular actions'), which has several meanings. In the seventeenth and the first half of the eighteenth century, it denoted plays performed by German touring companies. The plays, which were rather formless, presented tragic historical events in a bombastic and at the same time coarse and farcial way.
Secondly, this term can denote major political events. It was used in this sense by a trend in German historical science known as 'objective historiography'. Leopold Ranke was one of its chief representatives. He regarded *Haupt- und Staatsaktionen* as the main subject-matter of history.—280

337 *The Commonwealth,* No. 165 of 5 May 1866, carried an editorial statement to the effect that the editors bore no responsibility for the contributions printed below a certain line. The responsibility was to be borne by the authors themselves. The statement was directed primarily against Engels' series of articles 'What Have the Working Classes to Do with Poland?', which were printed below the line marked by the editors.—280

338 The crash of Barnett's bank in Liverpool was one of the first signs of the crisis of 1866 which led to the collapse of the leading houses of Overend, Gurney, and following this of other banks, including the Consolidated Bank.—281

339 No. 15 of *Le Courrier français* for 20 May 1866 carried an appeal of the Paris students to the students of Germany and Italy (*Aux étudiants des universités d'Allemagne et d'Italie, les étudiants de Paris*) in connection with the threat of war between Prussia and Austria. This appeal was strongly influenced by Proudhonists who ignored the historic tasks of the national unification of Germany and Italy. The meeting of the Central Council, which was held on 5 June 1866 in Marx's absence, discussed the appeal of the French Section in London in response to the appeal of the Paris students: 'To the Paris Students, to the Students and Young People of All Countries from the Workers of All Countries' (*The General Council of the First International. 1864-1866. The London Conference 1865. Minutes,* Moscow, 1961, pp. 337-39). Marx was dissatisfied with the content of the latter appeal. At the Central Council meeting of 19 June 1866, Marx gave an extensive criticism of the Proudhonist position on the nationalities question (see this volume, pp. 286-87).—281

340 A reference to the unsuccessful attempt on Alexander II's life made by the Russian revolutionary Dmitri Karakosoff on 4 April 1866.—282

341 An allusion to Bismarck's well-known expression about the unification of Germany by 'blood and iron'. He said at a sitting of the budget commission of the Prussian Chamber of Deputies in September 1862: 'The great questions of time are decided not by speeches and majority decisions—this was the mistake of 1848 and 1849—but by iron and blood'.—282

342 At a session of the Commons on 4 June 1866, Disraeli criticised Clarendon's activity as Foreign Secretary, in particular, his alleged lack of firmness during the Crimean war and at the Paris peace congress of 1856.—282

343 Engels is referring to Prussia's defeat in the war with Napoleonic France in 1806.—285

344 Part of this letter was published in English for the first time in Karl Marx and Friedrich Engels, *Correspondence. 1846-1895.* A Selection with Commentary and Notes, Martin Lawrence Ltd., London [1934]. The complete English translation was published in Karl Marx, *On the First International.* Arranged and edited, with an introduction and new translations by Saul K. Padover, New York, 1973.—286

345 This is a reference to Engels' intention to write articles for *The Manchester Guardian* on the Austro-Prussian war, which broke out in June 1866. He wrote a series of five articles, and they were published in the newspaper under the heading 'Notes on the War in Germany' (see present edition, Vol. 20).

The *Austro-Prussian war of 1866* put an end to the rivalry between Austria and Prussia, which had lasted for many years, and predetermined the unification of Germany under the supremacy of Prussia. Several German states (such as Hanover, Saxony, Bavaria, and Württemberg) fought on Austria's side.

Prussia formed an alliance with Italy. In June and July, hostilities were conducted on two fronts: in Bohemia and in Italy. After the grave defeat of her army at Sadowa, Austria began peace negotiations and signed a peace treaty in Prague on 23 August.—286, 290, 296, 298

346 A discussion on the Austro-Prussian war of 1866 took place at the Central Council meetings of 19 and 26 June, and 17 July 1866.

It was Marx's aim in the discussion to explain the necessity for the International to take an independent stand as a working-class organisation. This stand should have nothing to do either with the Proudhonists' nihilistic attitude towards the struggle for the national unification of Germany and Italy or with the British trade unionist tendency to embellish the unification policy of the ruling classes in Prussia and Italy, to neglect their expansionist and dynastic motives which played an important part in initiating the war conflict. Marx's critical speech persuaded the Central Council to refuse, on 17 July, to vote for the resolutions submitted earlier by Cremer and Dutton, as well as for Fox's resolution, because they failed to give precise formulations of the tasks of the proletariat. The Council unanimously adopted, with certain amendments, the following resolution which had been proposed by Bobczynski and Carter:

'That the Central Council of the International Working Men's Association consider the present conflict on the Continent to be one between Governments and advise working men to be neutral, and to associate themselves with a view to acquire strength by unity and to use the strength so acquired in working out their social and political emancipation' (*The General Council of the First International. 1864-1866. The London Conference 1865. Minutes*, Moscow, 1964, p. 213).—287

347 *Mutualists*, or supporters of mutual assistance, was the name adopted in the 1860s by the French Proudhonists, adherents of Proudhon's reformist ideas on the emancipation of labour by organising mutual assistance, equitable exchange of services and cheap credit.—287

348 A reference to the decisive battle in the Austro-Prussian war (see Note 345), which was fought at Königgrätz (Hradec-Králové) not far from the village of Sadowa (Bohemia) on 3 July 1866. The battle of Sadowa resulted in grave defeat for the Austrian forces. It is also known as the battle of Königgrätz.— 288, 537

349 At the end of 1865 and the beginning of 1866, Bismarck conducted negotiations with Napoleon III through the Prussian ambassador to Paris, von der Holtz. In the course of the negotiations, wishing to secure France's neutrality in the war against Austria which was being prepared by him, Bismarck sought to make Napoleon believe that the war would be extremely exhaustive for Prussia and hinted vaguely at the possibility of territorial expansion for France at the expense of Belgium and Luxemburg, as well as certain German territories on the Rhine.—289, 293

350 As a result of the resignation of the Russell Liberal government and in protest against the impending coming to power of the Conservatives headed by Derby and Disraeli, mass meetings took place in London's Trafalgar Square, on 27 June and 2 July 1866, which again demanded manhood suffrage. In March 1866 the Reform League abandoned this demand under the influence of bourgeois radicals (see Note 315), but in the situation its leadership had to return for some time to its former platform. These meetings, which began a new stage in the struggle for a second electoral reform in Britain, had virtually been organised by members of the Central Council of the International.—290

351 In referring to Thiers' criticism of the foreign policy of the Second Empire, Marx, apparently, had in mind his speech of 3 May 1866 in the Corps législatif to which Napoleon III responded with a speech in Auxerre on 6 May 1866 (see Note 332). On 6 July 1866 the government of Napoleon III submitted a project of a *senatus-consulte* to the French Senate in accordance with which it was the Senate's exclusive right to discuss any alterations in the Constitution; discussion of any such matters in the press was to be prohibited under the threat of heavy fines; and the clause in the Constitution of 1852 establishing a three-month term for the forthcoming session of the Corps législatif was to be abolished. The *senatus-consulte* was adopted by the Senate on 14 July 1866.

During the debates on the budget for 1867 in the Corps législatif on 14 June 1866, one of the leaders of the bourgeois-republican opposition, Jules Favre, criticised the Mexican expedition (see Note 270) which involved tremendous expenses. At the same session another member of the republican opposition, Deputy Glais-Bizoin, expressed support for the parliamentary system referring to the French as a nation living under a regime of despotism. For this he was called to order by Walewski, Chairman of the Corps législatif.— 290

352 On 4 July 1866, after the defeat of the Austrian army at Sadowa (see Note 348), the Austrian Emperor Francis Joseph sent a telegram to Napoleon III in which he informed Napoleon that he was ready to secede to him Venetia provided that Napoleon would then secede this region to Italy, and he asked Napoleon III to act as intermediary between the belligerent states. Italy and Prussia agreed to Napoleon's mediation. In accordance with the peace treaty with Austria signed in Vienna on 3 October 1866 the region was returned to Italy.— 291

353 Marx is referring to the bulbs that his daughter Jenny received from Johann Carl Juta, husband of her aunt Louise, in Cape Town and sent to Engels with detailed instructions on how to grow them.— 291, 294

354 '*Old Bess*' or '*Brown Bess*' were the names given to the flint-lock smooth-barrelled muzzle-loading gun used in the British army in the eighteenth and the beginning of the nineteenth century.— 291

355 A reference to Prussia's annexation of the Kingdom of Hanover, the Electorate of Hesse-Cassel, the Grand Duchy of Nassau and other territories as a result of its victory over Austria in the war of 1866.

According to a report published in the Augsburg *Allgemeine Zeitung* on 7 June 1866, the King of Naples Francis II Bourbon, who had been overthrown by the Garibaldist movement, was presented with an honorary shield at an election meeting of the Prussian conservatives in Berlin which was chaired by Count Stolberg; however, at the same meeting there were calls for Prussia's union with the Italian 'revolution'.— 292, 345

356 Certain South German states (such as Bavaria, Württemberg, and Baden) took part in the Austro-Prussian war of 1866 on the Austrian side.— 293, 295

357 A reference to the projected settlement of the Austro-Prussian conflict that was proposed by the government of Napoleon III on 11 July 1866 in response to Prussia's peace terms. According to the project, an independent South German Confederation was to be formed, consisting of states lying south of the Main, similar to the former Confederation of the Rhine. In this way Napoleon III hoped to prevent the unification of Germany and to subordinate South German states to his protectorate.

The *Confederation of the Rhine* (Rheinbund)—a confederation of states in

Southern and Western Germany that was formed in July 1806 under the protectorate of Napoleon I. Napoleon's creation of this military and political stronghold in Germany was made possible by his defeat of Austria in 1805. Initially the Confederation incorporated sixteenth states (Bavaria, Württemberg, Baden and others), and later on another five states (Saxony, Westphalia, and others), which virtually became vassals of France. The Confederation fell apart in 1813, after the defeat of Napoleon's army.—294, 297

358 A reference to the war that France fought against the Holy Roman Empire in the seventeenth and eighteenth centuries.—295

359 *Blue Books*—periodically published collections of documents of the British Parliament and Foreign Office. They have been appearing since the seventeenth century.

Marx is referring to five reports of the Children's Employment Commission (1863-66) and the Eighth Report of the Medical Officer of the Privy Council (1866) which was supplemented by Dr Hunter's report about the housing conditions of the workers; Dr Hunter's report was extensively used by Marx in Volume One of *Capital* (see the English edition of 1887, Part III, Chapter XXV and also Vol. 35 of the present edition).—296, 301, 383, 407, 551

360 The plan for *Little Germany* was a scheme to unite Germany without Austria under Prussia's supremacy.—297

361 In his letters of 30 June to Marx and of 16 July 1866 to Engels Paul Stumpf from Mainz said that Wilhelm Liebknecht held a pro-Austrian stance in the Austro-Prussian war. In these letters, as well as in his letter to Marx of 10 July, Stumpf asked for instructions on the stand to be taken by the International's members in Mainz with regard to the military events.—298, 299

362 On 16 July 1866, during the Austro-Prussian war, the free city of Frankfurt am Main, which sided with Austria, was captured by the Prussian army. An indemnity of six million guldens was imposed on it, the city senate was disbanded and the garrison and military organisations disarmed. On 19 July the Prussians raised the indemnity to twenty-five million guldens and demanded from the burgomaster Karl Fellner a list of the wealthiest and most influential citizens, whose property was to be a pledge for the payment of the indemnity. He hanged himself in protest on the night of 23 July.—299, 301, 333

363 *Eschenheimer Gasse*—the street in Frankfurt am Main where the Federal Diet was in 1816-66.—299

364 A reference to the *Slav Congress* which met in Prague on 2 June 1848. It was attended by representatives of the Slav regions of the Austrian Empire. The Right, moderately liberal wing, to which Palacký and Šafařík, the leaders of the Congress, belonged, sought to solve the nationalities question by achieving autonomy for the Slav regions within the framework of the Habsburg monarchy (Austro-Slavism doctrine). The Left, radical wing (including Sabina, Frič and Libelt) wanted joint action with the democratic movement in Germany and Hungary. The radical delegates took an active part in the people's uprising in Prague (12-17 June 1848) and were subjected to severe reprisals. On 16 June the moderately liberal delegates declared the Congress adjourned indefinitely.—299

365 On 11 July 1859 Austria and France signed a separate preliminary peace treaty in Villafranca which put an end to the war of France and Piedmont against

Austria. In accordance with the treaty, Lombardy fell to France, but later on Napoleon III ceded it to Piedmont in exchange for Savoy and Nice; Venice was to remain under the Austrian domination and the dukes of Tuscany and Modena were to be reinstalled to their thrones. Although some clauses of the preliminary treaty were never implemented (e. g. the clause on the restoration of the dukes of Tuscany and Modena) or were altered, on the whole it formed the basis of the final peace treaty signed in Zurich on 10 November 1859.

The peace treaty between Austria and Prussia was signed in Prague on 23 August 1866. Under its terms Austria ceded its rights on Schleswig and Holstein and recognised Prussia's annexation of Hanover, Electorate of Hesse (Hesse-Cassel), Nassau and Frankfurt am Main; the German Confederation ceased to exist and instead of it the North German Confederation was formed under the hegemony of Prussia which did not incorporate Austria. The peace treaty between Austria and Italy was signed in Vienna on 3 October 1866. In accordance with it the region of Venice was returned to Italy, but its claims to Southern Tyrol and Trieste were rejected because of Prussia's opposition.— 300, 345

366 On 23 July 1866 the Reform League (see Note 155) called a meeting in Hyde Park in support of manhood suffrage. Although banned by the government, the meeting took place; there was a clash between its participants and the police and several dozen workers were arrested. On 24 and 25 July tens of thousands workers, many of them armed, gathered round Hyde Park. The police and army units were sent against the demonstrators and a state of siege was virtually introduced in the capital; a threat arose of a clash of the people with the police and army. In this situation on 25 July a delegation of the League headed by its President Edmond Beales met the Home Secretary Spencer Walpole and promised to persuade the demonstrators to disperse if the army and police were ordered out of the park. Walpole agreed to this and did not object to another meeting in Hyde Park due on 30 July. However, during its preparation, Walpole denied his permission. His words were confirmed by Austin Holyoake, a member of the League Council, in his report about this talks with Walpole published in *The Times*. Fearing the mounting revolutionary activity of the masses the Council decided not to call any open-air meetings.—300

367 In May 1849, the republican Armand Marrast, President of the French Constituent Assembly, requested General Changarnier, a monarchist and commander of the Paris garrison, to bring in troops to defend the Assembly against the Bonapartists. Changarnier refused, declaring that he disapproved of '*baionnettes intelligentes*', i. e. soldiers meddling in politics.— 302

368 Part of this letter was published in English for the first time in K. Marx, *On History and People*, McGraw-Hill Book Company, New York, 1977. The full version of the letter was published in *The Letters of Karl Marx*, New Jersey, 1979.—303

369 A reference to a note handed to Bismarck in early August 1866 by the French Ambassador to Berlin Vincent Benedetti; it demanded the restoration of the 1814 frontiers as a compensation for France's neutrality during the Austro-Prussian war. This meant that the Saar Basin, the Palatinate, and the Rhenish part of Hesse-Darmstadt with the fortresses of Landau and Mainz were to be given over to France. The note also suggested that the Prussian garrison should be withdrawn from Luxemburg. The claims of Napoleon III were based on the secret promises made by Bismarck before the Austro-Prussian war not to

impede the annexation of the German territories between the Rhine and Mosel by France in case the latter did not prevent the formation of the Prusso-Italian coalition and defeat of Austria. However, following the victory over Austria, Bismarck, who planned a war with France, changed his stand and rejected the French government's demands on 7 August.—306, 352

370 This fact was later on cited by Engels in his unfinished work *The Role of Violence in History* which he wrote in 1887 and 1888 (see present edition, Vol. 26).—307

371 Part of this letter was published in English for the first time in K. Marx, *On Education, Women and Children*, McGraw-Hill Book Company, New York, 1975.—307

372 Marx was sending Engels a letter to him from Liebknecht of 10 August 1866 along with a few issues of the Leipzig *Mitteldeutsche Volkszeitung*. The newspaper was founded in 1862 by liberals but in August 1866, after it had lost most of its subscribers it was sold to Liebknecht. He tried to turn it into a democratic paper and use it, as he wrote to Marx, to publicise the ideas and documents of the IWMA in Germany. However, on 29 August the publication was stopped by the Prussian military authorities of the city and was never renewed again.—310

373 This letter was first published in English in K. Marx, *On Education, Women and Children*, McGraw-Hill Book Company, New York, 1975.—310

374 Marx is referring to his regular contributions to the *New-York Daily Tribune* which he made for over ten years, from August 1851 to March 1862.—311

375 The *Geneva Congress*—the first congress of the International Working Men's Association—took place between 3 and 8 September 1866. It was attended by 60 delegates from the Central (General) Council, various sections of the International and workers' societies in Britain, France, Germany and Switzerland. Hermann Jung was elected chairman. In preparing for the Congress Marx wrote 'Instructions for the Delegates of the Provisional General Council. The Different Questions' (see present edition, Vol. 20). This document was read as the official report of the Council.

The Proudhonists who enjoyed one-third of the votes at the Congress countered Marx's 'Instructions' with their own programme on all items of the agenda setting it out in a memorandum. Nevertheless, the Congress adopted a resolution based on six of the nine points formulated by Marx in the 'Instructions': on the international combination of efforts in the struggle between labour and capital, on limitation of the working day, on juvenile and children's labour, on co-operative labour, on trade unions, and on standing armies. A compromise resolution on Poland was moved by Johann Philipp Becker and was adopted.

The Geneva Congress approved the Rules and the Regulations of the International Association and elected its General Council (officially called Central Council before the Congress) mostly in its former composition. The Congress completed the formation of the International as a mass international proletarian organisation.—312, 314, 316, 326, 368

376 As a result of its victory over Austria in 1866, Prussia was able to embark on the unification of Germany under its aegis. Besides its direct annexation of certain territories (see Note 355), it compelled Austria to agree to the disbandment of the German Confederation, and also succeeded in signing alliance treaties with 17 North German states (north of the Main) which had

fought in the war on its side; later on Saxony and other German states joined alliance treaties. This form of union prepared the ground for the formation of the North German Confederation.—312, 349, 460

377 Judging by this letter, Engels left for Germany on 24 August 1866. Presumably he visited his home town and other places in the Rhine Province of Prussia, and stayed with his relatives. Engels returned to Manchester probably in the latter half of September.—313, 330

378 From the end of August till mid-September 1866, Jenny Marx was on holiday at the seaside.—314

379 At the meeting of the General Council (as the Central Council began to be called after the Geneva Congress) on 25 September 1866 Marx informed it that he had received £5, the annual contribution, from Samuel Moore in Manchester. The receipt issued to Moore by the Treasurer of the Council, William Dell, Marx sent to Engels enclosed with this letter.—317

380 As far back as in March 1865, the Central Council of the International adopted a resolution on the conflict in the Paris Section in which it opposed the Proudhonist thesis that only a worker was admissible as an official in the working men's organisation. During the discussion of the General Rules and the Regulations at the Geneva Congress (see Note 375), the French delegate Tolain declared that only a person directly engaged in manual labour could be a delegate to the congress. Tolain's statement met with stiff opposition. Cremer and Carter emphasised in their speeches the fact that many of the people to whom the International owed its very existence were not manual workers. They particularly noted the services of Marx who, as Cremer said, had made fight for the triumph of the working class the cause of his entire life. Tolain's amendment was rejected.—318

381 At the proposal of the French delegates Tolain and Fribourg, the Geneva Congress expelled Le Lubez from the General Council for his slander and intrigues. At the General Council meeting of 16 October 1866 the matter, at Le Lubez's demand, was referred to the Standing Committee, which at the Council meeting of 23 October confirmed the correctness of the report on Le Lubez's unanimous expulsion with the minutes of the Congress (see *The General Council of the First International. 1866-1868. Minutes*, Moscow, 1964, p. 51).— 318

382 To confirm his theory, Pierre Trémaux referred to the assertion of the Senegal missionary Santamaria that the black people descended from white people.— 320

383 The workers' congress in Baltimore was held from 20 to 25 August 1866. It was attended by 60 delegates representing 60,000 American workers organised in trade unions. The Congress discussed such matters as the legal introduction of an eight-hour working day, political activities, co-operative societies, the unification of all workers in trade unions, strikes, and housing conditions. It was decided at the Congress to form the National Labour Union.—326

384 In his letter to Marx of 11 October 1866 Kugelmann said that he had not received any letters from him since April of that year and that he believed that the subsequent letters might have been either lost or intercepted. Later on it turned out that Marx's letter to Kugelmann of 23 August 1866 (see this volume, pp. 311-12) was only received on 27 November 1866.— 327

385 In the first chapter of the first edition of Volume One of *Capital* Marx

summarised his *A Contribution to the Critique of Political Economy* which had been published in 1859 (see present edition, Vol. 29). In the second and subsequent German editions of Volume One of *Capital* and in the English edition of 1887, this chapter ('Commodity and Money') comprises Part I (see present edition, Vol. 35).—328

386 This letter is a reply to Kugelmann's letter of 23 October 1866. Kugelmann advised Marx to ask Engels for his help in arranging the loan; he also suggested that Marx should make the same request to a well-known doctor, A. Jacobi, a former activist in the Communist League, who lived in New York.—330

387 The *Code pénal* was introduced in 1811 in Napoleon's France and in the regions of Western and South-Western Germany conquered by the French. Article 2 of the *Code* says: 'Any attempt to commit an offence that manifested itself in practical acts and was accompanied by the *commencement of the commitment of the offence* and that was interrupted or was not carried out owing solely to circumstances that were beyond the control of the person in question shall be equivalent to an offence proper.'—333

388 Early in September 1866 the Prussian Chamber of Deputies passed an Indemnity Bill submitted by Bismarck. The Bill relieved the government of any responsibility for expenditures which had not been legally approved during the constitutional conflict (see Note 100). Thus the conflict ended with the complete capitulation of the bourgeois opposition to the Bismarck government. Deputies Karl Twesten and Frenzel, who belonged to the opposition and had more than once criticised the government, now voted for the Bill. Nevertheless, early in November 1866 they were once again put on trial on the basis of the Supreme Tribunal's decision of 29 January 1866 (see Note 292) for their former speeches in the Prussian Provincial Diet but were again acquitted.—333

389 Part of this letter was published in English for the first time in K. Marx, *On America and the Civil War*, New York, 1972, and in full in *The Letters of Karl Marx*, New Jersey, 1979.—334

390 Karl Marx's father, Heinrich Marx, owned a small vineyard in the Mosel region.—334

391 A reference to the commercial treaty between Britain and France of 23 January 1860. In accordance with the treaty the duties on British goods exported to France were not to exceed 30 per cent of their price; France had the right to duty-free import of most of her goods to Britain.—334

392 A reference to the defeat of the Democratic Party to which President Johnson belonged in the elections to Congress in November and December 1866. Johnson pursued a policy of compromise with the plantation-owners of the Southern states and opposed the granting of electoral rights to the Negroes. The elections were won by the Republicans who had received two-thirds of the votes in Congress.—334

393 Nos. 52 and 53 of the Berlin satirical weekly *Kladderadatsch* of 18 November 1866 carried a lampoon, *Die Frau in Weiß. Drama in 5 Acten mit freier Benutzung von Wilkie Collins,* which was directed against Marx and his comrades. Its author was Heinrich Bettziech, a German petty-bourgeois democrat, who wrote under the pen-name of Beta.

The *Brimstone Gang* was the name of a students' association at Jena University in the 1770s which was notorious for its members' brawls; subsequently, the expression 'Brimstone Gang' became widespread.

In his pamphlet *Mein Prozeß gegen die 'Allgemeine Zeitung'* which was published in 1859 the petty-bourgeois democrat Karl Vogt called Marx and his party comrades 'the Brimstone Gang'. However, this was a jocular name for a group of German émigrés that existed in Geneva in 1849 and 1850 with which Marx and his supporters were not connected. Marx exposed Vogt's slander in his pamphlet *Herr Vogt* which was published in 1860 (see present edition, Vol. 17).

Wilhelm Liebknecht was arrested in Berlin on 2 October 1866 after he had made an anti-government speech in the Berlin Printers' Union. He was sentenced to three months imprisonment.— 336

394 A reference to the letter to Engels of 6 December 1866 from the refugee Hossfeld who lived in Liverpool. He asked Engels to lend him some money.— 337

395 A reference to the seizure by the French authorities of letters written by members of the International, their confiscation of documents of the Geneva Congress and the pressure that the Bonapartist circles brought to bear on the British government in order to prevent the publication of Congress documents in *Le Courrier international.* Early in January 1867 the General Council published a statement entitled 'The French Government and the International Association of Working Men' in which it exposed the actions of the ruling circles of the Second Empire towards the International (see *The General Council of the First International. 1866-1868. Minutes*, Moscow, 1974, pp. 271-76).— 338

396 *Head Centre* was the code name of the leader of the Fenian secret organisation (see Note 257). At the General Council meeting of 4 December 1866 it was reported that James Stephens, the leader of the Irish Fenians who had been arrested late in 1865 but escaped from prison and emigrated to the United States, had joined the International.— 338

397 On 6 December 1866 Pius IX addressed the officers of the French regular forces before their evacuation from the Papal States on Napoleon III's order. In his speech the Pope virtually expressed his disapproval of this act by the French Emperor and asked for him to be informed that he should act 'as the head of a Christian state and a good Christian', in other words, he should take effective measures to prevent the incorporation of the Papal States into the Italian Kingdom.— 338

398 Marx used *A History of Agriculture and Prices in England* by James Thorold Rogers in Chapter VI of Volume One of *Capital* which later became a section (chapters XXIII and XXIV in the second and subsequent German editions respectively, chapters XXV and XXVII in the English edition of 1887; see present edition, Vol. 35).— 339

399 Part of this letter was published in English for the first time in K. Marx and F. Engels, *Literature and Art.* Selection from Their Writings, New York, 1947.— 339, 347

400 *Praetorians*—the privileged section of the army in ancient Rome, originally the generals' guards; in a figurative sense, mercenary troops propping up a system of government based on brute force.— 340

401 The *substitution system* was for a long time practised in the French army whereby members of the wealthier classes had the privilege of being able to free themselves from military service by hiring substitutes. During the French Revolution this was prohibited; however, Napoleon I introduced it again. Under the law of 1855, substitutes were to be selected by government bodies

and the payment for them was to be made to a special 'army donation' fund. The substitution system was abolished in France in 1872.— 340

402 Jules Gottraux, a Swiss-born subject of Great Britain and a member of the International, was detained by the French police on the Franco-Swiss border on 30 September 1866 when he was returning to London from Geneva. The police confiscated letters and printed matter which were to be handed to the General Council. The General Council made a public protest against this arbitrary act and other acts hostile to the International committed by the Bonapartist authorities and demanded the return of the seized documents (see Note 395). Receiving no reply from the French Minister of the Interior to its petition that the documents be returned, the General Council appealed to Lord Edward Stanley, the British Foreign Secretary, who through Henry Cowley, the British Ambassador to Paris, succeeded in returning the papers. At its meeting of 1 January 1867 the General Council passed a resolution in which it thanked Lord Stanley for his help.— 341, 346

403 A reference to the black-white-red flag of the North German Confederation which was founded in 1867 under the supremacy of Prussia (at the time the letter was written preparations were being carried on for forming it), and later of the German Empire.— 344

404 Marx used this information given by Engels in Volume One of *Capital* (see present edition, Vol. 35; English edition of 1887, Part IV, Chapter XV, Section 5, pp. 434-35).— 345

405 Article 4 of the *Peace Treaty of Prague* between Prussia and Austria recognised the independence of the German states lying south of the Main and their right to form a separate South German Confederation (Napoleon III's aim). At the same time it mentioned the national ties between the North and South German states and envisaged the possibility of their joining the planned North German Confederation under Prussia's supremacy. In August 1866 Bismarck made a secret defence alliance with the South German states which provided that in the event of war their armies would be placed under the Prussian high command.— 345

406 In his letter to Marx of 15 February 1867 Ludwig Kugelmann enclosed a notice from the Hanover liberal newspaper *Zeitung für Norddeutschland*, No. 5522, of the same day which reported Marx's intention to go to the Continent with the alleged aim of preparing a Polish insurrection. Sending the text of his refutation ('A Correction', see present edition, Vol. 20, p. 202) Marx considered its publication all the more necessary since he did plan to visit Germany to take the manuscript of Volume One of *Capital* to the publisher Otto Meissner in Hamburg and to agree about the terms of its publication.

On 21 February 1867 the *Zeitung für Norddeutschland* was forced to print a refutation of its fabrication about Marx's intention to take an active part in the preparations for a future insurrection in Poland. On 22 February Kugelmann sent the published refutation to Marx. This was probably what Marx told Engels in his letter of 25 February.— 346, 347, 352

407 The report on the Geneva Congress of the International (see Note 375) was published in English in *The International Courier*, Nos. 7-15 of 20 February, 13, 20 and 27 March, and 3, 10 and 17 April 1867 and in French in *Le Courrier international*, Nos. 8-16 of 9, 16, 23 and 30 March and 6, 13, 20 and 27 April 1867.— 346

408 This is a comment on the elections to the constituent North German Reichstag

which took place in Germany in February 1867. Two Saxon constituencies elected August Bebel who became the first ever working-class representative in the German parliament and the lawyer Reinhold Schraps, the candidate of the Saxon People's Party. Wilhelm Liebknecht had been in prison for three months until the middle of January and was therefore unable to organise an election campaign and to win the elections.— 348

409 A reference to the constituent North German Reichstag convoked on the basis of universal suffrage that had been proclaimed by Bismarck. The Reichstag held its sessions from 24 February to 17 April 1867; it approved the creation of the North German Confederation and its constitution, which became valid on 1 July 1867.— 349

410 The weekly *Hermann,* No. 426, 2 March 1867, reprinted from the *Volks-Zeitung* Stieber's statement which refuted the report published in the *Hermann,* No. 424, to the effect that in January 1860 he had attempted to bribe its editorial board in order to prevent the further publication of an article by Wilhelm Eichhoff exposing Stieber's activities as an *agent provocateur* during the Cologne Communist trial. Under this statement of Stieber's the editors placed a statement by R. Hirschfeld, the owner of the print-shop where at that time the weekly had been printed. Hirschfeld's statement cited facts showing Stieber's attempt to bribe the editorial board in January 1860. On 8 March 1867 the *Volks-Zeitung* carried a new statement by Stieber, in which he again denied his attempt.— 349

411 A reference to the secret peace negotiations between France and Russia in 1855 during the Crimean war (1853-56) waged by the Anglo-Franco-Turkish coalition and Tsarist Russia. They were conducted through Baron Seebach, Saxony's envoy to Paris, who had important connections at the Russian court.— 349

412 On 10 April 1867 Marx went to Germany to deliver the manuscript of Volume One of *Capital* to the publisher Otto Meissner. He arrived in Hamburg by boat on 12 April. Having made all the arrangements with Meissner, he came to Hanover on 16 April and stayed with Ludwig Kugelmann till the middle of May. On his way back to Britain Marx once again saw Meissner in Hamburg on 16 and 17 May and returned to London on 19 May 1867.— 350, 356, 366, 375, 379

413 In his note to Marx of 1 April 1867 Sigismund Borkheim told him that 'a continental friend' ('ein Freund vom Kontinent') had written to him about Marx's strained circumstances and his need of the Party's material support.— 350, 352

414 On 25 January 1867, the Paris Bronze-Workers' Credit and Solidarity Society (Société de crédit et de solidarité des ouvriers du bronze) sent a circular to its members calling upon them to prepare for a general strike of solidarity with Barbedienne's bronze-workers who demanded fixed rates. They went on strike in February. In response to this, the owners of 120 enterprises adopted, at their meeting on 14 February, a resolution threatening to impose a lock-out if the society were not dissolved. A general meeting of bronze-workers that was held on 24 February and was attended by nearly 3,000 people resolved to fight the employers. The General Council of the International was immediately informed of this by a delegation of the bronze-workers' society specially sent to London, consisting of Camelinat, Kin, and Valdun who were joined by Tolain and Fribourg. On the initiative of Jung, Dupont and other members of the General Council funds began to be raised to aid the Paris workers. The broad movement of solidarity, which had been organised by the General Council,

served to keep up the strikers' militant spirit and undermined the employers' position. Negotiations between employers and workers began at individual factories, and on 24 March representatives of the employers' association agreed to introduce fixed rates for separate jobs.—351

415 Early in 1867 a conflict broke out between the ruling circles of Prussia and France, since both sides had claims to the Grand Duchy of Luxemburg, which was connected by a personal union with the Netherlands (the King of the Netherlands was also the Grand Duke of Luxemburg) and was also a member of the German Confederation. However, after the latter was disbanded in 1866, Luxemburg refused to enter the North German Confederation which had been formed under Prussia's aegis. The government of Napoleon III and the King of the Netherlands agreed on the sale of Luxemburg to France, but Bismarck prevented it by making use of the Prussian garrison that was stationed in the duchy when the German Confederation still existed.

In May 1867 the Luxemburg question was discussed at an international conference in London which made it a duty of the European powers to guarantee the preservation of Luxemburg's former status and neutrality. Prussia was to withdraw its troops from the duchy. In both states the Luxemburg conflict entailed preparations for war and extensive militaristic propaganda and became a stage in the preparation for the Franco-Prussian war of 1870-71.—351, 352, 364, 459

416 In response to the protest of the Polish deputies to the North German Reichstag against the forcible incorporation of the Principality of Posen and other Polish territories in the North German Confederation, Bismarck made a demagogical speech on 18 March 1867 in the Reichstag in which he said in particular that the Polish peasantry trusted the Prussian and Russian authorities more than their own nobility.—351, 374

417 In his speech of 11 March 1867 in the North German Reichstag Bismarck said: 'Gentlemen! Let us quickly get down to work! Let us put Germany in the saddle, as it were! She will be able to ride.' On 23 March of the same year a conservative deputy to the Reichstag, Hermann Wagener ended his speech with the words Engels cites in his letter.—355

418 According to the arrangement with the publisher that Marx mentions in his letter, he planned after the publication of Volume One of *Capital* (appeared in September 1867) to publish Book Two and Book Three as Volume Two, and Book Four, which contained a critical history of economic theories, as a concluding Volume Three.

After Marx's death, Engels prepared for the press and published manuscripts belonging to Book Two and Book Three as Volumes Two and Three of *Capital*; he died before he could prepare for the press Book Four, *Theories of Surplus Value* (Volume Four of *Capital*) and have it published (see also Note 227).—357, 358, 367, 368, 371, 390, 402, 405, 407, 418, 436, 442, 509, 511, 515, 525, 544

419 Part of this letter was published in English for the first time in Karl Marx & Frederick Engels, *Letters on 'Capital'*, New Park Publications, London, 1983.—358, 386, 391, 402, 405, 409, 417, 425, 442, 487, 507, 511

420 *Guelphs* (Welfs)—members of a separatist party formed in Hanover following its annexation by Prussia in 1866. It consisted of supporters of the restoration of the independent Hanover monarchy headed by the house of Welfs which was once on the throne there.—361, 492

421 *Head-in-chief* (Haupt-Chef)—the name given by Wilhelm Stieber, one of the
     organisers of the Cologne Communist trial in 1852, to a police spy, Julian
     Cherval (real name Joseph Crämer). Stieber sought to represent Cherval as a
     dangerous conspirator and leader of the Communist League and make it
     appear that he was connected with Marx and the defendants (see K. Marx,
     Revelations Concerning the Communist Trial in Cologne, present edition, Vol. 11,
     pp. 407-19).—361

422 A reference to the subscription for Ferdinand Freiligrath that was started in
     the spring of 1867. The poet's admirers wanted to present him with a 'people's
     donation' since he had lost his post of manager in the English branch of the
     Bank of Switzerland after the latter's bankruptcy. With this aim in view,
     committees were organised in Britain, Germany and the United States through
     which funds were gathered. Reports about the subscription were regularly
     published in the London newspaper *Hermann.*—362, 378, 385, 425, 472, 532

423 A reference to the publicity Lassalle managed to achieve for his book about
     Heraclitus' philosophy, published in 1858. For this purpose he made use of his
     friends and officially joined the society of German Old Hegelian
     philosophers.—363

424 The 'nationalities principle' was put forward by the ruling circles of the Second
     Empire and was extensively used by them as an ideological smoke-screen for
     their plans of conquest and adventurous foreign policy. Seeking to pass himself
     off as a 'defender of nationalities', Napoleon III took advantage of the national
     interests of the oppressed nations with the aim of strengthening the hegemony
     of France and extending her frontiers. This principle was also used in the
     diplomacy of Tsarist Russia to spread Russian influence to the Balkans and
     Central Europe. The demagogical nature of the 'nationalities principle' used by
     the ruling circles of counter-revolutionary European states was exposed by
     Marx in his pamphlet *Herr Vogt* (see present edition, Vol. 17) and by Engels in
     the article 'What Have the Working Classes to Do with Poland?' (present
     edition, Vol. 20).—364

425 A reference to the second Reform Bill which was finally approved by
     Parliament on 15 August 1867. In accordance with the new law, the property
     qualifications for electors was lowered for lease-holders in the counties to
     12-pound rent a year, and in the towns franchise was granted to all
     householders, and house tenants, and those tenants who had held their place of
     residence for not less than a year and paid not less than £10. Although as a
     result of the 1867 reform the number of electors in Britain doubled, and
     suffrage was also extended to a section of skilled industrial workers, the bulk of
     the country's population remained disfranchised as before.—365, 384, 468

426 Part of this letter was published in English for the first time in K. Marx and
     F. Engels, *Correspondence. 1846-1895*, London, 1934. In full the letter was
     published in English in K. Marx and F. Engels, *Selected Correspondence*, Progress
     Publishers, Moscow, 1975.—366

427 Part of this letter was published in English for the first time in K. Marx, *On the
     First International*, New York, 1973. In full the letter was published in English
     in *The Letters of Karl Marx*, New Jersey, 1979.—367

428 Marx was first expelled from France in January 1845 by the Guizot ministry at
     the demand of the Prussian government. The pretext for this was Marx's part

in editing the newspaper *Vorwärts!* which violently criticised Prussian reactionary order. Early in February Marx had to emigrate to Belgium.

On 19 July 1849, Marx who was again in Paris—this time after the defeat of the German revolution—received a notice from the French authorities ordering him to leave Paris and move to the Department of Morbihan, a swampy and unhealthy part of Brittany. This prompted his departure to London in the second half of August 1849.—368

429 Marx's attempts to find somebody to translate *Capital* into French were unsuccessful at the time. On the French translation of Volume One of *Capital* see Note 539.—368

430 A reference to a cross given to Jenny on her birthday. Such crosses were worn by participants in the Polish national liberation struggle. Since the end of 1867 Jenny wore it on a green ribbon as a symbol of her mourning over the Irish Fenians executed in November 1867 (green colour was a symbol of struggle for the national liberation of Ireland).—369, 479

431 The *Manichaeans* were the followers of a religious trend current in the Middle East in the third century of the Christian era, its characteristics being asceticism and celibacy. In German students' slang the word Manichaean stood for a merciless creditor (in consonance with the German 'mahnender Gläubiger', i. e. a creditor demanding the payment of debt).—372, 436

432 The *National-Liberals*—a party of the German, above all Prussian, bourgeoisie which was formed in the autumn of 1866 after a split in the Party of Progress (see Note 99). Their policy showed that a considerable section of the liberal bourgeoisie had abandoned its claims to extend its political prerogatives and capitulated to the Bismarck Junker government after Prussia's victory in the Austro-Prussian war and the establishment of her supremacy in Germany.— 372, 421, 504

433 In June 1849 the right-wing liberal deputies of the Frankfurt National Assembly, who walked out after the Prussian King Frederick William IV had refused to accept the Imperial Crown, met in Gotha for a conference which resulted in the formation of the so-called *Gotha party*. The objective of this party, which reflected the sentiments of the big bourgeoisie and feared the victorious outcome of the revolution, was to achieve the unification of the Germany (with the exception of Austria) under the hegemony of Prussia. There was a certain continuity between the Gotha party and the National-Liberals.—372

434 In 1846 Marx and Engels negotiated through Joseph Weydemeyer the financing of the publication of their two-volume work criticising the German ideology (see present edition, Vol. 5) with the Westphalian publishers Julius Meyer and Rudolph Rempel. In July 1846, after a series of subterfuges and delays, Meyer and Rempel refused their promised assistance on the pretext of financial difficulties, the actual reason being the differences of principle between Marx and Engels, on the one hand, and the champions of 'true socialism', on the other, whose views both publishers shared.

In the spring of 1845 Hermann Kriege, one of the future exponents of 'true socialism', was recommended by Meyer to Engels and Marx and met the former in Barmen and the latter in Brussels.—373

435 In his speech in the North German Reichstag on 9 March 1867 Johannes Miquel demanded that a North German Confederation should be formed as a

single centralised state under the hegemony of Prussia and urged the other German states to sacrifice their freedom for Germany's unification.—373

436 *Cremorne gardens* existed in the 1850s-1870s in London; they were closed in 1877.—376

437 Marx stayed with Engels in Manchester from approximately 22 May to 2 June 1867.—377, 379

438 During his stay in Hanover in April and May 1867, Marx decided to write an appendix on forms of value for Volume One of *Capital*—an idea that was supported by Ludwig Kugelmann. Marx wanted to supplement and specify Chapter I of the main text on commodities and money. He implemented this idea in the first edition of Volume One (1867). In the second German edition of 1872 Marx revised this appendix and incorporated it in the relevant passages of the text. In the subsequent editions of *Capital*, including the English one of 1887 edited by Engels, the text was given in this form.—378, 384, 392, 396, 402, 423

439 A reference to the 'Report of the Commissioners on the Treatment of the Treason-Felony Convicts in the English Convict Prisons' by the police magistrate Alexander Knox and the medical officer George Pollock published in London in 1867 on Parliament's decision. The report dealt with the treatment of political prisoners, especially Irish Fenians (see Note 257) in the English prisons.—378, 383, 390, 394

440 *The Times* of 3 June 1867 carried a report by its Paris correspondent which stated that during the ceremony of welcome for the Russian Emperor Alexander II in Paris, there had been shouts of 'Long Live Poland' in the crowd. At the meeting of 18 June 1867 the General Council of the First International passed a resolution approving the mass demonstration of solidarity in Paris with the Poles suppressed by Tsarism. The text of the Council's resolution was published in *The Commonwealth*, No. 224 of 22 June 1867 (see *The General Council of the First International. 1866-1868. Minutes*, Moscow, 1974, pp. 129-30).—379

441 In Hegel's terminology, '*Knoten*' ('nodal points') are certain moments in movement when a sudden qualitative leap takes place as a result of gradual quantitative change (see G. W. F. Hegel, *Wissenschaft der Logik*, Erstes Buch, Dritter Abschnitt, Zweites Kapitel).—382

442 The Royal Commission to Make Inquiry Respecting the English Trade Unions was set up in February 1867 because the ruling classes were anxious about the mounting trade unions' activity and hoped that such inquiry would help to outlaw the trade unions or at least restrict the scope of their activity. At the same time an anti-trade union campaign was launched in bourgeois newspapers. The trade unions, supported by the General Council of the International, responded with meetings all over the country and a national conference in London on 5-8 March 1867. After the inquiry the Royal Commission failed to make any serious charges against the trade unions, but it hindered their complete legalisation (the legal protection of their funds, and the recognition of their right to fight strike-breakers and to support strikes organised by other trade unions).—384, 387, 426

443 The new inquiry into working conditions resulted in the law of 15 August 1867 which extended the validity of the factory acts to new industries. Now the

maximum working-day for women and children below eighteen years of age was restricted to $10\,^1/_2$ hours, not only at the factories but also at smaller enterprises and in the domestic industry.—384

444 Marx is referring to Chapter III of the first edition of Volume One of *Capital*; in the second and subsequent editions it corresponds to five chapters (V-IX) of Part III and in the English edition of 1887 to chapters VII-XI (see present edition, Vol. 35).

The note to the text of the first edition that is mentioned here stated that the molecular theory was advanced by Auguste Laurent and Charles Frédéric Gerhardt, and Charles Adolphe Wurtz was the first who scientifically elaborated it. Later on Marx made an additional study of the history of this problem and omitted his reference to Wurtz in the second German edition of Volume One of *Capital* (1872); in the third edition of the volume (1883) Engels also made a more precise assessment of the role that had been played by Laurent and Gerhardt (see the English edition of 1887, Part III, Chapter XI, and the present edition, Vol. 35).—385

445 Engels' *The Condition of the Working-Class in England* appeared in the spring of 1845. The part of the edition that had not been sold out was put on sale later on with a new title page dated 1848.—385

446 A reference to Chapter II ('The Transformation of Money into Capital') and Chapter III ('Production of Absolute Surplus-Value') of the first edition of Volume One of *Capital*. They correspond to Parts II and III in the second and subsequent German editions, and to Parts II and III (chapters IV-XI) of the English edition of 1887 (see present edition, Vol. 35).—386

447 One of the reasons for appointing the Royal Commission to Make Inquiry Respecting the English Trade Unions (see Note 442) was the excesses committed in 1865-66 in Sheffield, the centre of metal-working industry, by some trade-unionists against strike-breakers. The Commission, however, failed to make any serious charges against the trade unions, since these instances were few and far between.—387

448 Part of this letter was published in English for the first time in K. Marx and F. Engels, *Selected Correspondence*, Progress Publishers, Moscow, 1975.—388, 389

449 Between 5 July and early August 1867 Engels travelled in Sweden, Denmark and Germany and visited Ludwig Kugelmann in Hanover. His wife Lizzie Burns accompanied him during some part of the trip.—389, 391, 392, 395, 396, 399, 401, 444, 469

450 Marx is referring to the last section of Chapter V in the first edition of Volume One of *Capital*. It corresponds to Chapter XVII of Part VI in the second and subsequent German editions of this volume and to Chapter XIX of Part VI in the English edition of 1887 (see present edition, Vol. 35).—390

451 The paras mentioned in the letter, including the criticism of the theory of Nassau William Senior, were in Chapter III of the first edition of Volume One of *Capital*, and correspond to chapters VII and VIII of Part III in the second and subsequent German editions of this volume, and to chapters IX and X of Part III in the English edition of 1887 (see present edition, Vol. 35).—391, 392

452 A reference to the extremely negative reaction of the *Norddeutsche Allgemeine Zeitung* (in the articles published on 18 and 26 June 1867) to the statements by the British Foreign Secretary Stanley in the House of Commons on 14 June

and the Prime Minister Derby in the House of Lords on 20 June 1867. Stanley and Derby expressed their approval of the treaty on Luxemburg signed at the international conference in London on 11 May 1867. This treaty which guaranteed the former status and neutrality of Luxemburg put an end to the so-called Luxemburg crisis (see Note 415).—394

453 In his reply to Marx of 20 July 1867 Freiligrath evaded a direct answer to Marx's question (see M. Häckel, *Freiligraths Briefwechsel mit Marx und Engels*, Th. 1, Berlin, 1968, S. 181).—398

454 For the second German edition of Volume One of *Capital* (published by Meissner in Hamburg in 1872) Marx revised and enlarged the text and improved the structure of the book. In doing this he also took into account the suggestions Engels made in this letter. Instead of the original six chapters the second and subsequent German editions of Volume One contained seven parts comprising 25 chapters. Chapter IV, which is being discussed in this letter, became Part IV consisting of four chapters; Chapter XII was divided into five and Chapter XIII into ten sections. The text of this volume in the English edition of 1887, edited by Engels, was divided into even more chapters. Chapter IV of the first edition corresponds to Part IV, chapters XII, XIII, XIV (sections 1-5) and Chapter XV (sections 1-10) (present edition, Vol. 35).— 406, 407, 436

455 The reference is to Chapter VI ('The Process of the Accumulation of Capital') of the first edition of Volume One of *Capital* which corresponds to Part VII of the second and subsequent German editions, and to chapters XXIII-XXV of Part VII of the English edition of 1887 (see present edition, Vol. 35).—406, 409

456 Part of the Preface to Volume One of *Capital* was soon published in a number of German periodicals such as *Die Zukunft*, No. 206 of 4 September 1867; *Der Beobachter*, No. 210 of 7 September 1867; *Der Vorbote*, Nos. 9-11 of September-November 1867; and *Demokratisches Wochenblatt* of 4 and 11 January 1868. The English translation of part of the Preface done by Georg Eccarius was published in *The Bee-Hive Newspaper*, No. 308 of 7 September 1867; the French translation done by Paul Lafargue and Marx's daughter Laura appeared in *Le Courrier français*, No. 106 of 1 October 1867 and in the Belgian newspaper *La Liberté*, No. 15 of 13 October 1867.—407, 423, 428, 448, 450, 495, 527

457 A reference to Marx's work on Book Two of *Capital* in which he analysed 'The Process of Circulation of Capital'. By that time Marx had already finished the first rough version of the book, it being written presumably in the first half of 1865. From the latter half of 1865 to August 1867 he wrote another two manuscripts dealing with the subject. Between the end of 1868 and 1870 Marx wrote a second, complete version of this book, which, along with his later manuscripts, was subsequently used by Engels in preparing Volume Two of *Capital* for publication in 1885.—408

458 A reference to Marx's letter to Engels of 20 August 1862 and Engels' reply of 9 September 1862 (see present edition, Vol. 41).—408

459 This letter was published in English for the first time in Karl Marx & Frederick Engels, *Letters on 'Capital'*, New Park Publications, London, 1983.—410

460 In the summer of 1866 the Greek population of Crete (Candia) rose against Turkish domination demanding union with Greece. Despite the cruel punitive

measures taken by the Turkish troops against the insurgents and civilians, the struggle continued, supported by volunteers from many other countries.

The events on Crete brought about a new aggravation of the international contradictions in the Middle East. In November 1866 the Russian government proposed that the European powers should demand from the Turkish Empire the transfer of Crete to Greece. However, the western powers preferred Crete to remain under the Turkish rule since they were afraid that the position of Russia in the region might be strengthened and the national liberation movement of the nations ruled by the Sultan be further stepped up. The support of the Crete insurgents went no further than a joint statement made by Russia, France, Italy and Prussia of 29 October 1867 which recommended that the Turkish government should restrain from bloody excesses on Crete. In 1869 the insurrection was completely suppressed.—414

461 The *League of Peace and Freedom*—a pacifist organisation that was set up in 1867 with the active participation of Victor Hugo, Giuseppe Garibaldi and other democrats. The League owed its origin to the anti-war sentiments of the masses. However, its leaders held pacifist positions; they failed to see the social causes of war and often confined its anti-war activity to mere declarations.

The League's constituent congress was originally scheduled for 5 September 1867 in Geneva. Its organising committee, which enjoyed the support of a number of radical and democratic public figures like John Stuart Mill and the Reclus brothers, also counted on the participation of the leaders of the European proletariat. Therefore the committee sent invitations to the sections of the International and its leaders, Marx included, to attend the congress. It was also decided to postpone the opening of the congress until 9 September, so that the delegates of the Lausanne Congress of the International (due on 2-8 September) could take part in it too.

The International's attitude towards the League of Peace and Freedom was discussed both in the General Council and in local sections. Marx's speech at the Council meeting of 13 August 1867 and the resolution adopted at his proposal (see present edition, Vol. 20, p. 204) formulated the principles of the International's tactics in such a bourgeois-democratic movement. In contrast to the unconditional support of the League, which is what the leaders of the British trade unions inclined towards, the International's tactics envisaged both the joint participation with the democrats in the struggle against the threat of war, provided the class independence of the proletarian organisation was retained, and a revolutionary proletarian approach towards the questions of war and peace in opposition to bourgeois pacifist illusions. Marx believed that the International should not take part in the League's congress on an official basis because that would mean the International's solidarity with its bourgeois programme. However, it was recommended that the International's members should attend the congress privately in order to influence its decisions in a revolutionary-democratic way.—414, 424, 473, 517, 537, 581

462 The *Lausanne Congress* of the International was held from 2 to 8 September 1867. Marx took part in the preparations but he was unable to attend the congress, since he was busy reading the proofs of Volume One of *Capital*.

The Congress was attended by 64 delegates from six countries (Britain, France, Germany, Switzerland, Belgium and Italy). Apart from the report of the General Council (see present edition, Vol. 20), the Congress heard reports from the local sections which showed the increased influence of the

International on the proletariat and the growing strength of its organisations in different countries. The delegates holding Proudhonist views, especially those from France, sought to change the orientation of the International's activity and its programme principles. Having managed, despite the efforts of the General Council's delegates, to impose their agenda on the Congress, they sought to get the Congress to revise the Geneva Congress resolutions in a Proudhonist spirit. They did succeed in carrying through a number of their own resolutions, in particular the one on co-operation and credit, which they regarded as the principal instruments of changing society by means of reform.

However, the Proudhonists failed to achieve their principal aim. The Congress retained as valid the Geneva Congress resolutions on the economic struggle and strikes. The Proudhonist dogma on abstaining from political struggle was countered by the resolution on political freedom passed by the Lausanne Congress which emphasised that the social emancipation of the working class was inseparable from its political liberation. The Proudhonists likewise failed to seize the leadership of the International. The Congress re-elected the General Council in its former composition and retained London as its seat.—416, 418, 420, 425, 427

463 A reference to the printed sheets of Chapter VI, the last one, of Volume One of *Capital*.

In the second German edition of Volume One (1872) Marx, on Engels' advice, substantially enlarged the section on Ireland and wrote some additional notes (see the English edition of 1887, Part VII, Chapter XXV, Section 5).

The '*resumé*' on the expropriation of the expropriators' mentioned by Engels is placed at the end of Chapter XXIV in the second and subsequent German editions and at the end of Chapter XXXII (Part VIII) of the English edition of 1887 (see present edition, Vol. 35).—417, 432

464 *Der Social-Demokrat*, No. 102 of 30 August 1867 carried a report that J. M. Hirsch, publisher of a collection of songs, and two owners of the printing-house where it was printed had been arrested in Erfurt. Hirsch was charged with high treason.—417

465 The *Royal Society of Arts*—an educational and philanthropic organisation founded in Britain in 1754. It consisted mainly of businessmen and bourgeois intellectuals and enjoyed the patronage of aristocracy. Marx violently criticised the Society's attempts to act as a mediator in the conflicts between workers and employers with the aim of undermining the class struggle. At the same time he thought highly of its extensive library and its research publications of which he made use in his studies, especially in *Capital*. The Society's scientific material became available to him after he joined it in 1869.—418

466 This is apparently a reference to Emile de Girardin's articles in *La Liberté* of which he became the owner in June 1866. Girardin treated the situation in France at that time as similar to that during the pre-revolutionary years 1829 and 1847.—418

467 On 27 August 1867 during his visit to the French part of Flanders on the occasion of the anniversary of its annexation to France, Napoleon III made a speech in Lille in which he was rather pessimistic about France's situation at home and abroad.—418

468 When the Civil War ended, the movement for the legislative introduction of an eight-hour working day intensified in the USA. Leagues of struggle for the

eight-hour day were set up throughout the country; in California alone there were over 50. The National Labour Union, founded at a congress in Baltimore (see Note 383) in August 1866, joined the movement. Attaching great importance to the demand for the eight-hour working day Marx included it in the agenda of the Geneva Congress. In his 'Instructions for the Delegates of the Provisional General Council' he emphasised the need to raise it 'to the common platform of the working classes all over the world' (see present edition, Vol. 20, p. 187). This point as formulated by Marx was adopted as a congress resolution.

On 25 June 1868, the US Congress which was forced to reckon with the mass movement, adopted a law on an eight-hour working day for the employees of all governmental and federal bodies.—418, 452

469 Marx made a number of critical comments on the text of the speech prepared by Borkheim for the constituent congress of the League of Peace and Freedom in Geneva (see Note 461). Having delivered the speech at the congress, Borkheim then published it in French under the title of 'Ma perle devant le congrès de Genève' and also in German.—419, 435, 437, 441, 449

470 In addition to the ordinary footnotes for the first German edition of Volume One of *Capital*, Marx wrote nine notes in which he cited the latest facts from different sources. In preparing the second German edition (1872) he made some alterations in these additional notes and inserted them in the corresponding places of the main text.

On the appendix to Chapter I see Note 438.—419

471 A reference to Marx's speech on the International's attitude towards the congress of the League of Peace and Freedom (see Note 461) and the resolution on the issue proposed by him at the General Council meeting of 13 August 1867 (see present edition, Vol. 20, p. 204). Eccarius' brief report of the Council meeting was published in *The Bee-Hive Newspaper*, No. 305 of 17 August 1867; it was also cited in Lucien Dubois' article 'Les Conditions de la paix', published in *Le Courrier français* on 2 September 1867.—420

472 In his letter to Marx of 5 September 1867 Friedrich Lessner gave him extensive information about the beginning of the International's Lausanne Congress (see Note 462) and referred to the report published in the *Gazette de Lausanne*.—422

473 A reference to the first of Eccarius' series of articles about the Lausanne Congress of the International published in *The Times*, No. 25909 of 6 September 1867. The other articles of the series were published in *The Times*, Nos. 25911-25913 of 9-11 September 1867. In his articles Eccarius made ironical comments on the muddled views of the French Proudhonist delegates and their verbosity.—422, 425, 428, 434

474 Beginning from 5 September 1867 Vermorel's newspaper *Le Courrier français* published Henri Tolain's articles about the International's Lausanne Congress (see Note 462) in which he praised the French delegates' position at the Congress.—422

475 The activity of the Proudhonists at the International's Lausanne Congress (see Note 462) and the fact that they had some of their resolutions adopted, gave particular urgency to the struggle for the assertion of the main programme principles of scientific communism. In Marx's opinion, this task was to be carried out by the next Congress of the International which was to be held in

Brussels in September 1868. Thanks to the energetic preparatory work that was done by Marx and his followers, the decisions of the Brussels Congress, especially the one on the collective ownership of land, paralysed to a considerable extent the influence of the Proudhonists in the International Association.—424, 428

476 The *Berlin Workers' Association* was founded in January 1863 and was under the influence of the men of Progress (see Note 99), especially of Schulze-Delitzsch, and propagandised bourgeois co-operative societies. When the International Working Men's Association was set up, the advanced members of the Berlin Workers' Association were attracted towards it and sought to get rid of the liberals' protection. In October 1868 there was a split in the Berlin Workers' Association. Its radical members formed the Democratic Workers' Association which recognised the programme approved by the Nuremberg Congress of the Union of German Workers' Associations (headed by August Bebel and Wilhelm Liebknecht) based on the International's principles. The Democratic Workers' Association waged a vigorous struggle against the Lassalleans. In 1869 it joined the Social-Democratic Workers' Party which came into being at the Eisenach Congress.—424, 477

477 A reference to Lessner's letter of 7 September 1867 in which he informed Marx about the proceedings of the Lausanne Congress of the International (for Lessner's previous letter about the Congress see Note 472).—424, 429

478 Contrary to the position held by Marx and the General Council of the International towards the bourgeois-pacifist League of Peace and Freedom (see Note 461), the Lausanne Congress, largely owing to the efforts of Johann Philipp Becker and other members of the Geneva Section of the International as well as the French Proudhonists, decided by majority vote to send an official delegation from the IWMA to the constituent congress of the League. On 9 July 1867, before the Lausanne Congress, the general meeting of the Geneva Section of the International decided to join the League's programme and expressed their full confidence to its organisers; several members of the Section, including Becker and Dupleix, joined the League's Organising Committee.—425, 428

479 To break the conspiracy of silence with which official bourgeois academics met the publication of Volume One of Marx's *Capital*, Engels resorted to a kind of stratagem by writing a number of reviews for some bourgeois newspapers which looked as if penned by an unbiased bourgeois scholar. The reviews were published in *Die Zukunft, Elberfelder Zeitung, Düsseldorfer Zeitung, Staats-Anzeiger für Württemberg* and others (see present edition, Vol. 20).—427

480 In his letter to Marx of 9 September 1867 Johann Georg Eccarius informed him that he as well as Johann Philipp Becker, Ludwig Kugelmann, Sigismund Borkheim and others had been invited on 8 September to a preliminary conference of the German participants in the Geneva Congress of the League of Peace and Freedom (see Note 461). This conference made obvious the disagreements between participants in the workers' movement and the bourgeois democrats. Thus, in the discussion of the candidates to the presiding body of the Congress, the democrats Ludwig Simon and Jakob Venedey opposed the very principle of class representation and objected to Kugelmann, who had suggested that representatives of the proletariat be included in it. Nevertheless, as a result of the debates, Marx's followers Eccarius, Becker and

Borkheim and also Ludwig Büchner and Armand Goegg were elected German vice-presidents of the Congress.—429

[481] The *June days*—the proletarian uprising in Paris on 23-26 June 1848.—429

[482] From 13 September 1867, Marx and Paul Lafargue stayed for a few days with Engels in Manchester.—431, 432

[483] The reference is to the spot under the railway bridge in Manchester where on 18 September 1867 Fenians made an armed assault on a police van in order to free two arrested Fenian leaders (see Note 497).—431

[484] Wilhelm Liebknecht was elected deputy to the North German Reichstag by one of the Saxon constituencies on 31 August 1867; he delivered his first speech in the Reichstag on 30 September 1867.—432

[485] This misprint ('C' instead of 'B') also appeared in the second and all the subsequent editions of Volume One of *Capital* that were published during the lifetime of Marx and Engels.—432

[486] In his first speech in the North German Reichstag on 30 September 1867 that he made in the discussion on the passports bill, Liebknecht violently criticised the police and bureaucratic order. He proposed a number of amendments to the bill that would restrict the authorities' arbitrary rule. Liebknecht's bold statements about the political system and the government's policy were repeatedly interrupted by Simson, president of the Reichstag, and his proposals were rejected.

Apart from the reports in the newspapers, Liebknecht's speech was also published as a pamphlet, *Was ich in Berliner Reichstag sagte*, Leipzig, 1867.—433, 444, 445, 450

[487] A reference to Kugelmann's letter to Marx of 29 September 1867 which was written on his return to Hanover from the Geneva Congress of the League of Peace and Freedom. In this letter Kugelmann informed Marx that during the election of five German vice-presidents of the Congress (see Note 480) Karl Vogt was also nominated and that he (Kugelmann) objected giving as a reason the exposure of Vogt as a Bonapartist agent by Marx in his pamphlet *Herr Vogt*. In spite of the efforts of several democrats, in particular, Ludwig Simon, Vogt was not elected vice-president of the Congress.—433, 442

[488] Marx quotes from Paul Stumpf's letter to him from Mainz of 29 September 1867. In very vague terms Stumpf asked Marx to explain to him certain factors of the process of pauperisation and proletarisation of the petty bourgeoisie, artisans, etc.—434

[489] The decision to abolish the office of the General Council's President was moved on Marx's initiative by John Hales and adopted at the General Council meeting of 24 September 1867. The abolition of this post, which had been permanently held since 1864 by one of the British trade union leaders, George Odger, considerably weakened the positions of the reformist wing of the International. Odger did not get any post when the appointment of officers in the Council took place. Before this William Cremer had been dismissed from the post of General Secretary. The International's Basle Congress (September 1869) approved the General Council's decision.—434, 519

[490] The letter to which Marx refers was sent by Peter Fox to Johann Philipp Becker in Geneva on 29 August 1867, on the eve of the Lausanne Congress, and was marked as 'personal and confidential'. Fox's reason for suggesting that

the seat of the General Council should be transferred to Geneva was that, in his opinion, guidance of the international labour movement kept the British members of the General Council away from more effective participation in the activities of the International's organisations in Britain.—434

491 The editorial in *The Times*, No. 25917 of 16 September 1867, dealt with the Geneva Congress of the League of Peace and Freedom (see Note 461). It gave an account of the speeches by Garibaldi, Quinet, Dupont, Bakunin and others, and also mentioned speech by Borkheim who, according to the newspaper, suggested 'the abolition of classes'.—435

492 The title of this article which was published in *Le Courrier français*, No. 113 of 8 October 1867, contains an allusion to La Fontaine's fable *Les voleurs et l'âne.*—438

493 In his letter to Marx of 8 October 1867 Ludwig Kugelmann offered to publish short notes about Volume One of *Capital* and asked for the corresponding instructions.
    For Engels' efforts to popularise Volume One of *Capital* see Note 479.—438, 443

494 In February 1860 Marx who had started work on his pamphlet *Herr Vogt* wrote to Sigismund Borkheim, with whom he was not yet acquainted, asking him for any information that he could give about the so-called Brimstone Gang which existed in Geneva in 1849 and 1850 (see Note 393). Borkheim replied on 12 February and Marx used his letter in his pamphlet to expose Vogt's slanderous fabrications about proletarian revolutionaries. Ever since Marx and Borkheim had been friends.—441

495 The definition of *peonage* as a concealed form of slavery is given by Marx in Volume One of *Capital* (see the English edition of 1887, pp. 146-47 and present edition, Vol. 35).—442

496 A reference to Engels' reviews of Volume One of Marx's *Capital*, of which one was published with Kugelmann's help in *Die Zukunft*, No. 254 of 20 October 1867, Supplement (unsigned), while the other, meant for the *Rheinische Zeitung*, remained unpublished (see Note 523).—443, 445, 449

497 On 18 September 1867 in Manchester there was an armed assault on a police van in order to free Thomas Kelly and Michael Deasy, two Fenian leaders (see Note 257) who had been arrested after the suppression of the armed uprising of February and March 1867 organised by Fenians. Kelly and Deasy managed to escape but during a clash a police officer was killed and mass arrests followed. From 1 to 23 November a trial of the arrested Fenians was held in Manchester in the course of which false evidence and other disgraceful methods were used by the prosecution. In spite of all the efforts by the counsels for the defence, primarily by Ernest Jones, five Fenians were sentenced to death. One of them (Thomas Maguire) was subsequently pardoned; the death sentence of another (Condon), an American citizen, was commuted to life imprisonment; the other three (Michael Larkin, William Allen and Michael O'Brien) were hanged on 23 November.
    During the investigation of the case and the trial, the General Council of the International organised, on Marx's initiative, a broad campaign of the English workers in support of the Irish national liberation movement (see this volume, pp. 460, 464).—444, 460, 463, 466, 476, 479, 483

498 There is no further evidence about the letter which Engels intended to write to Carl Siebel.—445

499 The *Bill on Freedom of Movement and Settlement* was submitted on 3 October 1867 and passed by the North German Reichstag on 22 October. This was one in the series of legislative acts that were passed by the Reichstag from 1867 to 1870 with the aim of eliminating the obstacles to capitalist development in Germany that had been inherited from the period of feudal dismemberment. On 21 October 1867 in the debates on the bill Wilhelm Liebknecht proposed to abolish certain police obstacles to freedom of movement that remained in force.—445

500 A reference to *extradition treaties* which were concluded between various states and became especially widespread in the latter half of the 19th century.—446

501 The German-language weekly in London *How Do You Do?* published abusive allusions to Marx's family connection with the Prussian Minister of the Interior, Ferdinand von Westphalen (Jenny Marx's stepbrother). On 19 August 1851 Marx went with Ferdinand Freiligrath and Wilhelm Wolff to the editorial office of the paper and demanded satisfaction of the publisher Louis Drucker and the editor Heinrich Bettziech (Beta) (see present edition, Vol. 38, p. 432).—447

502 A reference to the *Illustrierte Familien-Kalender* which had been published by A. H. Payne in Leipzig annually, since 1857. The article by Heinrich Bettziech (Beta) 'Die Deutschen in London' was published there.—447

503 In his letter to Marx of 20 September 1867 a German émigré in New York, A. Nahmer, offered to translate into English Volume One of *Capital*. Marx asked some of his friends if they knew anything about Nahmer but none of them did, so he did not reply.—447, 450

504 In his letter of 8 October 1867 Wilhelm Liebknecht informed Marx that he and another Reichstag deputy, Reincke, intended to table the proposal that a commission should be appointed for inquiry into the workers' condition in Prussia. To substantiate this proposal Liebknecht wanted to acquaint himself with the powers of similar commissions in England and asked Marx to send him the relevant legislative acts.

Marx sent him the following acts: An Act for Facilitating in Certain Cases the Proceedings of the Commissioners appointed to make Inquiry respecting Trades Unions and other Associations of Employers or Workmen which had been passed by the British Parliament on 5 April 1867, and An Act to Extend the 'Trades Union Commission Act, 1867' which had been passed on 12 August 1867.—448, 456, 489

505 A reference to the letter that Ludwig Kugelmann wanted to send to Sigismund Borkheim. Kugelmann wrote about this to Marx on 13 October 1867 asking for Marx's opinion of his intention to persuade Borkheim to refrain from extensively advertising his published speech at the Congress of the League of Peace and Freedom since Marx's opponents claimed that Marx was the virtual author of this speech, which could damage his prestige as a serious researcher and the author of Volume One of *Capital*.—449

506 In his letter of 7 October 1867 addressed to Jenny Marx, Johann Philipp Becker told Marx about his strained circumstances, which was why he contemplated giving up his post as Chairman of the Central Committee of the German-language sections in Geneva and leaving the *Vorbote* editorial board.

With the help of his friends Becker managed to cope with the difficulties and continue his public activity.—450

507 On 14 October 1867, in the discussion in the North German Reichstag of the bill on the abrogation of the anti-coalition legislation which had been submitted by Schulze-Delitzsch, Schweitzer made a long demagogical speech. Although he did support the bill, he held a Lassallean stance denying the importance of strikes and coalitions in the workers' struggle against capitalist exploitation. He also made an attempt to expound some tenets of Marx's political economy but he did so in a primitive and distorted way. A report on Schweitzer's speech was published in *Der Social-Demokrat*, Nos. 122 and 123 of 16 and 18 October 1867.—450

508 The reference is probably to clippings from the *Hermann* which carried reports of the London committee for raising money for Freiligrath (see Note 422), in particular from the final address of the committee published in No. 459 of 19 October 1867. On this clipping which has been preserved among his papers Marx wrote a saying widespread in the Rhineland: 'If that's not champion drivel, I don't know what is.'—454

509 Engels wrote the review of Volume One of Marx's *Capital* for *The Fortnightly Review* much later, in May and June 1868. As can be seen from their subsequent correspondence, Marx and Engels exchanged opinions several times on the content and form of the article.

In spite of Professor Beesly's request, the review was rejected by the editorial board and has only been preserved in manuscript form (see present edition, Vol. 20).—455, 457, 463, 466, 512, 516, 518, 524, 526, 532, 533, 545, 555, 560, 583

510 In his letter to Marx of 14 October 1867 Eccarius told him that he and his family were hard-up. For his active work for the International he had been black-listed by his employers and was out of work.

For Becker's difficult financial circumstances see Note 506.—455

511 On 26 May 1849, in the discussion of the drafts for an Appeal to the German people in the Frankfurt National Assembly, W. Wolff made a vivid speech exposing the enemies of the revolution and the indefinite conciliatory stand of the liberals and moderate democrats. He described the Imperial Regent, Archduke John, as the betrayer of the people. The chairman hurriedly called him to order.—456

512 On 17 October 1867, during a discussion of the conscription bill in the North German Reichstag, Liebknecht, Bebel and others proposed that the standing armies should be abolished and the arming of the people substituted for them. In his speech Liebknecht described the North German Reichstag as 'the fig-leaf of absolutism'.

In the course of a discussion of the coalition bill in the North German Reichstag on 19 October 1867 (see Note 507), Liebknecht, Bebel and others submitted an amendment to Section 2 of the bill which would entitle the employer to hire workers of any trade and in any numbers; the amendment also proposed that Section 2 should not abrogate the laws on the limitation and protection of child labour at factories. The amendment was adopted by the Reichstag.—456

513 After Venetia was annexed to the Kingdom of Italy in 1866, the unification of the country would be completed if the Papal States were to be incorporated.

Garibaldi was the initiator of the struggle for their annexation. At first Victor Emmanuel's government turned a blind eye to his preparations for a march on Rome, but it suddenly arrested Garibaldi on the eve of the march. However, his volunteers did invade the Papal States and the patriots in Rome began to prepare an uprising against the Pope. On 18 October 1867, the government of Napoleon III promised its assistance to Pius IX and with this aim in view began to prepare an expeditionary corps to be sent to Italy. When Garibaldi (he escaped from under arrest on 14 October) and his men were on the approaches to Rome, the French corps sailed off for Italy and on 30 October marched into Rome. It was only with the help of the French interventionist forces that the Papal army was able to defeat Garibaldi's volunteers at Mentana on 3 November 1867. The Roman question remained unsettled till 1870.—457, 459, 468, 496

514 The *laws of primogeniture and entail*—feudal inheritance laws that were still in force in Britain in the 19th century. In accordance with them, the title and land were to be inherited by the elder son without the right of alienation.—458

515 A reference to the letter to Marx from the secretary of the German Workers' Educational Society in London (see Note 150) Carl Speyer of 6 October 1867. Speyer thanked Marx, on behalf of the society, for sending Volume One of *Capital.*—459

516 Atheistic societies of freethinkers became very active in Britain in the 1860s. Considerable influence on this movement was exercised by Charles Bradlaugh and other bourgeois radicals who grouped round *The National Reformer* and disseminated reformist ideas among the workers. In October 1867 a group of freethinkers, who thought the influence of Bradlaugh and those who were close to him burdensome, decided to convoke a conference in order to create a Central Association of Freethinkers for purely atheistic propaganda. Marx was also invited to join the preparatory committee for the conference but he declined the proposal.—459

517 Marx ironically uses here Karl Vogt's expression from his book *Mein Prozeß gegen die Allgemeine Zeitung*, Geneva, 1859 (see K. Marx, *Herr Vogt*, present edition, Vol. 17, p. 72).—459

518 The Franco-Italian agreement of 15 September 1864 guaranteed the inviolability of the Papal States and envisaged the withdrawal of the French forces brought there during the revolution of 1848-49 in Italy. In the autumn of 1867, when Garibaldi's detachments invaded the Papal States (see Note 513), secret negotiations for a revision of the September 1864 agreement began between the Kingdom of Italy and France, which, however, came to nothing. In connection with these negotiations Bismarck gave instructions in October 1867 to the Prussian ambassador to Florence, Count of Usedom, ordering him to maintain an observer's attitude in the Franco-Italian conflict and mark time.—460, 466

519 Marx is referring to the meeting between Napoleon III and Emperor Francis Joseph of Austria in Salzburg on 18 August 1867. Napoleon III tried to negotiate an agreement with Austria directed against Prussia and Russia. However, due to the mutual distrust of the parties and Austria's unwillingness to get into a new conflict with Prussia, the agreement was not concluded.—460

520 A reference to the letter which was written by Dupanloup on 15 September 1867, on the anniversary of the Franco-Italian agreement of 15 September

1864, guaranteeing the inviolability of the Papal States to the Italian Prime Minister Rattazzi calling upon him to fight Garibaldi's movement for their annexation to Italy. In a few days the letter was published in *La Gazette de France* and soon afterwards as a separate booklet entitled *Lettre à M. Rattazzi, président du conseil des ministres du roi d'Italie, sur les enterprises de Garibaldi*, Paris, 1867.—460

521 The meeting of the Reform League's Council (see Note 155) on 23 October 1867 discussed a letter of the Chairman of the League, Edmond Beales in which he vigorously condemned the Fenian movement. George Odger and Benjamin Lucraft, trade union leaders and members of the League's Council, objected to its publication and sympathised with the Irish liberation movement. This was the effect of the internationalist influence exercised by Marx and his close followers in the General Council of the International on trade union leaders. However, at subsequent meetings of the League's Council, those on 30 October and 1 November, Odger and Lucraft, under pressure from bourgeois radicals, renounced their former stance announcing that they had been misunderstood.—460

522 Part of this letter was published in English for the first time in K. Marx, F. Engels, *Ireland and the Irish Question*, Progress Publishers, Moscow, 1971.— 461, 463, 467, 474, 483, 505, 549

523 It is obvious from Kugelmann's correspondence as well as from Engels' letters to Marx of 10 November and 12 December (see this volume, pp. 470, 498) that Kugelmann sent this second review of Volume One of *Capital* to Heinrich Bürgers, a former member of the Communist League and an editor of the *Rheinische Zeitung*. Bürgers refused to publish it saying in his reply to Kugelmann of 4 November 1867 that, in his opinion, this work was purely academic and unfit for practical purposes of agitation. Bürgers believed that the level of the workers' consciousness was quite low and that therefore they were unable to understand *Capital*; he also disputed the idea expressed in the review by Engels that *Capital* would become the 'theoretical Bible' of the Social-Democratic Party.—462, 469, 471

524 On 1 November 1867, Moustier, the Foreign Minister of France, sent the Italian government a Note to the effect that the French government could by no means agree to the Italian intervention in the Papal States. On 4 November the French newspaper *La Presse* carried a report claiming that Napoleon III had given an ultimatum to the Italian government demanding the withdrawal of its troops from the Papal States. However, next day the report was refuted.—462

525 On All Saints' Day, 1 November 1867, a demonstration of supporters of Italy's independence and French republicans took place at Montmartre Cemetery in Paris. Wreaths were laid on the graves of the Italian patriot Daniele Manin and the French republican Godefroy Cavaignac. The police arrested some of the demonstrators.—462

526 A reference to the joint statement which was made by Russia, France, Prussia and Italy and sent to the Turkish government on 29 October 1867. The statement called upon Turkey to put an end to the violence against the population of Crete perpetrated by the Turkish troops who were suppressing the national liberation uprising (see also Note 460).—465

527 This note by Marx and the postscript from his daughter Laura were written on Kugelmann's letter to Marx of 6 November 1867.—470

528 In looking for ways to publish reviews of Volume One of Marx's *Capital*, Ludwig Kugelmann applied for help to the lawyer Ernst Warnebold who, as it turned out later, was one of Bismarck's informers, and the National-Liberal Johannes Miquel; both of them were prejudiced against proletarian revolutionaries.—471, 482

529 Engels' review of Volume One of *Capital* which was written for the *Frankfurter Zeitung und Handelsblatt* has not been found.

The review for the *Düsseldorfer Zeitung*, was published unsigned, with Carl Siebel's assistance, in No. 316 of 16 November 1867 (see present edition, Vol. 20).—471, 529, 532, 534, 536, 537

530 The *Barmer Zeitung* of 6 December 1867 carried a short review by Carl Siebel of Volume One of *Capital*, signed 'S'. Engels' review, which he had given to Siebel, was sent by Siebel, judging by his letter to Engels of 13 November 1867, not to the *Barmer Zeitung* but to the *Rhein- und Ruhrzeitung* in Duisburg. Its text has not been found.—471

531 The original of this letter, which was written by Marx on the copy of Volume One of *Capital* that he presented to Carl Siebel, is now not in the possession of the Institute of Marxism-Leninism.—472

532 A reference to the letter to Marx, dated 24 October 1867, from Joseph Dietzgen, a German self-taught philosopher then living in St. Petersburg and working at a tannery. He spoke highly of Marx's merits both before science and the working class and wrote about the deep impression Volume One of *Capital* had made on him and about his acquaintance with some of the earlier works by Marx, particularly *A Contribution to the Critique of Political Economy*. In his letter Dietzgen also outlined the basis of his own materialist world outlook. The letter was the beginning of a friendship between its author and Marx and Engels.

From Solingen Marx received a letter from Karl Klein dated 8 November 1867; he informed Marx about the activities of the local section of the International.—473, 497

533 On 16 October 1859 John Brown, a fighter for the emancipation of the Negroes in the United States, made an attempt to start a slave uprising. With a small detachment of his supporters he captured the state armoury in Harpers Ferry, Virginia. Brown's attempt to engage more people in the uprising failed. Almost all the participants in the uprising (22 people, five of whom were Negroes) who put up a stiff resistance to the government forces were killed. Brown and five of his comrades were executed.—474

534 In 1840, during an abortive attempt to carry out a coup d'état in Boulogne, Louis Bonaparte shot and wounded a government army officer.—474

535 Enclosed with his letter of 19 November 1867, Otto Meissner sent Marx two clippings (from unidentified newspapers) with new notices on the publication of Volume One of *Capital*. One of the notices enumerated the main points of the volume, the other gave an excerpt from Engels' review of Volume One that had been published in *Die Zukunft*, No. 254 (Supplement) of 30 October 1867 (see present edition, Vol. 20).—475

536 The first notice by Otto Meissner on the publication of Volume One of Marx's *Capital* was published in the *Börsenblatt für den Deutschen Buchhandel und die mit ihm verwandten Geschäftszweige*, No. 214 of 14 September 1867. Meissner's notice about Engels' pamphlet *The Prussian Military Question and the German*

Workers' Party was also published in this newspaper, No. 27 of 3 March 1865.—475

537 Appended to the pamphlet containing Wilhelm Liebknecht's speech in the North German Reichstag on 30 September 1867 (see Note 486) was a report of his speeches before workers in Berlin on 14 and 15 October which had been published in *Die Zukunft*, No. 242 (Supplement) of 16 October 1867. In these speeches Liebknecht said that to put forward the social question in the given situation was inexpedient because premature attempts to solve it could, in his opinion, only serve to strengthen the absolute monarchy and delay the victory of socialist principles.

In his letter to Marx of 23 November 1867, Ludwig Kugelmann criticised Liebknecht's point of view, emphasising that in practice this would give such people as the Lassallean Schweitzer and the conservative Wagener complete control over the social issue and the possibility of using it for demagogical aims.—477, 479, 488, 492, 499

538 A reference to the German workers' newspaper *Demokratisches Wochenblatt* which appeared in Leipzig from January 1868 and was edited by Liebknecht. Initially the newspaper was to some extent influenced by the petty-bourgeois People's Party; however, thanks to the assistance given it by Marx and Engels it soon came to play an active part in the development of the proletarian movement in Germany, spreading the ideas of the International and promoting the preparations for forming the Social-Democratic Workers' Party.—477, 479, 484

539 In his letter to Marx of 27 November 1867, Victor Schily informed him about Moses Hess' favourable opinion of *Capital* and the latter's intention to write an article about it for *Le Courrier français*. Schily also wrote about Hess' offer to translate, together with Elysée Reclus, Volume One of *Capital* into French and to publish it. Marx who attached great importance to the publication of *Capital* in French and saw this in particular as an important weapon against the influence of Proudhon's delusions (see this volume, p. 368) did not object to Reclus' participation in the French edition. However, the discussion which lasted for almost three years came to nothing. Later on, when it became clear that Reclus was one of the leaders of Bakunin's Alliance of Socialist Democracy, he could no longer be considered as a suitable translator of *Capital*. The translation of *Capital* into French which had been done by Joseph Roy and edited by Marx himself was published in Paris in 1872-75 by instalments.—478, 483, 488, 490, 528, 532, 533, 580

540 This was written by Marx on Kugelmann's letter to Engels of 25 November 1867.—482

541 The letter was published in English for the first time in the *Labour Monthly*, No. 11, London, 1932.—484

542 A reference to the address entitled 'The Fenian Prisoners at Manchester and the International Working Men's Association' which was written by Marx and approved by the special meeting of the General Council on 20 November 1867 (see present edition, Vol. 21). The document which was sent to the Home Secretary Gathorne-Hardy became an important part of the campaign organised by Marx in the autumn of 1867, for solidarity of the English workers with the Irish national liberation movement. The immediate aim of the address was to prevent the execution of the Fenians on whom the Manchester court had passed the death penalty (see Note 497).—485

543 At the meeting of the International's General Council of 5 November 1867 Peter Fox announced his intention of leaving his post as corresponding secretary for America and take a paid job at *The Bee-Hive Newspaper*. Hermann Jung, chairman of the meeting, condemned Fox's intention. Fox sent a letter to the next meeting which was held on 12 November reaffirming his resignation and accusing Jung of his alleged wish to remove Englishmen from the Council. All those present at the meeting supported Jung.—485

544 The draft resolution that had been proposed by Peter Fox read: 'That this meeting desires that a settled peace and amity between the British and the Irish nations should be substituted for the war of seven hundred years between Englishry and Irishry; and with a view to that end this meeting exhorts the friends of Irish nationality to bring their cause before the British people and advises the latter to accord an unprejudiced hearing to the arguments advanced on behalf of Ireland's right to autonomy' (*The General Council of the First International. 1866-1868. Minutes*, Progress Publishers, Moscow, p. 181). The draft was referred to the Standing Committee for consideration and for that reason it had not been adopted by the General Council.—486

545 The *Corn Laws*, which imposed high import duties for corn in Great Britain and which had been introduced in order to meet the interests of large landowners, were repealed in 1846.
From 1845 to 1847 a grievous famine blighted Ireland due to the ruin of farms and the pauperisation of the peasants, who were cruelly exploited by the English landlords. This had been caused by the almost total failure of the potato crop (potatoes were the principal diet of the Irish peasants). About a million people starved to death and the new wave of emigration caused by the famine carried away another million. As a result, large districts of Ireland were depopulated and the abandoned land was turned into pastures by the Irish and English landlords.—486

546 In 1849 Parliament passed the *Encumbered Estates Act* for Ireland, which was supplemented with a series of other acts in 1852 and 1853. The Act of 1849 provided for the sale of mortgaged estates by auction if their owners were proved to be insolvent. As a result, the estates of many ruined landlords passed into the hands of usurers, middlemen and rich tenants.—486

547 The reference is probably to the speech by Thomas Francis Meagher at a meeting in Dublin convoked on 15 March 1848 by the Irish Confederation. He said: 'If you do not give us a parliament in which to state our wrongs and grievances, we shall state them by arms and force.'—486

548 The upsurge of the Irish national movement caused by Britain's defeat in the War of Independence of the American colonies, forced the British Parliament in 1782 to pass an act which abolished the right of the British Parliament to pass laws for Ireland and granted this right to the Irish Parliament. The act was once more confirmed in 1783 in the form of a new 'Renunciation Act', which meant Irish autonomy in legislation. However, after the Irish national liberation rising of 1798 had been suppressed, the British government virtually nullified these concessions to Ireland by imposing on it a union with England. The Act of Union which came into force on 1 January 1801 put an end to the remnants of Irish autonomy and abolished the Irish Parliament. One of its consequences was the abolition of the protective tariffs for the emerging Irish industry which had been introduced by the Irish Parliament in the late 18th century; this led to a total decline of the national industry.—486

549 Marx apparently did not make a speech on the Irish question in the General
    Council as planned. In December 1867, the Council met twice, on the 17th and
    31st, and from January 1868, illness prevented Marx from attending the
    Council meetings for several months. His view of the Irish question, which
    reflected the position of the revolutionary proletarian wing of the General
    Council, was set forth in the detailed report he made on 16 December in the
    German Workers' Educational Society in London (see present edition,
    Vol. 21).—487

550 A reference to the sections of the first German edition of Volume One of
    Capital. They are given as chapters VIII, XI, XII, XIII and XXIV in the
    second and subsequent German editions of this volume, and as chapters X,
    XIII, XIV, XV and XXVI in the English edition of 1887 (see present edition,
    Vol. 35).—490

551 A reference to Ludwig Kugelmann's letters to Marx of 23 November and to
    Engels of 25 November (with enclosed reprints of Kugelmann's note on
    Volume One of *Capital* in the *Deutsche Volkszeitung*) and of 30 November 1867,
    and to Wilhelm Liebknecht's letter to Engels of 26 November 1867. In seeking
    to persuade German economists and philosophers to respond to Marx's book,
    Kugelmann sent reprints of his own and Engels' (from *Die Zukunft*) reviews of
    it to Faucher, Schulze-Delitzsch, Dühring, Roscher, Hildebrand and Rau, about
    which he told Marx in his letter of 23 November 1867.—492

552 Engels' letter to Liebknecht mentioned here has not been found. In his reply to
    this letter of 11 December 1867, Liebknecht said that he agreed with Engels'
    remarks on the policy pursued by the working-class representatives in Germany
    but that he had a different opinion on individual practical questions of
    agitation. In particular, he explained the reason for the address that he and
    Bebel had sent to the Vienna City Council by their confidence that Austria was
    on the eve of a revolution ('She has to experience her own 1789'), which was to
    have an impact on the whole of Germany.—492, 499, 503, 504

553 On 4 November 1867 Adelaide Macdonald who supported the Fenians made
    an attempt on the life of a policeman guarding the house of a witness at the
    Fenian trial in Manchester (see Note 497) who had given evidence against
    William Allen. She was arrested, put on trial and sentenced to five years' penal
    servitude.—492

554 With his letter to Marx of 3 December 1867 Ludwig Kugelmann enclosed his
    correspondence with Heinrich Bürgers (see Note 523).—493, 498

555 Engels fully accepted the draft of a review of Volume One of *Capital* for *Der
    Beobachter* that is being set out here by Marx and also used this letter in writing
    the review. The review was then published, with Kugelmann's assistance, in *Der
    Beobachter*, No. 303 of 27 December 1867, unsigned (see present edition,
    Vol. 20).
        The passage Marx mentions here is in a special additional note to Section 1
    of Chapter VI in the first German edition of Volume One of *Capital*, at the
    end of the book. Marx deleted this note when preparing the second German
    edition (1872).—494

556 In his letter to Marx of 26 November 1867, Wilhelm Liebknecht told him that
    he had the opportunity to make use of several German newspapers such as *Die
    Zukunft, Volkszeitung* (Hanover), *Oberrheinischer Courier* (Freiburg im Breisgau),
    Neue Baseler Zeitung, Correspondent (Leipzig), *Süddeutsche Presse* and *Deutsche
    Arbeiterhalle* (Mannheim).—495

557 A reference to No. 139 of *Der Social-Demokrat* of 29 November 1867 with its two supplements which carried a detailed report about the general meeting of the General Association of German Workers on 24 November 1867. Among the speakers was one of the publishers of *Der Social-Demokrat*, the Lassallean J. B. von Hofstetten, who included in his speech passages from *Capital* distorting their meaning and naming neither the work nor its author. Marx responded to this with an article, 'Plagiarism', which was published unsigned in *Die Zukunft*, No. 291 (Supplement) of 12 December 1867 (see present edition, Vol. 20).

The mentioned letter of Marx to Guido Weiß, the editor of *Die Zukunft*, has not been found.—495, 496

558 A reference to Section 4 of Chapter III of the first edition of Volume One of *Capital*. It is given as Chapter VIII of Part III in the second and subsequent German editions and Chapter X of the English edition of 1887 (see present edition, Vol. 35).—495

559 In his letter to Marx of 1 December 1867, Kugelmann asked whether Borkheim could make arrangements through his friend Lothar Bucher for the publication of Engels' review of Volume One of *Capital* in the *Norddeutsche Allgemeine Zeitung*. Since the newspaper was a semi-official mouthpiece of the Bismarck government, Kugelmann's offer was unacceptable to Marx and Engels.—497, 498

560 In his letter to Engels of 30 November 1867, Kugelmann asked him to write several reviews of Volume One of *Capital* by Marx. Kugelmann was going to arrange for their publication with the help of Lieutenant-Colonel Seubert, a writer and an official of the Württemberg War Ministry, to whose daughter he was giving treatment. Seubert promised his assistance in getting the reviews published in such newspapers as *Der Beobachter*, *Staats-Anzeiger für Württemberg* and *Schwäbischer Merkur*. For the first two Engels wrote reviews.—499, 510, 512

561 A reference to a legal action of the Schulze & Siebenmark firm against a woman home-worker accused of concealing wool. During the trial which took place in Berlin late in 1867, the employers' shady practices were brought to light: they provided their home-workers with dampened wool that lost weight while being processed, for which the workers were heavily fined by the firm. The case was given great publicity.—501

562 Part of this letter was published in English for the first time in the *Labour Monthly*, No. 11, London, 1932.—501, 504

563 On 13 December 1867 a group of Fenians caused an explosion in Clerkenwell Prison in London, their aim being to free the imprisoned Fenian leaders. The attempt failed, but the blast destroyed several neighbouring houses, a few people were killed and over a hundred wounded. The British bourgeois press took advantage of this to spread slanderous fabrications about the Irish national liberation movement and whip up chauvinistic anti-Irish sentiments among the English population.—501, 505

564 In his letter to Engels of 10 December 1867, Carl Siebel suggested that Otto Meissner should present Friedrich Albert Lange, a well-known philosopher, sociologist and democrat, with a copy of Volume One of *Capital* by Marx.—502

565 A reference to Marx's report on the Irish question which he made on 16 December 1867 at a meeting of the German Workers' Educational Society in

London (see Note 150); the meeting was also attended by members of other workers' societies of London as well as some members of the General Council. A detailed outline of the report which was written by Marx and a brief handwritten record of it by Eccarius (see present edition, Vol. 21) have come down to us.—504

566 The *Customs Union Parliament* was the guiding body of the Customs Union which was reorganised after the Austro-Prussian war of 1866 and the signing of a treaty between Prussia and South German states on 8 July 1867. The parliament consisted of members of the North German Confederation's Reichstag and specially elected deputies from the South German states— Bavaria, Baden, Württemberg and Hesse. It was to deal exclusively with problems of trade and customs policy; Bismarck's attempts to widen its jurisdiction met with the stubborn resistance of South German representatives.—505

567 On 6 December 1867 the Bismarck government submitted to the Prussian Chamber of Deputies draft treaties of compensation to be made to the King of Hanover and the Duke of Nassau whose possessions were annexed by Prussia after the 1866 Austro-Prussian war. In order to gain support from the Chamber, the government dismissed the unpopular Minister of Justice Lippe who had given Bismarck active help in carrying out his anti-constitutional measures, and appointed in his place Gerhardt Leonhardt, the former Minister of Justice for Hanover. Bismarck's calculations proved correct: the Prussian Chamber of Deputies approved the compensation treaties, thus sanctioning annexation of Hanover and Nassau.—506

568 A reference to Engels' reviews of Volume One of *Capital*. Engels intended to send them to Meissner so that he could compose and publish an advertisement of Marx's work.—507, 509

569 Ground rent is dealt with in Volume Three of *Capital* (present edition, Vol. 37).—508

570 A reference to Jenny Marx's letter to Engels of 23 December 1867 in which she thanked him for the wine he had sent them for Christmas and informed him about the state of Marx's health. She also told Engels about the popularisation of Volume One of *Capital* in Germany and about his reviews which played an important role in this campaign.—508

571 On 13 November 1867 Carl Siebel wrote to Engels that he had sent Engels' review, which had formerly been intended for publication in the *Barmer Zeitung*, to another newspaper, whereas he had sent to the *Barmer Zeitung* a short item on the subject that he had written himself (see Note 530). In another letter to Engels on 20 December 1867 Siebel enclosed a clipping from the *Barmer Zeitung* with his item, published on 6 December 1867.

In both letters Siebel suggested that the publication of a review of Volume One of *Capital* should be arranged in the *Kölnische Zeitung* with Meissner's assistance; he also named one of the contributors to the paper as a possible author of the review.—509

572 As Jenny Marx told Engels in her letter of 23 December 1867, the Lassallean J. B. von Hofstetten's answer to the article 'Plagiarism' (see Note 557) appeared in *Die Zukunft* on 18 December. Since 'Plagiarism' had been published anonymously, Hofstetten did not suspect that it had been written by Marx himself and ascribed the authorship to Liebknecht.—509, 529

573 In a letter addressed to Marx's daughter Jenny of 3 January 1868, Liebknecht said that he would like to ask Marx what he thought of his possible removal from Leipzig to Vienna.—512

574 Part of this letter was published in English for the first time in the *Labour Monthly*, Vol. 5, No. 3, London, 1923.—514

575 A reference to the section 'The So-Called Primitive Accumulation' of Chapter VI of the first German edition of Volume One of *Capital*. This section is given as Chapter XXIV, Part VII of the second and subsequent German editions and Chapter XXVI, Part VIII of the English edition of 1887 (present edition, Vol. 35).—514

576 A reference to the prospects for the distribution of Volume One of *Capital* in Austria, where an upsurge of the labour and national movement made itself clear in those years. This had been caused by the crisis of the Austrian absolute monarchy aggravated by the defeat of the Habsburgs in the Austro-Prussian war of 1866. This situation compelled Austria's ruling circles to reorganise in 1867 the empire into the dual state of Austria-Hungary and introduce a constitution which guaranteed certain bourgeois freedoms and provided for bourgeois reforms.—515

577 A reference to the help Marx gave Liebknecht when he was the London correspondent of the Augsburg *Allgemeine Zeitung*, i.e. from 1855 until 1862, when he moved to Berlin.—515

578 After his return from London to Germany in 1862, Wilhelm Liebknecht was at one time a member of the editorial board of the Berlin *Norddeutsche Allgemeine Zeitung*. Initially this was an opposition newspaper but after the formation of Bismarck's government it began to turn into its mouthpiece. When Liebknecht realised this, he left the newspaper.—516

579 Among the papers seized by the French police during the searches in the homes of members of the Paris Administration of the sections of the International late in 1867 was a letter to Murat, a member of the Paris Administration, from Eugène Dupont, the Corresponding Secretary of the General Council for France, of 23 November 1867. The letter informed the French members of the International about the campaign in support of the Fenian prisoners (see Note 542). The French authorities tried to use this letter to accuse the International of complicity in a Fenian plot. At a trial of the Paris Administration members which took place in March 1868, they were accused of forming an association without the sanction of the authorities. The court declared the Paris Section of the International disbanded and fined the Paris Administration members.—516, 520

580 A reference to the numerous articles by Engels in which he analysed the military operations during the siege and defence of Sevastopol and which were amongst his reports on the Crimean war of 1853-56 (present edition, vols 12-14), and to the series of articles he wrote about the progress of the Austro-Prussian war of 1866, 'Notes on the War in Germany' (see present edition, Vol. 20).—517

581 The expression 'treat like a dead dog' was first used by Gotthold Ephraim Lessing to describe the attitude of some of his contemporaries to Spinoza's philosophy. Hegel mentioned it in the Foreword to the second edition of his *Encyklopädie der philosophischen Wissenschaften im Grundrisse*.—520

582 Forestalling the General Council one of whose duties was to prepare the annual
congresses of the International, the Paris Administration published in *Le
Courrier français* on 11 December 1867 the programme for the next congress to
be held in Brussels. This programme which was markedly Proudhonist in
character would take away the congress' attention from urgent issues of the
working-class organisation.
At the General Council meeting of 21 January 1868 the agenda of the
Brussels Congress was approved. In spite of the efforts of the Proudhonists,
this programme outlined the ways of further consolidating the international
workers' organisation on the platform of proletarian socialism.—520

583 Marx was in Berlin from 17 March to 12 April 1861; he discussed starting a
joint newspaper in Germany with Lassalle; he also made unsuccessful efforts to
restore his Prussian citizenship (see Note 154).—520, 531

584 A reference to the moderate liberal interpretation of the popular demand for
the repeal of the Anglo-Irish Union of 1801 which deprived Ireland of the
right to have an autonomous parliament (see Note 548). Some of the leaders of
the Association of Repealers (i.e. supporters of the abolition of the Union),
which had been founded in 1840, such as D. O'Connell regarded agitation for
this demand merely as a means to obtain individual privileges for the Irish
propertied classes from the British government; they wanted Ireland to be a
country with limited self-government within the United Kingdom. A similar
stand was taken by their successors, the liberal wing of the Irish national
movement in the 1850s and 1860s, in contrast to the Irish radicals—the
Fenians—who sought to establish true independence for their country.—521

585 A reference to a copy of a bust of Zeus from Ogricoli which was presented to
Marx by Kugelmann.—521, 578

586 A reference to the letter to Engels from Liebknecht of 20 January 1868, in
which Liebknecht told Engels that, while sharing his critical attitude towards the
petty-bourgeois South-German People's Party and the League of Peace and
Freedom, he nevertheless did not believe it possible to break with them for
tactical reasons. Liebknecht also informed Engels about the steps he had taken
for the popularisation of Volume One of *Capital.*—525, 527

587 Engels' project was not fulfilled.—526

588 A reference to the letter from Kugelmann to Marx of 17-18 January 1868 with
which a letter was enclosed to Marx from a Hungarian writer, Károly Márie
Kertbény. In his letter Kugelmann said that Kertbény had seen him in Hanover
and showed an interest in the members of the revolutionary movement.
Kugelmann asked Marx to tell him what he thought of Kertbény and also to
receive a young banker from Hanover, Karl Coppel, who was going to London.
Judging by the letter from Kertbény to Marx of 17 January 1868, he wanted to
publish in the Leipzig *Illustrierte Zeitung* a short biographical note about Marx
and a portrait of him on the occasion of the release of Volume One of *Capital.*
Kertbény discovered this portrait by chance in the studio of a photographer in
Hanover and asked Marx to send biographical details. Kertbény's project was
not fulfilled.—527, 529, 531, 533, 536

589 This quotation from *The Saturday Review* given in English was partly used by
Marx in the afterword to the second German edition of Volume One of *Capital*
which appeared in 1872 (see present edition, Vol. 35).—529

590 The details from Marx's biography enclosed with this letter are being given according to the copy in Kugelmann's hand.—530

591 A reference to the lectures Marx delivered in the latter half of December 1847 at meetings of the German Workers' Society in Brussels. Early in 1848 he made an attempt to publish in Brussels a work that he had written on the basis of these lectures but was unable to do this because of his expulsion from the country. This work was first published in part as editorials in the *Neue Rheinische Zeitung* on 5-8 and 11 April 1849 under the general heading of *Wage Labour and Capital* (see present edition, Vol. 9). The publication of the editorials was first interrupted by Marx's temporary departure from Cologne and later because the newspaper ceased to exist.

The *German Workers' Society* was founded by Marx and Engels at the end of August 1847 in Brussels, its aim being the political education of the German workers who lived in Belgium and the spread of the ideas of scientific communism among them. With Marx, Engels and their followers at its head, the Society became the legally sanctioned centre rallying the revolutionary proletarian forces in Belgium. Its best activists were members of the Communist League. It ceased to exist soon after the February revolution of 1848 in France when the Belgian police arrested and banished many of its members.—530

592 Marx's pamphlet *Lord Palmerston* (see present edition, Vol. 12) was first published as a series of articles in *The People's Paper*, Nos. 77-81, 84-86 of 22 and 29 October, 5, 12 and 19 November and 10, 17 and 24 December 1853, signed by Dr Marx; in part it was published as editorials in the *New-York Daily Tribune*, Nos. 3902, 3916, 3930 and 3973 of 19 October, 4 and 21 November 1853 and 11 January 1854.

Some articles of this series were published in London in 1853 and 1854 in pamphlet form under the headings: *Palmerston and Russia* and *Palmerston and the Treaty of Unkiar Skelessy.*—531

593 A reference to Marx's help in publishing the series of articles by Engels *The Armies of Europe* (see present edition, Vol. 14) in *Putnam's Monthly. A Magazine of American Literature, Science and Art* in August, September and December 1855; Marx also helped Engels in collecting information on various European armies, in particular the Spanish and the Neapolitan, at the British Museum Library.

For the articles by Marx and Engels that were published in the *New American Cyclopaedia* in 1857-60 see present edition, Vol. 18.—531

594 A reference to Chapter III ('The Production of Absolute Surplus-Value') of the first German edition of Volume One of *Capital*. It is given as Part III in the second and subsequent German editions of Volume One and in the English edition of 1887 (see present edition, Vol. 35).—533

595 A reference to the article 'Das Preußische und das Schweizer Heersystem' published in the *Demokratisches Wochenblatt*, No. 2 of 11 January 1868. It was based on a series of articles by Karl Grün, 'Armées permanentes ou milices', that had been printed in *Les États-Unis d'Europe* at the beginning of 1868; the fourth article of the series (published in No. 7 of 16 February) dealt with the South German military system.—534, 540

596 A reference to the territories annexed by Prussia as a result of its victory in the Austro-Prussian war of 1866 (see Note 365).—534, 555

597 This letter is written on a form with the letterhead: 'Memorandum from *Ermen & Engels* to M'. Engels crossed out the words 'Ermen &' and filled in 'Mr Mohr' as the addressee.—537

598 In his letter to Marx on 26 January 1868 from Saint Louis Hermann Meyer told him about the death of Louise Weydemeyer, Joseph Weydemeyer's widow.—537

599 It is not known what happened to this article by Engels (the reference is probably to a review of Volume One of *Capital*).—537

600 A reference to the conversation between Bismarck and Karl Schurz, a German émigré in the United States who had taken part in the Civil War of 1861-65 and the editor of the newspaper *Die Westliche Post*, in January 1868 in Berlin. Schurz assured Bismarck that Napoleon III did not enjoy any popularity in America, and should Germany be drawn into a war with France, the United States would not support him. Marx and Engels satirised the earlier period of Schurz' activity in their pamphlet *The Great Men of the Exile* (see present edition, Vol. 11).—537

601 A reference to the forthcoming marriage between Marx's daughter Laura and Paul Lafargue, whose parents lived in Bordeaux; the wedding was in the early April 1868.—538, 544, 548, 551

602 At Marx's request, Engels wrote a detailed review of Volume One of *Capital* for the *Demokratisches Wochenblatt* in the first half of March; it was published in it unsigned, as two articles, in Nos. 12 and 13 of 21 and 28 March 1868 (see present edition, Vol. 20).—539, 540, 542

603 A reference to an article by Moses Hess about Volume One of *Capital* which he had started as early as November 1867 and intended to publish in the French press (see Note 539). In 1868 for several months, he made attempts to publish it in various papers, including *Le Courrier français* and *Morale indépendante*. Its further fate is unknown.—542

604 A reference to newspaper reports of lectures 'The Causes of Modern Trade Crises' read by Wilhelm Eichhoff from February to May 1868 in Berlin. These reports were published in *Die Zukunft* and the *Norddeutsche Allgemeine Zeitung*. In his lectures Eichhoff quoted from Marx's *Capital* and the *Manifesto of the Communist Party* by Marx and Engels.—542, 545

605 A reference to a report in *The Times* of 3 March 1868 that the Russian government had instructed its representatives in Turkey and in the Balkans to make every effort to refrain from conflicts with Turkey.—545

606 Engels sent Marx a letter from an Austrian journalist, W. Angerstein, dated 9 March 1868, in which he invited Engels to become a correspondent of a new workers' newspaper. On 11 March 1868, Angerstein sent a similar letter to Marx whom he invited to contribute to the Viennese newspapers *Telegraph* and *Arbeiter-Zeitung*.—546, 548

607 Engels' letter to Liebknecht has not been found. From Liebknecht's reply of 29 March 1868 it follows that his friends and he readily took Engels' advice to use *Capital* as a basis for the proletarian stance vis-à-vis a new crafts and manufactures code that was being prepared (the same was recommended in his review of Volume One of *Capital* for the *Demokratisches Wochenblatt*). When, in the spring of 1869, the North German Reichstag began to discuss the code bill, August Bebel and other working-class deputies, following Engels' advice,

resolutely criticised the bill and demanded that several amendments should be introduced into it that would meet the interests of the working class such as a ten-hour working day, the abolition of work on Sundays, the introduction of a factory inspectorate and the workers' right to coalitions. Although all these amendments were rejected by the bourgeois and Junker majority of the Reichstag, the speeches of the working-class deputies on this issue played an important part to unite the revolutionary efforts of the German proletariat.— 546

608 Part of this letter was published in English for the first time in Karl Marx, *Pre-capitalist Economic Formations*, Lawrence & Wishart, London, 1964.—547

609 This standpoint was expressed by Marx in 1859 in his *A Contribution to the Critique of Political Economy* (see present edition, Vol. 29) and also in Volume One of *Capital* (Vol. 35).—547

610 On 13 March 1868 Sigismund Borkheim informed Marx about Dühring's new book, *Die Schicksale meiner socialen Denkschrift für das preussische Staatsministerium*, in which he accused Hermann Wagener of plagiarism.—548

611 A reference to Article 11 of the French law on the press a draft of which was submitted to the Corps législatif by a group of deputies, Jean Dollfus included, on 11 February 1868. It was passed on 6 March 1868 and read as follows: 'Any publication in a periodical that may concern a fact of private life shall be an offence which shall be punished with a fine of 500 francs.'—550, 553

612 The publisher of *The Irishman*, Richard Pigott, and the owner of *The Weekly News*, Alexander Sullivan, were sentenced in 1867 and 1868 to various terms of imprisonment for the publication of articles in defence of the Fenians.—550

613 This is a quotation from the first German edition of Volume One of *Capital* (pp. 255 and 565 in the English edition of 1887).—552

614 A reference to the medical school at St Bartholomew's Hospital in London.— 553

615 Marx gives below an excerpt from *Lex Baiuvariorum*, X, 18—the code of common law of the Germanic tribe of Bavars, dating back to the 8th century.— 553

616 *Leges barbarorum* (laws of the barbarians)—written records of the customary law of various Germanic tribes compiled between the 5th and 9th centuries.—558

617 Engels came to see Marx in London on 1 April 1868 in order to be present at the wedding of Paul Lafargue and Laura Marx; he stayed there till 5 April.—560

618 *Straubingers*—German travelling journeymen. Marx and Engels applied the name ironically to some participants in the German working-class movement of the time who were connected with guild-based production and displayed petty-bourgeois sectarian tendencies.

The reference here is to the members of the Lassallean General Association of German Workers.—566

619 In his letter to Ferdinand Lassalle of 28 April 1862 Marx entirely denied the slanderous rumours which had been repeated by Lassalle besmirching the reputation of Johann Philipp Becker, and described him as 'one of the noblest German revolutionaries' (see present edition, Vol. 41, p. 356).—567

620 *Confessions*—semi-jocular questionnaires that were very popular in England in
the 1860s. Filling such questionnaires became a favourite pastime in many
families, including Marx's, in which relatives and friends participated. A
number of versions of *Confessions* belonging to Marx came down to us. In this
volume an early version is published which dates back to the spring of 1865
when Marx stayed with his uncle Lion Philips in Zalt Bommel (Holland). It is
somewhat different from the other two versions: the handwritten one included
in the album of his daughter Jenny (a facsimile of it is published in this
volume) and the one written in Laura Marx's hand. The latter version partly
coincides with the one that is being published here and partly with the one in
Jenny's album, except for the answer to the question: 'Your favourite
flower—Laurel' (instead of 'Daphne').
    Major divergencies between the version published here and the one in
Jenny's album are given in the footnotes.—567

621 A substantial extract from this letter was published by Johann Philipp Becker in
Der Vorbote, Jg. 1, No. 2 of February 1866 (present edition, Vol. 20).—568

622 A reference to a reprint of the first 1848 German edition of the *Manifesto of the
Communist Party* made in London probably in 1865: '*Manifest der Kommunisti-
schen Partei*. Veröffentlicht im Februar 1848. London, Druck von R. Hirschfeld,
English and foreign Printer, 1848, 24 S'.—571

623 Jenny Marx is recalling the meeting to celebrate an anniversary of the
International that was held on 28 September 1865. Marx was present at it with
his daughters. Speeches alternated with musical performances, singing and
dancing.—571

624 A reference to Jenny Marx's last trip to Trier in 1856 when she went to see her
dying mother. Then she stayed in Germany from 22 May to approximately
10 September 1856.—579

625 A reference to the letter to Marx from Card (Jósef Cwierczakiewicz) of
10 January 1868 in which he offered to translate *Capital* into French (see this
volume, p. 528).—580

626 This is an allusion to the explosion in Clerkenwell Prison in London which was
caused by a group of supporters of the Fenian prisoners in order to free
them on 13 December 1867 and also to the hanging of three Fenians in
Manchester on 23 November 1867 who had been captured in an armed assault
on a police van in order to release the arrested Fenian leaders (see Notes 563
and 497).—582

NAME INDEX

lower of Lassalle; President of the General Association of German Workers (1864-65), subsequently sided with the Eisenachers; delegate to the Hague Congress of the International (1872).—3, 15, 30, 33, 36, 51, 57, 58, 65, 68, 75, 82, 90, 104, 114, 135, 139, 140, 152, 154, 158, 161, 165, 170, 174, 175-76, 179, 191, 203, 205, 532, 548, 566

Becker, Hermann Heinrich (*'Red Becker'*) (1820-1885)—German lawyer and journalist; took part in the 1848-49 revolution; from 1850 member of the Communist League; one of the accused at the Cologne Communist trial (1852), sentenced to five years' imprisonment; member of the Party of Progress in the 1860s; later National-Liberal; member of the Prussian Chamber of Deputies (1862-66), then of the Reichstag (1867-74).—52, 53, 56, 75, 80, 94

Becker, Johann Philipp (1809-1886)— German revolutionary, participant in the democratic movement in Germany and Switzerland (1830s-40s) and in the 1848-49 revolution; organiser of the International's sections in Switzerland and Germany, delegate to the London Conference (1865) and all congresses of the International; editor of *Der Vorbote* (1866-71); friend and associate of Marx and Engels.—30, 163, 190, 191, 202, 207, 213-15, 219, 221, 314-15, 358, 425, 428, 434, 450, 456, 548, 567, 568, 571-72, 577, 580-82

Beesly, Edward Spencer (1831-1915)— British historian and politician; radical, Positivist; professor at London University; participant in the inaugural meeting of the International at St Martin's Hall on 28 September 1864; took an active part in the movement for the electoral reform (1867); in 1870-71 supported the International and the Paris Commune; was on friendly terms with Marx.—55, 60, 162, 185, 283, 291, 407, 423, 433, 455, 512, 516, 518

Beethoven, Ludwig van (1770-1827)— German composer.—571

Béluze, Jean Pierre (1821-1908)— French petty-bourgeois socialist; cabinet-maker; follower of Cabet; director of the Crédit du Travail bank (1862-68); one of the founders of *L'Association*, organ of the co-operative movement; member of the International; subsequently left the working-class movement.—118

Bender, H.—bookseller in London, publisher of the *Londoner Anzeiger* (1864-67), organ of the German refugees.— 50, 63, 66, 81, 114, 130, 133-34, 214, 447

Benedek, Ludwig von (1804-1881)— Austrian general, Commander-in-Chief of the Austrian army during the Austro-Prussian war of 1866.— 256, 263, 279, 288, 510, 517, 523

Bennigsen, Rudolf von (1824-1902)— German politician, advocate of Germany's unification under Prussia's supremacy; President of the National Association (1859-67); from 1867 leader of the National-Liberal Party (Right wing).—276, 340, 361

Berghaus, Heinrich (1797-1884)— German geographer and cartographer.—28

Berndes—German democrat, in the 1860s refugee in London.—151

Bernstorff, Albrecht, Count von (1809-1873)—Prussian diplomat, envoy to London (1854-61), Foreign Minister (1861-62), ambassador to London (1862-73).—355

Beta—see *Bettziech, Heinrich*

Bettziech, Heinrich (pen-name *Beta*) (1813-1876)—German democratic journalist; a refugee in London; follower of Gottfried Kinkel.—336, 447, 450

Beust, Friedrich Ferdinand, Count von (1809-1886)—Saxon and Austrian statesman, adherent of independence of small German states; held several ministerial posts in the Saxonian Government (1849-66); Foreign Minister (1866-71) and Chancellor (1867-71) of Austria-Hungary.—207, 349, 435

Beust, Friedrich von (1817-1899)—former Prussian army officer; took part in the Baden-Palatinate uprising (1849), emigrated to Switzerland; member of a section of the International in Zurich; professor of pedagogics; participant in the Congress of the League of Peace and Freedom in Geneva (1867).—433

Bille, Carl Steen Andersen (1828-1898)—Danish journalist and politician; liberal; editor and owner of the *Dagbladet* (1851-72); member of the lower chamber of the Rigsdag.—6

Biscamp (Biskamp), Elard—German democratic journalist; took part in the 1848-49 revolution in Germany, emigrated after the defeat of the revolution; member of the editorial board of *Das Volk*, organ of the German refugees in London published with Marx's collaboration.—135

Bismarck-Schönhausen, Otto, Prince von (1815-1898)—statesman of Prussia and Germany, diplomat; representative of Prussia in the Federal Diet in Frankfurt am Main (1851-59); ambassador to St Petersburg (1859-62) and Paris (1862); Prime Minister of Prussia (1862-71 and 1873-90); Chancellor of the North German Confederation (1867-71) and of the German Empire (1871-90).—7, 38, 53, 69, 71, 75-76, 77, 82, 83, 89, 95, 96, 102-05, 111, 113, 124, 126, 161, 169, 179, 182, 201, 204, 208, 211, 217, 226, 229, 254, 255-57, 258, 263-67, 270, 272, 275, 278, 280, 281, 285, 288, 292-94, 296, 297, 302, 303, 306-07, 328, 338, 339, 340, 345, 349, 351, 352-55, 361, 364, 372, 373, 374, 380, 417, 421, 426, 435, 456, 460, 461, 462, 466, 480, 494, 498, 505, 506, 523, 537, 545, 560, 566

Blackburn, Colin, Baron (1813-1896)—English judge.—462, 466

Blanc, Jean Joseph Louis (1811-1882)—French petty-bourgeois socialist, historian; in 1848 member of the Provisional Government and President of the Luxembourg Commission; pursued a policy of conciliation with the bourgeoisie; emigrated to England in August 1848; a leader of the petty-bourgeois refugees in London.—32, 33, 55, 270, 420, 429

Blank, Emil—Frederick Engels' nephew, son of Karl Emil Blank.—11, 337

Blank, Karl Emil (1817-1893)—German merchant; closely connected with socialist circles in the 1840s-50s; married Frederick Engels' sister Marie.—11, 77, 79

Blank, Marie—Frederick Engels' niece, daughter of Karl Emil Blank.—11, 313

Blind, Friederike (née *Ettlinger*)—Karl Blind's wife.—31, 34, 35, 274

Blind, Johann Adam—Karl Blind's father, owner of a tavern in Mannheim.—33, 41

Blind, Karl (1826-1907)—German democratic journalist; took part in the revolutionary movement in Baden (1848-49); in the 1850s-early 1860s, a leader of the German petty-bourgeois refugees in London; later National-Liberal.—27, 30, 31-38, 41-43, 44-46, 50-52, 56-57, 72, 78, 91, 97, 102, 107, 110, 115, 119, 120, 126, 129, 131, 134, 151, 182, 237, 273-74, 275, 278, 286, 380, 447, 518-19, 567, 581

Blind, Mathilde (née *Cohen*) (1841-1896)—English translator, author and poet; Karl Blind's adopted daughter.—35

Blum, Babette (c. 1791-1865)—Karl Marx's paternal aunt.—194

Bobczyński, Konstanty (b. 1817)—participant in the Polish uprising of

manufacturer and politician, a leader of the Free Traders and co-founder of the Anti-Corn Law League; leader of the Left wing of the Liberal Party from the early 1860s, held several ministerial posts.—15, 18, 44, 47, 71, 74, 130, 212, 253, 374

Bronner, Eduard—German physician; democrat; deputy to the Baden Constituent Assembly (1849); emigrated to England; supporter of Karl Blind.—32, 33, 41, 44, 51

Brown, John (1800-1859)—American farmer; took part in the Abolitionist movement, organised armed struggle against slave-owners in Kansas; tried to raise an uprising of Black slaves in Virginia in 1859; was put on trial and executed.—474

Bruhn, Karl von (b. 1803)—German journalist; member of the Communist League, expelled from it in 1850; supported the Willich-Schapper group; editor of the *Nordstern*, a Lassallean paper in Hamburg (1861-66).—26, 57, 116, 117-18, 130, 135, 165

Bucher, Lothar (1817-1892)—Prussian official and journalist; deputy to the Prussian National Assembly (Left Centre) in 1848; refugee in London, subsequently National-Liberal and supporter of Bismarck.—30, 53, 166, 202, 350, 352, 497, 498, 566

Büchner, Ludwig (1824-1899)—German philosopher and naturalist, vulgar materialist; liberal; member of the International, delegate to the Lausanne Congress (1867); participant in the Congress of the League of Peace and Freedom in Geneva (1867).—367-68, 433, 469

Buol-Schauenstein, Karl Ferdinand, Count von (1797-1865)—Austrian statesman and diplomat; envoy to St Petersburg (1848-50) and to London (1851-52), Prime Minister and Minister of Foreign Affairs (1852-59).—54

Bürgers, Heinrich (1820-1878)—German journalist; an editor of the *Neue Rheinische Zeitung*; member of the Communist League, from 1850 member of its Central Authority; one of the accused at the Cologne Communist trial; later supported the Party of Progress; National-Liberal; editor of the *Rheinische Zeitung* in Düsseldorf.—112, 207, 221, 430, 471, 493, 498, 502, 529

Burns, Lizzie (Lizzy, Lydia) (1827-1878)—Irish working woman, took part in the Irish national liberation movement; Frederick Engels' second wife.—27, 53, 67, 91, 99, 148, 158, 160, 177, 179, 181, 185, 193, 194, 205, 206, 208, 228, 237, 251, 254, 269, 283, 291, 301, 311, 341, 344, 357, 362, 374, 386, 389, 391, 394, 399, 408, 448, 455, 479, 495, 508, 517, 521, 559

Burns, Robert (1759-1796)—Scottish poet, democrat.—91

Burton—English house owner.—343

Butler, Benjamin Franklin (1818-1893)—American politician and general; a leader of the Left wing of the Republican Party; during the Civil War commanded the expeditionary Northern Army at the capture of New Orleans, military governor of New Orleans (1862).—199

C

Caesar (Gaius Julius Caesar) (c. 100-44 B.C.)—Roman general and statesman.—185, 558

Card, Ioseph (Cwierczakiewicz, Jósef) (1822-1869)—participant in the 1863 Polish uprising; journalist; émigré in Geneva; member of the International; co-editor of the *Journal d'Association Internationale des Travailleurs*; delegate to the Geneva Congress (1866).—528, 532, 533, 580

Carey, Henry Charles (1793-1879)—

refugee in Paris after the 1830-31 uprising; author of several works on the history and ethnography of Poland and Eastern Slavs.—163, 164, 305

Duller, Eduard (1809-1853)—German poet and historian, author of historical novels.—27

Duncker, Franz Gustav (1822-1888)— Berlin publisher and politician, member of the Party of Progress; founder and editor of the *Volks-Zeitung.*—328, 382, 384, 395, 543

Duncker, Friedrich Wilhelm August (b. 1797)—Prussian official, Police Superintendent in Berlin in the 1840s.—299

Duncker, Max (1811-1886)—German historian, professor in Halle and then in Tübingen; from 1859 Prussian government official; director of the Prussian state archives (1867-74).—27

Dunning, Thomas J. (1799-1873)— British trade unionist and journalist, reformist; leader of the bookbinders' union; member of the London Trades Council.—159

Dupanloup, Félix Antoine Philibert (1802-1878)—French politician; a leader of the Catholic party; Bishop of Orleans (from 1849).—434, 460

Dupleix, François—French refugee in Switzerland; bookbinder; a founder and president of the French section of the International in Geneva; delegate to the London Conference (1865), Geneva (1866) and Lausanne (1867) congresses.—190, 214, 215, 315

Dupont, Eugène (c. 1831-1881)—active participant in the French and international working-class movement; musical instrument maker; took part in the June (1848) uprising in Paris; from 1862 on lived in London; member of the General Council of the International (November 1864 to 1872), Corresponding Secretary for

France (1865-71), took part in the London Conference (1865), Geneva (1866), Lausanne (1867) (its Chairman), Brussels (1868), and the Hague (1872) congresses, London Conference (1871); associate of Marx and Engels; joined the British Federal Council of the International (1872); moved to the USA in 1874.— 140, 144, 149, 196, 250, 318, 334, 416, 428, 516, 520

E

Eccarius, Johann Georg (John George) (1818-1889)—prominent figure in the German and international working-class movement; tailor; member of the League of the Just and later of the Communist League; a leader of the German Workers' Educational Society in London; participant in the inaugural meeting of the International held on 28 September 1864 at St Martin's Hall, member of the General Council of the International (1864-72) and its General Secretary (1867-71), Corresponding Secretary for America (1870-72), delegate of all congresses and conferences of the International; follower of Marx; in the spring of 1872 joined reformist leaders of the British trade unions.—4, 15-17, 50, 74, 84, 90, 91, 101, 106, 107, 108, 114, 134, 150, 152, 163, 215, 219, 224, 249, 252-53, 255, 262, 314, 315, 339, 394, 416, 418, 420, 422, 423, 425, 428, 429, 433, 434, 438, 455, 456, 462, 519, 552

Eckardt, Ludwig (1827-1871)—Austrian democrat, took part in the 1848-49 revolution in Austria and Germany, emigrated to Switzerland; in 1865, a leader of the German People's Party and editor of the *Deutsches Wochenblatt*; opposed Germany's unification under Prussia's supremacy; returned to Austria in 1867.—198, 204

Egli, Johann Jakob (1825-1896)—Swiss geographer and teacher.—28, 188

Geffcken, Friedrich Heinrich (1830-1896)—German diplomat and lawyer; Hanseatic envoy to London (1866-69).—355

Geib, August (1842-1879)—German bookseller in Hamburg, Social-Democrat; member of the General Association of German Workers; participant in the Eisenach Congress (1869) and a founder of the Social-Democratic Workers' Party.—495

Gentz, Friedrich von (1764-1832)—Austrian statesman and writer; adviser and confidant of Metternich; Secretary at the Vienna Congress (1814-15) and congresses of the Holy Alliance.—478, 520

George II (1683-1760)—King of Great Britain and Ireland (1727-60).—487

George V (1819-1878)—King of Hanover (1851-66).—298, 506, 536

Gerhardt, Charles Frédéric (1816-1856)—French chemist.—385, 387

Giebel, Christoph Gottfried Andreas (1820-1881)—German zoologist and paleontologist.—28

Girardin, Émile de (1802-1881)—French journalist and politician; editor of *La Presse* (1836-66 with intervals) and *La Liberté* (1866-70); moderate republican during the 1848-49 revolution; deputy to the Legislative Assembly (1850-51); later Bonapartist, notorious for lack of principles in politics.—418, 424

Gladstone, William Ewart (1809-1898)—British statesman, Tory and later Peelite; leader of the Liberal Party in the latter half of the 19th century; Chancellor of the Exchequer (1852-55 and 1859-66), Prime Minister (1868-74, 1880-85, 1886, 1892-94).—269, 374

Glais-Bizoin, Alexandre Olivier (1800-1877)—French lawyer and politician, moderate republican, deputy to the Constituent Assembly (1848-49); member of the Corps législatif in the 1860s.—290

Gneist, Heinrich Rudolf Hermann Friedrich von (1816-1895)—German lawyer and politician; professor at Berlin University; member of the Prussian Chamber of Deputies (from 1858); representative of the liberal opposition in the early 1860s; National-Liberal from 1866.—154

Goegg, Amand (1820-1897)—German democratic journalist, member of the Baden Provisional Government (1849); after the revolution emigrated; took part in pacifist activities of the League of Peace and Freedom; joined German Social-Democracy in the 1870s.—433, 517, 519, 541, 581, 582

Goethe, Johann Wolfgang von (1749-1832)—German poet.—25, 355, 356, 455, 504, 568

Goltz, Robert Heinrich Ludwig, Count von (1817-1869)—Prussian diplomat, ambassador to Paris (December 1862 to 1869).—293

Gorchakov, Alexander Mikhailovich, Prince (1798-1883)—Russian statesman and diplomat; ambassador to Vienna (1854-56), Minister for Foreign Affairs (1856-82).—506

Götz (Goetz), Ferdinand (1826-1915)—German physician and politician; in the 1860s member of the Party of Progress and later National-Liberal; deputy to the North German and German Reichstags.—489

Gounod, Charles François (1818-1893)—French composer.—571

Gracchus, Cornelia—mother of Gaius and Tiberius Gracchus.—244

Gracchus, Gaius Sempronius (153-121 B.C.)—tribune (123-122 B.C.) in ancient Rome; stood out for agrarian laws in the interests of the peasants; brother of Tiberius Gracchus.—244

211, 266, 278, 282, 329, 379, 415,
417, 447, 493, 494, 516, 520, 526,
527, 532, 536, 548, 566, 567

Lau, Thaddäus (d. 1871)—German historian and teacher.—28

Laurent, Auguste (1807-1853)—French
chemist.—385

Law, Harriet (1832-1897)—a leading
figure in the atheist movement in
England, member of the General
Council (1867-72) and of the Manchester section of the International
(1872).—396

Ledru-Rollin, Alexandre Auguste (1807-
1874)—French journalist and politician, a leader of the petty-bourgeois
democrats, editor of La Réforme;
Minister of the Interior in the Provisional Government, deputy to the
Constituent and Legislative Assem-
blies (1848), where he headed the
Montagne Party; emigrated to England after the demonstration of 13
June 1849.—32, 33-34, 278

Lee, Robert Edward (1807-1870)—
American general, took part in the
war against Mexico (1846-48), during the US Civil War commanded
Southern troops in Virginia (1862-65),
Commander-in-Chief of the Confederate Army (February-April 1865).—
21, 39, 82, 113, 122, 123,
147

Lefort, Henry (1835-1917)—French
lawyer, journalist, republican;
member of L'Association's editorial
board; took part in the preparations
for the inaugural meeting of the
International held on 28 September
1864 at St Martin's Hall; dissociated
himself from the International in
March 1865.—85, 109, 118-19, 131,
140

Le Lubez, Victor (b. 1834)—French refugee in London, was connected with
republican and radical elements in
France and Britain; took part in the
inaugural meeting of the International held on 28 September 1864 at
St Martin's Hall, member of the

Central Council of the International
(1864-66), Corresponding Secretary
for France (1864-65), participant in
the London Conference of the International (1865); expelled from the
Council by the Geneva Congress
(1866) for intrigue and slander.—15-
18, 49, 66, 74, 92, 108, 118, 130,
131, 132, 140, 149, 155, 158, 170,
212, 214, 216-18, 250, 318, 519

Le Prince de Beaumont, Jeanne Marie
(1711-1780)—French   authoress.—
242

Lessing, Gotthold Ephraim (1729-1781)—
German writer.—568

Lessner,   Friedrich   (1825-1910)—
prominent figure in the German and
international   working-class   movement, tailor; member of the Communist League; took part in the
1848-49 revolution; prosecuted at the
Cologne Communist trial in 1852;
emigrated to London in 1856;
member of the German Workers'
Educational Society in London and
of the General Council of the International (November 1864 to 1872),
participant in the London Conference (1865), the Lausanne (1867),
Brussels (1868), Basle (1869) and the
Hague (1872) congresses of the International; member of the British
Federal Council; friend and associate
of Marx and Engels.—94, 118, 229-
30, 416, 424, 429, 477, 507, 571

Levy,   Joseph   Moses   (1812-1888)—
English journalist, a founder and
publisher of The Daily Telegraph.—86

Lewes, George Henry (1817-1878)—
English positivist philosopher, journalist, literary critic; editor of The
Fortnightly Review (1865-66).—455,
512

Lewis, Leon—American journalist; in
1865, in London, was elected
member of the Central Council of
the International and Corresponding
Secretary for America, did not take
part in the work of the Council.—
162

Felice Orsini's brother.—238, 242-43, 246, 250, 255, 259

Orsini, Felice (1819-1858)—Italian democrat, republican, a prominent figure in the struggle for Italy's national liberation and unification; executed for his attempt on the life of Napoleon III.—238, 242

Otto, L.—see *Breitschwert, Otto Ludwig*

Overbeck, Johannes Adolf (1826-1895)—German archaeologist.—28

Overstone, Samuel Jones Loyd, Baron (from 1860) (1796-1883)—English banker, economist, follower of the 'principle of money circulation' school.—186

Owen, Robert (1771-1858)—British utopian socialist.—326, 552

P

Palmerston, Emily Mary (c. 1787-1869) (previously *Countess Cowper*)—wife of Henry John Temple Palmerston.—374

Palmerston, Henry John Temple, Viscount (1784-1865)—British statesman, Tory, from 1830 Whig, Foreign Secretary (1830-34, 1835-41, 1846-51), Home Secretary (1852-55) and Prime Minister (1855-58, 1859-65).—36, 44, 45, 208, 269, 394

Pasteur, Louis (1822-1895)—French microbiologist and chemist, founder of microbiology.—284

Pauli, Reinhold (1823-1882)—German historian, author of works on the history of Britain.—28

Payne, A. H.—German publisher in Leipzig.—447

Petzler—German photographer, refugee in Manchester in the 1860s.—98

Petzler, Johann (d. 1898)—German democrat, refugee in England in the 1850s-60s.—49, 94, 98

Philips—Dutch maternal relatives of Karl Marx.—538, 542, 545, 548

Philips, Antoinette (Nannette) (c. 1837-1885)—Karl Marx's cousin, Lion Philips' daughter; member of the Dutch section of the International.—241-44, 567

Philips, Friedrich (Fritz)—Karl Marx's cousin; banker in Zalt-Bommel.—48

Philips, Lion Benjamin (1794-1866)—Dutch merchant, maternal uncle of Karl Marx.—46-48, 243, 249, 341

Pieper, Friedrich Ludwig Wilhelm (1826-1899)—German philologist and journalist, member of the Communist League, refugee in London; was close to Marx and Engels in the 1850s.—165

Pierre l'Ermite (c. 1050-1115)—French monk and preacher, headed peasants' volunteer corps during the First Crusade (1096-99).—452

Pigott, Richard (1828-1889)—Irish journalist, publisher of *The Irishman* (1865-79); sided with the British government in the 1880s.—550

Pius IX (Giovanni Maria Mastai-Ferretti) (1792-1878)—Pope (1846-78).—338, 460, 462

Platen-Hallermund, Adolf Ludwig Karl, Count von (1814-1889)—Hanover Minister for Foreign Affairs (1855-66); opposed unification of Germany under Prussia's hegemony.—307

Plon-Plon—see *Bonaparte, Prince Napoléon Joseph Charles Paul*

Pollock, George D.—British army doctor; member of the commission which in 1867 submitted to Parliament a report on the treatment of the political prisoners in the English convict prisons.—394

Polo, Marco (1254-1324)—Italian traveller and writer, made expedition to China (1271-95).—28

Potter, George (1832-1893)—a reformist

leader of the British trade unions, carpenter; member of the London Trades Council and a leader of the Amalgamated Union of Building Workers; founder and publisher of *The Bee-Hive Newspaper.*—18, 50, 154, 155, 156, 169, 173, 253, 259, 424

Preller, Ludwig (1809-1861)—German philologist, studied ancient mythology.—27

Prokesch-Osten, Anton, Count von (1795-1876)—Austrian diplomat, general and writer, envoy to Athens (1834-49), envoy (1855-67), then ambassador (1867-71) to Constantinople.—464, 520

Proudhon, Pierre Joseph (1809-1865)—French writer, economist and sociologist; a founder of anarchism.—67, 75, 102, 213, 218, 281, 287, 326, 368, 379, 455, 488, 557

Prutz, Robert Eduard (1816-1872)—German poet and historian of literature, liberal; publisher of the journal *Deutsches Museum* in Leipzig (1851-67).—484

Purdy, Frederick—English official.—53

Puttkamer, Elisabeth von—daughter of Prussian statesman Robert von Puttkamer, Otto Bismarck's niece.—390

Pyat, Félix (1810-1889)—French journalist, playwright and politician, democrat; took part in the 1848 révolution; from 1849 refugee in Switzerland, Belgium and England; opposed Marx and the International's leadership making use of the French section in London; member of the Paris Commune (1871).—474, 516

Q

Quenstedt—Wilhelm Liebknecht's acquaintance.—202

Quinet, Edgar (1803-1875)—French politician and historian; took part in the 1848 revolution, refugee in 1852-70; anti-Bonapartist; participant in

the League of Peace and Freedom Congress in Geneva (1867).—435

R

Racowiţa, Janko von (d. 1865)—Romanian nobleman; mortally wounded Lassalle in duel (1864).—19, 20, 31, 69, 162, 211, 415

Rasch, Gustav (1825-1878)—German lawyer and journalist, democrat; took part in the 1848 revolution in Berlin, later refugee in Switzerland and France.—33, 34, 119, 397

Rattazzi, Urbano (1808-1873)—Italian statesman of liberal-monarchist trend; Minister of the Interior in the Kingdom of Sardinia (1855-58 and 1859-60), headed Italian government (1862 and 1867).—460

Rau, Karl Heinrich (1792-1870)—German economist.—444, 490, 491

Ravenstein—refugee in England; secretary of the *Deutsche Freiheit und Einheit* society.—32

Réaumur, René Antoine Ferchault de (1683-1757)—French naturalist.—170

Rebour—French inventor.—254

Reclus, Jean Jacques Élisée (1830-1905)—French geographer, sociologist and politician, theorist of anarchism; member of the International, editor of *La Cooperation* (1866-68), participant in the Paris Commune (1871).—483, 487, 532, 533

Regnault, Élias Georges Soulange Oliva (1801-1868)—French historian and journalist, state official, Bonapartist.—163

Régnier, Mathurin (1573-1613)—French satirical poet.—453, 454

Reinach, Arnold (c. 1820-1870)—German democrat, took part in the 1848-49 revolution, emigrated to Switzerland.—63, 158, 164, 185, 208

Reincke, Peter Adolf (1818-1887)—German physician; member of the

General Association of German Workers who was elected deputy to the North German Reichstag in 1867; expelled from the Association; in June 1868 relinquished his deputy powers.—430

Reusche, Friedrich—German journalist; member of the General Association of German Workers, Lassallean, contributed to the Nordstern and Der Social-Demokrat (1864-65).—147, 548, 566-67

Reuter, Paul Julius, Baron (1816-1899)—founder of the Reuter telegraph agency in London (1851); German by birth.—267

Reybaud, Marie Roch Louis (1799-1879)—French writer and economist, liberal.—338, 340

Ricardo, David (1772-1823)—English economist.—137, 402, 457, 514, 543

Richelieu, Armand Jean du Plessis, duc de (1585-1642)—French statesman during the period of absolutism, Cardinal.—71

Richter, Eugen (1838-1906)—German politician, leader of the liberals (Left wing); a founder and leader of the party of free-thinkers.—211, 430

Richter, Heinrich Moriz Karl (b. 1841)—Austrian historian and journalist, liberal; professor at Vienna trade academy; worked in several Austrian newspapers.—512, 515, 518, 525, 537

Rimestad, Christian Vilhelm (1816-1879)—Danish teacher, politician and journalist, liberal; founder and leader of the Workers' Union (1860-79); editor of the Dags-Telegraphen (1864-75).—183

Ritter, Karl (1779-1859)—German geographer, professor at Berlin University.—28

Rittershaus, Emil (1834-1897)—German poet, democrat, belonged to the Party of Progress (Left wing) in the 1860s.—427, 433, 440, 471

Roberts, William R.—a leader of the Fenian movement in the USA, inspired an adventurist attempt of Fenians' invasion into Canada (May 1866) to arouse conflict between Britain and the USA.—485

Robespierre, Maximilien François Marie Isidore de (1758-1794)—Jacobin leader in the French Revolution, head of the revolutionary government (1793-94).—71

Robin, Charles Philippe (1821-1885)—French anatomist.—283

Röckel, August (d. 1876)—German musician, democratic journalist; took part in the 1849 Dresden uprising, sentenced to penal servitude for life, amnested in 1862; from mid-1866 was in the service of the Austrian government.—270

Rodbertus-Jagetzow, Johann Karl (1805-1875)—German economist and politician; leader of the Left Centre in the Prussian National Assembly during the 1848-49 revolution; later advocated 'state socialism'.—30, 54

Rode (Rohde)—German refugee in Liverpool.—152, 203, 281, 337, 338

Roesgen, Charles—employee in the Manchester firm of Ermen & Engels.—168, 192, 277, 451

Rogeard, Auguste Louis (1820-1896)—French democratic journalist, a founder and editor of La Rive gauche (1864); in 1865 was persecuted for his anti-Bonapartist pamphlet and emigrated to Belgium and then to Germany; a leader of the Paris Commune (1871).—216, 243

Rogers, James Edwin Thorold (1823-1890)—British historian and economist.—339, 340, 344

Roodhuizen, A.—pastor in Zalt-Bommel, subsequently husband of Karl Marx's cousin Antoinette Philips.—242

Roon, Albrecht Theodor Emil, Count von (1803-1879)—Prussian statesman and military leader, War Minister (1859-

publisher and bookseller, owner of a firm in Leipzig which published works of radical authors.—359, 363, 385

Wilke—Prussian army officer, refugee in London.—291

William I (1797-1888)—Prince of Prussia, Prince Regent (1858-61), King of Prussia (1861-88) and Emperor of Germany (1871-88).—12, 53, 67, 96, 103, 226, 236, 254, 257, 276, 278, 279, 290, 299, 302, 306, 338, 340, 355, 365, 374

William I (*The Conqueror*) (1027-1087)—King of England (1066-87).—299, 338, 365, 374

William, Prince of Orange (1840-1879)—Dutch Crown Prince.—293

Willich, August (1810-1878)—retired Prussian officer; member of the Communist League, participant in the Baden-Palatinate uprising of 1849; a leader of the sectarian group that split away from the Communist League in 1850; in 1853 emigrated to the USA, took part in the US Civil War on the side of the Northerners.—40, 147

Wirth, Max (1822-1900)—German economist and journalist, liberal.—467

Wolff, Luigi—Italian major; follower of Mazzini, member of the Association of Mutual Progress (organisation of Italian workers in London); participant in the inaugural meeting of the International held on 28 September 1864 at St Martin's Hall, member of the Central Council of the International (1864-65), participant in the London Conference (1865); exposed as an agent of the Bonapartist police in 1871.—16, 17, 55, 115, 131, 140, 162, 170, 243, 250

Wolff, Wilhelm (*Lupus*) (1809-1864)—German teacher; proletarian revolutionary, leading figure in the Communist League; an editor of the *Neue Rheinische Zeitung*; deputy to the

Frankfurt National Assembly (1849); emigrated to Switzerland in the summer of 1849 and later to England; friend and associate of Marx and Engels.—6, 19, 20, 31, 38, 44, 81, 115, 116, 125, 127, 188, 231, 378, 381, 402, 447, 456, 469

Wolffsohn—refugee in England, treasurer of the *Deutsche Freiheit und Einheit* society.—32

Wood—lawyer in Manchester.—127, 128

Worsaae, Jens Jacob Asmussen (1821-1885)—Danish archaeologist, moderate liberal.—8

Wrangel, Friedrich Heinrich Ernst, Count von (1784-1877)—Prussian general; one of the chief participants in the counterrevolutionary coup d'état in Prussia (November 1848); Commander-in-Chief of the allied Prussian and Austrian forces during the Danish war (1864).—121

Wurtz, Charles Adolphe (1817-1884)—French organic chemist, adherent of atomic-molecular theory.—385, 388

Wuttke, Johann Karl Heinrich (1818-1876)—German historian and politician, professor at Leipzig University; close to the Lassalleans in the 1860s.—348

Y

York—bookseller of the German Workers' Educational Society in London.—477

Z

Zamoyski, Ladislas (*Władysław*), *Count* (1803-1868)—Polish magnate, took part in the insurrection of 1830-31; after its defeat a leader of the Polish conservative monarchist refugees in Paris.—110

Zange—owner of a printing shop in Erfurt.—417

INDEX OF LITERARY AND MYTHOLOGICAL NAMES

INDEX OF QUOTED
AND MENTIONED LITERATURE

WORKS BY KARL MARX AND FREDERICK ENGELS

Marx, Karl

[*Address from the Working Men's International Association to President Johnson*] (present edition, Vol. 20)
— To Andrew Johnson, President of the United States. In: *The Bee-Hive Newspaper*, No. 188, May 20, 1865.—155, 159, 160

Capital. A Critique of Political Economy. Volume I (present edition, Vol. 35)
— Das Kapital. Kritik der politischen Oekonomie. Erster Band. Buch I: Der Produktionsprocess des Kapitals, Hamburg, 1867.—4, 22, 46, 71, 78, 130, 149, 153, 155, 160, 161, 163, 173, 174-76, 178, 192, 198, 199, 201, 213, 219, 221, 222, 223, 224, 225-28, 232, 233, 262, 269, 271, 278, 282, 289, 291, 295, 312, 319, 325, 328, 331-34, 336, 339, 343-44, 347, 348, 350-52, 357, 358, 359, 362, 363, 366, 367-68, 369, 371, 378, 380-85, 386-89, 390-94, 396, 399, 400, 402-07, 409, 415, 417, 419, 420, 424, 426-27, 431, 432, 436, 437, 439-43, 445, 449-51, 455, 456-58, 461, 463, 464, 467-69, 471, 472, 473, 477, 478, 480, 483, 487-88, 489, 490, 493-95, 497, 498, 502, 503, 504, 509, 511, 514-15, 518, 526, 527, 529, 531, 533-34, 536, 539, 541, 543-44, 546, 548, 551, 552, 553, 555, 565, 568-71, 572, 573, 575, 576, 577, 578, 582

The Communism of the 'Rheinischer Beobachter' (present edition, Vol. 6)
— Der Kommunismus des *Rheinischen Beobachters*. In: *Deutsche-Brüsseler-Zeitung*, Nr. 73, 12. September 1847.—97

A Contribution to the Critique of Political Economy (present edition, Vol. 29)
— Zur Kritik der politischen Oekonomie. Erstes Heft, Berlin, 1859.—328, 382, 384, 395, 531, 543

[*A Correction*] (present edition, Vol. 20)
— Berichtigung.—346

A Correction [To the Editor of the *Weiße Adler*] (present edition, Vol. 20)
— Berichtigung [An den Redakteur des *Weißen Adler*]. In: *Der weiße Adler*, Nr. 48, 22. April 1865 (signed: *H. Jung*).—143

[*Draft for a Speech on France's Attitude to Poland* (*Polemics against Peter Fox*)] (present edition, Vol. 20).—55

— Die Lage der arbeitenden Klasse in England. Nach eigner Anschauung und authentischen Quellen. Leipzig, 1848.—385

Herr Tidmann. Old Danish Folk Song (present edition, Vol. 20)
— Herr Tidmann. Altdänisches Volkslied. In: *Der Social-Demokrat*, Nr. 18, 5. Februar 1865.—68, 79, 94

Notes on the War in Germany, I-V (present edition, Vol. 20). In: *The Manchester Guardian*, Nos. 6190, 6194, 6197, 6201, 6204; 20, 25, 28 June and 3, 6 July 1866.—286, 296

[*Notice Concerning 'The Prussian Military Question and the German Workers' Party'*] (present edition, Vol. 20). In: *Berliner Reform*, Nr. 53, 3. März 1865.—111
— In: *Düsseldorfer Zeitung*, Nr. 62, 3. März 1865.—84, 111, 112, 119
— In: *Rheinische Zeitung*, Nr. 62, 3. März 1865.—84, 111, 112

Outlines of a Critique of Political Economy (present edition, Vol. 3)
— Umrisse zu einer Kritik der Nationalökonomie. In: *Deutsch-französische Jahrbücher*, hg. von Arnold Ruge und Karl Marx, 1-ste und 2-te Lieferung, Paris, 1844.—515

Po and Rhine (present edition, Vol. 16)
— Po und Rhein. Berlin, 1859.—365

The Prussian Military Question and the German Workers' Party (present edition, Vol. 20)
— Die preußische Militärfrage und die deutsche Arbeiterpartei. Hamburg, 1865.—70, 71, 76, 77, 78, 81, 83, 84, 87, 88, 94, 99, 100, 107, 111, 112, 114, 117, 119, 120, 125, 126, 130, 133, 134, 152, 154, 280, 348, 352, 363, 365
— In: *Rheinische Zeitung*, Nr. 68, 9. März 1865 (an extract from the pamphlet entitled 'Für die Arbeiterpartei').—126

[*Review of Volume One of 'Capital' for the 'Zukunft'*] (present edition, Vol. 20)
— Karl Marx, das Kapital. Erster Band. Hamburg, Meissner, 1867, 784 Seiten. 8°. In: *Die Zukunft*, Nr. 254, 30. Oktober 1867, Beilage.—443, 445, 449, 461, 467, 475, 497

[*Review of Volume One of 'Capital' for the 'Rheinische Zeitung'*] (present edition, Vol. 20)
— Karl Marx. Das Kapital. Kritik der politischen Oekonomie. I. Band. Der Produktionsprozess des Kapitals. Hamburg, O. Meißner, 1867.—444, 445, 449, 462, 471, 498

[*Review of Volume One of 'Capital' for the 'Elberfelder Zeitung'*] (present edition, Vol. 20)
— Karl Marx über das Capital (Hamburg, Verlag von Otto Meißner. I. Band. 1867). In: *Elberfelder Zeitung*, Nr. 302, 2. November 1867.—461, 463, 475, 529

[*Review of Volume One of 'Capital' for the 'Düsseldorfer Zeitung'*] (present edition, Vol. 20)
— Karl Marx. Das Kapital. Kritik der politischen Oekonomie. Erster Band. Hamburg, Meißner, 1867. In: *Düsseldorfer Zeitung*, Nr. 316, 17. November 1867.—471, 475, 529

[*Review of Volume One of 'Capital' for the 'Beobachter'*] (present edition, Vol. 20)
— Karl Marx. Das Kapital. Kritik der politischen Oekonomie. Erster Band. Hamburg, Meißner, 1867. In: *Der Beobachter*, Nr. 303, 27. Dezember 1867.—493, 495, 498, 500, 503, 507, 510, 511, 512

— An die Redaktion des *Social-Demokrat* in Berlin. In: *Neue Frankfurter Zeitung,* Nr. 60, 1. März 1865.—114
— An die Redaktion des *Social-Demokrat.* In: *Der Social-Demokrat,* Nr. 29, 3. März 1865.—96, 97, 98, 105, 106, 107, 108, 111, 113, 114, 116, 124, 126, 129, 135, 150, 175, 494

WORKS BY DIFFERENT AUTHORS

Alaux, J. E. *Une forme nouvelle du socialisme. Le Congrès ouvrier de Genève.* In: *Revue contemporaine,* t. 53, 15 octobre 1866.—338, 340

Alcott, L. *Little Women.*—370

Andral, G. *Clinique médicale, ou choix d'observations recueillies à l'hôpital de la Charité (clinique de M. Lerminier),* t. IV, Paris, 1827.—26

Arago, F. *Astronomie populaire.* T. 1-4. Paris-Leipzig, 1854-1857.—27

Baer, W. *Electricität und Magnetismus. Die Gesetze und das Wirken dieser mächtigen Naturkräfte und ihre Bedeutung für das praktische Leben.* Leipzig [1863].—27

Balzac, Honoré de. *Le chef-d'oeuvre inconnu.*—348
— *Le faiseur.*—348
— *Melmoth réconcilié.*—348

Becker, B. *Botschaft des Präsidenten.* In: *Der Social-Demokrat,* Nr. 3, 30. Dezember 1864.—65, 104
— *Rede des Vereins-Präsidenten Bernhard Becker, gehalten in der Versammlung der Hamburger Mitglieder des Allgemeinen deutschen Arbeiter-Vereins am 22. März 1865.* In: *Der Social-Demokrat,* Nr. 39, 26. März 1865, Beilage.—139, 140, 191

Becker, H. [Speech in the Prussian Chamber of Deputies on 11 February 1865.] In: *Der Social-Demokrat,* Nr. 22, 15. Februar 1865.—94

Becker, J. Ph. (anon.) *The International Working Men's Association.* In: *The Workman's Advocate,* No. 145, December 16, 1865.—214
— (anon.) *Rundschreiben der deutschen Abtheilung des Zentral Komites der Internationalen Arbeiterassociation für die Schweiz an die Arbeiter.* Genf, den 1. November 1865.—214
— *Zur Friedens- und Freiheitsliga.* In: *Der Vorbote,* Nr. 12, Dezember 1867.—581

Beesly, E. S. *Catiline as a Party Leader.* In: *The Fortnightly Review,* Vol. I, May 15 to August 1, 1865.—185

Berghaus, H. *Physikalischer Schul-Atlas.* Gotha, 1850.—28

[Bettziech, H.] *Die Frau in Weiß. Drama in 5 Acten, mit freier Benutzung von Wilkie Collins.* In: *Kladderadatsch,* Nr. 52 und 53, 18. November 1866.—336

Bible
  The Old Testament
    Genesis.—274
  The New Testament
    Luke.—509
    Matthew.—467, 578

Bismarck, O. [Speech in the North German Parliament on 11 March 1867]. In: *Der Social-Demokrat*, Nr. 33, 15. März 1867.—355
— [Speech in the North German Parliament on 18 March 1867]. In: *Der Social-Demokrat*, Nr. 35, 20. März 1867.—351

Blanc, L. *Lettres de Londres*. In: *Le Temps*, No. 1815, 23 avril 1866.—270

Blind, K. [*Address.*] In: *Der deutsche Eidgenosse*, Nr. 1, 15. März 1865.—119
— (anon.) *Bradford, 25. Oct.* In: *Der Beobachter*, Nr. 268, 17. November 1864.—41, 44, 45, 51, 52, 107
— *Ein Freundeswort an Deutschlands Arbeiter, Bürger und Bauer*. In: *Hermann*, 6. Juni 1863.—36
— (anon.) *German Democracy*. In: *The Morning Star*, February 24, 1865.—110
— [Letter to the American People.] In the article 'Bescheidenheit—ein Ehrenkleid'. In: *Der Beobachter*, Nr. 245, 21. Oktober 1864.—27, 44
— (anon.) [Regarding the Causes of Marx's and Engels' Breach with the *Social-Demokrat*.] In: *Neue Frankfurter Zeitung*, Nr. 64, 5. März 1865; *Der Social-Demokrat*, Nr. 31, 8. März 1865.—120, 126, 129
— (anon.) [A Republican Protest.] In: *Neue Frankfurter Zeitung*, Nr. 270, 29. September 1864.—30, 38, 41, 44
— (anon.) *Ein republikanischer Protest*. London, 17. September 1864. In: *Die Westliche Post*, October-beginning of November 1864.—30, 38, 41, 44, 57
— (anon.) *Republikanischer Protest*. In: *Hermann*, Nr. 2407, 8. Oktober 1864. 30, 38, 41, 44

Borkheim, S. *Ma perle devant le congrès de Genève*. Bruxelles, 1867.—419, 435, 436, 437, 440-41, 443, 446, 449, 452-53, 478, 513
— *Meine Perle vor dem Genfer Congress. Von einem literarischen Diplomaten*. Zürich, 1868.—435, 441, 478, 513

B[orkheim], S. *Russische politische Flüchtlinge in West-Europa*. In: *Demokratisches Wochenblatt*, Nr. 5, 6, 17, 20, 1., 8. February, 25. April, 16. Mai 1868.—539, 552

Bright, J. [Speech in the Birmingham Chamber of Commerce on 19 January 1865.] In: *The Times*, No. 25087, January 20, 1865.—71, 74
— [Speech on Parliamentary Reform delivered at a meeting in Rochdale on 3 January 1866.] In: *The Times*, No. 25386, January 4, 1866.—212

Das Buch der Erfindungen, Gewerbe und Industrien. 3 Bände. 3. Auflage. Leipzig, 1858.—188

Büchner, L. *Force et matière. Études philosophiques et empiriques de sciences naturelles*. Paris, Brüssel, Leipzig, 1863.—368
— *Kraft und Stoff. Empirisch-naturphilosophische Studien*. Frankfurt a. M., 1855.—368

Burns, R. *Is there for honest poverty.*—91

Caesar (Gaius Julius Caesar). *Commentarii de bello Gallico.*—558

Cervantes de Saavedra (Miguel de). *Don Quixote.*—313

Chaucer, G. *Canterbury Tales.*—246

Cicero (Marcus Tulius Cicero). *Oratio pro Sextio.*—136

Clement, K. J. *Schleswig, das urheimische Land des nicht dänischen Volks der Angeln und Frisen und Englands Mutterland, wie es war und ward*. Hamburg, 1862.—8

Cluseret, [G.-P.] *Mentana.* In: *Le Courrier français,* No. 173, 7 décembre 1867.—496

[Collet, C. D.] *Russia's Designs on the Pope.* In: *The Free Press,* Vol. XII, No. 12, December 7, 1864.—52, 54

Collins, W. *The Woman in White,* 2 vols. Leipzig, 1860.—336

Comte, A. *Cours de philosophie positive.* T. 1-6. Paris, 1830-1842.—292

Cotta, B. *Geologische Briefe aus den Alpen.* Leipzig, 1850.—28

Cuvier, G. *Discours sur les révolutions de la surface du globe, et sur les changemens qu'elles ont produits dans le règne animal.* 8th ed. Paris, 1840.—322, 323

Darwin, Ch. *On the Origin of Species by means of Natural Selection, or the Preservation of Favoured Races in the Struggle for Life.* London, 1859.—136, 304, 322, 323, 327, 494

Demokratische Studien. Unter Mitwirkung von L. Bamberger, Karl Grün, Moritz Hartmann, Friedrich Kapp, F. Lassalle, Michelet, H. B. Oppenheim, Ludwig Simon aus Trier, Adolf Stahr, Carl Vogt u. A., herausgegeben von Ludwig Walesrode. Hamburg, 1860.—365

Denis (de Chateaugiron). *L'Anti-Proudhon.* Rennes, 1860.—218

Denis, H. *La question polonaise et la démocratie.* In: *La Tribune du Peuple,* Nos. 41, 42, 43, 45, 46; 5, 26 mars, 17 avril, 29 mai, 30 juin 1864.—213, 223

Derby, E. [Statement on the Luxemburg Treaty, 20 June 1867.] In: *The Times,* No. 25843, June 21, 1867.—394

Diderot, D. *Le neveu de Rameau.*—34

Diogenes Laertius. *De vitis philosophorum.*—373

Disraeli, B. *Vivian Grey.*—300
— [Speech made at Oxford on 25 November 1864.] In: *The Times,* No. 25040, November 26, 1864. *Mr. Disraeli at Oxford.*—48
— [Speech in the House of Commons on 4 June 1866.] In: *The Times,* No. 25516, June 5, 1866.—282
— [Speech in the House of Commons on 24 July 1866.] In: *The Times,* No. 25559, July 25, 1866. *The Hyde Park Riots;* see also *Hansard's Parliamentary Debates,* Vol. 184, London, 1866, p. 1414.—300

Dubois, L. *Les Conditions de la paix.* In: *Le Courrier français,* No. 77, 2 septembre 1867.—420

Dühring, E. *Capital und Arbeit. Neue Antworten auf alte Fragen.* Berlin, 1865.—536
— *Kritische Grundlegung der Volkswirtschaftslehre.* Berlin, 1866.—544
— *Marx, Das Kapital, Kritik der politischen Oekonomie, 1. Band, Hamburg, 1867.* In: *Ergänzungsblätter zur Kenntniß der Gegenwart.* 3. Band. 3. Heft, Hildburghausen, 1867, S. 182-86.—511, 513, 514-15, 522, 536, 537, 543
— *Natürliche Dialektik. Neue logische Grundlegungen der Wissenschaft und Philosophie.* Berlin, 1865.—520, 544
— *Die Schicksale meiner socialen Denkschrift für das Preussische Staatsministerium.* Zugleich ein Beitrag zur Geschichte des Autorrechts und der Gesetzesanwendung. Berlin, 1868.—548
— *Die Verkleinerer Carey's und die Krisis der Nationalökonomie.* 16 Briefe. Breslau,

Grimm, W. *Die Deutsche Heldensage.* Göttingen, 1829.—168

Grimm, Brüder. *Kinder- und Haus-Märchen.* Bd. 1-3. Berlin, 1812-1822.—168

Grove, W. R. *The Correlation of Physical Forces.* 3rd. ed. London, 1855 (lst edition came out in 1846).—138

Grube, A. W. *Biographieen aus der Naturkunde, in ästhetischer Form und religiösem Sinne.* Stuttgart, 1850.—28

Grün, K. *Armées permanentes ou milices. IV. Ce que l'Allemagne du Sud a fait et ce qu'elle pourrait faire.* In: *Les Etats-Unis d'Europe,* No. 7, 16 février 1868.—534, 540-41

Guhl, E. und Koner, W. *Das Leben der Griechen und Römer nach antiken Bildwerken.* Berlin, 1862.—28

Harrison, F. *The Limits of Political Economy.* In: *The Fortnightly Review.* Vol. I, May 15 to August 1, 1865.—185

Harting, P. *Die Macht des Kleinen sichtbar in der Bildung der Rinde unseres Erdballs oder Uebersicht der Gestaltung, der geographischen und geologischen Verbreitung der Polypen, Foraminiferen und kieselschaligen Bacillarien.* Aus dem Holländischen übersetzt von Dr. A. Schwartzkopf, mit einem Vorworte von M. J. Schleiden, Dr. Leipzig, 1851.—28

Hebel, J. P. *Der Schwarzwälder im Breisgau.*—188

Hegel, G. W. F. *Encyclopädie der philosophischen Wissenschaften im Grundrisse,* Dritte Ausgabe. Heidelberg, 1830.—382
— *Phänomenologie des Geistes.* In: G. W. F. Hegel, *Werke.* 2-te Aufl., Bd. 2, Berlin, 1841.—522, 556
— *Vorlesungen über die Naturphilosophie als der Encyclopädie der philosophischen Wissenschaften im Grundrisse.* In: G. W. F. Hegel, *Werke,* 2-te Aufl., Bd. 7. Berlin, 1842.—138, 184-85
— *Vorlesungen über die Philosophie der Geschichte.* In: G. W. F. Hegel, *Werke,* 2-te Aufl., Bd. 9. Berlin, 1840.—370
— *Wissenschaft der Logik.* In: G. W. F. Hegel, *Werke,* 2-te Aufl., Bd. 3-5. Berlin, 1841.—138, 382

Heine, H. *Atta Troll, Ein Sommernachtstraum.*—32, 52
— *Den König Wiswamitra...* In: *Buch der Lieder. Die Heimkehr.*—242, 245
— *Deutschland. Ein Wintermärchen.*—52

[Heinzen, K.] *Der deutsche Hunger und die deutschen Fürsten.* In: *Deutsche Brüsseler Zeitung,* Nr. 49, 20. Juni 1847.—31

Herwegh, G. *An die Redaktion des 'Social-Demokrat'*—see Rüstow, W., Herwegh, G.
— *Zur Beachtung.* In: *Nordstern,* Nr. 303, 1. April 1865.—140

Herwegh, G., Rüstow, W., Reusche, F. *Protest.* In: *Nordstern,* Nr. 300, 11. März 1865.—134

H[eß, M.] *Paris, 10. Jan.* [*Arb.-Associationen. Internat. Arb.-Assoc. 'Avenir national'.*] In: *Der Social-Demokrat,* Nr. 8, 13. Januar 1865.—65, 66, 68, 80
— *Paris, 25. Jan.* [*Associationswesen. Clerus. Der oppositionelle Wahlsieg.*] In: *Der Social-Demokrat,* Nr. 15, 29. Januar 1865.—70
— *Paris, 28. Januar.* [*Internationale Arbeiter-Association.—Geldkrisis.*] In: *Der Social-Demokrat,* Nr. 16, 1. Februar 1865.—75

— *Paris, 4. Febr.* [*Neue Gesetzvorschläge betr. Cooperativ-Associationen. Die internationale Arbeiter-Association. Unterrichtsfrage.*] In: *Der Social-Demokrat*, Nr. 19, 8. Februar 1865.—83
— *Paris, 7. Febr.* [*Amerika.—Der Orient.—Italien.—Die Internationale Arbeiter-Association.*] In: *Der Social-Demokrat*, Nr. 21, 12. Februar 1865.—89, 95
— *Paris, 4. Mai.* [*Amerika. Internationale Association. Arbeiterindustrieausstellung. Städtisches Octroi. Italien und Rom. Militairfrage.*] In: *Der Social-Demokrat.* Nr. 57, 7. Mai 1865, Beilage.—157
— *Paris, 27. Aug.* [*Der Congreß der 'internationalen Arbeiter-Association' vertragt. Arbeitseinstellungen und Getreidepreise.*] In: *Der Social-Demokrat*, Nr. 130, 30. August 1865.—190

Heß, M. *Eine Warnung.* In: *Nordstern*, Nr. 320, 19. August 1865.—190

Hildebrand, *Camera obscura.* Haarlem, 1839.—242

Hirschfeld, R. [Statement.] In: *Hermann*, Nr. 426, 2. März 1867.—349

Der Hochverraths-Prozeß wider Ferdinand Lassalle vor dem Staats-Gerichts-Hofe zu Berlin am 12. März 1864. Nach dem stenographischen Bericht. Berlin, 1864.—30

Hoffmann, E. T. A. *Klein-Zaches, genannt Zinnober.*—230, 232, 233

Hofmann, A. W. *Einleitung in die moderne Chemie. Nach einer Reihe von Vorträgen gehalten in dem Royal College of Chemistry zu London.* Braunschweig, 1866.—382, 385

Hofstetten, J. B. [Speech at the General Assembly of the General Association of German Workers on 24 November 1867.] In: *Der Social-Demokrat*, Nr. 139, 29. November 1867, erste Beilage.—495

Holyake, G. J. *The Interview with Mr. Walpole.* In: *The Times*, No. 25561, July 27, 1866.—300

Horace (Quintus Horatius Flaccus). *Carminum*, III.—340
— *Carminum*, IV.—250
— *Satirarum*, II, III.—73

Hübner, O. [Address to the electors.] In: *Le Courrier français*, No. 81, 6 septembre 1867.—421, 422

Jacobs, F. *Hellas. Vorträge über Heimath, Geschichte, Literatur und Kunst der Hellenen.* Berlin, 1852.—28

Jones, E. *A Letter to the Advocates of the Co-operative Principle, and to the Members of Co-operative Societies* (present edition, Vol. 11). In: *Notes to the People*, Vol. 1, No. 2, May 10, 1851.—15
— *Co-operation. What It Is, and What It Ought To Be* (present edition, Vol. 11). In: *Notes to the People*, Vol. 1, No. 21, September 20, 1851.—15
— [Speech at the trial of the Fenians in Manchester on 8 November 1867.] In: *The Times*, No. 25964, November 9, 1867.—466

Juvenal (Decimus Junius Juvenalis). *Satirarum*—504

Kant, I. *Kritik der reinen Vernunft.* Riga, 1781.—238

Kekulé, A. *Lehrbuch der Organischen Chemie oder der Chemie der Kohlenstoffverbindungen.* Bände I-III. Erlangen, 1861-1867.—387

Kiesselbach, W. *Der Gang des Welthandels und die Entwicklung des europäischen Völkerlebens im Mittelalter.* Stuttgart, 1860.—28

— *President Lincoln and the International Working Men's Association* (signed: Charles Francis Adams). In: *The Express*, February 6, 1865.—86

Livy (Titus Livius). *Ab urbe condita libri.*—17, 52, 295

Longuet, Ch. *La question agricole, et le libre échange.* In: *La Rive gauche*, No. 15, 15 avril 1866.—281

Macaulay, Th. B. *The History of England from the Accession of James the Second.* 10th ed. 5 vol. London, 1854-1861.—28

McCulloch, J. R. *The Principles of Political Economy.* The first edition appeared in Edinburgh in 1825.—408

Macleod, H. D. *The Theory and Practice of Banking: with the Elementary Principles of Currency; Prices; Credit; and Exchanges.* In two volumes. Second edition. London, 1866. The first edition appeared in 1855-56.—511, 543

[Malthus, Th. R.] *An Essay on the Principle of Population, as It Affects the Future Improvement of Society, with Remarks on the Speculations of Mr. Godwin, M. Condorcet, and other Writers.* London, 1798.—136

Martin, H. [Preface to the report of the French delegates on the London Conference.] In: *Le Siècle*, 14 octobre 1865.—202

Maurer, G. L. *Einleitung zur Geschichte der Mark-, Hof-, Dorf- und Stadt-Verfassung und der öffentlichen Gewalt.* München, 1854.—547-49, 554, 557
— *Geschichte der Dorfverfassung in Deutschland.* Bände 1-2. Erlangen, 1865-1866.—547-49, 554, 557
— *Geschichte der Fronhöfe, der Bauernhöfe und der Hofverfassung in Deutschland.* Bände I-IV. Erlangen, 1862-1863.—547-49, 554, 557
— *Geschichte der Markenverfassung in Deutschland.* Erlangen, 1856.—547-49, 554, 557

Mazade, Ch. *La Russie sous l'empereur Alexandre II.—La société et le gouvernement russes depuis l'insurrection polonaise.* In: *Revue des deux Mondes*, T. 62, 15 mars 1866.—257

Metzner, Th., Vogt, A., Liebknecht, W. *Erklärung.* In: *Volks-Zeitung*, Nr. 145, 24. Juni 1865.—180

Mignet, F. A. *Histoire de la Révolution française, depuis 1789 jusqu'en 1814.* 2 vols. Paris, 1824.—28

Mill, J. S. [Speech in the House of Commons on 17 April 1866.] In: *The Times*, No. 25475, 18 April 1866.—269

Miquel, J. [Speech in the North-German Parliament on 9 April 1867.] In: *Der Social-Demokrat*, Nr. 45, 12. April 1867.—373

The Miller of the Dee.—241, 244, 249

Moilin, J.-A. (le docteur Tony). *Leçons de médecine physiologique.* Paris, 1866.—310, 319, 320, 324, 325, 327, 344

Moleschott, J. *Lehre der Nahrungsmittel. Für das Volk.* Erlangen, 1850.—28

Molière. *Les fourberies de Scapin.*—290, 296

Moltke, H. K. B. *Der russisch-türkische Feldzug in der europäischen Türkei 1828 und 1829.* Berlin, 1845.—520

Mommsen, Th. *Römische Geschichte.* 3 Bde. Berlin, 1854-1856.—27

Möser, J. *Osnabrückische Geschichte.* Theil 1. Berlin und Stettin, 1780.—547
— *Patriotische Phantasien,* Theil 3. Berlin, 1820.—558

Mozin-Peschier. *Dictionnaire complet des langues française et allemande.*... 4 éd. 4 vols. Stuttgart, 1863.—28

Müller, J. *Grundriß der Physik und Meteorologie. Für Lyceen, Gymnasien. Gewerbe- und Realschulen, sowie zum Selbstunterrichte.* 5. Aufl. Braunschweig, 1856.—27

Münster, G. H. *Politische Skizzen über die Lage Europas vom Wiener Congreß bis zur Gegenwart* (1815-1867). Leipzig, 1867.—520

Murchison, R. I., Verneuil, E. de, Keyserling, Count Alexander von. *The Geology of Russia in Europe and the Ural Mountains.* In two volumes. London, Paris, 1845.—164

Napoleon III. [Speech in Osere on 6 May 1866.] In: *The Times,* No. 25492, May 8, 1866.—274

The New American Cyclopaedia. A Popular Dictionary of General Knowledge. Edited by George Ripley and Charles A. Dana. Vol. 1-16, New York.—531

Nösselt, F. A. *Abriß der allgemeinen Weltgeschichte bis auf die neusten Zeiten.* Breslau, 1814.—27

Nouguès, L. *L'Art militaire et le progrès.* In: *Le Courrier français,* Nos. 123, 125; 18, 20 octobre 1867.—455

Österreichs Kämpfe im Jahre 1866. Nach Feldacten bearbeitet durch das K. K. Generalstabs-Bureau für Kriegsgeschichte. Bd. I. Wien, 1867.—510

Overbeck, J. *Pompeji in seinen Gebäuden, Alterthümern und Kunstwerken. Für Kunst- und Alterthumsfreunde.* Leipzig, 1856.—28

Pauli, R. *Bilder aus Alt-England.* Gotha, London & Edinburgh, 1860.—28

[Polo, M.] *Marco Paolo's Reise in der Orient, während der Jahre 1272 bis 1295.* Nach den vorzüglichsten Original-Ausgaben verdeutscht, und mit einem Kommentar begleitet von Felix Peregrin. Ronneburg und Leipzig, 1802.—28

Preller, L. *Griechische Mythologie.* Bd. 1-2. Leipzig, 1854.—27

Prokesch-Osten, A. *Geschichte des Abfalls der Griechen vom Türkischen Reiche im Jahre 1821 und der Gründung des Hellenischen Königreiches.* Bd. 1-6. Wien, 1867.—464, 520
— *Conference held on August the 27th, 1822, at Constantinople. From the Work of Baron Prokesch.* In: *The Diplomatic Review,* October 2, 1867.—464

Proudhon, R.-J. *Lettres inédites de P.-J. Proudhon sur les générations spontanées.* In: *Le Courrier français,* No. 121, 123, 124; 16, 18, 19 octobre 1867.—455

Prozeß gegen den Schriftsteller Herrn Ferdinand Lassalle, verhandelt zu Düsseldorf vor der korrektionellen Appellkammer am 27. Juni 1864 (Separat-Abdruck aus der *Düsseldorfer Zeitung,* Nr. 176, 177, 178). Düsseldorf, 1864.—12, 38

Pyat, F. *Addresse des Démocrates Français à leur Frères d'Irlande et d'Angleterre. Paris, 2 décembre 1867.* In: *The Times,* No. 26015, January 8, 1868. Under the general heading: *The French Democrats and the Fenians.*—516

— *Zur Aufklärung.* In: *Nordstern,* Nr. 303, 1. April 1865.—139, 140

Rüstow, W., Herwegh, G. *An die Redaktion des 'Social-Demokrat'. Zürich, den 4. März 1866.* In: *Der Social-Demokrat,* Nr. 31, 8. März 1865.—120, 126

Schiller, J. Ch. F. von. *Don Carlos.*—12, 53, 103
— *Das Eleusische Fest.*—242
— *Das Lied von der Glocke.*—299

Schilling, C. *Die Ausstoßung des Präsidenten Bernhard Becker aus dem Allgemeinen Deutschen Arbeiter-Verein und der 'Social-Demokrat'.* Berlin, 1865.—176, 179, 180, 181, 191

Schleiden, M. J. *Studien. Populäre Vorträge.* Leipzig, 1855.—27

Schlosser, Fr. C. *Weltgeschichte für das deutsche Volk. Unter Mitwirkung des Verfassers bearbeitet von Dr G. L. Kriegk.* Bd. 1-19. Frankfurt a. M., 1844-1857.—27

Schmeller, J. A. *Bayerisches Wörterbuch.* Theile 1-4. Stuttgart und Tübingen, 1827-1837.—554

Schoemann, G. F. *Griechische Alterthümer.* 2 Bde. Berlin, 1855-1859.—27

Schorlemmer, C. *Researches on the Hydrocarbons of the Series $C_n H_{2n+2}$.* In: *Proceedings of the Royal Society,* No. 94, 1867, No. 102, 1868.—560

Schulze-Delitzsch, H. *Die Abschaffung des geschäftlichen Risico durch Herrn Lassalle. Ein neues Capitel zum Deutschen Arbeiterkatechismus.* Berlin, 1866.—211

Schweitzer, J. B. (anon.) [Conclusion to Rüstow's and Herwegh's Statement on their refusal to cooperate on *Der Social-Demokrat.*] In: *Der Social-Demokrat,* Nr. 31, 8. März 1865.—120, 128-29
— (anon.) *Die deutsche Social-Demokratie.* In: *Der Social-Demokrat,* Nr. 19, 8. Februar 1865.—83
— *Der Kapitalgewinn und der Arbeitslohn. National-ökonomische Abhandlung.* Berlin, 1867.—417
— (anon.) *Das Kirchenthum und die moderne Civilisation.* In: *Der Social-Demokrat,* Nr. 5, 6. Januar 1865.—78
— (anon.) [Leader.] Berlin, 1. März. In: *Der Social-Demokrat,* Nr. 29, 3. März 1865.—114, 116, 124-25
— *Lucinde oder Capital und Arbeit. Ein social-politisches Zeitgemälde aus der Gegenwart. In drei Bänden.* Frankfurt a. M., 1863-1864.—25
— (anon.) *Das Ministerium Bismarck.* I. In: *Der Social-Demokrat,* Nr. 14, 27. Januar 1865.—104
— (anon.) *Das Ministerium Bismarck.* II. In: *Der Social-Demokrat,* Nr. 18, 5. Februar 1865.—104
— (anon.) *Das Ministerium Bismarck.* III. In: *Der Social-Demokrat,* Nr. 23, 17. Februar 1865.—104
— (anon.) *Das Ministerium Bismarck.* IV. In: *Der Social-Demokrat,* Nr. 24, 18. Februar 1865.—104
— (anon.) *Das Ministerium Bismarck,* V. In: *Der Social-Demokrat,* Nr. 28, 1. März 1865.—113
— (anon.) *Das Ministerium Bismarck und die Regierungen der Mittel- und Kleinstaaten.* In: *Der Social-Demokrat,* Nr. 6, 8. Januar 1865.—78
— (anon.) *Das Werk von Carl Marx.* In: *Der Social-Demokrat,* Nr. 10, 11, 12, 14, 22., 24., 26., 31. Januar; Nr. 15, 24, 25, 2., 23., 26. Februar; Nr. 30, 39, 8., 29. März; Nr. 49, 51, 24., 29. April; Nr. 54, 6. Mai 1868.—553
— *Widerlegung von Carl Vogt's Studien zur gegenwärtigen Lage Europa's.* Frankfurt a. M., 1859.—25

Shakespeare, W. *King Henry IV.*—177
— *The Merry Wives of Windsor.*—177

[Siebel, C.] *Carl Marx: Das Kapital. Kritik der politischen Oekonomie. Erster Band. Hamburg. Otto Meißner. 1867.* In: *Barmer Zeitung*, Nr. 291, 6. Dezember 1867.—471, 509, 529

Simon, L. *Deutschland und seine beiden Großmächte.* In: *Demokratische Studien.* Hamburg, 1860.—365

Smith, A. *An Inquiry into the Nature and Causes of the Wealth of Nations.* In three volumes. Edinburgh, 1814. The first edition in two volumes appeared in London in 1776.—514

Smith, W. *A Latin-English Dictionary. Based upon the Works of Forcellini and Freund....* London, 1855.—28

Spruner, K. von. *Historisch-geographischer Schul-Atlas.* 2. Aufl. Gotha, 1860.—28

Stalder, F. J. *Versuch eines Schweizerischen Idiotikon, mit etymologischen Bemerkungen untermischt.* Band I. Basel und Aarau, 1806; Band II. Aarau, 1812.—554

Stanley, E. [Statement on the Luxemburg Treaty made on 14 June 1867.] In: *The Times*, No. 25838, June 15, 1867.—394

Stein, L. *System der Staatswissenschaft.* Bd. I-II. Stuttgart und Tübingen, 1852-1856.—513
— *Die Verwaltungslehre.* Th. 1-7. Stuttgart, 1865-1868.—513

Stieber, W. [*Declaration.*] In: *Volks-Zeitung*, Nr. 48, 26. Februar 1867 and in *Hermann*, Nr. 426, 2. März 1867.—349

Stieler, A. *Hand-Atlas über alle Theile der Erde und über das Weltgebäude.* Gotha, 1859.—28

Struve, G. *Geschichte der drei Volkserhebungen in Baden.* Bern, 1849.—35
— *Die neue Zeit. Ein Volkskalender auf das Jahr 1 (Vom 21. März 1850 bis 20. März 1851 der alten Zeit).* Herisau, 1849.—33
— *Die 'Teig-Gesichter' in Deutschland.* In: *Der deutsche Eidgenosse* [No. 1], 15. März 1865.—119

Struve, G. und Rasch, G. *Zwölf Streiter der Revolution.* Berlin, 1867.—397

Swift, J. *Travels into Several Remote Nations of the World, by Lemuel Gulliver, First a Surgeon, and then a Captain of Several Ships.*—376

Tacitus, Publius Cornelius. *Germania.*—558

Terence (Publius Terentius Afer). *Andria.*—52, 498, 520
— *Heautontimorumenos.*—568

Ternaux, M. *Histoire de la Terreur 1792-1794 d'après des documents authentiques et inédits.* T. 1-7. Paris, 1862-1869.—27

Thornton, W. T. *Stray Chapters from a Forthcoming Work on Labour.* In: *The Fortnightly Review.* Vol. II. No. 10, October 1, 1867.—455

Thünen, J. H. *Der isolirte Staat in Beziehung auf Landwirtschaft und Nationalökonomie.* Th. I-III. Rostok, 1842-1863.—522, 543

Tolain, H. *Congrès de Lausanne.* In: *Le Courrier français*, Nos. 80-86, 5-11 septembre 1867.—422

Trémaux, P. *Origine et transformations de l'homme et des autres êtres.* Première partie. Paris, 1865.—304, 305, 306, 320, 322, 323-24, 327

Tschudi, Fr. von. *Das Thierleben der Alpenwelt. Naturansichten und Thierzeichnungen aus dem schweizerischen Gebirge.* Leipzig, 1853.—28

Tyndall, J. *Heat considered as a Mode of Motion.* London, 1865.—212

Urquhart, D. (anon). *Construction of the 'Kingdom of Italy'.* In: *The Free Press,* May 3, 1865.—154
— *Fall of Austria, and Its Consequences to the World.* In: *The Diplomatic Review,* Vol. XV, Nr. 3, March 6, 1867.—349

Vermorel, A. *La prochaine campagne de la Prusse.* In: *Le Courrier français,* No. 84, 9 septembre 1867.—426, 428

Vésinier, P. (anon.) *L'Association Internationale des Travailleurs.* In: *L'Echo de Verviers,* Nos. 293, 294; 16, 18 décembre 1865.—212-13, 214, 216, 218, 250
— *La Vie du nouveau César, Étude historique.* 1ère partie. Genève, 1865.—218

Virchow, R. [Speech in the House of Representatives on 9 December 1863.] In: *Stenographische Berichte über die Verhandlungen der* [...] *beiden Häuser des Landtages, Haus der Abgeordneten.* 13. Sitzung, Bd. 1. Berlin, 1864.—34

Virgil (Publius Vergilius Maro). *Aeneid.*—31, 276, 327, 371
— *Georgicon.*—281

Vogt, C. *Studien zur gegenwärtigen Lage Europas.* Genf und Bern, 1859.—364
— [On the Congress of the League of Peace and Freedom in Geneva in 1867.] In: *Neue Zürcher-Zeitung,* Nr. 254, 13. September 1867.—442

Voltaire, F.-M. A. *Candide.*—522

Völter, D. *Grundriß der Geographie.* Zweite verm. und umgearb. Aufl. der 'Elementargeographie'. Eßlingen, 1859.—27

Wagener, H. *Denkschrift über die wirthschaftlichen Associationen und socialen Coalitionen.* Zweite Auflage. Neuschönefeld an Leipzig [1866].—548
— [Speech in the North-German Parliament on 23 March 1867.] In: *Der Social-Demokrat,* Nr. 38, 27. März 1867.—355

Watts, J. *Trade Societies and Strikes: their good and evil Influences on the Members of Trades Unions, and on Society at large. Machinery: its Influences on Work and Wages, and Co-operative Societies, Productive and Distributive, Past, Present, and Future.* Manchester, 1865.—224, 228, 234

Weerth, G. *Es gibt nichts Schönres auf der Welt.*—521

Worsaae, J. J. A. *An Account of the Danes and Norwegians in England, Scotland, and Ireland.* London, 1852.—8

Wurtz, A. *Leçons de philosophie chimique.* Paris, 1864.—385, 388

DOCUMENTS OF THE INTERNATIONAL WORKING MEN'S ASSOCIATION[a]

L'Association Internationale des Travailleurs. In: *Le Siècle,* 14 octobre 1865.—199

---

[a] Documents written by Marx see in Section 'Works by Karl Marx and Frederick Engels; Marx, Karl'.

Aufruf an alle Arbeiter, Arbeitervereine und Arbeiterassociationen in der Schweiz zum Beitritt der 'Internationalen Arbeiter-Association'. Signed by Becker, Dupleix and other members of the Geneva Section. Genf, 1865.—119

Congrès de Genève. Société Internationale des Travailleurs. In: *Le Courrier international*, Nos. 8-16, 9, 16, 23; 30 mars, 6, 13, 20, 27 avril 1867.—346

Congrès ouvrier. Association Internationale des Travailleurs. Paris [1866].—259

Congrès ouvrier. Association Internationale des Travailleurs. Règlement provisoire. Paris [1864].—85

Congress of Geneva. International Association of Working Men. In: *The International Courier*, Nos. 7-15, February 20, March 13, 20 and 27, April 3, 10 and 17 1867.—346

Entwicklungsgang unserer Association. In: *Der Vorbote*. Erster Jg., Nr. 1. Januar 1866.—213

Great International Conference of Working Men. In: *The Workman's Advocate*, No. 134, September 30, 1865.—200

Great Meeting for Poland. In: *The Bee-Hive Newspaper*, No. 177, March 4, 1865.—143

International Working Men's Association. In: *The Bee-Hive Newspaper*, No. 305, August 17, 1867.—420

International Working Men's Association. In: *The Miner and Workman's Advocate*, No. 97, 7 January 1865.—60

Meeting of the General Council.— Mr. Beales on Fenianism.—Extraordinary Scene. In: *The Bee-Hive Newspaper*, No. 315, October 26, 1867 (in the section 'The Reform League').—460

Questions proposées pour le congrès de Bruxelles. Ier lundi de septembre 1868 (signed in the name of the Paris committee by Murat, Camélinat, Girardin). In: *Le Courrier français*, 11 décembre 1867.—520

The State Prisoners. An Appeal to the Women of Ireland. In: *The Workman's Advocate*, No. 148, January 6, 1866. Signed by O'Donovan Rossa and Luby.—228

To the Editor of 'L'Echo de Verviers'. Signed by H. Jung (present edition, Vol. 20). In: *L'Echo de Verviers*, No. 43, 20 février 1866.—250

To the Workmen of France from the Working Men of England. In: *The Bee-Hive Newspaper*, No. 112, December 5, 1863. In the article 'Address of English to French Workmen'.—15

The Working Men's International Association. In: *The Bee-Hive Newspaper*, No. 169, January 7, 1865.—60

The Workingmen's Movement in Europe. In: *St. Louis Daily Press*, Vol. I, No. 22, January 10, 1865.—73

DOCUMENTS

An Act for Facilitating in Certain Cases the Proceedings of the Commissioners Appointed to make Inquiry Respecting Trades Unions and other Associations of Employers or Workmen. 5th April 1867.—448

An Act for Regulating the Hours of Labour for Children, Young Persons, and Women employed in Workshops; and for other Purposes relating thereto [21st August 1867]. In: *The Statutes of the United Kingdom of Great Britain and Ireland.* London, 1867, p. 454.—401

An Act to Extend the 'Trades Union Commission Act, 1867'. 12th August 1867.—448, 489

Address of Germans to the American Nation. Signed by Blind, Freiligrath, Heinzmann, Juch, Kinkel, Berndes, Siemens, Trübner, Ravenstein. In: *The Times,* No. 25171, April 28, 1865.—151

Agricultural Statistics, Ireland. Tables showing the Estimated Average Produce of the Crops for the Year 1866; and the Emigration from the Irish Ports, from 1st January to 31st December, 1866; also the Number of Mills for scutching flax in each Country and Province. Presented to both Houses of Parliament by Command of Her Majesty. Dublin, 1867.—461

Ancient Laws and Institutes of Wales, Vols. I-II. 1841.—549

Artizans and Labourers' Dwellings Bill. 1866-1868.—401

Aux étudiants des universités d'Allemagne et d'Italie, les étudiants de Paris. Signed by Albert Fermé, Jules Carret, Robert Vaillant, Émile Richard, Robert Levasseur, Gibralle, etc. In: *Le Courrier français,* No. 15, 20 mai 1866.—281

Children's Employment Commission (1862). *Reports* (I-V) *of the Commissioners.*—224, 383
— *First Report of the Commissioners. With Appendix. Presented to both Houses of Parliament by Command of Her Majesty.* London, 1863.—384
— *Fifth Report...* London, 1866.—296

Code civil—see *Code Napoléon*

Code Napoléon. Paris und Leipzig, 1808.—422, 503

Code pénal, ou code des délits et des peines. Cologne, 1810.—332-33, 438

East India (Bengal and Orissa Famine). Papers and Correspondence relative to the Famine in Bengal and Orissa, including the Report of the Famine Commission and the Minutes of the Lieutenant Governor of Bengal and the Governor General of India. (Presented to Parliament by Her Majesty's command.) Ordered, by the House of Commons, to be printed, 31 May 1867.—401

East India (Madras and Orissa Famine). Return to an Address of the Honourable House of Commons, dated 4 July 1867. Ordered, by the House of Commons, to be printed, 30 July 1867.—401

Factory Reports—see *Reports of the Inspectors of Factories...*

Gewerbeordnung für den Norddeutschen Bund. 1869.—546

Grundrechte des deutschen Volkes. In: *Stenographischer Bericht über die Verhandlungen der deutschen constituirenden Nationalversammlung zu Frankfurt am Main.* Bd. I-II. Frankfurt a. M. und Leipzig, 1848.—276

Hunter, H. J. *Report by Dr. Henry Julian Hunter on the Housing of the Poorer Parts of the Population in Towns, particularly as regards the Existence of Dangerous Degrees of Overcrowding and the Use of Dwellings Unfit for Human Habitation.* In: *Public Health. Eighth Report of the Medical Officer of the Privy Council.* London, 1866.—296, 301

[Knox, A. A. and Pollock, G. D.] *Report of the Commissioners on the Treatment of the Treason-Felony Convicts in the English Convict Prisons.* London, 1867.—378, 383, 390, 394

Leges barbarorum.—558

Leges duodecim tabularum.—31

Lex Baiuvariorum.—553

Moustier [L.] [Note of 1 November 1867.] In: *Norddeutsche Allgemeine Zeitung,* 5. November 1867.—462

Public Health. Reports of the Medical Officer of the Privy Council.—224
— *Eighth Report. With Appendix.* London, 1866.—296, 301, 383

Report from the Select Committee on the Bank Acts. Together with the Proceedings of the Committee Minutes of Evidence, Appendix and Index. London, 1857.—185

Report from the Select Committee on the Bank Acts. Together with the Proceedings of the Committee Minutes of Evidence, Appendix and Index. London. 1858.—185

Reports of the Inspectors of Factories to Her Majesty's Principal Secretary of State for the Home Department [for the 1840s-1860s]. London, 1842-1867.—23, 224
— *For the Half Year ending 3lst October 1865.* London, 1866.—224, 230, 232

Resolutions de Paris. Paris, 1791.—71

Strafgesetzbuch für die Preußischen Staaten. Vom 14. April 1851. In: *Gesetz-Sammlung für die Königlichen Preußischen Staaten.* 1851. Nr. 10, Berlin.—77-78, 417

ANONYMOUS ARTICLES AND REPORTS PUBLISHED
IN PERIODICAL EDITIONS

Allgemeine Zeitung, Nr. 119 (Beilage), 29. April 1865: *Städtebuch des Landes Posen.*—156
— Nr. 1, 1. Januar 1866: *Deutschland. Berlin, 29. Dec.*—211
— Nr. 273, 30. September 1867: [Announcement about the publication of Volume One of *Capital* by Karl Marx].—437

The Athenaeum. Journal of English and Foreign Literature, Science, and the Fine Arts, No. 1902, April 9, 1864: [Notice concerning Karl Blind's joining of the Shakespearean Committee].—35

Augsburger Abendzeitung, Nr. 303, 4. November 1867: *Paris, 3. Nov., Morgens: Telegraphische Berichte der 'Abendzeitung'.*—466

Der Beobachter, Nr. 245, 21. Oktober 1864: *Bescheidenheit—ein Ehrenkleid.*—27, 41, 44
— Nr. 268, 17. November 1864: *Karl Blind.*—52

Börsenblatt für den Deutschen Buchhandel und die mit ihm verwandten Geschäftszweige, Nr. 27, 3. März 1865: [Announcement about the publication of *The Prussian Military Question and the German Workers' Party* by Frederick Engels].—475
— Nr. 214, 14. September 1867: [Announcement about the publication of Volume One of *Capital* by Karl Marx].—475
— Nr. 230, 3. Oktober 1867: [Announcement about the publication of Borkheim's speech at the Geneva Congress of the League of Peace and Freedom].—449, 452

The Commonwealth, No. 165, May 5, 1866: [Statement by the Editor].—280

Le Courrier français, Nos. 85, 86; 10, 11 septembre 1867: [Reports in the Section *Nouvelles*].—430
— No. 88, 13 septembre 1867: [Reports on the Geneva Congress of the League of Peace and Freedom].—435
— No. 106, 1 octobre 1867: *La Situation au Mexique.*—438
— No. 113, 8 octobre 1867: *Le Troisième larron.*—438

The Daily News, March 2, 1865: *The Late Polish Insurrection.*—143

The Daily Telegraph, No. 3249, November 17, 1865 (leader).—197

Demokratisches Wochenblatt, Nr. 2, 11. Januar 1868: *Das Preußische und das Schweizer Heersystem.*—534, 540

The Diplomatic Review, October 2, 1867: *Events of the Month.*—434

The Fortnightly Review, No. 37, December 1866 (leader).—338, 340

Die Gartenlaube, Nr. 10, 1867: [Article on Karl Vogt with his photograph].—365

Hermann, Nr. 426, 2. März 1867: *Herr 'Stieber' und der 'Hermann'.*—349
— Nr. 453, 7. September 1867: [Report on the course of money subscription for Freiligrath].—424
— Nr. 459, 19. Oktober 1867: *Für Ferdinand Freiligrath. Schluß-Aufruf.*—454

Journal de Saint-Pétersbourg, No. 140, 23 juin (5 juillet) 1866: *Nouvelles de L'extérieur* [On the Victory of the Prussian army over the Austrians at the battle of Sadowa on 3 July 1866].—293

Kölnische Zeitung, Nr. 63, 4. März 1865: [Announcement about the publication of *The Prussian Military Question and the German Workers' Party* by Frederick Engels].—116
— 8. April 1866: *Die Lage, Köln, 7. April.*—264
— 6. November 1867.—466

— Nr. 15, 29. Januar 1865: *Einsendungen von Arbeitern (Aus Asch in Böhmen).*—70
— Nr. 15, 29. Januar 1865: *Iserlohn, 25. Januar (Allg. Deutsch. Arb.-Verein).*—71
— Nr. 20, 10. Februar 1865.—88
— Nr. 21, 12. Februar 1865.—88
— Nr. 25, 22. Februar 1865: *Berlin, 21. Februar.*—106
— Nr. 43, 5. April 1865: *Vereins-Theil. Berlin, 4. April (Allg. deutsch. Arb.-Verein).*—141, 147
— Nr. 50, 21. April 1865: *Vermischtes (Gegen den Allg. deutsch. Arb.-Verein).*—150
— Nr. 58, 10. Mai 1865: *Feuilleton. Städtebuch des Landes Posen. Von Heinrich Wuttke (Aus dem 'Allgemeinen Zeitung').*—156
— Nr. 102, 30. August 1867: [Report from Erfurt].—417
— Nr. 107, 11. September 1867: *Unser Sieg im Barmen-Elberfeld.*—417
— Nr. 122, 123, 16., 18. Oktober 1867.—450

The Times, April 19, 1864: *General Garibaldi.*—34
— No. 25021, November 4, 1864: *Southern Italy (From our own correspondent). Naples, Oct. 30.*—47
— No. 25107, February 13, 1865: *Prussia. Berlin, Feb. 11.*—90, 95
— No. 25110, February 16, 1865: *The Prussian Legislature. Berlin, Feb. 15.*—94
— No. 25347, November 20, 1865 (leader).—199
— No. 25367, December 13, 1865: *Parliamentary Reform.*—215, 221
— No. 25368, December 14, 1865 (leader).—215, 221
— No. 25436, March 3, 1866 (leader).—236
— No. 25436, March 3, 1866: *The Outbreak in Jamaica (From Our Special Correspondent). Spanish town, Jamaica, Feb. 9.*—236
— No. 25437, March 5, 1866 (leader).—236
— No. 25468, April 10, 1866 (leader).—264
— No. 25469, April 11, 1866: *Austria and Prussia. Berlin, April 10.*—267
— No. 25827, June 3, 1867: *Paris, Saturday, June 1, 6 p.m.*—378-79
— No. 25917, September 16, 1867 (leader).—435
— No. 25974, November 21, 1867: *London Meetings.*—485
— No. 26074, March 17, 1868: *Prussia (From Our Own Correspondent), Berlin, March 14.*—555

Unsere Zeit. Deutsche Revue der Gegenwart, 2. Jg. 2. Hälfte, 1866: *Preußen in Waffen.* I-II, S. 161-77 and 321-43.—365

Der weiße Adler, Nr. 30, 11. März 1865; *Ein Meeting zu Gunsten Polens in London.*—143

Zeitung für Norddeutschland, Nr. 5522, 15. Februar 1867: [Report on Marx's intention to go to the Continent to take part in preparations for the Polish uprising].—346, 347, 352

Die Zukunft, Nr. 199, 27. August 1867, Beilage: *Englische Briefe.*—421
— Nr. 208, 6. September 1867, Beilage: [Advertisement about Käthe Freiligrath's engagement].—425
— Nr. 246, 20. Oktober 1867, Beilage: [Bebel's and Liebknecht's amendment to § 2 of the Combination Bill].—456

INDEX OF PERIODICALS

Die Gartenlaube. Illustriertes Familienblatt—a literary weekly published in Leipzig from 1853 to 1903 and in Berlin from 1903 to 1943.—365, 447, 580

La Gazette de France—a royalist paper published in Paris from 1631 to 1914 (first once and then twice a week, and from 1792 daily).—424

Gazette de Lausanne et Journal Suisse—a liberal-democratic daily founded in Lausanne in 1798.—422

Gewerbeblatt aus Württemberg—a weekly of the commercial and industrial circles, published in Stuttgart from 1849 as a supplement to the *Staats-Anzeiger für Württemberg*.—500, 503

The Glasgow Sentinel—a Scottish weekly, organ of the Tories, published in Glasgow from 1850 to 1877.—34

Guardian—see *The Manchester Guardian*

Hermann. Deutsches Wochenblatt aus London—a weekly of the German petty-bourgeois democrats published in London from 1859.—15, 33, 41, 50, 63, 70, 91, 114, 130, 134, 349, 378, 424, 447, 521

How Do You Do?—a humorous German-language weekly, published in London from 1796; in the 1850s it was edited by Beta (Bettziech).—447

Illustrierter Familien-Kalender—an annual magazine published in Leipzig by A. H. Payne from 1857 to 1874.—447

Illustrierte Zeitung—a German weekly published in Leipzig from 1843 to 1944; in the middle of the nineteenth century it was of a moderate liberal orientation.—533

L'Independance belge. Journal mondial d'informations politiques et littéraires—a liberal daily founded in Brussels in 1831.—215

The International Courier—a weekly published in London from November 1864 to July 1867 in English and French, its French name being *Le Courrier international*. In 1867, the paper was the organ of the International.—346

Internationale Revue—an Austrian bourgeois-democratic monthly published in Vienna in 1866-68.—464, 466, 484, 512, 516

The Irishman—a weekly published from 1858 to 1885, first in Belfast and then in Dublin; reflected the views of the moderate elements of the national movement; came out in defence of Fenians.—464, 485, 504, 521

Journal de l'Association Internationale des Travailleurs—a monthly of the International's sections in Romance Switzerland, published in Geneva from December 1865 to September 1866 with the participation of Johann Philipp Becker.—207, 214, 219, 220

Journal de Saint-Pétersbourg—a newspaper of the Russian Ministry for Foreign Affairs, published under this title in French from 1825 to 1914.—293

Journal des Débats politiques et littéraires—a daily published in Paris from 1789 to 1944; during the July monarchy, organ of the government; during the 1848 revolution, it voiced monarchist views; after the 1851 coup d'état, an organ of the moderate Orleanist opposition.—109

London in 1851 and 1852. Marx and Engels supported it and contributed a number of articles.—15, 531

The Observer—an English conservative weekly published in London since 1791.—35

Ostsee-Zeitung—a German daily published in Stettin (Polish name Szczecin) from 1835.—267

The Owl—a weekly published in London in 1864-69.—355

The People's Paper—a Chartist weekly published by Ernst Jones in London from 1852 to 1858. Marx and Engels contributed to it from October 1852 to December 1856 and helped with its editing.—531

Die Presse—a liberal daily published in Vienna from 1848 to 1896; in 1861-62, when the newspaper held anti-Bonapartist views, Marx was its London correspondent.—516

Preussischer Staats-Anzeiger—see *Königlich Preussischer Staats-Anzeiger*

Putnam's Monthly. A Magazine of American Literature, Science and Art—a Republican monthly published in New York from 1853 to 1857.—531

La Réforme—a daily published in Paris from 1843 to 1850, organ of the republican democrats and petty-bourgeois socialists; from October 1847 to March 1848 the newspaper published reports and statements by Marx and Engels.—530

Republikanisches Regierungs-Blatt—a newspaper of the petty-bourgeois democrats, founded by Gustav Struve and Karl Blind in Lörrach during the second Baden uprising in September 1848; only one issue appeared.—33

Revue contemporaine—a fortnightly published in Paris from 1851 to 1870; during the Second Republic represented the Party of Order; after the coup d'état of 2 December 1851 took a Bonapartist stand.—338, 340

Revue des deux Mondes—a literary and political fortnightly published in Paris since 1829.—257, 338, 340

Rheinischer Beobachter—a conservative daily published in Cologne from 1844 to the beginning of 1848.—97

Rheinische Zeitung—a liberal daily published under this title in Düsseldorf from 1863 to 1866, and in Cologne from 1867 to 1874.—52, 75, 84, 108, 111, 112, 114, 126, 134, 140, 148, 160, 207, 462, 469

Rheinische Zeitung für Politik, Handel und Gewerbe—a daily founded by the Rhenish bourgeois opposition and published in Cologne from 1 January 1842 to 31 March 1843. In April 1842 Marx became one of its contributors. In October of the same year, he became one of its editors, which gave the newspaper a revolutionary-democratic character.—530

La Rive gauche—a democratic weekly published from October 1864 to August 1866, first in Paris, and then in Brussels by a group of French Left republicans; it printed documents of the International. Its editor was Charles Longuet.—213, 219, 243

SUBJECT INDEX